THE IMPOSSIBILITY OF PERFECTION

THE IMPOSSIBILITY OF PERFECTION

Aristotle, Feminism, and the Complexities of Ethics

Michael Slote

OXFORD
UNIVERSITY PRESS

OXFORD
UNIVERSITY PRESS

Oxford University Press, Inc., publishes works that further
Oxford University's objective of excellence
in research, scholarship, and education.

Oxford New York
Auckland Cape Town Dar es Salaam Hong Kong Karachi
Kuala Lumpur Madrid Melbourne Mexico City Nairobi
New Delhi Shanghai Taipei Toronto

With offices in
Argentina Austria Brazil Chile Czech Republic France Greece
Guatemala Hungary Italy Japan Poland Portugal Singapore
South Korea Switzerland Thailand Turkey Ukraine Vietnam

Published by Oxford University Press, Inc.
198 Madison Avenue, New York, New York 10016

www.oup.com

Oxford is a registered trademark of Oxford University Press

Slote, Michael A.
The impossibility of perfection : Aristotle, feminism, and the complexities
of ethics/ Michael Slote.
p. cm.
ISBN 978-0-19-979082-1 (alk. paper)
1. Perfection. 2. Ethics. 3. Aristotle. I. Title. II. Title:
Aristotle, feminism, and the complexities of ethics.
BD233.S57 2011   170—dc22

1 3 5 7 9 8 6 4 2

Printed in the United States of America
on acid-free paper

In Memory of ISAIAH BERLIN

CONTENTS

ACKNOWLEDGMENTS

I would like to thank Kristin Borgwald, Brad Cokelet, Jennifer Etheridge, Virginia Held, P. J. Ivanhoe, Ben Yelle, and, especially, Otavio Bueno and Yang Xiao for their helpful comments. I am also very much indebted to two referees for particular points of criticism and for very useful suggestions about overall structure and presentation. As always, I owe a great deal to Peter Ohlin of OUP for his support of the present project and his general encouragement.

THE IMPOSSIBILITY OF PERFECTION

Introduction

This book defends the idea that perfection—whether of virtue or of personal happiness—is impossible in principle, an idea that was originally introduced by Isaiah Berlin, but that neither Berlin himself nor anyone subsequently has really *argued* for. But the argument I shall be giving here is also very different from anything that could have occurred or was at all likely to occur to Berlin himself because its main inspiration consists in ideas and examples derived from feminist thought and the recent and only partially successful history of "the women's movement." In my opinion, many of the implications of that thought and history have been philosophically under-theorized, and I want to show in particular that the wrenching choices regarding career versus family and regarding loving/committed sexuality versus adventurous sexuality *that both women and men face nowadays* help to illustrate Berlin's point about necessary imperfection more interestingly and poignantly than any of the examples that originally occurred to Berlin.

But if one comes to agree with the Berlin thesis, then it is no longer possible to accept the relatively harmonious or unified picture of ethical phenomena that we inherited principally from Aristotle and that still governs much philosophical thought about virtue and human good. Aristotle believed in the unity of the virtues (to have one virtue one has to have them all) and to that extent held that virtues cannot conflict with one another. But I shall be arguing not only that there can be conflict among the virtues and among life's goods, but (what will turn out to be a further point!) that those conflicts illustrate the impossibility of our ever having a perfect life or being perfectly virtuous. Moreover, once one moves away from the simpler unified conception of human (ethical) life that Aristotle and almost everyone else have offered us, we end up with a much more complex and, if I may say, more interesting (though also less ethically optimistic) picture of what human life is and has to be, one that, as I eventually will argue, is perhaps more appropriate to our more complex *age* than anything that could have been thought of in earlier times.

The book also has implications that are in some sense larger than anything suggested by its title and subtitle, because of the way its main themes and arguments tie in with work that I and others have done on care ethics and moral sentimentalism more generally. These latter philosophical developments call into question the rationalistic assumptions and arguments that underlie Greek and Enlightenment ethical thought, both in their historical embodiments and as they influence present-day (Kantian) liberalism and (neo-Aristotelian) virtue ethics. By contrast, the present book attacks historical and contemporary versions of Greek and Enlightenment thought from a *different* direction: not by criticizing their rationalism, but by arguing against their general assumption that ethical phenomena can be understood in a *unified harmonious way that allows for the possibility (in principle) of perfection.*

The later chapters of this book also bring out another theme that its title and subtitle, which are already long enough, leave unmentioned. Care ethics in its most ambitious form seeks to offer accounts of "masculine" concepts like justice and autonomy in terms of the "feminine" ideals of caring about and personal connection with others. This represents a kind of balance between male/masculine and female/feminine factors (as traditionally conceived), involving, as it does, a supposedly female *account* of *concepts* that are traditionally associated with men more than with women. But if we are to do care ethics or any other kind of ethics in an acceptable and fruitful manner, there *also* has to be a balance between those philosophical *methods* or *methodologies* that have been thought to come more easily to men and those that have been regarded as coming more readily to women. In particular, logical argument and philosophical analysis have to be balanced against or, better, integrated with emotional sensitivity and ethical intuition and insight, if we are to do ethics in the best way we can.

This is an idea I try to articulate in the Appendix to the present book (after the arguments for the impossibility of perfection have all been given). What I say there will depend on showing the philosophical importance of insight and good intuitions, and my efforts in that direction will, I think, rely on *personal examples and comparisons* in a way that I believe hasn't been previously attempted. The Appendix uses facts or assumptions about the different ways that Saul Kripke and David Lewis operated as philosophers to defend the importance of having good intuitions and of acknowledging that importance within the philosophical profession, and I also will mention facts about the reception of some of Annette Baier's ideas that I hope will illustrate and argue for the importance of philosophical insight in relation to philosophical analysis and argument. I also say something about how Nel Noddings's emotional sensitivity to and intuitiveness about ethical phenomena need to be supplemented by or completed in a more *analytical* approach to certain philosophical questions than she herself ever took.

Before I begin, in chapter 1, my main argument(s) for the impossibility of perfection, I think I need to say something (further) about why I shall be proceeding in the manner in which I have chosen to proceed. Berlin gives hardly any arguments for the impossibility of perfection, and the one case or example that, more than any other, Berlin mentions as illustrating his impossibility thesis seems to me and has seemed to others to do nothing of the kind. Berlin saw the clash between liberty and equality as exemplifying the idea that perfect justice or an ideal state (or society) is conceptually impossible, and, to be sure, if we seek to create a more equal society, we will almost certainly have to restrict the liberty of those more talented or driven individuals who would otherwise make disproportionately huge amounts of money or attain inordinate power over others. We will presumably have to tax those people, and such a society would then perhaps be less than ideal because the well-off would presumably be unwilling on their own initiative to share greater wealth with those who are less fortunate. If, however, we imagine a more ideal society in which people *are* willing to share equally with those who otherwise would have less money or wealth, we can see that (fully nontaxed) liberty and equality of goods or benefits could at least in principle be realized together, so Berlin's favorite illustration of the impossibility of perfection doesn't help at all with proving that thesis.[1]

More generally, since Berlin doesn't give any real arguments for the impossibility of perfection, I shall in chapter 1 proceed toward my own arguments for that thesis rather than consider Berlin's views on their own. Where my arguments touch on his ideas or examples (or those mentioned by others), I shall note that fact. But I think the idea of the impossibility of perfection needs to be given a new lease on life, and that is what I shall be trying to give it here. On the other hand, I clearly owe a great, great debt to Berlin, a debt that is only partially repaid by my having dedicated this book to his memory. Isaiah Berlin was the first person clearly to enunciate the impossibility thesis, and when he did so, he was going against the grain of long-standing philosophical tradition. So if we can actually give good arguments for that thesis, then we can credit him with amazing insight—even (dare I say it?) prophecy. But that is no substitute for the effort to work out and provide the actual arguments.

At this point, however, I think it might be useful if I offered a brief outline of the book chapter by chapter. Because I believe that the best or, in contemporary terms, most interesting illustrations of the Berlin thesis grow out of what we have learned from recent feminism, chapter 1 will talk about patriarchal ideas and values and about how feminist insights and ideals develop out of and in opposition to patriarchal notions, before I ease our discussion into a more direct consideration of the issue of necessary imperfection.[2] Patriarchy sees certain goods and virtues as gender-relative: for example, seeing adventurousness as a virtue in men, but not in women and regarding careers as good for men, but not for women. But feminism doesn't make these distinctions. Women who don't pursue a career are missing out on something, but by the same token, on typical feminist assumptions, men miss out on something important if they just have careers and are emotionally uninvolved with their families or with other people more generally. Chapter 1 maintains that this evenhandedness with respect to gender or sex generates Berlin-type problems for both men and women. Neither men nor women can combine real adventurousness with real prudence, or real adventures with real security, and chapter 1 argues that this entails the impossibility both of perfect virtue and of perfect happiness. It also argues that the choice between a personally fulfilling career and close personal relationships cannot be perfectly resolved. Adventure and security are merely "partial" goods, and to have either one of them is to be in a less than ideal situation vis-à-vis the other. Similarly, self-fulfilling accomplishment and intimate personal relationship(s) cannot be perfectly combined, and this too helps illustrate the impossibility of perfect happiness. Furthermore, and using a more traditional example that doesn't come out of either patriarchal thinking or feminism, the virtue of frankness and the virtue of tact(fulness) also cannot be ideally combined. These traits are thus merely "partial" virtues, but the illustrative example that helps us show this has to be a bit subtler and more complex than anything (along these lines) discussed in the previous ethics literature.

Chapter 2 relates the previous discussion more directly to Aristotle and Aristotelianism. The idea of partial virtues/goods/ values and the concomitant impossibility of perfect virtue or a perfectly happy life both contradict the Aristotelian picture of virtue and personal good. But we need to discuss that picture in greater detail in order to see the various ways in which it differs from any conception of the ethical that accepts the Berlin thesis. Also, since the argument I give for the impossibility of perfection makes such frequent use of the notion of a partial good or virtue (of a partial *value*), chapter 2 seeks, among other things, to compare this idea with the rather parallel notion of "partial denotation" that was introduced into the philosophy of language by Hartry Field. Chapter 2 also shows that the idea of partial values in no way entails ethical relativism or nonobjectivity. The theory that emerges from the impossibility of perfection is more complex or complicated than the Aristotelian view, but it makes just as strong a claim to objective validity or truth.

In chapter 3, I consider a variety of well-known views that differ less radically from Aristotelianism than acceptance of the Berlin thesis forces us to. But even if we have reasons of methodological conservatism to preserve as much of our Aristotelian tradition as we can, I argue that none of these other views is as realistic about and sensitive to ethical phenomena as what we get from arguing for and accepting Berlin's thesis. I then go on to discuss some significant (further) *objections* to our earlier arguments in favor of the impossibility of perfection. It can be argued, for example, that perfection is possible if one is allowed to consign different (and conflicting) values to different periods of a life, so that, for example, one lives adventurously and/for one's career early in one's life and then lives prudently and/or for personal/family relationships in one's later years. Chapter 3 seeks to answer this objection and a variety of other objections to the Berlin thesis.

Chapter 4 then compares what we have said about necessary imperfection with the philosophical literature on moral dilemmas and on (what Bernard Williams calls) moral cost. It might be thought that the possibility of moral dilemmas or cost would illustrate and argue in favor of Berlin's thesis, but our discussion will show that dilemma and cost don't *as such* favor the idea that moral/ethical perfection is impossible.

In chapter 5, I draw out some of the implications of our previous discussion in relation to care ethics and to the common philosophical ideas that underlie most of ancient Greek and modern Enlightenment philosophy. That philosophy claims and insists, first, that all our ethical values can be based in reason or rationality and, second, that this can be done in an ultimately harmonious and unified way; and whereas care ethics argues against the idea of basing our deepest values in reason, advocacy of Berlin's thesis represents a complementary challenge to the widely accepted idea of harmony or unity among such values. Together, then, what is said in the present book and what I and others have said in defense of care-ethical sentimentalism constitute a *joint challenge* to Greek and Enlightenment thought taken as a (bipartite) whole. We shall also see in chapter 5 that Romanticism occupies a kind of middle ground between Greek/Enlightenment thinking and the Berlinian approach I am advocating here.

In chapter 6, I step back from some of our main arguments and consider their positive implications for our total picture of ethical values. An ethical view or theory that allows for and insists on the impossibility of perfection sees ethical phenomena as much more complicated than Aristotelian approaches do. It agrees with Aristotle that some qualities or things are virtuous or good (for us) simpliciter, but it insists that there are also such things as partial goods and partial virtues, and that idea is clearly inconsistent with the unity of the virtues doctrine that Aristotle defended and maintained. So the Berlin thesis already leads to a more complex ethical picture than anything that comes down to us from Aristotle or any other Greek philosopher. But there are additional complications that are worth noting. Early in the book, I speak of dependent virtues, that is, of virtues whose status as such seems to depend on the presence of other virtues (one example is the way the virtue of conscientiousness seems to depend on the conscientious individual's having minimally decent or humane values). And I also early on mention the possibility of dependent personal goods, goods whose status as such depends on their possessor's possessing some other good as well. This category of dependency is not one that Aristotle or any Aristotelian has explored, and clearly it further complicates the/our ethical account of goods and virtues. But chapter 6 argues that things are actually more complicated than what I earlier said about dependent goods and virtues might lead one to think. Not only do some goods depend on others and some virtues on other virtues, but some goods depend on virtues and some virtues on goods. And, perhaps more surprisingly, it turns out that some virtues depend on vices or on certain personal evils and that some personal goods depend on personal evils or on certain vices. In fact, chapter 6 considers and argues for a number of *still greater* complications in our understanding of basic ethical values.

The Conclusion summarizes what has previously been said and attempts to put it in greater historical perspective, and the Appendix follows up on chapter 5 by arguing that in addition to involving a balance between male and female *content* (where this is understood in traditionalistic terms), ethical theory also requires a balance or integration of (what are traditionally conceived as) male and female *methods* of doing philosophy. But I have already spoken of this earlier in this Introduction, and it is time we proceeded to our main arguments.

Chapter 1

Feminism and Partial Values

INTRODUCTION

I want to begin this book by talking about some issues in feminist
ethics that I think are very interesting in their own right, but that
also advance us—at a somewhat leisurely pace—toward the main,
and the most controversial, issue in this book: the question of
whether perfection—either in terms of happiness or in terms of the
(possession of the) virtues—is a genuine possibility. The considerations I shall be discussing in what immediately follows were the
actual entry point of my thinking on the subject of perfection, and
we shall see how they naturally or inevitably lead in that direction.
But further along we shall also have reason to directly engage and
criticize Aristotelian views about happiness, virtue, and perfection,
and these criticisms will also support the diametrically opposed
conception of happiness, (the) virtue(s), and perfection that I will
be articulating and defending in these pages. So let me begin.

In her groundbreaking work *In a Different Voice: Psychological
Theory and Women's Development*, Carol Gilligan raised some very
important issues about whether gender is relevant to morality.[1] She
spoke of two different moral "voices," one that approaches moral
issues in terms of justice, rights, autonomy, and the invoking and
application of moral rules or principles; and another that approaches
them via a less rule-oriented personal connection with and concern

about others. Gilligan's work has been taken to imply or suggest that the first of these voices is associated more with men than with women; and the second more with women than with men. But various subsequent empirical studies (and some of Gilligan's own later work) have called this gender-correlation into question, and much of the interest nowadays in the second of these voices—the voice, as it is called, of caring and of the/an ethics of care—is relatively independent of any assumptions about the gendered character of the caring voice or moral "orientation."

Nonetheless, Gilligan did raise some important issues about the relation(s) between gender and (accepted or valid) morality. But neither her discussion nor the vast literature that evolved out of it focused (very much) on ethical issues that are not specifically related to morality. Ethics in the largest sense not only asks about moral right and wrong and moral good and evil, but also considers questions about the good life (what kind of life is good for us) and questions about various virtues that lie partly or wholly outside morality proper. Thus when we praise resourcefulness and strength of purpose as individual virtues, we don't necessarily think of these qualities of character as specifically moral. For a resourceful person can be a moral scoundrel; but most of us, nonetheless, think of his resourcefulness as a virtue, an admirable and praiseworthy quality of character. We are willing, so to speak, to give the devil his due. And similar things can be said about strength of purpose.[2]

I mention these other, nonmoral aspects or foci of ethics for a reason. Theoretical (as opposed to popular and/or psychological) discussions of the relevance or role of gender haven't paid sufficient attention to the possibility that gender, or thinking in terms of gender, might play a pervasive role in our understanding of ethical questions that are not specifically moral. But I believe that gender issues do, in fact, arise *very generally* with respect to questions about the good life (or human good) and questions about what sorts of character traits count as virtues, and to that extent recent theoretical discussion of the ethical issues that arise with respect to gender can be said to have proceeded much more narrowly than it makes sense for it to do. It will be my (immediate) purpose here to try to persuade you that this is so. (For simplicity's sake, my discussion won't take in issues about gays, lesbians, and the transgendered.) Our common or traditional attitudes and opinions about what is good for people and what counts as admirable or a virtue are very broadly contoured to considerations of gender, and we need to recognize that fact before we can move beyond such thinking in a way or ways that feminism would find desirable and that I myself completely endorse. The gendered way in which personal goods (ways of living a good life) and (nonmoral) human virtues are often conceived reflects patriarchal or sexist assumptions and attitudes, but some of the most important theoretical implications of this fact have somehow, surprisingly, been ignored, and the present chapter will attempt or at least begin to make up for that deficiency. Under patriarchy, various (nonmoral) values—various goods and virtues— are seen as gender relative, and I shall argue that a more enlightened feminist ethics needs to regard these values in a quite different, but somewhat unfamiliar, philosophical light.[3] This will require the introduction of certain philosophical/ethical distinctions into our discussion.

SOME ETHICAL PHENOMENA

Philosophical accounts of human good can roughly be classified into three categories. There are hedonistic views that try to reduce all the good things in life to pleasure; there are desire-satisfaction or preference-satisfaction accounts that reduce the good things in life to the satisfaction of our (rational) desires or preferences; and then there are "objective-list" theories that are essentially nonreductive and that try to allow, in intuitive terms, for the variety of important basic human goods.[4] It is easier to point out male-female distinctions if one focuses on the objective list theories, but in fact everything I am about to say can be carried over to the other two sorts of approaches to understanding human well-being/personal goods. However, those who have proposed objective list accounts of the (fundamental and intrinsically) good things in life—myself included—have made no mention of male/female differences in regard to such lists. Such things as pleasure, achievement, wisdom, security, love, and friendship have often appeared on those lists, but no one has ever pointed out that some of these items are more traditionally associated with women, some are more traditionally associated with men, and still others have (almost) never appeared to be anything other than general *human* goods.

Let's begin with the personal good of security. The psychologist Abraham Maslow mentions it as one of the basic human needs and conceives it as a basic human good; and Martha Nussbaum in her objective list approach to what is good in life also mentions security.[5] But the good of security is in fact more traditionally associated with women than with men. You may at this point ask whether men and women don't both need security, and, of course, in some degree they both do. But consider this. Adventure involves risk and danger (and novelty), and men are traditionally supposed to be interested in and/or to need adventure in a way women *aren't* supposed to. And adventure is the opposite of, or inconsistent with, security, so to that extent men (as a class or on average) are traditionally thought to need security less than women do.

Moreover, I have never seen an objective list that included adventure as a basic human good, and yet I think many men have over the centuries—over the millennia—regarded adventure as a good thing in their lives despite (or in part because of) all the insecurity and risk that adventure entails.[6] In fact, security and adventure constitute a rather naturally associated *pair* of opposites or contraries within the sphere of supposed human goods, and yet objective list accounts tend to ignore the adventure pole of that opposition and as a result treat security as if it were a human good *ueberhaupt* or in general—thus ignoring (what we could call) the feminine bias of including security without including adventure. And thus also ignoring the difference between such things as security and those items on the list—like pleasure and wisdom—that have always appeared to apply equally to males and females because (though this can't be the whole story) they seemingly *can't* be paired with some other putative basic human good that vies with or opposes them. (Pain and sometimes even ignorance can be instrumentally useful in life, but no one thinks of them as basic human goods.)

One irony of what I have just pointed out is that it in some measure runs counter to the common feminist (and realistic) assumption that traditional philosophy and traditional ethical theory are full of male bias. Nussbaum may not be subject to such bias, but it is interesting to see a male like Maslow ignore some putative traditional male goods in favor of an emphasis on a good that is traditionally, or in patriarchal terms, more typically and exclusively valued by women than by men. And why, more generally, do traditional male philosophers (though there may be exceptions I am not aware of) fail to mention adventure as something good in life? The Stoics can be seen as arguing for the importance of insulating ourselves from risk to our own well-being by becoming fully virtuous—since they held that virtue is sufficient for human good or happiness, and here, as with Maslow (and Nussbaum), the assumption seems to be that security is an important good; but, once again, adventure (not to mention novelty) is nowhere in the ethical picture. And I would want to argue (though not here) that one can detect a similar bias against adventure in Plato and Aristotle. What are we to make of this bias against a value that is traditionally associated with males rather than females?

Now we have just been talking about personal goods, the good things in human lives, but what we have said also carries over to views about the virtues, about what kinds of character traits are praiseworthy or otherwise. The distinction between things that are good for us and admirable features of our character—what we also call virtues—was somewhat obscured in ancient ethical thought by the idea that a trait doesn't count as a virtue unless it is typically useful to those who possess it. This last idea is sometimes called eudaimonism, and all ancient ethical theories were eudaimonistic; but we nowadays are not as inclined as the ancients were to see each virtue and the combination of all the human virtues as necessarily tending to produce (this-worldly) happiness for the person who has the virtue(s). After all, certain virtues seem to require self-sacrifice. So I am going to assume that there is a difference between what counts as a human good or good for us (conducive to our happiness) and what counts as an admirable trait or virtue. And in fact even Aristotle, who was every bit a eudaimonist, believed there was a distinction to be (conceptually) made between the two. In his *Eudemian Ethics* (1248b 17–27), he points out that health or a healthy constitution is considered a good thing, but is not regarded as admirable or praiseworthy. So I now want to apply the lessons of what has been said above about what is good for us or makes for happiness to questions about what is admirable or counts as a virtue.

For example, philosophers often use the term "prudence" or terms like *prudentia* that can be translated into English as "prudence" to cover the entire range or great swaths of human practical rationality, but consider the term in its ordinary sense. In ordinary English, it tends to imply a concern for long-term well-being (usually one's own) and a tendency or need to play things safe. In other words, if one is concerned with one's long-term well-being, one isn't supposed to take big chances; rather one is supposed to insure against risks to such well-being, and all this, I believe, is part of the meaning or connotation of the ordinary English term "prudence." But then someone who is prudent can't be a bold risk-taker and can't really, therefore, be *into adventures*. By the same token, someone who values adventure as a human good is likely to think that risk-taking boldness is not only acceptable but admirable, a virtue; and since prudence as ordinarily understood is inconsistent with such boldness, the typical or traditional male who values adventure will regard prudence as less than fully admirable. By contrast, traditional women who value security over adventure will have some tendency not to see risk-taking boldness as a virtue and to view prudence unequivocally as an admirable trait, as a virtue. And, of course, the opposition here has been played out in marriages since time immemorial, with husbands wanting to take risks that their wives try to rein them in from. (Obviously, this has something to do with wives' typically greater concern for actual or potential children, but I think it has also in some degree been independent of that factor.) What are we to make of all this?

So far I have just spoken of one familiar aspect or area of human goods and virtues where patriarchy sees or thinks it sees male/ female differences. But let me mention another such aspect or area, before we go on to try to account for or understand these supposed differences in philosophical *and feminist* terms. And let us talk now not about the goods that objective lists typically ignore, but about goods that are mentioned on (almost) all such lists. The typical objective list contains both love/friendship and achievement/success as goods—along with wisdom and pleasure as well. But wisdom and pleasure (or at least certain kinds of pleasure—of which more hereafter) aren't oriented toward one sex or gender more than the other, whereas love/friendship and achievement (in opposite ways) are traditionally thought to be. It is the stuff of pop-psychology and accounts of pop-culture that women are into friendships with one another and into close relationships with their children much more than men are and that one thing that prevents men from such "affiliative" interests is their preoccupation with their careers. There is much more talk of "distant fathers" than of "distant mothers"; and though there is lots of "male bonding" when men are young, female relationships are often said to last longer and be more emotionally intense than those of males. And, of course, men have traditionally been involved in/with their careers and with the achieving/accomplishing of certain career goals much more than women have been, and such involvement seems to some extent to be psychologically inconsistent with the preoccupation with and absorption in friendships and family love that (more) typically or traditionally have characterized women's lives.

So philosophically devised objective lists of human goods typically contain some goods that are traditionally regarded as gendered and others that are typically or traditionally thought of as applying fairly equally to both males and females: a fact that, I believe, has not previously been noted and that, more than any other consideration, led me toward the writing of the present book, *once I had noticed it.*[7] Now I could go on with further examples, but I think it will probably be more useful if, given the complexity of what has already been said, I try to sort things out a bit. The phenomena we have just been describing need to be conceptually and ethically clarified, and to that end I would like now to introduce some distinctions that take us beyond our previous discussion, but will help us toward a better understanding of the philosophical and ethical implications of what I have already said. Intuitively, or in commonsense ethical terms, certain virtues and goods seem (in a sense to be specified) to be *dependent* on other goods or virtues. On the other hand, certain goods and virtues *don't* seem to be relevantly dependent; and, as I shall now show, we need to be able to make such a distinction in order to get clearer about the philosophical/ethical issues raised by our previous discussion.[8]

DEPENDENT VALUES

The word "values" can be used as an overarching term to designate both personal goods and virtues, but I shall mostly be speaking of goods or virtues in particular; and let me explain the distinction between dependent and nondependent virtues and goods by describing some examples that are for the most part not tied to issues of feminism. Some people think conscientious adherence to duty is always and necessarily a (moral) virtue; but others disagree and say that where someone's conscience is really aberrant and inhumane, there is no virtue in adhering (rigidly) to it. Thus take the supposed conscience of the Nazi who feels it is his duty to eliminate, to help eradicate, all Jews and homosexuals. We think such a person is inhumane, monstrous, and certainly immoral, but do we give him some credit for at least being conscientious about his perverse values? Some will say yes. But others would certainly disagree and maintain that such conscientiousness is in no way virtuous, that conscientiousness is not a virtue when it is based on inhumane and indecent values. And this view is equivalent to saying that conscientiousness is a dependent virtue and that it depends on one's having relatively humane or decent values to be conscientious about. On such a view, in other words, the virtue of conscientiousness necessarily depends, for its virtuousness, on the (presence of the) virtue of humanity or the virtue of basic human decency.

Take another example. Many of us regard humility as a very important virtue, but is its status as a virtue really independent of someone's having other virtues? Is humility a virtue, for example, in someone who possesses no (other) attributes anyone could reasonably praise or be proud of? Quite possibly not; and in that case humility could be viewed as an inherently dependent virtue: dependent on having some other significant virtues, though perhaps not dependent on having any other *particular* virtues.

Finally, one can argue that civility and courtesy count as social virtues (virtues of the society in which they occur) only if the society they characterize is substantially a just one. The civility and courtesy that could be found in the antebellum American South, for example, seem rather empty, superficial, ironic, and hypocritical in the light of the massive injustice(s) that pervaded that society, and if we take this seriously, we have reason to say that social virtues like civility and courtesy necessarily depend, for their status as virtues, on (the presence of) the virtue of justice—that is, the justice of the society in which the civility and courtesy may flourish. And a parallel dependency may for similar reasons exist at the individual level as well. The courtesy or civility of any given person may seem to be or count as a virtue, as admirable, only if she or he is personally just (or moral) to a substantial extent.

Dependent *personal goods* can also be recognized or thought to exist in a number of contexts. Imagine, for example, someone who has just been fired from a job and who is with a male friend who is trying to console her. But the friend lets it somehow slip that he has doubts about how good his friend really was at the job she has just lost, and, as a result, his efforts at sympathy have the tone and character of condescension. The woman who has just been fired, seeing this, might very well angrily say to her friend: I want your respect, not your pity. And what I think she is saying, in part, to her friend is that mere pity, or sympathy without respect, isn't going to help her much in her present situation. In other words, putting the matter somewhat more objectively, we can say that given how demoralized the woman is feeling at present, sympathy can count as a good and be helpful to her only if it isn't mere pity, only if it is based in or accompanied by a relevant form of respect that can help her toward regaining her self-confidence. And if what she is saying makes sense, then it makes sense to suppose that the good of receiving sympathy can in some and perhaps in all cases depend on (being accompanied by) the good of being respected (or shown respect). (As I have indicated, we can also put this in terms of the idea that the good of receiving sympathy depends on that sympathy's not constituting a kind of mere or sheer pity.)

Finally, we find the idea of dependent goods in some widespread forms of thinking about the good of sexual pleasure. Many people would say that sexual pleasure is a good thing (in one's life) only if it occurs in the context of a committed or loving relationship, and this view amounts, in our terms, to the claim that the good of sexual pleasure depends on the good of having a committed or loving relationship.[9] But many people would disagree, and that disagreement might be thought to have a gendered character because at least traditionally it is women who think the good of sexuality depends on the presence of love, and men who think, or tend to think, otherwise.

And note the contrast with other forms of pleasure. Almost no one thinks aesthetic pleasure or enjoyment is more relevant to a particular sex/gender, and it is difficult, in addition, to see how the good of such enjoyment necessarily/inherently depends on any other particular form of personal good. Similarly with the pleasure of a hot bath or sauna or of a good meal. And though the idea that certain virtues aren't dependent on others is potentially a hostage to Aristotle's thesis of the unity of the virtues, certain virtues (e.g., patience?) may seem to be independent of others if we don't accept or (as I intend to do) offer arguments against that thesis. So there is a distinction to be made between dependent goods and virtues and goods and virtues that aren't or don't seem to be inherently dependent on other goods or virtues, and I propose to rely on that distinction in what follows.

Thus our final example of a (possibly) dependent good, the example of sexual pleasure, turns us back toward ethical issues concerning gender. But what we have said in this section on the whole also gives us some philosophical tools for better understanding what is happening and what is being (erroneously) thought, when people hold that there are gender differences with respect to human goods and human virtues. So let us now revisit some of the earlier-mentioned cases where gender differences might seem to be relevant or at least often are assumed—and let us see how the distinctions made in the present section can help us illuminate (our thinking about) such cases.

FROM PATRIARCHAL TO FEMINIST VALUES

I am going to argue now that some of the gender differences that have been thought to exist respecting various human goods and virtues reflect patriarchal values that need to be transcended or obliterated in the name of feminist ethical ideals and aspirations. The concept of dependent goods and virtues is useful in clarifying the social attitudes and thinking that prevail under conditions of patri-archy—though, as we have already seen, this notion also has a wider ethical application and usefulness. So let us return to our previous examples of supposed gender differences and see how the new notion, the new distinction, works to help clarify their ethical character. But first some preliminaries.

Under patriarchy, adventure isn't supposed to be *for women*, and adventurousness and a willingness to take bold risks are not sup-posed to be virtues in or for women. (Even apart from adventure in the strictest sense of the term, women aren't supposed to take risks or be bold and adventurous in their decisions, e.g., about whom to marry.) On the other hand, men are supposed to be willing to take risks, and prudence in its ordinary sense isn't supposed to be so univocally a male virtue as it is supposed to be a female one. And, of course, adventure (i.e., living adventurously) is widely considered quite proper and desirable for men at least in their relatively youth-ful years. In that case, we can say that patriarchy views adventure as a gender-relative good and adventurousness as a gender-relative virtue. These things are, respectively, good and virtuous only for or in men. And by the same token, patriarchal values see safety or secu-rity as clearly a good for women, but not so clearly one for men; and they regard prudence as clearly a virtue in or for women, but not so clearly one in or for men. Similarly, patriarchy considers career fulfillment to be appropriate and good for men, but not for women, and because of the difficulty most people have in pursuing a career while also being "family-oriented," it sees such family orientation as more unequivocally a good for women than for men. But now we need to bring in the notion of (ethical) dependency.

We earlier noted that some people think the good of sexual activity or pleasure depends on the good of love, the having of a loving or committed relationship in which the sexual activity or pleasure occurs; and we noted that others disagree. But these differences in fact (to some extent) reflect some patriarchal attitudes and ideas about gender differences and the role dependent goods play in those differences. For, very simply, patriarchy seems to regard the dependency of the good of sex on the good of love as itself holding only in relation to (relative to) the female gender. And in relation to males, it typically tends to hold that no such dependency exists. In other words, patriarchy appears to hold that *for women* the good of sexual pleasure (if it can really ever *be* a good thing for them) depends on the(ir having the) good of a loving relationship; but it holds that for men the good of sexual pleasure *doesn't* depend on the(ir having the) good of love.

However—and this is a new theme—I wouldn't want to deny that specifically moral assumptions/attitudes influence and help explain the patriarchal attitudes toward various goods and virtues that we have just been describing. If under patriarchy it is thought that uncommitted or "free" sexuality is not a good thing in women's lives, that is surely at least in part because it is thought that it is always wrong for women to enjoy sex in such circumstances, wrong in a way that is not presumed to be (universally) wrong for men. This is the so-called double standard understood in a strictly moral or moralistic sense. But it is also interesting to note that this moralism then seems to lend itself to attitudes about what is good for people that may not strictly follow from the original moral assumptions. Just because it is wrong, say, for a woman to engage in uncommitted sexual activity, it doesn't automatically or obviously follow that she gains nothing good for herself by or through such immoral activities. After all, we think a bank robber gets something good for himself if he steals money, and although the general tendency of eudaimonistic Greek philosophy has been to deny this rather commonsense view, it *is* a commonsense view. And so one would think that the transition from assuming something is morally wrong to assuming one doesn't derive some personal good (immediately) from it wouldn't be or have to be so quickly made as it seems to be made under certain patriarchal assumptions and attitudes. I don't think patriarchal views leave a whole lot of room for the possibility that women who engage in uncommitted sex are acting immorally but enjoying something very good for themselves. But I'm not sure. Perhaps the patriarchal idea is simply that it is wrong to enjoy the definite good of sex outside of committed relationships (specifically, marriage); and if it is, then the idea that the good of sex is gender-relative wouldn't really or necessarily be part of the patriarchal point of view. However, from what I have seen and heard (I came of age in the late 1950s), patriarchal or sexist attitudes at least sometimes involve the idea, the view, that sex isn't a good thing in women's lives if and when they indulge in it outside of marriage, and this is in effect to treat such sexual activity or sexual enjoyment as a gender-relative good.

Note too that the same issues basically arise with respect to all of the supposedly patriarchal attitudes or views we have been describing. The idea that adventure isn't a good thing for women may be influenced by the thought that (given the way things are in the world) adventure puts a woman's chastity, her honor, at risk, and so moral thinking would once again be influencing ideas about what is good for women. And here I don't think it at all plausible to assume that patriarchy sees unnecessary risk-taking and adventuring as morally wrong for women, but is happy to acknowledge that they gain a good thing in their lives, adventure, when they act thus immorally. Somehow in this case the assumed immorality and prob-ably other factors (e.g., ideas about how men should protect the "weaker sex") don't seem to allow for any slippage between moral goodness or acceptability and what is considered good or beneficial in personal terms. And in any event, adventurousness is clearly not traditionally considered to be any sort of virtue for women, even if that assumption is influenced by the thought that it is immoral for a woman to risk her honor by deliberately courting risk and adventure.

Similar conclusions hold, I think, with regard to the choice between career and family. The having of a career wasn't traditionally thought of as a good thing for a woman, but this attitude may very well have been influenced by the assumption that it is morally wrong for a husband or father to let his wife or daughter help support him and also morally wrong for a woman to seek a career outside the home when she has the opportunity (which is sometimes not the case) to be fulfilled and useful inside the home. The idea that a career is something that women can derive great benefit from, but that it is selfish or wrong for them to want to have isn't a particularly familiar one, and so I think that with regard to this example and the others we have discussed, patriarchal attitudes are pretty much as I have indicated. Moral considerations or moralism may feed the idea that certain goods and (putatively nonmoral) virtues are gender-relative, but the assumptions about gender relativity are nonetheless definitely *there* in much traditional thinking about men and women—even if not nearly as explicitly as the present discussion has attempted to make them.[10]

But surely we want to question all these patriarchal attitudes, values, and assumptions. The concepts and distinctions we introduced in the last section and have applied in the present section help us to understand what patriarchy is (or often is) committed to, but they don't seem to help us to criticize patriarchy or get beyond the typically invidious distinctions it makes between males/men and females/women. In order to do so, we of course have to put the specifically sexist or patriarchal (moral) assumptions I have just briefly discussed or alluded to entirely behind us. But what will also help us in philosophical terms to criticize and move beyond patriarchal views and attitudes and toward a feminist ethical picture of the basic values of our lives is some new ethical/conceptual distinctions I haven't yet mentioned. We need to introduce a new category of value, a new way of thinking about or parsing goods and virtues—we need the notion of a *partial* value, of a *partial* virtue or human good.

PARTIAL GOODS AND VIRTUES

I take the nomenclature, and to some extent the idea, of partial values not from the ethical doctrine of partialism (according to which we should accord more concern to those near and dear to us than to mere strangers or people we only hear about and never will meet), but from Sigmund Freud's notion that (e.g.) sadism and masochism are partial instincts.[11] We don't need to subscribe to any part of Freudianism in order to make conceptual use of what Freud has in mind here, and it turns out, in fact, that there is an interesting analogy between what Freud said about sadism vs. masochism and what can be plausibly said about certain human goods and virtues. The opposition between (the desire for the good of) security and (the desire for the good of) adventure mirrors or parallels the Freudian opposition between sadism and masochism, and this way of seeing things will turn out to help us formulate and justify some of the most important criticisms feminist theory wants to make and has made of patriarchal or sexist attitudes and traditions.

In Freudian theory, sadism and masochism are "paired opposites;" they both have a tendency to operate in any given individual in erotic/neurotic contexts, but those tendencies (obviously) work against one another in various ways. And something (conceptually) similar can be seen to operate in the sphere of ethics. However, rather than work at this point with our previous examples of security vs. adventure or career success vs. affiliative (or relationship) goods, I want to introduce a new kind of case, one that I believe illustrates the idea of (paired) partial values so clearly and forcefully that it can then be used as a basis for better understanding the ethical oppositions that we have previously been discussing.

Everyone recognizes that the virtues of frankness and of tact stand in some kind of opposition. They are naturally seen as paired and opposed because there are so many situations in which a choice has to be made between being tactful and being frank, situations in which one cannot exemplify both of these qualities of character. But an Aristotelian take on such issues would want to hold that whenever there is a choice between tact and frankness, there is a completely *right* choice in the matter. That is (at least in part) because Aristotle and many Aristotelians accept a doctrine of "the unity of the virtues" according to which one has to have all the virtues in order to possess any single one of them.

However, I don't believe that what we regard as virtues are as well-behaved as the unity doctrine and other aspects of Aristotelianism assume, and I think the issue of frankness vs. tact helps illustrate this point. On the Aristotelian view (and speaking rather roughly), frankness and tact never clash *as virtues*. In any case where tactfulness is called for, frankness (being frank) wouldn't count as virtuous or praiseworthy—quite the contrary. And in that case when one acts tactfully in response to situational ethical requirements, one's lack of frankness will simply not be open to ethical criticism. Now recent discussions of moral dilemmas and moral cost should make us suspicious of these Aristotelian ideas; but I would like to articulate my own suspicions by mentioning a case where it seems to me the Aristotelian take on frankness vs. tact doesn't hold water.[12]

Imagine that you have a friend who is always getting himself into abusive relationships that eventually turn sour and become intolerable for him. You have previously pointed this out to the friend; but he says he has no idea what you are talking about and enters into new and abusive relationships without seeming to have benefited in any way from what you or other friends have told him. (He also isn't willing to talk to a therapist about his problems.) So imagine further that your friend comes to you after his latest relationship has broken up and deplores the awful bad luck (as he puts it) that has led him once again into an unhappy and unsuccessful relationship. But he has no idea how abusively he has been treated (in this relationship or the others) and simply asks you, implores you, to tell him why you think this sort of thing is always happening to him. "What am I doing wrong?" he asks. However, you have told him in the past that he has a tendency to accept abuse, and you don't believe there is any chance he is going to change his ways or his thinking. (Assume he is an older man.) So what do you say to him?

Well, since he is imploring you to tell him what you think, you might (once again) be frank with him and explain the role he himself plays in bringing about these disasters (e.g., by accepting abuse, from the start, in the relationships he enters into). But you have every reason to believe (let's assume) that if you say this to him, it won't really register with him or make any difference to his future behavior; whereas, *if you just commiserate with him and say that you don't understand how he can be so unlucky,* he will feel much relieved or consoled by what he takes (or would like to take) to be your understandingness and what is clearly your sympathy vis-à-vis his situation. So what do you do? I don't think there is a right answer to this question. In other cases, there is reason to choose tact over frankness or frankness over tact, but in the present case I think ethical considerations are finely balanced, and one's eventual choice of either the tactful or the frank thing to say may show more about oneself than about the ethical issues operating in the particular situation I have described.

Moreover, and this is the main point, whatever choice one makes will be less than ethically ideal. If one is tactful, one will have compromised one's frankness (or honesty) with a friend who is imploring one to be frank, and to that extent one is open to the (mildish) criticisms that what one has done is less than ideal and that, more particularly, one has shown oneself to be somewhat lacking in the virtue of frankness. By the same token, if one is frank, one will have acted in a way that isn't entirely kind (or tactful), and, once again, what one has done will count as less than ethically ideal. Or so at least it seems to me. But if this take on the situation I have described is correct, the doctrine of the unity of the virtues is at the very least called into question; and, again more importantly for present purposes, we can see that—just as sadism and masochism war against one another as instincts according to Freudian theory—frankness and tact war against one another *as ethical virtues*. For if one is frank in the situation described above, one will be *lacking* with respect to tact or kindness; and if one is tactful, one will be *lacking* with respect to frankness or honesty (with or toward a friend). Aristotelianism cannot admit this kind of ethical possibility; and in the light of what we have said about the previous example, we can conclude that neither frankness nor tact can count univocally and unqualifiedly as a virtue. In that case, and on analogy with what Freud says about sadism and masochism, we can say instead that frankness and tact are both *partial virtues* and, therefore, *partial values*. For these two qualities are paired opposites, and in some situations where they clash, acting on either one of them will be ethically less than ideal.[13]

There are no exact precedents for the notion of a partial virtue in the literature of ethics. (As we shall see in more detail in what follows, previous work on moral dilemmas and moral cost doesn't in fact move us toward the idea of partial values and necessary imperfection.). But the idea of partial values not only helps us understand the paired opposition between frankness and tact, but can, I shall now show, be useful in clarifying some of the issues of gender that we have discussed above. I believe, for example, that security and adventure are best conceived as mutually opposed (and paired) *partial goods*, and that the opposition between the related virtues of prudence and boldness (or adventurousness) is likewise an opposition between what are best conceived as (paired) partial virtues.[14] Similarly, a life of careerism (in the best sense) may be a good life, but it undercuts or lessens the possibilities of good relationship; and the same, of course, holds in reverse. And rather than say that career success or achievement is an unqualified or unconditional good thing (in life), I think we should say that it is a partial good. For similar reasons, we should say that being involved in or cultivating good close loving personal (and, especially, familial) relationships is not univocally a good thing—since it detracts from the possibility or likelihood of significant achievements in a challenging career. Rather, it is a partial good, one that vies with or against this other partial good (and can be seen as paired with it).[15] And there is a contrast, therefore, to be drawn here between goods like affiliation and career success, on the one hand, and wisdom and aesthetic pleasure on the other. These latter don't seem to oppose either each other or other things we think of as fundamental human goods, and so there is no reason to regard them as anything less than personal goods simpliciter. So the objective lists of human goods that have been offered in fact contain some merely partial goods and other goods that are good in an unqualified way.[16]

Now this way of seeing things stands in marked contrast with the views or attitudes we earlier attributed to patriarchy. According to patriarchal attitudes or values, career success is good for men and not for women. But using the notion of a partial good we can oppose such patriarchal notions in the name of feminist ethical ideals. The feminist thinks careers should be as open to women as to men and so would want to repudiate the patriarchal or sexist notion that careers and/or career success are gender-relative goods. But feminists have not been as clear as I think they might be on what they positively think about the choice between career and an emphasis on affiliative goods. They have seen that women have to choose whether to give themselves fully to their careers and have seen that doing so will or can make it impossible to fully realize affiliative goods or values. They have wondered whether one can somehow balance and compromise these goods, and have often deplored the fact that men don't seem to face a similar hard choice.

But men in fact do have to face such a choice. If they go completely with their careers, they miss out on some deep affiliative values. They end up as "distant fathers" and "part-time husbands," and even if such men aren't capable of recognizing the grave loss that that entails in and for their lives, many women can. And that, perhaps, is why so many fewer women find it easy or acceptable to give themselves entirely to their careers.[17] The idea that the good of close, loving relationship(s) and the good of career success are (merely) partial goods that are equally relevant to men and women enables us to correct, and tells us what is wrong with, the patriarchal notion that these goods are (differently) gender-relative. And it also helps us to see why the choice between career and family/affiliation is such a wrenching and difficult one (even if or when men don't see it as such).[18]

And the idea of partial goods and virtues also helps us understand what is wrong with sexist values in other (though related) areas. The sexist thinks that women need security in a way that men don't; he (or she) values adventure for men, but not for women. And the same sexism sees boldness and adventurousness as male virtues but not as female ones. But, once again, the idea of partial values—of partial goods and virtues—enables us to articulate the or a feminist position about these matters. The feminist can and, I believe, should claim, rather, that both boldness/adventurousness and prudence are partial virtues that are equally relevant to men and women. Both men and women have to make the difficult choice or difficult choices between them; and, of course, they also have to choose between security and adventure.[19] And whatever they choose, they will lose out to a certain extent. If they choose security, they will miss out on adventure—and vice versa. If they choose prudence, they will seem to be ethically lacking in the virtue of boldness or adventurousness, but the completely bold and adventurous person will by the same token, I think, seem to us to be lacking in something we also think well of, to be lacking in a certain valued kind of prudence.[20]

In addition, the idea that we are here confronted with partial virtues and partial goods that are equally relevant to both men and women stands in marked contrast with the patriarchal opinion (as we have articulated it) that these virtues and goods are gender-relative. The idea of partial values thus allows us to *get beyond* the invidious gender-relativity of sexist thought and traditions, but of course one pays an intellectual/ethical price for recognizing the force and validity of this notion. For it makes us see that things can/could never be as good for us as we might wish them to be and that we ourselves could never be as virtuous, as admirable, as we would ideally like to be. But at least it makes this admission or concession in a gender-neutral and nonsexist way, and to that extent it exemplifies and furthers the feminist ethical vision of equality and justice between men and women.

But let me finally mention one further area in which the idea of partial values allows us to go beyond and in new terms criticize patriarchal/sexist attitudes and values. We spoke above about sexual activity and pleasure and noted the patriarchal/sexist view that for women, but not for men, these goods depend on the accompanying good of love and/or personal commitment. But young women these days (and over recent decades) have more and more explored the possibilities of sexual activity and pleasure that are based less on feeling and commitment than on a sense of (sexual) adventure, a desire for novelty and, yes, risk that has more typically characterized male sexuality in the past. And why not? In feminist terms, what's saucy for the gander should be saucy for the goose, and I would suggest, therefore, that there may (eventually) not be any gender relativity involved in the issue of whether sex has to be accompanied by love.

Does this then mean that sexuality is some sort of partial value? Well, I wouldn't put it quite that way. Sexual adventuring runs very deeply contrary to what we might call committed sexuality, i.e., the kind of sexuality that springs from and looks to some sort of foundation or inspiration in loving mutual commitment.[21] So maybe these two forms of sexuality and sexual pleasure can really be seen, then, as (paired) partial goods; and maybe that is what a more enlightened, feminist view of sexuality should say about the issues and values involved here. To think in this way is surely to go beyond the more confining and traditional patriarchal view that uncommitted sex is fine (and permissible) for men, but not for women. So, once again, the idea of partial values seems to enable us to advance beyond sexist notions, and the combination of that idea with the ideas of ethical dependency and gender-relativity that we used to articulate patriarchal views earlier on in this chapter thus allows us to say *in distinctively philosophical terms* how sexist attitudes invidiously differ from the ideas and ideals of a truly feminist ethics.[22]

CONCLUSION

Where patriarchy sees gender-relative dependent or nondependent values, feminist ethical thought sees or can see paired partial values that are equally relevant to men and women. That is one main conclusion of this first chapter; and, of course, it summarizes a variety of different illustrations and arguments concerning human goods and human virtues. Many, indeed most, of the particular examples I used in discussing patriarchal values and attitudes are familiar from the literature of feminism and more generally. But I have attempted to generalize and unify those examples in philosophical/ethical terms and to show, again in very general philosophical/ethical terms, how very *differently* patriarchy and feminism see or conceive those examples (and others like them).

Of course, we know that patriarchy (or sexist traditions and institutions) characteristically treats girls and women in disrespectful and unjust ways: they are deprived of opportunities and privileges that are accorded to males; their ideas and their complaints aren't seriously listened to; one could go on and on. But the present chapter has indicated another characteristic feature of patriarchy, the fact that it tends to see various personal goods and virtues in gender-relative ways; and I have argued further that a less biased and more accurate *postpatriarchal* and *feminist* view of things requires us to see various goods and virtues as partial rather than as gender-relative. Given these conclusions, it would, I think, be interesting and fruitful to be able to say how the two just-mentioned characteristic features of patriarchy interrelate or interact, but that is a large topic that is probably best left to another occasion.

What, then, about the idea of different moral voices with which we began, the idea, familiar from Gilligan and a host of subsequent discussions, that there are two different basic ways—only very roughly correlated with gender—in which people approach moral issues? How do our present findings, which largely refer to ethical issues that are not specifically moral, compare with Gilligan's and other views about moral differences?

Well, for one thing, what we have said here bears directly on feminist thought and values, and sheer talk of different moral voices doesn't bear a relevance to feminism on its face. The ethics of care that Gilligan mentioned and that was subsequently developed in the work of Nel Noddings and many others has been accused, in fact, of being retrograde and unhelpful from a feminist standpoint, because it sets up an ideal of caring that women are more likely to respond to than men, thus leaving women (once again) with an unequal burden of efforts and tasks in relation to men.[23] However, the/an ethics of care can be and has sometimes been deployed in a specifically feminist direction that allows one to *criticize* patriarchal/sexist attitudes and traditions (and whole societies)—I am thinking here of Gilligan's *In a Different Voice* and also, in fact, of my own work and that of Virginia Held and others over the past two decades.[24] A more specific and thoroughgoing comparison between care ethics and the concepts and conclusions of the present study must await a later chapter in the present book, but what should at least be clear at this point is that something like the idea of different voices can be applied to ethical topics outside the narrower moral sphere that Gilligan and many care ethicists have focused on. For better or worse, the issue of gender differences is as relevant to our understanding of ordinary human goods and (nonmoral) virtues as it has been to specifically moral questions.

But our discussion in this first chapter hasn't just been about issues of patriarchy vs. feminism. We have developed a notion of partial values that applies in a nonsexist fashion, but that also implies that things can never be as good for us as we ideally would like and that we ourselves cannot be as virtuous or admirable as we might hope to be. If, for example, we are adventurous, we not only aren't prudent, but can be seen as *lacking* in prudence, and if, we are prudent, there will seem to be something less than perfectly admirable about our lack of adventurousness. And so on through the various other examples we have described. One natural reaction to these results would be to say they show that "one cannot have everything" or that "one cannot have it all," but in fact such claims are, in the strictest terms, somewhat misleading. As will be explained in subsequent chapters, it doesn't immediately or obviously follow from the claim that one cannot have all the virtues or all the good things in life that one's life cannot be perfect in virtue or happiness. But our notion of a partial good or virtue does imply/entail such imperfection, and the examples we have discussed were all intended to show that perfection either of the virtues or of personal happiness or well-being is impossible.[25] It is high time, though, for us to focus *more explicitly* and *more exclusively* on the Berlin thesis that perfection is impossible.

Chapter 2

The Impossibility of Perfection

In the previous chapter, I considered some issues about patriarchy and its (ethical) problems, and the notion of a partial value was brought in to help us arrive at a postpatriarchal, feminist ethical picture of the nature of certain virtues and certain goods. Partial virtues are organized (if that is the right word) into pairs of opposing character traits, and exactly the same, mutatis mutandis, can be said of partial personal goods. But our discussion didn't seek to fully generalize these (supposed or argued-for) facts in philosophical terms. The focus, as I have just indicated and as was obvious, was on one limited, though very important, area of ethical thought and action.

However, in order to make the case for the existence of partial values, I had to use some illustrative examples that are not specifically relevant to feminist ethical issues. The opposition between tact and frankness characterizes certain areas or aspects of human life quite independently, I think, of questions about sexism and how sexism can be overcome. And here at the beginning of the present chapter, I would like to reconsider that opposition of (what I have committed us to calling) partial virtues. If we do so, we shall see that the issues raised in the last chapter and what we said there by way of treating those issues have a much more general philosophical application and import than anything explicitly said in that previous discussion. That discussion directly bears on Aristotelian views about the virtues (and about human good), and most particularly, or at least in the first instance, it bears on the central Aristotelian doctrine of the unity of the virtues. If frankness and tact conflict in important ways and yet both count as virtues, the idea of the unity of the virtues is at the very least called into question. But beyond that very specific doctrine there is also the Aristotelian and neo-Aristotelian idea that morality, or right and wrong, can be anchored in the notion of what an individual possessing all the ethical virtues (which is what Aristotelians think ideal or perfect virtue consists in) would do and feel. And I want to argue here that that notion and the assumptions on which it rests are also deeply flawed. The ideal of having all the virtues and the ideal of ethical perfection (as I have mentioned previously, they turn out not to be the same thing) are in fact absolutely unrealizable.

Now I am not the first person in recent years or decades to have suggested that perfection (of the virtues) is (in principle or noncontingently) impossible. This is a familiar, a major, theme in the work of the late Isaiah Berlin. But Berlin really doesn't *argue* for the impossibility of perfection. On the basis of a few of roughly described examples, he just *says* that perfection is impossible; and I think we want to do more than that. We want or should want a clearer analysis of the issues and better arguments, before we agree with Berlin that perfection is impossible. (Of course, once we have an argument or arguments for that conclusion, we can credit Berlin with having had an important *insight*.)

So I want in what follows to provide (or talk again about) some more carefully crafted examples and offer a further or reinforced argument for the idea that imperfection—whether of virtue or of happiness—is inevitable. And we will need to centrally consider the Aristotelian idea of the unity of the virtues, the idea that in order to fully possess any given virtue, one has to have them all. Many philosophers in the West have questioned this thesis, but if we can show that perfection is impossible, we can undercut that thesis more deeply than it has previously been possible to do—and we in fact end up with ideas that are *diametrically opposed* to the picture of virtue we associate with Aristotle (and with the unity thesis).

I want to begin (again) with an example we discussed in the previous chapter. Everyone recognizes that the virtues of frankness and tact (or tactfulness) stand in some kind of opposition. They are naturally seen as paired and opposed because there are so many situations in which a choice has to be made between being tactful and being frank, situations in which one cannot exemplify both of these qualities of character. Now Aristotelians want to say that whenever there is a choice between tact and frankness, there is a *right* choice in the matter, a choice not open to moral or ethical criticism. On their view (and speaking rather roughly), frankness and tact never clash *as virtues*: in any case, e.g., where tact is ethically called for, frankness wouldn't count as virtuous or praiseworthy—quite the contrary. So the Aristotelian will say that whenever one acts tactfully in response to (valid) situational ethical requirements, one's lack of frankness will simply not be open to ethical criticism. And similarly mutatis mutandis for acting frankly, when that is what a given situation calls for.

But as I argued in the last chapter, putative virtues like tact and frankness are not as well behaved as the Aristotelian picture of the virtues assumes, and the example I gave of the friend who is always getting involved in masochistic relationships but can't face that fact helps to explain why. Whatever choice one makes in that situation will be less than ethically ideal. If one is tactful, one will have compromised one's frankness with a friend who is begging one to be frank (and truthful), and to that extent one is open to the (mild) criticisms that what one has done is less than ideal and that, more particularly, one has shown oneself to be somewhat lacking in and with respect to the virtue of frankness (or honesty). By the same token, if one is frank, one will have acted toward one's friend in a way that isn't entirely kind (or tactful), and, once again, what one has done will count as less than ethically ideal. Or so, at least, it seems to me. But if this take on the situation I have described is correct, the Aristotelian doctrine of the unity of the virtues is very definitely called into question. For it will seem that one cannot possess the quality of perfect frankness and the quality of perfect tactfulness at one and the same time, and it will also seem that the virtues of tact and frankness conflict and/or war against one another *as ethical virtues.*

Defenders of the unity thesis have argued that when there is a choice between what are ordinarily considered virtues, one of those virtues trumps the other, and a failure to act on that other in no way, therefore, show any lack with respect to that virtue or with respect to virtue in general. If I have to choose between mercy and justice and if in this case, justice really should prevail, then if I do the just thing, I will not have shown myself to lack or be lacking in the virtue of mercy because it can still be true of me that I act mercifully whenever *that* virtue is appropriate or called for. Such examples don't undercut the unity thesis according to most contemporary Aristotelians, and I think I can agree about that. But the choice between tact and frankness is not like the one between mercy and justice as just described. In the former situation there is no one right answer, no path of action required by valid ethical values, and one will be ethically somewhat compromised, act in a way that is ethically to some extent unsatisfactory, no matter what one does. This is a far cry from what Aristotelians (and I) want to say about a situation in which the virtue of justice clearly trumps the virtue of mercy.[1]

On the unity thesis, in order to fully have one virtue, one has to have them all, and since we have seen via our example that someone who is completely tactful cannot also be completely frank, that thesis is very much open to question. But one can hold that ethical perfection, perfection with respect to the virtues, is possible without holding the unity thesis—one simply, or not so simply, needs to say that the virtues, even if they can be instantiated separately from one another to a substantial extent, can in principle be combined in one individual. If one says that, one will presumably then also say that such a person—someone combining all of the virtues—would be as ethically excellent as it is possible to be and count, in fact, as ethically perfect. But whatever choice one is inclined to make in the situation where tact clashes with frankness, one will be open to ethical criticism, and that, of course, entails that one will be less than perfect (or perfectly admirable). It doesn't immediately follow, however, that one will be less ethically admirable than it is possible to be, since, given the impossibility of virtue-perfection, the tactful person who is criticizable for not being fully frank may be as ethically admirable as it is possible to be—and similarly for someone inclined or disposed to be frank in the situation I described. For all I have said or want to say, they may, on grounds of their other admirable character traits and despite their ethical imperfection, be as *close* to ethical perfection as it is possible to be.

Now the situation I described is far from unique. There are other putative virtues that clash in the way that tact and frankness (sometimes) do, and I shall say more about (some of) them in a moment. But as a group such examples illustrate and argue for the main general claim I want to make in this chapter and in this book, the claim that perfection is impossible. Virtue is a dispositional notion—having a virtue is (roughly) having a disposition or tendency to act (and feel) in certain ways in various situations that may or may not arise. So even if the case I have mentioned and others to be mentioned hereafter are all hypothetical, they indicate, e.g., that there is a conflict or clash between complete or perfect frankness and complete or perfect tact as ethical dispositions. And that is all that is needed to show that one cannot be perfect in respect to virtue or the virtues.[2]

This "cannot" is intended as a strong "cannot." I am not just talking about human beings, but about any intelligent creature or creatures that could confront the kind of subtle, ethically important choice we described in our example. Indeed, if time allowed, I think it could be shown that even God or a god couldn't be ethically perfect. This goes against a long tradition of Western theological and religious thought, but I think the example used just a moment ago could readily be reconfigured in such a way as to target the familiar idea that God must be and can be perfect (or perfectly good).[3]

I also believe that some important *additional* conclusions can be drawn from the example of tact vs. frankness and others like it. But before we do that, let me just mention one other familiar case where virtues clash, a case that, once again, can be used to argue for the impossibility of perfection and the falsity of Aristotle's unity thesis. As I mentioned in the last chapter, some philosophers use the term "prudence" to cover just about all of practical rationality. But in ordinary English "prudence" refers (at least partly) to a tendency to play it safe with respect to long-term practical issues. People who take (unnecessary) risks with their safety or future well-being don't count as prudent, and yet anyone who is adventurous in the way they live or pursue their careers precisely does take such risks. So even if we think prudence is a virtue, we also think that adventurousness, a certain kind of boldness in practical affairs, is also something of a virtue. For the spirit of adventure is something we admire, even (or, sometimes, especially) when we ourselves insist on being prudent about our futures (or the futures of those we love).

And one can't (overall) be both a prudent person and an adventurous one. Prudence and adventurousness clash as dispositions with respect to any given area or subject matter and with respect to our lives more generally. One can't possess both these virtues, and, more importantly, one can't possess both these virtues *as virtues*. Nor can we easily say that one of them takes precedence as a virtue over the other, and in situations where they clash (and in fact they clash much more generally or holistically than tact and frankness do), one is to some degree ethically criticizable or lacking whichever way one chooses or is inclined to go. If one chooses or is inclined toward adventurousness and risk, one is criticizable for one's lack of (the virtue of) prudence; and if one chooses or is inclined toward being prudent, one is automatically lacking in something we find admirable or praiseworthy. So this pair of opposed virtues illustrates the impossibility of perfection and casts doubt on Aristotle's unity thesis in much the same way that our previous opposed pair of tact and frankness does.

However, I promised just a moment ago to draw some significant additional conclusions from our discussion, and we are now, I think, in a good position to do that. And let me begin with a point of methodology. In a famous article called "The Causal Theory of Perception," H. P. Grice sought to show that certain Wittgensteinian theses about the use of language were mistaken: in particular, he sought to show that when we say that something looks as if it is red, we don't have to be committed to holding that it actually *is* red—even though that implication usually attaches to our saying that something looks (as if it is) red.[4] In developing his argument, Grice didn't just rely on certain examples and certain subtle (and, to my mind, entirely justified) intuitions about those examples. He developed a somewhat larger theory of linguistic usage in which to imbed what he had to say about the Wittgensteinian examples and ideas.

And I propose to do something like that here. I want to show you that we can take the examples just used (and others analogous to them) to develop or work toward a larger theory about the nature of virtue and the virtues. If we can (begin to) do that, there will, I think, be more reason, more motivation, for us to rely on all the examples in arguing against various central tenets of Aristotelianism. After all, Thomas Kuhn tells us that it takes a theory to beat a theory, and the case against Aristotelianism will be more forceful, therefore, if we have something systematic and theoretical (though less neat or unified) to set against it (or replace it with).[5] And it is the notion of a partial virtue or value that moves us toward the more systematic picture that our examples cry out for and help to provide. Frankness and tactfulness are opposed partial virtues; and the same can be said about prudence and adventurousness; and in the last chapter we also spoke of various opposed and partial personal goods: e.g., adventure vs. security, career/creative fulfillment vs. fulfillment in (one's) intimate relationships. Now the reader may have some doubts about these last examples or, indeed, about what we have been saying about partial virtues. But I will discuss some further doubts and worries in the next chapter, and for the moment I ask the reader just to take the ideas I have been advancing on approval. For the moment, I just want to see—and I hope readers will be interested in my showing them— what the theoretical implications of those ideas may be.

In the previous chapter I argued that frankness and tact are both *partial virtues*; for these two qualities of character are paired opposites, and in some situations where they clash, acting on either of them will be ethically less than ideal. Similarly, prudence and adventurousness/boldness are paired opposites that deeply clash with respect to any human life (or period of human life), and so, once again, we can, and I believe we should, regard each of these character traits as a partial virtue, rather than as a virtue simpliciter or unqualifiedly.

But notice how this takes us beyond the core idea that virtues inevitably (to some extent) clash or conflict. Such a claim refers to the incompatibility of certain supposed or putative virtues, and to that extent it is merely or purely relational. It speaks, for example, to how frankness relates to tact, but it doesn't say anything about tact itself or in itself as a virtue. But Berlin's thinking and our previous discussion take us beyond merely characterizing how certain traits relate to one another and involve a further conclusion or conclusions about those traits taken singly or in themselves. They tell us that we should regard those traits as in themselves necessary to perfect virtue and/or as partial virtues rather than as virtues simpliciter, and this further move has a theoretical significance beyond anything that is immediately at issue when one (merely) talks of a clash or conflict between virtues (or personal goods). Perhaps the best way to see this would be to invoke the only other *philosophical* discussion of (something like) the notion of partiality I have been describing that I know of. And it is a discussion, interestingly enough, that lies entirely outside the field of ethics: Hartry Field's well-known treatment of the idea of partial signification or denotation.[6]

Field introduced the notion of partial signification in an article that considered W. V. Quine's views about the signification or denotation (or reference) of common nouns. Quine had argued that an anthropologist in the field seeking to translate some hitherto untranslated language would presumably point to various objects and try to elicit from some native speaker the word in that language for that kind of object. But as Quine noted, when the anthropologist points, say, to a rabbit, he is also always pointing to some undetached rabbit part, and since an undetached rabbit part isn't the same thing as a rabbit, there is a problem as to whether the native speaker who, say, utters "gavagai" in response to the anthropologist's ostension of a rabbit means by "gavagai" "rabbit" or "undetached rabbit part" (or even some other thing that is connected with rabbits but doesn't mean or refer to the same kind of thing as our "rabbit"). With respect to such a situation of "radical translation," it is going to remain indeterminate whether the native speaker means one thing or the other by "gavagai," and so, according to Quine, radical translation is radically underdetermined.

Now I don't propose to defend or further describe Quine's views in this area. The important point for present purposes is that Quine focuses on the fact or assumption that there are inconsistent hypotheses regarding the meaning of "gavagai" and claims that there is no way in principle to determine that "gavagai" denotes rabbits rather than rabbit parts (or the fusion of all rabbits). But Field takes these ideas in a new direction. Rather than focus on the mutual inconsistency of certain hypotheses concerning what "gavagai" really denotes or signifies, he introduces the idea that in the circumstances described by Quine, "gavagai" *partially signifies (or denotes)* rabbits and *also partially signifies (or denotes)* rabbit parts. (Similarly for the rabbit fusion, the "mereological object" that has all rabbits as its parts.) So rather than focus on the inconsistency of certain claims or theories about the signification of "gavagai" (together with other linguistic items), he proceeds to claim that "gavagai" partially denotes *each* of the entities that one or another of the mutually inconsistent theories or claims says "gavagai" unqualifiedly denotes. Rather than limit himself, like Quine, to speaking of how certain assumptions about the signification of "gavagai" (or any other general term) clash, he offers a single view of the signification of "gavagai." And this is like what we have done in offering a single view of the value status, say, of frankness as a partial value, rather than (merely) pointing out how that value clashes with others. (And just as we can talk of other values than frankness in that particular light, so too can Field apply his approach to *every other general term.*)

Thus the historically and currently somewhat familiar idea that certain virtues or values clash or conflict may to some extent point toward the conclusion that perfection is impossible, but it clearly doesn't itself tell us everything that can usefully be said about the (putative) virtues and goods we want to talk about. And the further step we have taken, involving as it does the concept of a partial value, can perhaps be better understood in the light of the parallel that can be drawn with Field's idea of partial denotation. To call some trait a partial virtue is not only to make the relational claim that it conflicts with a certain other (partial) virtue or virtues, but to characterize it as being in itself *so ethically important* that no one can be entirely admirable or perfectly virtuous in its absence.[7] And something parallel can, obviously, be said about partial goods and what we have said in describing them.[8]

However, Field also pointed out that his approach to denotation avoids a certain relativity that Quine's treatment has as one of its consequences. (The relevance of this to my own discussion of partial values was first brought to my attention by Otavio Bueno.) On Quine's indeterminacy view, the hypothesis or theory that "gavagai" refers to rabbits is true only relative to certain basic assumptions about translation, to a certain particular scheme of translation.[9] Relative to some other scheme, "gavagai" signifies undetached rabbit parts and relative to yet another, it signifies the fusion of all (whole) rabbits. But on Field's account, "gavagai" partially signifies rabbits, partially signifies undetached rabbit parts, etc., and this assumption, this fact, is not relative but absolute. And something similar can be said about the view of partial virtues and values introduced here. That frankness is (only) a partial virtue and that tact is a countervailing or opposed partial virtue is not relative to further assumptions, but counts as an absolute or objective ethical fact, given what we have said earlier. And to that extent there is no relativity in our account of the virtues—we are not committed to some sort of ethical relativism, far from it.

To say that frankness or adventurousness is a partial virtue is *not* to say that its ethical status is somehow relative to our cultural or social attitudes and beliefs about the importance and value of these traits, and even though I think our ethical intuitions about various cases give us reason to believe that frankness and adventurousness are partial virtues rather than virtues simpliciter, this is an epistemic/epistemological claim that simply doesn't translate into the relativistic idea or thesis that our cultural/social/intellectual attitudes/beliefs are what *makes* these traits and others into (partial) virtues. So the more complex and (one could say) richer picture of human virtue(s) that results when one admits the idea of a partial virtue is not committed to any sort of relativism. We may be impugning the Aristotelian picture of virtue and the virtues, but what we are substituting purports to be just as ethically objective as Aristotelianism has always claimed to be. Of course, we haven't yet spelled out the details of the new and more complicated picture of virtue and personal good, but I hope to do more and more of that throughout the remainder of the present book.

Now what I am trying to do—and what many, many other philosophers, including Aristotle, have also attempted to do—involves a certain risk. To avoid relativism and be willing to talk of objective values—even qualified ones—is to be willing to speak of certain people's views about what is good for us or what counts as a virtue as mistaken. And I am and have been willing to do that. I have said that patriarchal views of what is good for us are mistaken, for example, and I have specifically implied that those males who have been raised to think of relationship values as insignificant or relatively unimportant will tend to lack something important in their lives. A person who never has any close personal relationships is missing out on something good (in life) even if (because of the way they were raised or educated) they don't know or even suspect that that is the case. Similarly, someone who never ever has any sexual enjoyment is also missing out on something good, even if, again, they never suspect that they are missing something. Or so, at least, I am inclined to think. (A priest might well agree if he thought he had had to sacrifice something of some value in order to take up his higher calling.)

But isn't this arrogant? What right do I or anyone else have to claim to know more than others about what is good for us or a virtue? Well, moral philosophers frequently argue for specific moral views that they know many others—not just moral philosophers, but ordinary folk—will disagree with. It's part of the business, their business as moral philosophers, to do that sort of thing, and, of course, in doing so they assume a certain epistemological/epistemic (and ethical) burden and risk. In order to claim to know more or differently, they had better pay their dues in thinking more (and better) about moral matters than other people do or previous philosophers have. (Often this involves some standing on the shoulders of giants.) I don't think my situation in philosophizing about human goods and nonmoral virtues is really or substantially any different from that of someone doing normative moral philosophy in the strictest sense of the term. What we all do may sometimes and in some cases be arrogant—and certainly it may often be mistaken. But for philosophers not to pursue these issues and not to be willing to make judgments about other people's errors concerning what is good or virtuous in people's (or their own) lives own is to risk something other than arrogance. It is—if I may put it this way—to risk a kind of cowardice, to risk the (valid) accusation that we were so afraid of our moral shadows that we weren't willing to point out or argue for values that humankind has some reason to want to get clearer about. Someone who isn't willing to say that patriarchy is unjust may not (to that extent) be arrogant, but they can be accused of blindness, insensitivity, pusillanimity, and even, probably, of injustice. And if it turns out that perfect happiness is impossible but that saying so rains on some people's parades, that could well be because the impossibility of perfection is, at least for some of us, an unpleasant truth that it takes a certain amount of courage to face or even consider. All the more reason for the *philosopher* to push on with these ideas—even if they make or will make many people uncomfortable.

And speaking of unpleasantness, I think I should at this point mention (what strike me as) some rather intriguing, but also at least somewhat *unfortunate or unpleasant* further implications of some of the things I said earlier. A parent who is neither prudent nor adventurous is certainly not a very good model for their children. But we have argued that a parent who is prudent in their attitude toward important issues in life is flawed to some degree as a person, and the same can be said for one who is adventurous about such matters. That much follows from our previous analysis. But then *any* parent will be somewhat flawed or imperfect as a(n ethical) model for their children, and being a model for one's children is part of what parenting is all about. It follows that no one can (in principle) be a perfect parent, even if they are as good a parent as it is possible to be. It follows, further, that no *family* can be perfect (as a family); and since the family is in some (possibly nonpolitical) sense the foundational or cornerstone institution of any society, the notion of a perfect society is also in principle unrealizable. However, this may not imply that perfect *justice* or a perfectly *just* society is impossible. I can't think of any reasoning along the above lines to argue for *this* conclusion—though one can't be sure that no one will ever be able to give a good argument for it. Still, the implications of our discussion for our understanding of "family values" *are* pretty clear. And those implications are somewhat unpleasant or possibly (for some at least) disappointing.

But having said all that we have said in the past two chapters, it is time to retrace our steps. I want to spell out more of the implications of our approach, but in order to do so effectively, I think we first have to consider various objections to what I have already said. I want to do this in the next chapter, before we then go on (in subsequent chapters) to widen our perspective on the issues I have been raising and the approach I have been sketching.

Chapter 3

Alternative Views

Isaiah Berlin's idea that perfection of the virtues is impossible in principle seems to have largely slipped off the radar screen in recent moral philosophy. Under the influence of reviving Aristotelian virtue ethics, most of the focus of recent discussions of virtue has been on Aristotelian views that stand diametrically opposed (in a sense to be given fuller explication in what follows) to Berlin's conception of (the) virtue(s). In particular, the Aristotelian idea that the virtues constitute a unity, that one has to possess all the virtues in order to have any single one of them, has some currency at present. I have not criticized that view directly up till now and I don't propose to do it now. But my defense of a Berlinian conception of the virtues is implicitly a critique of the idea of the unity of the virtues, and if that conception can be made plausible, that will itself, I think, constitute the best possible argument against the unity thesis. Of course, on the face of it, the unity thesis seems wildly counterintuitive and goes completely against our prephilosophical ideas about virtue. But some forceful and interesting things have recently been said in defense of the unity of the virtues, and if we are to counter the (if I may say) attractive picture of virtue that the Aristotelian unity thesis offers us, I think we need to show how a realistic sense of the richness and complexity of ethical phenomena forces us to go in a quite different direction.

But has our previous discussion really accomplished that? Quite possibly not. I have discussed various examples and given a certain interpretation of their implications or significance, but I think other interpretations are possible, and that means that there are some ways of questioning our previous conclusions that we need to focus on and answer—in order for the defense here of a Berlin-like view of the virtues and human happiness to really be successful. And I want to begin by considering two fairly recent discussions of the virtues that make use of examples quite similar to the one we mentioned about the friend who is always getting into abusive relationships. Both Gary Watson and A. D. M. Walker discuss such examples, but show no tendency to move in the direction of Berlin's ideas.[1] Watson, in fact, never (completely) abandons the Aristotelian unity thesis, and, interestingly enough, even though Walker does reject that thesis and move in the *direction* of Berlin's views, he stops well short of the conclusion that virtue-perfection is impossible. I believe, in any case, that focusing on these related discussions can help us see why it is necessary to focus on the *particular* (*kinds of*) *examples* I examined in previous chapters, if one wants to make a strong case for the Berlin thesis.

Then, after we have considered Watson's and Walker's views, I want to consider some presumed or putative counterexamples to the claims I have made about the partiality of certain (personal) goods and virtues. For example, to hold that security is a partial good is to assume that one cannot be perfectly or ideally happy or well-off during some period of one's life in which adventure is absent; and someone might claim that a life in which there has been an earlier period of abundant adventure can be perfectly or ideally wonderful during some later period of nonadventurous safety and security.[2] Arguments of this sort challenge our earlier views, and I want to consider a number of such arguments (or counterexamples) later in this chapter. But first let us look at Watson and Walker.

Watson's is the earlier and the more Aristotelian of these two discussions. His article "Virtues in Excess" begins by speaking of the "straight view" of the virtues according to which various virtues can be possessed "in excess": as, for example, when someone is too honest or too generous. But Watson notes that "the straight view . . . sever[s] the connection we ordinarily suppose there to be between developing a virtue and moral [or ethical] improvement." And he concludes that the straight view is too simple to be plausible. Watson then moves on to consider what he calls the "due concern view" of the virtues, according to which a given virtue functioning as a virtue cannot lead to ethically bad actions. He takes it that this commits one to Aristotle's unity thesis, and he spends much of the rest of his paper talking about what can be said for and against the unity thesis and/or the due concern view. Along the way, however, he mentions an example that involves the "choice" between frankness and tact, and I think we need to look at that example because Watson doesn't take it to undercut the unity thesis or point us toward Berlin's views.[3] Without knowing more, we or the reader may wonder whether this gives us reason to be suspicious of what I said earlier based on an example that is at least somewhat similar to Watson's.

Watson's example involves someone A who asks two people B and C for an opinion of his book. B is said to be characteristically more frank and straightforward than C, and C is said to be more sensitive to others' feelings, more tactful, than B—and each responds accordingly. Watson says that each of B and C may be admirable in his or her own way; and he holds that in other circumstances, circumstances where there is a definite right choice between tact and frankness, both will or could do what was ethically required of them. But Watson treats the situation he describes as ethically "indeterminate" and holds that such cases reveal the moral/ethical individuality of individuals who might in other circumstances always do the same morally required thing. The difference of ethical "style"—as between frankness and tact—comes out in the case he introduces, but Watson makes it clear that (he thinks that) the two individuals needn't differ with respect to their virtuousness and also seems to assume that neither style is incompatible with *perfect* virtue. (He says each is admirable in his own way and never hints that either need be less than *completely* admirable, that either need be ethically criticizable in any way.)[4]

Watson ends with the unity thesis still, as he sees it, intact. He has mentioned many interesting problems with spelling out that thesis, but doesn't treat any of them as showing the nonviability of the thesis. And I certainly want to grant that the example Watson gave doesn't particularly lead us toward Berlinian conclusions. But that is exactly why I chose the particular example I used in previous chapters to argue for Berlin's thesis. It is different enough and specific enough to allow one to have the sense that whatever is done in the described circumstances will be to some degree ethically unsatisfactory, and Watson's case is not of the right kind, and in any event isn't spelled out in sufficient detail, to make one feel that something ethically important is lost whether one responds as *B* does or as *C* does. I don't think the unproblematic character of Watson's example as he describes it at all challenges what we have said about a somewhat, or perhaps very, *different* choice between tact and frankness. So let's move on to Walker.

Walker argues that certain pairs of virtues are mutually incompatible *as virtues* and so he clearly rejects Aristotle's unity thesis. His favorite illustrative example of virtue-incompatibility, borrowed, as he acknowledges, from Watson, is the choice between tact and frankness/openness/straightforwardness/truthfulness; but Walker provides even less detail about cases (or any given case) of conflict between frankness/openness and tact than Watson does.[5] He does, however, draw some theoretical conclusions from this kind of example and others like it. He thinks such conflicts or incompatibilities illustrate the plurality of incommensurable values, and he goes on to say that the person who "speaks openly while regretting that he must cause distress" may be in no way defective with respect to tact and may well have an entirely admirable character. And similarly for the person who "would resort to tactful evasion while regretting his lack of openness." In other words, and despite the talk of regret, Walker seems to hold that there is nothing ethically unsatisfactory or criticizable about someone who demonstrates tactfulness or who demonstrates frankness/openness in the kind of situation he describes; and he goes on to say that the tactful person and the open person may be equally admirable, but *in different ways*. So Walker is a kind of pluralist about admirability, but he doesn't take his examples of virtue-conflict to show anything about necessary or inevitable virtue-imperfection, and to that extent, then, he is a pluralist too about perfection (perfect virtue or admirability).

But the fact that Walker thinks the tactful person has reason to regret not having been frank or open and the open person reason to regret having to cause distress should give us pause with Walker's conclusions. We should at the very least suspect that or wonder whether an example of the tact-frankness conflict can be found where the sense or notion of regret rises to an explicitly ethical level; and the particular example I have relied on of the friend who falls into abusive relationships was supposed to be just such an example. If the person who is frank in the situation I described is appropriately regarded as having done something ethically somewhat unsatisfactory—and similarly for the person who is or would be tactful—then it would be a mistake to follow what Walker says about his less fully described example and say that they are both "entirely admirable" in what they have done; and it would be a mistake to assume that such cases and conflicts merely illustrate an interesting value pluralism. Such pluralism does indeed run counter to the Aristotelian unity thesis, but it doesn't acknowledge, what I think our example should lead us to acknowledge, that the inconsistency of certain virtues threatens the very possibility of someone's being *entirely* admirable, or ethically perfect.

So our discussion of Walker and, just before, of Watson should help explain the sense in which my own views and those of Isaiah Berlin go beyond or differ from other conceptions of human virtue. And I hope it also helps make it clear how or why one might be justified in taking the further step away from Aristotelianism that Berlin and I have taken. For even while disagreeing with Aristotle, Watson, and others about the (potential) viability of the unity thesis and even while subscribing to the idea of inconsistent or conflicting virtues—which Berlin and I also, of course, subscribe to—Walker seems to want to insist that people can in different ways be perfect in virtue. And his assumption that perfect virtue is possible, which Aristotle, Watson, and others also never question, is precisely what Berlin has called into question and what I have sought to argue against in this book.

In fact, there is another (very relevant) possible position about the virtues that I haven't yet explicitly mentioned. Walker points out that one can reject the unity thesis while holding, nonetheless, that the virtues are all mutually compatible—and he cites Peter Geach as an example of someone who holds such a view.[6] That conception of virtue obviously differs from Aristotle's, but it differs less than Walker's does and much less than Berlin's views and my own do. So there are in effect four different positions one can take on the general issues we have just been discussing. Aristotle holds that the virtues are all mutually compatible and in fact constitute a unity, and he also holds that ethical perfection is possible. Geach thinks the virtues don't form a unity but are completely compatible and he gives no reason to think that ethical perfection is problematic. Walker believes that the virtues neither form a unity nor are completely compatible, but he too doesn't question the possibility of ethical perfection. And finally, then, both Berlin and I deny the unity thesis, deny the compatibility of the virtues, and deny the possibility of ethical perfection.[7] This gives the sense, as I have expressed it earlier, in which Berlin's views and my own constitute the antithesis of Aristotelianism.

But in fact Berlin's ideas may be even more opposed to Aristotle's than my own clearly are. In particular, Berlin seems to have made the very un-Aristotelian assumption that various values are incommensurable or incomparable with one another and to have understood (his commitment to) pluralism to entail such incommensurability or incomparability; but my own argument for the impossibility of perfect virtue and happiness has in no way relied on such an assumption. For all I know, adventure and security (for example) may be *equally* important to (a good) human life, and my discussion of perfection has made no assumption(s) to the contrary. And even if security (say) is to a definite extent *more* important or valuable than adventure—or vice versa—our main arguments don't seem to be affected. So I don't think I need to invoke the ideas of incommensurability and/or incomparability in order to argue for necessary imperfection, and since Berlin thinks he does, his view is to that extent more anti-Aristotelian than my own.

In any event, both our views are further from Aristotle's than any other objectivistic ethical view that has ever been defended, and that fact, frankly, gives me pause. But we need to remember that Aristotle had less to work with than the embarrassment of ethical riches that we face and have to deal with nowadays. The riches I am talking about are facts and interrelated sets of facts about the complexities of human (and intelligent) life. Just think about it. Aristotle didn't know about as many different cultures as we do; and although he was well aware of the ways in which polities can conflict externally (e.g., by making war on one another), the societies he was aware of (Persia,

Athens, Sparta, Egypt, etc.) were culturally and ethnically much more uniform than modern-day pluralistic societies. The distinctive conflicts and issues of such societies were unknown to him, as were the issues of patriarchy vs. feminism and of individualism vs. collectivism (he arguably didn't have the idea of individual human rights). So what I am saying—and I agree this is somewhat superficial—is that we shouldn't be surprised if we nowadays want to countenance or can reasonably argue for countenancing a much more pluralistic and tension-full picture of human life and its ethical values than anything that could reasonably have occurred to Aristotle.[8] The kind of view Berlin defended and I am trying to expand on is *called for* in the modern or contemporary world in a way that it really wasn't in Aristotle's time. This is not (really) a philosophical argument for the philosophical conclusions I have been drawing contrary to Aristotle, but if one thinks the arguments I *have* given make sense, it should perhaps make one less reluctant to part ways with something as philosophically familiar and venerable as Aristotle's picture of the virtues. We can be nostalgic for a simpler/easier life and/or simpler/easier assumptions, but the way back seems, really, to be blocked, and I think we do best to reckon with, even struggle with, the more complex and richer (and, I think, less rosy) present and future that Berlin more than anyone else described and adumbrated for us.

But having now situated our approach in relation to other views, we still have to consider potential problems with or counterexamples to the ideas I have defended. It can be questioned whether the examples I have chosen have to be interpreted in the direction in which I have taken them—whether they show or justify as much as I have said they do. And so I want now to consider some very particular objections to what was said in chapters 1 and 2, beginning with an objection to what I said earlier about the roles of adventure and security in human happiness.

I argued in chapter 1 that security and adventure are partial goods. A life in which one or the other is absent is to some extent a less happy or good life, and I have said that no life can combine these (personal) goods. But is that really correct? After all, one might have security and adventure with respect to different aspects of one's life or at different times of one's life, and wouldn't or couldn't such a life combine these goods in a perfectly happy manner?

Here I am reminded of Flaubert's advice to be "regular and orderly in your life so that you may be violent and original in your work." And given our present purposes, the relevant thought is that one might have adventure in one's work while at the same time being secure or safe in one's life. But although I wouldn't want to deny that such a thing is possible, I don't think it helps the cause of those who want to argue—as against the thesis of necessarily imperfect happiness and against the idea of partial personal goods—that it is possible to combine adventure and security *in one's life*. The whole point of the Flaubert quote is that the violence and, presumably, adventure are in the work and *not* in the life. Of course, when this is the case, we may be able to say that (in some sense) there is adventure to be found *within* the given life, i.e., within the work that is part of that life. But what characterizes a part, the work, may not characterize the whole *tout court*, and that seems to be true in the present instance. The life Flaubert recommended and presumably (from what we know of his life) led himself is not an adventurous life—even if he was adventurous in his work. So I don't think this kind of example works against the idea that adventure and security are merely partial goods or in favor of the idea that they can be combined in a life that is perfect from the point of view of happiness. And similar conclusions are, I think, relevant to the associated partial virtues of adventurousness and prudence.[9]

However, I mentioned above the possibility that adventure and security might be exemplified at *different times* of a given life, might be exemplified seriatim, and one can ask whether this might not then allow for the possibility of a life of perfect happiness as far as these goods are concerned. Presumably and most plausibly, we are imagining a life in which a longer or shorter period of adventure is followed by a longer or shorter period of security, and of course such lives are a fairly familiar feature of the human landscape. But remember that we are assuming the importance of adventure as a human good; so we have to imagine that the earlier period of adventure, in the life we are talking about, was exhilarating, intense, fascinating, and fulfilling; and that a life of security won't or can't contain all these elements. In that case, the later period will be lacking in something valuable, and won't that then mean that it isn't *perfectly* wonderful (or even, perhaps, perfectly satisfactory) from the standpoint of happiness or well-being?

But, the reply might go, one may have had *enough* (of) adventure in one's earlier life and be more than happy to "retire" to a more secure and stable existence. Ask yourself, however, what the flavor of that "enough" actually, psychologically, is. Is the person who thinks this way merely reporting satiation, satiety, with respect to adventure in the way that someone who has eaten three slices of cake may stop being interested in cake and feel, in fact and for the moment, sated with (the experience of eating) cake? But the point about satiety or satiation is that it wears off, that one's appetite returns, so if the analogy with adventure is really to hold, we have to suppose that the person who has had enough adventure to want a life of (more) security will eventually look for adventure again—and be a bit dissatisfied if at that point the opportunity for it is denied him or simply impossible (given the choices he has already made). One doesn't yet have an example of perfect contentment and satisfaction in a life involving adventure and security seriatim.

But in speaking above of the person who feels they have had enough adventure in their life and who feels ready or more than ready for a life of real security, I asked the reader to consider what the psychological flavor of the enoughness might be. I suggested that it might just indicate satiety, and we found problems or a problem in using that interpretation of things to support the idea of perfect happiness serially containing adventure and security. But I actually think that the flavor of the enoughness is quite different from what I originally suggested. It seems to me that someone who expresses herself by saying that she has had enough adventure in her life and would like a little security is actually expressing a certain degree of revulsion with regard to her previous adventurous life. Adventure is scary and anxiety-inducing; and, as we know, it can *sometimes* to some degree be traumatic; and the feeling that one has had enough adventure (and a concomitant longing for safety and security) is most plausibly regarded as a sign of the negative features or factors that sometimes accompany or are part of adventure and adventurousness. But this then shows that in this instance the period of adventure wasn't entirely blissful and perfect (with respect to happiness or well-being) and helps support the idea that adventure and security are partial goods and that adventurousness and prudence are partial virtues—and that perfect virtue and perfect happiness are in principle impossible.

What also supports this is the thought that adventure, even if it induces anxiety, has many positive features that will be lacking in a life that combines adventure and security seriatim in a once-and-for-all way.[10] And if you try to vary the picture by imagining a *frequent alternation* between adventure and security, it doesn't really help matters much. If the alternation is (imagined to be) too frequent, then, and for a priori reasons, it doesn't make coherent psychological sense; and if it is infrequent, then every one of the points made above holds mutatis mutandis, and we still have no case for the possibility of perfection.

Finally, there is another possibility we haven't yet considered. Someone might want to argue that even if a period of life in which adventure (or security) was absent isn't ideal from the standpoint of happiness, a total life combining such a period with one in which there was, say, great adventure (or security) would or could be a perfectly happy one. This, clearly, is to appeal to and make particular use of the doctrine of organic wholes, and, of course, similar moves are familiar from attempts at theodicy within theology or the philosophy of religion: for it is often said, for example, that we can't appreciate the good without experiencing the bad and one might interpret that to mean that what is bad (e.g., pain) in the small actually makes for a better, or sometimes even perfect, whole. Now I shall be talking of this specific issue of theodicy in our next chapter, where we shall see more about how it bears on questions about how to argue for the possibility or for the impossibility of perfection. But prescinding from the analogy with theodicy, it does seem to me implausible to suppose, for example, that the anxiety/risk that characterizes a period of adventure and makes it less than an ideally happy period of life somehow doesn't affect the happiness of an overall life in the same basic direction. As I said, we shall discuss this kind of organicism further in the next chapter, but for the moment it doesn't seem plausible to hold that an adult life some of whose major periods or stages are less than perfectly happy can nonetheless be appropriately or plausibly characterized as being one that *on the whole was* perfectly or ideally happy.[11]

I would like to turn next to the somewhat different issue of the partial values/goods of career achievement and deep relationships with intimates. Here too one may think that there are possibilities for reconciling these goods and for showing them to be cotenable within an ideally happy life that I haven't considered—possibilities that challenge or undercut at least some of the things I have been saying about partial goods and the impossibility of perfect happiness. And as with adventure vs. security, some of these possibilities might be imagined to obtain by positing a division or partition of career achievement and deep affiliative goods into different parts of a person's life. One might think, for example, that someone could choose a career that typically peaks early—say mathematics or theoretical physics—then leaving herself free in later less intellectually fecund years for all the intimacy and devotion that were absent during the years when she was making her mark as a mathematician or physicist.[12]

But what are we supposing here? Is it really thinkable that someone should develop a desire and need for intimacy after spending years, decades, without those attributes? Or, assuming that that doesn't make much sense, could we suppose, instead, that the person simply represses or suppresses that desire in the knowledge or belief that they have to do everything they can while they are still capable of their best possible work in their chosen field and that they will later be able to make up for the absence of affiliative goods in their earlier life *and do so in such a way that that earlier absence in no way detracted from the overall goodness of their life*?

Well, for one thing, if they later develop or give expression to their capacity for intimate relationships and really enjoy and gain a sense of fulfillment from those relationships, won't they regret what they missed out on in their earlier years? If they have a wonderful husband and children later on, won't they regret not having had such full and fulfilling relationships earlier on with, say, their grandparents, their parents, their siblings, their college roommate? And won't this reflect an actual loss, through their having focused on career goals, that the later relationships cannot fully undo. Perhaps the later relationships will help make up for what they missed out on earlier, but what makes up for something bad doesn't erase it or make it somehow fail to count toward an intelligent reckoning of the value (for them) of their life overall. So unless one relies on the kind of organic view that I mentioned earlier, it seems hard to see how to make the case that such a person's life has been ideally happy on the whole. And if one does rely on the organic view and say that there is nothing (overall) regrettable about the fact that one didn't have good, close relations with one's family or friends or a partner/spouse during those early years, then one seems to be making light of—to be not taking really seriously—the loss one sustained through not having those relationships. Certainly, if one really loves those one later loves, one will not or may not spend time moping around and repining the early loss or absence. To do that would in fact derogate from the value and significance of the present relationships. But even if one doesn't spend time regretting the past, one might surely, if asked or pressed, acknowledge that one had missed out on something important. So I don't see how one could say that such a life was one of perfect or ideal happiness.

But there is another possibility, one not paralleled by anything said earlier about adventure vs. prudence. We can suppose that one's deep intimate relationships and one's career fulfillment are not segregated into different parts of one's life, but that they occur together—and that that is possible because achievements in one's chosen field come so easily to one that the energy and efforts that a career and career fulfillment normally demand of most of us are not necessary in one's own case. Think of Mozart, to whom musical invention seems to have come effortlessly and spontaneously. Couldn't a Mozart of physics or music have all the creative/career fulfillment any of us ever has while at the same time enjoying the deepest kind(s) of personal relationships? We could even imagine that this person cares much more about people and relationships than about their career, but that that doesn't in any way interfere with their creative/career success or fulfillment.

This doesn't, at first glance, seem particularly problematic (though in human terms it would have to be a rare phenomenon). But something is left out of this picture that in the end, I think, compromises the happiness, the fulfillment, of the person we are speaking hypothetically about. If someone is born with a talent and doesn't use it, we don't in the end envy them or think that the talent has really, ultimately, done them any good whatsoever. But Mozart, of course, made use of his talent and achieved great things, and let's not suppose that he didn't have to work hard to orchestrate his inspirations to completion in finished works of great art. Such hard work requires perseverance, strength of purpose, and so even a Mozart had to place great value on his career/artistic achievement/fulfillment. It's not easy to suppose that such a person cared much more about his relationships than about his artistic fulfillment. Now someone might say in response that we could in principle imagine a person who didn't have to work as hard and be as driven or committed as Mozart was in order to do or create important, fulfilling work: a super-Mozart, if you will. But this person, as we have now characterized him or her, does miss out on something very important in life, and let me try to explain what that is.

Most creative people—and perhaps this was true even of Mozart—have to *struggle* in order to create great work, achieve wonderful things; and though struggle may be painful or hard in various ways, the fact that one has, through struggle, overcome difficulties and obstacles to one's achieving things adds to the personal value, the personal good, one derives from such achievement. One naturally thinks that a fine achievement was worth all the turmoil, hard work, struggle, and even anguish that it took to make the achievement (finally) possible. Indeed, we tend to think that the hard work, struggle, etc., make the achievement *more* of an achievement and to that extent *more* of a life good. And if this thinking is granted any ethical weight, it tells against the view that a super-Mozart has an

ideally good life. Such a person hasn't "won through" to her accomplishments, to her fulfillment, and to that extent those fulfillments
mean less, constitute less of a good thing for her, than achievements
and fulfillment that *are* "hard won."[13] Once again, then, I believe
there is no reason to think that it is really possible to combine fully
creative career/artistic/scientific fulfillment and fully satisfying
deep intimate relationships in a single totally happy life.[14]

Now I earlier mentioned the possibility that the best life most of
us can lead may be one in which career involvement and personal
intimacy are traded off against one another—a life in which one is
only partly devoted to one's work and only partly involved in close
relationships. Such a life *might*, for various reasons, be better than
any life in which we were fully devoted to work and missed out in a
big way on the goods of personal intimacy and any life in which we
were totally involved with our intimate relationships and missed out
in a big way on career fulfillment. But I am far from sure of this, and
in any event I don't think we need to decide this particular question
here. However, we would normally characterize such a life as
involving a *compromise* between career/creative values and affiliative ones, and that very term, once again, suggests or even entails
that such a life isn't *ideally* good or happy (even if it is on the whole
reasonably *satisfactory*). I therefore think that the best objections I
have been able to come up with don't unseat our earlier conclusions
and leave us with the Berlin thesis not only intact but supported by
the sheer difficulty of finding any plausible strong objection to it.

But another point needs to be made—and from the standpoint
of relevancy to contemporary thinking and attitudes and their practical consequences, it may be the most significant point to be made
in this book. Most people today who think about the matter think
that the difficulty of balancing career and family—or, and more
generally, career and relationships—is an artifact of the way social

life is currently organized and perhaps will continue to be organized even if patriarchal (and other benighted) institutions and attitudes eventually loosen their grip on us. (As I have said, even men nowadays find it difficult to choose between or balance career and deep involvement with their families.) But if the preceding is on the right track, then the difficulty of balancing is conceptually, metaphysically, inevitable. (To my knowledge, Berlin never spoke of this particular predicament, but I think he might well have agreed with what I have just said: it certainly illustrates and helps to support his general theses about the conceptual impossibility of perfection.)

Perhaps, then, instead of beating our heads against the wall of current social arrangements and blaming ourselves or others or society when we find that we cannot have everything we want in or from our careers and (family or other) relationships, we should recognize the strong inevitability of this predicament, the deep impossibility of our situation in relation to our values, desires, and aspirations.[15] This might actually make it easier to accept the difficulties and impossibilities we face with respect to career/creativity vs. relationships. I certainly hope that this is the case (and that the present book might make a difference here); but of course one can't be sure. Seeing things as deeply inevitable and unavoidable doesn't always lead one to accept them—is it so clear that atheism makes it easy or easier to accept the inevitability of one's future nonbeing? So, as I say, it is not clear to me that the "message" of the present book—or at least the particular message I am now focusing on—will or would do people any good. But in any event, if the message is valid, is true, that has philosophical implications which are worth considering independently of any practical applications, and that is perhaps the only conclusion that we have any right to reach on the basis of the arguments that have been given here.

And let me now, finally, generalize what I have been saying about the issue of career vs. family or, perhaps more accurately, point to a generalization of that issue that has already implicitly operated in our discussion. If our previous arguments are on the right track, then the "choice" between creative fulfillment/accomplishment and deep relationship(s) constitutes *at a deeper level* what is typically presented or described as the "choice" between career and family (or between career and relationships). After all, not everyone who accomplishes significant things has a career (did Emily Dickinson, Kierkegaard, or Proust have a career?); and one doesn't have to literally have a family (think of some priests) in order to be involved in deep personal relationships. So I think the more superficial or "accidental" talk of career vs. family points us toward the more general or generalized choice between creative fulfillment/accomplishment and deep relationships and even toward the idea that ideal happiness is absolutely impossible, but it becomes easier to recognize and see the bases for that impossibility if one conceives things at the more general or less superficial and accidental level.

But now we have a new task. We have in this chapter discussed views that clearly contrast with those I have followed Isaiah Berlin in advancing. But there are other views and concepts that seem or might seem very much in line with, or in the spirit of, what Berlin has said about the impossibility of perfection. I am thinking, most particularly, of ideas about moral dilemma and moral cost that philosophers like Bernard Williams have defended. These ideas seem at first glance to fit well with and perhaps even to entail the impossibility of virtue-perfection, and I want to devote our next chapter mainly to discussing whether this appearance is or is not misleading. Does the possibility, if it is one, of moral dilemma or of moral cost (the latter in a sense to be defined in our next chapter) constitute another route to the impossibility of virtue-perfection beyond anything suggested in my own previous examples and arguments? Let us see.

Chapter 4

Perfection, Moral Dilemmas, and Moral Cost

Although he certainly was a brilliant and original ethical thinker in his own right, Bernard Williams was also in some measure a disciple of Isaiah Berlin. He was (I believe) Berlin's student, and Berlin did many things to advance his career. But, more importantly, some of his most important ideas in ethics develop Berlin's ideas in interesting and novel directions.

I am thinking here especially of what Williams has written on the subject of moral dilemmas, and also (though this has had less impact on the ethics literature) of Williams's notion of moral cost. Dilemmas in the now standard sense are situations where, through no moral fault of their own, agents cannot avoid acting wrongly, situations in which they cannot avoid violating some all-things-considered moral obligation; and Williams was one of the first philosophers to argue that such situations of dilemma not only are possible in principle but actually occur in our lives (or in situations described in literature). To be sure, many, many philosophers subsequently have argued that dilemmas as described by Williams and others are in fact impossible—they are said, for example, to entail the repudiation of certain basic deontic or moral principles that we have no reason to think we should repudiate. But I don't want to get into those debates here.[1] A virtue ethicist like myself may well have reason to agree with the critics, but for purposes of the present discussion, I shall assume that dilemmas are possible, because I want to consider how that possibility bears or would bear on the thesis of the impossibility of perfection that Berlin first introduced and that we have been defending.

The thesis that moral cost is possible is less controversial, because it doesn't seem to violate certain basic metaethical (or deep ethical) assumptions in the way that the idea of moral dilemma does. Serious moral cost occurs when one is in a situation, through no fault of one's own, where doing what is right will involve *wronging someone*. And this is a stronger notion than the idea that there are situations where one permissibly violates a prima facie duty to someone, but owes an apology to that person after the fact. If I promise to meet you for lunch at noon but am waylaid by an emergency situation in which I have to save a child from drowning, so that I end up late for our appointment, I have done nothing wrong, have acted permissibly, but I still do owe you an apology (and it will be wrong if I don't apologize). But if I do apologize, I can't really be said to have wronged you, whereas this is precisely what can be said in certain situations where I incur a moral cost by acting in a certain way.

For example, during World War II, Winston Churchill was told by the British intelligence services that they had decoded a transmission from Germany indicating that the Germans were about to launch an aerial attack on the town of Coventry. He decided not to warn Coventry because he judged that the value to the Allied war effort of the Germans' not knowing that their code had been broken outweighed the human cost of allowing Coventry to be bombed. And we may think he was right about this, so that we regard Churchill as not having acted wrongly in failing to alert the citizens of Coventry and allowing many to die who wouldn't have died if that city *had* been alerted. Still, Churchill did something morally very distasteful, and he or the government he headed can, not implausibly, be said to have wronged the citizens of Coventry.[2] They will then be owed more than an apology, and more even, perhaps, than monetary reparations (how does one really make reparations for lost lives?). Cases of moral cost are not moral dilemmas because they don't involve anyone in having to act immorally, but they are direr, morally, than situations in which one merely owes an apology. They lie in a moral area between these two kinds of cases, and I believe Williams was the first person to bring such cases to our notice.[3] They involve the idea that one can wrong *someone* without having acted (overall) wrongly, and this is certainly a very, very interesting moral concept (though, as I said, it has been largely neglected in recent ethics). And in the present chapter, in addition to relating moral dilemma to what we have been saying about perfection, or the necessity of imperfection, I want to consider how the idea of moral cost also bears on that issue. In particular, I want to show you that the sheer ideas of moral dilemma and moral cost don't in fact point toward the impossibility of virtue-perfection (much less toward the idea of necessary imperfection in regard to happiness or living well).

This may be somewhat surprising—especially in the light of Williams's strong intellectual relationship to Berlin's ethical thought. Like Berlin, Williams is very much a pluralist. But more significantly, the idea of moral dilemma in particular seems to partake of much the same structure as that of the necessity of virtue-imperfection. Berlin's thesis holds that there is a certain inconsistency among (what are properly conceived of as) the virtues, and the idea of moral dilemmas entails that there can be an inconsistency among our all-things-considered obligations. So one might well expect that (the existence of) moral dilemmas would count as a confirming instance of Berlin's thesis of necessary virtue-imperfection; that the existence of dilemmas would help to show that Berlin's thesis is correct—in which case the brilliant student or disciple would have provided new and additional resources as support for what the teacher had claimed. But to my knowledge Williams never said as much, never said that moral dilemmas support the impossibility of perfect virtue (of perfection with respect to the virtues), and as I shall argue in what follows, Williams was probably right not to do so. Facts or assumptions about moral dilemma and/or moral cost don't seem to support Berlin's original contention, and if that is so, then we were right to use our previous arguments to support it, rather than relying on anything to do with dilemma or cost considered as such. The cases mentioned in previous chapters, especially the case of frankness vs. tact, may well illustrate the idea of moral cost, for example, but, I shall argue, there can be moral cost and dilemma that don't bring necessary imperfection in their train; so with respect to those previous cases it isn't the fact that they may involve moral cost (or even dilemma) that is relevant to supporting Berlin's thesis, but other facts about them that we mentioned in our previous discussions—facts, most especially, having to do with partial values or partiality of values. But all of this needs to be shown. Let us begin by focusing on moral dilemmas.

Perhaps the purest and most convincing (putative) example of moral dilemma that can be found in literature occurs not in Greek tragedy, but in the more recent book *Sophie's Choice* by William Styron.[4] A Nazi official makes Sophie choose which of her two children is to be sent to a concentration camp, and she is told that if she refuses to choose, both will be sent. Eventually, Sophie commits suicide over what she has done—in choosing to send her daughter rather than her son. And, as I have indicated, I don't so much want to consider whether this was indeed a moral (or ethical) dilemma, but rather to ask how such a (putative) tragic choice (or others like it) bears on the issue of inevitable or necessary ethical imperfection. (Also, Sophie seems to have had some sexist reasons for "preferring" her son, but let us as best we can remove them from the example—they are hardly inevitable elements in such a forced choice.)

The bearing of such examples on the issue of necessary imperfection concerns the attitude or disposition that (I think we can assume) Sophie inevitably displays in choosing one of her children over the other. In so choosing, she shows herself to be disposed to choose one or the other of them rather than let both be sent to concentration camps, and we must ask whether there is anything ethically criticizable in such a disposition. And my brief answer is that there isn't. Some philosophers have maintained that in making any choice between her children, Sophie shows herself to be willing to "cooperate with evil." Were she to refuse to choose, the choice to send both children to concentration camps (or to one camp) would be entirely the choice of the perverse Nazi who set up the dilemma she was confronted with, and some have concluded that that is or would have been the better choice to make—the refusal to cooperate with evil—rather than to choose or pick one of them for hardship and likely extermination. But I hope you don't agree with this. Most people who see her as facing a dilemma see her situation as dilemmatic precisely because she can't in all conscience refuse to cooperate with evil in a case like this, and I shall assume as much in what follows.

In that case, then, can we, should we, say that she manifests an ethically criticizable disposition in being willing to choose one of them for the camps? I am inclined not to think so. But I am not entirely sure about this because those who say it is never right to cooperate with evil could claim that an antecedent willingness to cooperate with evil is always ethically criticizable—and presumably such people would want to say that a willingness to enter into a nuclear test-ban treaty with a genuinely "evil empire" would also manifest an ethically criticizable disposition on the part of any nation that was willing to do such a thing. However, this strikes me and perhaps it will strike others as extreme, and so I believe that there is nothing about Sophie's somewhat similar disposition to criticize in ethical terms. In other words, I am saying that if someone, in advance of being in a situation like Sophie's, has the disposition to choose one or the other of her/his children for hardship and possible extermination rather than let them both be sent to the death camps, given that she or he is ever in a situation like Sophie's—and I think this is a disposition most of us have—we wouldn't be inclined to call that an ethical failing or imperfection. (Of course, I am assuming here that the disposition in question isn't a disposition in favor of a *particular one* of one's children, and is, quite simply, the disposition to choose *one or the other* of them for hardship and possible extermination. How one on that basis would actually decide which child to choose is a complicated issue, but not one we need to discuss further here.)

What we are saying about the Sophie case stands in subtle but definite contrast, I think, with what most of us would want to say about the example mentioned in Chapter 1 of the person who has to be either tactful or frank with a friend who is masochistic in relationships but can't (we assumed) face that fact about himself. In that kind of case, and as I said earlier, if the person has the disposition to be frank and tell the truth, we think they are not as sensitive and kind as they ideally ought to be. And if they are disposed, instead, to be tactful, even when their friend is begging them to be frank, there is also something ethically regrettable in their attitude (and dispositions toward) their friend. In some sense they will be seen as falling short of our ideal of true friendship, of being a true and genuine friend; and, in fact, this can be plausibly said whatever they are inclined to do and actually do.

So I think our earlier type of example (and the notion of a partial virtue or value that we used to clarify or explain it) offers a stronger case for the inevitability of ethical imperfection than anything that derives from the sheer/mere supposition of the possibility or actuality of moral dilemmas. Even if the example of the friend *is* a case of moral dilemma (and I am not saying either that it is or that it isn't), it is not the fact of dilemmatic status as such that yields the inevitability of imperfection, but rather the aspects of that case that were focused on in earlier chapters.

Something similar, I believe, can be said about moral cost. If a political leader is willing and has the disposition not to warn some city or town of impending aerial bombing *given that a huge war effort (in a just war in which the future of humanity seems largely at stake) requires that one not alert the town,* I don't believe we are inclined to think that there is or must be something ethically regrettable or unsavory about that leader in virtue (excuse me!) of the fact that they possess such a disposition. And, once again, this contrasts with what we are inclined to think and say about the example of frankness vs. tact(fulness). So the sheer fact of serious moral cost (and even of the *inevitability,* as perhaps in the present case, of *either* moral cost *or* wrongdoing) doesn't entail the impossibility of virtue-perfection.

On the other hand, the case of the friend, even if it doesn't involve a moral dilemma, arguably does involve moral cost. If one is frank, one (knows in advance that one) is going to hurt one's friend a great deal (at a point where he needs or craves your support and reassurance); and if one is tactful, one knowingly refuses to tell a friend the truth when that is precisely (at least *de dicto*) what he is begging one to do. But the most we can conclude from this (and I am not sure, on the basis of our one example, that we should accept such a conclusion) is that the necessity of virtue-imperfection may or does entail the possibility or inevitability of moral cost. The reverse implication, as we have seen, simply doesn't hold.[5] If a case is to support the idea of inevitable ethical imperfection, it has to involve something more than or different from moral dilemma or cost, and I have argued that that (or one such) more or different something is most clearly described in terms of the notion of a partial virtue.

But let us now consider another possibility. Public and private concerns and commitments are sometimes in tension, and perhaps in that signally important area of moral choice and possible conflict, we can find examples or an example that supports the idea of necessary ethical imperfection without leaning on the ideas of partial virtue and partial value that we have discussed earlier.

Let me begin with an example that I discussed years ago in the book *Goods and Virtues*. Imagine a public official living in Italy during the period of the "Brigate Rosse" and their attacks on the state or its government. Imagine further than his son has committed murder under the auspices of the Brigades and that, further, he has killed someone who is entirely innocent and in any event did not deserve to be killed. Given his position of power, the father is in a position to spirit his son out of the country and in fact chooses to do so.

Now in *Goods and Virtues* I argued that this may well be an example of justified immorality. It would count as immorality because (let us assume) the state is just enough and the son's deed heinous enough so that it would be wrong, morally wrong, for the official to use his powers to help his son evade Italian justice. (It might not be wrong of him simply not to *tell* authorities of his son's whereabouts, but that is another matter.) On the other hand, given his relationship with and love for his son, it wouldn't necessarily be irrational for the father to do what he does. What he has most reason to do might in such a case run counter to morality.[6] And I hasten to mention that this conclusion, however plausible it may seem with regard to the case just described, goes against the familiar and wide-accepted "overridingness thesis" that claims that moral reasons, and especially the fact of acknowledged moral wrongness, override in rational terms (in terms of good reasons for action) any other reasons or rational considerations that may favor doing what is immoral.

Now some philosophers, some ethicists, will want to invoke the overridingness thesis precisely to counter what I have said about the case of the Italian father. But if we allow the case to be described in the way I described it above, that will make it easier (if it is possible at all) to argue against what I have been saying and want to say here, namely, that it is only the kinds of examples I discussed in earlier chapters that support the Berlin thesis about the impossibility of perfection. So let us assume that the father in our example acts in a justified but immoral way. (After all, the case isn't like weakness of will because the father may well be willing to *stand by* what he has done long after he does it, and in cases of weak will, the weak-willed person typically shows regret for what he or she has done after the fact.) Our assumptions here make things more difficult, not less difficult, for the thesis I want to maintain, so let us continue to make them.[7]

We have to consider, then, whether, in the light of those assumptions, ethical imperfection is inevitable with respect to cases like that of the Italian father. And my thought is that it isn't inevitable because if the father had been unwilling to spirit his son out of the country, there would have been nothing ethically criticizable in that disposition or tendency. Now if the father hadn't been willing to break the law for the sake of his son, he might have shown himself to love his son less than he might. A father willing to break the law for his son may evidence or embody a greater love for his son than a father whose love was limited by such moral considerations.[8] But that doesn't necessarily show that this latter kind of father is ethically criticizable, deficient, or suspect. Love is a great and wonderful thing, and there are moral and ethical imperatives and ideals that form an important part of our conception of real or true or great love. But we don't think there is anything suspect in there being limitations to a given love. If one loves both one's children equally, then one may love each of them less than one would have loved a given one of them, if one had had an incredibly strong attachment to that one and a lesser, merely affectionate relation to the other. But no one thinks that is a reason for holding a father who loves both his children equally, and less than he might have loved a particular one of them, to be ethically deficient or suspect.

Similarly, the fact that a father is unwilling to do a grave injustice in order to save a delinquent or criminal son from just punishment doesn't show him to be ethically deficient, even if it *may* show him to lack the greatest possible love for that son.[9]

And the same point can be made with less philosophical controversial examples. If I give money to Oxfam rather than spending it to give my daughter private German lessons that she is very interested in having, then perhaps I show myself to love her (dote on her) less than if I forgot about Oxfam and its mission. But if these are the only two choices I have, the presumed lesser love for the daughter doesn't seem to imply or indicate any ethical failing on my part. Sometimes the larger or more important needs of distant others can take precedence over interests and desires closer to (or at) home without there being anything ethically regrettable or criticizable about this ethical preference.

Once again, then, we haven't identified any really plausible route to Berlin's ideas other than the one that goes through the idea of partiality and the sorts of examples we have used to move us in that direction. The thesis of necessary imperfection grows in a very special soil, and issues of moral dilemma, of moral cost, and also of justifiable immorality largely bypass that terrain. This may be surprising, and when I first thought of the examples we used earlier, I imagined that Berlin's thesis would receive further support from our understanding of moral dilemma and the like. But that didn't, that doesn't, turn out to be the case.

However, I do want finally to mention a way of arguing for the impossibility of perfect *happiness* or *well-being* that doesn't bring in—or doesn't seem to bring in—the idea of partial goods or values. It has sometimes been said that what is bad can help us to appreciate what is good, so that, in fact, a world without pain would inevitably be a less happy place than certain possible worlds where pain was present. Such views are often part of theodicy, part of an attempt to show that despite the fact of pain and hardship our world may be the best of all possible worlds—in which case God's existence and goodness may not be impugned or undercut by the pain and hardships that clearly do exist in the world.

But if the greatest possible human happiness depends on there being pain and suffering, how does that show that our happiness is necessarily imperfect or incomplete, or that a perfectly good or happy life is impossible? Couldn't one claim, rather, that the existence of pain, say, in a given life is necessary to that life's greatest happiness and might help ensure that that life was perfect in happiness. To be sure, pain considered in itself is a bad thing; but we all know the doctrine of organic wholes according to which something that is bad out of context or in one context may count as or contribute to good in another. So one might say that the pain we experience isn't at all a bad thing in the context of a sufficiently pleasurable overall life (I am simplifying in order to make a point); and one might go on to claim that such a life would or could in fact (if one were ever so lucky) be *perfectly* happy. In that case, it wouldn't be at all clear that this kind of theodicy will entail the impossibility of perfect happiness; rather, it would seem to show us that and how perfect happiness *is* possible.

But we, and the person arguing in the manner just mentioned, are forgetting a lesson from chapter 2. We saw there that there is a difference between something being as good as possible and something being perfect, for if imperfection is necessary and inevitable, what might count as the best possible might invariably *not be perfect*. In that case, the sheer fact that a life is as good as possible doesn't entail that it is perfectly good, and the assumption that pain is necessary to the best and highest possible appreciation and enjoyment of the good doesn't show that pain is compatible with a *perfectly* happy or good life. The best possible may simply not be, may inevitably not be, perfect.

So if pain is necessary to the best possible life but inevitably to some degree mars such a life and makes it count as less than perfectly good, then the above theodicy would actually tend to show that the world can't be perfect at least with regard to happiness. (This would represent a serious but metaphysically inevitable limitation on God's powers.) However, above we mentioned the doctrine of organic unities, and according to such a doctrine, as relevantly applied in the present case, pain doesn't or needn't at all mar a life or its happiness. And I agree that if one accepts this application of the just-mentioned doctrine, then pain cannot be used to argue for the inevitability of less than perfect happiness.

But is it really plausible to say that the pain that is presumed to help us to appreciate life better than we otherwise could is in no way a bad thing in the context of that life, that it in no way or to no degree mars that life with respect to its happiness? This doesn't seem at all plausible to me, and if we reject the idea, then we are indeed faced with an argument for the impossibility of perfect happiness that in no way borrows from what we have been saying about partial values. Substantial pain may be necessary to the best *possible* life, but since it also arguably mars that life's happiness, the life, whatever else may happen in it, cannot be perfect with respect to happiness. And that is the thesis we have earlier argued for in other ways.

But is it really true that one cannot appreciate the good (things in life) without having one's share of bad things happen to one? I for one am somewhat skeptical about this. I don't see that someone has to have experienced pain in order to enjoy the pleasures of a good meal or a good swim or a good concert or a good conversation.[10] Certainly, if we never experienced pain, we might be unable to empathize with the pain that others feel and (for empirical reasons) our moral capacities might never fully develop. But I think we should be able to leave this particular issue aside in the present context and just consider how plausible it is to say that someone has to experience pain in order to (otherwise) enjoy life. This doesn't seem all that plausible, but that doesn't necessarily exhaust the issues that are relevant here. Enjoying life is one thing, but having an overall good life is or may be something different and larger, and our discussion of the partial good of achievement in chapter 3 argued (in a way obviously influenced by Romantic thought) that the good of a life's achievement or accomplishment is diminished if it all comes too easily, that struggle is essential to the overall life-goodness of great or fine achievements. But there is surely something less than perfectly happy about a life that involves struggle, so if certain goods are necessary to an ideal life but require struggle, that in itself constitutes an argument against the possibility of perfect happiness.

However, even if this dialectic is persuasive—and it tends to persuade me—it doesn't undercut what I want to say about the role the idea of partial values plays, and I think must play, in understanding and explaining the necessity of imperfection. If perfect happiness is impossible because the full good of accomplishing something important or significant depends on a certain amount of struggle, we are still talking about what is only a partial good, of something that precludes the fullest value of deep, intimate, personal relationship(s) in an ethically regrettable way. So the idea of partial value is built into the picture of what is inevitably less than perfect about a life in which achievement occurs at the cost of struggle, because that achievement occurs at some cost to personal relationship as well.[11] Thus in a perhaps surprising way, the old theodicean claim that (fully appreciating) the good requires (experiencing) the bad lends support to the Berlinian idea of the necessity of imperfection and to our attempt here to explain and justify that idea by reference to the concept of partial values.[12]

Chapter 5

Connections with Care Ethics and Romanticism

The present project didn't begin with Isaiah Berlin and the thesis of the impossibility of perfection. It's true that for many years the example or idea of frankness vs. tact had rolled around in my mind and that I had thought it might indicate that perfection at least of the virtues was impossible. But I believe I was at best only dimly aware, through those years, of what Berlin had claimed; and to the extent I was aware of it, I didn't see that Berlin had any better arguments for the impossibility of perfection than I did. And I had precious little: as I say, I had the idea of tact vs. frankness and hopes and suspicions about it, but nothing more.

If the reader won't mind a little personal intellectual history, what finally got me to the point of wanting to argue for the imperfection thesis and of having some actual arguments for that thesis was a consideration of issues having to do with feminism and patriarchy. I had noticed the seemingly gendered character of certain objective list theories of human goods: of the lists themselves and of particular items on the list. I saw that according to patriarchy certain things were good only for (or relative to) men and certain others only for (or relative to) women, and I realized that a more enlightened, feminist view of these matters would recognize a certain clash between the goods, or the virtues, in question, but wouldn't regard them as gender-relative in the traditional fashion. All this *reminded*

me of the clash or possible inconsistency between tact and frankness that had preoccupied me for so long, and the fact that I now
had so many examples of paired but opposed goods or virtues led
me to push the issue of frankness vs. tact much harder than I had
previously. I then came up with a specific example of how these
traits can clash that seemed to show (as Isaiah Berlin had held) that
ethical perfection is impossible, and this led me to the explicit idea
of partial virtues, goods, values. It then was relatively easy to apply
this thinking to the paired and opposed goods and virtues that patriarchy relativizes to gender, and I was off and running (in some directions Berlin had never spoken about).

Of course, this sequence of events is recorded in chapter 1 in a
more philosophically objective or argumentational fashion. But
chapter 1 also noted that those academic feminists who had spoken
of or argued about gender differences in how people approach
moral issues hadn't really spoken of values outside of morality narrowly conceived. So as I was developing the ideas of chapter 1,
I was implicitly comparing and contrasting what I was coming up
with and what I was doing with what (other) feminists had said
about specifically moral issues of right and wrong, moral goodness
and moral badness (or blameworthiness). I mentioned some of
this in chapter 1, but having now more fully stated what I want to
say about the impossibility of perfection and its relevance to feminist ideas or values, I also want to say more about how what I have
been doing relates to feminist, and especially care-ethical, views of
morality. There seems in fact to be a tension between the two, and
since I am a committed care ethicist, I think I need to say more
about how what I have been arguing in the present book relates to,
and is not really in tension with, what I have said about care ethics
in two previous books: *The Ethics of Care and Empathy* and *Moral
Sentimentalism*.[1]

Let me first describe the seeming tension. Care ethics originated with Carol Gilligan's 1982 book *In a Different Voice: Psychological Theory and Women's Development.*[2] The different voices she spoke of were a voice of caring and a voice of justice, and at least initially she associated those two moral voices, respectively, with women and with men—though she maintained from the beginning that the significance of (the difference between) the voices transcended any issues of sex or gender. According to Gilligan and most subsequent care ethicists, those two voices constituted two different ways of approaching moral issues or problems. The care voice sees such issues in terms of caring for and direct connection to or with other people; the justice voice approaches moral questions in terms of justice, rights, individual autonomy, and a reliance on (citing and applying) principles or rules in making moral decisions. And when I first explored the questions I dealt with in chapter 1, I realized or at least thought that the idea of different voices could also be applied outside the specific realm of morality to questions about human good or well-being and to questions about virtues that were not specifically moral. This is something that no one had previously pursued in any kind of scholarly way, but it seemed clear that just as caring might be traditionally associated with women's treatment of moral questions, the personal good of security (to choose just one example) was traditionally associated with women more than with men. And just as justice might be more traditionally associated with male or masculine approaches to morality, so too was the personal good of adventure more traditionally associated with men than with women. So, as I have indicated, I initially believed I had unearthed a difference of voice(s) outside the area of morality that corresponded at least roughly with the difference of voice(s) that care ethicists had argued for in and for the realm of morality.

But there also seemed to be a clear difference between the inferences care ethics had drawn about the voices and what I was prepared to say about the application of that notion to extramoral, but ethical questions about human good(s) and virtues. Care ethics treated one of the voices, the voice of care or caring, as determinative of how one should ultimately and validly think about morality; and this tendency was clearly visible in the work of the first person to write specifically about what an ethics of care could or should be. Nel Noddings's *Caring: A Feminine Approach to Ethics and Moral Education* focused on caring and how it would or could operate in moral contexts and pretty much ignored (except to criticize) supposedly masculine ways of dealing with moral issues.[3] And by and large care ethics, as it has developed in recent decades, has tended to stress the voice of caring over the voice of justice.

By contrast, the approach taken in the present chapter 1 stressed the importance and validity of both voices with respect to issues of human good and virtue. It rejected the idea that certain goods are relative to gender, and it argued, for example, that both security and adventure are equally valid (partial goods) for both genders. To that extent what I have done here is gender-neutral in a way that care ethics doesn't seem to be, and one can wonder, therefore, whether the approach taken here really fits in with or can accommodate care ethics as a view of the moral. The answer to this question, this problem, is that ultimately the two approaches are compatible and much less different with respect to issues of gender or gender-neutrality than might appear. I say "ultimately" because I think the approach we have taken and the conclusions drawn in chapter 1, above, do require us to rethink care ethics to a certain extent. But once we have done so—and in a moment I shall explain how and why I think we can and ought to do so—I believe that care ethics and the ideas of the present book will really not be in any tension. There will be differences of *implementation* as regards the issue of gender neutrality (or balance), but neither care ethics nor the present view of the virtues and personal good/well-being needs to be biased in favor of one gender or the other, even if the ways in which they achieve such neutrality will—I think interestingly—be somewhat different. But all of this will require a good deal of explanation.

I think some of the things I said in chapter 1 should lead us to object to certain familiar, but ultimately inessential, features of care ethics. Both Nel Noddings and Virginia Held, another very prominent care ethicist, have treated care ethics as involving not only a direct (principle-unmediated) concern for the welfare of others, but also a general desire to promote, maintain, and enhance caring relationships.[4] And I have no objection to such a view or approach *as far as it goes*. But the question can arise why caring relationships are stressed to the exclusion of other good things in human life.

In chapter 1, I argued that deep (caring) relationships and individual creative/career achievement and fulfillment are complementary partial goods, but a care ethics that stresses the relationships but not such things as individual achievement and self-fulfillment effectively treats these latter as less important goods than the relationships, and as I mentioned earlier, that smacks of patriarchy and the values it assigns predominantly to women. If you remember, patriarchy treats intense close relationships as more important for women than for men, treats them, in effect, as gender-relative goods *for women*, and I think and said that it is objectionable from a feminist standpoint to treat relationships in this way. And it is also objectionable from that standpoint to stint on the value assigned to career goals: rather, such goals should be and are validly seen as important for both men and women and as comparable in their overall importance to traditionally conceived feminine goods like close personal relationships. But this is precisely what the kind of care ethics that stresses (the promotion, maintenance, and enhancement of) relationships and says nothing similar about career fulfillment implicitly denies, and I think this aspect of previous care ethics is therefore quite objectionable.[5]

Care ethics has previously come in for a great deal of criticism not only from traditionally minded moral philosophers, but from feminists. Previous objections have included the claim that care ethics, in retrograde fashion, encourages women to keep doing most of the caring (for others) that is done in society and leaves us with no way to criticize such a state of affairs. They have also included the claim that care ethics can't handle issues of autonomy and justice that any systematic or complete and contemporaneously relevant approach to ethics needs to be able to deal with. But previous work of my own and of others has addressed these criticisms and, I believe, has done so pretty effectively.[6] So I don't propose to dwell on those criticisms of care ethics at any length here. However, the criticism I have just myself made of care ethics is at least somewhat different from these others, and rather than attempt to rebut it, I think we should instead attempt to incorporate it into care ethics: that is, change care ethics so that it no longer is open to the criticism. More particularly, if care ethics, as it has often been articulated, tells us we should be concerned about promoting, maintaining, and enhancing relationships and doesn't limit this to relationships that we ourselves are or will be involved in, it should also tell us to be concerned with *generally* promoting, maintaining, and enhancing the fulfillment of individual careers and vocations.[7]

Now care ethicists might object at this point that they have never said that individual self-fulfillment is unimportant, and this is, strictly speaking, probably correct. But to set the enhancement and preservation of relationships as an explicit general goal and *not to do the same* for individual career/creative fulfillment or accomplishment is at the very least implicitly to downplay the importance of such fulfillment or accomplishment, and I think care ethics should stop doing that. Of course, the care ethicist might once more object on the grounds that care ethics is supposed to be a feminine ethics, that it is supposed to stress and articulate the (traditionally) feminine side of morality. But if care ethicists move in that direction, then they are granting that their views are one-sided and in need of supplementation. And indeed many care ethicists have said that care ethics needs to be supplemented by justice ethics in order to represent a complete normative conception of morality. But when care ethicists have said this, they have meant that there are *moral issues* (especially regarding politics and society) that care ethics cannot treat on its own, and my point here, then, is that *what care ethics says and understands about (the promotion, etc., of) human good is also in need of supplementation.* When the care ethicist says, e.g., that we should seek to enhance our own and others' relationships and doesn't say we should enhance both our own and others' individual fulfillment, s/he stresses what is traditionally, or in patriarchal terms, viewed as a good thing for women—and does so at the expense of what is traditionally viewed as a good thing for men.[8] So it is not just with respect to moral questions, but also with respect to questions about human good (and about nonmoral virtues) that care ethics needs to be supplemented. And this last point is one that care ethicists haven't, I think, been aware of.[9]

My own preference, and I think this makes the most sense in philosophical terms, is to develop care ethics in a way that *doesn't* require supplementation by some different, putatively masculine way of thinking about morality. This means showing the relevance of care ethics to issues of justice and autonomy, something my own work and, more recently, Noddings's, have sought to accomplish.[10] But—and this is the main point here—it also means emphasizing *both* relationships *and* career fulfillment in spelling out the moral aims or goals of caring.[11] And in order to do that, we as care ethicists have to put an end to the exclusive emphasis on the goal of maintaining or developing caring relationships that has been so characteristic of previous care ethics.

A related point also needs to be made. There has been much criticism in recent decades of (Kantian) liberalism's atomistic view of individuals, of people, and not only care ethicists, but communitarians and many others have joined in this chorus of criticism.[12] What care ethicists and communitarians have wanted to replace the atomism with is a conception of individuals that treats their relations to or with others as at least partly constitutive of their identity, of who they are, and one finds such a relation-emphasizing view of personal identity, for example, in the work of Nel Noddings and Virginia Held that I have previously cited.

But doesn't this privilege our relationships with others over, say, our connection(s) with our own career/creative aspirations and achievements in a way that the discussion of chapter 1 should warn us against? If individual self-fulfillment is just as much a partial good as deep personal connection with other people, shouldn't we expect each to play a fairly equal role in constituting our personal identity? The care ethicist or communitarian who stresses the importance of relationships to individual identity and says nothing analogous about an individual's (relation to their own) creative aspirations and fulfillment (again) stresses a good that is traditionally associated with women more than men over another good that is more associated with men, and it seems to me that, at least from a feminist standpoint and with an eye to the broadest and more objective view of what counts in a human life, we should be stressing the importance of both relationships and career choices to constituting identity.[13] In other words, if atomism is wrong, then we shouldn't make up for its metaphysical/ethical faults in a way that favors traditional female values over male ones, but should recognize that both sets of values have their importance and validity. If we tie the metaphysics, so to speak, of individual identity to certain ethical values, we should do so in a way that is even-handed with respect to gender issues or gender assumptions, and I think this point can be made not only on an abstract level, but more concretely.

There may be some, or many, individuals whose relationships are the most important thing about them, the thing from which they get their principal joys and disappointments, and for such individuals relationships may be more individuating (though what a paradoxical way to put it!) than anything they seek or achieve in any career they may have. But other people are different. Think, for example, of the antisocial Beethoven. Do we really want to say that his identity was constituted by his (arguably rather poor) relations with others? Doesn't it make more sense to see his identity as deeply entangled with his artistic aspirations, efforts, struggles, and accomplishments? And may there not be others whose personhood is more *equally* entangled with career issues and relationship issues? So if the care ethicist or communitarian insists that liberalism gives us an unrealistic or impoverished picture of personal identity and its conditions, then I think they had better be more gender-neutral and take in more kinds of factors than they have previously done. And in what follows I shall assume that care ethics is or has been adjusted in the ways I have been suggesting.

Nonetheless, there remain differences between care ethics and the Berlin-like view of goods and virtues adopted and defended here, and those differences might still worry us—make us think the two sets of views don't fit well with one another and make us think, therefore, that if the ideas defended earlier are valid, care ethics has to be abandoned—*or vice versa*. After all, I have just criticized previous care ethics' views about personal identity and the goals of caring on the grounds of their being biased in favor of values traditionally associated with women (that is, traditionally thought of as more relevant to women than to men). And one can summarize this criticism by saying that, for the reasons and in the ways we have just been describing, previous care ethics seems (almost) as prejudiced against men as patriarchy and its values seem prejudiced against women.

But can't the same thing be said about the core concepts of care ethics, about its basic approach, independently of the assumptions we have just criticized and claimed to be inessential to care ethics? Isn't it, by contrast, absolutely essential to care ethics that it privilege care or caring over justice promulgated or instantiated in accordance with moral rules or principles, and isn't justice traditionally associated with men and caring more typically associated with women? How, in the light of that basic and irrecusable fact, can care ethics escape the charge of (a certain kind of) gender bias, of a preference for things female or feminine over things male or masculine? The approach taken in the present book clearly (I hope) doesn't arouse such worries or suspicions, so we can put the issue that needs to be faced in the following terms. How can someone who has pushed, as I have here, for a gender-neutral approach to the virtues and the good things in life accept a care-ethical approach to morality proper (i.e., narrowly conceived) that seems to grant so little value and validity to things (traditionally associated with the) male?

Well, I think the answer, in a nutshell, is that care ethics places more value on supposedly or traditionally male or masculine values than might appear, so that even if it is neutral or even-handed about gender in a somewhat different way from the way in which the approach of the present book is, the two are more congruent, less out of sorts, than the criticisms aired above would have us believe.

For one thing, many care ethicists hold that care ethics can't completely cover the realm of morality and that it needs to be supplemented by or to supplement some form of "justice ethics" in order to do justice (excuse the expression) to moral phenomena generally. Such care ethicists sometimes say that the care ethics part of what should eventually be an integrated whole is the more important part, but I have heard others say that neither part of the eventual integrated whole has any moral precedence over the other—with the significance of care ethics then being that it emphasizes an area of our overall morality that has been given short shrift within traditional philosophical/ethical theory and theorizing.

This would be a fairly easy way to show that and how care ethics fits with the gender-neutral arguments and conclusions of the present book, but it also would come at a price: the price being the admission or assumption that care ethics can't cover the whole waterfront of morality and needs to look to justice ethics to deal with issues of autonomy, rights, and, of course, justice. And the further assumption here is that care ethics and justice ethics *can*, in fact, be integrated and/or harmonized. This is an assumption that many prominent care ethicists and others (including myself at one time) have been willing to make, but it is also an assumption that I (now) believe to be deeply mistaken. Care ethicists say that their approach stresses human connection rather than separateness and claim that the justice approach or "voice" stresses separateness (e.g., autonomy rights as against others) at the expense of connection to or with others. But is it really to be supposed that two such opposing or contrary approaches would never conflict about important moral issues? This doesn't in fact make much sense, and my recent book *The Ethics of Care and Empathy* sought precisely (this was the principal raison d'être of the book) to show that an emphasis on connection of the sort characteristic of care ethics and an emphasis on separateness (and autonomy rights) yield different and incompatible conclusions about certain highly important moral issues.

I argued there that with respect to "Skokie-type" examples of potential hate speech, the Kantian/liberal ethicist of justice will insist on the autonomy rights of those who wanted to demonstrate and make neo-Nazi speeches in a town where numerous Holocaust-survivors were living, whereas a care ethics that emphasizes our empathic concern for and connection to others will place much more weight on the potential damage to—and retraumatizing effects on—the Holocaust survivors that the neo-Nazi presence and activities were likely to cause. This is something that the neo-Nazis who wanted to march in Skokie were presumably well aware of—why else choose that particular town? But, as I pointed out in my book (drawing on previous work by Susan Brison), the liberals who have discussed this issue ignore those grievous effects, and I believe that makes them take a different position regarding what should or should not have been allowed in Skokie (the march never occurred) from what the care ethicist would advocate. For the care ethicist, serious potential human damage can trump or outweigh rights of autonomy—that is precisely what it means to treat connection with others as more important, ethically, than our separateness from or autonomy rights against others.

So in this case and in fact in many others, care ethics and justice ethics disagree;[14] and the idea, therefore, that they can be integrated or harmonized doesn't really make sense. Justice ethics has taken on moral issues at every level—individual, social, legal, political, international—and since care ethics can't be integrated with that approach or rely on it for answers to questions about legal/political morality, it has to stand on its own with respect to such questions; and in recent years more and more care ethicists have realized this. Care ethicists like Nel Noddings, Daniel Engster, and myself have realized that in order to represent a genuine alternative to justice ethics, to Kantian liberalism, care ethics needs to offer its own account of justice—and we have provided or begun to provide accounts of that concept and (at least in my own case) of relevant other notions like autonomy and respect.[15]

Therefore, let us ask ourselves whether what has been said, so gender-neutrally, in the present book fits comfortably with a care ethics that takes on moral issues across-the-board, the kind of care ethics I myself strongly favor. Such care ethics treats caring as basic not only to issues of personal or family morality, but to larger questions of social, and even international, justice, and doesn't our previous objection resurface with respect to such an overall approach to morality? In basing *everything* on caring, doesn't such an ethic show a bias in favor of what is typically associated with women rather than men? And does this fit at all with the gender-neutral approach of the present book?

I think, in fact, it does, and the reason why has to do with what care ethics has to do if and when it takes on issues of social justice that extend beyond the individual and family spheres that Noddings, for example, first focused on. Justice ethics has its own notion of or ideas about justice in relation to assumptions about individual autonomy and personhood that have at least been accused of being atomistic. But care ethics presumably cannot conceive justice in such terms: it clearly needs to rethink the idea of justice in its own terms, come up with its own distinctive conception of justice; and that reconfigured view of what justice involves will have to handle cases and deal with objections and offer explanations that on the whole do as well as or better than what traditional ("justice-ethical" or liberal) approaches to justice have to offer. And many of us care ethicists have in recent years been trying to do just that. And the reconfiguring needs to occur and has occurred not only with respect to justice but with respect to the notion of autonomy as well. Care ethicists and feminists have recently argued, for example, that autonomy is better conceived *relationally* than in the ahistorical and atomistic way that Kantians have treated it.

But notice what this means about care ethics. It means that care ethics is dealing with issues and concepts that have traditionally been (conceived as) the territory or purview of men. Rather than avoid (thinking about) issues of justice that typically occupy, or historically have occupied, males more than females, care ethics is now focusing on such issues, but giving its own distinctive connection-emphasizing interpretation of these issues and the notions they centrally involve. So this broader sort of care ethics combines what is typically or historically associated with women—namely, a stress on caring and connection—with what is typically or historically associated with men and not with women—namely, a keen interest in questions about and the concepts of autonomy and justice (and rights). Considered on the whole, this *isn't* a bias in favor of female things over male things, but of course the way this gender-even-handedness is achieved isn't quite the same way that such evenhandedness occurs or is instantiated in the present book. However, these are merely differences, not incongruities, so I think there is nothing in the present approach to goods and (nonmoral) virtues that should make us question care ethics as an approach to individual and political morality.[16] Thus there is no real tension between care ethics and the views of the present book, and I can see no problem with accepting them both.[17] But, of course, the reader may well not have seen care ethics defended in any full-blown way, and in that case I can only refer her or him to what I have said in *The Ethics of Care and Empathy* and in the more metaethically oriented *Moral Sentimentalism*—or, perhaps better, to the classic works on which my own work and other work in care ethics are in important ways based: namely, Carol Gilligan's *In a Different Voice*, Nel Noddings's *Caring*, and (for historical depth and some of the metaethics) Hume's *Treatise of Human Nature*.

But there is more to be said. The ethics of classical antiquity and the modern-day Enlightenment saw the world as intellectually and practically organizable in a unified, harmonious fashion under the aegis of reason, and both the ethics of care and the Berlinian ideas of the present book question this vision. To that extent, they side with Romanticism (the Romantic Movement) in *its* rejection of Enlightenment values and of the unified rational vision of human values that the philosophers of classical antiquity (starting with Socrates) sought to work out. Romanticism put feeling and emotion ahead of reason and rationality and was to that extent similar to most versions of care ethics.[18] But in the present book the emphasis hasn't so much been on the (importance of the) emotions as on the complexity, tensions, and, ultimately, inconsistencies that exist between and among our deepest and most considered ethical values. This, too, clearly contradicts the ideas of rational ethical harmony and unity that were accepted by the (nonskeptical) philosophers of classical antiquity and by the Enlightenment or neoclassical thinkers of the modern period and today.

But what we have said here also *goes beyond* Romanticism (and care ethics) in a very important way. By and large the Romantics never questioned the "perfectibility of man," never questioned the possibility of ideal virtue or happiness, and the main purpose of the present approach has been to do just that. Of course, the Greeks and the philosophers of the Enlightenment saw human perfection in rationalistic terms (e.g., the perfect virtue of the Stoic sage was supposed to consist in being perfectly rational), and (some of) the Romantics had a very different vision of how human perfection might be promoted or attained.[19] But it is only with the work of

Isaiah Berlin that one arrives at the clear and explicit idea that perfect virtue and/or perfect happiness are impossible in principle, and to that extent our arguments here have taken us in a direction not previously explored by Greek/Enlightenment thought, by care ethics, or by Romanticism.[20]

However, the fact that care ethics and the present book are both opposed to the classical, rationalist view of human life and ethics may help us to see how and why it is possible and makes sense to hold the views of the present book in tandem with some form of care ethics. The two represent, in effect, a two-pronged attack on the overall (and unified) ethical view or picture one finds in ancient Greek ethics and in those forms of modern or contemporary ethics that are rooted in Enlightenment thought. That picture sees all ethical value as in principle harmonizable under the aegis of reason, and care ethics objects to the "aegis of reason" part of that description, whereas the arguments offered here seek to undercut the somewhat different idea of harmonizability (whether understood rationalistically or Romantically). I believe these two ways of objecting to classical/Enlightenment views have more critical force taken together than they do taken separately, and that is at least part of what makes it natural and sensible to accept both care ethics and the Berlinian thesis of the impossibility of perfection (or complete ethical harmony).[21]

I might just add, too, that the opposition between care ethics and the present book, on the one hand, and classical/Enlightenment views, on the other, to some extent parallels the opposition between Dionysian and Apollonian values that Nietzsche describes in *The Birth of Tragedy*. But Nietzsche doesn't make much use of analytic philosophical arguments, so, as we have done with Isaiah Berlin, the present book seeks to give rational analytic arguments for ideas that have previously been expressed (only) passionately, impressionistically, intuitively, or very approximately.

Perhaps it is ironic that my argument for disunity in human good and virtue should be expressed via a theoretical approach that itself (I hope) isn't disunified or lacking in unity (any more than Greek or Enlightenment ethical views are lacking in unity *as views*). But in the area of theoretical or epistemic rationality, skeptics try to convince us, via theoretical reason, of such reason's own impotence, its inability to deliver conclusions that many or all of us believe to be true; and even if skepticism fails as a rational enterprise, the idea of using epistemic or theoretical reason to defeat such reason (via a kind of reductio ad absurdum) is certainly not ruled out ab initio. By the same token (and perhaps more obviously), the use of systematic or unified intellectual/ethical reasoning (mixed, I can only hope, with some measure of insight and emotional/psychological sensitivity) to call ethical rationalism and the unity of ethics into question also isn't ruled out from the start. That is what I have been to a certain extent doing here, and the only question is whether that effort, and our arguments and assumptions, have really been convincing. But one final point.

My reference just now to my own desire as an ethicist to combine intellectual/theoretical reasoning with some measure of insight and sensitivity raises an issue that sits quite comfortably alongside the question of whether care ethics can or does combine traditionally masculine and feminine elements, but that needs to be addressed in its own right: the issue of masculine vs. feminine ways of *doing philosophy in general*. Gilligan and Noddings have pointed out that certain ways of approaching moral issues can be associated with various differences between men and women that exist at least under patriarchy, but certain ways of *doing philosophy* can also be associated more with traditionally masculine or with traditionally feminine traits, and I want to suggest not only that care ethics should contain an (as traditionally conceived) feminine approach to concepts that are (traditionally) more associated with men than with women, but that it should also be pursued via methods, philosophical methods, some of which are more associated in our minds with women and others of which we associate with men. Care ethics needs to be insightful and emotionally/psychologically sensitive, but it also needs to address various philosophical issues making use of all the analytic and theory-building skills it can muster. But I won't pursue this thought right here and want to leave it for discussion in a separate appendix to this book.

Chapter 6

Relational Profiles of Goods and Virtues

We have offered a complex picture of human goods and virtues, but things are about to get more complicated. I earlier mentioned and used the notion of a dependent good/virtue—and the further and (for our purposes) central concept of a partial good/virtue was also introduced. But at a certain point in thinking about these topics, it occurred to me that our talk of dependency in particular was rather limited or regimented. Earlier in this book and in my 1983 book *Goods and Virtues*, I spoke of some virtues' being dependent on others, and some (personal) goods' being dependent on others— but there was never any talk of goods' depending on virtues or virtues' depending on goods, never any mention of the possibility of what (since goods and virtues are both ethical categories) we can call transcategorial ethical dependencies. Yet some of my own work on virtue ethics and its history had assumed such transcategorial dependencies without explicitly making use of that (precise) notion.

The Stoics believe, for example, that overall human good or happiness depends on one's being (totally) virtuous, and that is, in our new terms, a kind of transcategorial dependency. And one doesn't have to take as extreme a view as Stoicism in order to find examples of such ethical dependency. As I suggested earlier, one cannot really *accomplish* anything unless one has worked with strength of purpose (or perseverance), and here we have an example where a *particular* personal good, accomplishment or achievement, is seen as dependent on a *particular* human virtue, strength of purpose or perseverance. But are there transcategorial ethical dependencies in the opposite direction, plausible instances of virtues that depend on particular human goods? Well, I think there are, but before I say more about that, let me just say a bit more about what I propose to do in the present chapter.

There have been many comparative studies of the virtues in recent years. But the most prominent of these—and I am thinking in particular of the work of Thomas Hurka and Christine Swanton—tend to focus on the content of particular virtues and to put less emphasis on how the virtues relate to each other.[1] More specifically, although these studies have been pluralistic about the virtues, they haven't spoken (at least explicitly) about how various virtues depend on each other, and they certainly haven't focused on the relations of dependency that exist *among* (a plurality of) human goods or on those that exist *between* individual goods and individual virtues (what I am calling transcategorial ethical dependencies). To that extent, the (differing) pictures or profiles of the different virtues that other authors have offered have been largely *internal* to the various individual virtues they have focused on, and I am proposing to discuss a number of virtues and goods as they relate to *other* virtues or goods.[2] I hope and believe that such *relational* profiles both of the virtues and of personal goods will complement, rather than (in principle) conflict with, what internal(ist) approaches have said, and we will see that what we have to say in relational terms is actually quite complex. However, the complexity is not, as I shall argue, imposed or gratuitous, but (once again) simply reflects the diversity and richness (and interestingness) of ethical phenomena.

Before I get back to the topic of virtues' depending on goods, I would like to say more about transcategorial dependencies that move in the opposite direction. Just above, I mentioned two potential examples of goods' (or a good life's) depending on virtues or virtue, but there are many, many more, and we should say something about the other examples. In chapter 1, I mentioned a couple of instances where goods putatively depend on other goods, but I think the instances in which particular human goods depend on particular virtues may in fact be more numerous.

Thus the good of personal relationships seems to depend on one or another relevant form of caring—because we don't accord any particular value as such to relations of hostility or to relationships based on purely utilitarian (in the ordinary sense) considerations. Of course, the good of civic friendship will depend on a different (and less intimate) kind of caring from what ordinary friendship requires, but we think well of both kinds of caring and to that extent can regard both kinds as virtues, and in general the relationships we think of as among life's good things all entail one or another form of virtue. Consider next the personal good of deep knowledge or wisdom (we can also think of wisdom as a virtue, but let us put that point mainly to one side). We may not place a value on having sheer information, but we do tend to think that someone is better off for being wise, even if the wisdom is hard-won and makes one unhappily aware of how bad or inexplicable things are in human affairs or in the universe overall or in one's own life. And, as I have argued at great length elsewhere,[3] wisdom (either as a human good or as a virtue) seems to require us to have a certain kind of courage: not battlefield courage, but the courage to face unpleasant facts about oneself, about the human condition, and/or about the nature of the universe. It originally required courage (and I suppose for some it still requires courage) to believe in the theory of evolution, and it can certainly take courage to recognize the difficulty of justifying (or the epistemologically problematic character of) theistic belief. It also takes courage to face one's own inner demons, and yet all of these things seem necessary to being a wise person.

Now objective list accounts of human good vary to some extent among themselves as to what basic goods they say are to be included on an accurate objective list. But almost all such lists include wisdom, achievement, and friendship/love as among the basic goods of human life. And we have just seen that all of these basic goods depend on given virtues, different ones depending on the good in question. Objective lists almost all include one further human good, the good of appetitive (or aesthetic) pleasure, and one might wonder whether this (final) basic human good also depends on some particular virtue. It might not seem so, since pleasure seems so primitive and basic and virtue so high-falutin', but we shouldn't be misled by this appearance. It is quite possible that for a pleasure to constitute or give rise to a human good, to something that makes our life go at least temporarily better, we have to be to some extent *satisfied* with that pleasure. And in order to be satisfied with a given amount of appetitive pleasure, we can't be totally immoderate in our desires or appetites. Since being to some degree moderate in one's desires is regarded by many as a virtue (possessed to at least a minimal degree), it could therefore be argued that the good of pleasure depends on the virtue of moderation. I have elsewhere argued for this conclusion at considerable length—and attempted to show that this is also Plato's view of the good of pleasure.[4] However, it is enough for present purposes to indicate that in addition to the less controversial transcategorial dependencies mentioned above, there is another important putative or potential example as well. But having now (in the present book) discussed the intracategorial dependency of goods on goods and virtues on virtues and the transcategorial dependency of goods on virtues, it is time to consider whether virtues can transcategorially depend on goods.

Well, what about being modest about one's possessions? Presumably, the possessions are good things to have, things that make one's life more comfortable and better, and modesty about such possessions therefore seems to be a virtue that depends on one's having or enjoying certain goods.[5] But if one can be modest about the goods one possesses oneself, one can also have attitudes about the goods possessed by others, and if someone who is envious of others' possessions can be said to have the vice of envying others, surely someone who is entirely free of such envy can be said to have a virtue—though it is a virtue for which there is no commonplace and conventional name in English. Here, however, the dependency crosses the boundary between persons: one is virtuously unenvious of the good(s) enjoyed or possessed by others, and in fact this is the first time we have spoken of any sort of transpersonal dependency. Every kind of dependency I have spoken of so far in this book— whether of goods on goods, of goods on virtues, of virtues on goods, or of virtues on virtues—has been *intrapersonal*, has involved only one person. But the example of unenviousness (of being unenvious of the goods that others possess) clearly crosses the boundary between persons, and that means that a full account or picture of various ethical dependencies needs to be expanded. In addition to the distinction between transcategorial and intracategorial dependencies, we also need to distinguish between transpersonal and intrapersonal dependencies.[6]

Moreover, once we make this further distinction, we suddenly have a good deal more to say. We just saw that the virtue of being unenvious with respect to others' goods (or, if you will, the virtue of lacking covetousness with respect to such goods) transcategorially and transpersonally depends on the good(s) possessed by others.

(I suppose one could also virtuously lack envy for goods one mistakenly thought others possessed, but I will not consider such cases further.) But perhaps goods can also transpersonally depend on virtues, and virtues on virtues, and goods on goods, as well.

For example, the good of friendship, the good of having a good friend, depends to some extent on the friend's attitude. I earlier mentioned that to enjoy the distinctive good of being someone's friend, one needs to care about the friend, to have in some substantial degree the virtue of being a caring person—and that is an intrapersonal kind of transcategorial dependency. But if one's supposed friend doesn't care about one, then there is something illusory or worse about the relationship, and I think most of us would be inclined to say that where one isn't loved or well liked in return, being friends with a given person isn't a good thing for one (or is at best only a means to the enjoyment of other goods), even if one's own caring or love for the friend is part of the situation. Unrequited love and unreciprocated feelings and acts of friendship are not in themselves human goods; or so, at least, it seems intuitive to say. So if unenviousness is a virtue that depends transpersonally on the good(s) that others enjoy, then friendship is a good that depends transpersonally on the virtuous caring of another person; for a totally one-sided friendship doesn't count as a good thing for the person who has the friendly feelings—or, indeed, for the person who doesn't reciprocate those feelings.[7] (I shall have more to say about one-sided friendships later in this chapter.)

Given that we have examples of the transpersonal dependency of a virtue on a good and of a good on a virtue, can we also find instances in which a personal good transpersonally depends on someone else's good and other cases in which a virtue in one person depends on the existence of virtues in others? Let's return to the good of friendship. We think of friendship (between two individuals) as a reciprocal relationship, and I believe part of that reciprocity involves the good that each derives from the friendship. I believe that for a friendship (or love relationship) to be good for one of the friends (or lovers), it has to be good for the other, but one has to be careful when one says this. Friends typically say that their good depends on the good of the other, but what is typically meant is that anything bad that happens to one of them independently of their friendship, counts as bad for the friend as well. And I am not talking about that kind of dependency of goods, but rather of the good that each derives from the existence of the friendship itself. The friendship cannot be a good thing for one of the friends and not the other—as, for example, if the one friend generally takes advantage of the other or if one of the friends (assuming this is consistent with their really being friends) generally resents the way they are treated by the other. Friendship thus involves not only a reciprocal *relationship*, but also a reciprocity (or mutuality) in the good that each derives from the fact or reality of that close and mutually caring relationship (a good that may include, but is far from limited to the good and pleasant things they do with or to one another). So this is an example of how goods can transpersonally depend on other goods.

But I have not been able to find any complementary example of virtues transpersonally depending on other virtues. We naturally think of certain goods (and feelings) as reciprocal, but don't seem to have any use for or familiarity with the notion of a *reciprocal virtue*. Even in one-sided friendships, the caring concern one of the parties has for the other seems still to be to some extent admirable, to count as something of a virtue. We might think that the person who never gets any help or affection from his or her supposed friend would be entitled to stop caring about and doing things for such a friend, but if someone continues to care about someone who doesn't reciprocate, there is something at least a bit lovely (though, of course, also sad) about their attitude and motivation. (I am assuming that such continued caring doesn't have to be masochistic.) So I am loath to say that such cases give us an example of a virtue (of caring) whose status as such depends on its being virtuously reciprocated by another person. Similarly, cooperativeness, a willingness to cooperate with others on condition that they are willing to reciprocate, is a virtue. But this virtue doesn't depend on anyone else's actually being virtuously willing to cooperate in return. Someone living in a world of uncooperative narcissists (or worse) who has the disposition to (relevantly) cooperate with anyone who might be willing to reciprocate has a disposition we think well of and can call virtuous. After all, virtue is a dispositional notion, and a virtue doesn't actually have to be exercised in order to count as such. So such a person's possession of the virtue of cooperativeness doesn't depend on anyone else's possessing that virtue or, it would seem, any other. In fact, and as I have already indicated, I can't think of *any* halfway plausible case of one (person's) virtue's transpersonally depending on another (person's).

Nor do I have an explanation of why the interpersonal mutuality that seems to attach to certain personal goods doesn't seem to apply to anything we would call a virtue. And in the absence of such an explanation, one can't be sure that someone (perhaps a reader of this book) won't sooner or later come up with a plausible case where a virtue *does* transpersonally depend on a(nother) virtue. But for the moment, I don't know what more to say and have to leave the asymmetry of transpersonal dependencies (the fact that some goods transpersonally depend on certain virtues, that some virtues transpersonally depend on certain goods, that some goods transpersonally depend on certain goods, but that no virtues seem to transpersonally depend on any virtues) something of a mystery.

At this point, however, we come to what may well be the most interesting or surprising aspect of our study of ethical dependencies, of the relational profiles of various goods and virtues. We have spoken of goods depending on other goods or on virtues and of virtues depending on other virtues or on goods, and these dependencies in many cases cross the boundaries of self and other. But all the interrelated values we have spoken of are positive ones: goods, virtues, not evils/harms or vices, and there is no reason why we shouldn't expand our discussion to take in the latter. There are two ways, however, of doing so: one less interesting, one (to my mind) extremely interesting. We have spoken, for example, of how certain virtues depend on other virtues, and it would be possible at this point to expand our discussion to take in (the) ways in which vices depend, either intrapersonally or transpersonally, on vices or evils— and then go on to say how certain personal evils, or bad things, depend transpersonally or intrapersonally on vices or other evils.

All this, as I say, would be possible. But I don't think it would be all that interesting. If instead of talking further of the dependency relations of certain virtues, we spoke of the dependency relations of the vices that correspond to those virtues, I believe we would end up repeating some of the thinking that went into our previous discussion of the virtues. And similarly for any expansion of our discussion of goods to take in corresponding personal evils and what depends on them. Nothing very surprising is likely to come of such a discussion—and I think that in the end it would seem and be somewhat repetitive of what we have already done.

But there is another, much more interesting way in which we can expand our discussion to take in vices and evils (i.e., bad things in people's lives—I am not talking about moral evils). We have so far examined how goods and virtues relate to other goods and virtues, and the discussion has to that extent remained completely within the realm of (what we can call) positive values. But what about the possibility that certain virtues may depend on certain vices, or on evils, either intrapersonally or transpersonally? What about the parallel possibility that certain goods might depend on certain evils or on certain vices? Such *transvalent* dependencies (as we may call them) would be very interesting if we could find them, and surprisingly enough there turn out to be quite a few of them. So rather than focus on vices and personal evils and ask what they depend on, let us continue to focus on virtues and personal goods, but ask ourselves the new questions of whether and to what extent such positive values can depend on negative ones.

In the light of our earlier distinctions between transpersonal and intrapersonal and between transcategorial and intracategorial dependencies, this gives us quite a large *spielraum* for investigation. Given that everything we have described up till now has related to *intravalent* dependencies, the possibilities for transvalent dependencies include the possibility of goods transvalently and intrapersonally depending either on personal evils or on vices, the possibility of goods transvalently but transpersonally depending either on personal evils or on vices, the possibility of virtues transvalently and intrapersonally depending either on vices or on personal evils, and the possibility of virtues transvalently and transpersonally depending either on vices or personal evils. This constitutes quite a large number of conceivable "slots" for transvalent ethical dependencies to fit into, but we shall just have to see how many of those constitute plausible or realistic ethical possibilities. Moreover, and as I said, the idea that virtues could depend on vices or personal evils/ills may seem a bit surprising at first, and so one has to cast about a bit when one starts looking for examples of transvalent dependency. I have myself been thinking quite a bit about this topic recently, and what follows here is what I have been able to come up with.

We have actually already mentioned—not in this chapter, but in chapters 3 and 4—the possibility that a personal good might depend on a personal ill or evil. The view that one cannot, for example, fully enjoy the pleasant things in life unless one has experienced personal evils like pain or heartache clearly entails the existence of an intrapersonal, intracategorial, but transvalent ethical dependency. But I continue to be somewhat skeptical about that particular view, and I think some of the other discussion in chapter 3 can help us toward a more compelling (though related) example of good depending on personal ill or evil. Chapter 3 argued that the full good of personal achievement depends on having struggled with and overcome difficulties, disappointment, obstacles, and frustration on the way to fulfillment and/or success. But if this is plausible, then we have a reasonable example of intrapersonal, intracategorial, transvalent ethical dependency. And having found one, we turn out to be in a good position to find others, for some very plausible further examples emerge immediately and unproblematically from our discussion of partial goods and virtues in chapters 1 and 2.[8]

Adventure is a (partial) good that comes at the cost of some insecurity; and by the same token adventurousness is a (partial) virtue that depends for its instantiation on the person in question's being less than fully prudent. We have similar reason to believe that the (partial) good of career fulfillment depends on one's having (at least) slightly superficial relationships with other people. And reason likewise to believe that the (partial) virtue of frankness depends on one's being less than completely tactful; and so on for all the partial goods and partial virtues we have considered. Each such good or virtue is paired with another and depends for its full instantiation on that other's not being fully instantiated,[9] and in every case this will involve intrapersonal, intracategorial, but transvalent ethical dependency.

In fact, then, the new categories for relationally profiling goods and virtues that we have been exploring in this chapter help us better see the nature and implications of the arguments and conclusions of earlier chapters. For we can now say that it is characteristic and even definitional of what it is to be a partial virtue/good that it be transvalently, but intrapersonally and intracategorially dependent on the ethically negative *absence* of another partial virtue/good. In fact, our earlier talk of the pairing of and opposition between partial goods or virtues can be unpacked or cashed out in terms of what we have just been saying about the transvalent, intrapersonal, and intracategorial dependencies that exist between such partial goods or virtues.

But the sheer abundance of such examples of transvalency raises an interesting question about the possibility of *different* kinds of examples. Every example of transvalent dependency that arises out of the existence of partial goods and virtues involves intracategorial and intrapersonal dependency. A partial virtue depends on the noninstantiation of an opposed virtue in the same person who has the partial virtue. And similarly for partial goods. So we have to ask whether the category of transvalent dependency is or has to be confined to intrapersonal and intracategorial examples. Could there be a virtue whose possession depended on that person or *someone else's* possession of some personal *evil*? Could there be a good whose possession depended on that person or *someone else's* possession of some *vice*?

Perhaps forbidden fruit can taste better than fruit one is allowed to have. I am not sure that Adam or Eve had any sort of thrilling taste experience eating their apple, but consider the La Rochefoucauld bon mot that there are delicious affairs, but no delicious marriages. *Such* forbidden fruit might be thought to be tastier or in some other way better than the permissible, and consider more particularly the following example drawn from Ingmar Bergman's *Scenes from a Marriage* (TV miniseries version): The formerly married main characters Marianne and Johan initiate an affair with one another after each has remarried, and as they are driving off to an "illicit" weekend together, one of them says that what they are doing is indecent, and the other replies: "that's what's so nice about it." This illustrates the idea that a heightened level of enjoyment or satisfaction may depend on the vicious (non-virtuous) character of the enjoyment or satisfaction and so represents a form of (assumed) transvalent transcategorial dependency. And the dependency here may be both intrapersonal and transpersonal, because it seems as if (the couple may be agreeing that) the heightened pleasure that each feels may depend not only on betraying their own spouse but on the fact that the other is betraying *theirs*. (I must say, though, that I am not entirely persuaded by this kind of example.)

However, before we move forward, it might be interesting to make some explicit comparisons and draw some contrasts that have so far have been merely implicit in our discussion. We have made a good many claims about different forms of ethical dependency, have offered brief and (no doubt) partial relational profiles of a good many individual virtues and personal goods, but I think it would now be interesting briefly to compare and contrast what we have said about some of those different virtues and goods.

For example, earlier in this book, in chapter 1, I mentioned the way in which conscientiousness seems to depend on the possession of basic humane values, and this means that the virtue of conscientiousness intracategorially, intrapersonally, and intravalently depends on the virtue of humaneness. I also pointed out in chapter 1 that the social virtue of civility seems to depend for its status as a virtue on there being a certain level of justice in a given society. For example, the civility and good manners of the antebellum American South may not strike one as embodying any sort of genuine social virtue given (in the light of) the near-total injustice of Southern society, so once again we have one virtue (albeit a social one) intracategorially, (in some sense) intrapersonally, and intravalently depending on another.[10] By contrast, the virtue of adventurousness intracategorially, intrapersonally, but *transvalently* depends on the vice of imprudence; and similarly for the relationship between the virtue of frankness and the vice of being to some extent lacking in tact. (Parallel claims can obviously be made mutatis mutandis for the virtues of prudence and tactfulness.)

Next, consider how the good of (receiving) sympathy intracategorially, intrapersonally, and intravalently depends on the good of being respected—an example we mentioned in chapter 1; and contrast this with the way in which the good of adventure intracategorially, intrapersonally, but transvalently depends on the evil or ill of insecurity and the way in which the good of creative fulfillment (likewise) intracategorially, intrapersonally, but transvalently depends on the evil or ill of struggle and frustration. Then contrast all these examples with the way in which the full good of the forbidden is supposed to depend—transvalently, *but also transcategorially*—on one or another vice (e.g., infidelity).

But, as we have just seen, such transvalent transcategorial dependencies can also be either intrapersonal or *transpersonal*, and our earlier discussion brought in a number of other kinds of transpersonal dependency. We saw, for example that the good of friendship for any given person depends on their friend's deriving some good from the friendship (on the friendship's being a good thing for the friend as well). And this is a case of transpersonal, but intravalent, and intracategorial dependency. But the good of friendship for a given person also depends transpersonally and intravalently, but *transcategorially* on the virtuous caringness of their friend. Similarly, the virtue of unenviousness depends transpersonally and intravalently, but also transcategorially on the good(s) enjoyed by others— though in this case the dependency is of a virtue on a good, rather than in the opposite direction. But all the examples in this paragraph are transpersonal, so every one of them stands in more or less marked contrast with the cases with which we began this review discussion.

As you see, this is all quite complicated. We have a plurality of (bimodal) categories for classifying ethical dependencies, and the possibilities of comparison and contrast may be even greater than what I have just offered you. Still, I think I have said enough to indicate why I think our tools of comparison are rather useful and yield illuminating results. The distinctions we have drawn with regard to (issues of) ethical dependency include the difference between intrapersonal and transpersonal dependencies, the difference between transcategorial and intracategorial dependencies, the difference between transvalent and intravalent dependencies, and (what has been implicit all along) the difference between talking of what a virtue depends on and talking of what a good depends on. (The other distinctions are in some sense relational ones, but this last distinction is one, so to speak, in where one starts.) And there is one further complication.

I have spoken of giving various individual goods and virtues relational profiles, and those profiles have involved speaking of what a given good or virtue ethically depends on. But the full relational profile of any given (qualified) good or (qualified) virtue will also have to include claims about what depends (intracategorially or transcategorially, etc.) *on it*.[11] So I hope you can see that the task of offering profiles of the virtues (and goods) involves much more than Swanton, Hurka, and others have spoken of. It involves relational profiling in addition to the kind(s) undertaken by these other philosophers, and relational profiling turns out to be a highly complicated matter. I also hope the reader will have found the above to be of at least theoretical or philosophical interest. It opens up some new possibilities of ethical exploration and comparison, and, I believe, adds to what philosophers like Swanton and Hurka (and others in recent times or earlier on) have said about the richness and complexity of ethics.

But having said all this, let me finally—yes really, finally—speak about one further dimension of the complexity or complexities of ethics. At the miniconference on neo-Confucian thought that was held at the Pacific Division meetings of the American Philosophical Association in Vancouver in 2009, I heard a very interesting talk by Yang Xiao (of Kenyon College) in which he spoke of certain values as being deviant. I thought his most forceful example was cultural relativism, which he claimed was a deviant version of the notion and value of authenticity. This makes sense to me, and I think one might also say that to treat authenticity as a matter of simply being true to *whatever values one has* (no matter how perverse or malign) constitutes a distortion of the ideal of authenticity and so constitutes another deviant form or version of that ideal.

After hearing Xiao's talk, it also occurred to me that there is an interesting distinction to be made between deviant forms of an ideal or activity and *variant* forms of an ideal or activity. Collegiate wrestling and Greco-Roman wrestling are not deviant forms of wrestling; they are simply variants of or on that sport or activity. But wrestling on television really is deviant as an example of wrestling—it betrays or distorts the traditions of wrestling by substituting showmanship and deception for a genuine test of "combat" skills. And I think (though Xiao himself didn't say this) that cultural relativism and the idea that any set of values can be authentically adhered to both distort the ideal of authenticity by treating it as it weren't limited or conditioned by other values.

By contrast, the idea of variant forms of some valued activity or institution can be seen in the example of civic friendship. Civic

friends may not be as close as intimate, personal friends are supposed to be, but civic friendship is in many ways analogous to ordinary friendship, and the ways it which it differs from ordinary
friendship don't betray or distort the values we find in ordinary
friendship or, for that matter, in the kind of just society in which
civic friendship is supposed to occur and be nourished. Civic friendship can therefore reasonably be called a variant on or of (the idea or
ideal of) friendship.

On the other hand, a one-sided friendship in which one person
gives and the other only takes seems deviant as a form or instance of
friendship. Of course, some will say that such a friendship really is
no friendship at all, and perhaps that is correct. But in saying that
such a friendship is a deviant form of friendship we are not necessarily supposing that it is a genuine kind of friendship—"deviant"
might be considered an *alienans* adjective like "counterfeit" in "counterfeit dollar." But we probably don't have to decide on the issue of
whether "deviant" is an *alienans* adjective or on the question whether
a one-sided friendship is really a friendship in order to say that a
one-sided friendship is a *deviant form* of friendship. The claim that it
is deviant says less than the claim that it is no friendship at all, but it
says *something*, something that we in fact would or might like to be
able to say and express about one-sided friendships. And to that
extent the notion of a deviant form of friendship is or can be useful
to us.

Let me give you another example where the notion of deviance
can seem to apply and where using the notion can be of some use to
us. In *Reasons and Persons*, Derek Parfit says that ethical egoism has
in recent times been extruded from the class of theories or views we
think of as moral,[12] and if the egoist tells us (merely) what we have
most reason to do—namely, advance our own self-interest—then
he doesn't use any specifically moral concept and his view is fairly

clearly then not a moral one. But some egoists say that it is our *moral obligation* always to advance or promote our own self-interest, and this claim clearly does use or purport to use a specifically moral notion. However, the notion of obligation involves, for most of us, some sort of binding tie to other people (the Latin root of the word "obligation" contains the idea of tying or binding), and any purely egoistic theory of moral obligation distorts the whole idea of what morality is about because it totally fails to recognize any such ties. Once again, though, we can say that an egoism of moral obligation is a *deviant* form of morality or moral theory without having to commit ourselves to claiming that it is *not* a kind of morality, and this may be what, in all circumspection, it makes the most sense for us to say about it.

Note further that what is extreme or exaggerated (and mistaken) is not necessarily deviant—at least by our common lights. Pacifism may take the imperative of not harming to an extreme, but I don't think we would ordinarily regard it as a deviant form of morality: misguided perhaps, yes, but not, I think, deviant. That is because its exaggerations don't run counter to the spirit of morality; rather, if anything, they are exaggerations *both of and in* that very spirit. And the same might be said about the belief that torture is wrong in all conceivable circumstances. Again, this takes morality to an extreme and is a (limited and probably mistaken) form of absolutism, but the extremity seems more an exaggeration of and in the very spirit of morality, than a distortion of that spirit.[13] So I think that, in addition to all the distinctions we made earlier about the relations among the virtues and human goods, it is also useful for us to have the just-introduced distinctions among variant, deviant, and exaggerated forms of an ideal, institution, etc. But note this:

If "deviant" isn't an *alienans* adjective, then deviant values may be real values in some qualified sense, and that would mean that the category of qualified values (virtues or goods) would contain not just partial values and dependent values, but also deviant ones. In other words (for example), it might turn out that a commitment and disposition to act in accordance with one's belief in cultural relativism was not only a kind of deviant (or distorted) virtue, but also counted as a *qualified kind* of virtue, and that would mean that we had unearthed yet another kind of qualified value and were moving even further from the Aristotelian picture of virtue and value.[14] But, then, we might also want to say that pacifism (or a refusal to torture under any circumstances) represents an exaggerated or extremist form of (real) moral virtue, so we would in fact end up with four different types of qualified values in our general scheme of things: partial values, dependent values, deviant (or distorted) values, and exaggerated (or extreme) values.[15] What we have said (following but expanding on Yang Xiao's ideas about deviance) allows us to add to the ethical picture of human life and values that we have been drawing in this book, and that is why I thought it made sense to introduce the new notions of deviant and exaggerated value(s) before bringing our main discussion to a close.

Conclusion

Most philosophers who focus on the virtues have been beholden to Aristotle. They may not have accepted the Aristotelian doctrine of the mean—indeed few present-day Aristotelians are comfortable with that doctrine—but to a considerable extent they accept an Aristotelian conception of the virtues. They don't reduce the virtues to purely instrumental notions; they treat the virtues as objective features of the human ethical landscape; they accept or at least don't explicitly reject the idea of the unity of the virtues; they accept the view that perfect virtue and well-being/happiness are possible in principle, and they certainly don't go in for qualifying or conditionalizing the virtues in various ways.

I said earlier that any attempt to criticize such a basically Aristotelian picture or to replace it with something supposedly more adequate needs to present a systematic alternative picture. With all due apologies (again) to Thomas Kuhn, it takes a picture to beat a picture—and that is something Kripke taught us in *Naming and Necessity*, where he argued not only point for point against the description theory of proper names, but also presented what he explicitly said was an alternative picture of what naming is all about.[1] Now I haven't covered the field of the virtues and human goods nearly as thoroughly as I would like, and certainly not as thoroughly as Kripke covered the basic problems of reference that any theory of naming has (or then had) to deal with. But my criticisms of Aristotle and others *have* been embedded in a larger picture—one that emphasizes the complexity and tensions within our understanding of ethical phenomena in a way that Aristotle never did and perhaps never was in a position to do. Aristotle wasn't aware of many of the complex issues that distinctively characterize the modern world—with questions about feminism, about individualism, about intrasociety pluralism, and about large-scale international relations occupying us recently in a way they didn't in Aristotle's time (or the Middle Ages).

Now I haven't questioned the nonreductive and objective character of the Aristotelian picture of human goods and virtues; nor would I wish to criticize the Aristotelian approach to certain important virtues like (battlefield) courage and temperance. But I have presented reasons for thinking that the nexus of human good and virtue is much more complexly contoured than modern-day Aristotelians and Aristotle himself ever thought (or imagined). That complexity fits in well with the ethical issues that occupy us today. To take just one of the examples we have mentioned, the difficulty or difficulties of balancing and even of properly valuing career/self-fulfillment and personal relationships is glaringly obvious to us today, and some, though hardly all, of what I have been saying stems from a belief that we have to better understand those difficulties and can't easily blink them away. The idea that those difficulties are not an artifact of particular social arrangements or of certain people's failings or inadequacies and that they indicate something very deep about our (or anyone else's) ethical condition, the idea that the best explanation or account of those difficulties leads us, if we take into account our own intuitive ethical understandings and sensitivities, to the thought that perfect happiness is in principle impossible, certainly represents a radical break with traditional or Aristotelian understandings. And that is something that, other things being equal, we are and should be intellectually or philosophically reluctant to commit ourselves to. But our radical conclusion here also has something attractive about it, for it could be in some measure consoling to know that the heartache, handwringing, personal and family tension(s), and hard-working practical excogitation that have accompanied our thinking and worrying about how to balance career/creative fulfillment and relationships are not due to our own inadequacies or our society's but are basic to the condition of any set of intelligent beings who live in (what we would call) an advanced society. (As I mentioned earlier, they are also not due to "the human condition," if by that phrase is meant something that characterizes humans but might not hold for other intelligent or "higher" beings.)

But the idea of the impossibility of perfection and the applicability of the notion of a partial value extend, as I argued, far beyond the general area of career vs. family. That area marks an area of special feminist ethical concern, but we also spoke of other issues that engage feminist ethics and of issues that extend well beyond any specifically feminist concern(s) in making the case for the impossibility of perfect virtue and happiness and in using and applying the concept of a partial virtue/good/value. If you recall, I argued that the question of whether sex with emotional/personal commitment is better than uncommitted (adventurous) sex(uality) also calls out for treatment in terms of the notion of a partial good, and the position I took on that question, in addition to illustrating the idea of partial goods and the impossibility of perfect happiness, is also responsive to feminist ideas and values and critical of patriarchal "double-standard" sexist views about this issue. Similarly, for our discussion of adventure vs. security as values in a human (or any other kind of intelligent) life.

But the issue of frankness vs. tact doesn't directly concern any issue that feminism or feminist ethics feels called on to deal with, and our discussion of various kinds of dependent vs. nondependent values takes us beyond the sphere and interests of feminist ethics and makes us focus on issues of general human ethical significance. The offered picture as a whole isn't confined to any one point of view or sphere of ethical concern, but is really very general in its ethical implications, and that is why I am saying that it counts as a general alternative to Aristotelian views. Of course, and as a matter of personal history, I got my effective start with this alternative picture through a consideration of some questions about patriarchy vs. feminism; and those questions and their importance for (many of) us today do much (I hope) to move us in the direction of the alternative picture. But what I have offered as an alternative to Aristotle is based on much wider considerations, and, I might add, this alternative is not *just* an alternative, but, as we saw in chapter 3, is a *diametrically opposed* conception of ethical values. That is all the more reason, I suppose, to be hesitant and even suspicious, so a great deal of this book rests on the assumption that what I have had to say about specific examples is intuitively plausible—together with the case that can be made for saying that those claims about examples have been organized via ethical categories and distinctions which, while somewhat or totally unfamiliar, are philosophically and ethically worth making. So, as I have said, the reader will have to judge for herself or himself whether the radical suggestions, the recommended alterations in how we see and classify things, are really worth it.

Even apart from those more radical alterations, if the idea of dependent values seems to be worth working with, if the notion that our profiling of the virtues ought to have a relational dimension in addition to the more familiar internal one seems reasonable, and if it also seems plausible to suppose that such profiling should be applied to goods and not just to virtues—then much of what I have been doing will also be worth it. However, I believe and hope that this book will have a larger significance through its attempt to present an alternative, (largely) anti-Aristotelian view of the virtues and human well-being in which Isaiah Berlin's original ideas about the impossibility of perfection can comfortably fit.

The idea of an alternative or alternatives to Aristotle is hardly a new one, however. In the seventeenth century Aristotelianism lost its hegemony over European ethical thought when it became increasingly clear that it was inadequate (as then formulated and understood) for dealing with the kinds of religious and cultural conflicts that at that time were besetting Europe. The ideal of human or political rights and an increased emphasis on legal structures (or analogies) then emerged as a better way of handling the new, distinctive modern political/legal challenges, and, as we know, Aristotelianism went into a deep decline that wasn't even partially reversed till the recent (re)emergence of virtue ethics.

Recent Aristotelianism has sought and claimed to be able to deal better with the problems that the notion of human rights was invented to deal with, and I don't want to question that ability here.[2] Rosalind Hursthouse, for example, has presented a basically Aristotelian picture of social justice in which many, but not all, of our most familiarly claimed human rights are included, and the present book hasn't taken on and at this late point surely doesn't want to take on the issue of whether Aristotelianism is an adequate form of morality.[3] Aristotelianism may now be getting a good second wind on the moral/political front, but, as I have said all along here, the criticisms that derive from the Berlin thesis and the considerations that support it are not distinctively or particularly moral. They stem rather from ideas about the (largely nonmoral) virtues and about the good life that challenge the way Aristotle and most Aristotelians see those topics—and this really is a far cry from the sorts of criticisms that brought down Aristotelianism in the seventeenth century and subsequently.[4] So what I am and have been saying here is largely independent of those earlier criticisms and focuses on a different aspect of Aristotelianism from what so greatly occupied the Dutch jurists and others in the seventeenth century.

However, there is another issue—which I don't believe surfaced much in seventeenth-century discussions—that divides my Berlinian approach from Aristotelianism, one that I haven't really focused on up till now. As a eudaimonist, Aristotle thought (roughly) that if one acts virtuously over a full lifetime one will inevitably flourish, do well in life, and many of today's Aristotelians are also eudaimonists. But most modern moral philosophers don't accept eudaimonism, and I don't accept it either. I think self-sacrifice, sacrifice of one's own good or welfare, is possible and sometimes morally necessary and virtuous (as when men went off to war during World War II). However, I don't want to get into my reasons or give arguments for this rejection of eudaimonism, because, for one thing, what I have said earlier about goods and virtues doesn't (*I think*) depend on that rejection.

Of course, if one does, explicitly, reject eudaimonism, there is less of a necessary overall connection between human happiness and human virtue than Aristotle and most ancient philosophers supposed, and so the rejection of eudaimonism represents another or additional way in which one can argue that Aristotelianism has too simple a picture of virtues and goods. But the theses and arguments of the present book go well beyond anything that a rejection of eudaimonism entails in the way of challenging the simplicity of the Aristotelian picture. The rejection of eudaimonism doesn't entail that perfection of virtue or well-being is impossible, and on its own that rejection doesn't offer us a way of dealing with the complex social/human issues I have been focusing on. It says nothing, for example, about the distinctively modern problems of career vs. relationships or of committed vs. uncommitted sexuality. And similarly, if one thinks about it, for almost every other issue we have spoken of here. So although the denial of eudaimonism further calls into question the unity of the Aristotelian picture of virtue and human good, I think it does so less radically than the arguments of this book do. For better or worse, the idea that eudaimonism may be false is far more familiar and acceptable to most philosophers than Berlin's "extreme" views have ever been. What we have offered, therefore, is a picture of virtue and good that is diametrically opposed to Aristotelian views of virtue and good, and the rejection of eudaimonism on its own doesn't move us in anything like such a radically new direction.

It is perhaps no accident that this book is appearing when it is appearing—and not before. Most of our good examples of partial values emerge from consideration of feminist issues that weren't on the front burner of social or philosophical concern in earlier times— even, for example, during the not-so-distant past when Isaiah Berlin was enunciating his thesis of the impossibility of perfection. (That just adds to my sense of how prophetic his contribution really was.) Certain wrenching choices having to do with sexuality and more generally with how to lead one's life were earlier on not vivid for (many) people in the way they are today, and I see the purpose or function of this book as at least in part an attempt to bring some of these issues to a kind of philosophical self-awareness that has, in my estimation, been lacking or absent up till now. The complexities that feminism and the rejection of patriarchy bring in their train affect all or many of us in our practical concerns vis-à-vis others or vis-à-vis the shape and content of our own lives.[5] But as far as I know the present book represents the first attempt to make us aware of (what

129

I take to be) the most general philosophical/ethical implications of all these complexities of contemporary life.[6]

To be sure, and as I have indicated earlier, some issues of partial values lie beyond the sphere of feminist ethics—e.g., the choice between frankness and tact or between dependability and spontaneity. But in my case at least, it was easier to recognize the force of the more "neutral" examples once I had seen the force of the issues that derived from or related to feminist ethical goals and aspirations. Those issues are assailing and perplexing us all the time these days, and they seem to me to compel us toward a recognition of partial values and of the impossibility of perfection. But at that point we can also recognize that the same kinds of issues were facing us all along with examples like tact vs. frankness (though these questions were probably less central to our lives). So the present book, abstract and philosophical as it is, is also very much of and for its time. I don't think it would ever have occurred to me to think along present lines (and follow up with arguments what Isaiah Berlin had so peremptorily stated), if I hadn't been living at a point in history where feminism is making us aware of wrenching (and divisive) issues that are potentially relevant to all our lives. Nonetheless, the conclusions I have reached are supposed to characterize not just the present time, but the irrecusable ethical situation of human beings and of intelligent beings more generally; and to that extent the philosophical enterprise of the present book has really been quite traditional.

Men's Philosophy, Women's Philosophy

In chapter 5, I spoke about the (as traditionally conceived) feminine and masculine elements that are combined within an ethics of care that seeks to be normatively systematic or comprehensive. Such a care ethics takes in and takes on philosophical concepts, like justice, autonomy, and respect, that supposedly interest men more than women, but it gives a distinctively care-ethical account of those concepts, and the terms of that account (or of the different accounts that invariably are offered within any given general approach) are distinctively (as least by patriarchal or traditional association) feminine: for the emphasis is all on caring, on empathy, and on emotional sensitivity and connection more generally. But at the end of chapter 5, I mentioned the fact that there are also (as traditionally conceived) distinctively male/masculine and distinctively female/feminine ways of doing philosophy in general and, therefore, of working up or developing any ethics in philosophical terms.

I believe—and I shall say more about this in just a moment—that care ethics was initially approached and developed more in an intuitive than in a philosophically analytic or theoretical manner, but there is no reason why those who do care ethics shouldn't combine (masculine) analytic skills with (feminine) emotional sensitivity and intuitiveness. And in fact if care ethics is true or on the right track, there is more reason for it to combine these "methods" than for other approaches to do so, if one assumes that they are the right way to think about ethics. If Kantians are right about the rational roots and grounding of morality, then emotional or psychological sensitivity may just be less relevant and helpful to someone pursuing Kantian ethical theory than it is or would be, if care ethics is or were the right way to go and one were pursuing ethical theory in that direction.

But even Kantian theory cannot do or live without insight and intuition. I don't think of Kant, for example, as showing, in his moral philosophy, very much emotional sensitivity. However, one cannot deny that Kant's philosophy contains important, even amazing moral insights. Kant was an incredibly creative thinker, and at least part of the creativity involved his intuitions and/or insights about moral matters. For example, his distinction between categorical and hypothetical imperatives corresponds to something very deep in us but never previously articulated by any moral philosopher. So one can certainly say, in this instance and many others, that Kant was intuitively insightful about some of our deepest moral convictions or understandings. This is one form (but only one form) of Kant's philosophical creativity, and there are certainly other Kantian issues and/or concepts that also illustrate this kind of intuitive insight and creativity. (I am thinking most particularly about Kant's distinction between *das Gute* and *das Wohl*, a distinction which, I have elsewhere argued, he was the first to make clearly in the entire history of philosophy.)[1]

But it isn't just creativity in the field of theoretical ethics that requires intuition and insight.[2] It helps to have good intuitions and to have insights if one is doing philosophy of history or philosophy of mathematics, and some feminist thinkers have suggested that even in the latter field *emotional* sensitivities may play a role (perhaps one that is even comparable to their role in ethics). And in fact many of the things I have been and shall be saying here have been said by others—notably by feminists—in other contexts. But I shall also be making some new, some not previously anticipated, further points about the role of masculine and feminine elements in ethical theorizing and, especially, in approaching ethics from a care standpoint that places emotion and feeling at the very center of the moral life (and of moral thought).

Let's consider what actually goes on and is said in the field of philosophy. People give talks and write papers or books, and these things are evaluated to a large extent—and more than I think is entirely appropriate—in terms of how well they stand up to analytic philosophical criticism. But, you say, if they can be knocked down in analytic terms, they aren't likely to be true or insightful, so why am I (or other feminists) making such a fuss? Well, let me give you an example that might help to show why a fuss needs to be made.

In 1985, Annette Baier published an article called "Cartesian Persons" that argued that we are all "second persons," that we have to be a "you" for some nurturing other before we can be an "I" for ourselves.[3] She took this to show that there is something profoundly wrong in the Cartesian/Kantian view of personhood/autonomy that sees us as atomistic units that can be defined or understood independently of all relation to other people. But many philosophers immediately leaped on her argument and accused her of some kind of genetic fallacy. Just because our autonomy and personhood causally require the presence and actions of others in order to develop doesn't mean that it is philosophically best to understand these things *in themselves* (and once they have developed) in terms of those earlier facts and relationships. And I remember having similar thoughts myself when I first read (I'm not sure when) about Baier's views on this topic. But despite the availability of the genetic fallacy retort, despite the fact that her ideas can be easily subjected to the just-mentioned form of analytic criticism, it is quite possible that Baier's idea here contains a genuine philosophical insight. In fact, I am inclined to believe it *does* contain an insight, but I think that insight could only be generally recognized once some further and very creative philosophical developments had occurred.

In 1989, a short time after the publication of Baier's essay, Jennifer Nedelsky became to first person to explicitly advocate a relational conception of human autonomy, and since that time the idea that autonomy should be understood relationally has become a quite standard way of dealing with or treating that concept.[4] But in the light of this subsequent development, it is possible to see Baier's idea about second personhood for what it is and was: an anticipation of and an insightful way of encapsulating what eventually emerged as the theory of relational autonomy. So an idea can be knocked down or knocked about in strictly analytic terms and be seen, not entirely incorrectly, as involving some sort of standard fallacy, yet turn out to anticipate, insightfully and/or intuitively, a whole new and (to my mind) promising way of understanding traditional philosophical concepts (and assumptions). In placing as much emphasis as we tend to do in the field of philosophy on analytic arguments and criticisms (and the ability to answer such criticisms), we tend to skimp on the value of insight and good intuitions (and the kind of creativity they involve or require). And yet new ideas and insights and creativity are in fact the life blood of philosophy and every other field I know of. In musical comedy and opera, the music is considered much more important than the lyrics (that's why it is Rodgers and Hammerstein and Rodgers and Hart, not Hammerstein and Rodgers or Hart and Rodgers—it's also why practically no one remembers the names of Verdi's or Puccini's librettists). But in the field of philosophy—somehow and much of the time—the lyrics are stressed and sought after much more than the music. One is much more interested in pointing out analytic weaknesses than in ferreting out the insights that just might be contained within those analytically weak or undefended frameworks—the example of Annette Baier is only one instance of this pervasive tendency.

But let's for a moment also talk about intuitions (which are not the same thing as insights). We have intuitions about what is moral or immoral in particular cases, and sometimes people's intuitions clash about such matters. When that happens and is known to have happened, those outside the situation and perhaps even some of those within it are quite likely to give up (to some extent) on the probative value, in the given circumstances, of the intuitions on one side or the other of the issue at hand; and sometimes it is said that one needs to do some (better) theorizing in order to come to a resolution of the given issue where intuitions clash. But in fact some people have better intuitions than others, are more intuitive than others. Some people are better in touch with their linguistic intuitions than others are, and the same holds true for moral intuitions and even intuitions about what makes sense in the fields of logic and metaphysics.

However, no one, or almost no one, ever speaks this way. Almost no one says that some people have better intuitions than others or is willing to name names on that score. And when two people come up with different intuitions, say, about some practical moral question, it rarely happens (as far as I know) that one of the two tells the other that they don't have very good intuitions about the relevant questions. That kind of thing seems or would seem arrogant or like pulling rank (though what rank would it be?); and one doesn't hear of this kind of thing happening. But why shouldn't it?

Well, for one thing, because it would sound arrogant and would probably count as rude (though perhaps not if a teacher does this sort of thing to a student). But in some circumstances it may be rude to speak (what one knows to be) *the truth*. One person's intuitions *may* be better (in a certain area) than another's, but we have developed a philosophical culture in which it does indeed seem rude to question the intuitional capabilities of another person. I think that is at least in part because in our field we don't officially or publicly or educationally place any emphasis on having good intuitions. Of course, there is or seems to be an important difference between criticizing someone's argument and criticizing their intuitions. When, as so frequently happens, we criticize someone's argument(s), we leave it open to them to criticize our criticism(s), to argue right back. But if and when we tell someone that they have bad intuitions, we seem to leave them nothing to say—except to outright deny the accusation—and that seems philosophically unfair.

However, the matter is philosophically a bit more complicated than has just been suggested. If someone accuses me of having bad intuitions, there *are* in fact things that can or could be said in reply. To take just one example, one could point out to the person who is saying one lacks good intuitions that one's intuitions are much more in line with other people's intuitions than are the intuitions of the person who is criticizing one. If one could support *that* claim, one would have a relevant response to the person who had started things by criticizing one's intuitions. And why shouldn't claims like this be supported?

Well, you might say, it would take an entire new field of theoretical research, one targeting people's or philosophers' intuitions and proposing and even theorizing about various factors that may interfere with having good intuitions, in order for people to be able to support claims like this. Yes, but what stops us from pushing ahead with and in such a field? Arguably, it is because we as philosophers don't feel comfortable talking about how good people's intuitions are that we don't inaugurate a field in which the quality of intuitions would be the subject matter under investigation. And we don't feel comfortable about this because we don't place all that much intellectual/philosophical *value* on having good intuitions. We may *rely* on intuitions and to that extent think them important, but we don't think the *quality* of intuitions is (an) important (issue). However, once we acknowledge the value of having good intuitions, then such a field could come into being and, more significantly, we could achieve or come to a more balanced and realistic view of what is important in doing philosophy. And I am going to stick my philosophical neck out a bit further now by mentioning what I take to be a prime personal example of the importance of having good intuitions.

Everyone in philosophy knows, or ought to know, that the young Saul Kripke had, at least in contemporary times, unique powers of philosophical analysis and argument. Robert Nozick called him the sole acknowledged genius in the profession of philosophy, and that genius was manifested not only in his precociously proven theorems in modal logic, but in philosophical conversations with him on almost any topic. He was simply in a different intellectual class from everyone else he argued with—and, believe me, I felt this as much as others did, when I engaged in philosophical conversations with him. What I am saying, then, in order (eventually) to make the point I want to make, is that Kripke's argumentational powers exceeded those of everyone else who was around, including some people, like W. V. Quine, Hilary Putnam, and David Lewis, whose (creative) contributions to the field of philosophy might be thought to be comparable to Kripke's. But what does all this have to do with having good intuitions?

Just this. One can say that Kripke was analytically more forceful and acute than even David Lewis. (Kripke was acknowledged as a genius, but William Lycan once said that Lewis's intellectual powers were simply at the very extreme end of normal human intelligence.) But what may be almost as remarkable about Kripke—and in comparison with Lewis—was the quality of his philosophical intuitions. His (original) philosophical ideas seemed *unencumbered* by his knowledge of and contributions to logic, but, if I may say so, there was something logically or metaphysically muscle-bound about Lewis's philosophical thinking. However, no one ever makes this kind of comparison. Differences with respect to genius, with respect to analytic powers of mind, are spoken of (sometimes quite reverently), and certainly Lewis's ideas about real possible worlds (or about there being, in the actual world, many cats roughly in the same place as any given cat) are sometimes said to be totally counterintuitive and/or to show a deficient sense of reality. (So when enough people disagree strongly enough with a given person's intuitions, that can get mentioned and talked about.)

But as far as I know, no one ever talks about how remarkably intuitive Kripke was as a philosopher. And yet, despite known and even self-acknowledged personal quirks and idiosyncrasies, Kripke's intuitions were (perhaps they still are) remarkably free of personal bias, remarkably *limpid*. Again, as I have suggested, this doesn't get mentioned because having good intuitions isn't considered important to philosophical practice and education, and, of course, I am saying it should be. But this then means that in the field of ethical theory (and assuming that we are working in the care ethics tradition), we need insight/creativity, emotional/psychological sensitivity, *and* good intuitions.[5] However, that doesn't mean that we don't also need to be analytically or logically alert as critics of what we and others think, say, and argue. So I am claiming that we need both methods associated (traditionally) with men and methods associated (traditionally) with females if we are to do ethics, or care ethics, successfully and well.[6]

When care ethics was getting off the ground, it focused on such female concepts/interests as caring and direct connection (unmediated by rules or laws) with other people, and in chapter 5, I suggested that it would do better to work with a mixture of male and female elements (understood in traditional terms): it needs to apply its more feminine approach to concepts and ideals that are more traditionally associated with masculine thinking and with men as such. But I want to say in addition that care ethics now needs to emphasize philosophical analysis/criticism and ethical theorizing more than it did in its earliest days. In *Caring*, the first book written specifically on care ethics, Nel Noddings gave us an insightful and in many ways a highly intuitive and sensitive picture of some important and previously neglected aspects of the moral life. Previous ethical theory had skimped on issues about (and the details of) the moral psychology of intimate relationships, and Nodding's book, along with a great deal of relevant later work by other thinkers, helped to make up for the previous lacunae. Still, *Caring* and much subsequent work in the care-ethical tradition (as it was becoming) have skimped on philosophical analysis and criticism and have shied away from general or systematic theorizing.

For example, although Noddings (somewhat obliquely) mentions the traditional philosophical problem of justifying deontology, she approaches the whole topic in an impressionistic and, to my mind, inconclusive way, and someone who is more analytically minded can then be left wondering whether care ethics can say anything plausible (in its own terms) about this central, indeed crucial, ethical topic. Similarly, Noddings brings up the issue of whether moral claims state facts and seems ready to assume that they don't. But she never considers the philosophical and intuitive problems that arise for any theory that denies the objectivity and truth of moral claims. Moreover, in her earlier work (though not in her later), Noddings says that caring doesn't apply to large-scale social/political issues, and this means or meant leaving the topic of social justice (or rights) for others to deal with.

I think those who pursue and develop care ethics at this point need to pay (more) attention to the tasks or possibilities of philosophical/analytic criticism and systematic theorizing (this is something I have tried to do in my own work)— without losing touch with the insights and intuitions about the emotional and psychological dimensions of the moral that helped make care ethics so appealing to so many people in the first place. If they or we do so, then there can and will be a balance between (traditionally) male and female elements or factors both as regards the content of care ethics (feminine takes on what are to a substantial extent masculine concepts) and as regards the methodology employed and valued by those who work on such ethics (a combination of sensitivity and intuitiveness with analytic philosophical criticism and theorizing). The balance between male and female that care ethics seeks and exemplifies is not the same as what was unearthed with respect to the issues of necessary imperfection that Isaiah Berlin first explored—there is no issue of partial values in its notions of right and wrong, and though it tells us to aim for better relationships and also better self-fulfillment on the part of those whose lives we can affect and these goods are themselves only partial, that aim doesn't itself necessarily exemplify any partiality of value or constitute a less than perfect form of moral imperative or morality. So what I am suggesting about philosophical and moral-philosophical methodology doesn't, I think, smack of partial value or necessary moral imperfection, and I am thus not saying that when we combine philosophical analysis with sensitivity, etc., we somehow fail to achieve or exemplify some sort of perfect moral theorizing. (There are enough other reasons why we won't achieve or exemplify *that*.) Rather, I am saying that the best kind of ethics and perhaps the best kind of philosophy involve two kinds of content (feminine normative thinking and masculine concepts as a sizable portion of the terrain of such thinking) and two kinds of method (the kind of analytic/theoretical thinking traditionally associated with men and with philosophy done by men, on the one hand, and explorations based in emotional/intuitive sensitivities of a kind we would tend to associate more with women than with men, on the other).[7]

Of course, if what I am saying about method in particular is on the right track, then the field of philosophy is in a sorry position—and women's place in the field is unjustly restricted or devalued. Even though there are probably more women than men working in ethical theory nowadays (at least in the United States), most of those women and men work in philosophy departments dominated by men and by traditional male philosophical thinking. So insight, intuition, and sensitivity to emotional/psychological nuance are devalued even for those (women) who do ethics, because they are judged for tenure and promotion (largely) by men who don't value or even think about such things. Of course, we see bias and mistakes in the opposite direction when those who attend conferences on one or another aspect of feminist thought get criticized for being too analytic or critical if and when they raise objections to points made in one or another paper being given at such a conference. Sometimes the analytic methods and criticisms that get criticized can be or can be seen as ways of fighting (underhandedly or surreptitiously) against feminist goals and aspirations. But they can also be useful and, even, insightful. It is intellectually and humanistically helpful to get things straight, to state an argument or theory in a really cogent and non-confusing way, and those who stress intuition and emotion need to take—or can benefit from taking—this other kind of philosophical value into account (in a nondefensive way).

Philosophy is and always has been a very masculine profession or field. But I am advocating a more balanced or even-handed way of doing philosophy—and of teaching the younger generation how to do philosophy.[8] If more emphasis were placed on having good intuitions and on emotional or psychological sensitivity, women would be more comfortable in philosophy departments, and those departments, in honoring something philosophically valuable that has been undervalued in the past, would be rectifying or starting to rectify a good deal of previous injustice toward women as philosophers.[9] I can only hope that some of these developments are more likely to occur now than in previous times because of the ways in which feminist thought has been articulated and has achieved increasing influence on our culture and politics over the past several decades. (The very fact that everyone talks about caring nowadays—every HMO says "we are the caring folks"—is some evidence of this, but many feminists think they aren't winning or likely in the future to win all their major battles.) Perhaps, this essay, written by someone coming originally from standard analytic philosophy but seeking to accommodate other methods and values, can make a small bit of difference to these desirable potential developments.

NOTES

Introduction

1. What I am saying here is rather similar to what Ronald Dworkin has said about the supposed conflict between liberty and equality. Neither of us thinks Berlin's favorite kind of case moves us in the direction of his general conclusion about the impossibility of perfect ethical virtue (or ideal justice). Dworkin also talks about conflicts between one's work projects and one's family commitments and seems to believe that such conflicts might be thought to illustrate Berlin's impossibility thesis and/or do so better than liberty vs. equality does. But Dworkin is somewhat vague about this and in any event speaks as if the work vs. family conflict is *not inevitable*. My own discussion will argue, however, that it is. And I shall consider objections and relate the whole discussion to feminist themes in a way that Dworkin never does. See his *Justice in Robes* (Cambridge: Harvard University Press, 2006), ch. 4.

2. In *Reason's Grief: An Essay on Tragedy and Value* (NY: Cambridge University Press, 2006), George Harris discusses themes and examples that are in many ways similar to those of the present book. I didn't learn of Harris's book until work on the present book was already completed, but let me just mention some important differences between our approaches. Harris discusses the conflict between real values—like creative achievement vs. social equality, being a good parent vs. being a creative thinker or artist, and security vs. liberty—and claims that such conflicts entail that life has a tragic dimension. But his arguments largely rely on empirical/contingent assumptions (like the facts of human physical vulnerability and of large differences in human intelligence and talent), and the point of the present book, and the gravamen of Berlin's original claims, is that perfection is

impossible *in principle* (for some reason Harris doesn't frame his discussion in terms of the notion of perfection). In addition, Harris doesn't make use of the history and ideals of feminism in anything like the way I shall be doing here—and he also is much readier than I am to interpret inevitable conflicts and hard choices as showing the tragic nature of life and as inconsistent with thinking of our lives and our character as good or good enough (even if they aren't perfect). The arguments I shall be presenting are not the same as those offered by Harris, even if somewhat similar considerations enter the picture at various points, and since the force of my arguments here doesn't depend on undercutting those given by Harris, I shall leave his views largely to one side in what follows.

Chapter 1

1. Carol Gilligan, *In a Different Voice: Psychological Theory and Women's Development* (Cambridge: Harvard University Press, 1982).

2. But probably not, for example, about courage. Philippa Foot in her book *Virtues and Vices* (Berkeley: University of California Press, 1978), pp. 15ff., argues (roughly) that we wouldn't call a scoundrel courageous for engaging fearlessly or daringly in nefarious activities. To that extent, courage (unlike resourcefulness) *is* regarded as a moral virtue.

3. Even though patriarchy has assumed many different forms in many different places over the millennia, I shall be mainly focusing on the forms it has taken in English-speaking countries over the past couple of centuries.

4. For some examples of objective list approaches to human (or personal) good, see James Griffin, *Well-Being: Its Meaning, Measurement, and Moral Importance* (NY: Oxford University Press, 1986); David Brink, *Moral Realism and the Foundations of Ethics* (Cambridge: Cambridge University Press, 1989); and my own *Morals from Motives* (NY: Oxford University Press, 2001). The term "objective list" comes from Derek Parfit, *Reasons and Persons* (Oxford: Clarendon Press, 1984).

5. Martha Nussbaum, *Frontiers of Justice* (Cambridge: Harvard University Press, 2006), esp. pp. 178–86. Abraham Maslow, *Motivation and Personality*, 2nd edition, (NY: Harper & Row, 1970), ch. 4.

6. However, the idea that adventure is a significant human good (or value) is sometimes suggested in passing in philosophical/ethical discussions that don't focus primarily on the nature and variety of human goods. See, for example, Christine Korsgaard, "Two Distinctions in Goodness," *Philosophical Review* 92 (1983): p. 185; and Bernard Williams, "A Critique of Utilitarianism" in J. Smart and B. Williams, *Utilitarianism: For and Against* (Cambridge: Cambridge University Press, 1973), p. 112.

7. For what it is worth, this idea first dawned on me when, seated in an airport waiting to board a plane, I noticed various women approach one woman, who

was pregnant and accompanied by a toddler, and start making conversation with her about her pregnancy and the toddler. It struck me how different all this was from anything that was likely to occur among men, and I started thinking about the causes or nature of the differences. Having offered an objective list theory of human goods myself, it then somehow dawned on me that one item on my list, friendship/love/affiliation, was much more typically emphasized by women and that men's strong orientation toward another item on my list, namely, career success or achievement, had something to do with the lesser emphasis they placed on the first item. It then also occurred to me that such gender-bias didn't or couldn't be said to characterize the other items (wisdom, pleasure) that I had also put on the list. Finally, and still in the airport, I realized that I had stumbled on new kind of difference in voice between males and females: not the familiar difference with respect to morality or moral issues that Gilligan (and others subsequently) had spoken of, but an as yet philosophically unexamined gender difference or traditional gender bias with respect to important human goods and (nonmoral) virtues.

8. My discussion of dependent goods and virtues will to some extent be taken from my earlier book, *Goods and Virtues* (Oxford: Clarendon Press, 1983), esp. ch. 3.

9. For some historical background on the idea that sex is a good only in the context of a committed relationship, see Roy Porter and Lesley Hall, *The Facts of Life: The Creation of Sexual Knowledge in Britain, 1650–1950* (New Haven: Yale University Press, 1995), esp. pp. 218–23; and Ornella Moscucci, "Clitoridectomy, Circumcision, and the Politics of Sexual Pleasure in Mid-Victorian Britain" in A. Miller and J. Adams, eds., *Sexualities in Victorian Britain* (Bloomington: Indiana University Press, 1996), esp. p. 71.

10. To the extent patriarchy sees (deliberate) adventuring as immoral for women, it will see adventurousness as a moral vice in women. But since we reject such moral assumptions nowadays, there is no reason for us not to regard adventurousness as a *nonmoral* virtue. Note too that to the extent sexism or patriarchy tends to make one think that what it is immoral for women to do (like go adventuring or engage in uncommitted or extramarital sex) can't in any way really benefit women, it is committed to what we might usefully call *sexist eudaimonism*. And such eudaimonism can usefully be seen as analogous to the tendency (e.g.) to regard sadistic pleasure at the suffering of others as really or ultimately not making the life of the person enjoying such pleasure (go) better. Even apart from any general or philosophical commitment to eudaimonism, we have a tendency to think of totally immoral pleasures as somehow not benefiting those who enjoy them (wishful thinking?). So it isn't surprising and there is some reason to think that Victorians and others who regarded emotionally uncommitted female sexual pleasure as fundamentally immoral also tended to regard such sexuality as no sort of genuine personal good. The analogy with sadistic pleasure is clear, and all this supports what we said in the text: that patriarchy tends to see uncommitted female sexuality as offering nothing (personally)

good to women—sees female sexual pleasure as (at most) a good dependent on the accompanying good of having a committed (preferably marital) relationship and sees this dependency itself as gender-relative.

11. For discussion of partial instincts and relevant references to Freud's works, see Franklin Maleson's "Masochism and Sadism" in Edward Erwin, ed., *The Freud Encyclopedia: Theory, Therapy, and Culture* (NY: Routledge, 2002), pp. 331ff.

12. On moral dilemmas and moral cost, see, e.g., Bernard Williams's *Problems of the Self* (Cambridge: Cambridge University Press, 1973), ch. 11; and his *Moral Luck* (Cambridge: Cambridge University Press, 1981), chs. 2 and 4. We shall have more to say about dilemmas and cost in later chapters.

13. The analogy with what Freud says about sadism and masochism is not perfect, however, because Freud thinks both these partial instincts are at work in everyone, and I am certainly not saying that everyone is, say, both frank and tactful. (Some people, in fact, may be neither: for example, they can be just plain taciturn.) But one can still naturally say that frankness and tact are paired and opposed, and this is just what Freud says about sadism and masochism.

14. The contrast between adventurousness and prudence, which Berlin never specifically talks about, is very similar to another familiar contrast that Berlin does refer to, that between freespiritedness/spontaneity and dependability/reliability/prudence/carefulness. See his "The Pursuit of the Ideal" in H. Hardy and K. Hausheer's collection of his writings entitled *The Proper Study of Mankind*, (NY: Farrar, Straus and Giroux, 1997), pp. 10ff. This second contrast can involve interpersonal (moral) issues much more directly than the first does, though many similar things can be said about both of them. However, I don't propose to discuss the opposition between freespiritedness/spontaneity and dependability, etc., any further here. Finally, let me just mention the contrast George Harris draws between security and liberty in *Reason's Grief* (NY: Cambridge University Press, 2006). He treats the opposition between these two values as dependent on contingent facts about human vulnerability, so that opposition or conflict isn't as deep or necessary as what I have argued exists between security and adventure. (Harris doesn't explicitly mention this latter conflict.) Also, the contrast between liberty and security doesn't illustrate and promote feminist themes in the way that the contrast between adventure/adventurousness and security/prudence does.

15. But one has to be careful here. Even if career success of her own is not treated by patriarchy as a good thing for a woman, her husband's (or father's or brother's) career success is supposed to be good for her, to enrich her life. Similarly, even if men are not supposed to go in for or benefit from stressing close personal relationships of their own, it is often thought that they benefit (somehow) from having wives, mothers, etc., who are deeply invested in such relationships. So these relevant goods and virtues complement one another interpersonally even if they are thought of as segregated according to gender within given individuals. Of course, once we see both career and personal intimacy as equally relevant to

both men and women as individuals and see them as *opposing* each other within every given individual, we can still see them as to some degree complementary and mutually supportive as *between* individuals. (If couples could be regarded as genuine individuals, most of the claims made in this book would be thoroughly undercut.) Similar points also hold for sadism and masochism: although they are regarded by Freud as opposed forces within each individual, they are obviously to be treated as complementary and mutually supportive as between individuals. (However, with some of the other partial values we shall be discussing, things are a little more complicated.)

16. In saying this, I don't mean to imply that pleasure (or even wisdom) can't have ill-effects. But philosophers can call something intrinsically good without denying it may have bad effects—and one can say of aesthetic pleasure, for example, that it is always good *as such* and independently, therefore, of its consequences. (I here ignore the problem of sadistic pleasure.) My point in the text above has been, in effect, that the opposition between career and enduring emotional connection with others runs deeper than any opposition or inconsistency of "mere effects;" strong personal connection and career creativity are inherently opposed; and I don't think there is any comparable opposition between wisdom or aesthetic pleasure and the other things that figure in objective lists of human goods.

17. Some women who deplore the ease with which men are allowed to choose career over close, loving relationships may themselves place greater value on (having a) career than on close relationships, and to that extent they show themselves to envy the ease with which men are able to have (and are not criticized for having) what they themselves would prefer to have. In addition, of course, they may very well deplore and resent the widespread sexist social *values* that make such a choice easier for men. (I won't cite the vast literature, feminist and otherwise, on these issues.) Note further that if, under patriarchy, men don't always recognize what they are missing or losing out on when they emphasize their careers and downplay personal relationships, then it can equally be said that patriarchy leads many women not to appreciate what they are missing out on when they (more or less consciously and/or voluntarily) choose to forgo careers. (Of course, I am assuming here that we can attain a larger and more accurate perspective on valid ethical values if we free ourselves from patriarchal/sexist assumptions.)

18. Of course, if patriarchal men don't see anything particularly valuable in affiliation or loving relationship(s) and accordingly miss out on a great deal of what life has to offer, one can say it is their own fault. After all, that lack or absence can be said to be mainly due to an oppressive and unjust situation they themselves have largely created (for their own purposes and their own benefit). By contrast, what women miss out on (e.g., career fulfillment) tends to result from injustices that have been imposed on them by men. But my main focus in this book has been and continues to be issues of human good or virtue, not of justice or injustice and its subspecies oppression, lack of respect, violence, etc.

For discussion of how difficult *some* men find it to choose between career and family relationship(s), see Kari Palazzari, "The Daddy Double-Bind: How the Family and Medical Leave Act Perpetuates Sex Inequality across All Class Levels," *Columbia Journal of Gender and Law* 16 (2007): 429–71.

19. To simplify the exposition here, I am talking of virtues as if it made sense to think of (actively or deliberately) choosing between them. But those who recognize the problem here will know how to correct it. Also, someone can be prudent (or adventurous) in some matters, but not others; and such a person may very well not be prudent (or, alternatively, adventurous) overall or simpliciter, i.e., may not be a prudent (alternatively, an adventurous) *person*. In the main text I am talking about whether someone counts as having the virtue of prudence (or adventurousness) in this larger sense and saying that such prudence excludes boldness or adventurousness as a general character trait (just as overall adventurousness, adventurousness simpliciter, excludes prudence as a general character trait). Similar qualifications need to be made for some of the other virtues and personal goods I am speaking of. But I should also perhaps add that although the virtue of prudence is typically or often correlated with the good of security and the virtue of adventurousness with the good of adventure, someone who isn't at all adventurous may have adventure(s) thrust on them—and deal with it/them in a prudent manner. In addition, what *counts* as adventurous/adventure for women will differ factually from what counts as such for men—in part, but not merely because men are stronger than women and women are more vulnerable to men (and their desires) than men are to women. But that is consistent with adventure/adventurousness being a partial value for both genders.

I should also mention Philippa Foot's claim (*Virtues and Vices*, pp. 17f.) that prudence isn't a virtue in everyone because some people are *too* attached to safety. This seems to be correct and it certainly points toward the idea of the partial-virtue status of prudence. However, it doesn't make its valid point with all the generality and extrapolatablity that the explicit idea of partial virtues and values enables us to achieve.

20. Adventurous people are more likely, I think, to be innovative and independent of others than prudent people are. But the issue of adventurousness/adventure vs. prudence/security remains even after one notes these further connections, and the connections do nothing to undermine the relevance here of the idea of partial values. (I am indebted on this point to Kristin Borgwald.) Note too, by the way, that adventurousness doesn't entail and may even preclude recklessness.

21. The talk of sexual adventuring here is meant to suggest that the issue of sexual adventure vs. committed sex(uality) can to a substantial extent be subsumed under the issue of adventure vs. security. If the latter two represent paired and opposed partial goods, then sexual adventuring and committed sex can be viewed as representing paired and opposed partial goods that *fall under* and *instantiate* the larger pairing of partial goods. However, in speaking of sexual adventure, I have also ignored the possibility that adventuring (tinged with a

degree of emotional insecurity) can be part of a loving couple's sexuality—perhaps they agree to involve third parties in their sexual doings with one another or agree to swing with other couples or individuals in sexual activities that are no longer (immediately) shared. Open marriage may stretch these ideas even further, but my main point is that sexuality can derive some of its value from the quality of a relationship. That is what I mean to be referring to when I speak of the good of committed sexuality, and that good is to some degree undercut if, say, one member of a couple, against all the understandings and commitments of the couple, engages in (adventurous) sexual activities without the other member's knowing it. So having the good (let us assume) of cheating sex undercuts what we tend to think of as a source of what is good about committed sexual activity, namely, the quality of the relationship in which the latter occurs. This gives the sense in which (roughly speaking) the good of *purely* adventurous sex is at odds with the full good of committed sex.

And it also supports the idea that they are (merely) partial goods. When men give up uncommitted sexuality for a committed relationship, they may well be and think they are better off than if they had remained unattached. But they may nonetheless feel or recognize that they are missing out on something, that things are less than *perfect* in their lives, when they (have to) limit their sexuality to a single relationship or to terms agreed on in a committed relationship. And if this is true for men, it seems to me that the same holds for women. If emotionally unencumbered sexual adventure really was a good thing early on in their lives, then there is something less than ideal about later having to live without it, even if on the whole they have a lot to gain by doing so. But of course this doesn't mean that men or women have to *dwell* on what they are missing out on (e.g., variety or pure adventure) when they are involved in committed relationships. One can be satisfied, even *entirely* satisfied, with less than perfection. On this point see my *Beyond Optimizing* (Cambridge: Harvard University Press, 1989), ch. 3.

22. In a paper called "Oppression," which can be found in her book *The Politics of Reality* (Trumansburg, NY: The Crossing Press, 1983), Marilyn Frye points out that today's women face a kind of double bind: if they are sexually conservative, they will be thought of as prudish, cold, or uptight (in a way that wouldn't so frequently have occurred in earlier, more patriarchal times); if they are sexually adventurous, they will be accused by many of being loose or sluttish (in a way that reflects lingering patriarchal values). (Also, the sexually adventurous contemporary practice of "hooking up" seems to benefit males much more than females, and one has to wonder whether this disparity can ever be eliminated.) Similarly, and going now beyond what Frye says, women are in a double bind about career vs. family because if they choose career, they will be said to have forgotten or repressed what they are as women, and if they choose family, they will be accused of depreciating the sacrifices other women have made in order to make it possible for women in general to have full career opportunities (they will

be accused of having "let down the side" or of betraying female solidarity and/or the ideals of feminism). But these double binds in different ways reflect and express (what we can only hope is) the *transitional* nature of what is going on nowadays, the fact that our society and we ourselves are moving from (benighted) patriarchal to (enlightened) feminist values. By contrast, I have in effect been claiming that the choices between partial values like adventure and security and like career and loving relationship(s) are built into the human condition and represent a more *ultimate* or *fundamental* double bind for us because they *don't* depend on the existence of distorted ideas or values (in some people). But what Frye (and others) have said about present-day double binds needs to be more thoroughly related to and interpreted in terms of the more general/abstract ethical conclusions discussed in this chapter, and I hope to say more about this on another occasion.

23. Nel Noddings, *Caring: A Feminine Approach to Ethics and Moral Education* (Berkeley: University of California Press, 1984).

24. Virginia Held, *The Ethics of Care: Personal, Political, and Global* (NY: Oxford University Press, 2006); and my own *The Ethics of Care and Empathy* (NY: Routledge, 2007).

25. There is another area of human goods (at least) where patriarchal values seem mistaken, but where one doesn't have to infer that "one can't have everything" or make use of the notion of a partial good. Patriarchy seems to hold that certain consumables are more for women than for men, and others more for men than for women: men are supposed to like whiskey more than chocolate, and just the reverse for women. Men are supposed to enjoy cigars and women are not. And there are even certain drinks that are deemed appropriate for women but not for men: e.g., creme de cacao and "White Russians." But recently some women have started being interested in cigars, and in the British Commonwealth at least there is some precedent for women liking things like single malt whiskey; and I am inclined to think that there will be more equalizing in the area of gustatory consumption in the future. Perhaps this will even mean that men won't feel like "sissies" if they prefer "White Russians" to straight whiskey and admit a liking/craving for chocolate. In any event, there is no reason why both men and women can't both fully enjoy every consumable that patriarchy used to assign exclusively to one sex or the other. (You know, whiskey, cigars, and chocolate go very well together.)

Chapter 2

1. I am ignoring the possibility that certain clashes between justice and mercy may not be so easily resolvable in ethically acceptable terms, and in fact such clashes might even sometimes illustrate the impossibility of ethical perfection. This is something that Berlin seems to have believed (see his "The Pursuit of the Ideal"

in *The Proper Study of Mankind* [NY: Farrar, Straus and Giroux, 1997], esp. p. 10), and he may have been right. It is entirely possible that justice and mercy could turn out to be merely partial virtues; but I am not going to pursue that theme here because I haven't been able to think of any really good examples to use in illustrating and arguing for such a view.

2. It may not show, however, that it is impossible to have all the virtues. I can imagine someone (even an Aristotelian?) arguing that the presumed fact that it is impossible to be both perfect in frankness and perfect in tactfulness doesn't show that one can't be both frank simpliciter and tactful simpliciter. The person, for example, who is disposed to be tactful with his friend in the situation I described may be frank enough on enough other occasions to count as a frank person, and similarly mutatis mutandis for someone with the disposition to be frank with a friend in the kind of situation we have described. So the issue of whether one can combine all the virtues may not be crucial to determining whether virtue-perfection is possible, and so I am putting much more emphasis on the latter idea in the present context.

   However, note this. Even if we think that, whichever way someone is inclined to choose with respect to their friend in the case I described, they can still be frank and tactful simpliciter, the issue of adventurousness vs. prudence (and all our other feminism-related examples) may seem to us quite different. In the case of frankness vs. tact, it is very difficult to think of a case where they clash as virtues (I had been trying for many years to think up such a case), so since the vast majority of potential situations don't involve this kind of problem, one can think that frankness simpliciter and tact simpliciter could be sufficiently exemplified to be combined in a single individual. But adventurousness and prudence seem to clash more frequently and broadly (and deeply) than this, so I really do think that these partial virtues cannot be combined in any individual (though chapter 3 will give further arguments to this effect). In any event, I want to argue that all the cases we have discussed are the same with respect to the issue of perfection.

3. Some theologians have argued that a perfect God, a God with all perfections/ virtues, couldn't make a stone too heavy for him to move. But I am inclined to think that omnipotence involves the capacity to render oneself less than omnipotent. So even if a God who rendered himself unable to move a certain stone would lack all perfections, that God (for all the theologians have really shown) may have had all the perfections "before" he decided to make himself less than omnipotent. I don't think, therefore, that we can argue for the impossibility of perfection along these particular lines.

4. H. P. Grice, "The Causal Theory of Perception," *Proceedings of the Aristotelian Society* supplementary volume 35, (1961): 121–53.

5. Thomas Kuhn, *The Structure of Scientific Revolutions*, 2nd edition (Chicago: University of Chicago Press, 1970).

6. See, for example, his "Theory Change and the Indeterminacy of Reference," *Journal of Philosophy* 70 (1973): 462–81, and his "Quine and the Correspondence

Theory," *Philosophical Review* 83 (1974): 200–28. Relevant references to Quine's work occur in those articles.

7. Berlin never makes this specific kind of claim and in fact never explicitly brings in the notion of a partial virtue or good; but what we are saying here in fact *follows* from things Berlin said about the impossibility of perfection. So we are pointing to implications of his views that Berlin himself may not have recognized.

8. Not every good that is inconsistent with some other good counts as a partial good. The goods may not, for example, be paired in any significant way, but more importantly, neither good may seem or be necessary to perfect happiness. A fully successful lifetime career as an architect is incompatible with a fully successful one as a doctor, and both constitute large-scale personal goods; but (almost) no one thinks an architect's life cannot be perfectly happy because they didn't have time to also be a doctor. Similarly, having a satisfying Japanese dinner on a given evening may be inconsistent with having a satisfying French meal on the same evening, but almost no one thinks that means one can't have a perfect meal on a given evening or, for that matter, have a perfect evening. Once again, therefore, the goods in question aren't merely partial. By contrast, adventure and security *are* partial goods: they are incompatible with one another, and both a life lacking in adventure and one lacking in security will seem to us less than perfect.

9. The scheme will have to make assumptions, for example, about the signification of a term or terms that might be thought to refer to identity, but could be interpreted in what to us is a more complex fashion. Thus if the anthropologist points to two parts of the same rabbit and tries to ask whether the two ostended objects are the same thing, he or she may initially assume that some native term (call it) "ohtoh" means or has the same signification as "is the same as." In that case, if the native answers his question in the affirmative, he may decide that "gavagai" signifies rabbits and "ohtoh" the identity relation. But another anthropologist, on Quine's assumptions, could think of "gavagai" as denoting rabbit parts, and when s/he points to two different parts of the same rabbit and asks whether "ohtoh" applies, an affirmative answer needn't entail that "gavagai" denotes rabbits. The anthropologist could always adopt a translation scheme or manual according to which "gavagai" signified rabbit parts and "ohtoh" denoted the relation of being part of the same thing as. This too would be consistent with the native's affirmative responses, so, more generally, the assumption that the native is referring to rabbits is valid only relative to the assumption that "ohtoh" refers to the relation of identity or sameness, together with a whole host of other assumptions about signification that allow one to square one's overall translation scheme with all the data the native is giving one. And the assumption that the native is referring to rabbit parts is valid only relative to the assumption that "ohtoh" refers to the relation of being part of the same thing as. (Of course, the idea here that ostension is unambiguous is a dubious one, but if one *doesn't* make use of it, it becomes all the easier for Quine to prove his point.) In any event, what I have just said may help the reader better understand how, for Quine, assumptions about signification have a merely relative validity or truth.

Chapter 3

1. Gary Watson, "Virtues in Excess," *Philosophical Studies* 46 (1984): 57-74; A. D. M. Walker, "The Incompatibility of the Virtues," *Ratio* 6 (1993): 44-62.

2. Incidentally, "perfectly happy" is ambiguous as between a psychological interpretation equivalent to "perfectly contented" and an ethical one equivalent to "ideally happy," and I mean to be invoking the latter notion throughout our discussion.

3. One of the sections of Watson's article is called "The Incompatibility of the Virtues," but Watson doesn't *defend* such incompatibility in the article—in fact, quite the contrary; but I shall ignore the details.

4. At one point in "The Pursuit of the Ideal" (in H. Hardy and R. Hausheer, eds., *The Proper Study of Mankind* [NY: Farrar, Straus and Giroux, 1997], p. 10), Isaiah Berlin speaks rather vaguely of the choice between telling a destructive truth and telling a white lie and indicates that he thinks the possibility of such a choice supports his view about the impossibility of perfect virtue; but since philosophers like Watson and Walker speak of situations involving such a choice in which the possibility of complete virtue doesn't at all seem to be compromised or undercut, one has to say more than Berlin did if one is to use the choice, essentially, between frankness and tact in support of the thesis of the impossibility of perfection. The example I used in chapters 1 and 2 was supposed to support Berlin's thesis by including a detailed description of a situation that it is difficult to make intuitive ethical sense of in non-Berlinian terms. But that was just the point—one needs a better example than Berlin ever gave us and a different and more detailed example than anything considered by Watson or Walker, if one wants to show how and why our ethical understanding of things must move in the direction of Berlin's thesis. Of course, our argument for the Berlin thesis and the existence of partial values didn't depend on this one example: what we said about prudence vs. adventurousness, security vs. adventure, career/creative fulfillment vs. the fulfillment that comes from deep personal relationships, etc., also illustrated and argued in favor of those ideas.

5. Actually, Walker never once uses the term "frankness;" but since he uses all the other terms just mentioned and says he is borrowing from Watson, who does focus specifically on frankness, I won't treat this omission as relevant to our discussion.

6. See Peter Geach, *The Virtues* (Cambridge: Cambridge University Press, 1977), pp. 160-68.

7. In his writings, Berlin seems sometimes to run together the idea of the inevitable clash of values/virtues and the idea that perfection is impossible: that is, he doesn't always clearly (enough) distinguish between Walker's kind of pluralism and the more radical pluralism that denies the possibility of perfection. However, he sometimes *does* make it clear that he is committed to the more radical view. Keep in mind too that, as we are understanding it, the idea of (objective) values

clashing, conflicting, or opposing one another *doesn't* entail either the denial of the principle of noncontradiction or any other radical notion of the requirements of sheer logic. And, finally, let me refer the reader back to note 8 of chapter 2, where I mention some cases of clashing/conflicting goods that don't entail the impossibility of perfect happiness and are thus not partial goods in the sense of this book.

8. I am defending a kind of complex objective list theory of human goods and virtues, and objective list theories are automatically pluralistic in some sense. But I don't think *such* pluralism necessarily entails the incommensurability or incomparability of values. Berlin, however, did think of (his kind of) pluralism as entailing the incommensurability of various values.

9. I have seen a television advertisement that says that the biggest risk in life is not to take risks, and at least superficially it might seem that this idea could be used to show that risky adventurousness and prudence are compatible: the idea being that one has to take risks in order to be really prudent. Now I can agree that if someone has taken huge risks and they have paid off, then, from the standpoint of that later good fortune, one might see that one would have had a much worse life if one hadn't taken the risk, so that, from that later standpoint, it would have been imprudent not to have taken the risk. But the practical standpoint with respect to action is not a retrospective one, and the attribution of imprudence here is really a nonstarter. And the paradoxical idea that prudence requires one to live or act in a risky or adventurous manner doesn't really hold water if one examines it carefully. Take some would-be academic, a married graduate student working with an eminent professor at a prestigious university who has found a dissertation topic his professor is highly enthusiastic about, but who has thought of another potential topic that promises more exciting and novel results but that is likely to be disapproved by his supervisor. Is it really the prudent thing for him to take on the more exciting topic, given the likely possibility that he will get a less good job recommendation and less good job as a result? Even if the more exciting topic is likely to win him eventual prestige and good job offers, it also puts obstacles in the path of his career success, and if his wife has traditional values and (as we described this in chapter 1), a penchant or preference for security over adventure, she is not going to advise him to go with the more novel topic. Now she may be mistaken to advise him so (even from the standpoint in medias res); perhaps he really should persevere with that topic. But no one could reasonably say that in doing so, he was being prudent and/or cautious. Rather, that course of action seems to throw caution to the winds, and even if it is wrong for his wife to cling so firmly to her (patriarchy-induced) preference for security, she is indeed opting for security and prudence in preference to other potential values. So this is definitely *not* the way to undercut the examples and arguments offered in this book.

10. If the person whose life is no longer adventurous is *consoled* by the thought of all the previous adventure, that just shows that she has something to be consoled

about and indicates, therefore, that her more secure life is lacking in something inherently valuable. By the way, someone might hold every life should contain some element or period of adventure, but also claim that once one has had "one's adventure," further adventure doesn't add anything good to one's existence. And there would be analogies then here with what some Stoics said about virtue—namely, that one's life as a whole will be perfectly happy if one is ever, even for a moment, perfectly virtuous—and with the romantic Japanese notion that when a couple has had perfect happiness, they might as well commit suicide. But these analogies are so implausible that they cast doubt on the idea that having one adventure is ideal for a life. And would someone who had had and was looking back on their one great adventure not be a little wistful about what they could no longer (fully) experience? (Compare what the mother says about her earlier life in the movie *National Velvet*, a movie in which the preadolescent Elizabeth Taylor made a rather startling early appearance.) That would be a sign that there was something not entirely perfect about their later life.

Finally, even if there are differences between how much value different people place on adventure relative to security, that won't affect the issue of whether perfect happiness is possible. Some value adventure more than security, some value security more than adventure, but we don't have decide who is right in this matter or even decide whether there has to *be* a right answer on this issue, in order to see that both sides can or should place *some* value on both security and adventure. In that case, and however they may otherwise disagree, both will have reason to grant that *there will be something lacking* whichever of these values someone "chooses" to emphasize and/or whichever is more exemplified in someone's life.

11. I say "adult life" here because of some possible objections that might come from my own book *Goods and Virtues* (NY: Oxford University Press, 1983). In that book I argued that we don't take childhood happiness or achievement very seriously from the standpoint of our lives overall, and it isn't clear to me that someone couldn't use that argument to argue that a perfectly or ideally happy overall life could contain a fairly unhappy childhood. But I don't think I would (now) want to argue this way myself.

12. In *Reason's Grief* (NY: Cambridge University Press, 2006), George Harris considers the choice between individual creativity/achievement and good parenting and argues against the possibility of (easily) combining them. But he doesn't consider the kind of "different periods of life" objection I shall be discussing in what follows.

13. What I have been saying is somewhat reminiscent of things Nietzsche says about creative fulfillment/achievement, but I am limiting my claims here to what (I believe) has intuitive commonsense appeal, and Nietzsche doesn't put such limits on what he says on this topic or others. Notice too how far the present conception is from traditional "aristocratic" values that univocally prefer leisure over work. Creative or career achievement definitely requires work, and it is one

of the most distinctive characteristics of modern thought that it places such a positive value on work and struggle and achievement. One could discuss how all this relates to the Protestant Ethic, to Romanticism, and to Hegel's ideas about master and slave ("Lordship and Bondage") in the *Phenomenology of Spirit*, but the important question is whether we are really right to place so much value on the just-mentioned things or whether, in fact, a life of leisure is better or just as good. Again, I am going to take a risk on behalf of the modern age and myself and say that we have become sensitive to values that earlier philosophers (perhaps even Plato and Aristotle, though that is a complex subject) *just didn't get*. This is the kind of thing feminists say about those brought up to think in patriarchal or sexist terms, and perhaps we moderns can say something analogous about the kind of thinking about work and achievement that was more characteristic of earlier periods of human history. A life mainly of leisure may simply be, to a certain extent, unfortunate.

14. William Butler Yeats's thought that one must choose between "perfection of the life, or of the work" seems somewhat tangential to what I have been saying about the choice between career/creative fulfillment and affiliative values. But it is surely also *related* to what I have been maintaining here.

15. Those who speak of "the human condition" or "the human predicament" are typically referring (or intending to refer) to tragic problems and limitations that (as that very language suggests) may not beset all possible intelligent beings in all possible circumstances. But what I have been saying about partial values and what both Berlin and I have said about the impossibility of perfection is in fact supposed to hold for every possible rational or intelligent being and not just for humans. The impossibility of making a perfect choice between career/creative fulfillment and affiliative values and the other ethically frustrating problems/situations that arise out of the assumption of various partial values do deeply characterize the human condition, and to that extent they are an important part of the human condition or predicament. But no intelligent or higher beings could ever be free of these difficulties—so they are not *just* due to the human condition or to our humanity.

Chapter 4

1. However, I can't resist mentioning that the idea that moral dilemmas are inconsistent with the principle that "ought" implies "can" is almost certainly mistaken. If one denies that obligations agglomerate, one can accept moral dilemmas and at the same time hold that "ought" implies "can." On this point, see Williams's "Ethics and Consistency" in his *Problems of the Self* (Cambridge: Cambridge University Press, 1973).

2. If you aren't convinced that the citizens of Coventry have really been *wronged* in the example just mentioned (after all, everyone in England had, one might say,

implicitly signed on to a concerted war effort), consider the following, arguably better example of moral cost. You and your husband can afford to adopt an orphan, but only one orphan, and you go to the orphanage to find and choose a child (this is in the bad old days when adoption involved less screening and wasn't in any way difficult). You see two children, Janet and Janine, who might be potential adoptees, and officials at the orphanage tell you that in order to take home one of them, you save to spend two or three hours with each one on her own: they want you to have some basis for choosing between them, lest the whole thing quickly turn into a fiasco. The children know what is going on—how could they not? But at the end of the day or weekend, you have to choose one of the girls over the other, and you do choose one of them, let us say it is Janine. But won't you feel, rightly feel, terrible about having to disappoint, to dash, Janet's newly aroused hopes? Won't you, after the fact, feel that you have wronged her in a nontrivial way? Yet the situation doesn't seem dilemmatic because it can hardly be said to be morally wrong to choose between them, when one really can't afford to clothe and feed both girls and when the alternative to making such a choice would to be to adopt neither. (This really does seem different—doesn't it?—from the cases of putative dilemma, like Sophie's choice, that have been discussed in the ethics literature—on which see more below.) I am indebted here to discussion with Jennifer Etheridge.

3. See Williams's "Moral Luck" and "Politics and Moral Character" in his *Moral Luck* (Cambridge: Cambridge University Press, 1981).

4. William Styron, *Sophie's Choice* (NY: Random House, 1979).

5. However, any approach to morality (like my own) that gives primacy to inner states and motives needs to explain how such an internalist approach is consistent with the idea or possibility of moral cost. But I don't want to get into issues about virtue ethics as a systematic approach in the present book. (Because perfection with respect to all the virtues, moral or otherwise, is not [just] a moral notion, the idea of necessary virtue-imperfection doesn't raise the same problems for a virtue-ethical account of morality that the issue of moral cost does.)

6. In "Are Moral Considerations Overriding?" in her *Virtues and Vices* (Oxford: Blackwell, 1978), Philippa Foot says that one may have reason on balance to do something immoral in order to stave off disaster to one's family, but my discussion in *Goods and Virtues* sought to be more specific about possible cases of this than Foot was.

7. For some reasons to doubt whether the Italian father case is a genuine counterexample to overridingness, see my "How Important Is Overridingness?" forthcoming in the first volume of the series *Ethics and Morals*, published by Tectum.

8. In saying this, I am indicating a (possible) disagreement with what Richard Lovelace in the poem "To Lucasta, going to the Wars" says about love: "I could not love thee, Dear, so much, Loved I not Honour more."

9. In *Two Cheers for Democracy* (NY: Harcourt Brace, 1962), E. M. Forster says—in a very Bloomsbury manner—that if he had to choose between betraying his best

friend and betraying his country, he hopes he would have the courage to betray his country. This implies that he would be ethically deficient, if he betrayed his friend and presumably, too, if he merely didn't help his friend, given the alternative of betraying his country. Clearly, what I am saying in the text disagrees with this judgment, and the fact that Foster seems to intend this claim as iconoclastic and as defying or tweaking common (or traditional) opinion indicates that most people would or do find his idea distasteful or unappealing. All I am saying is that I disagree with that idea and think most of us would as well. Let me just mention (again) that I am not taking sides on whether the Italian minister has a moral obligation to actually *turn his son in* to the police.

10. Many or most ancient philosophers seem to have thought that the enjoyment of food was based on the pain of lacking and wanting food—such pleasure was therefore considered impure or "mixed." But nowadays we commonsensically don't believe this sort of thing. The enjoyment of food may to some degree depend on having *an appetite*, but who says that appetite and a keen anticipation of the joys of a meal one is about to have are in any way painful? (I say "to some degree" because a friend of mine once said—I think convincingly—that the true measure of great food is whether one can enjoy it without having any appetite left.)

11. We could even say that the full good of achievement is (in a limited sense) *doubly* partial because it entails both struggle and the absence of fully satisfying deep personal relationships and because each of those facts or factors detracts from ideal happiness. Note too that I am not assuming that struggle entails suffering (something I believe Nietzsche did assume). But we can still say that happiness is to some degree marred or made less than perfect by the fact of struggle—perhaps that is because struggling may have to be to some degree unpleasant. It is also worth noting that the paired opposite of creative achievement in a career, namely, intimate personal relationship, may also be doubly partial. It may not only undercut full creative accomplishments, but also intrinsically involve a certain sort of emotional vulnerability, risk, and danger. If love or friendship is by its very nature insecure, then it lacks something that, as we have already argued, is essential to ideal or perfect happiness. So (the fullest kind of) intense personal closeness involves the partial evil/bad of insecurity and also precludes the partial good of full-blown creative (career) achievement. (The insecurity can be a matter of possible dangers to those we love or of the possibility of their ceasing to love us or of the possibility of our being unable to be or share things with them.) Notice then, finally, how our somewhat separate earlier discussions of relationship vs. career and of security vs. adventure come together in what we have just been saying. There can be ethical interaction effects between partial goods that are not *paired* with one another, and I hope to be able to say more about this on some future occasion.

12. Note that some of what I have just said about achievement as a human good that requires something bad to happen could be applied to what we earlier said about

adventure. Adventure involves risk and/or danger, and if such things are bad, then the partial good of adventure illustrates the old theodicean theme about good requiring bad or (nonmoral) evil. But (again) spelling out the precise nature of the requirement in this case necessitates a reference to the partiality of the value or good of adventure, so our general picture remains intact.

But what about wisdom, which I have treated as an unqualified good? Doesn't wisdom require pain, suffering, or (at the very least) struggle, and don't we, therefore, at least in this one instance have a case of necessary imperfection that has nothing to do with partial value(s)? Even if it is conceptually possible that someone should be born wise, wouldn't such a person have to have quasi-memories of painful events (occurring to themselves or others), and wouldn't the having of such memories, if they were felt like genuine memories, involve a certain amount of pain or sadness? Perhaps so, and therefore in this case and perhaps others, it would seem that the impossibility of perfect happiness could be based in something other than partial value—and have its roots, rather, in something akin to the old familiar thesis about good things requiring (the appreciation of) something bad. Ultimately, then, there might be two different bases for the necessity of imperfection, but I am certainly far from confident about the assumptions about wisdom I have just been making for the sake of argument.

Chapter 5

1. *The Ethics of Care and Empathy* (London: Routledge, 2007); and *Moral Sentimentalism* (New York: Oxford University Press, 2010). Incidentally, my defense of care ethics (and sentimentalism) involves a (mentally) internalist criterion of right and wrong and is to that extent also a defense of a certain form of virtue ethics. (See especially ch. 7 of *Moral Sentimentalism*.)

2. Carol Gilligan, *In a Different Voice: Psychological Theory and Women's Development* (Cambridge: Harvard University Press, 1982).

3. Nel Noddings, *Caring: A Feminine Approach to Ethics and Moral Education* (Berkeley: University of California Press, 1984).

4. See Held's "The Ethics of Care" in, D. Copp, ed., *The Oxford Handbook of Ethical Theory* (Oxford: Oxford University Press, 2006), pp. 537–66, and Noddings, *Caring*.

5. In *Beyond Good and Evil* and other works, Nietzsche makes the opposite "mistake" of stressing (solitary) individual creative fulfillment/accomplishment at the expense of ordinary relationships. On the present view, both care ethics (developed and articulated in a certain way) and Nietzsche hold *one-sided* views about the importance of achievement and relationships; and in effect our efforts to avoid such philosophical one-sidedness have led us to say that both achievement and affiliation are *themselves* one-sided, that is, partial, values. However, it is also worth noting that Nietzsche seems to be clearer about the (at the very

least) intrinsic tension between creative fulfillment and intimate relationships than any care ethicist appears to have been.

6. See, for example, my *The Ethics of Care and Empathy*, chs. 4–6.

7. For an example of someone who lays fairly equal stress on the value of relationships and personal achievement/fulfillment, see Bernard Williams in "A Critique of Utilitarianism" in J. Smart and B. Williams, *Utilitarianism: For and Against* (Cambridge: Cambridge University Press, 1973). Williams speaks of projects and commitments with fairly equal emphasis, and the projects are treated as connected with individual self-fulfillment, whereas the commitments involve personal (or larger group) relationships.

8. It can also seem retrograde or even antifeminist for care ethics not to emphasize helping (other) people—(other) women—toward the good of individual career/creative self-fulfillment (in the way it emphasizes the goal of building and maintaining good relationships).

9. By way of summary, then, certain forms of care ethics have previously stressed the importance of someone's accommodating and advancing their own career goals, but the idea of helping other people with their careers or creative aspirations hasn't been mentioned, and this stands in marked contrast with the emphasis some care ethicists have placed on maintaining/enhancing relationships *generally*, a goal that includes relationships one is not oneself directly involved in. A more gender-neutral or feminist care ethics ought, therefore, to place as much emphasis on the general promotion of career/creative fulfillment as it places and has placed on the general promotion of relationships.

10. See my *Ethics of Care and Empathy* and *Moral Sentimentalism*, and Noddings's *Starting at Home: Caring and Social Policy* (Berkeley: University of California Press, 2002).

11. But if care ethics emphasizes both relationships and creative fulfillment as things morally to be aimed at, won't our claim here that these are paired merely partial goods create problems concerning whether or when to prefer one of them over the other? Yes, it will; but if the present book is correct, then every normative moral view that recommends or mandates concern for people's welfare or aspirations will generate similar problems. So this is not a problem for care ethics in particular or for the assumption that it can be combined with the ideas and arguments we have advanced here.

12. For the communitarian critique, see, e.g., Michael Sandel, *Liberalism and the Limits of Justice* (Cambridge: Cambridge University Press, 1982).

13. The care ethicist who stresses the importance of relationship(s) to individual identity doesn't necessarily assume that we are stuck with (most of) the relationships we have if we wish to retain our own identity (and improve *our own* lives). For example, in her book (not the article) *The Ethics of Care: Personal, Political, and Global* (NY: Oxford University Press, 2006), p. 84, Virginia Held argues that care ethics allows a caring person to break off or disavow abusive relationships and forge new and better ones—though she doesn't specifically address the

question of how personal identity can or could survive some of the changes in personal relationships that care ethics and any form of feminism would recommend. (For example, a woman who has no birth-family or children of her own and who is over the years abused by both her husband and his family presumably should make a break with such people—assuming she can't reform them. But how, exactly, and according to care-ethical views about personal identity, does her identity survive such a radical break with her past?) But even where care ethicists see certain relationships as inessential, that is not because they think *something other than relationships* can help to make up the difference in or to someone's identity or individuality. Held and others talk about the abused or mistreated individual forming new relationships, but not about the resources, say, in someone's career or artistic life that can carry an individual, and their deepest identity, forward in their life. Once again, this seems one-sided.

14. Among the other kinds of moral issues where care ethics can conflict with the typical Kantian/liberal emphasis on autonomy rights is over the rights of abusive spouses and boyfriends. Questions of how soon and/or on the basis of what sort of evidence courts should issue restraining orders will be answered differently depending on whether one mainly emphasizes individual rights of autonomy or places more emphasis on protecting or ensuring the *welfare* of individuals. And if the liberal too quickly allows courts to intervene on behalf of the (potentially) abused in such cases, they will owe us an explanation of why autonomy rights are less important in such cases than they have claimed they are in Skokie-type cases.

15. See Noddings, *Starting at Home*; Daniel Engster, *The Heart of Justice: Care Ethics and Political Theory* (NY: Oxford University Press, 2007); and my *Ethics of Care and Empathy* and *Moral Sentimentalism*. I am using "justice ethics" to refer mainly to modern-day Kantian liberalism, rather than (say) to utilitarianism, because that is how care ethicists use the expression. And that usage reflects the fact that when Gilligan originally contrasted two moral voices, the voice of justice was conceived in terms that arguably fit Kantian liberalism better than they fit any other normative moral view.

16. Anyone with lingering worries about whether care ethics is biased in favor of traditional female values should remember, too, that the kind of care ethics I am talking about is theoretical and systematic in a way that is much more reminiscent of male intellectual tendencies than of anything historically associated with women('s thinking). However, that doesn't mean that a morally good and caring person needs to think theoretical thoughts or to appeal to some overall ethical theory of caring when they do caring things for other people. A theory of moral justification or rightness can justify what some or many people do independently of (thinking about) that very theory. (On this point, see my "Caring Versus the Philosophers" in my *Selected Essays* [NY: Oxford University Press, 2010], pp. 260–70. But what I say there needs to be expanded on in the light of the later *Moral Sentimentalism*.)

17. Both care ethics and the Berlinian ethical approach of the present book can allow
that there may turn out to be some intrinsic or "essential" differences between
males and females (not that those are particularly clear categories at this point).
For example, and as I have argued in *Moral Sentimentalism*, care ethics may
validly apply to both males and females even if male testosterone levels to some
extent interfere with empathic tendencies (and make aggressiveness more
likely). Similarly, there might be some differences between the genders as
regards, e.g., sexual adventurousness or the desire for sexual variety. But such
differences also exist between individuals of a given gender, and I don't see how
any of this undercuts the (partial) goodness of enjoying sexual variety or
adventure.

18. However (as Benjamin Yelle has reminded me), Romanticism also frequently
viewed individual passion and accomplishment as *taking precedence over* concern
for group (or family) welfare and/or over moral norms themselves; and care
ethics would want to have nothing to do with such a view of human values.
(Romanticism can *idolize* a Byron or a Gauguin in a way that care ethics never
could.) Note too that the idea (defended earlier in this book) that struggle can
make an achievement count for more is very definitely derived from Romanticism.
If it seems plausible, that is because many or most of us find certain Romantic
notions quite persuasive.

19. For discussion of ancient, Enlightenment, and Romantic views of the perfectibility of man, see John Passmore, *The Perfectibility of Man* (London: Duckworth,
1970).

20. Here (as earlier in this book) I am distinguishing Berlin's thesis that perfect happiness and virtue are impossible from the pluralist view that there is *no single
model* of (perfect) happiness or virtue (no such thing, for example, as *the* good
life). One can believe the latter while holding that *various* (mutually incompatible) ways of life and forms of human activity are in no way ethically lacking,
unsatisfactory, or criticizable. But someone who wants to claim that perfection is
impossible must hold that every conceivable way of life is to some extent ethically criticizable or lacking.

21. What also helps make it natural and sensible is that both the Berlinian understanding of human goods/virtues and the sort of sentimentalist care ethics
that seems most capable of standing up to and defending itself against ethical
rationalism accept the objectivity of (the) values (they respectively deal
with). We have said enough to indicate why a belief in partial values (alongside
unqualified ones) needn't call the objectivity of those values into question;
but my *Moral Sentimentalism* explains how care ethics can and why it should
adopt a semi-Kripkean reference-fixing empathy-based account of the
meaning of moral terms that allows moral judgments to be fully objective
(more objective than any strictly Humean moral semantics, even an ideal
observer view, allows them to be). Of course, such a view of moral terminology makes empathy central to all moral judgment, and most of the human

goods and virtues we have spoken of in the present book don't involve empathy (friendship and love relationships are an exception, but no one thinks an unempathic narcissist can't have interesting adventures or create great art). But rather than counting against the acceptance of both care ethics and the Berlinian picture of values, the just-mentioned difference helps make sense of what we ordinarily think is so special or distinctive about morality as compared with other values.

Chapter 6

1. See Thomas Hurka, *Virtue, Vice, and Value* (Oxford: Oxford University Press, 2000); and Christine Swanton, *Virtue Ethics: A Pluralistic View* (Oxford: Oxford University Press, 2003). Swanton's book is partly based on a prior article entitled "Profiles of the Virtues."
2. However, whenever Swanton compares and contrasts the profile of one virtue with that of another, she is in effect characterizing each of those virtues in relational or external terms, and, given my own nomenclature, this means that she is to that extent giving a relational profile of the virtue that she has already profiled in internal terms. But she doesn't herself count such external characterizations as part of any given virtue's profile, so I am in effect saying that it makes sense to widen the notion of a profile to include factors that are relational with respect to a given virtue. If we do, then some of Swanton's comparisons and contrasts will count as part of a virtue's profile, but, in any event, she doesn't talk about dependency relations as such, and so the present account takes us beyond or substantially adds to what Swanton says about given virtues. Moreover, Swanton doesn't (explicitly or deliberately) offer either external or internal profiles of human *goods*, and Hurka deliberately avoids the whole concept of a human or personal good (except to criticize and express the kind of skepticism about it that one finds, e.g., in G. E. Moore's *Principia Ethica*). To that extent, what we are doing in the present chapter is much broader in explicit categorial scope than Swanton's groundbreaking discussions (just) of the virtues. Note, finally, that I will for simplicity's sake sometimes speak, say, of a given virtue's depending on a certain good, when it would be more accurate to say that a given *qualified* virtue depends on a certain *qualified* good, etc.
3. See my "The Opposite of Reductionism" in my *Essays on the History of Ethics* (NY: Oxford University Press, 2010).
4. I discuss this further in "The Opposite of Reductionism."
5. Someone could have the disposition to be modest about possessions even while lacking any possessions and while never *displaying* that modesty. But the phrase "modest about his possessions" entails that the person actually has possessions, and if we can say that it refers to a (highly specified) virtue, then that virtue is a transcategorially dependent one. In general, however, I shall focus on (the

possession of) virtues rather than on their being displayed in certain ways, so one can't really say, for example, that the virtue of fortitude transcategorially depends on one's suffering or having suffered certain ills, because presumably someone can (unbeknownst to anyone) have that virtue without having yet had occasion to display it. By contrast, the virtue of conscientiousness doesn't seem to have to be displayed in order to depend on humaneness: if someone's values are inhumane, then *any conscientiousness they would display* in the name of those values (arguably) wouldn't be admirable, and I think that means that such conscientiousness seems to be lacking in admirability independently of whether it is actually displayed in particular situations.

6. The utilitarian (arguably Benthamite) claim that a trait like benevolence counts as a virtue only if it actually produces an overall balance of human good involves seeing that virtue as transpersonally and transcategorially dependent on the good of those who benefit from it. This may include the agent herself, but it clearly and most importantly takes in the good of others. However, the idea that this virtue depends for its virtue status on actual results is controversial and far from obvious.

7. It is often said that psychopaths, who lack the capacity for emotional empathy, also lack (full) moral concepts. Sentimentalists like myself say this sort of thing (see my *Moral Sentimentalism* [NY: Oxford University Press, 2010]), but the lack of empathy may have other implications as well. Most of us assume that psychopaths are incapable of love and genuine friendship. But if it takes empathy to understand what it is to care about another person, then the psychopath won't really be able to *understand what friendship or love is* and also won't be able to understand why or how *or even that* it is a good thing (apart from its contribution to other life goods the psychopath is presumably capable of understanding).

In addition, if the good of friendship depends on the caringness of one's friend, then it may depend on one's friend's being a good friend and, other things being equal, be proportional to how good a friend that friend is. But our arguments earlier showed that every friend has to be ethically lacking with respect to their dispositions vis-à-vis a given friend (they are disposed to be either disturbingly frank or disturbingly lacking in frankness). This in effect means that no one can be a perfect friend (compare what was said about perfect parenting in ch. 2), and in the light of what has just been said, it would seem to be impossible for anyone to enjoy the good of perfect friendship. For no one's friend can be perfect *as a friend*. This is one more reason for thinking perfect happiness is impossible.

8. There is also the possibility (mentioned in the notes in ch. 4) that the nonpartial and unqualified good of wisdom may depend on having had and/or containing within one the unhappy experience/sense of sorrow. This would then count as an example of a transvalently, intrapersonally, and intracategorially dependent good, and if wisdom also (or mainly) counts as a virtue, we would also then have

an instance of a transvalently, intrapersonally, and *transcategorially* dependent virtue. But I won't discuss any of this further right here.

9. For simplicity's sake, I am here blurring the distinction between the noninstantiation of, say, a given virtue and the instantiation of its opposite. But adventurousness not only rules out the full instantiation of prudence, but entails some degree of imprudence as well, and similarly for our other examples. I believe that we are inclined to think this way about such cases.

10. Two more possible examples (not previously mentioned) of the intracategorial, intrapersonal, and intravalent dependency of one virtue on another: courage and resourcefulness on (relevant) strength of purpose. Arguably, a person won't count as courageous if they lack strength of purpose with respect to the goals or activities dictated by or appropriate to courage. Similarly, a person isn't resourceful if they ingeniously think of ways to solve practical problems but don't follow through. Both courage and resourcefulness may also depend on a certain amount of patience and/or self-control.

11. Given our notion of transvalent dependency, once one includes what depends on a given virtue or good and not just what it depends on in its relational profile, one is probably going to have to talk about what given vices and evils depend on much more than we have here. For nothing then automatically precludes a vice or evil's depending on some virtue or good and our having to talk about that sort of dependency in specifying what depends on a given virtue or good (and is therefore part of its relational profile). I don't think every vice or evil will come into consideration in this way, and an absolutely exhaustive treatment of this area would require one to focus much more on evils and vices than we have. But at least for now, let us spare ourselves these particular complications.

However, note one thing. Above, we briefly contrasted the relational profiles of certain different goods and certain different virtues, and we could have said a lot more about the ways in which various virtues or goods differ from or resemble each other with respect to how they relate to, and in particular depend on, other values. But such comparisons are relational in a *second-order way*, for they compare and contrast some pair of values (two virtues, two goods, or, even, one good and one virtue) with respect to their relations of dependency. This means that value x is compared and contrasted with value y, with something external to it, and that is to characterize both x and y in relational terms. But what one is then relating is the way x and y depend on and so externally relate to various other values. To compare or contrast two values is to characterize each externally or relationally, and so to say, for example, that two values differ from one another with respect to the way(s) they depend on other values is to bring in relationality in a double way. And the relationality of the comparison or contrast between the values is second-order because it focuses on similarities or differences in *how the values relate to (depend on) other values*.

12. Derek Parfit, *Reasons and Persons* (Oxford: Oxford University Press, 1984), p. 129.

13. In *Plural and Conflicting Values* (NY: Oxford University Press, 1990), Michael Stocker calls the unwillingness ever to torture a kind of "moral immorality." That supports the idea that such unwillingness is (exaggeratedly) in the spirit of morality and doesn't constitute a form of deviant morality.

14. In addition, we could perhaps regard certain masochistic experiences as deviant *personal goods*.

15. Variants on a given value are just different forms or kinds of the value, and I don't think such differences really represent qualifications of a given value or virtue. Humanitarianism and devotion to one's family could, for example, be said to be variant forms of caring about others, but I don't think this particular fact in any way *qualifies* their status as virtues or values. So I am not (at least for the moment) including variant values as a kind of qualified value.

Conclusion

1. Thomas Kuhn, *The Structure of Scientific Revolutions*, 2nd edition (Chicago: University of Chicago Press, 1970); Saul Kripke, *Naming and Necessity* (Cambridge: Harvard University Press, 1980).

2. Part of that greater adequacy comes from the rejection, by most recent Aristotelians, of the notion that the doctrine of the mean governs all moral issues.

3. Rosalind Hursthouse, "After Hume's Justice," *Proceedings of the Aristotelian Society* 91 (1990–91): 229–45. I think I should mention, however, that Hursthouse doesn't emphasize or seek to justify rights of full political participation—e.g., voting rights—in her account of justice. That strikes me as a real limitation, in contemporary terms, to her approach.

4. On these historical issues and developments, see Jerome Schneewind, "The Misfortunes of Virtue" in R. Crisp and M. Slote, eds., (Oxford Readings in) *Virtue Ethics* (Oxford: Oxford University Press, 1997), pp. 178–200.

5. Under patriarchal or sexist assumptions many values we can now see as clashing *for everyone* were (as I have argued) widely viewed as relative to sex or gender and therefore as not really clashing *for anyone*. So feminism not only helps us (we hope) overcome patriarchy, but also makes it easier to see the noncontingent complexities and clashes of ethically intelligent living and thereby recognize the deficiencies of Enlightenment or ancient Greek views about the ultimate harmony and unity of our values. And these forms of awareness clearly have potential practical implications for how we (decide to) live our lives.

6. George Harris's *Reason's Grief* (NY: Cambridge University Press, 2006) grapples with various complexities or disharmonies of modern life, but there is only a very partial overlap between the complexities he talks about and those discussed here. And, more significantly, Harris doesn't diagnose the modern conditions he focuses on as pointing toward the in principle impossibility of perfection.

Appendix

1. See my "Kant for Anti-Kantians" in my book *Essays on the History of Ethics* (NY: Oxford University Press, 2010).

2. I realize that in speaking of "theoretical ethics," my very language suggests— misleadingly on my view—that reasoning and argument play a greater role in the field than insight, intuition, and emotional/psychological sensitivity. But I don't know what better term would be available here and am loath to introduce a neologism—I'd rather make my points without having to do that. (Similar problems arise with respect to the use of the term "intellectual.")

3. See her *Postures of the Mind: Essays on Mind and Morals* (Minneapolis: University of Minnesota Press, 1985), pp. 84ff.

4. See Nedelsky's "Reconceiving Autonomy: Sources, Thoughts, and Possibilities," *Yale Journal for Law and Feminism* 1 (1989): 7–36; and for some of the subsequent literature that follows Nedelsky's lead, see C. MacKenzie and N. Stoljar, eds., *Relational Autonomy: Feminist Perspectives on Autonomy, Agency, and the Social Self,* (NY: Oxford University Press, 2000).

5. The present discussion doesn't take in issues that have been raised about the (possibly) gendered character of people's philosophical(ly relevant) intuitions. (On this point, see, for example, Wesley Buckwalter's as yet unpublished "Gender and Epistemic Intuition.") I think one has to separate out any pure gender effects from questions about better and worse intuitions—though it might turn out that one gender or another had better intuitions in one area or another. But this is a topic that requires much further consideration.

   For interesting discussion of general skeptical doubts about the value or validity of intuitions, see the exchange between Ernest Sosa and Stephen Stich in D. Murphy and M Bishop, eds., *Stich and His Critics* (Malden, MA: Wiley-Blackwell, 2009), pp. 101–112, 228–36. But I don't think either Sosa or Stich takes seriously enough the possibility that some people may be more (philosophically) intuitive than others (and the relevance of that possibility to explaining putative disagreements).

6. For reasons discussed in chapter 5, I think that systematic theory-building should be included—alongside analytic criticism, etc.—as among the "methods" traditionally associated more with men than with women.

7. Care ethics emphasizes our connection(s) with others, rather than our autonomy or separateness from others. But the making of *theoretical* connections (as when care ethics draws on results from psychology to help it make its points) is also something valuable, and that kind of theoretical work may, at least in the past, have come more comfortably to women than purely logical deduction or philosophical analysis—which does, after all, involve *separating out* elements in a subject matter treated, for at least the moment, in *isolation* from other intellectual considerations. However, the ability to make intellectual connections (as in the example mentioned above) seems to go beyond sheer intuitiveness or

emotional/psychological sensitivity (as described in the text above), and if (a big "if") that ability has come less easily to men, we might need to add a reference to it in our description of the feminine side of ethical (or philosophical) methodology. Alternatively, and perhaps more plausibly, this might be a (unique?) respect in which men and women have been *equally* comfortable with connecting and connection.

8. Annette Baier notably urges something similar in her "What Do Women Want in a Moral Theory?" (reprinted in R. Crisp and M. Slote, eds., *Virtue Ethics* [Oxford: Oxford University Press, 1997], pp. 263–77). But Baier doesn't accept care ethics as a comprehensive approach to moral philosophy, and I have also been advocating a number of theses and distinctions that Baier doesn't consider. Thus (to take just one example) when Baier calls for a present-day Tiresias to combine the male and the female in the pursuit of a really adequate overall ethical theory, it isn't clear whether she is referring to an integration of content or of method or of both. But having above distinguished between male vs. female method and male vs. female content, I think this Tiresias is definitely going to have to pursue and give expression to both sorts of integration.

9. As a reader for OUP has pointed out to me, the injustice or injustices here have not been a matter merely of an unwillingness or inability, on the part of male philosophers, to recognize the value of intuitiveness and emotional/psychological sensitivity, but have also involved a tendency, again on the part of male philosophers, to dismiss feminist thought out of hand as too ideological or politically activistic to be taken (philosophically) seriously. (But I won't say more about this here.)

INDEX

HOSTAGES AND HOSTAGE-TAKING IN THE ROMAN EMPIRE

Hundreds of foreign hostages were detained among the Romans as the empire grew in the Republic and early Principate. As prominent figures at the center of diplomacy and as "exotic" representatives, or symbols, of the outside world, they drew considerable attention in Roman literature and other artistic media. Our sources discuss hostages in terms of the geopolitics that motivated their detention, as well as in accordance with other structures of power. Hostages, thus, could be located in a social hierarchy, a family network, in a cultural continuum, or in a sexual role. In these schemes, an individual Roman, or Rome in general, becomes not just a conqueror, but also a patron, father, teacher, or generically masculine. By focusing on the characterizations of hostages in Roman culture, we witness Roman attitudes toward ethnicity and imperial power.

Joel Allen earned his Ph.D. at Yale University and currently is Assistant Professor of History at Queens College, City University of New York.

HOSTAGES AND
HOSTAGE-TAKING
IN THE ROMAN EMPIRE

JOEL ALLEN
Queens College
City University of New York

CAMBRIDGE
UNIVERSITY PRESS

CAMBRIDGE UNIVERSITY PRESS

Cambridge, New York, Melbourne, Madrid, Cape Town, Singapore, São Paulo

Cambridge University Press
40 West 20th Street, New York, NY 10011-4211, USA

www.cambridge.org
Information on this title: www.cambridge.org/9780521861830

© Joel Allen 2006

First published 2006

Printed in the United States of America

A catalog record for this publication is available from the British Library.

Library of Congress Cataloging in Publication Data

Allen, Joel, 1970–
Hostages and hostage-taking in the Roman Empire / Joel Allen.
p.   cm.
Includes bibliographical references and index.
ISBN-13: 978-0-521-86183-0 (hardback)
ISBN-10: 0-521-86183-7 (hardback)
1. Rome – Foreign relations.   2. Hostages – Rome.   3. Ethnicity – Rome.
4. Politics and literature – Rome.   I. Title.
DG214.5A45   2006
937 – dc22   0508200600

ISBN-13   978-0-521-86183-0 hardback
ISBN-10   0-521-86183-7 hardback

For my parents and stepparents,
Linda and Jim Williams,
Doug and Lynn Allen

CONTENTS

LIST OF FIGURES

Figures follow page 170.

NOTE ON ABBREVIATIONS
AND TRANSLATIONS

Ancient sources are abbreviated in keeping with the third edition of the *Oxford Classical Dictionary*. Translations are my own, although most were checked against and improved by the Loeb Classical Library.

ACKNOWLEDGMENTS

Many people have had an influence on this book, both in its first incarnation as a doctoral dissertation and in its current, substantially revised form. I owe John Matthews the greatest debt of gratitude, not just for the initial idea and for years of advice in seeing it through but for taking me on as a student in the first place. Even as the project went in a different direction from his specialty in Late Antiquity, he remained supportive and encouraging. Susan Mattern-Parkes also has been generous with her time and assistance, sharing her research, serving as an outside reader of the original thesis, and enduring repeated requests for her thoughts. Over the years, various other colleagues have offered insights in a number of settings, from seminars to dinner parties, from emails to elevator rides; even job interviews, torturous at the time, clarified key issues. I am grateful to Barbara Burrell, Tom Carpenter, Carlos Galvao-Sabrinho, Mario Erasmo, Andrew Gregory, Veronika Grimm, Ann Ellis Hanson, Donald Kagan, Diana E. E. Kleiner, Lynne Lancaster, Bentley Layton, Joel Lidov, Ramsay MacMullen, Bill Metcalf, Ellen Oliensis, Bill Owens, Holt Parker, C. Brian Rose, Susan Treggiari, Gordon Williams, and Zvi Yavetz. The anonymous reviewers at Cambridge University Press also were rigorous and helpfully unforgiving, and the project benefited enormously from their suggestions, as well as from the efficient supervision of the manuscript by Beatrice Rehl. Ultimately, of course, decisions about what to do and how to do it were mine to make, which means that any errors herein are mine to claim.

A number of institutions provided financial support. Most important, a fellowship at the Center for the Humanities at the Graduate

Center of the City University of New York, supported by the Mellon Foundation, gave me a year off from teaching in 2002–2003. I also received funding in various forms from the Research Foundation of the Professional Staff Congress at CUNY and from the Ohio University Research Council. I was itinerant for several years after graduate school, which meant ambling through one library after another, finding my way to the DGs and the PAs anew each time; I should therefore thank the uniformly affable staffs of the libraries at Ohio University, Wake Forest, Duke, Yale, New York University, Columbia, Queens College, and my favorite, the New York Public Library. Also, the chair of the History Department at Queens College, Frank Warren, a good friend, has been patient and supportive and has created a department that is the model of collegiality.

Over the years, my family has also been warmly encouraging. They know that I was transformed by a remarkable Latin teacher, Maureen O'Donnell, now deceased, who inspired me in countless ways, and not just with regard to ancient Rome. As I pursued these studies, my parents and stepparents opened doors and created numerous opportunities, as well as welcomed me home whenever I needed a break. Finally, although Andy Rich (a professor of American politics) calls the Pantheon the Parthenon and thinks Augustus is a restaurant in the Village, he still delivers dead-on criticism and sends me back to the drawing board time and again; in the end, such a pleasant companion makes anything enjoyable.

I

INTRODUCTION

When Titus Quinctius Flamininus returned to Rome in 194 BCE from his campaigns in Greece, he treated the city to a magnificent show. The senate granted him permission to celebrate a triumph for several victories, most notably for the one over Philip V of Macedon, who had supported Hannibal during the Second Punic War and who had struck a little too close to home when he tried to conquer the Greek coast across from the Italian peninsula.[1] As Livy tells it, the festivities lasted for three days, with a parade of the usual riches and spectacles of a Roman triumph, but here at hyperbolic levels.[2] Works of art, weapons caches, and wagons loaded with ingots of precious metals and mounds of coins were carted through the streets. Brightly colored placards and tableaux would have depicted events in the war, as well as conquered territories, city walls breached by the Romans, and unfamiliar fields, rivers, and mountains. A horde of prisoners of war would have choked the streets, hundreds of them destined for slavery.[3] Such an array of conquest must have been deeply impressive

---

[1] The principal victory had come in 197 BCE, but Flamininus did not return to Rome until after evacuating Greece three years later. On the activities of Philip in Illyria during the Second Punic War, see Dorey and Dudley 1971, 120–121 and Gruen 1984, 373–379. For the origins of the so-called Second Macedonian War, characterized by caution and a reliance on Greek allies on the part of the Romans, see Gruen 1984, 437–447. For Flamininus's role in driving the campaign and the negotiations, see Eckstein 1987a, 269–277.

[2] Livy, 34.52. Phillips 1974 discusses the formulaic nature – and artistry – of Livy's references to triumphs.

[3] For the history and common characteristics of Roman triumphs, see Versnel 1970; Warren 1970; Künzl 1988. For the theatricality of the triumph, see Beard 2003.

to the audience: most of the people in the crowd would have never been to Greece, much less ever traveled beyond Italy, and the images of a distant place and the troves of its artifacts represented their first, or only, experience of an Hellenic landscape and culture. They would have been aware of few details of the campaign itself and would have reveled in the knowledge, here newly created, of a mysterious enemy now thoroughly reduced.[4] Confidence in Rome's opportunities must have been pervasive: the crops of another world would grow for the first time at the behest of the Romans, and prisoners of war would soon be enslaved and their activities thus diverted from the defense of Greece to labor for Roman masters.[5] In the Roman world, triumphal processions were fundamentally optimistic; the display of conquest was as much about imminent glory as it was about the general's past success.[6]

The climax came on the third day when dozens of Greek boys trudged along in front of Flamininus, who, as the *triumphator*, would have appeared as a near-god, decked in purple and with his face painted red as he rode in a four-horse chariot up to join Jupiter on the Capitoline Hill. The Greek youths before him were about twenty-five in number; Polybius calls them ὅμηροι and Livy calls them *obsides*.[7] The conventional English translation for both terms is "hostage," as the

---

[4] On the informative aspects of the triumph's display, see Mattern 1999, 162–168. On paintings in triumphal processions and their didactic quality, see Holliday 1997.

[5] Flamininus had just evacuated Roman troops from Greece and proclaimed Greek freedom from oversight, and so no formal tribute could have been expected at the time. Nevertheless, the image of conquest and control was unmistakable. In Livy, 34.50.4 the Romans expected *officium*, or duty-bound reciprocity from Greece. According to Livy, 34.51.6, Flamininus had hand-picked the new government there, on which Cf. Eckstein 1987a, 294–295.

[6] Versnel 1970, 371, compares the *triumphator*'s function as the bearer of good fortune with festivals in ancient Greek, Israelite, and Norse cultures. Compare Polybius, 6.54.3, who discusses the Roman funeral procession in terms of its forward-looking, inspirational effect on the audience.

[7] Five were from Sparta and the rest from Macedon. Sparta: Livy, 34.35.11, 34.40.4. Macedon: Polyb. 18.39.5; Livy, 33.13.14, 33.30.10; App. *Mac.* 2; Plut. *Flam.* 9.5; Cass. Dio, 18.60. Our sources do not mention a number for the Macedonian hostages. It would be reasonable, and conservative, to estimate about twenty, given the greater size of Macedon relative to Sparta and the fact that forty hostages were taken from the Aetolian League in 189, and twenty were taken from Philip's principal, and comparable, Hellenistic rival Antiochus III in 188 (see later).

boys had been taken from their families in Greece in part to serve as
assurances for the postwar settlement. One of them was Demetrius,
the son of Philip V; another was Armenes, the son of the tyrant Nabis
of Sparta. Demetrius had been about ten years old when his internment began in 197, so he was about thirteen when he took part in
the triumph in 194; we do not know the names of the others but they
would have been of similar age and aristocratic pedigree.[8]

Viewed together, they formed a memorable entourage: as children
of the nobility, all of them would have been well dressed; as adolescents,
many of them would have been gangly and uncomfortable, both in
Rome and in their own skins. Speaking to each other in Greek (if
they spoke at all), failing to understand the Latin cries all around them,
making their way before Flamininus's chariot, which bore down on
them from behind, and perhaps stumbling in the awkwardness of their
early teenage years, the hostages must have seemed utterly pathetic and
powerless. That appears to have been the point: here at the very zenith
of the triumph, the man responsible for it all came shepherding a final
and peculiar asset for Rome's future, a next generation. Demetrius had
been a young, healthy prince with a famous father and a potentially
glorious career ahead of him as an heir to a faraway kingdom – that
of Alexander the Great, no less – until Rome intervened; now he
was firmly, and spectacularly, under Roman control. His position at
the front of the *triumphator*'s chariot was a meaningful place for him
to march; he and his peers were occupying a space that was typically

---

[8] According to Livy, 40.6.4, Demetrius was born around 207 BCE. Polyb. 18.39.5 and Livy,
33.13.14 say that he served as a hostage for a four-month truce in 197 while terms were
negotiated and ratified in Rome. In Livy, 33.30.10, Demetrius is included as a hostage
for the final settlement of 196. It is uncertain whether Demetrius stayed with Flamininus
on campaign in Greece until 194 or if he had been sent to Rome immediately after
Cynoscephalae. Plut. *Flam.* 9.5 weakly implies the latter, but Walker 1980, 97–99 notes
examples where Roman generals are said to hold on to their hostages until the triumph.
For the timing of events from the victory to the settlement, see Baronowski 1983. No
source explicitly states the ages of the other Macedonian hostages, nor of Armenes and
the other Spartans. Polyb. 18.39.5 and Livy, 33.13.14 say that the Macedonian hostages
were taken from among Philip's "Friends" (τινας ἑτέρους τῶν φίλων, *ex amicorum
numero obsides*). Walker 1980, 50 suggests this may refer to the children of these powerful
associates of the king, although it is possible that the "Friends" themselves, obviously
adults, were in the entourage. Once again, comparable episodes from this period would
suggest that the very young were the principal targets of Roman policy (see later).

reserved for the most valuable catch of the campaign.[9] Unlike their compatriot prisoners of war who plodded through the streets *en masse*, these boys held positions of respect, on par with the conqueror's own social milieu. The presence of the hostages – the first in Rome from the Greek mainland – alongside the leaders of the city demonstrated that the Romans had entered onto an international stage. Through possession of Demetrius, Armenes, and the rest, Flamininus and the Roman celebrants who watched them implicitly staked a claim to that cultured land that had, to the Roman mind, produced giants of history and human intellect, as well as made fundamental contributions to their beliefs and legends. The scene was a dramatic verification of the success of the campaign. This crowd of boys, when so starkly shown in captivity and respectful submission, would have enlivened an already raucous pageant of civic pride, nationalistic superiority, and hopes for the future.

In the Rome of the early second century BCE, there appears to have been a fascination for the experiences of the foreign traveler in a land not his own. Watching from the windows and rooftops of a packed city, the spectators would have been exhilarated by the sight of the hostages, but they would not have been surprised. Such detainees had been part of prior triumphal processions, and only recently a much larger band of them, brought to Italy from Carthage, had conspicuously taken up residence in and around the city.[10] The Carthaginians had agreed less than a decade earlier, under the terms of an armistice in 203 BCE and again under the compulsion of their defeat at Zama in 202, to submit hundreds of hostages.[11] All of them were intended to fit a profile that was specified by the Romans in a formal treaty: they were to be between fourteen and thirty years of age; they were to be of noble

[9] Versnel 1970, 95; Phillips 1974, 271. Compare Edwards 2003, 62–64, who sees the inclusion of images of the enemy in the triumph as potentially honorific for the defeated. See also Chapter 4.

[10] Other than the Carthaginian example outlined below, note also the hostages taken from the Samnites (Livy, 9.16.1; 9.20.4; 10.11.13) and the Boii (Polyb. 3.40.7; Livy, 21.25.7; Frontin. *Str.* 1.8.6), and, perhaps mythically, from the Etruscans (Livy, 5.27; Dion. Hal. *Ant. Rom.* 9.17.3; Frontin. *Str.* 4.4.1) and the Volsci (Livy 2.16.9; 2.22.2; Dion. Hal. *Ant. Rom.* 6.25.2; 6.30.1).

[11] For a complete discussion of the evidence for the Punic hostages, collected at Moscovich 1974a, see Chapter 2.

families; and a group of them was to be present in Rome, apparently, as long as the war indemnity payments were required, or a period of fifty years.[12] Every now and then, at the discretion of the senate, hostages who had grown up in Italy could be sent back to Carthage and swapped for a new batch of young aristocrats.[13] Again, speaking in an unfamiliar language and wearing their distinctive Punic clothing, and most important, under the close supervision of the senate, these hostages must have drawn the gossipy attention of the Roman public, as well as of the ruling elite. Residents abroad embodied the honor and identity of their native origins; their differences made them exotic and larger than life. Any visitor, be he a hostage or not, was charged with symbolism; an insult directed toward him could carry a broader message of disrespect to all of his countrymen and would be assumed to reflect the general attitude of the host. Likewise, if he were honored and treated favorably, he could serve as a living token of peace and accord. Both sides, Roman and non-Roman, weighed the traveler's reactions to his peculiar surroundings, whether they be of assimilation or resistance, in forming their general opinions about each other. The way the host treated the hostage and the way the hostage responded to either hostility or embrace affected entire populations in multiple areas of life.

The subsequent career and behavior of Demetrius of Macedon serves as an extended case in point. After six years as a hostage, he was released in 191 as a gesture of gratitude by the senate for Philip's assistance in a war against the Seleucid king, Antiochus III.[14] Of course, a child's years from ages ten to sixteen are witness to acute physical, social, and psychological transformations in any context, whether at home or abroad, and not surprisingly our sources suggest that Demetrius returned to Pella a changed man. Having spent

---

[12] In addition to later in Chapter 2, see Polyb. 15.18.7–8; Nepos, *Hann.* 7.2; Livy, 30.37.6; App. *Hann.* 54, 79; Cass. Dio, 17.82. No source explicitly links the hostages to the indemnity; on the problematic relationship between hostages and indemnity payments, see Chapter 2.

[13] Livy, 40.34.14 suggests a rotation for 181 BCE, and Livy 45.14.5 suggests the same for 168 BCE. The practice has been called *mutatio obsidum*, on which see note 46.

[14] Polyb. 21.3.3, 21.11.9; Diod. Sic. 28.15; Livy, 35.31.5, 36.35.13, 37.25.12; Plut. *Flam.* 14; App. *Mac.* 5, *Syr.* 20.

his formative years under the tutelage of Flamininus and other senators, Demetrius appeared to have developed a capacity for communicating well with the Romans. When, in 184 BCE, several of Macedon's neighbors gathered before the senate to accuse Philip of plotting to extend his territory against Roman wishes, Philip chose Demetrius to deliver the response in Rome. At the age of twenty-four, then, he made the trip back across the Adriatic and reentered the familiar buildings of his youth.[15] Memories of his first arrival, when he was a boy, as part of a rambunctious and noisy triumph could not have escaped him.

Our sources suggest that Demetrius's transformation continued to have larger political ramifications. The senators, along with Flamininus, gave their former ward a warm reception, the complaints of Philip's neighbors were dismissed, and Demetrius's mission was presumably a success.[16] But, according to Polybius, word got out among the Macedonians, helped by Roman sources, that the grant of indulgence by the senate was a favor to Demetrius specifically, and not to his father. Livy adds that the senate claimed still to hold Demetrius's soul hostage even though they had returned his body.[17] Our historians thus imply that the Roman embrace of Demetrius had behind it an insidious purpose and that Flamininus was deliberately reestablishing the relationship that he had formed during Demetrius's hostageship in order to win him over and thus to interfere with Macedonian politics.[18] The tactic is said to have had its intended effect on the Macedonian people at large: not wanting war with Rome, they allegedly pinned their hopes on Demetrius as the leader who would avoid it, and he became the center of a political movement against Philip V.[19] As Polybius and Livy construe it, just one former hostage, who gave the impression of an affinity for Rome based on his childhood acquaintance with

---

[15] Polyb. 22.14.10; Livy, 39.35.3.

[16] Polyb. 23.2.9–11; 23.3.6; 23.7.1.

[17] Livy, 39.47.10: *obsidum enim se animum eius habere, etsi corpus patri reddiderit.*

[18] Polyb. 23.3.7–8; Livy, 39.47.10. Cf. Edson 1935, 193 and Aymard 1961, 141. Gruen 1984, 221 sees the action as only Flamininus's undertaking and not a part of Roman policy. For our purposes, the perception of Demetrius's malleability, as described by our sources, takes precedence over the reality, whatever it was.

[19] Polyb. 23.7.2–3; Livy, 39.53.1–10; 40.5.2.

Roman senators and Roman life, had enhanced the Roman-friendly environment under a diplomatically unfriendly regime. By singling out a symbolic foreign resident in their midst, Roman senators had polarized a community at their periphery and had exacerbated already existing ideological rifts therein.

At this point, Polybius's narrative becomes fragmentary and we are left with Livy to recount the famous story of the suspicions of Demetrius's older brother Perseus.[20] Perseus believed that Demetrius had begun to plot with Flamininus for the overthrow of Philip with the plan of taking Perseus's place in the succession and installing himself on the throne as a vassal of Rome. For Livy's Perseus, a mountain of circumstantial evidence began to pile up: Demetrius appeared to spend an inordinate amount of time with Roman ambassadors in Pella, and he defended Rome and the Roman way of life in conversations with his family.[21] At no time is Demetrius said to have acted on any royal ambitions, but his brother's and father's perception of his demeanor condemned him nonetheless. First Perseus, and later Philip as well, planted spies to verify, or in some cases to fabricate, evidence of Demetrius's betrayal.[22] Eventually two of Philip's ambassadors produced a letter from Flamininus to Philip stating that Flamininus doubted that Demetrius would plot against the royal family, but that if he did, Flamininus would not have any part in it.[23] Although there was no accusation in the letter, Flamininus's tone still left open the possibility that Demetrius was a traitor, and this was enough for Philip to order one of his men to kill his son. Livy says that the letter was revealed to be a forgery, but by then the damage had already been done.[24] Demetrius's bizarre, lifetime journey, split between Macedon and Rome – and all the rumors, paranoia, espionage, deceit, and betrayal

---

[20] Cf. Polyb. 23.10.13–16; 23.11. For the literary quality of the story of family dysfunction and Demetrius's demise, see Walbank 1938.

[21] Livy, 39.53.11; 40.5.7–8.

[22] Livy, 40.7.4; 40.20.3–4; 40.21.10–11; 40.23.1–2.

[23] Livy, 40.23.7–8.

[24] For the forgery, see Diod. Sic. 29.25; Livy, 40.55. For Philip's call for Demetrius's execution, see Polyb. 23.3.9; Diod. Sic. 29.25; Livy, 40.24, 41.23.11; Plut. *Arat.* 54.3. On the authenticity of the letter, forgery or not, see Walbank 1940, 250–251.

that such travels are said to have elicited in Perseus and Philip – came to an end when Demetrius was poisoned and smothered in 181 at the age of twenty-six.

From his early childhood, Demetrius seems to have been swept up in a maelstrom. At the root of both his failures and what little success he achieved, according to our sources, was his status as a hostage and his unique trait of having spent extended periods of time in two competing realms. According to Polybius and Livy, Demetrius himself was unable to do much on his own. When he was part of the embassy pleading on behalf of Philip against his Greek neighbors, he is said to have bungled his presentation to the point that senators intervened out of sympathy and granted his requests regardless.[25] Demetrius does not seem to have been savvy in politics, but rather he is depicted as a pawn in events that taxed his capabilities and as a symbol of relations between two great powers. As a hostage, he was at the center of high level negotiations in international diplomacy, and as a hostage, he was privy to both the Roman and the Macedonian ways of life. His connections in Macedon made him appealing to Flamininus; his connections in Rome made him appealing to Philip. His Greekness made him suitable for display before the greedy eyes at the triumphal procession; his Roman-ness made him a magnet for a faction of pro-Romanists in Macedon. His Roman qualities also drew the fatal envy of his brother.

All of these various fears and hopes reflect certain exigencies in the international relations of Roman antiquity. By holding Demetrius at a young age and by exercising their influence over him, the Romans believed they had an undeniable opportunity in geopolitics. In societies where legitimacy to rule was passed through blood, an opposing faction, outside of power, could make significant inroads with merely a warm body with a good name, if he (or, more rarely, she) was shown to represent their cause. Diplomacy naturally did not entail simply a bilateral relationship between two states; under a more complex rubric, it involved the various factions in internal struggles on either side. Monarchies, by virtue of their centralized authority, could be subject to manipulation through dynastic alternatives. Even in the cases of nondynastic regimes, like the more democratic or

---

[25] Polyb. 23.2.2–9; Livy, 39.47.1–9.

oligarchic leagues of Greece, hostages and other types of travelers in
Rome could wrinkle the cloth of diplomacy, either by actively pursuing their own ambitions or in being used by others. Young men,
potentially impressionable, potentially ambitious, whose stay in Rome
was finite and who were within reach of major political responsibility could have a heavy influence on political opinion down the
road. As a hostage Demetrius was seized on as a valuable commodity
more than once; tugged back and forth, he never had control over his
future.

It would be fair to say that Roman writers – historians and otherwise – were obsessed with hostages. Many stories from Greco-Roman
antiquity are strikingly similar to that of Demetrius, and hostages
recur frequently as contentious figures at the center of momentous
events. According to one source, a mythical hostage was a foremother
of the Roman race: Dionysius of Halicarnassus says that one version for the parentage of Latinus, the king whose daughter married
Aeneas, claimed that he was the son of Heracles and a hostage girl from
the north, with whom Heracles was traveling.[26] Roman legends are
packed with courage-in-the-face-of-adversity moments, embellished
over centuries, which feature bold heroes who ignore their shackles.
Cloelia famously swam the Tiber to escape her obligation as a hostage
to the invading king Lars Porsenna in the early days of the Republic,
only to be returned by the Romans who upheld their diplomatic vow;
as a prisoner of war Mucius Scaevola willfully thrust his right hand
into the fire before the same Etruscan king, showing that he would
suffer any amount of torture before assisting his enemy.[27] As we shall
see, such tales, bandied about by Augustan age authors, may have had
more to do with events contemporary with the time of composition
than with the international negotiations of the early Republic. Nevertheless, numerous references to hostages in the early skirmishes with
Rome's neighboring tribes – the Etruscans, the Volsci, the Samnites –
suggest that hostage-taking was seen as widespread at an early stage

[26] Dion. Hal. *Ant. Rom.* 1.43.1.
[27] Cloelia: Livy, 2.13, 2.15.6; Dion. Hal. *Ant. Rom.* 5.33; Verg. *Aen.* 8.651; Val. Max.
3.2.2; *De vir. ill.* 13; Juv. 9.264–265; Plut. *Mor.* 250D, *Publicola* 19.2; Cass. Dio, 45.31.1.
Scaevola (as a hostage rather than a prisoner of war): Dion. Hal. *Ant. Rom.* 5.31.2. See
also later, Chapters 3 and 7.

in Rome's development.[28] One does not have to look far into other periods and regions to find that the practice was an integral component of all ancient warfare, Rome aside. Demetrius's own predecessor in the Macedonian royalty, Philip II, had spent time as a hostage in Thebes from 367 to 364 BCE with important consequences, long before Rome held international attention; the stories of detainees in the Peloponnesian War, whether they be of Spartans on Sphacteria or of Mytileneans following their revolt against Athens, gave Thucydides opportunities for his most significant set speeches.[29] An interest in the experience of hostages (mythical though they are) is arguably at the very origins of recorded history: Herodotus, in his first book – his first passage, in fact – tells the story of Io, a princess of Argos, who was seized by Phoenician traders.[30] For Herodotus, the event was loaded with significance, as it set off a chain reaction of retaliations in kind: the Greeks responded by "kidnapping" Europa from Tyre, and then Medea from the shores of the Black Sea, and the "East," or rather Troy, then came back to steal Helen. The seesaw of vengeful kidnapping was brought to an end when the Greeks, instead of abducting yet another princess, launched their thousand ships. So ran the string of events that, according to Herodotus, defined the international tensions of the Persian Wars in the fifth century BCE and lingered in the minds of Darius and Xerxes, Miltiades and Leonidas.

Most of the major initiatives in foreign policy and warfare during the Roman Republic and early Principate involved hostages in some way. The first hostages to receive serious attention in the literary sources are those that arrived in the decade or so following the end of the Second Punic War in 202 BCE. Several high-profile triumphs made their way down the Via Sacra during this generation, and detailed reports of hostages are preserved in treaties with the Aetolian League in Greece in 189 and with the Seleucid monarchy in Syria in 188, and incidental references are made to hostage groups from Spain, northern Italy,

[28] See earlier, note 10.
[29] Philip II: Diod. Sic. 15.67.4; Dio Chrys. *Or.* 49.5; Plut. *Mor.* 178C, *Pel.* 26.4; Just. *Epit.* 6.9.7, 7.5.1–3. On Mytilene and Sphacteria: Thuc. 3.37–48 and 4.17–20. On the hostageship of Philip II, see Aymard 1954 and later and on hostages in Greek history in general, see Amit 1970 and Panagopoulos 1978.
[30] Hdt. 1.1–4.

Sardinia, and Corsica, in addition to Carthage, Macedon, and Sparta, already mentioned.[31] A crest in the wave ultimately came after the Battle of Pydna in 167, when, according to Polybius who was himself among the detained, the Romans transported to Italy one thousand hostages from the various *poleis* of the Achaean League which the Romans had only recently "freed" from Philip V in the prior generation.[32] After the Third Punic War, hostage-taking was common in Rome's effort to gain control of both the Iberian peninsula and Numidia in North Africa.[33] In the first century BCE, Pompey brought back crowds of royal hostages from his campaigns in Asia Minor; it is this achievement that Julius Caesar, Pompey's rival, seems deliberately to address and surpass in his repeated stories of the detentions of hundreds of hostages from Gaul and Britain in the 50s BCE.[34] In the subsequent generation of competing statesmen, Mark Antony held many high-profile hostages at his court at Alexandria, and Octavian took 700 from Dalmatia in 33 BCE.[35] During Octavian's ensuing reign as *princeps*, hostage-taking was worked on an even wider geographical spectrum, including every corner of the empire: Western Europe, the Balkans, Asia Minor, Parthia, Armenia, Judaea, and North Africa. The nature of detention, or at least the attitude toward it, changed markedly under the Principate of the Julio-Claudians and Flavians, as we shall see throughout and revisit in the epilogue, but elite foreign youths continued to visit Rome from all over and to receive significant attention from historians and other writers as a way of explaining Rome's shockingly sudden ascendance in the Mediterranean; they embodied the vulnerability of the periphery and thus enabled Rome's

[31] Aetolian League: Polyb. 21.32.10–11; Livy, 38.11.6–7. The Seleucids (Peace of Apamea): Polyb. 21.42.14 and 22; Livy, 38.38.9 and 15; 42.6.9; App. *Syr.* 39. Spain: (in 195) App. *Hisp.* 41; Polyaenus, *Strat.* 8.17.1; (in 179) Livy, 40.47.2 and 10; (for wars from 152–151) App. *Hisp.* 48–54. Liguria: Livy, 40.28.6 and 40.38.5. Boii: Livy, 36.39.3 and 36.40.3. Sardinia: (in 176) Livy, 41.17.3. Corsica: (in 181) Livy, 40.34.12. See the appendix in Walker 1980, 215–243.
[32] On the issue of the terminology for these hostages, see later and Chapter 8.
[33] Spain: Diod. Sic. 33.16.1 and App. *Hisp.* 72, 73, 77, 79. Numidia: (in 109) Sall. *Jug.* 54.6; (in 108) Cass. Dio, 26.89.1; (in 90) App. *BCiv.* 1.42. See the appendix in Walker 1980, 215–243.
[34] Pompey: App. *Mith.* 103, 117; Cass. Dio, 37.2.5–7; Plut. *Pomp.* 45.4. On Caesar's many references to hostages, see Moscovich 1979–1980 and Walker 1980, 236–241.
[35] Antony: Cass. Dio, 51.16.1–2. Dalmatia: App. *Ill.* 28.

invincibility. Deployed again and again in our sources, the hostage became iconic of a successful type of diplomacy and of an emerging universal, yet hegemonic culture.

This book examines how authors of the Roman era viewed the figure of the hostage and others like him who moved to Rome from the outside world and were said to develop a fluency with Roman culture, ultimately coming to be represented as figures who had a split, or hybrid, identity as a result. Our objective is to understand the essence of the Roman hostage; in short, to get some sense of what may have been going through the minds of the Romans at, for example, the triumph of Flamininus when they saw the thirteen-year-old Demetrius of Macedon being led, or driven, through the streets. What did it mean to the Romans for Flamininus to possess the hostage? What did it mean for Philip to give him? In what ways did writers imagine the hostage's predicament and consequently, the evident superiority of Rome? What was expected of Demetrius and those with uniquely dual identities? What was thought to be possible? It is the principal contention of this book that by examining the impressions of hostages and hostage-taking as revealed in literary sources, the reader can discover trends in how the elite Roman viewed entire non-Roman populations. It should be pointed out that this study is not so much about what the hostages did or what happened to them, which has been the subject of numerous previous studies, as about how they were constructed in our sources.[36] Given the significance of the hostage as a representative of another culture in a Roman setting, to whom great

[36] There have been many general studies of hostage-taking in the Roman world: Matthaei 1905, Phillipson 1911, Lécrivain 1916, Aymard 1961, Moscovich 1983, Braund 1984a, Lica 1988, Elbern 1990, Ndiaye 1995, Noy 2000. There also are several studies of individual hostage episodes that review some of the basic trends: Aymard 1953, Moscovich 1974a, Moscovich 1979–1980, Rose 1990, Guidobaldi 1993, Lica 1993, Scardigli 1994, Kuttner 1995, esp. 111–123, and Lica 2000, 251–257. Several studies have focused on late antiquity, outside the time frame of this book: Matthews 1989, Lee 1991, Speidel 1998. The overlap among them all is considerable. By far the most thorough examination is a dissertation completed by Cheryl Walker at the University of North Carolina at Chapel Hill in 1980, which was consulted here and by Braund 1984a; in 2005, it was made available online by the Center for Hellenic Studies. None of these, however, has looked at the rhetoric of the practice at great length. Walker 1980, iii mentions that the legendary material on hostage-taking in the Roman monarchy provides "insight into the practices of the times in which our sources were written" and that this material

political meaning is attached, by focusing on the expectations of the hostage's behavior and experience as expressed in Roman culture, we can learn something about the Roman understanding of international relations, their attitude toward other groups of people, and the ways in which they thought they should interact with non-Romans, or exercise power over them.

OVERLAPPING CATEGORIES

A number of scholarly studies, mainly in the form of journal articles, have noted trends in Roman hostage-taking.[37] Although the current inquiry into the perceptions and expectations of hostages differs in approach from previous scholarship, it is useful to review some of the fundamental characteristics of hostages, which others have identified. When the hundreds of episodes of hostage-taking from Roman history are considered together, some basic patterns emerge, with hostages generally fitting the same demographic profile based on the categories of sex, age, and socioeconomic status. The sex of hostages was most frequently male, although the taking of females is not unheard of.[38] The target age for hostages was spelled out in detail in three prominent cases of the early second century: in the treaties with Carthage, with the Aetolian League, and with Antiochus III of Syria, the hostages were required to be between fourteen and thirty, twelve and forty, and eighteen and forty years old, respectively.[39] Exceptions to these parameters, however, were possible; for example, Antiochus IV of the

"affords us a glimpse of the possibilities envisioned by our sources," but she does not pursue the question at length.

[37] See the previous note. Walker 1980 includes a prosopography of 257 hostage episodes from the Roman Republic and the Hellenistic East, plus a list of 14 instances of the use of the figure of the hostage rhetorically or as a metaphor. Elbern 1990 includes a catalog of 125 cases, only from the Roman world, but extending into late antiquity.

[38] Aymard 1961, 137–139; Walker 1980, 28–35; Lica 1988, 42; Elbern 1990, 108–109; Scardigli 1994, 128. Phillipson 1911, 401 and Ndiaye 1995, 158 point out exceptions. For more on the gender of hostages, see Chapter 7.

[39] Carthage: Polyb. 15.18.8; Livy, 30.37.6. Aetolian League: Polyb. 21.32.10; Livy, 38.11.6. Antiochus III: Polyb. 21.42.22. With Antiochus III, Livy, 38.38.14–15 alleges an age range of 18–45. On ages of hostages, see Matthaei 1905, 233–234; Aymard 1961, 141; Walker 1980, 35–42; Ndiaye 1995, 157. Elbern 1990, 108 points out that the age parameters allow for adults to be detained as well.

Seleucids was only in his early teens when he arrived in Rome in 188, well below the stated cut-off age of eighteen.[40] In other, less detailed accounts of hostages, ambiguous expressions of age — writers may identify hostages as the *"liberi"* or "τέκνα" (children) of the donor — preclude precise conclusions, but still at least imply a nearly universal attribute of hostages: that they were not yet at the peaks of their public careers when they were taken to Italy.[41] Their socioeconomic status was invariably of the highest level; they came from royal or noble families, or from the equivalent within their respective societies, depending on the nature of the political regime.[42] The number of hostages taken at one time also depended on the nature of the donor state's political structure. Monarchies or highly centralized oligarchies would typically submit a small group of around ten to twenty hostages, but when Rome was dealing with a region that was governed by oligarchies in multiple city-states, the number could swell to several hundred.[43] Carthage, for example, surrendered hundreds following the Second Punic War, whereas Sparta gave only five in 195 at a time when it was ruled by a single tyrant; the Seleucids, a monarchy, submitted twenty in 188.[44] The duration of a hostage's detention tended to be stated explicitly at the outset, although the evidence suggests that it varied in practice. In several treaties, the length of internment seems to have been linked with the schedule of payments toward a war indemnity

---

[40] Mørkholm 1966, 38, on the contrary, suggests Antiochus IV had been born around 212, judging from numismatic images of 170 BCE in which Antiochus seems to be "at least 40 years of age" at the time, making him in his early twenties at the start of his hostageship. However, as Mørkholm concedes, the estimate may be too early, considering that "the Seleucid princes were generally initiated into public life at an early age," and yet Antiochus's hostageship is the first we hear of him. A better date for Antiochus's birth may be after 202, when Antiochus III returned from his campaigns in the East, in which case he would have been fourteen when his hostageship began. See also Walbank 1979, 162, pointing out that Demetrius, Antiochus's nephew who replaced him as a hostage, was also below the minimum age requirement.

[41] Walker 1980, 35; Elbern 1990, 108.

[42] Lécrivain 1916, 128; Aymard 1961, 141; Walker 1980, 48–52; Elbern 1990, 105–109; Ndiaye 1995, 153–154.

[43] Matthaei 1905, 234; Phillipson 1911, 400–401; Lécrivain 1916, 127–128; Walker 1980, 42–48 (including a chart that illustrates the trend); Elbern 1990, 103–105; Ndiaye 1995, 156–158.

[44] On Sparta, see note 7. On Carthage, see note 12. The Seleucids: Polyb. 21.17.8; 21.42.22; Diod. Sic. 29.10; Livy, 37.45.16; 38.38.14–15; App. *Syr.* 38, 39.

where the hostages were released once the financial obligation had been met, but this is not universal. With the Aetolians in 189, the duration was for six years; with Antiochus III in 188, it was for twelve; and with Carthage in 201, it was presumably for fifty.[45] Individual hostages could be replaced at certain intervals, which would be necessary in cases of lengthy internments either because of the aging or death of hostages or because of changes in the political situation of the donor state. The treaty with Antiochus III in 188 called for a rotation of hostages every three years, with the exception of the king's son who was to remain throughout; as we have seen, evidence in Livy hints at occasional replacements from Carthage following the Battle of Zama, although they were not regularly scheduled.[46]

Few restrictions were placed on hostages' everyday lives, and minimal security measures guarded against their escape. They were free to move about in public spaces, as well as outside the city of internment, and they could communicate regularly with ambassadors from their native states without interference or participation by the Romans.[47] Demetrius Soter of Syria, for example, a hostage from 178 to 162 BCE, was able to escape from captivity in part by telling his overseers that he was on a hunting trip outside the city, which was presumably allowed.[48]

---

[45] Aetolians: Polyb. 21.32.10. Antiochus III: Polyb. 21.42.19, 22; Livy, 38.38.13–15; App. *Syr.* 38. Carthage: Polyb. 15.18.7; Livy, 30.37.5; App. *Lib.* 54.

[46] Antiochus III: Polyb. 21.42.22; Livy, 38.38.15; App. *Syr.* 39. Carthage: see earlier, note 13. As Moscovich 1974a points out, given the fifty-year period of the treaty at Zama, regular rotation on three-year intervals, which Aymard 1953 argued was the case based on the system of rotation in the roughly contemporary treaty with Antiochus III, would have required thousands of hostages, an unlikely scenario; rather, in this case the Romans proceeded according to what was expedient. On *mutatio obsidum*, see also Matthaei 1905, 244–245; Aymard 1961, 140; Moscovish 1974b; Walker 1980, 67–72; Ndiaye 1995, 161.

[47] Matthaei 1905, 235–236; Lécrivain 1916, 130–132; Walker 1980, 107–116; Elbern 1990, 110–114; Ndiaye 1995, 159.

[48] Polyb. 31.14.1–5. Throughout this book, Demetrius I of the Seleucids will be called by his later epithet, Soter, so as to distinguish him from Demetrius of Macedon. The date of the start of Demetrius's hostageship is problematic: App. *Syr.* 45 implies that Demetrius was sent by his father, Seleucus IV, to replace Antiochus IV, who was released. The original terms of the treaty called for Antiochus to serve for twelve years, which would put his release at 176, and yet an inscription reveals that he was in Athens as early as 178/7. Paltiel 1979b, 42 suggests the exchange recorded in Appian took place in 178. See also Gruen 1984, 646. On Demetrius's hostageship in general, see Polyb. 31.2; 31.11–15; 33.19; Diod. Sic. 31.18; Livy, *Per.* 46; Just. *Epit.* 34.3.6–9; App. *Syr.* 45–47.

Livy says that after a rebellion of Carthaginian slaves in Italy after the Second Punic War, the Carthaginian hostages were placed under confinement, but he presents this as an anomaly.[49] A hostage's household, complete with spouse, children, and a retinue of slaves, could accompany him to Italy, and he could bring material possessions with him and receive more luxuries from the Romans themselves. The Carthaginian hostages following Zama had slaves with them, and ambassadors from Carthage successfully petitioned for an improvement in their conditions.[50] A house was famously built in Rome for Antiochus IV, a hostage from 188 to 178/7, at public expense, and Demetrius Soter of Syria was lavishly entertained at Roman banquets.[51] Some have seen the hostage as sacrosanct.[52] Apart from the occasional story of an attempted escape, for many hostages it must have been a physically comfortable life, even when the separation from home and the political indignity could be appalling.

A major difference between this book and previous work done on hostages, apart from approach, is that the figures who are labeled specifically as "hostage" in Roman literature (ὅμηρος or *obses*) are not the only ones to be considered here. I would argue that the figure of the "hostage" was not exclusive or well defined in Roman antiquity: other categories of foreign residents in Rome or the Roman world shared remarkably similar experiences, and more importantly, our sources are not consistent in how they use the label. Past scholars have attempted to classify hostages as if with calipers, in accordance with what is perceived as different types of treaties[53] – *foedus aequum, foedus iniquum, deditio*, armistices, and informal, imperial rule – but a significant problem with such an endeavor is that our sources themselves do not seem to be aware of any such subcategories of hostageship; our sources do not correlate particular characteristics of one "type" of hostage with

---

[49] Livy, 32.26.18. See Walker 1980, 112–115, countering Aymard 1953 who argues that the record of the rebellion is an invention.

[50] Livy, 32.2.4; 32.26.5.

[51] Antiochus's house at public expense: Asc. *Pis.* 12k; Demetrius at senatorial banquets: Polyb. 31.13. For more on the expectations among Roman writers concerning hostages' living conditions, see Chapter 3.

[52] On the question of the religious or legal inviolability of hostages, see Chapter 3.

[53] Matthaei 1905, 227–229; Lécrivain 1916, 125–126; Elbern 1990, 98–103.

just one "type" of diplomatic relationship. Rather, there are frequent instances of overlap, where, say, a hostage of a so-called *foedus aequum* is treated no differently from one of a so-called *foedus iniquum*.[54] Moreover, the label of ὅμηρος or *obses* meant different things to different authors at different times, such that one author's hostages are another's students, or exiles, or brides, or prisoners, or recruits, and so on. For example, Plutarch refers to the rape of the Sabine women as a case of hostage-taking (ὅμηροι), but he is the only one.[55] Similarly, many authors identify the sons of Phraates IV who were sent to Augustus from Parthia in 10/9 BCE as hostages, but Augustus himself, in his *Res Gestae*, does not.[56] *Obses* or ὅμηρος was just one of many labels that could be assigned to the same type of figure. Moreover, formal treaties were not necessary in articulating the terms of detention, nor were leverage or coercion crucial characteristics of a hostage's stay with a recipient, as we shall see.

The very translation of the ancient terms ὅμηρος and *obses* as "hostage" (or ôtage, ostaggio, Geisel) presents some initial problems: to the twenty-first-century reader, the word conjures a set of impressions, mostly negative, that would differ considerably from the connotations evoked in ancient Rome.[57] Modern episodes of hostage-taking typically involve allegations of terrorism or "war crimes" where one group retaliates against another by inflicting some kind of pain or deprivation on innocent prisoners. On a smaller scale, hostage-taking can be a criminal's device in forcing some kind of petty demand – a personal ransom or safe passage from a besieged position. Sensational "hostage

---

[54] For example, Elbern 1990, 139–140 classifies the treaty with the Seleucids of 188 as a case of *foedus aequum* and the treaty with the Aetolian League as *foedus iniquum*, yet both have similar stipulations for their hostages. Gruen 1984, 14–15 argues that the terms *foedus aequum* and *iniquum* do not occur frequently enough in our sources to justify their use as a category of analysis, which has become the consensus today, in spite of the oft-cited Livy, 28.34.7–10. For example, Baronowski 1990 discusses the arbitrary nature of the execution of so-called *foedera aequa*.

[55] Plut. *Rom.* 16.2.

[56] *Mon. Anc.* 32; they are called *pignora*. The conventional vocabulary of hostage-taking is used at Strabo 6.4.2, C288 and 16.1.28, C 749; Vell. Pat. 2.94.4; Joseph. *AJ* 18.46; Suet. *Aug.* 21.3 and 43.4.

[57] Matthaei 1905, 226–227; Lécrivain 1916, 115–116; Elbern 1990, 157. Braund 1984a, 12–13 with notes, points out that etymology of the words raises the possibility of mistranslation.

situations" recur frequently in popular culture: some helpless character is typically held with a gun to his head and the hero must overcome tremendous odds. The practice is associated with ruthlessness, blackmail, cowardice, suspense, and despair. It is the sign of an unfair fight; it can make the weak stronger than they deserve to be. If this is the case, the word "hostage" turns out to be only a rough, and ultimately misleading, translation of the ancient Greek and Latin vocabulary. As we have seen, negotiations concerning hostages were part of standard postbattle business; the surrender and detention of hostages followed strict protocols and were sanctioned by international treaties. They were typically taken from the weaker party by the stronger one, not the other way around, and the circumstances of their detention could even be benign and far from hostile. The Greek word for hostage, ὅμηρος (it is the same word as the name of the epic poet Homer), is derived from ὅμοιος, meaning "similar" or "like"; such an etymology would imply something closer to "companion" than "prisoner."[58] The Latin word, *obses*, comes closer to our notion of the hostage as a guarantee of compliance; it is related to words involving siegeworks, such that the *obses* is one who, etymologically speaking, "constitutes a siege" or is "the mechanism of a siege." Even in this case, however, linguists have seen the roots of *obses* as indicating one who "stays with" the other side rather than being detained by it.[59]

In terms of word origins, at least, the sense of coercion embedded in our term "hostage" was not crucial to the ancient conception of ὅμηρος and *obses*. Of course, etymology is not an ideal way to get at the meaning of a word and how it was used in context: ὅμηρος and *obses* often *do* express an element of coercion, despite their possibly docile origins. The critical point to make here is that such a connotation was not universal. Juba II, the prince of North Africa who was largely raised in the Augustan imperial court, is called a hostage in one source, although his father had been killed at the moment of his detention and

---

[58] The observation is made in several etymological dictionaries: Boisacq 1950, Hofmann 1971, Chantraine 1984.

[59] Tucker 1985, Ernout and Andre 1985. Walker 1980, 19 sees a military and diplomatic meaning to *obses*, which she believes did not necessarily apply to the more flexible ὅμηρος of Greek. As we shall see, however, *obses* was used throughout the Principate in metaphorical ways, just as the Greek term.

his home kingdom, Numidia, ceased to be autonomous, such that the rationale of coercion cannot be applied to his tenure in Rome.[60] More than anything else, the period of Juba's life in Rome is remembered as one of intense education in literature and science, and on coming of age, he was sent back to North Africa as a king, but to the completely different realm of Mauretania, west of his native Numidia.[61] Those who refer to him as a "hostage" therefore could not have been thinking that he served as collateral against another state, but as something else, yet to be understood in modern scholarship. Moreover, in cases in which coercion was clearly the motivation for detention, the label of ὅμηρος/*obses* may *not* have been used. For example, the "thousand" Greeks of the Achaean League, including the historian Polybius, who were detained by Rome and brought to live in Italy in 167 BCE are never called ὅμηροι or *obsides* in our sources; they are called simply "those detained in Rome," or "exiles."[62] Nevertheless, like other ὅμηροι/*obsides*, they were kept as leverage against their families back home, they were dispersed to towns around Rome, and periodic embassies were sent to Rome to negotiate for their release. Numerous scholars have rightly referred to the thousand Achaeans as hostages;[63] reasons for the shift in label in this particular case will be discussed in Chapter 8, but at least an initial observation is clear: just as the terms ὅμηροι and *obses* did not necessarily imply coercion in the case of Juba II, stories of coercion – like that involving Polybius – did not necessarily demand such conventional vocabulary. The hospitality and general benevolence inherent in Roman hostage-taking has seemed ironic to modern readers in the past who have expected the phenomenon to be associated with conflict. Some Roman historians today, noting the absence of coercive intent in certain cases of detention, have said that the characters under question are "not formally hostages" or that the

---

[60] Ael. *NA*, 7.23.

[61] Plut. *Caes.* 55; Cass. Dio, 51.15.6. Roller 2003, a recent, thorough examination of Juba, notably does not refer to him as a hostage. For another biographical sketch of Juba II, see Coltelloni-Trannoy 1997, 33–45.

[62] For example, Polyb. 31.23.5; 32.6.4; 33.1.3; 35.6 (= Plut. *Cato* 9.2–3). See Chapter 8.

[63] Matthaei 1905, 234; Lécrivain 1916, 136; Gruen 1976, 48; Elbern 1990, 127; Foulon 1992, 10; Ndiaye 1995, 153; Champion 2004, 17. Walker 1980 does not include the Achaeans in her study, hewing exclusively to cases that use the specific ancient terminology.

ancient label of hostage is "hardly appropriate."[64] Perhaps in the end they speak correctly: these figures are not hostages; they are ὅμηροι, or *obsides*, and we are the ones, not the ancient writers, who have failed to understand the circumstances of this shifting category.

Given the inconsistency in labeling, one is justified in expanding the objects of analysis beyond simply ὅμηροι and *obsides*. If Juba II is conflated with the hostage when sources about him emphasize the theme of education, it stands to reason that stories of foreign students in Rome are relevant to discussions of attitudes toward or interpretations of hostage-taking even if that vocabulary is not present. Some scholars have already drawn links between the sudden proliferation of hostages in the second century BCE and the arrival of formal students of Roman culture at about the same time.[65] The oft-cited examples of students are Ariarathes V of Cappadocia, Charops of Epirus, Jugurtha of Numidia and the sons of Herod the Great, whose fathers or guardians – often classified by moderns as client kings – sent their sons to Rome for education and training.[66] The students in question were of elite status; their residence in Rome was only temporary; and they were received honorably in the city – often there was little to distinguish the two categories of hostage and student, apart from the conditions under which their tenure in Rome began. Whereas political hostages were compelled to make the trip, these others came of their own volition. But perhaps not even this distinction is valid: if not forced to visit Rome, these students at least faced a less tangible form of compulsion in that they could not function in the new reality of Rome's hegemony

---

[64] Walker 1980, 127–128 and Lee 1991, 367, respectively. Kokkinos 1992, 25 and Kuttner 1995, 113 use scare-quotes over the English "hostage" to call attention to its difference from *obses*. Cf. Aymard 1961, 141: "non pas otage." Scardigli 1994, 130 says that the label may be "richtig oder falsch." On the Parthians of 10/9 BCE not being true hostages in the modern sense, see Furneaux 1896, 292; Ziegler 1964, 52; Goodyear 1981, 188–189; Braund 1984a, 12–13; Nedergaard 1988, 108; and Gruen 1996, 160.

[65] Badian 1958, 105–106 suggests that the phenomenon of sending sons to Rome for an education grew from hostage-taking. Brizzi 1982, 217–219 includes both hostages and students in a single category, and both Millett 1990, 37–38 and Elbern 1990, 120 compare them as similar figures. Braund 1984a, 9–21 explores the connection more fully. Gruen 1984, 194, note 234 keeps a distinction between hostages and students.

[66] Ariarathes V: Livy 42.19; Charops: Polyb. 27.15; Jugurtha: Sall. *Jug.* 9.3 and 101.6; Herod's sons: Joseph. *AJ* 15.342–343; 15.52–53; 17.80, and *BJ* 1.435; 1.573; 1.602–603. See especially Braund 1984a, 9–17.

without learning the language, understanding the politics, and essentially negotiating their place in the empire.[67] As quickly as Rome's importance grew in the Mediterranean, so too did it become the very *locus* of opportunity and advancement in international relations, and other kinds of informal coercion seem to have forced non-Roman youth to function in Roman contexts. Non-Roman soldiers were at times pressed into service with Roman auxiliaries; such recruits, having been incorporated into the army when they were young, could receive Roman citizenship and a new name – a cultural identity that, in some cases, had an effect on subsequent international relations. In the *Annals*, Tacitus describes Flavus along these lines: he was a German of noble lineage who served Rome with his brother Arminius early in Augustus's reign, and although Arminius defected to become one of Rome's most notorious enemies, Flavus stayed behind; notably Tacitus later compared Flavus's son, who was raised in Rome and given the telling name Italicus, with an *obses*.[68] One also could refer to other categories where the terms ὅμηρος and *obses* were used intermittently in apposition – brides in marriage alliances, refugees who fled political intrigue at home, and certain elite prisoners of war (which is what Juba II essentially was).[69]

[67] One could locate the decision on the part of the periphery to embrace Roman culture through students in recent theories that the phenomenon of Romanization was driven by the non-Romans themselves, with little agency from the center: Garnsey 1978, 252–254; Millett 1990 (with a model outlined at page 38; reviewed by Woolf 1992); Jones 1991; and MacMullen 2000, 134–137. Compare Whittaker 1997, esp. 152–156, arguing that Rome's role in foreign assimilation was more active. Cf. Brunt 1990, 268: "everywhere it was the Roman policy to win over, and to enfranchise, the local leaders." One could argue that the Roman ways of thinking about hostages indicate that they took an *active* interest in the transformation of the periphery (see Chapter 6). Good overviews of the debate on the motivations of Romanization are at Hingley 1996 and Woolf 1998, 1–23. Webster 2001 introduces the notion of creolization to Roman studies, and Ando 2000 discusses Roman methods of building *consensus*.

[68] Tac. *Ann.* 2.9–10 and 11.16. Cf. Vell. Pat. 2.118.2. Elbern 1990, 126 discusses recruits as a type of Roman hostage, whereas Scardigli 1994, 130–131 excludes Italicus from the study of hostages. Speidel 1998, 503–504 argues that when Ammianus Marcellinus (admittedly out of the time frame of this study) mentioned the killing of Gothic hostages after the Battle of Adrianople in 378 CE, the victims in question were actually military recruits.

[69] On brides: Lécrivain 1916, 116; Elbern 1990, 124. On refugees: Kuttner 1995, 115, citing the example of Adherbal, son of Micipsa and rival of Jugurtha. On prisoners of war and captives, see Braund 1984a, 167–173. Arguing for a distinction from hostages is Scardigli 1994, 122–123. On the ambiguities of the category of "hostage," generally, see Kuttner 1995, 112–113.

All of these types of presences of non-Romans in Rome might be attributed to a "patron-client" relationship between Rome and the periphery, but such a construct is also fraught with problems. A debate has been ongoing since Badian published *Foreign Clientelae* in 1958, arguing that the Romans viewed the states on their periphery as collective clients under their own patronage. Scholarly responses have suggested that we should be conscious of using such language as "client state" and "client king" only metaphorically, given that the Romans themselves did not use the word *clientes* in reference to other states.[70] The debate, in essence, concerns the proper terminology with which to describe peaceable Roman international relations, but we simply will never be able to generalize the endlessly polyvalent phenomenon of geopolitics. In the end, no one term from antiquity will be satisfactory in covering what to the Roman mindset was a complex identity, contested and redefined *within our sources:* even after we have chosen a label for a given object of study – say, "hostage" – and have supported its use with reference to relevant source material, we must still be aware that while some accounts may agree with us, others may not. In short, our attention in this study will be directed at a "type": the characters under study here are the young, elite figures who crossed into another world, were technically autonomous, yet betokened the subordinate role in a hegemonic, reciprocal relationship. While those described as hostages (that is, ὅμηροι and *obsides*) will be the main focus of this book, at times attitudes toward them are compared with attitudes toward other, similar figures. As a single category of highly symbolic foreign travelers, they all function as unusual representatives of the interaction and overlap between two worlds.

THE EVIDENCE

Writers in the Roman world had an abiding interest in hostages, but they did not have perfect information about them, as Livy

---

[70] A recent discussion of the significance of the vocabulary of patronage is Eilers 2002, 2–18. The debate is reviewed by Rich 1989, who, following the lead of Saller 1982, finds evidence for *de facto patrocinium*, regardless of the language in our literary sources and in spite of Harris 1979, 135, note 2; Gruen 1984, 158–200; and Braund 1984a, 23, 29–30. In reference to hostageship, Lica 1988, 44 sees it as a sure sign of clientage, and Elbern 1990, 120 compares hostages with the sons of client kings.

pointedly complains in reference to Scipio's Spanish campaign of
209 BCE:

Scipio ordered the hostages of the cities of Spain to be assembled; I do not
wish to record how many there were, given that I find in one source that
there were nearly 300, while in another, 3,724.[71]

The modern reader of Roman history may find it alternately unsettling
and comforting that their original forebears experienced just as much
frustration over the unreliable or confusing nature of source material as
we do today. Recurring obstacles confront any historian of antiquity
seeking to recover the details of "actual events" in the Roman past –
exaggerated accomplishments, divine intervention, contradictory
accounts, and, as earlier, the inflation of or imprecision concerning
the size of crowds, whether they are of hostages or, more famously, of
war casualties. Our sources at times confess to reporting fiction amid
what purports to be real: the Augustan age geographer Strabo was
quoting Polybius when he said that "one can make a lie more persuasive if one mixes in some amount of truth."[72] In antiquity, history was
a literary and rhetorical genre with a Muse just like poetry and drama,
and "non-fiction" often appears to be blatantly exaggerated, polemical, apocryphal, or anecdotal. While it is rare for a historian to admit
that the "truth" is lost or altered, as Livy, Strabo, and Polybius imply
earlier, such disclosures happen frequently enough that today's Roman
historians must tread carefully in recovering certain details and sorting
through the sources. Previous scholars working on Roman hostage-
taking have done much to untangle the records of those episodes that
are relatively well (though not always accurately) documented, such as
the hostages taken (or received) from Carthage after the Second Punic
War, from Gaul during Caesar's campaigns, and from Parthia at the start
of Augustus's reign. In the case of Livy's conundrum, quoted earlier, for
example, the problem has been "solved" with reference to *comparanda*
of similar events, to the likely extent of the Roman deployment in

---

[71] Livy, 26.49.1.
[72] Strabo 1.2.9, C 20 = Polyb. 34.2.2: ὡς εἰκός, ὡς πιθανώτερον ἄν οὕτω τις ψεύδοιτο,
εἰ καταμίσγοι τι καὶ αὐτῶν τῶν ἀληθινῶν.

Spain at the time, and most important, to a comparison with Polybius's version: Scipio probably took the smaller number.[73]

But more is at stake in Livy's problem, as it is expressed, than simply the number of hostages. We might not be able to see, right away, the "truth" about Scipio's Spanish hostages, but we certainly do see an anxious historian, fretting about the details. Before Livy came to write about Scipio and Spain, at least two others, apparently, had published different versions of events; the fact that Livy's sources saw fit either to uncover the truth or to fabricate some other scenario and the fact that Livy himself researched the question doubly show, at the least, how much the phenomenon mattered in the Roman world. As we read of hostage-taking in Rome, we often find that we can learn as much about the writers as about their subjects. For example, our two principal sources on Demetrius of Macedon, namely, Polybius and Livy, tell different tales: Polybius's account includes a greater role for Flamininus and the Roman senate in the tragedy of the Macedonian dynasty, whereas Livy portrays Flamininus as a meddler, but not a kingmaker. One wonders why such a discrepancy exists.[74] What did Polybius think of the figure of the hostage, given not only his own hostage status but also the fact that he wrote for a dual audience in Rome and in Greece? What did Livy think of the practice of hostage-taking, given that he was writing more than a century after Polybius at a time when Roman leaders – Pompey, Caesar, Octavian/Augustus – were relying on the practice in unprecedented ways? In attempting to answer these questions, one almost sets Demetrius himself to the side; it is how he is characterized that is more urgent. Of particular interest here is the manner in which information about hostages is conveyed: we are not discussing when, or if, a particular hostage was killed, but how the writer viewed the killing; not the extent to which a hostage was reeducated, but how the writer conceived of the process of reeducation; not how a hostage became the victim of rape, but how the writer explained the crime or reported it in context.

---

[73] Cf. Polyb. 10.18.3. Cf. Klotz 1936, 78.

[74] Walbank 1940, 247 states simply that Livy has "embellished" Polybius's account. Gruen 1974, 223–224 ascribes the difference to an interest on the part of Livy to exonerate the Romans of wrongdoing. One could also point to the nature of hostage-taking and the *Pax Romana* in Livy's day, and to Polybius's own status as a Greek hostage (Chapter 8).

Because our primary interest is in the attitudes of the authors, it is they who determine the time frame of our study. It should be noted that "empire" in the title of this book refers to Rome's territorial expansion, and not to the political regime inaugurated by Augustus, which throughout is called the Principate. Our earliest text for hostage-taking is an inscription from the tomb of the Scipios, dating to around 200 BCE, but the histories of Polybius are the earliest source used extensively, and they date to the mid-second century.[75] Most of the other authors come generations after him, with serious interest in hostages picking up in the late Republic and early Principate. Many writers of the second century CE were also interested in hostage-taking; at times they respond directly to trends articulated by their predecessors, and so they too are considered. The bracket closes when the nature of our source material changes drastically and falls off sharply, around the turn of the second to the third century CE, during the reign of the Severans. The sources of this highly active four-hundred-year period – roughly 200 BCE to 200 CE – unsurprisingly are not homogenous in their attitudes toward hostages. Some suggestions concerning continuity and change in attitudes toward hostage-taking will be made in the epilogue, where special attention is paid to certain watershed moments, such as the Roman civil war, Augustus's new regime, and Trajan's reinvigoration of the military.

It bears repeating that the time frame for this study – roughly 200 BCE to 200 CE – refers to the dates of composition of the stories about hostages and not to the dates during which the stories are set. Thus, the reader will find episodes dealing with earlier times, with non-Roman cultures, and with cases of hostage-taking that are only hypothetical or legendary, so long as they are told by Greco-Roman authors in the era that concerns us. When Dionysius of Halicarnassus wrote about hostage-taking in the legends of Rome's foundation, for example, we take it as evidence of how writers in the Roman world were thinking about hostages during his own lifetime in the late first century BCE. Moreover, we include stories of hostage-taking that are set outside of Roman contexts, especially in Greece and the Hellenistic world, just as

[75] On the date of the inscription, see Chapter 4.

art historians are increasingly rethinking the "Roman copies of Greek original" sculpture as evidence for Roman sensibilities and points of view.[76] When Dio Chrysostom uniquely reimagines the hostageship of Philip II of Macedon in Thebes, which took place in the fourth century BCE, we view it as information about the expectations of Chrysostom's own day in the late first to early second century CE. Because this is not a political history but a history of expectations – something like a history of the history of hostage-taking – we also focus on texts in which authors offer general comments on the practice of hostage-taking, such as when an author describes a decision *not* to take hostages, or records a *plan* to take hostages that never materializes, or refers to a nefarious general who displays false hostages to an audience for the sake of heightening his prestige. Such texts would not appear in a prosopography of hostages in Rome, yet satisfy our aim of learning about writers' conceptions of hostages in Roman antiquity.

A wide range of sources are brought together here for the sake of establishing as complete a body of evidence as possible, and no one literary genre is privileged over others. To use Lendon's words, this method leads to the inclusion of what might seem "perfectly dreadful" sources, at least to the view of a positivist.[77] Conventional historiographical genres, such as annalistic narrative, biography, political oratory, and military commentary, are naturally useful, but one also can draw profitably from works of nonhistorical literary genres, such as epic and lyric poetry, drama, satire, epideictic oratory, and novels. All works of literature, whether self-avowedly fictional or not, were intended by their authors to resonate with a contemporaneous audience such that when trying to acquire a sense of conventional wisdom, one cannot say which is a "good" source and which is a "bad" one. It is an increasingly common observation of Roman historians working today that "falsehoods are always an integral part of the world in which they are disseminated"[78] and that it is thus defensible "to use the data we have not as sure indications of motive in individual

---

[76] For example, Marvin 1993; Bergmann 1995; Gazda 1995; and most recently Stewart 2004, 136–180. Perry 2005, 24 defines "Roman art" chronologically rather than on the basis of ethnicity.

[77] Lendon 1997, 28.

[78] Bowersock 1994, 6.

instances, but as clues to how observers expected things to work; that is, to treat *all* evidence as a kind of fiction, but as fiction that gives the historian legitimate insights into norms and broader realities."[79] The texts discussed here thus include, for example, a study of marine biology (Oppian's *Halieutika*) and a work of science fiction (Lucian's *True Histories*), because they both (if only briefly) demonstrate ways of thinking about hostages.[80] The latter, Lucian's *True Histories*, is an eccentric parody of the rather outrageous tropes of ancient historiography. As a work of "history," it includes battle narratives, records of treaties, and ethnographies of exotic lands, but when one notes that the battles are between winged centaurs, a treaty is inscribed on electrum and magically suspended in midair, and the exotic land is in the belly of a whale, one sees the point of Lucian's idea of the "truth": history's legitimacy may be grounded in nothing more than its own genre.[81] In the end, of course, Lucian's work says more about ways of thinking in the Rome of Marcus Aurelius than on the moon, where many of the scenes are set.

A common denominator to all of the sources for this study is the fact that they were produced from elite perspectives in the Roman world, which constitutes both a limitation and an opportunity. Ideally we would be able to consider many different vantage points – not only those of the recipient and the donor but also of their respective

[79] Lendon 1997, 28, italics included. The way in which Barton 1993, 4 defended her use of varying genres of literary evidence to understand the Roman view of gladiators can be applied to this study of hostages: " . . . for my purposes, the 'truth,' 'sincerity,' 'authenticity' of the ancient statements or stories that I repeat is largely irrelevant. I am concerned with mapping Roman ways of ordering and categorizing their world, and of transgressing, denying, or obliterating those orders. What made things seem real or unreal to a Roman at a particular moment is of greater concern to me than what was (or is) real. As possible clues to a 'physics' of the emotional world of the Romans, the metaphor, the fantasy, the deliberate falsehood, the mundane and oft-repeated truism, the literary topos, the bizarre world of school declamations, and the 'cultural baggage' taken over from the Greeks are as valuable as a report of Tacitus or an imperial decree. For my purposes, all of the sources are equally true and equally fictive."

[80] On classifying the *True Histories* as "science fiction," see Georgidou and Larmour 1998, 44–48.

[81] Many have considered Lucian's attitude toward history as expressed not only in the *True Histories* but also in his *How to Write History:* Anderson 1976b, 23–40; Jones 1986, 46–67; Bowersock 1994, 4–7; Georgidou and Larmour 1994, 1478–1482; Fox 2001; and Whitmarsh 2001, 252.

populations, not to mention of the hostages themselves. Unfortunately, in addressing our questions we are confined almost entirely to the opinion of the elite male in the Roman world, who was the only one with the wherewithal to write about anything, much less the hostage in particular. Very occasionally, a hostage's voice may be present in epigraphy, and Polybius's long history of Rome from the perspective of a hostage constitutes a special case that is treated in its own chapter, but still, the vast majority of those directly involved in, or targeted by, hostage-taking are silent. Nevertheless, the voices we do hear are not insignificant: left as we are with an exclusively elite point of view, we at least can isolate and concentrate on the opinions of those with massive responsibilities. Mattern has shown how the emperors, generals, and senators who governed and conducted foreign policy were of the same social milieu as the historians, poets, dramatists, satirists, and other authors, if they were not authors themselves.[82] Given that the same men who wrote all of our literary sources also constitute "the decision-making elite," their opinions should delineate the motives, and explain the execution, of imperial policies that affected both the center and periphery in profound ways. Our study of perceptions and expectations thus may complement other studies of international relations that have focused on more measurable modes of imperial activity; decisions concerning the location of garrisons and supply routes, the manpower of legions, and the conduct of diplomacy all fell under the purview of the same men who spoke about hostages. This study is meant to reveal the backdrop against which such decisions in geopolitics were made.

HYBRID IDENTITIES AND EMPIRE

The basic thesis of this book – that Romans expected to exercise authority over their hostages in ways that both reflected and reinforced their attitudes toward the periphery – is generated by two forces at work in Roman relations with non-Romans: first the appropriation and transformation of the hostage himself, and second, the act

---

[82] Mattern 1999, 2–4.

of reporting the results by simplifying the phenomenon in accordance with different metaphors for describing power relationships. In the case of the first, social psychologists have observed that prolonged periods of detention or oppression, particularly when characterized by a paradoxical admixture of menace and hospitality, may cause crises in the personal world of the hostage or the oppressed, whereby he may alter his identity to accommodate competing ways of thinking – those of his origins and those imposed from without. In the Roman world, hostage-taking may be seen as bringing a very small population of the non-Roman elite closer in orbit around the center of power; the practices thus can be seen as having helped to forge a new imperial "overclass" across the Mediterranean, which colluded in the exercise of power, yet also abided by a hierarchy that benefited Rome. In the second case – the reporting of hostage-taking as opposed to the running of policy – literary scholars have noted that the cultures of various empires have often been predicated in part on the depiction of the "Other" as helpless and savage yet also welcoming of a process of civilization. Applying this approach to Roman sources, one notes that the way in which the complex hybrid quality of the hostage was commonly reduced to an undemanding tale of the powerful controlling the powerless seems to be part of a larger imperial agenda. Our sources often remove the hostage from the byzantine geopolitical events which motivated his or her detention and possible realignment of loyalties and instead assign him to a position in some other, comparable structure of power, figurative or literal, as a way of articulating the hostage's general inferiority. A writer may locate the hostage in a social hierarchy, or a family network, or a cultural continuum, or a sexual role. In these schemes an individual Roman, or Rome in general, becomes not just a conqueror, but also a host, or a father, or a teacher, or a "male," and so on. The hostage was thus at the center of Roman thinking about empire: he both helped to acquire it when he was alive and then afterward, the memory of him, expressed mainly in literary texts, assisted in prolonging it.

Roman hostage-taking was clearly very different from the activities of extranational or terrorist groups in the twentieth and twenty-first centuries, yet the psychological research carried out on these more recent episodes of hostage-taking may provide a useful parallel

for the discussion of evidence from the ancient world.[83] Beginning
in the 1970s, psychologists took a keen interest in what motivated
captors and how they, their hostages, and society in general reacted
to episodes of detention. One of the more significant hypotheses to
emerge from this research was that detainees were potentially susceptible to a "hostage identification syndrome," or as it is more commonly
called, the Stockholm Syndrome.[84] As the symptoms of the syndrome
are described, initial fear on the part of the detainee turns to sympathy, which grows to an appreciation for his captors, which eventually
evolves into a fanaticism that is, according to psychologists, not of the
hostage's choosing. Something about the intimacy of forced detention
by hostage-takers and the unending, intense exposure to their way of
life is said to have a profound effect on the outlook of those under
guard. One's natural resistance to alien ethics and attitudes is broken down and worn away, until the mind becomes a blank slate onto
which an entirely new moral code or point of view can be inscribed.[85]
Psychologists have suggested that a number of factors may determine
the extent to which the syndrome is realized in a hostage. Time is
seen as especially critical: the longer a hostage is detained, the more
likely it is that he will identify with his captor.[86] Also, the age of the
detainee plays a role, with younger hostages being more susceptible
to transference.[87] Facility of communication between the hostage and
his captor also is thought to contribute to the condition so that if
the hostage and captor speak the same language, if the hostages are

[83] Ager 1998 is the first ancient historian as far as I know to discuss the psychology of
hostage-taking in reference to her work; specifically, she looks at an inscription, *IG*
12.3, no. 328, which mentions the detention by pirates of farmers from Crete in the
mid-third century BCE.
[84] Miller 1980, Strentz 1982, Symonds 1982, Turner 1985, Harkis 1986, MacWillson 1992.
The common name for the syndrome is derived from an episode in which two men held
up a bank in Stockholm in 1973 and held four hostages for nearly six days (Miller 1980,
45; Strentz 1982, 149–150; Turner 1985, 706; Card 2002, 214). One of the detainees,
Kristin Ehnmark, entered into an intense relationship with one of her captors, having
consensual sex with him and, from captivity, criticizing both the police and the prime
minister of Sweden as responsible for the siege.
[85] Symonds 1982, 99–100 speaks of "pathological transference" and "traumatic psychological infantilism," which compel the victim to think of his captors as heroes, teachers,
or even parents. Cf. Ager 1998, 90–91.
[86] Miller 1980, 42; Strentz 1982, 154–156; Turner 1985, 705; MacWillson 1992, 59.
[87] Miller 1980, 46; Harkis 1986, 50–51; MacWillson 1992, 61.

not too numerous, if both sides share similar cultural backgrounds, and if they live in the same space during the hostage's detention, some amount of identification is likely.[88] The psychological research has had some influence in recent historical studies. Many historians working on colonial or imperial systems in a wide variety of regions and time periods have noted the role of politicized detention or indoctrination in international power struggles. Demos tells of a seven-year-old girl who was seized by Mohawk Indians in 1704 and taken from her home in Deerfield, Massachusetts, to be raised as a member of the tribe; Kertzer tells of the kidnapping and indoctrination of Edgardo Mortara, a six-year-old Jewish boy, by the Catholic Church in nineteenth-century Bologna; and Viswanathan has shown that the academic discipline of English, as it exists today, has its origins in colonial India, where teachers prepared curricula to train upper caste boys.[89] These are not formal hostages in the Roman sense, but they faced compulsion nonetheless as they were forced to accommodate, or at least listen to, an outside hegemon.

The first studies of hostage identification syndrome (the Stockholm Syndrome) in the 1970s emphasized the shock of detention, the fear of imminent death, and the promise of deliverance as mitigating factors in transference. Recent considerations of the condition, however, have argued that longer term, institutionalized forms of oppression, which are not as immediately diabolical as acts of terrorism but which nag on the powerless over a lifetime, may yield similar results. Card has cited

---

[88] Languages: Turner 1985, 705. Smaller groups: MacWillson 1992, 59. Cultural affinity: Miller 1980, 41; Turner 1985, 705; MacWillson 1992, 60. For all of these see Strentz 1982, 156–158. Criminologists advise that negotiators in situations involving hostages should view the hostages themselves with mistrust (Miller 1980, 42; MacWillson 1992, 58). It is also argued that the expectation of transference has led terrorist groups to place hoods over the heads of detainees, or to wear masks themselves, in order to diminish the potential for sympathy to emerge between detainee and captor (Turner 1985, 708). All of this research, it should be noted, predates the conflicts of the late twentieth, early twenty-first centuries.

[89] Demos 1994; Kertzer 1997; Viswanathan 1989. To these one could add many more, including works on deliberate cross-cultural education in colonial situations: Marks 1987 presents the correspondence of an African girl seeking a British colonial education in South Africa in the 1940s and 50s; Skard 1961 and Heald and Kaplan 1977 examine the Fulbright and Rhodes scholarships as serving the function of formal cultural communication through the temporary relocation and exchange of students.

a number of studies that illustrate the role of transference in the emergence of uneven social relations, be they governed by race, gender, class, or sexual orientation. As Card sees it, when W.E.B. du Bois observed that, as an African American, he possessed a "double consciousness" as a result of straddling two cultures, his identity, in essence, had been "smothered, rendered inoperative through a combination of fear and hope of being able to deflect dangers by learning to perceive and think as one's oppressor does."[90] One identity thus existed alongside a radically different one, and the subject became adept at shifting between the two. Card sees the phenomenon of transference as inherent and inevitable over the long term in social relations characterized by inequality. It is as if the syndrome described by psychologists is the result of some kind of equation in which multiple variables contribute and occasionally offset each other in determining the intensity of the identification: a short but intense detention, such as is practiced by terrorists, may achieve the same results as a slow, lingering, yet less immediately terrifying oppression.

The kinds of power discrepancies explored by Card are more relevant to studies of Roman hostage-taking than those apparent in late-twentieth-century terrorism. As we have seen, Roman hostage-taking was neither surprising nor abrupt but was a means of maintaining imperial authority, used for centuries; it is not characterized by "frozen fright."[91] Card's cases of gradual domination match in essence the creeping influence exercised by the Romans over young detainees from weaker neighbors over long stretches of time. But even so, the relationships in Roman hostage-taking are different from Card's cases in that there is a third level in the hierarchy. The hostage recipient and the hostage occupied the rarefied world of the elite; behind the hostage, to

---

[90] Card 2002, 215, quoting "double consciousness" from W.E.B. du Bois, *The Souls of Black Folk* (New York: New American Library, 1969), 45. In other cases, Card points to studies that observed that in "training" new prostitutes, pimps were found to isolate indigent women, deprive them of sustenance, and gradually reward them with privileges until they became more than simply loyal to their overseer but also saw their fate as tied to his (pp. 139–146). In terms of sexual orientation, she sees the participation of Roy Cohn, the closeted gay aide of Joseph McCarthy, in the House un-American Activities Committee as an ironic homophobia brought on by the same kind of "pathological transference" (p. 216).

[91] Symonds 1982, 97.

the Roman mindset, there lingered large, subordinate groups, which, in building an empire, is where the Romans ultimately set their sights.[92] By holding the hostage for years and by judiciously applying the threat of violence with a promise of salvation, the Romans essentially invited him to collaborate with them and in effect cause a shift (or so they expected) in the attitudes of his entire state. The hostage alone was geared for transference; the people he might some day command would follow his example.

In this sense, Roman hostage-taking can be compared with an approach to empire characterized by the empowerment of an "overclass." The term overclass has been increasingly used by public intellectuals in observing new realities of modern globalization.[93] It refers to a community of elites with profound economic and social advantages, isolated and exclusive, yet exercising tremendous influence over most public institutions. The overclass, it is argued, propagates itself through marriage connections, educational background, and professional opportunities; its members are mutually recognizable through language, dress, and residence. Some have understood the term also to imply a homogenous clustering, with racial overtones, and it is in this sense that it has appeared in ancient history, in reference to Sparta and the power and unity of the Spartiates over both *perioikoi* and helot populations.[94] Recently, however, writers have conceived of the overclass as more international in scope and more racially heterogeneous.[95] The multinational, or global, overclass is no longer thought to be uniquely American, but may transcend borders – a power elite founded on status whose members easily commingle in a world delineated by class and seamlessly shift from one nation to the next, from one culture to the next. The overclass helps to maintain a new kind of empire, one not as reliant on physical domination as in the past but instead controlled through wealthy individuals.[96]

---

[92] See Brunt 1990, 277–280 on elites serving as translators of vernacular languages.

[93] Especially Lind 1995, used polemically. See also Phillips 2002, 12 and Wu 2003, 19. Compare Spivak 1988, 284 on the layers of elites at the center, elites at the periphery, and finally, the subaltern. Barber 1996, 271 similarly discusses the relationships among elite nations in globalization.

[94] Hanson 2001, 17. Cf. Lind 1995, 100–102.

[95] Wu 2003, 18–32, noting that racism persists, in spite of the model.

[96] As articulated recently at Hardt and Negri 2000.

It cannot be argued that the Roman conceptions of social rank corre-late with modern economic notions of "class" as we know it, yet the experiences of hostages do seem to have been influenced by prevailing attitudes toward order and status, which cut across borders and cultures and which inspired a whole host of rights and privileges for certain hostages, yet not for their native populations.

In talking about hostages, the Romans seem to congratulate them-selves on their imperial accomplishment, perpetually glancing over the hostage's shoulder at the world that he might someday help them to control. In this sense, the texts themselves perform an imperial func-tion in addition to reflecting one. As Bhabha has argued, when an author of an imperial center propagates a "stereotype" of the Other as one who "mimics" the center's institutions, that author pursues "a complex strategy of reform, regulation, and discipline."[97] By neces-sity, the "difference or recalcitrance" of the periphery is highlighted, or even created, as a way of justifying the imperial enterprise.[98] Yet the text cannot represent reality: the ideal of the monolithic periphery, open to a process of civilization, ignores the heterogeneity of the mass population and thus is impossible "on the ground"; the texts instead reveal only the desires and anxieties of the imperial power.[99] One might compare Roman accounts of hostage-taking with texts describ-ing the creation of hybrid identities in the age of the European empires. As an example, Pratt has shown that European travel writing of the eighteenth and nineteenth centuries promoted the reeducation of the local populations in the new colonies as a kind of "anti-conquest," in which the empire is seen as the result of a mission of condescending philanthropy, characterized by peace yet yielding benefits chiefly for the conquerors.[100] In John Barrow's *Travels to the Interior of Southern Africa* (1801), the defeated are no longer portrayed as savages; instead the image shifts to one of "benign, ingenuous, childlike victims," thus establishing both the innocence and effectiveness of the travel-writer

[97] Bhabha 1994, 66 and 86.
[98] Bhabha 1994, 86.
[99] Cf. Spivak 1988, 285.
[100] Pratt 1992, 38–85.

and his regime.[101] By contrast, Roman texts do not seem as preoccupied with asserting their innocence, yet their interest in the hostage's hybrid qualities and in the different forms they could take does assert Rome's undeniable domination.

Writers and artists working in the Roman period deployed a common set of motifs and metaphors in describing their hostages, which placed the hostages in easily conceptualized and thoroughly justified positions of subordination. Six chapters in this book take their titles from common themes in our sources' descriptions of hostages and hostage-taking. I have chosen a thematic organization because no one source or time period seems to have viewed hostages in one particular way; rather, writers seemed to pick and choose from a number of characteristics, depending on what they are trying to achieve in their narrative.[102] Chapter 2, "Creditor-Collateral," considers the role of hostages that is most in keeping with modern instincts about the practice: coercion and blackmail. It examines the prevalence of the language of contracts and finance in descriptions of hostage-taking, where the hostage is implicitly compared with property used to secure an agreement. An array of concessions could be guaranteed as a result of the transaction, and a variety of threats could be leveled against hostages, from death to slavery, in order to ensure compliance. The imagery suggests that the Romans had a legalistic view of their hegemony and saw themselves as overseeing a series of obligations from the outside world. Coming right after discussions of violence and leverage, the chapter called "Host-Guest" may come as a surprise; it

---

[101] Pratt 1992, 65. One also may compare Randall 2000, 2–4, who discusses Rudyard Kipling's characterization of hybrid boys in *The Jungle Book* and *Kim* as an imperial act, "encoding hierarchies" and substituting "a production of bodies for a genealogy of cultures, provid[ing] a metonymic physiology for the transformation of codes and values."

[102] The first incarnation of this study, a doctoral dissertation, was organized geographically – a chapter on hostages from Gaul, then one on hostages from Greece, then hostages from Judaea, from Africa, and so on. But as I revised, I grew increasingly concerned with the repetitive nature of accounts of hostage-taking, and so the themes of such stories now hold center stage. To be sure, there are obvious differences among hostages from places in the West and from various kingdoms of the East, and these differences may be fruitfully explored in the future.

demonstrates that commonly held views of hostages in Roman antiquity could seem contradictory. This chapter looks at the rhetoric of hostage-taking, that invokes the ancient norms of hospitality and in so doing, paints the hostage as a respected guest who is entitled to kindness, security, and even luxury. The relationship still privileges Rome, but the hierarchy, so imagined, presents the Romans as part of an honorable network of allies in which international law and notions of reciprocity hold sway. The next chapter, "Conqueror-Trophy," explores how foreign residents in Rome or in Roman contexts were featured as symbols of conquest through public appearances that were carefully orchestrated to enhance the prestige of the hostage recipient. Hostages were an indispensable component of the Roman triumph, and they thus became contentious in public disputes: one could advance his career by presenting false propaganda of hostage-taking, or one could discredit a rival by alleging that his hostages were fabricated. With such a mentality, the Romans view the detention of the hostage as a means of achieving personal success in domestic contexts and not as a collectively supported objective.

Such an image of the hostage as conquest was tempered, however, especially during the early Principate, with filial representations of the hostage experience. Chapter 5, "Father-Son," points to the significance of adult adoption in Roman antiquity and the frequent equation of the marriage alliance with hostage submission and argues that individual hostage-takers viewed their wards as being grafted onto their extended family. Such an expectation bespeaks a paternalistic view of the outside world, and given the powers of the Roman *paterfamilias*, the metaphor puts the Romans in a position of irresistible, although dutiful, authority in geopolitics. Continuing in the vein of seemingly benevolent conceptions of hostage-taking and hierarchy, "Teacher-Student" notes occasions where the Romans think of hostages as eagerly embracing their culture and susceptible to indoctrination. The chapter shows that the Romans at least expected their cultural identity to be a compelling factor in maintaining their empire and saw hostage-taking as a potential means of reaching a larger population. Various "cultural products" of former hostages, such as the urban commissions of Antiochus IV in Syria and Juba II in North Africa and the coins of the Parthian Vonones, show that hostages seem to have accommodated Roman culture rather than subscribed to it completely. The final thematic chapter, "Masculine-Feminine," looks at how the Romans assigned a gender to the participants in episodes of hostage-taking. Keeping in mind the obvious power discrepancies in both sex and imperialism, it is perhaps predictable to find that hostages were said to be penetrated in sexual relationships, often as victims of rape. The sexual rhetoric rejects hostage-taking as a useful instrument of imperial policy and implicitly calls for a more forthright method of domination of foreign territories that was in keeping with Rome's imagined past.

The last two chapters look closely at two authors in particular whose views of hostages are unique in respect to the six metaphors described earlier. Chapter 8 considers Polybius's attitude toward his own hostage-ship, analyzing the historian's self-referential passages that serve to *deny* his and other hostages' subordination to Rome. Chapter 9 demonstrates that Tacitus uses the common perceptions of hostages and hostage-takers in constructing certain historical personages, but ultimately rejects the effectiveness of the device in governing the empire: in the *Annals*, those who are said to view themselves as "fathers" and "teachers" of hostages – Augustus and his Julio-Claudian successors – fail utterly and are corrected by those who are disdainful of the acculturation of hostages, like the more heroic Germanicus and Gnaeus Domitius Corbulo. Tacitus's apparent need to challenge and undermine the rhetoric of hostage-taking is taken as further evidence of its pervasiveness in the Principate.

2

CREDITOR-COLLATERAL

The phenomenon of human collateral in Rome is at least as old as the Laws of the Twelve Tables, the legal code that took shape around 450 BCE during the early Republic. Debt bondage (*nexum*), in early Rome as in Greece, was a penalty for one who defaulted on a loan; either his family or the debtor himself might enter into the service of the creditor to compensate him for his lost resources.[1] The defaulting bondsman was not quite a slave, as Table III allowed for him to live at home if he wished. Nor was his son enslaved if the debtor hired him out for the purposes of repayment: Table IV granted a son freedom from his father's authority if he had been "sold" in such a way three times, implying the detention, or service, was not expected to last indefinitely.[2] Labor performed for a creditor on a temporary basis could offset, or satisfy, the debtor's obligation. It is a sensibility that persisted in the later Roman Republic: even after the penalty of debt bondage was abolished for Roman citizens in 326 BCE, the code was still memorized as part of a Roman boy's education, remembered fondly by a Cicero nostalgic for his youth.[3] Holding a person as security for a financial obligation thus remained more than

---

[1] Watson 1975, 111–124; Cornell 1995, 280–283, with notes. The debtor could also be sold into slavery outside of Rome. Another clause of the law – that the creditor may "cut pieces" – has been interpreted variously as a metaphor for the liquidation of the debtor's estate or a magical device of restitution. In any case, the codification of the law has been seen as a boon for the creditors: Eder 1986.

[2] For more on *nexum*: Cornell 1995, 280–283.

[3] Cic. *Leg.* 2.23.59. On the *Lex Poetelia*: Cornell 1995, 332–333. On the role of debt in the history of the early Republic, see esp. Savunen 1993 with references.

a reasonable proposition down into the Principate: it was among the strongest forms of coercion, the most intense verification of trust.

A common view of hostage-taking in Roman literature is in keeping with such notions of human collateral and has affinities with the conventional motives of the practice today: hostages were secured in order to coerce some kind of desired behavior from hostage donors. Accordingly hostages occasionally carried epithets such as *pignus* and ἐνέχυρον, meaning security or guarantee.[4] Even when there is no direct juxtaposition of such vocabulary, the narratives involving ὅμηροι and *obsides* still often imply a system of credit and collateral. The language is reminiscent of financial contracts and duty, with the result that the Romans may be thought of as overseeing a kind of great lending bank, from which non-Roman states "borrow" an allowance of autonomy that they "pay back" with loyalty. Hostages in these cases are the collateral: should the "debtors" default on their end of the bargain, the hostages would be forfeit and would pass under the legitimate control of the Romans.

The financial metaphor works by replacing the economy of wealth with one of human anxiety: the value of the human security in international hostage-taking was not based on material equivalence, nor on any quantifiable measure for that matter; the hostage's worth was based on the emotions felt for an irreplaceable figure or on an intangible service that the hostage could have provided for the donor – as an heir, for example – had he not been surrendered. Hostages thus embodied the potential for peace but implicitly reminded their possessors that a contingency plan was necessary and wise. They gave teeth to trust; blackmail and coercion may have lingered in the background as two states that were bound by hostages began to learn a new settlement and to abide by a new peace. The hostage was ever threatened, a marked man. It is a simple point, but it is critical for understanding, by the extension described in the introductory chapter, the Roman view of the non-Roman world as represented by hostage-taking. When Roman eyes fell on a hostage in the street, whether in a triumph or,

---

[4] *pignus:* Cic. *Cael.* 78; Livy, 24.31.13; 36.40.3; 40.47.10; 43.10.3; Lucan, 8.131; Suet. *Aug.* 21.2; Gell. *NA* 16.10.11. ἐνέχυρον: Dion. Hal. *Ant. Rom.* 6.84.2; App. *BCiv.* 1.44 (cf. Aen. Tact. 5.1). For examples of the juxtaposition with *pignus,* see Moscovich 1979–1980, 126. Walker 1980, 1, 6 mentions other vocabulary: *arrabo* and ἀνάδοχος.

years later, in a banquet or at the games, memories of past conflict must have been conjured, and fears, or at least expectations, of future perfidy could not have been far behind. Others have shown that in the scheme of Roman hegemony, which hostage-taking undeniably articulates, the idea of peace was defined as a lopsided state of affairs, requiring violence in order to be sustained.[5] This chapter examines the coercive nature of hostage-taking in such conceptions of peace – what conduct was ensured by the hostage recipients, what repercussions were promised to recalcitrant donors, and how such a marriage of trust and brutality informs our understanding of the Roman view of their periphery.

INSURANCE

Just as family members might secure private, lower level debts and commercial transactions, hostages were occasionally identified as collateral for schedules of tribute and indemnity payments or for other, specifically financial obligations. Livy, for example, writes of Roman ambassadors to Pineus of Illyria who were told to take hostages if the king was unable to honor his tribute schedule.[6] In referring to Athenian history, Plutarch says that Pericles, after defeating the island of Samos in 440, took hostages as an assurance for their war indemnity; presumably there was no need to ensure against aggression, given that Pericles had already destroyed their walls and navy.[7] Plutarch also assigns such a view of hostages to Pericles's younger contemporary Nicias who, on facing the defeat of his invasion of Syracuse, offered to surrender his own men as a guarantee that the Athenians would pay to repair the damage they had done.[8] Tribute and indemnity were not the only financial debts that could require hostages. Polyaenus,

---

[5] Note, for example, Woolf 1993. For a survey of nineteenth- and twentieth-century scholarship on the relationship between Roman war and peace, beginning with Mommsen, see Linderski 1984.

[6] Livy, 22.33.5.

[7] Plut. Per. 28.1. Plutarch argued against one source, Duris, who said that Pericles had acted unjustly against the people of Samos, suggesting that Plutarch himself viewed Pericles's conduct as generous: Wardman 1974, 173. See also Stadter 1989, 256–257.

[8] Plut. Nic. 27.2. cf. Thuc. 7.83.2.

Plutarch's younger contemporary in Rome during the second century CE, recounts how Antigonus the One-Eyed of Macedon gave hostages in 306 BCE to his mercenaries as an assurance that he would pay them their wage.[9] In these cases the detainees are unambiguously necessary for the loan: cash was required in payment before the hostages would be released.

In some of the famous cases of Roman hostage-taking, hostages are not specifically tied to tribute and indemnity, but they seem to be closely linked. As we have seen in the Introduction, according to several sources – Polybius, Diodorus Siculus, Livy, and Appian – after Philip V of Macedon helped Rome against the Aetolian League and Antiochus III in 191 his son Demetrius was freed from hostageship; simultaneously, he was forgiven the remainder of the fine imposed on him five years earlier at Cynoscephalae.[10] It is possible that the hostage was conceptually "attached" to the debt, and detention became irrelevant when there were no payments to be made. But it is also possible that the two encumbrances – indemnity and hostage son – were separate, and that Philip V received both back as a result of total forgiveness. Similarly, in the records of treaties with the Aetolian League in 189 and with Antiochus III in 188, the duration of the hostages' internment in Rome is identical with the length of time stipulated for tribute payments; it is possible that they were mutually dependent obligations.[11] None of the sources are specific on this matter, however, and the question is complicated by cases where hostages continue to be detained after the financial terms of the contract have been satisfied. Such is the case with Demetrius Soter of the Seleucids, who arrived in Rome as a hostage around 178 and stayed long after the final payment of the

---

[9] Polyaenus, *Strat.* 4.6.17.

[10] Polyb. 21.3.3; 21.11.9; Diod. Sic. 28.15.1; Livy, 35.31.4–6; 37.25.12; App. *Syr.* 23; *Mac.* 5. In several references to the release, the cancellation of indemnity is omitted: Livy, 36.35.13; Plut. *Flam.* 14.2; App. *Syr.* 20.

[11] Aetolians: Polyb. 21.32.10; Livy, 38.11.6–7. For the discrepancy between Livy and Polybius, see Walbank 1979, 134–135. Antiochus: Polyb. 21.42.22; Livy, 38.38.15; App. *Syr.* 39. Moscovich 1974a, 420–421, note 14 argues that the hostages of Antiochus III were tied to his indemnity payments although it is never explicitly stated as such. See also Matthaei 1905, 232; Lécrivain 1916, 133–134.

indemnity was delivered in 173.[12] It would thus be a mistake to assume that hostages only secured financial debt.

More commonly and more explicity, the objective secured by hostage-based coercion was simply the cessation of fighting on a large scale, or the avoidance of it in the first place, with the substitution of a Roman-defined peace in its stead. Repeatedly the stories of hostage-taking are told with the language of peace-keeping. Livy provides an example in his description of relations between Rome and Cephallonia in the Ionian Sea in 189 BCE.[13] Marcus Fulvius Nobilior crossed to the island after defeating the Aetolian League and formally presented the Cephallonians with the option of surrendering or facing war. The Cephallonians capitulated, we are told, on the spot and submitted hostages. Livy is grandiloquent on this score: in his language the hostage submission amounted to an "unexpected peace," which "radiated on Cephallonia" like a conjured sun.[14] According to Livy, only one town, Same, offered resistance:

> Because the city had been founded in a strategic location, the Sameans said that they feared that they would be forced by the Romans to relocate. It has not been determined whether some of the Sameans themselves invented the story – and thereby aroused a sleeping evil with an empty fear – or if the plan had been boasted among the Romans and reported back to Same. It is only known that even after hostages had been surrendered, they suddenly closed their gates and chose not to desist from their enterprise even when implored by the prayers of their own people, for the consul had sent the hostages up to the walls to test the pity of their parents and friends. When there was nothing of peace in the Sameans' response, the city came under siege.[15]

The historian reports the justification of the Samean rebellion as ambiguous, as it depends on the origins, right or wrong, of the Sameans' paranoia ("it has not been determined"). But by framing the episode with allusions to peace in conjunction with hostage-taking,

---

[12] For the completion of the indemnity payment, see Livy, 42.6.6–7. On the dates of Demetrius Soter's detention and release, see Chapter 1, note 48. Elbern 1990, 99 argues that the financial aspect of hostage-taking was more pronounced in cases of *foedus aequum,* but Walker 1980, 66 believes the evidence is too sparse for firm conclusions.

[13] Livy, 38.28–29. For chronology, see Warrior 1988.

[14] Livy, 38.28.7: *insperata pax Cephalloniae adfulserat.*

[15] Livy, 38.28.8–10.

Livy manages to decide against the Sameans. As he tells it, Fulvius achieved *pax* by taking hostages (an "unexpected peace") and reasserted it by parading them before their families' eyes. In this sense the act of ignoring the hostages on the part of the Sameans, then, is construed as the very denial of peace ("there was nothing of peace in the Sameans' response"),[16] and the Sameans thus become the agents of their own destruction. The act of bullying the Sameans with hostages to reach a peace is an irony that Livy does not acknowledge. For the historian, peace was imposed by the Romans and was constituted primarily by two phenomena: the Roman possession of hostages and the Sameans' respect for that possession. By means of hostage submission, one state of affairs was believed to be exchanged for another: success in warfare weighed evenly in the balance with a peace accompanied by hostages. The Romans are obviously ahead in both scenarios, but, in the latter, they demonstrate an alleged magnanimity and suffer no great military expenditure.

A similar equation appears in several other authors in different contexts, where the Romans forego a military victory provided that the resultant peace is secured by hostages. In Appian's account of the Spanish wars of 152 BCE, the Roman siege of one town, Ocilis, only came to a peaceful end when hostages were submitted along with 30 talents of silver.[17] Just as Livy's Fulvius, by accepting hostages, delivered a refulgent peace to the Cephallonians, Appian sees the Romans' action in Iberia as convincing Ocilis's neighbors, the Nergobriges, to seek a similar settlement (εἰρήνη). A brief overview of similar examples demonstrates how many authors expected this to be the case. In Polyaenus's analysis of Alexander the Great's strategies in the East, his demand for hostages in one episode was answered by the inhabitants of an unnamed city in India with an olive branch, the unmistakable emblem of peace.[18] For Sallust, hostage-taking was what ended the raids of Metellus on the North African countryside in 108 BCE and thus converted Numidia from a land of war to one of peace, where Jugurtha,

[16] Livy, 38.28.10: *nihil pacati respondebatur.*
[17] App. *Hisp.* 48. On the campaigns of Claudius Marcellus in Spain, see Richardson 2000, 144–147.
[18] Polyaenus, *Strat.* 4.3.30.

painted as having an innate hatred for Rome, became anathema at the very instant when his fellow Numidians surrendered hostages.[19] One could point to similar episodes throughout Roman historiography.[20] It was clearly a convention of ancient historians and writers that peace, in its nascent stages, could easily hinge on the submission of hostages as a resolution that was as acceptable to the Romans as a military victory, a *sine qua non* for arguments whereby the weaker state was allowed to remain intact.

In domestic politics as well, both the language and the practice of hostage-taking were evident in the formation of coalitions, the settlement of disputes, and the easing of tensions, all with the same coercive quality of the institution's foreign manifestations. The rift between plebeians and patricians in the Struggle of the Orders in the early Republic was thought to be remediable through hostage possession. Dionysius of Halicarnassus presents the patrician Appius Claudius's arguments for a resolution of the first secession of the plebs in 494 BCE as irresistible:

We have as hostages (ὅμηρα) their fathers and wives and the rest of their relations; even in prayers to the gods we could not have chosen better hostages than these. Let us station them in view of their relations, threatening that if they dare to attack, we will destroy them in utter disgrace (ὡς ταῖς ἐσχάταις λώβαις διαχρησόμενοι). And if they understand this, you should well expect them to beg and mourn and surrender themselves without even their shields, submitting entirely. For such natural ties (αἱ τοιαίδε ἀνάγκαι) can distract these outrageous plots and bring them to nothing.[21]

---

[19] Sall. *Jug.* 54.6. On Sallust's construction of the character of Jugurtha, see Claassen 1992–1993.

[20] At Diod. Sic. 21.18, the submission of four hundred hostages from Syracuse to its mercenaries ends a war. Joseph. *AJ* 18.96 says that Tiberius instructed Vitellius not to finalize a treaty with Artabanus unless it included hostages, especially Artabanus's son (cf. Cass. Dio, 59.27.3). At Plut. *Mor.* 248E, Hannibal lifts his siege of Salmantica in exchange for three hundred hostages and as many talents (cf. Polyaenus, *Strat.* 7.48.1). At Just. *Epit.* 7.3.2, the Persians of 490 BCE abandon an invasion of Thrace only when the king, Amyntas, surrenders hostages. At SHA, *Ant. Pius,* 9.10, the submission of hostages from the Tauroscythians to the people of Olbiopolis manages to preserve a fragile peace. In Cass. Dio, 37.2.6, an account of Pompey's wars with Artoces of Iberia in Asia Minor in 66 BCE, the submission of hostages is singled out as a necessary condition for peace. Cf. Flor. 1.40.28, in which Artoces's act of giving the hostages is part of a pardon granted by Pompey (*ignovit Hiberiae*).

[21] Dion. Hal. *Ant. Rom.* 6.62.5. Cf. Dion. Hal. *Ant. Rom.* 6.53.

Patricians needed plebeians in order for their Rome to survive as a unified state, but because they possessed hostages they had the upper hand in trying to coerce a settlement that benefited themselves.[22] The striking plebeians were *obliged* to submit; the duty was not specifically contracted, but was in effect naturally, through family ties. The result was equilibrium, mutually beneficial yet favoring one side: the patricians would be allowed to rule and the plebeians would be allowed to live. The lives of the hostages were viewed as the collateral for stability, for peace.

Cicero identified the phenomenon of hostage obligation as a catalyst for the smooth workings of Republican institutions, where power is loaned out based on the figurative collateral of a statesman's family and position. In his fourth speech against Catiline, Cicero puts his son, his daughter, and wife in the category of hostages: they are assurances against him, held by the Roman state so that he should continue his duties as a consul and stamp out the (purported) threat posed by Catiline.[23] It is a fawning statement to the Roman people, asserting Cicero's subordination to propriety and deflecting any criticism that he is working out of spite or ambition. Moreover, the description of his family members as hostages with their lives in the balance becomes a rhetorical device by which Cicero heightens the anxiety of a grave situation. Just as a foreign enemy would respect the terms of a treaty when there were hostages, likewise a consul (or praetor, or tribune) would only avoid corruption and maintain order when something they valued was out of their hands. Giving hostages, even figuratively, was thought to make magistrates trustworthy in the exercise of power. In *Against Caecilius*, Cicero refers to his livelihood with the vocabulary of hostage-taking: the "people" could easily "kill" his career as a public figure if he failed to do well by them:

The Roman people hold many hostages (*obsides*) from me, and I must struggle in every possible way in order to keep them safe, and to guard, secure, and

[22] For hostages in domestic politics, see also Lécrivain 1916, 135 and Elbern 1990, 128–131. For the debate as to whether sufficient numbers of plebeians were of the hoplite class to pose a military threat to the patricians, against which their hostages guarded, see Brunt 1971, 47; Raaflaub 1986; and Cornell 1995, 257–258.
[23] Cic. *Cat.* 4.3.

ultimately reclaim them. Namely, they hold the office I seek, the goals which I set for myself, and my reputation, which has been acquired with sweat, hard work, and vigilance. If I prove my duty and diligence in this case, I will be able to preserve them, and by the will of the Roman people, they will be safe and uncorrupted. If there should be one offense or error, however small, I would lose in an instant these things which have been built up for a long time, piece by piece.[24]

As Cicero sees it, the Roman people have lent him his status, and by holding his title, rights and privileges as figurative hostages, they ensure that he does work that is in keeping with their conception of a public servant.[25] Cicero is in their employ; he is charged with maintaining a *status quo* of political tradition, and he may survive, or even advance, as an elected official as a result, but he is not sovereign.

The same kind of ideology of the equalizing quality of hostage possession in political power can be seen in the Principate, although as power is concentrated in the hands of one man, the practice involves fewer people and not the entire electorate. As the empire grew, civil conflicts became increasingly analogous to international warfare, with provincial generals posing as great a danger to any given regime as a foreign aggressor. Hostage-taking naturally became a part of life at the imperial court. Josephus makes sense of Nero's selection of Vespasian as the general to take care of the troublesome but lucrative East in 66 CE on the grounds that Vespasian's sons would be his hostages in the city.[26] Also in reference to Vespasian's sons, Tacitus says that Titus was sent to Galba after Nero's death for complicated reasons: on the surface, it was to begin Titus's career and to pay respect to Galba's regime, but a popular rumor, hardly quashed by a disclaimer from Tacitus, was that Titus was to be adopted as an heir. On hearing of Galba's death, Titus then fled to his father lest he become a hostage to either Vitellius or Otho.[27] As reported by Tacitus, Vespasian's decision to offer his son to

---

[24] Cic. *Caec.* 72.
[25] The passage should have a bearing on recent debates, such as at Millar 1998 and Morstein-Marx 2004 for example, surrounding the extent of democratic qualities in the politics of the late Republic.
[26] Joseph. *BJ* 3.3.
[27] Tac. *Hist.* 2.1. On the nature of Tacitus's polemics against Otho and Vitellius, see Chilver 1979, 161–162.

a potential ally but to guard him from rivals at a sensitive time when one dynasty was dying out bespeaks the power of hostage-taking in building political coalitions. Titus's life could become the fulcrum by which his father was forced to obey; the obligation could be either voluntary in the case of Galba, expressed in quasi-filial terms to be discussed in Chapter 5, or involuntary, as blackmail, in the case of Vitellius and Otho.

Herodian records the same kind of politicking via hostages, also in the context of a change of dynasty. He says that Commodus kept hostages of his provincial governors to hold them in line and that Septimius Severus's success in the civil war of 193 after Commodus was overthrown was a result of similar decisions: he held the children of Aemilianus, the governor of Asia, as hostages and encouraged them to write to their father to ask him to follow Septimius lest they be harmed.[28] Moreover, Septimius is said to have removed his own sons from Rome so that they could not be used as leverage against him.[29] In thinking about Roman politics, writers thus conceived of the stronger, entrenched power as holding hostages from its competitors. The nature of the regime determines the nature of the hostage relationship. The patricians could hold plebeians; the res publica could hold aristocrats; and imperial dynasts could try to nab the families of their generals. Hostages were thought to ensure public service or personal loyalty and to defend against the subject's natural proclivity to greed and ambition.

Shorter-term objectives apart from lengthy peace treaties or political détente were also typically accompanied by hostages, which could be held for a matter of just days or even hours. For example, they could ensure that a diplomatic conference among leaders was held without mishap.[30] The phenomenon occurs frequently in the context of civil war, in which formal treaties did not apply. According to Appian, Lucius Scipio received such hostages from Sulla in 83 BCE to guarantee a conference.[31] Likewise, Julius Caesar demanded the son of Lucius Afranius as a hostage before agreeing to meet him at a spot

---

[28] Hdn. 3.2.3–4.
[29] Hdn. 3.2.4.
[30] Phillipson 1911, 399; Lécrivain 1916, 133; Walker 1980, 9; Elbern 1990, 101. For late antiquity: Lee 1991, 370–371.
[31] App. BCiv 1.10.

that was not easily accessible to Caesar's own troops and bodyguard.[32] And Antony and Lepidus famously gave their sons to Caesar's assassins in order to convince them to come down from the Capitol and accept amnesty.[33] Conferences between states also frequently required *ad hoc* hostage submission. According to Plutarch, Philip V asked for hostages from Flamininus in 197 BCE before a conference, given that the Macedonians had arrived without a guard and the Romans had come with troops.[34] According to Livy, Philip's son was on the giving end of a similar exchange years later: this time Perseus was the one who traveled with too large a retinue and thus offered his two closest advisors to certify his good faith before meeting with Quintus Marcius Philippus.[35] Individual missions or embassies that were risky for involving deception or betrayal on the part of a double agent of some kind also were thought to be more reliable if hostage-taking were involved. According to Livy, two men of Nequinum in Umbria, which was under siege in 299 BCE by the Romans, offered to betray the town; one was kept as a hostage while the other led the Roman troops through their secret tunnels.[36] Multiple hostage-based missions drove the plot of the biblical story of Joseph (of the many-colored coat fame), as retold in the Roman empire by Philo.[37] After Joseph had been freed from the slavery into which his brothers had sold him and had risen to prominence in the Egyptian bureaucracy, he confronted the same brothers years later, who failed to recognize him. Demanding that the brothers return to Canaan and bring back their (his) youngest brother to prove that they were not spies, Joseph detained the second eldest as

---

[32] Caes. *BCiv* 1.84.

[33] Livy, *Per.* 116; App. *BCiv* 2.142; Cass. Dio, 44.34.6. Several authors mention only Antony's sons, and not Lepidus's: Vell. Pat. 2.58.3; Plut. *Brut.* 19.2 and *Ant.* 14.2. Cicero uses the submission as an opportunity to vilify Antony as both an uncaring father and failed patriot: *Phil.* 1.13.31 and 2.36.90. Cf. Octavian, as quoted by App. *BCiv* 3.15. On the polemical nature of Dio's account: Freyburger-Galland 1997, 136.

[34] Plut. *Mor.* 197A.

[35] Livy, 42.39.6–8. See Chapter 4.

[36] Livy, 10.10.4–5. Compare App. *Hann.* 47, in which the senate detained the son of a man of Salapia in southern Italy, to whom they had given troops for a mission against Hannibal. Note also Curt. 7.2.12–18: when Alexander the Great intended to send Polydamas along with Arab guides to sabotage his general, Parmenio, he held on to the brothers of Polydamas and the wives and children of the Arabs as hostages.

[37] Philo, *On Joseph* 168–169, 185–190, 201.

a hostage. When the brothers then reached their father and asked to be allowed to bring his youngest son to Egypt, the father refused until one of the brothers offered *his* sons as hostages for this second mission. The remaining brothers were thus caught in a double bind with Joseph holding one brother and their father holding his own grandsons, until their plight was resolved, as coerced, in the successful completion of both missions and a reunion of the entire family.[38] Hostage detention thus was not only the device of grand geopolitics, but was thought, at least in this legendary context, to work on temporary, even personal levels, as well.

The several different manifestations of coercive hostage-taking – indemnities, armistice, conference, treaty, domestic alliances – are present simultaneously in the records of Roman and Carthaginian relations following the treaty of Zama at the end of the Second Punic War. The incomplete and contradictory sources on the matter have been sorted out convincingly by Moscovich; the result is a complex scenario of multiple, flexible exchanges and detentions, which were manipulated for generations. The first demand for hostages came in 203, after the Romans defeated Hasdrubal and Syphax in Africa, when the Carthaginians were considering a peace in a quickly arranged armistice.[39] But the Carthaginians rejected the peace in the following year and thus forfeited their hostages. After the ultimate victory at Zama in 202, the two sides arrived at a second armistice for which the Romans took additional hostages while what would become the final treaty was being ratified in Rome.[40] The treaty strongly privileged the Romans, requiring, among other things, the payment of 10,000 talents, made in installments covering fifty years, or down to

---

[38] On Philo's characterization of Joseph and the blend of positive and negative qualities: Bassler 1985, Gruen 1999.

[39] Our source for this is indirect: Polyb. 14.8.7, describing the diplomatic situation of 202, makes an oblique reference to a prior hostage submission as already having happened a year earlier, or 203; his record of it must have been in one of his lost books. See Moscovich 1974a, 423.

[40] Polyb. 15.8.7; Livy, 30.37.6; App. *Lib.* 54; Cass. Dio, 17.82. Moscovich 1974a, 417–418 clarifies the vagueness of Polybius and Livy on the question of the timing of this submission by associating it with Appian's more specific account and with precedent: the second batch of hostages was given at the start of the (successful) armistice of 202. See also Walbank 1967, 470–471.

152 BCE, and the detention of one hundred hostages between fourteen and thirty years of age, who were to be held in Rome presumably for the duration.[41] The total population of Punic hostages in Rome as of 201 cannot be known, but given the hostage submissions from the first and second armistices, Moscovich suggests that it was around 250.[42]

From incidental references to these hostages in Livy, we can piece together some details of what their life was like in Italy and gauge the intensity of their coercion. A few years after the hostages had arrived, in 199, Carthaginian ambassadors came to Rome to make an installment of their indemnity. According to Livy, in response the Romans returned one hundred of the hostages and also granted a request of the ambassadors that the remaining hostages be moved from Norba – a place they thought was "hardly appropriate" (*parum commode*) – and restationed in Signia or Ferentinum, which are near Norba, just southeast of Rome in Latium.[43] From this episode in Livy, we can observe that the hostages were in contact with Carthage and not kept entirely sequestered, that their living conditions in the Latin periphery were less than ideal, but they could presume to complain about them, and that the Romans cared enough to respond by moving them to other towns. We also learn from a subsequent episode in Livy that the hostages traveled with their own slaves. In 198, an uprising of Carthaginian slaves in Italy, both those of the hostages and those of the Romans, took place at Setia, Norba, and Cerceii.[44] One of the objectives of the rebellion, apparently, was to free the hostages.[45] The revolt was suppressed, but according to Livy:

The state feared that the Carthaginian hostages and prisoners of war had plotted these events . . . so letters were sent by the praetor around Latium

---

[41] Polyb. 15.18; Livy, 30.37.5–6. App. *Lib.* 54 says the indemnity was 250 Euboic talents. Again, no source explicitly links the hostages with the indemnity. The evidence is inconclusive, as Moscovich 1974a, 421 points out that the last date for which the Punic hostages are reported to be in Italy is 168 (Livy, 45.14.5, later).

[42] Moscovich 1974a, 426. See also Aymard 1953.

[43] Livy, 32.2.3–5. Nepos, *Hann.* 7.2–3 says they were moved to Fregellae. For possible archaeological evidence for the hostages' housing, see Guidobaldi 1993. See also Matthaei 1905, 240–242.

[44] Livy, 32.26.5–8.

[45] Livy, *Per.* 32 says as much, but the full account, Livy, 32.26.5–18, does not make the point explicitly, instead just describing the war. On the status of the slaves and the theories for the origin of the rebellion, see Briscoe 1973, 216.

saying that the hostages should be kept in private and permission to go out in public should not be granted.[46]

By this point, the treaty had been in effect for only four years, yet in terms of the status of the hostages, it had undergone stark highs and lows, to Livy's understanding. From the return of hostages and the improvement of their housing in 199, to their confinement in 198, the Romans used the hostages as vehicles for either reward or punishment.

The next reference to the group of Carthaginian hostages comes for 181 BCE, when Livy says that one hundred more hostages were released.[47] Given the time frame and the large number of hostages returning to Carthage – one hundred in 199 and one hundred more in 181, eighteen years later – Moscovich raises the possibility that there had been some kind of submission of new hostages in the interim that is not recorded by our sources.[48] If the treaty required relatively young hostages, in their late teens and twenties, there must have been some kind of movement; otherwise by 181 the original hostages would have been between thirty-five and fifty. Some would have died of natural causes, or at least would no longer have held as dramatic a sway on the conscience of their families back in North Africa. For coercion to remain effective over the long term, new hostages had to be cycled through Rome. This requirement made the institution available to political leaders in Carthage as a strategic device, which they could use to govern in a domestic context. Livy's last extant reference to the hostages refers to 168 BCE, when Masgaba, a Numidian prince whose kingdom abutted Carthaginian territory, asked the Romans to take as a new hostage a certain Hanno, the son of Hamilcar.[49] The Romans did not follow Masgaba's advice, but the fact that he asked them to do so in order to improve his own political position in the region resembles hostage-based strategies for civil disputes in Rome, from the Republic through the Principate. Masgaba wanted some control

[46] Livy, 32.26.16–17.
[47] Livy, 40.34.14.
[48] Moscovich 1974a, 426–427.
[49] Livy, 45.14.5.

over Hamilcar via hostage-taking, just as Nero sought Titus in order to ensure Vespasian's loyalty.

A large number of people from many walks of life were affected by the presence of the Carthaginians in Rome. Obviously the two signatories of 202 (the governments of Rome and Carthage) were involved in the process, but also the youth of Carthage – even those born decades after Zama – grew up under the specter of a hostage future; rural Italians on the outskirts of Rome were charged with controlling the hostages and adjusting to their status, which was in constant flux; and the Numidians near Carthage, like Masgaba, preyed on their neighbor's obligation to Rome as a weakness. Even theatergoers in Rome felt the influence of the Punic hostages: Plautus's play, *The Little Carthaginian* (*Poenulus*), of 191 BCE may owe aspects of its plot involving a Punic child far from home to the belief that young hostages were the targets of reeducation or indoctrination (see Chapter 6). The detention of hostages was meant to guarantee a peace, yet like a machine with many parts, it needed to be tended to and periodically and alternately reinforced and relaxed. The coercion based in hostage-taking was neither foolproof nor static, but demanded constant attention from the hostage recipients and remained an object of concern even to satellites of the transaction.

THE PRESENCE AND ABSENCE OF VIOLENCE

What was at stake in an agreement secured by hostages? What fate was expected for a hostage when his donor state forfeited him by violating the recipient's conditions? When a Roman thought about a hostage's status as blackmail against a foreign population, in what ways did he think a hostage's life would change, or even end, should circumstances call for retaliation against that hostage's homeland? The answer is complicated by a discrepancy between, on the one hand, the lenient treatment of the hostages of the defaulted in practice, as reported in our literary sources, and, on the other hand, the expectations of hostage-taking, which were rather more violent.

By definition, it would seem that coercion would require physical harm against forfeited hostages, but it has been pointed out that the actual execution of hostages by the Romans is very rarely attested in our sources. Only three examples are recorded.[50] Dionysius and Livy say that when the Volscian towns of Cora and Pometia revolted in 495 BCE, one of the consuls, Appius Claudius ordered their three hundred hostage boys to be beaten publicly in the forum and beheaded;[51] Livy reports that the hostages of Thurii and Tarentum in southern Italy were tossed from the Tarpeian Rock after they unsuccessfully tried to escape in 212 BCE during the Second Punic War;[52] and according to Plutarch, the renegade Sertorius killed hostage Iberian boys in 73 BCE when their families abandoned him to the Romans who were hunting him.[53] The rarity of examples of execution would seem to indicate that the Romans did not normally react so harshly. Even in the three examples summarized earlier, the executions were extralegal and anomalous, and perhaps had nothing to do with the conduct of the donor states in question. The historicity of the case of Cora and Pometia has been challenged, but in any case, as Dionysius tells it, the mass execution was meant to act as a deterrent, not as revenge; it was a lesson that abandonment of hostage obligations would be answered with force, directed not to the people of Cora and Pometia, but to others who had donated hostages under similar conditions.[54] In the case of the Thurians and Tarentines, given that they were punished for their own misdeeds – an attempted escape – and not those of their donor states, coercion is not applicable as an explanation for the hostages' death. One also might note that these hostages were

[50] Matthaei 1905, 234–237; Walker 1980, appendix 1.B; Elbern 1990, 116–117. See also Moscovich 1979–1980, 126 and Ndiaye 1995, 163–164. Ammianus Marcellinus's story of the slaughter of Gothic hostages following the Battle of Adrianople is outside the time frame of this study; see Speidel 1998. On another possible example from late antiquity, based on a Syriac text that was unpublished at the time, see Lee 1991, 372.

[51] For the punishment: Livy, 2.16.9; Dion. Hal. *Ant. Rom.* 6.30.1. For the initial detention: Livy, 2.22.2; Dion. Hal. *Ant. Rom.* 6.25.3 (who says the hostages were adults). Livy's chronology is confused, putting the execution before the detention. Moscovich 1979–1980, 126, n. 34, doubts the authenticity of the episode, whereas Elbern 1990, 116–117 does not.

[52] Livy, 25.7.11–13.

[53] Plut. *Sert.* 25.4.

[54] Dion. Hal. *Ant. Rom.* 6.30.1. Cf. Livy, 2.16.9, which is more vague as to the motivation for the executions: "the wrath of war did not hold back from . . . even the hostages," *ne ab obsidibus quidem . . . ira belli abstinuit.* Livy's *ne . . . quidem* ("not even") implies an element of astonishment.

executed when Rome was in a state of emergency, with Hannibal having won many of his famous Italian victories just earlier. In this case, the reader is led to conclude that the Romans were reacting to a sacrilege at a time of great distress and hysteria, not administering justice in international relations. And Sertorius's slaughter of the hostage boys is seen in Plutarch as the act of a despot, not the proper, regular conduct of a Roman; he calls it "cruel and desperate."[55] Readers are thus left without a single example in which Romans carried out the execution of a hostage per the specific terms of a contract.

Occasionally we catch glimpses of other possible responses toward noncompliance, which are nonviolent. We have already seen how the Carthaginian hostages of the Second Punic War were simply confined and more closely monitored following a rebellion; it was the Carthaginian slaves and prisoners of war who were crucified in retaliation. But like the case of the Thurians and Tarentines, the punishment was in response to the hostages' activities, not to any misdeed by the Carthaginians in general. In some cases of rebellion by the donor state we know no more than that the Romans simply took more hostages. As Livy tells us, when Iberian tribes turned on Gnaeus and Publius Scipio in the Second Punic War in 218 BCE, they managed to regain control and only took more hostages; the fate of the originals is not recorded.[56] In the final years of the same war, as we have seen, the Romans received hostages from Carthage for an armistice in 203 and then took more for a second treaty in 202, probably keeping the originals for future negotiations. Appian reports that one town in Spain, Talabriga, had become known by Roman commanders for donating hostages and then abandoning them on repeated occasions.[57] In 137, Sextus Junius Brutus took hostages from them once again, and then

---

[55] Plut. *Sert.* 10.3: ὠμότητος καὶ βαρυθυμίας. The word σοφιστὴς, at *Sert.* 10.2, may also refer to an evil disposition: Duff 1999, 174. On Plutarch's attempts to salvage Sertorius's fundamentally respectable reputation, nonetheless: Wardman 1974, 134 and Konrad 1994, 205–208. On the paradox of Sertorius's behavior, as channeled by Plutarch: Swain 1989, 66–68 and García Moreno 1992, 136.

[56] Livy, 21.61.5–8. Likewise in Sardinia, Titus Manlius suppressed a revolt in 215, two years after the Romans had taken hostages from them; his only recorded retaliation was to ship more hostages back to Rome: Livy, 22.31.1 and 23.41.5.

[57] App. *Hisp.* 73.

went so far as to threaten to destroy the town entirely if they disregarded their obligation. The Talabrigans then backed down, decided to honor the hostages, and remained cowed thereafter; apparently the hostages were never actually in jeopardy. It should be pointed out that in the vast majority of cases of hostage-taking, we do not know what became of the detainees, whether the donor state complied with the terms or not. In short, the evidence for Roman *policy* concerning forfeited hostages is both slight and inconclusive; if anything, what exists might suggest a general policy of clemency with regard to the hostages.

A study of the rhetoric associated with hostage-taking, however, reveals a different attitude. As rarely as the execution of hostages is recorded as an event, it is very common as a threat. To hold a hostage was to adopt a menacing position. In Dionysius's account of the secession of the plebs, quoted earlier, the patricians find comfort and strength in the fact that they can kill the families of plebeians in order to get them to obey. Moreover, Livy repeatedly supports the notion that large groups of people could be swayed by the fear of death for hostages. In his story of the Sameans of Cephallonia, also quoted earlier, he believed it was plausible that the hostages, exposed to their families who were watching from behind their walls, were in a precarious situation, liable to arouse pity. In a separate episode, the emotion inspired by hostages was intense enough to calm a rampaging army: Livy describes the Roman soldiers who sought to avenge the humiliation of their defeat at the Caudine Forks in 321 BCE by pillaging Samnite towns in 320; their consul is said to have ordered them to desist:

A speech was hastily delivered among the soldiers who became enraged that the sweetness of their revenge had been interrupted. The speech assured each soldier that the consuls did not fall short, and would not ever fall short, of any of the men in their hatred for the enemy, and that just as they had been leaders in war, so would they be in the insatiable quest for slaughter. However, thoughts of the 600 *equites* who were held as hostages at Luceria were like shackles to their anger because an absence of restraint on their part would induce their enemies into beheading the hostages, choosing to destroy them before they perished themselves. The soldiers praised these words and were elated that the consuls had blocked their anger and confessed that anything was preferable to forsaking the safety of so many princes of Roman youth (*principum Romanae iuventatis*).[58]

The imagination of the hostages kneeled over for beheading was as strong as if physical restraints prevented (*praepedisset*) the Romans' vengeance; the youth of the hostages made the feelings for them more intense. Again in Livy, in an episode set in Spain during the Second Punic War, two chieftains who had previously submitted hostages rebelled against Scipio (not yet Africanus) and were defeated. The two, Mandonius and Indibilis, then sought clemency and attempted to arrange a new treaty. As told by Livy, Scipio ultimately, in this case, decided *not* to take hostages:

> The Romans had the following old custom for those with whom they were not joined in friendship either by treaty (*foedere*) or shared laws (*aequis legibus*): not to exercise power over them as if pacified until they had surrendered everything divine and human, and until hostages had been taken and arms had been seized and guards had been stationed in their cities. Scipio, having inveighed in a long speech against the present Mandonius and the absent Indibilis, declared that they had, in terms of true justice, relinquished their lives by their own transgressions, but that they would go on living by his own kindness and by the kindness of the Roman people. But he would not seize their arms, nor demand hostages, because these were the assurances of one fearing a rebellion; rather, he would leave them with their arms free and their spirits unencumbered, and if they rebelled, he would not take it out on innocent hostages, but on themselves; he would exact penalties not from the unarmed, but from the armed.[59]

According to this calculus of international justice, as Livy tells it, Scipio would have been expected, indeed nearly required, to kill any abandoned hostages, but, he is made to say, would have derived little benefit from it. According to Livy, in an ideal scenario, fighting back against a rebellion was a privilege that was *denied* to the recipients of hostages; if the hostage donor violated the agreement, the hostage was to be the surrogate for all violence.[60]

---

[58] Livy, 9.14.13–16. On the detention of the Romans see Livy, 9.5.5; App. *Sam.* 4; Gell. *NA* 2.19.8, 17.2.21; Cass. Dio 8.19–20.

[59] Livy, 28.34.7–10.

[60] In similar fashion, after a Roman legate, Gnaeus Octavius, was murdered in Antioch in 162 BCE, the Romans refused to receive the person of the murderer as a prisoner

The notion of hostages in danger recurs frequently in Roman literature, whether in historiography or in retold legends and folk tales. The potential for brutality against hostages exists in Caesar's account of Gallic intrigue and in an episode in Diodorus Siculus concerning Hellenistic Thrace.[61] In Philo's treatise on Joseph, summarized earlier, Joseph threatens to kill the hostage in his possession, and the brothers, having given their sons to their father on the other end in Canaan, tell him to murder those hostages if they failed to return.[62] Plutarch's biography of Theseus includes the story that the hero was compelled to turn over Daedalus to the Cretans after he had fled the labyrinth, lest hostages of Athens, still left behind, be killed.[63] And Polyaenus tells of Queen Tirgatao of the Ixomatae, north of the Black Sea, who killed her hostage when her opponent, the hostage's father, sent assassins to kill her.[64] Given the frequency of hostage-taking, the variety of donor states, the longevity of the practice over time, and its place in a wide range of literary genres, it is not surprising that there is no consistency in the responses, *in practice,* to states that forfeit hostages. It is safe to say, however, that *in theory,* the hostage was in danger, liable, or at least able, to be killed with impunity according to a contract, whether unspoken or real.

BEYOND THE TREATY

The power enjoyed by a hostage recipient over his wards and, by extension, over the hostage donors encouraged an attitude of invincibility

because it would mean that justice could be worked against him, rather than against the Antiochenes as a group: App. *Syr.* 47.
[61] Philo, *On Joseph* 169, 187–189.
[62] Plut. *Thes.* 19.5.
[63] Polyaenus, *Strat.* 8.55.
[64] According to Caes. *BGall* 1.31, the Aedui had been reluctant to seek help from Rome against the Sequani and Ariovistus in 58 BCE because the hostages in Ariovistus's possession, as a result, could be tortured. Diviciacus is said to have been chosen as the one to seek aid because he alone was not bound by hostages, but even so, he feared that word of his embassy would set Ariovistus to killing. Diod. Sic. 33.15.1–2 reports that Diegylis of the Thracians began to torture and then slaughter hostages when their families defected from his side to that of Attalus II of Pergamon in 145 BCE. Similarly, Plut. *Mor.* 215B states that King Agesipolis of Sparta was happy to be taken hostage, rather than Spartan women and children, because he should be the one to suffer for the state's mistakes, implying that a hostage's death was an expected risk.

that drove the Romans to consider hostage-taking as useful beyond the parameters of any treaty. Roman writers thought it was possible, and common, to step out of an agreement and to employ hostages either to attain a full friendship on a faster time table by releasing them prematurely or to bully their donors into conceding more ground by unduly threatening them. Rather than reflecting and assuring a new *status quo*, hostages could be manipulated to change the relationship, either for better or for worse.

An especially kind treatment, or an early release of hostages before the time allotted in the agreement, or a refusal to take them in the first place, could indicate the degree to which two states had developed shared interests. Hostages were borne of suspicion, and once suspicion waned, they could become irrelevant. In the Roman mindset peace with hostages thus had the potential to graduate over time to a true and solitary peace where coercion was unnecessary. An excerpt from Dionysius of Halicarnassus demonstrates the Roman point of view on the role of hostages in the different gradations of peace. Here he is describing the options considered by the Romans in their early relations with the city-state of Tusculum, to their south, which had rebelled from Rome in 381 BCE, yet had been defeated:

Looking for a way that such a thing would not happen in the city and that they [the Tusculans] would not find a pretext for rebellion, the Romans thought it was not necessary to station a garrison on their acropolis, nor to take hostages from the most prominent men, nor to disarm their soldiers, nor to send any other signal that they distrusted their friendship. Thinking that the one action to bind all people who are related to one another by blood or friendship was an equal partnership in prosperity, they decided to grant citizenship to the defeated, sharing every right that was the Romans' by birth.[65]

To hold hostages, among other things, would be a sign of distrust, which was judged inappropriate in the case of near neighbors and was rejected in favor of the building blocks of peace that came from shared citizenship: alliance, intermarriage, the acknowledgment of a

[65] Dion. Hal. *Ant. Rom.* 14.6.2–3. Cf. Livy, 6.25–26. Note also Arr. *Anab.* 2.12.2, where Arrian preserves the same notion in a story of Alexander the Great, who returned hostages to the people of Soli when they lent him aid in a battle.

common lineage, probably commerce. It cannot be known if this was the Roman way of thinking as early as 381 BCE; what is important here is that Dionysius, writing at the time of Augustus, assigns these qualities to a state which in his own day was self-consciously negotiating the complexities of a multinational empire and periphery and using hostages to do so. The *absence* of hostages mattered in diplomacy; the decision *not* to take them could be counted as a show of genuine friendship. We have already seen how Philip V was rewarded for his support in the wars in Greece with the premature return of his son; in his record of the event, Livy goes to great lengths to associate the release of the hostage with the revolutionary transformation of Philip V himself, not just of his son, into an abrupt and unlikely Romanophile. Alone of the half-dozen writers who mentioned the release, Livy says that Philip's ambassadors went so far as to sacrifice to Jupiter Optimus Maximus on the Capitoline.[66] Livy is also alone in suggesting that other states at war with Rome on the Greek mainland bristled *at the release of Demetrius* because it meant that the Roman-Macedonian alliance had reached a higher plateau.[67] Indeed, Philip is depicted as remaining a friend even after he had Demetrius back: later that year, he facilitated the passage of Roman troops through his kingdom, on their way to the Hellespont to take the war to Antiochus III in Asia. To hold on to Demetrius would have been an insult that could have spun the Romans back into a duel with Philip. As time passed, an international relationship could change, but the treaty, inconveniently, could not; the manipulation of hostages allowed for greater flexibility, creating shades of gray for a black and white arrangement that may have grown obsolete.

The release of hostages was also thought to be able to forge a peace, rather than just reflect one. Releasing hostages was, at times, seen as part of a strategy of persuasion, intended to convince the donor state of Rome's generosity. Polybius, followed by both Livy and Appian, tells

---

[66] Livy, 36.35.12–13. See Briscoe 1973, 273 on the blend of annalist with Polybian material here.

[67] Livy, 35.31.4–6. However, on the informal nature of Rome's ties to Philip, see Gruen 1973.

of a letter sent by Publius and Lucius Scipio to Prusias of Bithynia, which cited the release of Demetrius of Macedon as proof of Rome's benevolence in foreign affairs.

> Having defeated Philip in battle and hobbled him with hostages and tribute, they now seized upon his slightest show of goodwill and gave back his son together with the other young hostages.[68]

The Romans here, as reported by Polybius, are pointing to a policy of releasing hostages and exaggerating it (for Philip had done considerably more than the "slightest show," βραχεῖαν ἀπόδειξιν) for the purpose of advertising an image of magnanimity to a potential new ally in Asia Minor.

Several episodes show that the Romans, or at least Roman writers, believed that releasing hostages back to the donor society had this proactive quality beyond securing a treaty. In most of these cases, the Romans constituted a third party, intervening in others' foreign affairs and charitably returning the hostages that they found in an enemy's possession.[69] Polybius provides an extended example.[70] Hannibal, before leaving Spain for Italy, gathered hostages to assure the loyalty of the Iberian tribes under Carthaginian control, and stationed them in Saguntum under the guard of Bostar. An Iberian, Abilyx, who was formerly loyal to Carthage, decided in secret to shift his allegiance to Gnaeus and Publius Scipio, respectively the uncle and father of the more famous Africanus. Abilyx's plan, as Polybius tells it, was to trick Bostar into giving him the hostages by saying that he would return them to their homes throughout Spain and thus enhance Spanish loyalty to Carthage. But when Bostar accordingly turned over the hostages, Abilyx gave them to the Scipios, instead, who themselves distributed the hostages to their homes just before

---

[68] Polyb. 21.11.9. Cf. Livy, 37.25.12 and App. *Syr.* 23.

[69] Phillipson 1911, 405; Walker 1980, 183–185. Walker 1980, 189 notes that this was easy generosity, given that the original agreements were sealed between two states through hostages, and when one of those states was defunct and a third party entered the scene, the hostages served no technical purpose.

[70] Polyb. 3.98–99. Cf. Livy, 22.22.6–21. Matthaei 1905, 239 and Elbern 1990, 101–102 accept the account, whereas Walbank 1957, 432 argues that the episode is exaggerated in its importance.

the end of the campaigning season, reaping the benefits for Rome.[71] Being able to release the hostages himself was considered a windfall (ἐκ τῆς τύχης) for the Scipios, and it had the desired effect as the Spanish towns are said to have joined the Roman cause. The returning of hostages was perceived to be a material benefit for whoever pulled it off, whether it was Bostar, who believed Abilyx's promise and trusted its potential outcome, or the Romans, who attributed a boost in their position to their hostage manipulation. Polybius and others record that the younger Scipio (eventually Africanus) accomplished a similar feat later in his Spanish campaigns when he returned a hostage bride to her fiancé, complete with a dowry in the amount of the ransom she was to fetch; as a result, her entire tribe was said to ally with Rome.[72] Similar stories occur in the context of the late Republic and early Principate: Caesar won the support of Ambiorix, according to his own commentaries, by recovering Ambiorix's son and nephew from the Aduataci, who were mistreating them as hostages.[73] In Alexandria, Octavian is said to have pondered the hostages that had been held by Antony and Cleopatra, releasing some and holding on to others according to expedience.[74] Such a practice occurs in legend as well: in Plutarch's version of Athenian mythology, when Ariadne replaced Deucalion on the throne in Crete, she returned hostages to Theseus as the first act of diplomacy in building a new alliance.[75] In all these cases, the return of hostages prefigures a new friendship.

---

[71] Polyb. 3.99.9. Cf. Livy, 22.22.4–18. Eckstein 1987a, 212 questions how valuable the return of the hostages was for the older Scipios.

[72] Polyb. 10.19. The dowry is in Livy, 26.50 and Val. Max. 4.3.1; cf. Gell. *NA* 7.8. As with many stories of hostage-taking, this episode should be taken with a grain of salt: that it is probably a trope is demonstrated by an identical story in Frontinus (*Strat.* 2.11.6), where Alexander the Great returned a hostage bride to her fiancé in unnamed tribes. Cf. also Curt. 3.12.21, 4.10.24; Amm. Marc. 24.4.27. On the significance of paying a hostage's dowry, see Chapter 5. See also Eckstein 1987a, 200 and Hoyos 2001, 73–74, arguing against the notion that two episodes of benevolent hostage restoration by Africanus are doublets of a single event. Similar stories can be found at Polyaenus, *Strat.* 7.23.2, about Mausolus of Caria returning hostages to Latmos in order to win their trust, and in Polyb. 30.17 and Livy, 45.42.6–11 the Romans return Bithys to Thrace to secure an alliance.

[73] Caes. *BGall* 5.27.

[74] Cass. Dio, 51.16.1–2. On Octavian's entrance into Alexandria and Dio's conflation of him with Alexander the Great, see Freyburger-Galland 1997, 20.

[75] Plut. *Thes.* 19.7.

To see a hostage in the city of Rome was to witness difference: whatever donor state had given the hostage by definition had not yet reached the level of trust achieved by Tusculum or by Philip V or by Scipio's Spanish allies, and so on. Another means of pushing the hostage donors toward a relationship that was more appealing to Rome was to do the opposite of releasing the hostages: we often find episodes in which hostages were held to abuses that were illegal by the word of the treaty. The Romans thus were seen to exercise a secondary phase of coercion in their possession: hostages defended a settlement first, but then later were used by the recipients to reach beyond it. In this way, hostages could become devices with which to add to the empire rather than to secure that which was already won. Polybius clearly viewed the prolonged detention of Demetrius Soter of Syria along such lines.[76] Demetrius seems to have been given in 178, when he was about ten years old, to substitute for his uncle, Antiochus IV, who was released after about a decade of hostageship.[77] Demetrius's father, King Seleucus IV, died soon after, with Antiochus IV ultimately assuming the throne. For years, Demetrius was the child hostage for Antiochus IV though the two had perhaps never laid eyes on each other. As Polybius tells it, when Antiochus IV died in 164, Demetrius, having grown to maturity, saw his continued detention as a case of imperial overreach. He appeared before the senate to request his release, but the senate declined, and Polybius supplies the reason:

It seemed best to the senate to retain Demetrius and to join in promoting the rule of the remaining heir [in Syria]. They did this, in my opinion, out of suspicion for the industriousness of Demetrius, deciding instead that the youth and frailty of the child who had ascended to the monarchy was more expedient for their affairs in the East.[78]

On strictly legal grounds, given the deaths first of Demetrius's father and then of his (unfamiliar) uncle, his hostageship had become absurd. The Romans were ignoring the conventions and purposes of the practice and using Demetrius's presence in Rome for strategic reasons.

---

[76] Polyb. 31.2. See Phillipson 1911, 403–404; Lécrivain 1916, 131.

[77] On the dates, see Chapter 1.

[78] Polyb. 31.2.6–7. Cf. App. *Syr.* 46. Paltiel 1979b, 43 argues that Demetrius's detention was not used as leverage against Antiochus IV.

Later on in 162 BCE, a Roman legate to Syria, Gnaeus Octavius, was murdered while on a mission to Laodicea. Believing that discontent with such affairs within the senate would make the senators more amenable to his release, Demetrius sought to try his luck again; Polybius recommended against it because the request would only make Demetrius seem ambitious and untrustworthy and thus prolong his detention.[79] Demetrius persisted nonetheless and was turned down again, because, as Polybius reports, the Romans preferred the policy of supporting Antiochus's young heir.[80] In this case, the historian sees the Romans as capable of utterly amoral conduct on the question of hostage-taking and its practice in international law.[81]

A more sustained and critical comment on Rome's hostage-taking abuses comes in various historians' accounts of the origins of the Third Punic War.[82] The Carthaginians had defended themselves in 150 against their neighbor Masinissa, who was an ally of Rome. This was alleged to be an affront to the Romans, and they demanded three hundred hostage boys from elite families to keep the peace. On the matter of what this new peace exactly entailed, Appian presents the Romans as guilty of a colossal double-cross: they promised that the Carthaginians would be allowed their freedom, autonomy, and African territory as long as they surrendered hostages and followed other orders.[83] The ambiguity of these "other orders," however, gave the Romans a loophole: after the hostages were deported to Lilybaeum in Sicily, the Romans demanded, at first, complete disarmament, and then, the destruction of the city and the relocation of its citizens to

---

[79] Polyb. 31.11.5: he tells Demetrius "not to trip on the same stone" (ὁ δὲ παρεκάλει μὴ πρὸς αὐτὸν λίθον πταίειν). Walbank 1979, 466 suggests the opinion would have been shared by Polybius's fellow detainees. On the significance of Polybius's self-representation, see Chapter 8.

[80] Polyb. 31.11.11–12. Cf. App. Syr. 47 and Just. Epit. 34.3.6–7. Livy's account exists only in summary: Per. 46.

[81] For the debate on "Machiavellian" aspects of Polybius's histories, see Eckstein 1995, 105–108, noting that Polybius also disapproved of Demetrius and his bid for the throne owing to his personal problems such as excessive drinking. See also Chapter 8.

[82] Polyb. 36.3–6, 11; Diod. Sic. 32.6.1–4; App. Pun. 76–93. Again, Livy's account is only summarized: Per. 49.

[83] App. Pun. 76. In Diod. Sic. 32.6.1, the Carthaginians are promised their laws, land, sanctuaries, tombs, freedom, and property.

any new site provided it was ten miles from the coast.[84] This famously led to a new war.[85] To Appian, the scandal hinged on what was typically expected from hostage submission, with which the Carthaginians expressly complied and which the Romans betrayed. The following is Appian's version of a speech given to the Romans by a Carthaginian envoy:

> The senate told us, as did you, that if you received the hostages you were calling for, you would allow Carthage to retain its autonomy. If it was added that you would issue further commands, it was not likely, given that there were hostages as you demanded and promises for the city to be autonomous, that you would move beyond the hostages to turn Carthage into a gravesite (κατασκαφήν).[86]

Clearly, Appian has imagined the Punic resistance as having its basis, first and foremost, in the violation of the sanctity of the hostage submission; the Romans are in the wrong. Appian may have had a source in common with Diodorus Siculus, who also attributed a secret plan to the Romans in their seizure of the three hundred hostages.[87] Polybius, the earliest extant account, is more subtle, yet also damning. He first summarizes the cases for and against Rome in this episode, ultimately believing (so he states) that Rome's technicality was justifiable, namely that Carthage had given itself completely to Rome, unlike in the past, and thus should not have resisted the orders, nor complained about broken trust concerning the hostages.[88] But immediately following this report, Polybius registers some discomfort with the tactic nonetheless. He employs an anecdote of his own experience in the Punic hostage-taking in order to comment on the Romans implicitly: he says that he was called by the Romans to witness the war, but decided to turn back at Corcyra and returned home when he heard that the three

---

[84] App. *Pun.* 80–82.

[85] For Polybius's view of the causes of the war and the Romans' search for a "pretext" (πρόφασις), see Baronowski 1995. Cf. Yavetz 1974a, 875–876 on Rome's decision to fight the war long before the detention of new hostages. On the Roman anxieties concerning Carthage, see Welwei 1989. On the power of the catchphrase, *delenda est Carthago,* and its indication of Rome's determination, see Dubuisson 1989.

[86] App. *Pun.* 83.

[87] Diod. Sic. 32.6.1.

[88] Polyb. 36.9.2–17.

hundred hostages had been surrendered. He says that he assumed that the hostage submission meant that the war was over, as was typical.[89] But Polybius was proven wrong, as hostilities obviously erupted from there: the hostages, as told by Polybius, were dispatched to Rome, enclosed in a warship – accommodations that were at odds with the properly dignified treatment of hostages.[90] By stating his mistaken assumption concerning the hostage-based peace and by recording their odd living conditions – an unusual comment for an ancient historian – Polybius has implied Roman guilt without explicitly labeling the Romans as traitors. According to Polybius, in this case the Romans were anything but typical, anything but just, and it is interesting to see him put distance between himself and this betrayal.

Hostage-taking was thus seen in our sources as susceptible to abuse, where hostage recipients might ignore their own obligations and try to coerce more in their own interests on the backs of the hostages. One can point to several other examples. We have already seen in Livy how, in Same in Cephallonia, the Sameans were surprised that in addition to giving hostages they also might be ordered to relocate. Appian piles up similar stories: Lucius Licinius Lucullus took hostages from Cauca in Spain, but then annihilated the town, killing nearly all the adult males; Sextus Junius Brutus demanded hostages from Talabriga in exchange for peace and then surprised them with further demands for horses, supplies, and cash; Mithridates's general Zenobius accepted hostages from the island of Chios as a settlement and then surprised them by levying an additional 2,000 talents; Octavian took fifty hostages from a town in Illyria and then surprised them by calling for complete disarmament.[91] Julius Caesar offers a suspiciously similar scenario in which he manages, just barely, to exonerate his Romans: his lieutenant, Servius Galba, took hostages from Helvetian tribes to assure his winter quarters, but later faced resistance when a rumor circulated among the natives that the Romans intended to stay for much longer and to seize

---

[89] Polyb. 36.11.2–4.

[90] Polyb. 36.5.9. See also Chapter 8. On the lacuna in the text, see Walbank 1979, 657–658. Morgan 1990, 43–44 sees Polybius as "pro-Roman" on this question, but see Eckstein 1995, 217–218.

[91] App. *Hisp.* 52 and 73 (earlier); *Mith.* 47; *Ill.* 21.

more strategic positions.[92] Caesar devalues the rumor and attributes the Helvetians' resistance to their own anger and barbarous qualities, yet Caesar's own conduct in securing Gaul on a permanent basis makes his account dubious – Servius Galba probably did plan to stay longer, over and above the terms of the first hostage-based settlement.[93] Dio records how Metellus took hostages from Jugurtha in exchange for peace, only to keep "upping the ante" unexpectedly with demands for his weapons, elephants, and Roman captives and deserters.[94] In all of these cases the hostage donors got considerably less than what they bargained for.

It is in these examples of Romans overstepping the bounds of the treaty that we find the stiffest resistance on the part of the donors to agreements coerced by hostages. Demetrius Soter's escape from captivity was a form of resistance, undertaken when the Romans failed to abide by the justice of hostage-based relationships. The Carthaginians of the Third Punic War as well went to war with Rome in spite of their hostages. The Sameans of Cephallonia also continued to resist; the Illyrians faced by Octavian in Appian are said to have made a defiant last stand, burning themselves in their citadel; the Helvetians ultimately succeeded in driving off Julius Caesar's lieutenant; and Jugurtha prosecuted a full war against Metellus and then Marius in spite of hostages in Roman possession. Perhaps this resistance should be expected: the document secured by the hostages had proven to be valueless, and the Romans revealed as confidence men in their international relations. When the peace ordained by hostages was overturned by the behavior of the recipients, the parties returned to a state of war. The act of using hostages as coercion for more than what was agreed upon thus had the ironic affect of rendering the practice worthless as a coercive device.

---

[92] Caes. BGall 3.1–2.

[93] On Caesar's deliberate construction of his officers' images in this episode, see Welch 1998, 93.

[94] Cass. Dio, 26.89.1. Polyaenus, Strat. 1.47.2 also discusses an episode from Greek history, in which Thrasyllus received hostages from Byzantium and then made a surprise attack at night. See also SHA, Prob. 14.2–3, where the emperor Probus took hostages from nine Germanic princes, and then proceeded to require grain and livestock after the fact.

3

HOST-GUEST

A classic example of the significance of hospitality in antiquity comes in Homer's *Iliad,* when Diomedes, a Greek, meets Glaucus, a Trojan, on the battlefield. Diomedes recognizes his opponent as a descendant of a man who had been a guest in the house of one of his ancestors long before the war. Bound by a custom of reciprocity between host and guest, the two exchange armor rather than fight, with Glaucus famously on the losing end as he gives up gold in exchange for bronze.[1] Each then returns to his troops, still on opposite sides, still at war with each other. Although the writers of the Roman empire were far removed in time from the Dark Age epics, the significance of hospitality for travel, communication, and international relations has been shown to have persisted in Roman contexts.[2] A host was expected to provide a refuge and basic comforts to a worthy traveler, and the traveler was expected to be grateful and was informally indebted to his host as a result. In writing about hostage-taking, Roman historians and other literary figures occasionally applied the simple analogy of host and guest to the hostage recipient and the hostages themselves, especially, but not only, in the contexts of peaceful, friendly, or allied submissions. The attendant requirements

---

[1] Hom. *Il.* 6.119–236. On Diomedes's profit in the exchange, and the implication of his superiority, see Traill 1989, Donlan 1989, Scodel 1992, and Fineberg 1999, among many others.

[2] On proposed categories of hospitality in antiquity and their application in Rome (especially according to Livy), see Bolchazy 1977, 1–54. Cf. Badian 1958, 154–155 and Saller 1982, 160. Burns 2003, 101 links hostage-taking with guest-friendship when the detainees are adults.

of reciprocity then held sway. As the hostage stood in for his country-men, hospitality, as a governing force of interaction, was thought to have wide repercussions in geopolitics.

Plutarch provides a brief example of the host-guest dimension of hostage-taking in an anecdote concerning the relationship between Philip II of Macedon and Philo of Thebes. Philip II had spent years as a hostage in Thebes during his adolescence, where he evidently ben-efited from Philo's sustenance. Like Homer's Diomedes and Glaucus, they later meet:

Philo the Theban was [Philip's] benefactor and guardian when he was living as a hostage in Thebes. Later he would not accept any gift from him; whereupon Philip said, "Do not rob me of my invincibility by letting me be bested in benefactions and gratitude" (εὐεργεσίας καὶ χάριτος).[3]

Plutarch does not provide any setting for this vignette, but the economy of the situation would have clearly privileged Philip had he not been bound by the rite of his prior hostage status to assume a position of subordination. The hostage, in addition to suffering the years spent from home and the sometimes menacing environment of his travels, must also repay the kindness of the hostage recipients in a debt of gratitude. Wherever they were in this story, Philip figuratively left with bronze, and Philo with the gold, yet Plutarch does not imply resentment on either side; his Philip jokingly seeks only to balance the scales, not to break free from an excessive burden. The hostage and his caretaker are presented as too familiar with each other for any bitterness or animosity.

The submission of hostages often had nothing to do with aggres-sion, opposition, or threats. In many episodes, hostages arrived in Rome before there was any fighting. They came not to end a battle, but to forestall it; not the guarantee of a truce, but as the emblem of an alliance that was undertaken from the ground up before troops were even mobilized. Rather than focusing on the coercive func-tion of hostage-taking, in these cases Roman writers emphasized a benign relationship, where the fact of the hostage proved an affinity (not a conflict) between the states in question. The mutual exchange

---

[3] Plut. *Mor.* 178C.

of hostages, where two sides both traded detainees, signaled an equiv-alency in international status. But in cases in which there is just one hostage recipient – the overwhelming number of examples in Roman stories of our period – the hostages of this type represented a benevo-lent hierarchy that was dominated by the hostage-taker. Power on the international scene remained a bone of contention, just as it had when hostages were viewed primarily as collateral, but the relationship was settled without resort to arms. Thoughts of blackmail thus receded into the background (if they were not forgotten completely), and Rome accordingly traded the image of prison guard of the Mediterranean for that of its host, gracious but still in charge. If the hostage can be viewed as a surrogate for entire populations, then readers of these sto-ries, where hostages are like guests, encounter a world in which the Romans are overwhelmingly powerful, yet universally loved.

Understanding the host-guest analogy in hostage-taking helps to resolve certain enigmas of the practice, such as the strict sense of deco-rum that is sometimes present in descriptions of hostage-taking, and how any departure from that decorum flagged the perpetrators not simply as dishonest, but also as barbaric or animal. Taking hostages was often seen as a marker of civilization and order, and the experience of the hostage was accordingly used to gauge the level of culture and sophistication of the parties involved. Even despite his foreign iden-tity and the potentially hostile circumstances surrounding his presence among the Romans, a hostage in a proper and just context was afforded a degree of respect and compassion. And while the early release of hostages was seen as a sign of goodwill in the context of blackmail as discussed in the previous chapter, under the rubric of hosts and guests it connoted the opposite: if holding hostages bespoke friend-ship, then releasing them could spell the displeasure of the hostage recipient. A proper grasp of the Roman mindset on matters of foreign policy depends on unraveling what, for us, may seem a paradox: how newly established friendships could coexist with a ruthless application of blackmail. With the host-guest contrivance, the Romans seem to be applauding their brand of empire: taking hostages is a gesture of clemency, and when non-Romans themselves are said to embrace that clemency, Roman prestige soars, and the notion of creditor-collateral is conveniently or momentarily displaced.

A HIERARCHY OF ALLIES

A conventional model of coercion and blackmail in hostage-taking might be thought of as a series of basic steps: (1) some disagreement between two states leads to hostility, which (2) leads to warfare, which (3) leads to a Roman victory (according to our predominantly Roman-friendly record), after which (4) hostages are taken out of suspicion, and (5) donors regret their obligation to submit. But in many episodes, as reported in our sources, this process could be truncated. One or more of the "steps" could be absent to the point that the practice implied something very different from coercion. For example, in some cases warfare led to a Roman victory and to the demand for hostages out of suspicion, yet far from regretting their obligation, the hostage donors are said to welcome it with celebration, and the general who took the hostages is seen as exceedingly generous. When Diodorus Siculus describes how the Carthaginian Hanno dealt with a defeated town in Sicily, he labels his decision to take three thousand hostages as evidence of the general's kindness, because a more violent retribution, we are told, would have been justified.[4] Similarly, Livy portrays the consul Quintus Marcius Philippus's levy of hostages following the surrender of Agassae in 169 BCE as a conciliatory maneuver, a substitute for direct rule by a garrison, which allowed him to "charm the hearts of the remaining Macedonians."[5] According to Josephus, Antiochus VII Sidetes was extolled by the Jews as their benefactor for taking hostages from Jerusalem when he could have exacted harsher penalties. He was feted throughout the city and attended festivals while his troops were fully supplied.[6] Hostage-taking could thus be seen as a happy alternative to what was seen as the victor's by right: hegemony, extirpation, or even genocide. The conquerors in all of these cases – Hanno, Marcius Philippus, Antiochus VII – are seen as especially kindhearted given the preceding combativeness and resistance of the donor societies, and although they hope to control states that had only recently been defeated, the defeated are grateful for a concession.

---

[4] Diod. Sic. 24.10.2.
[5] Livy, 44.7.5: *ut reliquorum Macedonum animos sibi conciliaret.*
[6] Joseph. *AJ* 13.247–249. Antiochus VII Sidetes's accommodating attitude toward the Jews is contrasted with that of Antiochus IV Epiphanes: *AJ* 13.243.

This sense of celebration in hostage-taking may account for other episodes in which the series of steps in conventional coercion is abbreviated even further. If the chance exists for hostage-taking to be welcomed, then it stands to reason that a weak state in a disagreement with a strong one may attempt to avoid warfare entirely and hasten to the conclusion. In other words, a common scenario in our sources is that an initial disagreement between two states gave way to immediate hostage submission, without any fighting, but still with the element of suspicion. Livy and Dionysius of Halicarnassus both speak of the Roman treaty with the Lucanians of southern Italy, dated to 298 BCE, along these lines.[7] The Lucanians had distanced themselves from Rome despite an old alliance, and relations between the two had soured. But now wanting Roman assistance in a war against the Samnites, they sought to patch the rift, and thinking that mere persuasion would not be enough to win over the Romans, hostages were offered not only to prove, but also to *create* their own loyalty in the eyes of the Romans.[8] Our authors thus describe a situation in which warfare, as a step in the model of hostage-taking, was dropped, but where suspicion between the recipient and donor still lingered. The resulting alliance was said to be strong, as the Romans, hostages in hand, declared their support for Lucania and went to war against the Samnites. In these cases, coercion is still a powerful element in the hostage relationship, but is has been scaled down in its intensity. The ambience of the recorded submission is very different from episodes where threats of violence are prominent; the animosity between the states has softened, with hostages as the agents of – the very reason for – the less turbulent relationship.

Coercion ceases to be a central explanation for Roman hostage-taking when even the element of suspicion is lost, and the gap between two states is closed without war, without victory, without skepticism on the part of the recipient, without remorse on the part of the donor, and only with hostages, given over in a supreme act of alliance. Often the (self-professed) reputation of a Roman general's

---

[7] Livy, 10.11.13; Dion. Hal. *Ant. Rom.* 17.1.2–3; 17.3.1.

[8] Livy, 10.11.13; Dion. Hal. *Ant. Rom.* 17.1.2. For another view of the Lucanian hostages, see Chapter 4.

previous accomplishments provided the impetus for donor states to give hostages in such a way. In Julius Caesar's commentaries on the Gallic wars, for example, when word of Caesar's success in Gaul traveled north, tribes from across the Rhine were said to send hostages in droves as a sign of a new alliance.[9] Likewise, Caesar says that he knew of the loyalty of the Remi, the sole Belgic tribe to support him, only because they had given him hostages unprovoked.[10] In Livy ambassadors from 120 Iberian tribes rushed (*legati concurrerunt*) to Gnaeus and Publius Scipio in 217 BCE in order to offer them hostages after they had conquered the Balearic Islands and landed on their shores.[11] And in Tacitus's *Agricola*, the British tribes are so impressed with the Romans' civilization and strength and with Agricola himself (of course, the author's father-in-law) that they embraced the practice of hostage-submission as an opportunity to join his side.[12] The notion of coercion in hostage-taking is not raised by the various commentators in these episodes; the role of hostages as guarantees evaporates, and the fact of the submissions exists only as an acknowledged symbol of hierarchy. The situation is not only one of peace or a cessation of fighting but of active friendship and of shared responsibilities, with Rome as the more powerful partner. This type of hostage acts as a bridge connecting sovereign states rather than a token of blackmail. The metaphor of the hostages as "shackles" that bind the contracting parties, seen earlier, for example, in Chapter 2, when the Romans were held at bay by hostage-wielding Samnites, would not be appropriate in this context.

Authors of the early Principate share the idea that hostages could be given in unwarlike settings and could have nothing to do with coercion. It is how Strabo at one point characterizes the submission of Parthian princes by Phraates IV to Augustus's care in 10/9 BCE:

As for the Parthians, although they are powerful neighbors of Rome, they have nevertheless yielded to the superiority of the Roman people and of our rulers to such an extent that they have not only sent back to Rome

---

[9] Caes. *BGall.* 2.35.1.
[10] Caes. *BGall.* 2.3. See also Barlow 1998, 145 and Burns 2003, 124.
[11] Livy, 22.20.11. For chronology: Hoyos 2001.
[12] Tac. *Agr.* 20.3. For comment on the rhetorical nature of this passage, see Chapter 6.

the standards which they once raised as a monument over the Romans, but Phraates also entrusted his children to Augustus, and his children's children, thus obsequiously giving hostages for his friendship (φιλίαν).[13]

Strabo's Phraates IV, in his relationship with Augustus, thus comes to resemble the Gallic tribes confronted by Caesar: Phraates IV here used hostages to court an international ally.[14] Tacitus refers back to Strabo's interpretation of the Parthian hostages in his account of the Neronian wars in the East. He reports that the Romans in 54 CE encouraged Vologaeses of Parthia to give hostages to Gnaeus Domitius Corbulo before any conflict and thus choose peace as his predecessors had.[15] Ultimately, according to Tacitus, Vologaeses had other reasons for surrendering his sons, which have to do with protecting his throne from rivals, a theme to be discussed in Chapter 5. Nevertheless, Tacitus at least preserves the notion that a benevolent hierarchy with Rome at the top could be *expected* as a settlement orchestrated through hostages – that is what Corbulo hoped to achieve.[16] And the rhetoric appears in other places. In Lucan's *Pharsalia*, hostage-taking is deployed as a metaphor to describe Pompey's relations with the island of Lesbos after he sent his wife Cornelia to live there during his civil war with Caesar. Addressing the people of Lesbos, Lucan's Pompey says:

Not only by a promise had I shown to you that no land in the world is more pleasing to me; Lesbos also held my affection with my wife as a hostage (*obside*); my sacred home and my cherished family gods were here; here was my Rome.[17]

The metaphor does not include any notion of compulsion to submit; on the contrary, Pompey sent his wife willingly, and the result was to transform Lesbos into what Lucan suggests was an equivalent to

---

[13] Strabo, 6.4.2.

[14] On the domestic tensions within Parthia at the time, see Nedergaard 1988, 102–105; Campbell 1993, 222; Kennedy 1996, 82–83, 88; and Drijvers 1998, 289. On the other motive that Strabo attributes to Phraates IV at 16.1.28 – that of eliminating his dynastic rivals – see Chapter 5.

[15] Tac. *Ann.* 13.9. On the chronology, see Wheeler 1997.

[16] On Tacitus's construction of Corbulo's character in the *Annals* through discussion of his attitudes toward hostages, see Chapter 9.

[17] Luc. 8.129–133. In Sklenár 2003, 121, the fact that Lesbos, a non-Roman place, counts as a second Rome demonstrates the upheaval of the civil war.

Pompey's hometown. Later in the passage, Lucan uses another metaphor to describe Cornelia's status on Lesbos, calling her a *hospita*, or guest.[18] In none of these cases does the reader find hostility or wariness or regret in hostage transactions, and the device is repeatedly reported as successful in sustaining alliances.

As hostages guaranteed the trust, or *fides*, between Rome and the hostage donors, they became the human manifestation of a critical concept in Roman foreign relations. A temple to *Fides* stood on the Capitoline Hill, which, though attributed to Numa by tradition, seems to have been first dedicated by Atilius Calatinus, a consul of 258 and 254 and *triumphator* of 257, at a time when the Romans were beginning to engage in warfare overseas, beyond the Italian peninsula; it was then rededicated by a Marcus Aemilius Scaurus, who could be either the consul of 115 or his son, the curule aedile of 58.[19] *Fides* thus had a home at the pinnacle of the city, and its construction and refurbishment coincided with Rome's blossoming imperial fortunes. That the "trust" revered here had a specific application in foreign relations is proven by the treaties and other documents pertaining to Rome's allies, which seem to have been posted on the temple's walls, or at least nearby.[20] The diplomatic significance of *fides* also was acknowledged by the various kings themselves and by the cities belonging to Rome's network of allies: near the temple stood a long statue base, which was decorated with dedications from Asia Minor. All that remains of the monument are several fragmentary inscriptions, some in Latin, some in Greek, and some bilingual; these mention gifts of statues of Roma or of the Roman People, donated out of gratitude for Roman benefactions and generous relations.[21] Anyone wandering into this precinct of the Capitoline

---

[18] Luc. 8.157.

[19] See Richardson 1992 and the entry by Reusser in the *Lexicon Topographicum Urbis Romae*.

[20] *LTUR* (Reusser) cites a dedicatory inscription from Thasos dating to c. 80 BCE and a reference in Cassius Dio to the damaging of inscriptions posted at the temple in 44 or 43 BCE (45.17.2–3; one wonders if this is a rhetorical harbinger of the crisis of the time). Some soldiers' *diplomata* were also apparently posted there. The *Lex Antonia de Termessibus,* concerning the grant of freedom to Termessus and the levying of tribute there, was found nearby; see H. B. Mattingly 1997. See also Freyburger 1986, 259–273.

[21] The inscriptions (*CIL* I² 725–731) are discussed and placed in historical context at Mellor 1978, with references. The dedications, at least on this monument, seem to have begun shortly after the Battle of Pydna and extend into the early first century BCE

would have been struck by the extent to which promises and good faith seemed to govern Rome's foreign affairs; hostages signified, or even reified, the same notion.

The function of the hostage as the talisman of trust is especially vivid in cases where *obses* or ὅμηρος were used as metaphors to describe the role of children in cementing the bonds of extraordinary families. It was a common conceit in Roman literature for a man and a woman who produce offspring to be described as parties agreeing to a contract for which their children are the security. In language in keeping with the financial transactions between a creditor and debtor, the newborn child helps to maintain an otherwise contentious bond; the depiction of children as hostages is particularly common when the parents form an unusual pair that must be reminded of a force beyond their coupledom to keep them together. In Propertius, when the deceased Cornelia addresses her husband, Paullus, from the grave she says that their obligation to one another still holds by virtue of the security embodied in their two sons and one daughter.[22] In Ovid's *Heroides,* when a brother and sister – Macareus and Canace – produce a child from an incestuous union, the son is called a pledge of their love that will unite them in spite of the circumstances and the hostile reaction of others.[23] Also in the *Heroides,* when Medea wants to accentuate Jason's faithlessness, she refers to their sons as twin pledges whom Jason has ignored.[24] All of these couples are remarkable in some way: a deceased woman and her widower, a sister and her brother, and a jilted wife whose revenge on her disloyal husband is notoriously violent. In these cases the status of the children as pledges is in the forefront: at the moments in question the need for a security, or guarantee, is acute, and the one who best fits that role is a biological progeny. Another strained couple uses a daughter in the same way in one of the staged

and possibly a little later. Among the dedicators are the Lycian League; the cities of Laodicaea, Ephesus, and Tabae; and Mithridates IV of Pontus (ruled 169–150) and Ariobarzanes (I or II) and Athenais of Cappadocia. The entire monument was rebuilt, and the inscriptions recarved, under Sulla – the result of a fire and Sullan ideology (Mellor 1978, 329–330).

[22] Prop. 4.11.73.

[23] Ov. *Her.* 11.113. Cf. the despair between Jupiter and Ceres when Proserpina, their daughter – and hostage between them – is taken by Hades: Ovid. *Met.* 5.523.

[24] Ov. *Her.* 6.122, 130.

ethical debates in the *Controversiae* of Seneca the Elder.[25] The mother
and father have become catastrophically estranged: the reader is told
at the start that the mother has poisoned and killed her stepson who
was born to her husband in his first marriage. As she is about to be
executed, she reveals that their daughter (the father's second child) was
her accomplice in the murder and therefore should be executed as
well. The father defends the daughter on the grounds that the wife,
disgruntled to say the least, was using the girl as a hostage against her
father. The result is an odd kind of *fides*-by-coercion, which is to say,
not true *fides* at all.

Finally, in a second-century novel by Chariton, the identification of
a child as a hostage between two parents is critical to the plot of mistaken identities and confused parentage. The story is as sensational as
most Hellenistic novels: Callirhoe is taken from her husband Chaereas
by pirates and sold into slavery to Dionysius. Dionysius falls in love
with her and marries her, and seven months later she gives birth to a
son whom the reader is told belongs to Chaereas. Overcome with joy,
Dionysius calls out to Aphrodite:

Callirhoe was a delight to me – sweeter than country or parents. I also love
this child and how he makes his mother more securely bound to me; I now
have a hostage of her good will (ὅμηρον ἔχω τῆς εὐνοίας).[26]

Again, the "marriage" is unusual – a master and the slave he purchased
from pirates, who herself is still married to another – and Dionysius
finds the legitimacy of their union in his son/hostage. For readers
who know the child is not his, this expression points out the characters' plights: Dionysius's ignorance and Callirhoe's deception. For
our purposes, it is enough to note the language of hostage-taking in
Chariton's portrayal of the crux of conflict: the hostage may betoken
fides, even when it should not truly exist.

MUTUAL EXCHANGE

Just as hostage submission from the weak to the strong articulated
and cemented a hierarchy, the mutual exchange of hostages one to

---

[25] Sen. *Controv.* 9.6.3.
[26] Chariton, *Chaereas and Callirhoe* 3.8.4.

another proclaimed equal status in international relations. In this kind of pact, coercion is an unlikely prospect: the execution of hostages on one side would, by reason, be answered in kind on the other, resulting in a losing situation for both parties. Instead, the mutual exchange of hostages served as the manifestation of a common bond. It is particularly prevalent in Roman accounts of diplomacy within Gallic communities. For example, according to Tacitus, Julius Civilis prepared his rebellion in Gaul first through the mutual exchange of hostages.[27] Earlier, Julius Caesar cited a similar physical exchange of hostages in Gaul – the movement required in the logistics of exchange and the rumors it triggered constituted the very evidence of a nascent rebellion:

While Caesar was in his winter quarters in nearer Gaul . . . frequent rumors were brought to him, and likewise he was informed by letters from Labienus, that all the Belgae, whom I have already said made up a third of Gaul, were swearing oaths against Rome and exchanging hostages among themselves.[28]

Similarly, the Carnutes, we are told, chose *not* to exchange hostages in their alliance of resistance "lest the plot thus be revealed" to the Romans through rumor.[29] The theme that intelligence gathering in the non-Roman West depended on the visibility of the mutual hostage exchange also appears in Appian. He describes how a secretive alliance among Italians was revealed before the Social War:

They secretly sent embassies to each other, banding together over these matters and exchanging hostages for mutual trust (καὶ ὅμηρα διέπεμπον ἐς πίστον ἀλλήλοις). The Romans did not learn about these for a long time because of the disputes and factions in the city. When they did learn about it, they sent to the cities men who were suitable for each in order to learn what was happening without being detected. When one saw a young hostage (μειράκιον ὅμηρον) being led from Asculum to another town, he alerted Servilius, the praetor in that region.[30]

---

[27] Tac. *Hist.* 4.28.

[28] Caes. *BGall.* 2.1. Cf. Caes. *BGall.* 1.19, when Caesar similarly learns of a conspiracy among the Helvetii and Sequani through the evidently cumbersome movements involved in mutual hostage exchange, on which see also Burns 2003, 100–101.

[29] Caes. *BGall.* 7.2: *ne res efferatur.* On Caesar's confidence in the intelligence, see Austin and Rankov 1995, 22.

[30] App. *BCiv.* 1.38.

The movement of hostages in Gaul and Italy, swapped back and forth, was a precursor to the movement of troops in a unified assault. The act of mutual exchange registered a strong and determined effort at attaining shared objectives. By extension, alliances without hostages must have seemed cruder, or flimsier: in these regions, hostages were seen by Roman writers as a necessary part of friendship.

The Romans in the period under study are never said to have engaged in mutual exchange themselves, perhaps because it would entail an admission of weakness or at least equality with a foreign regime.[31] The closest example of such behavior on the part of the Romans involves mythology: according to Dionysius of Halicarnassus the Trojans, led by Aeneas, and the indigenous Italians, led by Latinus, gave each other their children as reciprocal hostages when they were preparing to fight Turnus and the Rutulians.[32] Dionysius mentions that previous authors thought that Romulus and Remus were included among the Trojan entourage of hostages as grandsons of Aeneas (and not grandsons of Numitor, as it appears in Livy's famous account). According to this alternate version of the myth, it is from this position – as friendly hostages – that the brothers left to found their cities.[33] The mutual exchange in this story is presented as proof of the shared interests, deeply felt, which existed between the Trojans and the Latins. The act unites the two peoples rhetorically in a way that allows for the unique identity that the Romans cultivated in the Augustan age as rustic warriors (Latins), yet also heroes of a storied and cultured past (Trojans): Romulus and Remus, in this version, *were* Trojans, and they were supported by Latins, in whose land they founded Rome.[34]

Far from marking a state of unease or temporary distrust, hostage exchange could be seen as proof of a kind of symbiosis, as if two

---

[31] Elbern 1990, 128. Mutual exchange occurred more frequently in late antiquity, perhaps because Roman power was waning: Phillipson 1911, 399; Lee 1991, 373.

[32] Dion. Hal. *Ant. Rom.* 1.59.2.

[33] Dion. Hal. *Ant. Rom.* 1.73.2. On Dionysius's use of Fabius Pictor, see the debate at Poucet 1976 and Verbrugghe 1981.

[34] On the history and significance of identifying Romulus (and sometimes Remus) as Trojans, see Gruen 1992, 35–39; Miles 1995, 137–178; Cornell 1995, 65 and 70–71. On later rites that celebrated the bond between Aeneas and Latinus: Galinsky 1969, 147. Wiseman 1995, 55–56 suggests that the anonymity of the father may be meant to imply divine parentage. On the filial aspect of their hostageship, see Chapter 5.

parties could be made kindred if they had hostages of one another. A fantastic illustration of this point comes oddly in a second-century treatise on marine biology by Oppian, who uses certain phenomena of humankind as metaphors to explain sealife. Of course, it is Oppian's understanding of the human *comparanda* that is interesting here. In this prayer to Zeus, the hostage exchange of fish and birds explains the interconnectedness of the ocean and the sky:

With such affection have you separated and divided each from the other, the radiant sky and the air and the flowing water and the earth, mother of all. Yet you also brought them together in an unbroken bond of amity and, as a matter of necessity, you join them under a shared yoke, not to be removed. For the sky does not exist without the air, nor the air without water, and the water is not indifferent to the earth, but they are born of each other, all on one path, all unfolding in a single cycle. For this reason they also exchange hostages (ὁμηρεύοσαι) in the shared races of amphibians: some come up from the sea to the land; others dive from the air to mingle with Amphitrite, such as the cormorants and the lamenting tribes of kingfishers and the mighty, rapacious ospreys and whatever else that plunges into the water to hunt and fish. Likewise there are those that live in the deep yet cut through the sky: the calamaris, the race of seahawks, and the underwater swallow. When these fear a stronger fish at hand, they leap from the sea and take to wing in the air.[35]

Flying calamaris notwithstanding, Oppian's metaphor, when worked in reverse – the hostage of humankind is a "cultural amphibian" who can function in two different worlds – elevates the hostage beyond a Limbo between two separate worlds to a space where cohabitation is the norm. As Oppian understood it, the hostage is more than an oddity; he (it) is a crucial link and the key to equilibrium; the stopgap against chaos, which keeps radically different realms "all on one path, all unfolding in a single cycle." The hostage is a special kind of hybrid figure, such that if one world became threatening, he could find refuge or asylum in the other without undergoing radical change. The essence of hostage exchange here is very different from the violence discussed in the previous chapter with respect to coercion. The hostage might

[35] Oppian, *Halieutica* I.412–430.

even be seen as having a revolutionary identity to which the partners in the agreement ultimately aspire.

GUEST OR COLLATERAL? THREE CASES OF CONTRADICTORY ACCOUNTS

Roman writers were aware of a difference between hostage-taking for the sake of alliance and hostage-taking for the sake of coercion. An episode in Livy shows how the discrepancy could alter the path of Roman foreign policy: the entire interpretation of international relations surrounding the Battle of Pydna depended on which of the two roles for hostages – collateral or guest – one assigned to Bithys, son of King Cotys of Thrace. Thrace had had nominally good relations with Rome in the recent past, but it had sided with Perseus of Macedon in the war.[36] Livy records that after the Romans defeated Perseus they discovered Bithys living at the court in Pella as a hostage. Owing to Thrace's switching sides, they took possession of Bithys and sent him back to Rome as a hostage of their own. Shortly thereafter, envoys from Cotys appeared before the senate to ask for Bithys to be released and simultaneously to justify and apologize for Thrace's support of Perseus:

When [the ambassadors] were introduced into the senate, and when they offered as the basis of their plea the specific argument that Cotys did not help Perseus in the war of his own volition because he had been forced to give hostages, they begged them to allow [the hostages] to be redeemed at whatever price the senators deemed appropriate. The response offered by the authority of the senate was that the Roman people remembered the friendship that had existed with Cotys and his ancestors and with the people of Thrace, but that the giving of hostages was itself the charge, not a defense of the charge, because the people of Thrace had had no reason to fear Perseus when he was at peace, let alone when he was occupied in a war with Rome.[37]

Livy's Cotys was arguing that he had been forced to follow the orders of one who held his son hostage; the senate countered by claiming

---

[36] Chiranky 1982, 462–465 describes Cotys's close relationship to Perseus before Pydna and identifies possible periods of *amicitia* with Rome preceding that.

[37] Livy, 45.42.7–10. Polyb. 30.17.1–4, by contrast, makes no mention of the argument that Cotys's hostage to Perseus constituted friendship.

that Bithys was not *that* kind of hostage, but was dispatched to Perseus prematurely by Cotys as a token of loyalty.[38] The senators had a decision to make; the fate of all Thrace hinged on whether Bithys's father had sent him to live with Perseus voluntarily or under duress, both of which were viable but distinct options in Livy's understanding of hostage-taking. The implication is that the most acceptable option for Cotys would have been a third path: to give Bithys *to Rome* as a hostage, even though Rome and Thrace were already (informally) friends. In a previous story, after all, Livy records that before Pydna, the Penestae and Parthini, which like Cotys were allies of Rome and also weaker neighbors of Macedon, had given hostages to Rome unsolicited and in spite of a preexisting friendship.[39] The senate ultimately decided that Cotys gave Bithys to Perseus in the same spirit; although the Romans thus concluded that Cotys had acted treasonously, they opted not to punish him "as he deserved," and sent Bithys home.[40] Still, to Livy's senators, Bithys alone was evidence of Cotys's place in Perseus's network of allies. The discrepancies between various attitudes toward Bithys illustrate the potential for the figure of the hostage in Roman culture to endure a split identity, taking on different meanings at different times. The nature of his detention was contentious and open to interpretation, and yet utterly crucial in accounting for geopolitical alliances, obligations, and vendettas.

For the controversy surrounding Bithys's hostageship, Livy records a debate in the senate; in another case, we see historians, not senators, disagreeing over the same question of whether hostage donors should be construed as friendly or hostile. In telling the story of Cloelia – the Roman maiden who served as a hostage to Lars Porsenna, the invading Etruscan king – Plutarch allows the benevolent qualities of hostage-taking to dominate the series of events.[41] He even fabricates new details (or else includes ones otherwise unattested in extant sources) in order to shoehorn peaceable hostage-taking into a tale that is, universally

---

[38] Walbank 1979, 440; Lica 1988, 35–36.

[39] Livy, 43.21.2–3. On an alliance with the Parthini, in 205, see Polyb. 2.11.11; 7.9.13 and Livy, 29.12.13.

[40] Livy, 45.42.10: *quid merito eius fieri posset*. See Braund 1984a, 16 on Bithys's education in Rome.

[41] Plut. *Publicola* 18–19 and *Mor.* 250 B-F.

among prior authors, one of warfare between enemies.[42] In all other
versions but Plutarch's, Lars Porsenna attacked Rome in order to help
the exiled king Tarquin retake his throne and took hostages after conquering the city or after deciding to withdraw of his own volition.[43]
But, according to Plutarch, Porsenna first broke off all ties to Tarquin
because of his villainy and became a *friend* of Rome instead.[44] He
then accepted (not demanded) ten hostage boys and ten hostage girls,
including Valeria, the daughter of the consul, as tokens of alliance. It
is another case of proactive, diplomatic hostage submission, with no
fear and no distrust.

Because Plutarch's hostage-taking is devoid of any sense of coercion, in his case when Cloelia famously led the hostages in an
escape to freedom, the Romans – particularly the consul Publicola –
were accordingly angered (not inspired) by the hostages' deed as it
made them "less honorable," and they decided to send Cloelia and the
other hostages back.[45] When the hostages were sent back to Porsenna,

[42] Different narratives of Cloelia can be found at Livy, 2.13.1–11; 9.11.6; Dion. Hal. *Ant.
Rom.* 5.31–34; Val. Max. 3.2.2; Sil. *Pun.* 10.490–502 and 13.828–830; and Flor. 1.4.7–
8. Many others mention Cloelia but refer only to her bravery without any additional
narrative: Cic. *Off.* 1.61; Verg. *Aen.* 8.651; Sen., *ad Marc. de Consol.* 16.2; Plin. *HN*
34.28–29; Juv. 8.265; *De vir. ill.* 13; Polyaenus, *Strat.* 8.31; and Cass. Dio, 45.31.1. Tac.
Ann. 11.24 adds a reference to Porsenna's hostages to Claudius's speech on behalf of
Gallic citizenship, of which there is a famous inscribed version (Dessau, 212); on Tacitus's change see Griffin 1982, 410; Williams 2001, 181–182. Variations in the story are
discussed in the footnotes below. On other historical discrepancies in the *Life of Publicola*:
Affortunati and Scardigli 1992. On historical traditions for Porsenna: Gagé 1988 and
Cornell 1995, 216–218. On the characterization of Cloelia, see Walker 1980, 263–270,
especially 265 on the role of the annalist, Valerius Antias, in changing aspects of the
story, particularly in making Valeria, not Cloelia, the chief heroine.
[43] Livy, 2.13.1–4 says Porsenna demanded hostages in order to withdraw because he was
frightened by an assassination attempt. Dion. Hal. *Ant. Rom.* 5.31.4 says he demanded
hostages because his Etruscan noblemen were weary of war and because he lost a minor
skirmish. In other accounts the implication is that Porsenna had nearly defeated the
city and was still threatening Rome: Val. Max. 3.2.1–2; Sil. *Pun.* 10.485–490; and Flor.
1.4.2.
[44] Plut. *Publicola,* 18.1–2 and *Mor.* 250B. Dion. Hal. *Ant. Rom.* 5.34.1 says the falling out
with Tarquin did not occur until *after* the debacle with the hostages.
[45] Plut. *Mor.* 250 D: ἐν πίστει χείρονες. Also Plut. *Publicola,* 19.2. In Livy, 2.13.7, it is
Porsenna who is angry at the betrayal, and he rebukes the Romans as dishonest (cf.
Livy, 9.11.6). Similarly, in Dion. Hal. *Ant. Rom.* 5.33.2, it is Tarquin who rebukes the
Romans, who in turn reply that Cloelia acted alone and not at their instigation. In
both these versions, it is only after the Romans have already been criticized that they

as Plutarch tells it, Tarquin tried to ambush them; Valeria then escaped *to* Porsenna (not from him), and the rest were rescued (not detained) by Aruns, Porsenna's son.[46] And in response to Cloelia's courage, Porsenna gave her a war horse, a version which disagrees with others that say she stole the horse during her escape.[47] Hostage-takers here were like the heroes in a melodrama, not the villains; Porsenna provided a service for which the Romans generally were grateful. According to Plutarch, Cloelia and the others were treated well; the Romans took pains to maintain their new friendship; and Tarquin was excluded as a mutually despised outsider to the alliance.

The various possible interpretations of hostage-taking in antiquity could lead to confusion among the various authors commenting on a single individual. The many accounts of Cloelia present different interpretations of hostageship, which in turn lead to different understandings of early Rome. Or, rather, the authors have in mind particular impressions of the Etruscan war and make the hostages "fit" accordingly. In either case, the mutability of the *figure* of the hostage is evident. For example, Livy and Plutarch both record that a bronze equestrian statue of Cloelia stood on the Via Sacra in the Roman forum (although it was gone by their lifetimes), but each interprets the statue in a different way. Livy believed that the statue honored Cloelia's valor at having swum the Tiber and for having maintained sufficient composure in the presence of Porsenna to retrieve the boys who were hostages.[48] Plutarch admitted of a debate surrounding the meaning of

send back the hostages in order to maintain the treaty. None of the episodes in other authors refers to the fact that Cloelia was sent back to Porsenna, but in their accounts, she is praised for freeing her country by means of her flight: Val. Max. 3.2.2; Sil. *Pun.* 10.499–500 and 13.828; Sen. *ad Marc. de Consol.* 16.2; Juv. 8.263–265; and Flor. 1.4.7–8.

[46] Plut. *Publicola*, 19.3 and *Mor.* 250E. Dion. Hal. *Ant. Rom.* 5.33.3–4 essentially agrees with this version, except that Tarquin's men arrive too late to effect a serious ambush. None of the other sources mentions the ambush, although Pliny, *HN* 34.29 believes Tarquin succeeded, somehow, in laying his hands on all of the hostages except Valeria.

[47] Plut. *Publicola* 19.4 and *Mor.* 250 E-F. Dion. Hal. *Ant. Rom.* 5.34.3 again agrees, saying Porsenna gave her the horse. For the theft of the horse: Val. Max. 3.2.2; Flor. 1.4.7. Plut. *Mor.* 250 D and F refer to the tradition that Cloelia stole the horse, but he does not subscribe to it. Sen. *ad Marc. de Consol.* 16.2 says she was given a horse, but does not say by whom. For the bronze equestrian statue of Cloelia, see later.

[48] Livy, 2.13.11; Sen. *ad Marc. de Consol.* 16.3 interprets the statue along similar lines: it testifies to Roman courage in *escaping* an enemy.

the statue, but he ultimately believed that it commemorated Porsenna's friendship, in reference to his decision to give Cloelia a horse for Rome's integrity in returning so brave a girl.[49] The bronze image itself was obviously fixed, but its meaning as an icon was fluid and ever changing; Cloelia was able to be appropriated and deployed according to any historian's plan. At times, the guest identity of hostage-taking could be recorded and emphasized, while at others it could be denied.

In addition to the discrepancies in the stories of Bithys and Cloelia, one further example of competing claims demonstrates the extent to which a definition of the hostage – collateral or guest – affects our understanding of critical episodes of Roman foreign policy. There are conflicting and obscure reports about Augustus's first encounter with a Parthian hostage as well. The surrender of four princes by Phraates IV in 10/9 BCE is famous and has received much attention in modern scholarship. Less well known is the detention of an older sibling of these four – an unnamed son of Phraates IV who was in Augustus's possession in the mid-twenties BCE. The two accounts – one in Justin's epitome of Pompeius Trogus and the other in Cassius Dio – differ in several details, but what is agreed between them is that a Parthian nobleman, Tiridates, fled Parthia and sought refuge with the emperor after Phraates IV had returned from exile to claim his throne.[50] According to Justin, the event occurred in 25 BCE, when Augustus was in Spain. He says that Tiridates arrived with a large retinue of political allies and, in exchange for asylum, offered Augustus both his assistance in leading a campaign against Parthia and possession of a son of Phraates, whom he had kidnapped before his escape. Phraates then sent an embassy to Augustus, either still in Spain or in Rome, to demand the return of "his slave Tiridates" and his hostage son.[51] In an effort to delay choosing sides in the Parthian civil war, as Justin tells it, Augustus sent back the child but decided to maintain Tiridates among the Romans in an opulent lifestyle.

---

[49] Plut. *Publicola,* 19.5 and *Mor.* 250F. Plin. *HN* 34.28–29 does not comment on the statue's purpose. He also says that Annius Fetialis said that an equestrian statue of Valeria similarly stood next to the Temple of Jupiter Stator. Dion. Hal. *Ant. Rom.* 5.35.2 mentions a statue but does not say specifically that it was equestrian.

[50] Just. *Epit.* 42.5.6–9; Cass. Dio, 51.18.2–3 and 53.33.1–2.

[51] Just. *Epit.* 42.5.7: *servum suum Tiridaten.*

Dio's story is different. In his version, Tiridates fled to Augustus twice, first when he was in Syria in 30 BCE (still Octavian at that point), and again around 23 BCE in Rome. In neither case had Tiridates kidnapped a son of Phraates; instead, Dio says that in 30 BCE Phraates's son passed from Tiridates's care into Octavian's, at which point he became a formal hostage (ἐν ὁμηρείᾳ) in Rome; the receipt of the hostage is described as an "act of kindness" directed at Phraates.[52] Some time around 23 BCE, then, Tiridates appealed to Rome for a second time. The senate referred both Tiridates and Phraates's envoys to Augustus, who decided to continue holding Tiridates, but to return Phraates's son with the result that Parthia restored the captives and standards taken from Crassus and Antony.[53]

There is an obvious discrepancy between Justin's hostage, who was unwillingly kidnapped, and Dio's hostage, whose submission was received as a benefaction for Phraates. The comment in the *Res Gestae* that Tiridates had come "as a suppliant" (*supplices*) to Augustus to ask for his support confirms the Romans' role in mediating the dispute but lacks any details concerning the hostage.[54] Both Justin and Dio say that Augustus returned Phraates's son to him, but his motivation in doing so is contested as a result of the different possible understandings of the initial detention. Justin's version is a story of involuntary creditor-collateral, where it is implied that Phraates's son was in jeopardy. As we have seen, if this is the case, the act of returning the hostage is a sign of goodwill, an act of diplomacy that reveals, or forges, close ties between the parties involved. Dio's version, by contrast, is one of

[52] Cass. Dio, 51.18.3: ἐν εὐεργεσίας μέρει. Sherwin-White 1984, 323, note 1 points out that the language of kidnapping is missing from Dio's version.
[53] Translating "ἐπὶ τῷ" as "with the result that" differs from the Loeb's "on the condition that," which implies a contractual arrangement that would seem odd given the three-year lag before the retrieval of the standards. Cf. Ziegler 1964, 47.
[54] *Mon. Anc.* 32.1. The other of the *supplices* mentioned in this passage is an unidentifiable Phraates, son of Phraates IV. Tarn 1932, 831; Oltramare 1938, 129; Karras-Klopproth 1988, 137 and Sullivan 1990, 468, note 134 suggest that he is the kidnapped son (Oltramare argues that Augustus received him as a hostage but was pretending in the *Res Gestae* that he was a refugee), but that is unlikely, since the *Res Gestae* says that he came after (*postea*) Tiridates, as pointed out by Timpe 1975, 157. Of little help are two references to the conflict in Horace's poetry. *Odes* 1.26.5 has Tiridates on the throne, while *Odes* 2.2.17 refers to the reinstatement of Phraates, but neither can be securely dated: Nisbet and Hubbard 1978, 47; West 1995, 120; in spite of Oltramare 1938, 124–127.

host-guest, where the hostage prince betokens friendship rather than staves off resistance. In this scenario, the return of the hostage should signal a breakdown in the alliance. It is an important conundrum to resolve, as both of our sources attribute Augustus's earliest dealings with Phraates as having an influence on the later, more momentous settlement of 20 BCE, when the Parthians returned the lost standards.

Numismatic evidence may help somewhat: Tiridates and Phraates were both minting coins simultaneously from early 26 to at least May of 25 BCE, suggesting that the two were engaged in a civil war; one of Tiridates's epithets on his coins, ΦΙΛΟΡΩΜΑΙΟ, shows that he at least advertised his Roman connections.[55] Justin's version does not seem to fit with this epithet: he says that Tiridates came to Rome for military support in 25, yet never received it and was kept, presumably, among the Romans thereafter.[56] In Dio's account, Tiridates's appeals to Rome occurred first in 30 and then again in 23 BCE. With the coins in mind, one might interpret Dio as follows: Augustus took over the hostage in 30 as a favor to Phraates, agreeing not to help Tiridates, but when Tiridates resurfaced in the East a short time later, at least claiming Rome's support, and was again forced to flee, the emperor gave back that which had marked the earlier agreement, namely Phraates's son. It seems likely, then, that Justin, who was working from the larger history of Pompeius Trogus, invented the kidnapping of 25 BCE to explain Augustus's possession of a hostage at that time, which may have been omitted by Trogus or neglected by the epitimator.[57] Either way, the flexibility of the figure of the hostage is what is important for this

---

[55] On the coins, see McDowell 1935, 185 and 222. Wroth 1903, 135 and Timpe 1975, 156–157 point out that another epithet, ΑΥΤΟΚΡΑΤΟ, is meant to draw a link between Tiridates and the Hellenistic Seleucids.

[56] The suggestions of Sherwin-White 1984, 322 that Tiridates made the claim without "material Roman support" reconciles this discrepancy.

[57] Develin 1994, 5–6 discusses Justin's tendency to diverge from Trogus. Alonso-Nuñez 1987, 60–61 has suggested that his entire section on Parthian relations from 30 to 10 BCE has been shortened at the expense of the chronology of Trogus's account. However, note Tarn 1932, 832 who accepts Justin's account, because a flight from Syria to Spain is simply stranger than fiction.
   I cannot pretend to have resolved the controversy surrounding the facts of the first Parthian hostage, which is not as pressing here as the representation of his detention anyway. Timpe 1975, 155 observed that no two scholarly opinions on the matter agree in every detail. Tarn 1932, 834 suggests Augustus had backed both Tiridates and the mysterious son as co-rulers, dismissing the story of the kidnapping (cf. Sullivan 1990,

study: the status and experience of a hostage could be manipulated by different historians to channel different interpretations of the past. With Justin, the return of the hostage freed Phraates from a situation of blackmail and constituted an alliance between Augustus and Parthia (partially, given Rome's simultaneous sheltering of Tiridates); the standards were returned only after Augustus shifted policy and intimidated Phraates with troop movements in the East.[58] With Dio, the emphasis is on a host-guest paradigm – a friendly possession of a hostage – whose deterioration stemmed from Rome's support of Tiridates; it was then the release of the hostage that led to Phraates's fear. The true sequence of events may never be recovered, but for our purposes it is sufficient to observe that the critical Roman relations with the East could not be understood *in antiquity* without considering the first Parthian hostage, who was in the shadows even then as he is now.

THE CULTURE OF HOSPITALITY

Descriptions of the living conditions of hostages suggest that the Romans expected hostages to be well cared for, even coddled, in their internment. Hostages had a special status from the moment they came into Roman possession: according to Hyginus's treatise on the layout of the basic Roman camp, they were housed in the same place as the ambassadors of the enemy, at the inner *praetorium*.[59] As for their accommodations once they arrived in Rome, we have a handful of famous references. According to Livy, hostages from Thurii and Tarentum lived in the so-called *Atrium Libertatis* during the Second Punic War.[60] The name, House of Freedom, is hardly appropriate

---

318). Debevoise 1938, 136 believes Dio's second story in Book 53 actually refers to the same event of 30 BCE, told in Book 51, and so there was no second flight of Tiridates in 23. Oltramare 1938, 131 interprets the return of the son (in Dio) as evidence for Augustus's prudent diplomacy and skill in winning back the standards, but Ziegler 1964, 47 denies that the evidence substantiates a link between the Tiridates matter and the standards. Nedergaard 1988, 105 simply omits Dio's later reference to the hostage and its impact on the retrieval of the standards. Timpe 1975, 166–167 suggests Augustus's handling of the affair played a role in his receiving the *tribunicia potestas*.

[58] Just. *Epit.* 42.5.10–11.
[59] Hyginus, *De munitione castrorum* 18.
[60] Livy, 25.7.12. cf. Purcell 1993.

if one were to hew to the aggressive or coercive interpretation of hostage-taking.[61] The location of the building is controversial, but it seems that it stood on the eastern slope of the Capitoline Hill. The reference to the Thurian and Tarentine hostages is the earliest mention of it, but it probably began life in the Struggle of the Orders between plebeians and patricians: it was mainly known as an archive for laws and other documents pertaining to the censors. Nevertheless, its connection with resident non-Romans in the city continued (at least according to our patchy sources): it was completely rebuilt by Gaius Asinius Pollio in 40 BCE, at which point a library was included in its walls; it is the same Pollio who housed the sons of Herod the Great, Aristobulus and Alexander, who were sent to Rome for, among other things, an education.[62] Moreover, German soldiers stayed at the *Atrium Libertatis* in the last days of Galba's reign in 69 CE (though not as formal hostages).[63] The building was later replaced in grandiose fashion by the Basilica Ulpia of Trajan's forum, whose library apparently continued to be called the *Atrium Libertatis*.[64]

Varro mentions briefly that the Carthaginian hostages who came to Rome after the Second Punic War drew enough attention to inspire a new name for the district on the Esquiline where they lived, the *Vicus Africus*.[65] Nothing else is known about their living conditions, although it has been suggested that an offering to "*Dea Caelestis*" from the Esquiline may refer to a Romanized version of Tanit, an important Punic goddess, and thus a remnant of the Carthaginian

[61] Elbern 1990, 113. It should be admitted, however, that *libertas* in the Roman sense need not have any association with international relations.

[62] Pliny, *HN* 35.10; Suet. *Aug.* 29.5. On Herod's sons, see Joseph. *AJ* 16.6 and Chapter 5.

[63] Tac. *Hist.* 1.31.

[64] The preceding discussion has preferred the arguments of Coarelli 2000 and the *LTUR* (Coarelli) against those of Purcell 1993, who associated the *Atrium Libertatis* with what topographers have long misleadingly called the "*Tabularium*." Briefly, the most convincing piece of evidence seems to be the fragment of the *Forma Urbis* that labels the eastern apse of the Basilica Ulpia in Trajan's forum (known to have been a library) with "*Libertatis*"; presumably the diagram of the western apse, now missing, read "*Atrium*" (cf. Clarke 2003, 39). Moreover, the claim of Purcell 1993, 143 that the detention of hostages (and other prisoners) in the Atrium meant that it must have been like a "fortress" – and therefore to be associated with the massive "*Tabularium*" – is not in keeping with what we know about the freedoms of many hostages in the city.

[65] Varro, *Ling.* 5.159.

presence there.[66] Long after the Punic detentions, the porticus of Livia, a lavish enclosed garden and gallery, was built nearby.

Asconius gives us the oft-cited, oblique reference to an expensive house on the Palatine that was built from public funds for Antiochus IV of the Seleucids and later used by the wealthy satirist Lucilius.[67] It was located on the Palatine Hill, the elite residential district of the Roman Republic. We do not know where Antiochus's replacement as a hostage, Demetrius Soter, lived, but Polybius tells us that he was allowed to join Roman hunting parties, to attend banquets, and to travel unaccompanied around the environs and periphery of Rome.[68] Diodorus Siculus offers an anecdote that Demetrius, when a hostage, met his cousin Ptolemy IV Philometor, who was coming to Rome on a diplomatic mission from Egypt to plead for assistance against his brother, Physcon, who had usurped his throne.[69] Ptolemy was intentionally dressed down in order to convey an image of desperation before the senate, and Demetrius, not privy to the details of the plan, offered some of his own clothes that were more fitting for a royal personage, thus demonstrating his relative opulence.

In more cases, we see hostages dispersed to towns surrounding Rome, although even these were expected to provide a comfortable setting, as we have seen with the Carthaginian hostages who were allowed to move from Norba in Latium, southeast of Rome, to the nearby towns of Signia and Ferentinum, in order to improve their living conditions.[70] In the remaining examples, we know little more than names and locations of towns. The hostages from the Penestae and Parthini, who were given over to the Romans without provocation as a sign of alliance before the war with Perseus, were kept in Apollonia and Dyrrachium, respectively, on the Illyrian coast.[71] Bithys, the son

---

[66] *LTUR* (Palombi).

[67] Asc. *Pis.* 13.16–17. On the house, see Marshall 1985, 105–106; Gruen 1992, 279.

[68] Polyb. 31.11–15.

[69] Diod. Sic. 31.18.1.

[70] Livy, 32.2.4. They also are said to have been kept at Setia (Livy, 32.26.5) and at Fregellae (Nep. *Hann.* 7.2), still in central Latium, and at Cerceii (Livy, 32.26.5), on Latium's coast. All of these are plotted on map 44 in the Barrington Atlas (Talbert 2000). Cerceii is also where Demetrius said he was headed when he was plotting his escape (Polyb. 31.14.2); it is also where Lepidus was detained after his fall from the Second Triumvirate.

[71] Livy, 43.21.3.

of Cotys, who had moved to Italy from the hostageship of Perseus, was housed along with other hostages at Carseoli just east of Rome, half way to Alba Fucens and just north of the Carthaginian hostages.[72] Polybius says that the "thousand Achaeans" were scattered to other towns outside Rome although he stayed in the city, presumably at the household of Aemilius Paullus.[73] The obscurity of most of these towns and the anonymity of their hostages would lead one to think that, in practice, not all hostages would have had a luxurious, or even eventful, stay in captivity. But whenever the reporting of hostage accommodations is specific and detailed, the overwhelming tendency on the part of our sources is to emphasize their collocation with powerful, wealthy Romans. The aura surrounding hostageship, regardless of the reality, could easily be one of privilege.

The allegation by a Roman source of another people's barbarism is often predicated on their denial of the ideal version of hostage justice. The mistreatment of hostages, like the mistreatment of guests, was a cause for shame for the civilized and an expected characteristic of the barbaric.[74] In Polybius, Scipio's generous treatment of hostages in Spain in 209 BCE during the Second Punic War – he gave presents to the children and protected the women from rape – is sharply contrasted with their former plight under Carthaginian control, which was reported to him by Indibilis, a Spanish chieftain:

When Indibilis finished his speech, Scipio replied that he believed his accusations and that he knew well of the hubris of the Carthaginians from their brutality against other Iberians and against the wives and daughters of Indibilis and his friends, whom he recently found not holding the rank of hostages, but of prisoners and slaves (οὐχ ὁμήρων ἐχούσας διάθεσιν, ἀλλ' αἰχμαλώτων καὶ δούλων). He said that he guarded them with a loyalty that they, their fathers,

---

[72] Livy, 45.42.5, 12.
[73] Polyb. 31.23.5. In terms of detainees who resided in the city with prominent Romans, it is interesting to consider also the case of Tigranes, a son of a king of the same name who was installed in Armenia by Pompey: he was living with the praetor, Lucius Flavius, when Publius Clodius Pulcher stole him away (Cass. Dio, 38.30.1–2). Other details of the story are at Cic. *Dom.* 66; *Mil.* 18 and 37; and Plut. *Pomp.* 48.6. Tatum 1999, 170 refers to him as a hostage, although he is universally called a prisoner in our sources: Cicero, *hostem captivum* (*Dom.* 66); Plutarch, αἰχμάλωτον; Cass. Dio, ἐν δεσμοῖς.
[74] Compare Phillipson 1911, 406 who believed the Romans actually *were* more civilized than non-Roman communities by virtue of their hostage-taking practices.

could not match. After expressing their agreement, honoring him, and saluting him as king, they applauded him, and Scipio humbly told them to take courage, for they would enjoy all the generosity of the Romans.[75]

Polybius's explicit placement of hostages at the other end of a spectrum from prisoners and slaves, which is how Carthage had treated them, underscores their social importance, and the experience of the hostage was understood as a primary source for an international reputation; Polybius goes on to say that the Carthaginians suffered materially by comparison with Rome because of their hostage policies, as the Iberians joined the war against Hasdrubal on that account. The same kind of enhancement of Roman prestige through a comparative analysis of hostage policies comes in Caesar's commentaries. The Aduatuci are barbaric in their policy of holding the son and nephew of Ambiorix "in slavery and bondage" when Ambiorix had given them as hostages and thus expected better.[76] Caesar recognized this as a sacrilege and, like Polybius's Scipio, came to the rescue. Moreover, in Livy the consul Flamininus invoked the memory of a mass execution of hostage boys by the Spartan tyrant Nabis, addressing him in a reproving and sarcastic tone.[77] The slaughter of the hostages was the most prominent entry in a list of *facinora,* or moral crimes, perpetrated by Nabis and was grounds for Sparta's dismissal from Roman allies. After the ensuing war between Nabis and Rome, Livy then sets up a telling contrast: whereas Nabis is immoral in his treatment of hostages, Flamininus holds them in a dignified way, in keeping with proper diplomatic traditions.[78] The message to the reader in these stories is that the abuse of hostages is unconscionable to the Romans, yet typical for others.

Some Roman versions of Greek myths demonstrate a collective anxiety about the experience of hostages. Early in Ovid's *Metamorphoses,* Jupiter addresses an assembly of the gods in order to discuss the

---

[75] Polyb. 10.38.1–3. Cf. Livy, 26.49.4: the hostages were treated "as if they were the children of allies" (*ac si sociorum liberi essent*). Cf. Diod. Sic. 26.21; App. *Hisp.* 23.

[76] Caes. *BGall.* 5.27: *in servitute et catenis.* Moscovich 1979–1980, 127 notes that the discrepancy between Roman and non-Roman behavior may be attributed to a "stark editiorial contrast" on Caesar's part.

[77] Livy, 34.32.11–12. Cf. 34.27.7–8, where Livy describes the circumstances under which the boys were detained by Nabis.

[78] Livy, 34.52.9 and 37.25.12. cf. Polyb. 21.3.3–4 and 21.11.9–10.

depravity of the human race and the need to take action to correct them.[79] To illustrate his point, he reports on a mission that he undertook to investigate the human race: disguised as a mortal, he wandered throughout Greece and then revealed himself as a god to the people of Arcadia. King Lycaon, not believing the stranger's divinity, decided to test him by killing a hostage from the Molossians and then serving him to Jupiter in a banquet.[80] This version is unique to Ovid; in other accounts, Lycaon kills either his own son, his grandson, or an unidentified child (not a hostage).[81] Outraged, Ovid's Jupiter turned Lycaon into a wolf and decided, based on this sole transgression, to flood the earth and eradicate all mortals.[82] It is unmistakable that Ovid's Jupiter, seated on a throne and addressing the assembled gods, is meant to resonate with the newly enthroned and senate-friendly image of the *princeps*, Augustus: the gods who attend Jupiter's speech are said to gather in what the poet calls "the Palatine in the sky," and Jupiter's reaction to their approval is specifically likened to Augustus's gratitude for the support of the Roman people in the civil war against Caesar's assassins.[83] The conflation of Jupiter and Augustus makes it all the more significant that Ovid has created a new story whose focus is on the propriety of hostage-taking, which was a prevalent device of diplomacy during Augustus's reign. Ovid is making an implicit comment on the nature and rectitude of Roman foreign policy with respect

[79] Ov. *Met.* 1.164–252.
[80] Ov. *Met.* 1.226–227.
[81] Son: Nonnos, *Dion.* 18.20–24. See also Arn. *Adv. Nat.* 4.24 and Clem. Al. *Protr.* 2.36. Grandson: Hyg. *Poet. Astr.* 2.4; Eratosth. [*Cat.*] 8. Other child: Apollod. *Bibl.* 3.8; Stat. *Theb.*, 11.128; Paus. 8.2.3 (Arcadia). In Hyg. *Fab.* 176 and Nic. Dam. fr. 43, Lycaon's sons kill the boy and serve it to Zeus. See Grimal 1963. Anderson 1997, 174 notes the uniqueness of the hostage submission and the gravity of the concomitant notions of hospitality.
[82] Some say that Zeus blasted Lycaon with a thunderbolt instead: Apollod. *Bibl.* 3.8; Hyg. *Fab.* 176. Ovid does not say explicitly that Jupiter was responsible for the metamorphosis; Wheeler 1999, 180 suggests the silence makes the heinousness of the crime and the appropriateness of the penalty "more credible."
[83] Ov. *Met.* 1.176 (*Palatia caeli*) and 1.200–207. Solodow 1988, 85 emphasizes the sycophantic conduct of the gods/senators, whereas Wheeler 1999, 181 suggests that the emphasis on Lycaon's disbelief warns the audience of the poem against the disbelief of Augustan authority. For readings of the episode as subversive to Augustus: Mueller 1987, 277–281; Anderson 1989; and Segal 2001–2002, 85 (with Lycaon's crime as a "violation of the sanctity of guests").

to its hostages: just as Jupiter honors and protects the obligations of hostage-taking, so does Augustus. Ovid's Lycaon, an obvious villain, thus falls into the same category as Polybius's Carthaginians, Caesar's Gauls, Livy's Nabis, or any other Roman enemy of the moment.

One could likewise compare Seneca's treatment of Atreus's crime in his tragedy, *Thyestes*. Thyestes had seduced his brother Atreus's wife, and so was banished (details that are not in the play).[84] Yet Atreus is determined to punish him further, feigning clemency in order to draw Thyestes into a trap. In a twist on the Greek myth, Seneca has Atreus at first accept the sons of Thyestes as hostages as a way of redressing their past disputes.[85] The pronounced domesticity of the scene sets the stage for the tragic denouement, which would have been well known to the Roman audience. Atreus's kindess toward Thyestes once the hostages had been accepted is, of course, an act, and Atreus famously murders the boys and feeds them to their father, just as Lycaon tried to do with Jupiter. In other versions of the story, Atreus manages to abduct and murder the boys rather than receive them as hostages by Thyestes.[86] But Seneca has intensified the atrocity by adding the violation of a hostage-based trust to the crime of cannibalism. The crime had wide repercussions: just as Lycaon's sin leads to the drowning of most of the human race, Atreus's results in the curse by which his household is turned upside down: father kills daughter (Agamemnon and Iphigenia); wife kills husband (Clytemnestra and Agamemnon); son kills mother (Orestes and Clytemnestra). Order in both religion and family life, an important concept in Roman thought, is articulated in part in these stories through proper respect for hostages' dignity.

Observing the generous treatment of hostages and the distinction made in the sources between them and regular prisoners and between the civilized and the barbaric, some scholars have argued that hostages were formally sacrosanct, protected from harm and deserving of respect through partly religious, partly legal strictures.[87] Our

---

[84] For the mythography of Thyestes, see Grimal 1963.

[85] Sen. *Thyestes*, 519.

[86] Apollod. *Epit.* 2.13; Hyg. *Fab.* 88; Paus. 2.18.1 (Corinth). See Grimal 1963.

[87] Lécrivain 1916, 130; Moscovich 1979–1980, 127; Elbern 1990, 109–110; Ndiaye 1995, 159.

sources, however, are by no means explicit on this score. The nearest case is in Dionysius of Halicarnassus: in describing how Tarquin ambushed Cloelia and the other hostages as they were being returned to Lars Porsenna (discussed earlier), he says that Tarquin violated the hostages' "sacred bodies" (ἱερά σώματα).[88] Some have also pointed to the story in Livy where Scipio (soon to be Africanus) orders his men to treat the hostage-women of Spain, whom he has commandeered from the Carthaginians, as if they were the wives and mothers "of guest-friends" (*hospitum*), which category certainly benefited from quasi-sacred status.[89] In the case of the former, Walker suggests that the truly sacred entity was the agreement which Porsenna swore to uphold and which Tarquin violated.[90] More important, one could note that both of these stories exist in multiple versions and in both cases, no author other than the one cited uses the specific vocabulary of the sacred: what we have are authors changing the terms (if only slightly) in pursuit of their arguments, whether it be to villainize Tarquin or to exalt Scipio. Moreover, none of the hundreds of other references to hostages implies that they held a sacred status. In some cases, of course, reviewed earlier, the hostages are well treated, but Walker points out that there are many others where they are not: if anything, the captor of the hostage was governed by expediency rather than by any "law of war," to which those who allege sacrosanctity must anachronistically allude.[91] In short, it is often the author's choice whether his written hostages will be sacrosanct or not.

---

[88] Dion. Hal. *Ant. Rom.* 5.34.1.
[89] Livy, 26.49.16; the reference to guest-friendship is not present at Polyb. 10.18.
[90] Walker 1980, 15.
[91] Walker 1980, 16. Note Ndiaye 1995, 159: *le droit de guerre.* In Elbern 1990, 109–110, sacrosanctity did not apply to hostages who came as a result of *deditio,* but did to those who were part of a treaty; in the latter case, if the treaty was violated, rights to sacrosanctity were waived implicitly.

4

CONQUEROR-TROPHY

R umor, in Vergil, has a life of its own, and a terrifying one at that: in the *Aeneid, Fama* appears as a gruesome bird, whose feathers conceal thousands of eyeballs, which peer out at the world from under cover.[1] By the very act of flying, it grows larger and larger: as the metaphor implies, vision leads to stories that prompt further inquiries and a broader audience, with more sets of eyes, yielding additional stories, and so on. The participants in rumor-mongering, by definition, ever increase in number, resulting in the creation of new knowledge. Vergil's Rumor "grows as it goes."[2] The fact that Vergil makes Rumor into a monster and not something more pleasant highlights the Roman anxiety concerning the indomitable nature of one's reputation.[3] Prestige, a very rough translation of the Latin *auctoritas*, carried an inestimable weight in the Roman world: it could account for one's political power even more than a formal magistracy; it could enhance one's social standing in the form of a large base of clients; and it could give one economic clout beyond the level of his true personal wealth.[4] A public figure's image was thus carefully orchestrated for the

---

[1] Verg. *Aen.* 4.173–195.

[2] Verg. *Aen.* 4.175: *viresque adquirit eundo.*

[3] Néraudau 1993 argues that Vergil chose a horrific image in order to reflect the role of rumor in the civil war. Rutherfurd 1989 argues that the eyes belong not to the monster but to the people watching it. For the distinction between *fama* and *existimatio:* Yavetz 1974b.

[4] The single word, "prestige," of course, is not enough to encapsulate the complex meaning of *auctoritas*; a fuller discussion is at Galinsky 1996, 10–41. Zecchini 1996 discusses the derivation of the epithet "Augustus" from *auctoritas*, the significance of which, however, is downplayed in Lacey 1998. See also Luetcke 1968.

benefit of all those thousands of eyes on the streets, in the temples, behind the helmets, and gazing out from the senatehouse. With this in mind, one begins to understand the supreme value of the triumphal procession in Roman politics during which generals were honored as gods for the performance of their duty to Rome. It is hard to think of a more attention-getting entrance into the city than a triumph, as described in the Introduction to this book, and yet this is how most hostages would have had their first exposure to the Roman people, arriving at the apex of festivities, which in some cases lasted for several days.[5] In such a way, hostages were closely associated with the individuals who brought them there. As they were introduced in the context of military achievement, they represented that aspect of the hostage-taker's career even long after the triumph had ended and the booty dispersed. They were proof, especially vivid, of the force of the victor's accomplishment: unlike a pile of gold, hostages could walk, talk, and express emotion. The possessor of the hostage stood much to gain from the detention of this type of foreigner.

The previous two chapters have argued that when hostages marched through Rome in a triumphal procession or passed through the streets as temporary residents, they helped Romans to think about the world beyond their city. We have seen how a Roman would understand, through the hostage, the obligations of the defeated in virtual contracts of international relations; we have also seen how the possession of the hostage articulated Rome's own honorable place in an international society. This chapter focuses on the role of the hostage in shaping the *individual* character of the general or emperor responsible for the hostage's internment. Specifically, we see how the hostage determined one's military reputation, which in turn translated into political influence. In short, this chapter examines a simple syllogism: if power comes

---

[5] Elbern 1990, 102–103 and Scardigli 1994, 126–127 discuss the importance of hostages in a triumph. It is an understatement to say that triumphs were contentious in Republican politics. On the availability of the rite to praetors, see Richardson 1975 and Brennan 1994, and on the political motivations for triumphs on the Alban Mount, see Brennan 1996. Flory 1988, 498–499 notes that the lavishness of Pompey's triple triumph necessarily triggered a response from Caesar, and Gurval 1995, 22 discusses the competitive nature of the pageantry. For Nero's manipulation of the triumph to recall Augustan associations, see Miller 2000, 415–419. The setting up of any trophy was critical in politics: Rawson 1990, 159–162.

from victory, and if victory comes from hostages, then in some cases it makes sense to see that power could be derived directly from hostages, skipping the "step" of victory. The associations of hostage-taking had the effect of offering a shorter path to power. The hostage became a prize in and of himself; Romans are said to brag about them, lie about them, and compete ferociously for them.

VICTORY AND HOSTAGES

For Roman writers, hostages were an integral part of triumphal processions. They offered something unique to the overall presentation and are therefore often singled out. Although hostages and royal prisoners of war probably marched in the same position in the parade, just in front of the chariot carrying the *triumphator,* their roles were clearly differentiated in our sources. We have already seen how Livy isolates the hostages in his account of Flamininus's triumph over Macedon: he draws attention to the presence of Demetrius and Armenes over and above the prisoners of war whom they accompanied.[6] Demetrius's march, in Livy, comes in sharp contrast to that of his older brother, Perseus, who was a prisoner of war after the Battle of Pydna nearly thirty years later and whose plight is repeated over and over in Livy's record of the triumph of Aemilius Paullus.[7] Similarly Appian and Plutarch, in their accounts of Pompey's triple triumph, make an effort to distinguish between prisoners of war on the one hand and hostages on the other within the crowd of 324 detained satraps, princesses, royal children, and defeated generals: the prisoners included the wife, son, daughter-in-law, and granddaughter of Tigranes; the sister and five children of Mithridates; the leaders of the Mediterranean pirates; Aristobulus, the king of the Jews; and groups of Scythian women, while the hostages included groups from Asian Iberia, Albania, and Commagene.[8] The distinction communicates an added dimension to Pompey's accomplishment: the group of detainees is divisible and

---

[6] Livy, 34.52.9.

[7] Livy, 45.35.1; 45.39.1; 45.40.6; 45.41.10–11; 45.42.4. Cf. Plut. *Aem.* 37. Cf. Reiter 1988, 142.

[8] App. *Mith.* 117; Plut. *Pomp.* 45.4. App. *Mith.* 103 says that Pompey took hostages simultaneously from Oroezes of Albania, Artoces of Iberia, and from an Amazonian race;

complex, and Pompey's work abroad is seen as all the more varied, flexible, and strategic.

Livy manipulates the fact of hostages and their visual role in triumphs to tell the story of the fall and rise of Roman fortunes in the Battle of the Caudine Forks in 321 BCE and its aftermath. When Livy attempts to describe the nature of the defeated Romans, he does so by setting up a kind of anti-triumph, a photograph's negative of a proper triumphal procession, as the soldiers in his account "imagined to themselves . . . the return to their *patria* and to their parents, where often they themselves and their ancestors had returned in triumph."[9] Hostages were surrendered here, whereas they ought to have been detained, and the soldiers' progression thence continues.[10] Whereas *triumphatores* typically wore a special cloak, the generals were stripped by the Samnites; whereas victorious armies usually marched in pride through the city, the soldiers passed beneath the yoke unarmed and half-naked; whereas convention had it that the Romans gazed upon the defeated, here they were taken in by "enemy eyes."[11] According to the early historian Claudius Quadrigarius, the news of the hostages detained by the Samnites caused their relatives to run wailing through the streets.[12] For Livy, who had access to this account, the *loss* of hostages is as important visually in a procession of the defeated as their inclusion is in a better outcome.[13] Of course, Livy wrote this narrative with full knowledge of the Roman recovery: the defeat is later corrected by a reversal of fortunes where the rescue of the hostages is highlighted over and above the humiliation of the Samnites:

Seven thousand men were sent under the yoke, and a huge amount of booty was captured in Luceria, with all the standards and weaponry which had been lost at Caudium retrieved, and what was more important in all of their

Plutarch demotes the Amazons ("Scythian women") to prisoners and adds the hostages from Commagene.
[9] Livy, 9.5.8–9. Crawford 1973 and Horsfall 1982 discuss the fictive qualities in Livy's account of the Samnite Wars and settlement.
[10] Livy, 9.5.11–9.6.3.
[11] Livy, 9.6.3: *per hostium oculos.*
[12] Quoted in Gell. *NA* 2.19.8.
[13] On Livy's use of Claudius Quadrigarius and the latter's occasional exaggerations, see Walsh 1961, 120–121.

rejoicing (*quod omnia superabat gaudia*), the *equites*, whom the Samnites had stationed to guard Luceria as guarantees of peace, were recovered.[14]

The retrieval of hostages, to Livy, constituted the climax of the affair; the sight of Romans *not* in captivity as hostages was the visual reassertion of Rome's hegemony over southern Italy.

A victory, no matter how absolute in terms of subduing the enemy, could go unacknowledged, or somehow be downplayed, if no hostages were taken. According to Livy, Quintus Minucius Rufus was denied a triumph in 197 BCE for his campaigns against the Ligurians because he did not have hostages to back up the claim that he had conquered a number of towns.[15] Livy says that without approval from the senate Minucius was forced to celebrate a private triumph on the Alban Mount in Latium.[16] Likewise, Dio shows disdain for Mark Antony's negotiations with Antiochus of Commagene in 38 BCE based on the paltry number and nature of his hostages; the fact that he had received only two, low-ranking ones proved, to Dio at least, that nothing of value had come from the campaign.[17] Without a significant crowd of hostages, a victory could be brought into question. Roman generals thus needed them for more than just the guarantee of a settlement: they reflected back on the general's dignity and were indispensable evidence of victory.

In some episodes, our sources suggest that the possession of foreign hostages was nearly a precondition for a triumph: if a general's accomplishment was in doubt in the senate, then the revelation of his hostages, among other trappings of victory, could confirm his right to public esteem. For example, Livy tells the story of Publius Cornelius Scipio Nasica, who asked the senate for a triumph after defeating the Gallic tribe of the Boii in 191 BCE, having taken half of their land and killed half of their men.[18] A tribune, Publius Sempronius Blaesus,

---

[14] Livy, 9.15.7–8.

[15] Livy, 33.22.9. The absence of hostages (if that is what is meant here by "*sine ullo pignore*") was cited by the opposition as a clue that the *deditiones* were false (*falsas*). On the question of the "criteria" for triumphs in this period, see Richardson 1975, 60–62. See also Gruen 1995, 63.

[16] On the Alban triumph as an act of protest, see Brennan 1996, 324–325.

[17] Dio, 49.22.2.

[18] Livy, 36.39.3 and 36.40.5.

had intervened to argue that Nasica was not worthy of a triumph until he also had defeated the Ligurians, who were the Boii's partners in warfare and who would surely repair the setbacks that Nasica had inflicted if left unchecked. In response, we are told, Nasica pointed to his Boan hostages which he had taken "as a guarantee of future peace."[19] Nasica's rebuttal continues in Livy as he recounts the "much greater" matter (*illud multo maius*) – his feats in battle and the large number of enemy casualties. The hostages were thus only one part of Nasica's resumé, but it would be reasonable to speculate that they were present, at the very meeting at the Temple of Bellona where Nasica had convened the senate. Nasica naturally would have wanted to avoid the criticisms that had been leveled against Minucius, as seen earlier. In the end, Blaesus was compelled to withdraw his veto, and Nasica was awarded the triumph.[20]

The display of hostages in the quest for prestige could have a foreign audience as well as a domestic one. Livy tells the story of a diplomatic conference between Perseus and the Roman legate Marcius Philippus in the Third Macedonian War. Perseus's goal in the negotiations was to avoid an outright war:

As they stood facing each other, the river flowing between them, a minor delay transpired in the exchange of messages about who should cross to the other side. Some thought that some privilege was owed to Perseus's royal dignity, others thought the right belonged to the name of the Roman people, especially because Perseus had asked for the meeting. Marcius also convinced those who were delaying with a joke: he said, "Perseus ought to cross over to him as a younger man approaches an elder or as a son to his father" – for his cognomen was Philip. The king was easily persuaded. Then there was more indecision about how many should cross. The king thought it was fair to cross with his entire entourage; the envoys, however, ordered him to come over with just three, or if he was going to bring across so great a line, then to give hostages that there would be no treachery in the meeting. Perseus assigned Hippias and Pantauchus, the best of his friends, to be hostages; he had already sent them as ambassadors. But these hostages were not sought by the Romans as a security of trust so much as to prove to the allies that the king

---

[19] Livy, 36.40.3: *pacis futurae pignus*. The reference to the hostages punctuates (Livy's) Nasica's summary of the Boan campaign and victory.

[20] Livy, 36.40.10. cf. Gruen 1995, 63.

and his legates did not arrive from the same level of dignity (*nequaquam ex dignitate pari*). The greeting was not at all hostile, but was kind and hospitable and when seats were brought out, they sat down together.[21]

Livy here sees the Roman demand for hostages as having a symbolic function entirely separate from the assurance of a safe meeting.[22] Philippus's call for hostages constituted a bald show of power, orchestrated, so Livy tells us, to impress the large crowds in attendance on either side.

HOSTAGES IN SELF-REPRESENTATION

The power of the images of hostages can be inferred from the few texts from Roman antiquity in which individuals refer to themselves. So far, we have seen examples of writers who describe the hostage-taking activities of others, but we gain a better sense of the triumphant quality of the practice from those who are boasting for their own gain or to propagate their own memory. Three inscriptions and two sets of letters (of a sort) demonstrate that in the ongoing competition for prestige, the contribution that a group of hostages could make was substantial.

That the first epitaph here cited is arguably the second oldest extant verse inscription in Latin points out the antiquity as well as the significance of hostage-taking in an aristocratic military career. It comes from the tomb of the Scipios on the Appian Way, and it honors Lucius Cornelius Scipio Barbatus, a consul for 298 BCE and censor for, perhaps, 280:

Lucius Cornelius Scipio Barbatus, born to Gnaeus, his father, was a brave and wise man whose appearance was equal to his courage. A consul, censor, and aedile among you, he seized Taurasia/Cisauna from Samnium, conquered all Lucania, and detained hostages.[23]

---

[21] Livy, 42.39.4–7.

[22] Cf. Braund 1996a, who discusses the symbolism of rivers as boundaries between two realms in Roman historiography. Note also that *Lucius* Marcius Philippus, consul in 56 BCE, was Octavian's stepfather (Suet. *Aug.* 8); perhaps the story in Livy redounded to the credit of the *princeps*.

[23] Dessau, 1: *Lucius Cornelius Scipio Barbatus Gnaivod patre / prognatus, fortis vir sapiensque, quoius forma virtutei parisuma / fuit, consol censor aedilis quei fuit apud vos Taurasia Cisauna /*

The war with the Lucanians mentioned here is a mystery that raises questions about the mutability of hostage-taking in the quest for *auctoritas*. It is uncertain to which war with Lucania the inscription refers.[24] One possibility is that the inscription commemorates the same event as recorded by Livy and Dionysius of Halicarnassus: as we have seen in Chapter 3, the historians record that the Lucanians came to Rome in 298 BCE, when Barbatus was consul, to ask for help against the Samnites; they offered hostages to mark the alliance.[25] The fact of the hostages from Lucania would seem to bring all of these texts into line, except that there is a discrepancy between them: the verbs in the inscription – *cepit, subigit, abdoucit;* he seized, he subdues/subdued, he detains/detained – are at odds with the tone of the two historians who see the relationship more as one of host and guest.[26] Marcotte plausibly believed that the absence of any "degradation" in the literary accounts suggests that these were different hostages entirely, but one could also

Samnio cepit, subigit omne Loucanam opsidesque abdoucit. The translation of *Taurasia Cisauna / Samnio* is controversial: La Regina 1968, 176; Silvestri 1978, 174–179; Marcotte 1985, 727; Radke 1991, 73–75. The date of the inscription is also debated. Several scholars argue that it was carved long after the sarcophagus was made and long after not only Barbatus's death (c. 270), but also that of his son (c. 230), who was entombed nearby. The language of the son's epitaph seems more archaic and the shape of the letter G in the father's suggests it is later. Moreover, the erasure of a little more than one line of text on Barbatus's sarcophagus seems to be the remnant of an earlier epitaph, which our inscription replaced at a later date. Wölfflin 1890 believed the inscription was, in effect, commissioned by Scipio Africanus at the height of his prestige after Zama, around 200. His chronology (if not his identification of the very poets who wrote the verses) is followed by Frank 1921, 169; Coarelli 1973, 234; and van Sickle 1987, 43, note 9. Other scholars agree that the text is later than that of the son, but cannot pin it to 200 and allow that it may have come before that, in the last quarter of the third century BCE: La Regina 1968, 175; Silvestri 1978; Marcotte 1985, 724. These views are all vehemently contested by Wachter 1987, 301–342 and Radke 1991, who argue that the text was carved soon after Barbatus's death. Kruschwitz 1998, 282–283, although leaning toward this opinion, concludes that the available evidence is insufficient. Cf. *LTUR* (Zevi). What follows is based on Wölfflin's scenario; even if this should be somehow unambiguously refuted in the future, the larger point – that mention of the hostages helped to fashion the memory of the honorand – would still hold.

[24] Possibilities are reviewed by La Regina 1968, 177–187; Silvestri 1978, 170–171; Marcotte 1985, 728–731; Radke 1991, 75–76.

[25] Livy, 10.11.13; Dion. Hal. *Ant. Rom.* 17.1.2–3; 17.3.1.

[26] Radke 1991, 76 argues that *subigit* does not necessarily demand a military action, but the power differential between captor and donor is clear.

make the case that the inscription and the literary texts are using the fact of one hostage episode for different effects, playing on the ambiguity of hostages as either blackmail (the inscription) or guests (the prose historians), as discussed earlier in Chapter 3. What concerns us here, however, is that the epigraphic reference to the hostages comes in the context of underscoring one man's lifetime accomplishments. Just like the verbs of action, the hostages mentioned in the inscription are meant to inspire awe and reverence in the reader; Marcotte, although not believing that the inscription and the literary histories deal with the same event, did conclude that the epitaph sought to compensate Barbatus with extra glory after his co-consul, Gnaeus Fulvius Maximus Centumalus, had been the only one to celebrate a triumph for their consular year.[27]

When it is noted that although the sarcophagus dates to around 270 BCE, the original inscription was erased and the verses as we have them may have been carved well after the death of Scipio Barbatus, around 200 BCE, another aspect of the prestige-value of hostage-taking becomes apparent.[28] Around the time of carving, Scipio Africanus was active in overseas warfare and had dealt with hostages, famously, in both Spain and Carthage. In the generation before, Africanus's father and uncle, Gnaeus and Publius, had similarly acquired a reputation for the shrewd management of hostages, also in Spain. Moreover, Africanus and his younger brother, Lucius, were instrumental in winning the war against Antiochus III in 189, which also yielded significant hostages, especially Antiochus IV. As we have seen, Scipio Nasica was said to have argued effectively for a triumph over the Boii based, in part, on his possession of hostages in 191. The act of remembering one Scipio's hostages from a century earlier – Barbatus's from Lucania – would have reflected back and magnified the more recent feats of his descendants. Barbatus's sarcophagus was in the center of the family tomb, expertly and expensively carved from a single block of stone and uniquely decorated with architectural elements. His descendants,

[27] Marcotte 1985, 740–742, noting the *Fasti Triumphales*. Cf. La Regina 1968, 175. On the inscription as an indication of "the ideology of *nobilitas*," see Hölkeskamp 1993, 26–27. It may be that the poem on the stone was remembered from Barbatus's eulogy: van Sickle 1987, 44.
[28] See note 23, on the question of the date.

piling up an impressive record of hostage-taking themselves, may have highlighted anew the exploits of their oldest ancestor with the newer inscription. In short, a family's accomplishments in hostage-taking in the past could enhance similar success in the present, even if that past were a new creation, or new interpretation.[29] Right around the early second century BCE, the clan of the Scipios on the one hand and the idea of hostage-taking on the other were intersecting in multiple locations; both were powerfully associated with military conquest.

The second inscription to mention hostage-taking does so in a different context and describes the submission of the hostages with less martial tones. The *Res Gestae,* or *Accomplishments,* of Augustus was written in the first person and was set up outside the emperor's new mausoleum on the northern edge of the Campus Martius, as well as copied, translated into Greek, and distributed throughout the empire for public display.[30] In reviewing Roman affairs in the East and elsewhere under his regime, Augustus begins with a long list of foreign kings who bowed to him in search of some kind of assistance or other; the long names would have stood out to the Roman reader for their exotic qualities: Tiridates, Artavasdes, Artaxares, Dumno-bellaunus, and others.[31] He then mentions the sons and grandsons of Phraates IV, who were given to his care in 10/9 BCE:

Of the Parthians, Phraates son of Orodes sent all his sons and grandsons to Italy, not conquered in war, but seeking our friendship through his children as securities (*pignora*). Many other tribes experienced the good faith of the

[29] Cf. Brennan 1996, 322, discussing Gaius Papirius Maso's decision to hold a triumph on the Alban Mount in 231 on the same day, March 5, on which his most illustrious ancestor, Lucius Papirius Cursor, triumphed over the Samnites nearly a century before, in 324; it was a move to enhance his own glory for the present. For the competitive nature of politics at the time and the place of the Scipios therein, see, in general, Gruen 1995 and Cornell 1995, 359–360.

[30] Augustus had written a literary – that is to say, nonepigraphic – autobiography in thirteen volumes, of which only a few fragments survive. The inscription is shorter by necessity, of course, but also by design: Yavetz 1984 with notes.

[31] See Barnes 1974 for Augustus's acclamations as *imperator.* Yavetz 1984, 13 discusses the sloganeering quality of literary propaganda: in a largely illiterate society, the rhythm of the words, or even their shape in a line, could matter more than content. On the monumentality of the words, see Elsner 1996.

Roman people with me as *princeps,* even when there had been no prior exchange of embassies and friendship with the Roman people.[32]

Augustus, or the writer of the inscription, explicitly denies the use of force in receiving the Parthian princes, and he calls them *pignora* (assurances) rather than *obsides.* In this way, his description is unlike that of the hostages recorded in Barbatus's epitaph and is more in keeping with Livy's and Dionysius's literary characterization of Barbatus's Lucanians as guest-hostages. Although the writer of the inscription does not make any pretense of military victory and instead focuses on "embassies and friendship," Augustus nevertheless reaps the benefits and legitimacy of the hegemonic associations of hostages, or even *pignora,* which allow him to earn *auctoritas* all the same. In the section of the *Res Gestae* immediately preceding this one, he says that he "compelled" the Parthians to return the standards lost by Crassus a generation before, and in the subsequent section, he talks about how he controlled the eastern states to such an extent that he could appoint their kings from among the batches of heirs who had been surrendered.[33] What Augustus wants readers to learn is not that he did not fight others, but that he did not *have* to fight others; he furthered Rome's interests by sheer intimidation, and the sons of Phraates IV and their families constitute living proof.

The ironic message of peaceful conquest would have been further articulated for the visitor to the mausoleum complex by its proximity to the Altar of Peace (Ara Pacis), which had been constructed nearby. Turning from the tomb and walking in a southeasterly direction down the Via Flaminia to the pavement of an enormous sundial (another kind of trophy), one would come upon the northwestern side of the sculpted frieze surrounding the altar, which depicted a procession of senators

---

[32] *Mon. Anc.* 32: *Parthorum / Phrates Orod(i)s filius filios suos nepot(esque omnes misit) in Italiam, non / bello superatu(s), sed amicitiam nostram per (liberorum) suorum pignora / petens. Plurimaeque aliae gentes exper(tae sunt p.R.) fidem me prin / cipe, quibus antea cum populo Roman(o nullum extitera)t legationum / et amicitiae (c)ommercium.* For a discussion of the language of the text and the use of the first person, see Ramage 1987, 21–28.

[33] *Mon. Anc.* 29, 33.

and members of the imperial family (Figures 1 and 2).[34] Prominently featured in the center of the panel facing him, at eye level, would be a surprising sight: a bare-footed child looking distinctly un-Roman with his buttocks showing from beneath a too-short tunic, with long curly hair and a twisted torque necklace around his neck, smiling as he tugs the toga of the man in front of him (Figure 2). Moving around the building to the opposite, southeastern side, the visitor would see another non-Roman child, also with long curly hair and a slightly different kind of torque necklace, but who, in addition, wears a diadem, has shoes on, and seems to be accompanied by an adult woman behind him; he is older than the child on the northwestern side, and the Roman before him, whom he also pesters by pulling on his toga, is Agrippa himself, Augustus's son-in-law, one-time heir, and most trusted general (Figures 3 and 4). Much scholarly debate has been devoted to identifying these children.[35] Some have suggested both are eastern princes; some have suggested both are western princes; but the differences in clothing are significant enough to conclude that they come from opposite geographic extremes, with the southeastern child wearing eastern dress and the northwestern one appearing as a "barbarian" of western Europe.[36] It may be possible to assign names and historical events to these figures – the southeastern boy and woman could be Iotape and Antiochus III of Commagene, or Dynamis of Pontus and an unnamed son, possibly Aspurgus; I would argue that the boy may, in any case, have evoked the recent detention of the Parthian hostages.[37] The northwestern child may be a prince of Gaul accepted

[34] On the meaning of *pax*, so displayed, see Kuttner 1995, 105. Rose 1990, 459 and Clarke 2003, 19–22 also discuss the connection of the altar to the *Res Gestae* and mausoleum. On the horologium as a trophy, see Favro 1996, 264. For Augustan social policy as it relates to the altar, see Kleiner 1978.

[35] Rose 1990 and Kuttner 1995 are recent, successful studies of both figures; they also review earlier scholarship.

[36] Both eastern: Simon 1967, 18 and 21 (she says the boy on the northwestern side "brings to mind the barbarian child," but also suggests that he is a son of Julia, dressed as a camillus). Both western: Pollini 1987, 27; previously suggested at Kleiner 1978, 757–758, note 15. But see also Kuttner 1995, 264, n. 25. On the identification of the two boys as Gaius and Lucius Caesar, grandsons and heirs of Augustus, and the ambiguous, filial relationship between foreign hostages and their captors, see Chapter 5.

[37] Iotape and Antiochus III: Kuttner 1995, 104. Dynamis: Rose 1990, 458. The Parthians have usually been quickly ruled out by virtue of timing in that the altar was ordered in

by Augustus when he visited Lugdunum, an episode unrecorded by literary sources but suggested in other monumental commissions.[38]

But perhaps they are none of these: the various arguments of identification may miss the point of the impact of the image on the average Roman viewer, who would have had only a notional understanding of geopolitics. The parallel placement of the boys on opposite sides of the monument, the diametric nature of their clothing, and the coordination of their ethnic identity with points on the compass all signal that the generic was meant to take precedent here over the specific.[39] These are the *types* of children Augustus referred to in his neighboring epigraphic self-portrait as *"pignora."* The altar's message is that the children are in Rome as a result "of peace"; similarly, the inscription repeats that Parthian children had come to him "not conquered by war." The guest aspect of foreign children in Rome is thus emphasized in two proximate structures. To the Roman pedestrian, three shared attributes of these children would have mattered the most: they are foreign; they are young; and they are under control, even peaceful. They are abstractions of the periphery, both as many Romans would have preferred to view it and as Augustus would want to present it.[40] Suetonius reported that Augustus once appeared with the Parthian

---

13 BCE, and the Parthians did not arrive until 10/9 BCE, and Agrippa, whose toga the boy in question is gripping, died in 12 BCE. But when one notes that the altar was not finished until January of 9 BCE, the possibility emerges that the boy inspired comparison with the newly arrived Parthians. As Kuttner 1995, 274, note 100 points out, the fact of Agrippa's portrait does not freeze a *terminus ante quem* for the figures in question.

[38] Kuttner 1995 associates the northwestern boy with the children on the Boscoreale cup, itself a possible "quotation" of a lost monument. Cf. Rose 1990, 461.

[39] This is not to say that the "specific" identity is altogether unimportant: Kuttner 1995, 122 points out that the images must originally have referred to actual persons. But Favro 1996, 267, in her refreshingly creative, hypothetical image of a girl and grandfather confronting the monument in 14 CE, points out that twenty years after that altar was completed, "a more global message" characterized the frieze, as the girl, illiterate and unfamiliar with the details of political history from a generation before, primarily recognizes the fact of *pax*. Cf. Clarke 2003, 22–28 on the response of the "ordinary" Roman viewer. Simon 1967, 18, followed by Rose 1990, 461 suggests the images of the children could have been connected with the personifications of provinces in the interior of the altar. See Billows 1993, 91 on Augustus's *supplicatio* of 13 BCE, arguing that the foreign children are generic "guests."

[40] A similar conclusion is reached at Severy 2003, 110. Cf. Augustus's and Agrippa's map of the world set up in the Porticus Vipsania: Nicolet 1991, 110–114.

hostages in public, bringing them into the theater with him and having them sit behind him.[41] It was by accentuating the hostages that Augustus was proven to have achieved the same result as, say, Scipio Barbatus, even though he kept the peace on an international scale. Augustus's celebration of a victory over Parthia is well known: coins showed kneeling Parthians surrendering the standards; the breastplate of the Prima Porta statue depicted the same event (although with the Parthian standing, not kneeling); and even a victory arch seems to have gone up next to the Temple of Divus Julius.[42] But it is a strange kind of victory: the unequivocal message of the *Res Gestae* is that Augustus conserved Rome's resources and avoided the tensions of warfare that had beleaguered the Roman state in the previous generations in the form of internecine conflicts, yet did not sacrifice Rome's international reputation and did not let up on the foreign enemy, who despite being unknown, was ever viewed in Roman culture as a threat that needed suppressing. In the Augustan Campus Martius, the guest identity of hostages afforded as much prestige as that of the blackmail emphasized in the tomb of the Scipios.

The final inscription to mention hostages presents yet another type of boast that could be grounded in hostage possession. The epitaph for Tiberius Plautius Aelianus dates to the late seventies CE, and it honors a man who was consul under two very different emperors: Claudius in 45 and Vespasian in 74 (as co-*suffectus* with Vespasian's son, Titus). It was set up outside the large cylindrical tomb of Plautius's family on the road between Rome and Tivoli. The inscription mentions his various magistracies and posts, yet devotes its majority to his record as governor of Moesia:

To Tiberius Plautius Aelianus, son of Marcus, . . . governor of Moesia, in which he led more than 100,000 from the multitude of the Transdanubians

---

[41] Suet. *Aug.* 43.4. Their oddity is what was emphasized: Suetonius also describes Augustus's display of a stentorian dwarf, a rhinoceros, a tiger, and a gigantic snake. Cf. Nedergaard 1988, 109.

[42] On Augustus's depiction of victory over Parthia, see Rich 1998 (note page 73: "an ostentatious display of modesty"); Mattern 1999, 172–176; Campbell 2002, 122–132. This, in spite of Augustus's refusal of a triumph: Hickson 1991, 135–137. Simpson 1992 believes that the arch was never erected; Rich 1998 argues that an existing arch was given new decoration. The new temple of Mars Ultor referred to revenge against Parthia as well as against the conspirators: Galinsky 1996, 111.

across the Danube to pay tribute, with their wives and children and leaders or kings. He suppressed an initial uprising of the Sarmatae although he had sent a large part of his army on an expedition to Armenia. He drew kings who were previously unknown or hostile to the Roman people to the bank of the Danube, which he was guarding, in order to pay homage to the Roman standards. He sent back sons to the king of the Bastarnae and Rhoxolani and the brother (or brothers) to the king (or kings) of the Dacians, who had been captured or rescued from the enemy. He received hostages from some of these and through these actions he confirmed and extended the peace in Moesia...[43]

Hostage-taking is just one small part of a large dossier of triumph-worthy activity, but it is still something that Plautius is sure to include.[44] The inscription goes on to explain that Plautius's honors for all this activity were late in coming. It was upon Vespasian's suggestion, six years after the fact, that Plautius was granted triumphal ornaments for his tenure in Moesia and was simultaneously given his second consulship. Proper honors, it implies, had been denied by the megalomania of the late Julio-Claudian emperors, particularly Nero, whom Plautius had served. The inscription thus had a double task: not only did it record the honorand's deeds for posterity, it also redressed the public's current ignorance, which stemmed from the suppression of the "truth" by other emperors before Vespasian.[45] Echoes of Augustus's *Res Gestae* can be heard in Plautius's claim to have suppressed the Sarmatae even

---

[43] Dessau, 986: *Ti(berio) Plautio M(arci)... legat(o) pro praet(ore) Moesiae / in qua plura quam centum mill(ia) / ex numero Transdanuvianorum / ad praestanda tribute cum coniugib(us) / ac liberis et principibus aut regibus suis / transduxit; motum orientem Sarmartar(um) / compressit quamvis parte<m> magna<m> exercitus / ad expeditionem in Armeniam misisset; / ignotos ante aut infensos p(opulo) R(omano) reges signa / Romana adoraturos in ripam quam tuebatur / perduxit; regibus Bastarnarum et / Rhoxolanorum filios et regi (or regibus) Dacorum fratrem (or fratres) / captos aut hostibus ereptos remisit; ab / aliquis eorum opsides accepit; per quae pacem / provinciae et confirmavit et protulit.*

[44] Compare Dessau, 985, in which Tampius Flavianus also boasts of triumphal ornaments which he won, in part, as a result of taking hostages from across the Danube. The epitaph is shorter and more fragmentary. It is the same Tampius Flavianus, governor of Pannonia and political ally of Vespasian in 69 CE whose name is the last word in Tacitus's *Histories* before it breaks off (Tac. *Hist.* 5.26). See also Tac. *Hist.* 2.86; 3.4; 3.10. On the background of Moesia and Balkans generally, see Conole and Milns 1983; Lica 1988, 37–38; and Scardigli 1994, 197–198.

[45] Conole and Milns 1983 see the inscription and Vespasian's awarding of the triumphal ornaments as a rebuke to Nero.

without much of his army, to have exposed formerly unknown people to Roman diplomacy, to have performed favors for neighbors, and to have received hostages, all in the name of peace. The mention of hostages provided the reader with an additional way of thinking about the honorand in terms of his contributions to Rome's glory. Partly by means of his hostages, Plautius Aelianus was tied conceptually to Augustus, elevated materially by Vespasian, and distinguished from the "bad" emperors who had come in between.

Self-aggrandizing references to hostage-taking could appear in literary form as well, in published pamphlets or letters. Cicero, for example, is infamous for calling for a triumph following his stint as governor in Cilicia in 51 BCE and his highly questionable military activity there. Cato the Younger was opposed to the senate granting him any such recognition, but that did not keep Cicero from trying for a *supplicatio,* the first step in securing a triumph.[46] Not a seasoned soldier, Cicero had complained bitterly about the provincial assignment, which was the site of the death in battle of his grandmother's brother and which was forced on him by the senate. He had harsh words for the governor preceding him and repeatedly called for reinforcements to strengthen his position.[47] We know from Cicero's correspondence that at the start of his term, Parthian armies of indeterminate size marched into Syria and threatened to invade his own province next. Cicero's response was to move to Cybistra, with a mountain range between him and the opposing Parthians, and to send a detachment to the border at Epiphania to fight them in the interim.[48] After this division's initial success, he ascended into the Amanus mountain range on the border with Syria. By contrast with his dilatory conduct during the early fighting of the war, in a later context he records a siege of Pindenissus, a town (*oppidum*) of the "Free Cilicians"; his prose in a letter to Cato is clipped and intimidating, suitable for announcing his military acumen:

---

[46] See Hickson 1991, 130 on the process of requesting triumphs and *supplicationes* in the late Republic.

[47] Fuhrmann 1992, 122–123, who points out that Cicero viewed his service abroad as a "second spell of exile."

[48] Mitchell 1991, 227 sees this as a move to defend Cappadocia.

I surrounded the town with a wall and ditch; I enclosed it with six forts and substantial fortifications; I attacked with earthworks, mantlets, and towers; using many catapults and archers and at great personal toil; without any damage to or expense from our allies I finished the task on the 57th day, so that, with every part of the city in ruins or burned, they were driven to surrender to my authority. The people of Tebera are nearest to these and are equal in their savagery and fearlessness; once Pindenissus was captured, however, I received hostages from them. I then dispatched the army to its winter camp.[49]

In appealing for official recognition from the senate, Cicero made assertions of his own tactical ingenuity, which was so impressive that Tebara gave hostages without a fight.[50] Without these, presumably, a *supplicatio* would have been more difficult to obtain: they were proof of success beyond Pindenissus alone. The hostages were an important part of the boast; the detained Cilicians could *produce* an excellent reputation with respect to the military, an area of Roman politics in which Cicero had heretofore been lacking. In the fifties BCE, a public figure needed military honors in order to operate at the upper levels of politics. We have already seen that Pompey celebrated a triple triumph in which hostages played a prominent role, at least in Appian's and Plutarch's accounts. After him Crassus, Pompey's co-consul in 55 (and in 70 before that), made his ill-fated journey to Parthia in 53 in search of similar glory – an expedition that famously ended in utter defeat and Crassus's own demise.[51] In this context, Cicero's epistles, written two years later in 51, make sense as a way of furthering one statesman's ambitions. Whether one tried to wrest difficult hostages from Parthia or snatch easy ones from Cilicia, an enhancement in *auctoritas* was expected as a result. Cicero, after all, was awarded his *supplicatio*, although it was not followed by a triumph.[52]

---

[49] Cic. *Fam.* 15.4.10.
[50] On the self-glorifying nature and purpose of the letters, see Steel 2001, 192–202. For Cicero's attitude toward the proper conduct of a governor in general, see Braund 1998, 17–18, 21–23. Generous assessments of Cicero's military activity exist, based largely on the evidence of his own letters: Sherwin-White 1984, 290–297; Mitchell 1991, 228.
[51] On Crassus's efforts to compete with Pompey at home, see Parrish 1973.
[52] Cic. *Fam.* 8.11.1–2; 2.15.1; 15.5.1–2. On the vote, see Mitchell 1991, 235–236.

A fourth player in this game, Julius Caesar, also took large crowds of hostages; with him we again have the benefit of a personal voice in the form of his reports to Rome from the battlefield in Gaul. Throughout these, his *Commentaries on the Gallic War*, Caesar refers to the taking of hostages from thirty-seven different tribes.[53] He was keen to write about his campaigns because, with potential rivals in charge of the senate hundreds of miles away in Rome, he could not otherwise be assured of a career-defining triumph. It is perhaps for this reason that he also kept the hostages close to him in Gaul, rather than sending them to Italy for the senate to manipulate on its own.[54] In some cases, Caesar did more than record the simple fact of hostage submission; he manipulated the circumstances of the detention in order to elevate his own accomplishments. For example, hostages were said to be the sticking point in the negotiations between Divico of the Helvetians and Caesar in a particularly tense exchange in 58 BCE. Caesar says that he told the Helvetians that they could enter a peace with Rome as long as they surrendered hostages. Caesar's words have Divico boasting that among the Helvetians, the custom is to *take* hostages, not to submit them.[55] Hostilities ensued, and the Helvetians were eventually conquered. Caesar's narrative pointedly reports that the Helvetians were then compelled to surrender hostages.[56] Divico's spotlighted refusal to give them at the start of the digression is thus answered with Caesar's almost mechanical success, as the detention of hostages punctuates the end of the episode; the hostages have lent a dramatic arc to his campaign, such that Divico was not only defeated but also humiliated. Judging by Caesar's own account, one finds that the written boast of hostages along with all of the other trappings of victory won him real advances in politics back home. In referring to his victory over the Arverni at the Battle of Alesia, Caesar says that "he acquired a great number of hostages," among other concessions. At the moment when the announcements were made in Rome concerning this victory,

---

[53] Moscovich 1979–1980, 122.
[54] Elbern 1990, 111.
[55] Caes. *BGall.* 1.14. Cf. App. *Gall.* 15.
[56] Caes. *BGall.* 1.28. See also Lécrivain 1916, 126; Moscovich 1979–1980, 127–128; and Ndiaye 1995, 150–151, n. 9.

he was rewarded with a *supplicatio* for the entire package, hostages included.[57] This is the final statement in his final book before Aulus Hirtius took over for Book 8. When persuasion of victory to the masses was critical for political survival, hostages played a prominent role in self-representation.

The potential for writers to interpret hostages and to gauge their value for prestige in different ways can be seen in the case of Caesar's record of his demand and manipulation of hostages from Britain from 55 to 54 BCE, and the ensuing reaction of later authors. As in his story of the hostages of Divico, Caesar at first asked for hostages in Britain with little success. As he reports, word of his preparations to cross the Channel in 55 BCE prompted several tribes to offer hostages, a promise that Caesar says he encouraged. Nevertheless, he never received any hostages and met with stiff resistance on attempting a landing. After winning a difficult victory, he again heard promises for hostages from the defeated, but the tribes delayed and eventually regrouped. The cycle becomes familiar: Caesar scored additional victories and then doubled the number of hostages that he was demanding, but winter found him back on the mainland with detainees from only two of the tribes.[58]

What Caesar was seeking, at least, was the basic acceptance of Roman hegemony in the region. In his narrative, hostages come to stand for not only the guarantee of success on this score, but the very manifestation of his authority. As he prepared to return to Britain in the next year, he says that he doggedly collected hostages from unruly tribes in Illyricum and Gaul to maintain peace during his absence.[59] From this point, Caesar's account of his campaign in Britain proceeds with characteristic brio, as the Romans are able not only to defeat the enemy, but also, in the spirit of imperial writing, to map their island, to observe their ethnic habits, and to gauge their degree of civilization.[60] His success is all the more pronounced by comparison with

---

[57] Caes. *BGall.* 7.90.
[58] Caes. *BGall.* 4.21, 27, 31, 36, 38. See also Braund 1996b, 61–66.
[59] Caes. *BGall.* 5.1 (the Pirustae), 5.4 (the Treveri).
[60] Caes. BGall. 5.12 (ethnography), 5.13 (geography), 5.14 (the inhabitants of Cantium are the "most humane," *humanissimi*).

the problems he reported for 55: now, in 54, he is receiving hostages from the Trinobantes, the "strongest" tribe (*firmissima*), and then he completes the record of the expedition with reference to even more hostages:

Because he had decided to spend the winter on the mainland on account of recent uprisings in Gaul, and because not much of summer remained, and because he judged that it would be possible for it to be easily effected, Caesar demanded hostages and decided on how much tribute should be charged each year to Britain for the Roman people. He forbade Casivellanus from harming Mandubracius and the Trinobantes. Once the hostages were received, he led the army back to the sea.[61]

As in the account of Divico, the entire story has begun with a refusal by the enemy to give hostages and has circled back with Caesar's abrupt contravention of that very refusal.

A number of other writers clearly have read this passage.[62] In evaluating Caesar's accomplishment, they each give attention to the hostages, as he did, and interpret them in their own way. The following five references to the hostages of Caesar's British adventures are presented in chronological order of composition.[63]

Cicero: On 24 October I received letters from my brother Quintus and from Caesar sent from the shores of nearer Britain, 25 September. With the campaign in Britain finished, with hostages received, and with no booty, but with some funds demanded, they reported that the army had left Britain.[64]

Strabo: The deified Caesar crossed over to the island twice, but he hastily returned having accomplished nothing great (οὐδὲν μέγα διαπραξάμενος) nor having penetrated into the further reaches of the island . . . he conquered (ἐνίκησε) the Britons in two or three victories, although he had just two

---

[61] Caes. *BGall.* 5.22–23. Cf. Ndiaye 1995, 163.

[62] On the publication and distribution of Caesar's commentaries in Rome, see White 1997.

[63] Allen 1972 argues that Catullus 11 also may refer to Caesar's British campaign (no hostages are mentioned, however). For the history of the campaigns as opposed to their representation, see Ellis 1980; Braund 1996b, 61–66.

[64] Cic. *Fam.* 4.18.5 (*Att.* 92).

legions of his army, and he brought back hostages, slaves, and a huge quantity of the remaining spoils.[65]

Suetonius: [The deified Julius] advanced as far as the Britons, too, who had been previously unknown, and after they were conquered (*superatis*) he demanded funds and hostages.[66]

Plutarch: After sailing over to the island twice from the facing coast of Gaul, and having harried the enemy in many battles more so than benefiting his own men – for nothing was worth taking from this impoverished and wretched people – he brought an end to the war in a way not as he intended (οὐχ οἷον ἐβούλετο). But taking hostages from the king and arranging tribute payments, he abandoned the island.[67]

Cass. Dio: Caesar then forced [the Britons] (ἠνάγχασε) to abandon their fortifications by an overwhelming assault and after this, extricated (ἐξήλασε) them from their defenses by a siege, as others drove off a marauding band from the harbor. [The Britons] then became frightened and capitulated, giving hostages and succumbing to an annual tribute.[68]

With the connection between hostages and victory in mind, all of these authors measure Caesar's contribution by referring to the nature of the hostages, but they do so in subtly different ways. Cicero, who was referring directly to letters and not to the commentaries themselves, sees the hostages as suggestive evidence that something good came out of Caesar's campaigns: with hostages and tribute, he says, Caesar (and Quintus Cicero) at least had two out of three. Perhaps they all – Caesar, Cicero, and his brother – understood that booty would have been the greatest prize. But the essence of victory, for Cicero, had been achieved: Cicero later worked on an epic poem celebrating the invasion.[69]

Strabo, by contrast, stresses the lackluster quality of the campaign (Caesar "accomplished nothing great") and cites the hostages only as a kind of saving grace. The reason for his relatively subdued

[65] Strabo, 4.5.3.
[66] Suet. *Caes.* 25.2.
[67] Plut. *Caes.* 23.3.
[68] Dio, 40.3.2.
[69] Cf. Braund 1996b, 66. On the poem: Lossman 1962, Byrne 1998. Albertson 1990, 804 sees an image of Cicero building walls on the frieze of the Basilica Aemilia as a parody of Cicero's opportunistic obsequiousness to Caesar after the defeat of Pompey. On Cicero's ambivalent attitude toward Caesar later in life, after 46 BCE, see Dyer 1990.

treatment of the hostages may have to do with an interest in promoting Augustus's image by contrast: his account of Caesar in Britain
is immediately followed by a record of the Briton kings who came to
Rome to pay obeisance to the *princeps,* practically "giving the entire
island to the Romans."[70] Strabo gives an impression of Caesar's success
without it seeming overwhelming; he strikes a balance by mentioning the hostages but also by citing the overall shortcomings of the
whole enterprise. Like Strabo, Plutarch also presents the hostages as
a saving grace for a flawed campaign, but he has more interest in
absolving Caesar of any culpability: he doubts that there was anything of value in Britain and implies that the hostages were taken
out of habit by a man flummoxed as to how to deal with such a
savage land.[71]

Suetonius and Dio are the least cynical about the invasion of Britain,
and they present it as an unqualified victory for Caesar. The Britons
were "extricated from their defenses" (Dio) and "were conquered"
outright (Suetonius) by Caesar. Dio, whose account is more thorough
than any of the other summaries, also preserves Caesar's notion of
revenge in winning hostages from the recalcitrant: he says that Caesar's stated reason for returning in 54 was that the hostages had not
been received; he calls it a "pretext" (πρόφασιν), covering for Caesar's true ambition to subdue the entire island.[72] Although Caesar did
not succeed (which Dio admits), Dio's account ends with a flattering appraisal. Such enthusiasm might be attributed to imperial wishful
thinking or to the mystique of Caesar, compounded by generations of
emperors claiming descent. In any case, it is interesting to find both
Suetonius and Dio relying on the fact of the hostages in order to convince their readers of their point of view. Hostages would connote
military victory, even if no lasting impression had been made on the

---

[70] Strabo, 4.5.3. Clarke 1999, 327 sees Strabo's account as asserting that "Rome has *chosen*
not to conquer Britain" (italics included), because its subordination is apparent in other
ways.

[71] Relative to others of his *Lives,* with the *Caesar,* Plutarch took a keener interest in
domestic rivalries and politics as opposed to biographical anecdote (Pelling 1986), which
may explain his enthusiasm in this case.

[72] Cass. Dio, 40.1.2. McDougal 1991 points out that his account of the Gallic wars blends
Caesar's commentaries with a second, unknown source.

ground; they were one ingredient in a recipe for success and prestige, which were craved alike by Pompey, Caesar, Crassus, and Cicero in the late Republic, and by generals and *principes* after them.

COMPETITION

Another sign that hostages themselves were tickets to glory comes in stories where Romans vie with one another specifically for the possession of hostages and the attention they bring. When Publius Clodius Pulcher sought to challenge Pompey in 58 BCE, he, as tribune, requisitioned Tigranes, a son of the Armenian king who had been installed in Pompey's eastern campaigns.[73] Clodius tried to ship him back to Armenia, but Tigranes was forced by a storm to land at Antium. Pompey's loyalists raced to recover him there, as did friends of Clodius; both bands came to blows on the Appian Way, resulting in the death of one of Pompey's men. The fate of this Tigranes is unknown, but it is clear by the lengths to which the general and the tribune went to secure him that he afforded his possessor some real value.

As a further example, in Josephus, when Vitellius received hostages from Artabanus of Parthia in 37 CE, a virtual race was on between Vitellius and Herod Antipas, the Judaean tetrarch, to be the first to inform Tiberius:

Herod, wanting to be the first to send word of the receipt of the hostages (τῶν ὁμήρων τῆς λήψεως) to Caesar, wrote precisely about everything in a letter and sent couriers such that he left nothing for the proconsul to announce. When letters had been sent by Vitellius, and Caesar told him that everything was made clear to him by the earlier news of Herod, Vitellius was furious and took greater offense than appropriate . . .[74]

Earlier, Josephus records that Tiberius's explicit instructions were to ignore any treaty that did not include hostages; accordingly, the hostage had become the most important piece of information from the negotiations, although the author is ultimately mystified by the desire of Vitellius to be the first to announce it to the emperor

[73] For references and for his identity as a prisoner, rather than a hostage, see Chapter 3, note 73. On Clodius's motivations, see Tatum 1999, 170–171. Cf. Braund 1984a, 169.
[74] Joseph. *AJ* 18.104–105. Cf. Cass. Dio, 59.27.2–6; Suet. *Calig.* 14.

(the offense was judged not to be as bad as Vitellius's anger indicated).[75] It has been suggested that Antipas acted quickly because he feared that Vitellius would downplay his role in the peaceful (and profitable) mediation; with the emperor Tiberius's (or Caligula's – the date is in question) favor, Antipas may have stood a better chance of being granted the territory of his recently deceased brother, Philip.[76] In any case, as Josephus records it, just telling a superior about a hostage was a coveted opportunity.

According to Tacitus the possession of a hostage was the cause of a minor feud between the Neronian generals in the East, Gaius Ummidius Quadratus and Gnaeus Domitius Corbulo, in 54 CE. Four legions were divided between them, making the possession of supreme *imperium* ambiguous; Quadratus was governor of Syria, and Corbulo of Cappadocia-Galatia.[77] Each is said to have wanted to detain the hostages of the Parthian Vologaeses, and in order to avoid a dispute, they agreed to an unusual solution:

Each warned Vologaeses via messengers [to give hostages]. . . . The centurion Isteius, sent by Quadratus, received them, because by chance the king had gone to him concerning a prior matter. When [the submission] was later made known to Corbulo, he ordered Arrius Varus, the prefect of his cohort, to go and take command of the hostages. At this point an argument erupted between the prefect and the centurion, and lest it become a spectacle any longer before non-Roman eyes, the right to settle the matter was granted to the hostages themselves and the envoys who escorted them. They preferred Corbulo by virtue of his recent glory and because of a certain proclivity toward him, even though they were enemies. At that point, a rift opened up between the leaders (*unde discordia inter duces*) . . .[78]

Because this was a bloodless victory of diplomacy, hostages would have been the sole evidence of success against the Parthians, and the physical possession of them thus became critical for receiving due

[75] On the instructions: Joseph. *AJ* 18.96. Cf. Cass. Dio, 59.27.3. Cf. Paltiel 1991, 156.
[76] Hoehner 1972, 253. On the controversy surrounding the date, see Edmondson 1992, 180 and Paltiel 1991, 154–155.
[77] Vervaet 1999b, 579.
[78] Tac. *Ann.* 13.9.

recognition.[79] The Parthian audience was also of concern: the reason for the odd decision to let the hostages decide their fate, according to Tacitus, was to avoid humiliation in front of the enemy.[80] The dispute was not an inconsequential matter: Tacitus goes on to say that Nero was forced to give both generals credit in a public declaration in order to settle their quarrel.[81] The historian himself uses hostages to make his own distinction; as he construed it, the decision of the hostages to go with Corbulo, based on his *gloria,* reveals the truth behind Nero's compromise: Corbulo is said to have been chosen because hostages "fit" better with the general with the greater military prowess; Quadratus held them, after all, only "by chance" (*forte*). Corbulo is Tacitus's hero in this narrative: the episode opens with a contrast between the empty and forced adulation exhibited by Romans toward Nero and their *bona fide* respect for Corbulo. Moreover, Tacitus had reported in the passage before the hostage episode that the eastern kings had been more impressed with Corbulo than with Quadratus.[82] The message thus is that a general must earn his trophies, not be given them. Tacitus reveals that he had access to Corbulo's memoirs as a source for his history;[83] it would be a reasonable assumption, then, that Tacitus's attention to Corbulo's hostages reflects a concern of the hostage-taker himself to win credit and explain thoroughly his victory, as with the Scipios, Caesar, Augustus, and the others.

A law recorded in the Digest suggests that emperors were anxious about the control that their underling generals exercised over hostages and the perception of power that went along with it. The Julian law on treason, or *maiestas,* states that it would be a crime against the emperor to plot "to kill hostages without his command."[84] The charge is followed by a list of other subversive activities, including taking up

---

[79] Eck 1984, 138–139 discusses the end of senatorial triumphs under Augustus, long before Corbulo was fighting and Tacitus was writing.

[80] On the nature of the (expected) humiliation, see Gilmartin 1973, 588–589.

[81] Tac. *Ann.* 13.9: *quo componeret diversos.*

[82] Tac. *Ann.* 13.8. On the characterization of Corbulo as a model for *Trajan* to follow: Vervaet 1999a. As a foil to Nero: Syme 1958, 579. Comparing Corbulo's eventual courage in suicide with that of Socrates is Allison 1997. For more on Tacitus's manipulation of narratives involving hostages, see Chapter 9.

[83] Tac. *Ann.* 15.16.

[84] Dig. 48.4.1: *quo obsides invisu principis interciderent.*

arms in assembly, killing a magistrate, or plotting with foreign enemies; one thus sees that robbing an emperor of a hostage is seen as the equivalent of issuing a challenge. The law is not concerned so much with the safety of the hostage; rather, manipulating hostages was the privilege of the highest political office, and others who interfered were thought to be dangerously out of line. To an emperor, then, it could also seem threatening for a general to take hostages on his own in the first place. According to Dio when Vitellius received the hostages of Artabanus, he drew the envy and ire of Caligula, who called for his execution, a fate which he is said to have narrowly avoided by pandering to the emperor.[85] Similarly, in the biography of Agricola, Tacitus says that the governor's success in Britain, including the taking of hostages from the Boresti, annoyed Domitian who supposedly had not been able to take real prisoners in Germany, but had dressed up slaves to appear as such.[86] Domitian is said to have responded by cutting short Agricola's career and, if the rumor reported by Tacitus is true, by regularly sending one of his imperial freedmen to poison him slowly.[87] Much of this is clearly a polemic against Domitian, but the formulation of the polemic, based on achievements in hostage-taking, suggests that hostages were a prerequisite in an individual's, or emperor's, reputation, or even survival.

FALSE HOSTAGES

Roman leaders and the writers who discussed them naturally understood that their world was one of imperfect information and that misrepresentation and distortion of the truth could be both simple and enormously effective. When the power derived from conquest was a primary objective, but the timetable was short or true campaigning was unsavory for whatever reason (expense, inconvenience,

---

[85] Cass. Dio, 59.27.3–5.

[86] Tac. *Agr.* 38.3–39.1. With respect to the negative assessment of Domitian's triumph over the Chatti, Rives 1999, 281–282 argues that Tacitus contradicts himself at the *Germ.* 29.3, in which he discusses roads that had been built under Domitian. Hanson 1987, 180–181 points out that Frontinus approved of the campaign. For further rehabilitation of Domitian's memory in general, see Jones 1992.

[87] Tac. *Agr.* 43.2.

cowardice), an ambitious Roman could put false hostages on display in order to sway public opinion in his favor. For example, as Appian tells us, Quintus Pompeius, failing repeatedly in his siege of Numantia in 140 BCE and desiring some sign of success in order to save face back in Rome, offered generous terms to the Iberians in private, but in public demanded a complete surrender; in the end he left with cash and hostages but without taking the city.[88] Hostage-taking was excellent fodder for propaganda, and according to our sources, the early *principes*, masters of their media, readily took to "faking it." We have already seen how Tacitus believed that Domitian dressed up slaves as prisoners of war as a way of massaging his public *persona* and holding his own against more capable generals, such as Agricola. Suetonius assigned similar behavior to Caligula on two occasions. First, he describes Caligula's delusional conquest of Britain, and repeatedly the emperor's campaign, as imagined, involves false captures and detentions. When Adminius, a son of the Briton chieftain Cynobellinus, was banished by his father and deserted to the Roman side, Caligula is alleged to have sent a missive to the senate equating Adminius's presence among the Romans with the defeat of the entire island.[89] Moreover, Suetonius has his Caligula forcing numbers of his German prisoners to hide among the trees on the opposite side of a river and pose as enemies, whom he soon rushes off to fight.[90] His Caligula also has preexisting hostages removed from the school where they were studying and sent ahead of his train so that he could "recapture" them and put them in chains.[91] In the end, he lined up his army on the beaches of Gaul, prepared to cross to Britain, only to call it off and have the soldiers collect seashells to be used as trophies in the celebration back home.[92] In all, Suetonius exposes four acts of deception

---

[88] App. *Hisp.* 79.

[89] Suet. *Calig.* 44.2. On the unreliability of Suetonius's obvious invective, see later.

[90] Suet. *Calig.* 45.1.

[91] Suet. *Calig.* 45.2. On the "schools" of hostages, see Chapter 6.

[92] Suet. *Calig.* 46.1. Cf. Cass. Dio, 59.21.3, 59.25.2–3. Some scholars have attempted to absolve Caligula of guilt, particularly with respect to Britain. Woods 2000 argues that the "seashells" collected in Britain were actually small boats called *conchae*. Flory 1988, 501 says that they were pearls and thus a valuable haul, given the Julio-Claudians' descent from Venus. Benediktson 1988–1989 attributes his behavior to a form of epilepsy, neglecting the rhetorical nature of the passages. Malloch 2001 suggests that Caligula

in Caligula's portrayal of his European campaign; three of the four involve falsely redefining detainees under his power.

Perhaps more infamous is Suetonius's second example of fabricated hostages (also recounted in Dio, although slightly differently) – those in Caligula's fanciful "triumph" over Neptune, staged in the form of a procession over a bridge of ships spanning the Bay of Naples.[93] According to Dio, Caligula led Darius, the Parthian hostage whom Vitellius had received from Artabanus, across the bay as if Darius had been captured in battle. Suetonius's version is slightly different: he says that on the second day, on the trip back across the bay, Caligula, dressed as a charioteer, acted as Darius's driver, not his master. In making Caligula the slave to his hostage, Suetonius portrays the emperor's insanity as even more pronounced: not only is he faking a triumph, but he is also ceding the more respectable status to the underling who is both a false hostage in this context and a true hostage, won by someone else.[94] Caligula, as so characterized, is said to desecrate the reputation of Rome, reversing the logic of hostage-taking that was to have Rome on top.

These episodes in Gaul and on the Bay of Naples are listed in the catalog of Caligula's madness, but on one occasion, in Justin's epitome of Pompeius Trogus, the ruse of hostage-taking was said to backfire in a dangerous way. He reports that Ptolemy Ceraunus, a short-lived king of Macedon in the early third century BCE, was under attack by the Gauls in 279 BCE. The Gauls, taking mercy on him, offered to let him bribe his way to safety.[95] According to Justin, Ptolemy was prepared to settle, but in the outward portrayal of the negotiations, put on for the benefit of his people, he claimed that the Gauls were standing down out of fear. He made a show of demanding hostages in order to enhance his prestige; the Gauls were amused at first, but soon grew angry to the point of withdrawing from the peace. Justin reports that they took Ptolemy by storm, murdered him, and paraded

downgraded the celebration of the British adventure to an ovation in recognition that it was incomplete.

[93] Suet. *Calig.* 19; Cass. Dio, 59.17. Cf. Sen. *Brev. Vit.* 18.5–6; Joseph. *AJ* 19.5–6.

[94] Kleijwegt 1994 suggests that, with the event at Baiae, Caligula was trying to build a stronger alliance with his soldiers. See also Edmondson 1992, 163–165.

[95] Just. *Epit.* 24.5.1–6.

his decapitated head on a stave before the eyes of his people, who later remembered him as a madman.[96] The ending is a moral to an ethical tale: deception in hostage-taking – the contravention of truth in such a way – could have deadly repercussions for the perpetrator and his state.

Writers of the second century CE seem especially attuned to the notion that hostages could be fictitious and manipulated with deliberate intent. The accounts of Caligula and Domitian in Suetonius and Tacitus can be supplemented with examples of similar analyses from their near contemporaries, Plutarch and Pliny the Younger. In a piece of historical criticism, Plutarch assails the father-historian Herodotus for making a false claim concerning hostages in order to skew his narrative to his own tastes.[97] According to Plutarch, Herodotus tried to discredit the polis of Thebes by saying that the only reason that the Thebans were present at the Battle of Thermopylae – a defining event for Spartan glory against a huge Persian army – was because four hundred of them were detained as hostages by Leonidas and the Spartans in order to prevent Thebes from rebelling. Plutarch attempted to rehabilitate the nature of the Theban contingent at the battle by arguing that they were not hostages but had fought of their own volition. He points out that (1) there were only three hundred Spartans and so they could not have detained four hundred Thebans against their will; (2) Leonidas had earlier ordered the Thebans to leave, far from keeping them involuntarily; and (3) if the Thebans had been hostages, they would have tried to escape when they had the chance. The validity of Plutarch's interpretation of the role of the Thebans at Thermopylae does not concern us here so much as Plutarch's *accusation* that Herodotus had knowingly changed the status of the Thebans, who were actually allies in the battle, and refashioned them as fictive hostages.[98] Just as Suetonius exposed Caligula's "texts" of phony hostages, Plutarch suggests that Herodotus had falsely colored the Thebans with the hostage stigma in order to portray the Spartans

---

[96] Just. *Epit.* 24.5.11.

[97] Plut. *Mor.* 865B–D, commenting on Hdt. 7.222.

[98] Seavey 1991 believes Plutarch's critique is an epideictic exercise. Marincola 1994, 199 discusses Plutarch's motivations and methods in his negative appraisal of Herodotus. For the Thebans at Thermopylae, see Hammond 1996.

as stronger and braver than they deserved. For Plutarch, himself a Boeotian, such reinvention was unacceptable.

Pliny's *Panegyric* to Trajan exemplifies the new attitude to the "victory theater" of the recent past. Here he is praising the new world order under Trajan and expressing disdain for the policies of preceding "bad" emperors:

> Now terror has returned to all [of our enemies] as well as awe and a vow to do what is commanded of them. For they see a Roman leader who takes after the great men of old to whom the fields, covered with blood, and the waves, stained with victories, granted the title *imperator*. Therefore we receive hostages rather than purchase them (*accipimus obsides ergo non emimus*), nor do we attain peace through huge expenses and enormous gifts in order to seem like we have conquered.[99]

As Pliny tells it, Trajan would have been appalled at Caligula and his sham triumphs and at Domitian and his slaves in disguise. By this logic, Augustus could also be faulted, in that he minted coins with kneeling Parthians, erected an arch in celebration of victory, and had the scene of their submission carved onto the breastplate of a military portrait, when in reality all he had done was negotiate the return of the standards and later received hostages without resort to arms. At the start of the second century, it was believed that all of these emperors should have been more like Tacitus's Corbulo, who, while eschewing war in 54 CE and taking hostages instead, is said at least to have deserved them: the hostages chose him based on his *gloria*.

In the end, it is difficult to know if certain emperors really did dress up counterfeit hostages. The record of fictive hostage-taking is common enough, and the tone sufficiently vitriolic, for the motif to be challenged as a trope of Roman invective historiography. As the formula goes, some corrupt emperor or other dresses up someone (usually a slave) as a hostage from some exotic nation. All that was left for a historian in pursuit of a specific agenda was to fill in the blanks with a new perpetrator and a new source for false hostages. It is the filling in of the blanks that is interesting here. Not only Roman

---

[99] Pliny, *Pan.* 12.1–2: On the significance of this passage in relation to Trajan's campaigns in Dacia, see Lica 1988, 40 and Lica 2000, 202.

leaders, but also Roman writers, were adept at manipulating hostages. Just as hostages could serve as trophies to enhance one's prestige, they could be manipulated by our sources as the opposite of trophies, as the evidence of bad character. Suetonius himself admits that previous sources on Caligula's mock triumph over the Bay of Naples argued that he had staged the event for legitimate reasons – either to impress the Germans and Britons with Roman engineering or to emulate Xerxes, the Persian king who bridged the Hellespont on his way to Athens. Suetonius, however, chose to accentuate an unflattering story of delusion and deception. Once again, we see hostages as symbols whose identity is flexible: some viewed Caligula's hostages, however fake, as having real value in the intimidation of non-Romans; others, like Suetonius himself, saw them as signs of a dangerous insanity. If we think of hostages as a window for Romans onto the outside world, then the ability for them to be trophies, or simply trophy-ized, shows that the periphery and its subjugation was thought of as a means to an end – success in domestic politics – rather than the prevailing objective itself. When Romans saw hostages on the street, at least by the Principate and perhaps earlier, they might not have given any thought to the periphery at all and instead focused on the leader in charge, their minds racing to figure out if the hostages were legitimate.

5

FATHER-SON

Roman family relations were surprisingly flexible given the society's close monitoring of the power and significance of a Roman father in both his immediate family and in his extended clan. In theory, the *paterfamilias* had the ultimate power of life and death over children still under his authority, as stories of fathers calling for the execution of cowardly or disloyal sons in the Roman past attest.[1] In practice, however, the authority of the Roman father was hardly limitless, but was circumscribed by significant restrictions, both legal and social.[2] Moreover, an individual father might face competition for authority over a younger generation from men in other categories of fatherhood. A father-in-law, for example, could wield a tremendous amount of influence, especially if he were high-ranking. The practice of fosterage was also widespread, whereby a son could be raised or mentored by, or

---

[1] E.g., Lucius Junius Brutus, the first consul, executing his sons for plotting to restore the monarchy; see Hanson 1999, 26–27; Eyben 1991, 121–124. Shaw 2001 discusses the background and rhetorical nature of the stories. Eyben 1991 cites evidence of the father's concern for his children, as opposed to steely overlordship. On the possible connection between patriarchal family structures and patriarchal political institutions, see Lacey 1986. On the survival of the right of *patria potestas*, at least rhetorically, see Arjava 1998.

[2] Saller and Shaw 1984, 136–137 note the absence of commemorations of senior patriarchal figures in tombstones. Saller 1987, 32–33 notes that a large majority of adult men and women would have been *sui iuris*, given relatively shorter life expectancies. Saller 1991a and Saller 1994, 114–132 defines the power of *patria potestas* and gauges its application in practice as opposed to theory. Slater 1988 demonstrates how Terence's *Hecyra* subverts the ethic of deference to the *paterfamilias*. Plescia 1976 argues that the challenge and erosion of patriarchal authority by younger generations precipitated the disorder of the late Republic.

simply linked informally to, a surrogate father figure, usually a prominent social ally of an older generation.[3] Also, one's birth father could
cede authority to a new adoptive father to whom a Roman son could
be given "in exchange" for the social, financial, or political clout that
the new father could offer.[4] Under *adoptio*, the transference of a son
from the biological to the adoptive was negotiated by the two fathers;
under *adrogatio*, the son himself, if he was *sui iuris*, made the decision
to join another family.[5] Adoptions could occur within an extended
family, to bring distant cousins closer in relation or to bring later generations closer in time; they could occur among in-laws (*adfines*) in
order to reinforce existing marriage alliances. In all of these cases, the
adoptee would have been an adolescent or older: if the motivations
for adoption were to protect an estate or to make a social alliance, it
stands to reason that, given the low survival rates of childhood diseases
in antiquity, a grown son was much more valuable than an infant.[6] In
that the adoptee was meant to assist in building a relationship between
two groups, he took on a completely new identity comprised of both
families, a change that was reflected by a new, double name in which
the birth name was demoted to an adjective and tacked onto the name
of the adopting father.[7] Famously, Gaius Octavius became Gaius Julius
Caesar Octavianus.

Aemilius Paullus, the victor over Perseus and the Macedonians at
the Battle of Pydna in 167 BCE, gave away two of his sons in adoption for multiple reasons. First, according to Livy, he had remarried
and had had two additional sons from the union, and so giving away
sons in adoption helped to preserve his estate by reducing the number of beneficiaries.[8] Moreover, the sons helped to link the Aemilii
with other prominent families: one went to Quintus Fabius Maximus

---

[3] Corbier 2000 discusses the differences between adoption and fosterage. See also Gardner
1998, 114–208.
[4] Corbier 1991a and 1991b; Gardner 2000. Hopkins 1983, 49 points out that over a two-
hundred-year period (249–50 BCE), fifteen, or 4 percent, of consuls had been adopted.
[5] Corbier 1991a, 63–76; Gardner 1998, 126–132.
[6] Cf. Gardner 1998, 148 and 165.
[7] On naming strategies and deviations from the model, see Salomies 2000. On the significance of the *nomen* designating the all-important male line, see Saller 1991b, 31–32.
See also Corbier 1991a, 69.
[8] Livy, 45.41.12; cf. Plut. *Aem.* 5.5.

Cunctator, the general who had memorably harried Hannibal in Italy during the emergency of the Second Punic War (he took on the new name Quintus Fabius Maximus Aemilianus), and the other went to Paullus's nephew, Publius Cornelius Scipio, whose parents, otherwise childless, were Scipio Africanus, the great champion at the Battle of Zama, and Aemilia, Aemilius Paullus's own sister (his new name, of course, was Publius Cornelius Scipio Aemilianus).[9] The new emphases were on the "Fabius" and the "Scipio": the Aemilian prestige was subjoined; the Fabian and Scipionic reputations were sustained; and a new family network emerged linking Roman generals who were all but a part of the Roman pantheon – two conquerors of Hannibal and the victor over Macedon. It was an impressive political core, wholly manufactured, to which, as we shall see in Chapter 8, Polybius referred in shaping his own identity in the Roman world as an associate of Scipio Aemilianus. In short, the adaptable rules of family transformations worked to keep the state's premier "fathers" – one of the names the senatorial elite called themselves – at the head of viable, perpetual dynasties, linked and cemented by mutual filial interests.[10] Relationships by blood remained the most compelling bond, but the notion of "fatherhood" in Roman antiquity had other stops along a sliding scale; "fatherhood" could be shifted and manipulated for the purpose of arranging and maintaining political and social alliances.[11]

Keeping in mind both the flexibility of fatherhood as a concept and its significance in the exercise of power, one is better equipped to examine the intersections of the rhetoric of family relations and the practice of hostage-taking in Roman geopolitics. Our sources occasionally view the formation of international alliances by means of hostage-taking as analogous to the construction of a network such as that of the Aemilii-Fabii-Cornelii through the exchange, or donation,

[9] Thus, in the case of Scipio Aemilianus, his adoptive father had already been his first cousin; see the family diagram at Corbier 1991a, 71. On Aemilius's financial problems and on the ambiguous, physical problem that beleaguered the son of Africanus, see Astin 1967, 13. For the closeness of the new families, see Bannon 1997, 123–124.

[10] On the term *patres*, see Lacey 1986, 130–133. But also see Mitchell 1986 on the priestly associations of the term in its early application.

[11] See Dixon 2000 and Sigismund Nielson 2000. On the difficulty of tracing the meaning of family ties over time in the Roman period, see Dixon 1997.

of sons. Under this rubric the hostage is seen as a special kind of family member with either individual Romans or the entire collective society playing the role of his new "father" and the hostage donor seeming like one who offered his son for adoption for the purposes of advancement. Literary texts may not present hostages as explicitly adopted, but several imply that hostages had sufficiently insinuated themselves into the close-knit family structure of their guardian, especially after a lengthy period of detention, so as to become heirs to the overseer's estate, to marry into the overseer's family, or to submit to a legalistic, paternal authority. The hostage's hybrid identity, as a unique figure who was both non-Roman and Roman at the same time, in essence mirrored that of the Roman adult adoptee who crossed from one elite family network to another. Although not claiming that hostages became actual members of Roman families through formal channels, this chapter argues that the *representation* of hostage-based diplomacy in filial terms and metaphors betrayed a paternalistic view of the outside world on the part of the Romans. As foreign hostages came to serve similar functions as sons, sons-in-law, or adoptees in an international "family" of elites, new Roman "fathers," as they were depicted – generals, senators, emperors – were seen to exercise a greater facility in international relations. The power discrepancies between notional father figures and surrogate sons articulated the nature of hegemony and the strength of alliances formed by hostage-taking. To put it simply, when a Roman saw a hostage in the street, he might think of him as a kind of younger brother in a uniquely Roman sense, and by extension, all of Mauretania, or Judaea, or Parthia, for example, fell into a recognizable, easily conceptualized, inferior role.

ONE OF THE FAMILY

Just as within Roman society, fatherhood could be negotiated and reassigned on the level of the international elite through hostage-taking. Dionysius of Halicarnassus provides an initial example from the legends of Rome's beginnings. As we have seen in Chapter 3, one tradition for the founding of Rome held that Romulus and Remus were sons or grandsons of Aeneas who were given to Latinus as hostages to seal the alliance between the Trojans and Latins before the war against the

Rutulians. Years later, as Latinus was dying without an heir, they were counted as veritable sons and given a part of Latinus's territory as their patrimony, which is where they eventually founded their city.[12] Although Dionysius presents this as only one of many different versions of an epic legend, his account demonstrates that it was plausible for hostages to be welcomed into another ruling dynasty, with the hostage inheriting from his host's estate. In this case, the correlation between international hostage-taking and the concept of an international dynasty has implications for our understanding of Roman national identity. As argued in Chapter 3, proponents of this version of Rome's origins – that is, whomever it was that Dionysius was citing – blended the two major strands of Roman native ethnicity as preserved by other writers – the Trojans and the Latins – through the device of hostage-taking. Although the exchange was mutual in this case, the filial notion of hostage-taking effectively arranged the competing identities into a hierarchy. As the sons, the Trojans were subordinate to the Latins, yet they ultimately led the Latin race to a new beginning. As constructed by Dionysius's source, Latin ferocity "adopts" a Trojan nobility, which prepares the Roman race for an international role.

In a more historical text, Polybius uses the metaphor of family to describe Scipio (Africanus)'s conduct toward his Iberian hostages during the Second Punic War. Polybius records an extended exchange between Scipio and the wife of Mandonius, who was the brother of Indibilis, a major chieftain in Iberia.[13] After Scipio had taken control of the Iberian hostages from Carthage, the woman, who was herself a hostage along with her daughters, appeared before Scipio and pleaded for the safety of the girls. Polybius lets the reader know that her chief concern was that they be protected from rape, but that her own sense of decorum prevented her from speaking bluntly with Scipio. She hints at her concerns through circumlocutions, struggling to find a delicate way to put it, but the hints are lost on Scipio, who is sketched as to be so guileless that he could never fathom such a crime; he thinks she

---

[12] Dion. Hal. *Ant. Rom.* 1.58.5–59.2; 1.73.2–3.
[13] Polyb. 10.18.7–15.

is only worried about food.[14] Soon an epiphany comes, and realizing that rape is her fear, he sheds tears out of respect for her compassion and dignity. As Polybius tells it, Scipio promises in the end that he will treat the girls "as if they were his own sisters and daughters."[15] Later in the narrative, when Scipio meets with Indibilis himself, Polybius has Scipio declare that, unlike when the girls were in Carthaginian possession, the hostages under Rome's supervision were treated with a respect that "even surpasses the conduct of the hostages' fathers."[16] To Polybius, the hostage-taker properly steps into the role of father figure, if not through formal adoption (naturally) then through attitude and emotion.

The metaphor of hostage as son recurs in Polybius's history when he gives indirect speech to Demetrius, the hostage of Seleucid Syria who was detained in Rome from the mid-170s to 162. As mentioned in Chapter 2, the hostage appeared before the senate to ask for his release on the grounds that both his father and uncle, for whom he was a security, were deceased, and therefore his use as collateral made little sense. According to Polybius, Demetrius failed in his attempt to convince them to release him, in spite of assuming the attitude of a Roman son:

After he had delivered a long speech and had come on particularly strong with the principle they were looking for – namely that Rome was like his fatherland and nurse (πατρίδα καὶ τροφόν) and that he thought of all the sons of the senators as his brothers and of the senators themselves as his fathers, since he arrived there as a mere whelp (νήπιος) and was now 23 years old – all of his audience was moved.[17]

The senators thus reportedly agreed with Demetrius that a new kind of kinship bound them to him (the "audience was moved"), but in spite of their feelings, as Polybius goes on to say, they decided not to

[14] On Polybius's approval of Scipio, see Eckstein 1995, 182; and on his casting of Mandonius's wife as the paragon of feminine virtue, see Eckstein 1995, 152.
[15] Polyb. 10.18.15: ὡς ἰδίων ἀδελφῶν καὶ τέκνων. Elbern 1990, 102 and Ndiaye 1995, 152 accept Polybius's account without comment on its rhetorical nature.
[16] Polyb. 10.38.1–3: πατέρας.
[17] Polyb. 31.2.5–6. Cf. App. Syr. 46. On Demetrius's continued detention, see Chapters 2 and 8.

return Demetrius and instead to pin their hopes on the child who was already on the throne and who was more malleable in international relations. The filial quality of hostageship is problematic in this case: as Polybius tells it, Demetrius says that the senators were like fathers to him, and their sons like brothers, but Demetrius does not believe it himself (he goes through the motions, telling them what "they were looking for," and of course, he later escapes). Moreover, the senators trust his affection (they are moved), but their deeds do not reflect as much; ultimately they rejected the interests of this "son" in favor of the expediency of existing geopolitics.[18] The filial quality of hostage-taking may be only on the surface in this episode, but the fact that it deserved comment in the first place demonstrates that it was a possible way of thinking about hostages in historiography as early as the second century BCE. In other words, Polybius would not have been surprised at the version of Rome's founding that included Romulus and Remus as hostages-turned-sons of Latinus, but he would have been skeptical about the depth of the emotion so described.

Like Polybius, Livy also betrays an interest in the rhetoric and legitimacy of the hostage as a quasi-son to Roman captors. He adds the filial quality of hostage-taking to his version of the story of Demetrius of Macedon, who, as we have seen, was a hostage for his father Philip V from 197 to 191 BCE, and is said to have developed close ties to Roman senators, particularly Flamininus, both during his hostageship and after his release, when he served as his father's ambassador and negotiator.[19] Livy goes on to report that the rift that opened between Perseus and Demetrius over the question of Rome was predicated on Perseus's perception of a specifically filial relationship that had emerged between Demetrius and Flamininus. He stages a debate between the brothers in front of their father over charges of Demetrius's disloyalty. His Perseus has a set speech in which he hurls accusations at Demetrius, in the midst of which he makes the following assertion (addressing their father, Philip, in the second person):

---

[18] On Polybius's negative attitude toward Roman *Realpolitik* in this situation, see Eckstein 1995, 105–108 and Chapter 8.

[19] Polyb. 23.3.4–9; Livy, 39.35.2–3, 39.47.

Titus Quinctius [Flamininus] is now the leader and teacher of all matters for [Demetrius]. Once you, his father, have been removed (*abdicato patre*), he substituted Flamininus in your place.[20]

Livy's Demetrius denies the charge by drawing a sharp line between a hostage and an adopted son, and claims never to have crossed it, always acting on behalf of his true father (*pro patre*).[21] He goes on to state that he has not been *impius* – a specific term in Latin referring, in this context, to the sacred bond of loyalty and duty that a son feels for a father.[22] The fact of the rumor itself is of more interest to this study than the true relationship, whatever it was, between Demetrius and Flamininus. Livy expected Perseus's slander to make sense to an audience that understood the nature of the closeness between a hostage recipient and his ward. Demetrius passed into Flamininus's care as a youth; he spent years in Rome; and even after his release, he was reportedly coddled by Flamininus when he was in Rome for the second time. It was not preposterous, at least to Livy, for the suspicion to arise that Demetrius had replaced Philip with Flamininus as a primary father figure. In this sense, (Livy's) Demetrius's defense *had* to be crafted in a way that asserted his filial obligation to Philip as a foil to his hostageship.

Contemporary readers of Livy's account of his debate between Perseus and Demetrius may have been reminded of the new monument that had gone up in Rome to great fanfare at about the same time. As I have argued earlier, the Ara Pacis, on its northwest and southeast sides, presents foreign children who served as generic symbols of hostages. In the frieze, they parade along side the children of the ruling family, similar in age and demeanor, but different in dress (Figures 1–4). On the southeast panel, three Roman children, ascending in height and presumably in age, are all wearing togas as they march behind the "Parthian" or "eastern" child; on the northwest panel (much more

---

[20] Livy, 40.11.2.
[21] Livy, 40.15.7.
[22] Livy, 40.15.9. Saller 1991a, 146–151, argues that *pietas* referred to "obligations shared by all family members," marked by reciprocity. See also Bannon 1997 for the *pietas* among brothers, which Livy's Philip is made to trumpet in the same episode. Chaplin 2000, 80–81 discusses Livy's departure from Polyb. 23.11 in recording Philip's admonition to his sons: Livy adds Roman *exempla* for them to follow.

fragmentary), two Roman boys and a Roman girl are escorted behind the "Gallic" or "western" child. Several of these children have been identified as children of the imperial family, such as Gaius Caesar, Julia the Younger, and Lucius Caesar, three of the grandchildren of Augustus by Julia and Agrippa.[23] The proximity of the foreign children on the frieze to the fully Roman sons and daughter of the imperial family led numerous scholars to suggest that the *foreign* children were Gaius and Lucius Caesar themselves, dressed in foreign garb.[24] An ancient viewer could be expected – perhaps intended – to make a similar association (although probably not so extreme as to identify them as Augustus's very grandsons). The sculptor was ambiguous in suggesting a picture of an international family, a quality which formed the backdrop of Augustan foreign policy, as Severy has shown.[25] With this kind of mentality among the Romans, Perseus's accusations against Demetrius as portrayed by Livy could carry weight: Livy's Perseus was essentially imagining his own Ara Pacis, fictitiously depicting a procession in which his brother marched along with Roman toddlers, tugging at Flamininus's toga. In both cases, the Romans appear to be appropriating the best and brightest youth of the non-Roman world, guaranteeing a future that, in the case of Macedon, would not include Demetrius's true father Philip V. In the case of the Ara Pacis, the *absence* of the *native* fathers of the foreign children would have been equally as striking.

Compared with Polybius, Livy (and also Valerius Maximus, who followed him in the age of Tiberius) can be shown to have intensified the fatherly qualities of the hostage recipient. Livy also wrote about Scipio and his conduct with the Iberian hostages during the Second Punic War, but in one case he went a step further than Polybius in alleging Scipio's role as father to the detainees.[26] According to

---

[23] Rose 1990, 463–464. See also the alternative identifications of Torelli 1982, 50; Pollini 1986 and 1987. Again, the precise identification of the children is not terribly crucial for this argument; the idea and ideal of the Roman family are clearly conveyed by the frieze, regardless of who is represented. Cf. Severy 2003, 110.

[24] Torelli 1982, 48; La Rocca 1983, 30; Zanker 1988, 217–218.

[25] Cf. Kuttner 1995, 112–115 and Severy 2003, 110 on the inclusion of hostages in the *domus* of the emperor. Kleiner 1978 compares the boy's tugging on the toga with representations of filial scenes on Attic grave reliefs.

[26] Livy, 26.50; Val. Max. 4.3.1; cf. Polyb. 10.19.3–7.

him, when Scipio appropriated the Spanish hostages that were held by Carthage during the Second Punic War, he took pity on one of the girls who had been on the verge of marriage at the time of her detention. As we saw briefly in Chapter 2, Scipio decided to return her to her fiancé and, what is more, supplied her with a dowry in the amount of the old ransom. Setting the dowry in Roman antiquity was among the father's primary responsibilities toward his daughter; Livy's (and Valerius's) Scipio thus demonstrates what to the Roman eye would have been obviously paternalistic behavior.[27] The story of the ransom-turned-dowry seems apocryphal as it neatly circles the narrative in a ring composition from the girl's status as a bride to her hostageship and back to her wedding, complete with a happy ending. Notably, Polybius also tells of Scipio restoring the fiancée but he does not include the provision of a dowry. In general, Polybius's account of Scipio in Spain involves figurative language to imbue hostage-taking with a filial quality; his Scipio is "fatherlike." By contrast, Livy and Valerius, perhaps products of their time in the Julio-Claudian era, elevate metaphor to truth, embellishing the narrative to the point at which Scipio's fatherhood is literal; their Scipio *has become* the father, unequivocally.

Much later than Livy, Tacitus also was aware of the reception of hostages as virtual sons, as he included speeches in his narrative of Parthian hostages that referred to the paternal qualities of the hostage-taker. The Parthian hostages who traveled to Rome under Augustus in 10/9 BCE brought their families with them, and their descendants, Phraates IV's grandchildren, lived in Rome well into the next generation. In 35 CE, a group of dissident Parthian ambassadors came to Rome to call on the emperor Tiberius to install one of these grandsons, Tiridates, on the throne.[28] Vitellius was the Roman general for the campaign, and according to Tacitus, before arriving in Parthia, he

[27] On fathers and dowries, see especially Treggiari 1991, 323–364. See also Hallett 1984, 99; Dixon 1986; and Saller 1994, 207–224 (with Saller 1984).
[28] It is not certain whether Tiridates was a son or grandson of Phraates IV, but Tacitus's description of Tiridates's "boyishness" (*Ann.* 6.43: *pueritiam Tiridatis*), forty-five years after the initial submission in 10 BCE, implies that he had been born after the Parthian families settled in Italy. Tiridates's older ancestors, Vonones and Phraates V, had already been called to Parthia; see Chapter 9.

135

advised Tiridates to take as his role models both his grandfather, Phraates IV, and his "foster-father," (*altor*) Tiberius.[29] In the end, Tiridates was driven out by the sitting Parthian king, Artabanus, despite some initial successes, but some years later in 47 CE, the Romans tried again, this time sending Meherdates, another descendant of Phraates, who most likely was born in Rome. In Tacitus's narrative the emperor Claudius speaks publicly before Meherdates's departure and explained his expectations, again with the language of fosterage:

Claudius began a speech about Roman dominance and the obsequiousness of the Parthians, and he equated himself with the divine Augustus, pointing out that a king had been sought from him, as well (the memory of Tiberius was omitted, although he too had sent one). Because Meherdates was present, too, he added some guidelines: Meherdates should view his situation not as a dictatorship with slaves but as a ruler with citizens, and he should practice clemency and justice which, being unknown to the barbarians, would be especially pleasing. Turning to the legates, he praised the foster-son of the city (*alumnum urbis*) . . .[30]

Meherdates turned out to be a colossal disappointment; nevertheless, Tacitus demonstrates that Romans had a prevailing sense of ambition and optimism in wielding former hostages, dictating their careers, and through them, effectively ruling foreign territories as absent patriarchs, or at least trying to do so.[31]

Plutarch, a near contemporary of Tacitus, was also interested in a hostage's potential entrance into a foreign family. In his biography of Pyrrhus, the third-century BCE king of Epirus, he recounts that at the age of seventeen, Pyrrhus was deposed and forced to flee to his sister's husband, Demetrius I Poliorcetes. When Demetrius was defeated at Ipsus in 301 BCE by Ptolemy I of Egypt, Pyrrhus was surrendered to Ptolemy as a hostage for the new treaty. Far from suffering in his confinement or bearing any resentment, Pyrrhus is said to have excelled in Alexandria in hunting expeditions and exercises at the *gymnasium*. We are told that he so impressed Berenice, Ptolemy's queen, by his "orderly

---

29 Tac. *Ann.* 6.37. Again, on the language of fosterage, see Corbier 2000.
30 Tac. *Ann.* 12.11.
31 On Tacitus's evaluation of this ideology, see Chapter 9.

and restrained demeanor" that she gave him her daughter Antigone in marriage.[32] Ptolemy, the hostage recipient, became the father-in-law of the detainee, and just as Romulus and Remus received Latinus's largesse in Dionysius's story, and just as the Parthians were backed by the Julio-Claudian emperors, Pyrrhus, along with Antigone, received material support (money and troops) in an attempt at retaking the Epirote throne. Hostageship was thus viewed by Plutarch as a possible first step, treated as commonplace and requiring no leap of imagination, for a would-be Hellenistic dynast to gain entry into the crucial network of intermarried families; now with both Antigonid and Ptolemaic associations, he could stake a doubly compelling claim to the inheritance of Alexander the Great.[33]

The motif of hostages as sons also had a prominent place in Roman mythographers of various genres. Poets of the Roman empire expected their readers to understand a one-for-one correlation between hostages and sons. The equivalence between the two gave writers the opportunity to make substitutions, as hostages often stand in for sons in stories involving human moral transgressions. As seen in Chapter 3, when Ovid told the story of Lycaon in the *Metamorphoses,* he replaced the son or grandson, who in earlier versions was the one who fell victim to Lycaon's near cannibalism, with a hostage and yet the story did not lose any of its criminal intensity; Jupiter still flooded the earth. The murder of a son and the murder of a hostage were seen as sacrileges of the same category. Again, Augustan readers of Ovid might be reminded of the children on the Ara Pacis, or of Livy's story of Demetrius's ties to Flaminius, or of Livy's account of Scipio and the dowry for the hostage fiancée in Iberia. A hostage also took the place conventionally belonging to a son in the story of Antheus told by Parthenius of Nicaea in the first century BCE.[34] The poem follows a common tragic scenario: while Antheus was a hostage at the court of Phobius, Phobius's wife, Cleoboea, conceived a passion for him and tried to

[32] Plut. *Pyrrh.* 4.4: κόσμιος δὲ καὶ σώφρων περὶ δίαιτιαν. Cf. Lécrivain 1916, 120.
[33] On reading Plutarch's *Pyrrhus* as a companion piece to his *Alexander,* see Mossman 1992.
[34] Parth. *Amat. narr.* 14.

seduce him. Antheus rebuffed her advances, and so she killed him out of frustration by stoning him to death as he went down a well to fetch something she had lost.[35] After realizing her crime, Cleoboea hung herself. This little-known story borrows its central motif from better-known myths involving the attempted seduction of a stepson by a stepmother: Potiphar's wife failed to seduce Joseph and had him sent to prison, and Phaedra's secret passion for Hippolytus was revealed to him, and, in embarrassment, she killed herself and framed him of rape, such that Theseus fatally cursed his son.[36] Although the story in Parthenius pivots around a hostage and not a stepson, the intensity of the tragedy is undiminished.

The Romans clearly had a propensity to think of their hostages as pseudo-sons in a vast, notional family. Viewing the phenomenon from the perspective of the hostage, however, we have just one example of a first person assertion of quasi-adoption into the family of his captors, although it is not literary. Portraits of Juba II, the former hostage who became king of Mauretania in the age of Augustus, suggests at least the desire for a public understanding of filial relations between him and the emperor. As reviewed briefly in Chapter 1, Juba had been taken as a child from Numidia after his father committed suicide following his defeat by Caesar in 46 BCE. He arrived in Rome as part of a triumphal procession and received an extensive education, developing interests in literature and philosophy and drafting treatises on geography, drama, botany, and painting, among others.[37] Presumably, Juba spent much time in the Julian household, as he clearly had close ties to Octavian,

---

[35] Parthenius says that he is reporting two earlier versions of the story, one supposedly from Aristotle and the other from Alexander Aetolus. He tells us that in Aristotle, Antheus is told to retrieve a partridge whereas in Alexander Aetolus he is sent after a gold cup. See Lightfoot 1999, 454–455 for the significance of the well as a confining space, just as incest confines a victim to his or her family.

[36] Potiphar: *Genesis* 39; Phaedra: Eur. *Hipp.* For other references, see Grimal 1963. On the theme, generally, and for other examples, see Yohannan 1968. On the significance of the wicked stepmother in Rome, see Gray-Fow 1988 and Barrett 2001.

[37] The triumph: Plut. *Caes.* 55; App. *BCiv.* 2.101. Gurval 1995, 23 says Juba II was emphasized in the triumph to remind the crowd of Juba I and thus distinguish the victory from one of civil war. On possible candidates for Juba's instructors, based on a survey of scholars known to have been in Rome simultaneously, see Roller 2003, 65–68. His literary fragments are collected at *FGrH* III A 275 and discussed extensively at Roller 2003.

accompanying him on campaign, perhaps at the Battle of Actium but more likely on his Spanish expedition from 27 to 25 BCE.[38] If Juba was in Spain in 25, then he did not have far to travel when he was given the kingdom of Mauretania that year, just across the Straits of Gibraltar.[39] At the time, he had spent twenty-one years with Octavian/Augustus, from the time of his earliest memory. By 20 BCE — the precise date is uncertain — Juba, in his late twenties, had been married to Cleopatra Selene, the orphaned daughter of Antony and Cleopatra nearly ten years his junior.[40] He had probably first seen her when she entered Rome on the last day of Octavian's triple triumph in 29 BCE. Since she was the half-sister of Antonia the Elder and Antonia the Younger, Augustus's nieces, Juba was thus brought even closer to the throne. After Cleopatra's death, Juba married Glaphyra, a former daughter-in-law of Herod the Great.[41] He was thus enormously well connected in the court that was emerging in Rome.

In his public image, Juba expressed a loyalty to the Julio-Claudian dynasty that took on filial dimensions. In one portrait, Juba's crown signals his difference from the ruling Roman family, but overall, his visage appears distinctly Julio-Claudian, sharing with Augustus and the rest the tendency to borrow heavily from Hellenistic prototypes (Figure 5).[42] It is a reasonable assumption that the images of Juba were also set up in public places alongside those of his wife and in

---

[38] On the Julian household, see Severy 2003, 150 and Roller 2003, 61–64. On Juba's presence on campaign, see Cass. Dio, 51.15.6 and Desanges 1984–1985; Coltelloni-Trannoy 1997; and Roller 2003, 74. On Dio's possible use of Juba's history of Africa as a source for his own work, see Moscovich 1997.

[39] Strabo, 6.4.2, C288; 17.3.7, C828; Cass. Dio, 53.26.1–2.

[40] The two appear together on coins dating to 20/19 BCE: Braund 1984b, 175; Coltelloni-Trannoy 1997, 36. Roller 2003, 86–87 plausibly suggests they were married before Juba took over Mauretania. A poem in the Palatine Anthology (9.235), likely written by Crinagoras, celebrates the union; see Braund 1984b. Plut. *Ant.* 87 says Octavia had promoted the match. Cf. Cass. Dio, 51.15.6.

[41] The date of Cleopatra's death is not known, although a poem of the Palatine Anthology (7.633) associates the passing of a "Selene" with a lunar eclipse, which may be datable astronomically to certain days in 9, 8, or 5 BCE: see Roller 2003, 250. Of course, the eclipse in the poem may be figurative. On the marriage to Glaphyra, see Roller 2003, 248–249.

[42] Poulsen 1951, 321–322; Fittschen 1974; Simon 1986, 223; Coltelloni-Trannoy 1997, 161; Roller 2003, 146–148. On the related issue of the portraits of Cleopatra Selene, see Grenier 2001.

association with imperial portraits.[43] The most famous example of the latter is the so-called Cherchel torso, presumably a portrait of Augustus (the head is lost), in military regalia that seems to have adorned the theater at Iol/Caesarea.[44] Juba seems to have defined himself as a Julio-Claudian son and even found power in it. Any viewer of Juba's portrait in these contexts, be they Mauretanian, Roman, Numidian, or Hellenistic Egyptian, would naturally have been aware of the king's non-Roman origins; looking at these images then, they would have developed the impression of a radical transformation for Juba – one that went deeper than merely his outlook or ideology, but which also altered his very body, creating, in a sense, a brand-new Roman. This portrait of a member of the Julio-Claudian dynasty was predicated on the expectation of the quasi-adoption of foreign hostages and their subordination to an authority at times cast as specifically patriarchal.

THE IMPERIAL *PATERFAMILIAS* AND DYNASTIC DECISIONS

When Strabo ends a long digression on the state of the empire in 23 BCE, he says that the senate, unable to rule the entire domain as it had during the Republic, gave the empire to Augustus "as to a father."[45] In the Roman world, the nature of geopolitics was such that Strabo's interpretation need not be taken only metaphorically. Owing to the socially restricted nature of ancient politics, international relations in

---

[43] A controversy exists over whether certain female portrait heads depict Selene or her mother: Roller 2003, 139–142.

[44] Fittschen 1979, 232–234; Galinsky 1996, 107–111; Roller 2003, 144. The image on the breastplate depicts Victory crowning a man; Galinsky 1996 sees it as either Julius Caesar or Gaius Caesar, whereas Roller 2003 suggests it is Augustus himself. On the city of Iol/Caesarea as Juba's "capital," see Chapter 6.

[45] Strabo, 6.4.2, C288: ὡς πατρί. Severy 2003 discusses the rhetoric of family in Augustus's regime, and the filial metaphor in foreign affairs is acknowledged at Braund 1984a, 23 and Edwards 1993, 60. On Strabo's "universalism" and the centrality of Rome in his geography, see Clarke 1999, 307–315. The image was prominent in poetry, too: Toll 1997, 42 points out that Aeneas is called "*pater*" more often than "*pius*" and Nicolet 1991, 114 discusses Ovid's conception of Augustus as "*pater orbis.*"

the empire depended to a large extent on the contacts among a set of important families both abroad and at Rome. Whether a single dynasty ruled a kingdom or a few extended clans hoarded their privileges in an oligarchy, one's bloodline was as crucial a determinant of political clout as wisdom, or courage, or eloquence, or other leadership qualities. Leaders would thus guard their family identity and manipulate access to their relations with calculation and negotiation: newly forged family connections could lead to alliances between states, or *vice versa,* preexisting alliances could determine the nature of, say, a new "adoption" or a new marriage. An elite family on the periphery heightened its prestige and influence whenever it "went international"; likewise whenever such a family was connected to Rome, the emperor benefited from a higher position of authority. For Augustus or any emperor to rule the empire, he had to oversee the network and act generally as an imperial *paterfamilias.* Hostage-taking was thought to provide them with access to foreign regimes such that they could manipulate their wards, or at least try to do so, as if dictating their own family affairs.

When a king wanted to draw closer to Rome – if he depended on Roman assistance to survive in his domestic politics, even at the expense of his own autonomy – he submitted his very best heirs to Roman control. In effect, the hostage donor who gave the son of the highest rank could be interpreted as welcoming the hostage recipient into his own dynastic politics; the king's rivals at home, the donor would hope, would realize that they would have to overcome not only a sitting monarch but also his international coalition, which held critical dynastic assets. An adoption, or quasi-adoption, in a sense created new fathers as well as new sons and thus Roman hostage recipients, could acquire foreign authority of their own, in addition to their military domination.[46] A thoroughly realized example of the expectation of a hostage recipient's quasi-fatherly dalliance in foreign dynasties can be found in Josephus's extensive description of Augustus's treatment of the sons of Herod the Great. According

[46] Cf. Romer 1979, 201, observing that Augustus's possession of the Parthian hostages gave him "nominal custody of the ... succession."

to Josephus, Augustus received several heirs of Herod at the imperial court throughout the course of the king's bumpy reign and practically dictated changes to Herod's will based on his favorites. These were not hostages, *per se*, but their experiences are similar in that they were young, abroad for a finite period of time, and most important, their very presence in Rome constituted and reified a diplomatic pact. In this long, operatic saga, the sons who were sent to Rome – six in all, born of four mothers who were themselves of four different backgrounds and factions – passed in and out of favor with Herod as the competition among various branches of the ruling dynasty led to intense court intrigue.

Josephus's account suggests that the ultimate power in choosing successors rested with Augustus, who, as Octavian and with the cooperation of Antony, had declared Herod king of Judaea in 40 BCE.[47] In 22 BCE, Augustus received Alexander and Aristobulus, sons of Herod's first Hasmonaean wife, Mariamme, whom Herod had executed in 29.[48] Soon after, according to Josephus, Augustus gave permission to Herod to leave his kingdom to whichever of his heirs he wished, but the emperor's affinity for the two Hasmonaeans was taken as obvious.[49] The very act of granting Herod permission to act independently bespeaks Augustus's power (as it was perceived by Josephus).[50] But the boys' promotion did not go unopposed in Judaea, and Herod's Idumaean family sought a greater role for Antipater, Herod's son by his Idumaean wife. The way the Idumaean faction chose to increase Antipater's clout was to turn him over to Augustus in 13 BCE, via Agrippa who was acting on Augustus's behalf in the East. As Josephus describes it, Rome had become a kind of dynastic court of law for

[47] Herod took command three years later, in 37, after capturing Jerusalem: Joseph. *AJ* 14.470–480.
[48] For the controversy surrounding the date of the submission of the sons, see Hoehner 1972, 9 and 13, suggesting that the boys had to have been just past thirteen years old and completed their Bar Mitzvah.
[49] Joseph. *AJ* 15.343. See Feldman 1985 on the accommodations of the brothers at the house of Asinius Pollio (consul of 40 BCE). Cf. Joseph. *BJ* 1.454, implying Alexander was given precedence. The following account of Herod's various wills owes much to Hoehner 1972, 269–272, also with Richardson 1996, 33–40.
[50] Braund 1984a, 139–140.

the Judaeans: as Herod grew suspicious of the Hasmonaean heirs and came to prefer Antipater, he went to Rome in order to accuse the Hasmonaeans formally in a trial, rather than risk suspicion of impiety (ἀσεβείας) by ordering their execution outright.[51] Josephus presents an imaginary transcript of the trial in which Alexander defends his loyalty to Rome; the result is that Augustus compels Herod to include all three heirs in his will.[52] Herod later managed to execute the Hasmonaeans but only after holding a new trial in Berytus (Beirut) and not in Rome, out of Augustus's oversight.[53]

With the Hasmonaeans removed, other sons of Herod from other branches of his family rose to contest Antipater's status, and again, the submission of sons to Rome was the ironic way of achieving leverage in the Judaean court. Josephus mentions, without much elaboration, that other sons were brought up in Rome: Antipas and Archelaus, sons of a Samaritan woman named Malthace, and Philip, a son of a Jerusalemite named Cleopatra.[54] The historian never mentions why or when these youths were sent to Rome or any other circumstance of their time there, but they came to serve as obvious substitutes for Antipater when he too fell from Herod's favor. In 6 BCE, Herod had sent a will to Augustus to be "ratified," in which Antipater was to be his sole heir,[55] but as Herod was dying, evidence came to light that Antipater was conspiring to have him killed, and so Herod sent Augustus a replacement will designating Antipas as his principal heir.[56] Antipater was eventually found guilty and executed shortly before Herod's own death in 4 BCE. According to Josephus, at some point in the week between Antipater's execution and Herod's own demise, yet another will was drafted for Augustus, shifting the bulk of the estate in accordance with primogeniture: namely to Archelaus, the elder Samaritan son, who would be the overarching ruler, with his

---

[51] Joseph. *AJ* 16.90.
[52] Joseph. *AJ* 16.106; 16.129.
[53] Joseph. *AJ* 16.133; 16.392–394.
[54] Joseph. *AJ* 17.20–21. On the ages, with Antipas being the youngest, see Hoehner 1972, 11–12.
[55] Joseph. *AJ* 17.53.
[56] Joseph. *AJ* 17.146–147; *BJ* 1.646. Hoehner 1972, 3–14: they were summoned back from Rome when Antipater's alleged plot was made known to Herod.

brothers receiving lesser territories.[57] Augustus at first adhered to Herod's final will, but in 6 CE he judged Judaea, at least in part, to be more easily ruled as a province and transferred Archelaus and his wife to Gaul.

Josephus tells the story as if the successors of Herod were being decided and arranged in detail by Augustus alone, as some kind of Judaean patriarch. In sum, Augustus meddled in the drafting of Herod's will five times before he made a sixth and final decision with regard to the regime by reassigning Archelaus.[58] Choosing and deleting heirs and approving wills are obviously the father's activities. Residence with the imperial family was seen, at least by Josephus, as critical to a would-be dynast's success, as traditional rights of patrimony were supplanted by an emperor's quasi-fatherly *dicta*. Much depended on the attitude of the hostage donor and his relationship with his own hostages: if the donor was amenable to Roman interference, the filial quality of hostage-taking could have the effect of drawing the hostage recipient into the dynastic politics of the donor state.

Given the filial aspect of the power that Roman hostage recipients could be expected to wield over their detainees, one may understand a common trope of Roman hostage-taking, namely that if hostage donors, unlike Herod, sought to guard their independence and keep their distance from Rome, then they tended to protect their first born or their most valuable heir from the institution, and instead submit their youngest offspring, or those who had the least relative legitimacy to rule. The record preserves multiple examples: Philip II was chosen as the hostage to be sent to Thebes by Amyntas in 369 BCE because he was the youngest son; years later, Philip V gave Demetrius to Flamininus and held on to his older son, Perseus; likewise in 188 Antiochus III of Syria sent the Romans his adolescent son Antiochus

---

[57] Joseph. *AJ* 17.188–190; *BJ* 1.664. Cf. Romer 1979, 203 on Augustus's inclusion of Gaius Caesar in making these decisions.

[58] The following is a summary of Josephus's history of Augustus's role in the wills: 22 BCE: he favored Alexander and Aristobulus; 12 BCE: he allowed Antipater to be promoted; 7 BCE: Herod executed Alexander and Aristobulus, and the will with Antipater as sole heir was sent to Augustus shortly thereafter; 4 BCE: Herod sent Augustus a replacement will with Antipas as heir; but later, still in 4 BCE, he hastily substitutes Archelaus.

IV and kept the elder Seleucus in Antioch.[59] In the Roman conflict with Sparta in 195 the same phenomenon applies: when Nabis, the tyrant of Sparta, was compelled to surrender hostages, he sent his son Armenes, among others, but retained his son-in-law Pythagoras who had proven to be his most capable heir.[60] Tacitus also demonstrates the protective sentiment for politically significant heirs when he tells how Germanicus's troops in Germany abandon their mutiny when they realize that their treasured "foster son" (*alumnus*), the young Caligula, could become a hostage (*obses*) to the Gauls as a result. According to Tacitus, the very sight of the precious great-grandson of Augustus headed to a foreign city for safekeeping, it would seem, was all that calmed the soldiers.[61] Fathers or father figures who were interested in maintaining their autonomy deliberately shielded their best prospects for the succession and submitted the least important in a practice that was, by expectation and nearly by definition, a means of changing one's family identity.

A related historical trope presents another dimension of the notion that the least favorite heirs were given as hostages by enemies of Rome: in several episodes a king on the periphery is said to discard his untrustworthy or potentially treasonous heirs as hostages before they could do harm at home. As the logic goes, hostage donors could change the filial status of a "bad" heir by sending him abroad, effectively removing him from the dynasty. Such motivation is attributed on occasion by some ancient sources to Phraates IV of Parthia. Strabo, who, as seen in Chapter 3, at one point refers to the Parthians as guest-hostages, in another section gives a discrepant account, saying that the sons were

---

[59] Amyntas: Diod. Sic. 15.67.4; Just. *Epit.* 7.5.2–3; Plut. *Pel.* 27.3. For Philip V and Antiochus III, see chapter 1. On the phenomenon of the detention of "second sons," see Walker 1980, 276–280.

[60] Livy, 34.25.5; 34.29.14; 34.30.4; 34.39.9; 34.40.2–3. In the negotiations leading up to the war with Sparta, Flamininus dealt primarily with Pythagoras, and according to Livy, it was Pythagoras who, after the Romans had breached the walls, rallied the troops and organized them in burning the buildings nearby as a distraction.

[61] Tac. *Ann.* 1.44. Compare Suet. *Calig.* 48.1 and Cass. Dio, 57.5.6 which imply that the *troops* held Caligula hostage, soon releasing him. On the Tacitean passage as a "pro-Germanicus" version, see Barrett 1989, 9–10.

given away because they were Phraates's potential *rivals*.[62] Because of
the Parthians' long-standing loyalty to the Arsacid dynasty, no political opponent could act against Phraates without at least an Arsacid
figurehead to legitimize his claim to power. As the argument goes,
Phraates must have appreciated from personal experience the problems that came with having too many sons, as he himself had killed
his father and had fought against his brothers for power.[63] Not only
were the troublesome heirs removed from the region, thus making
it logistically difficult for them to challenge the throne, but they also
were given a Roman quality in the process, which could reduce their
Arsacid legitimacy. Sending his sons to Rome was thus seen in this
context primarily as a convenient way for Phraates to preserve order.

Following the second of Strabo's interpretations of the hostages –
that they served as smoke-screens – Josephus and Tacitus both present
the submission of Parthian hostages as part of dynastic management.
Josephus assigns agency to Phraates's consort, Thesmusa, an Italian
woman who had been given to Phraates as a gift from Augustus in
gratitude for the return of the standards.[64] As Josephus tells it, she
sought to promote the interests of her own son, who was kept at
court, at the expense of her stepsons, who were fully Arsacid and therefore more legitimate heirs. Tacitus believes the tactic was employed
by a later Parthian king: Vologaeses is said to have agreed to give
hostages to Corbulo in 54 CE so that he could either buy time to prepare for war or remove his rivals for the throne.[65] Here the hostages
are again a distraction, thrown up to conceal unfriendly plots, and
the Romans were thus said to suffer from hostage-taking strategies,
rather than profit from them. This way of thinking about hostages
equates the practice with exile; transferring sons to Rome was thought
to protect the king's position. It should be remembered that these

---

[62] Strabo, 16.1.28, C749. Contrast Strabo, 6.4.2, C288. Drijvers 1998, 289 also notes
the discrepancy, arguing that the earlier reference along the lines of host-guest is a
"Romano-centric view."

[63] Just. *Epit.* 42.5.1; Plut. *Ant.* 37.1; Cass. Dio, 49.23.4.

[64] Joseph. *A.J.* 18.39–42.

[65] Tac. *Ann.* 13.9. In an additional example, Josephus (*AJ* 20.36–37) records that Izates, a
king of Adiabene, dispatched his brothers as hostages, some to Claudius in Rome and
others to Artabanus in Parthia, in order that they pose less of a threat.

interpretations of the Parthian hostages may be rhetorical: other accounts of the Parthians do not include this motive for the submission, and Strabo is inconsistent; Josephus and Tacitus may be employing a trope in order to develop the characters in their stories in accordance with a foregone agenda. For example, Josephus's account is a clear polemic against Thesmusa and deploys the literary motif of the wicked stepmother, and Tacitus's account emphasizes the failure of the practice of hostage-taking in general, a theme that is evident throughout his corpus, especially the *Annals*, and which serves the larger purpose of commenting on his Julio-Claudian forebears (see Chapter 9). Depending on the writer's point of view, the same hostage in Rome could either have been despised and sent away to end his career in the dynasty, or loved and sent away to promote him. In the former conception, the donor comes off as emphasizing his autonomy; in the latter, he is a true vassal.

As a final example of discrepancies in the reporting on hostages on this score, one could consider Sallust's monograph on the Roman war with Jugurtha. He says, on the one hand, that the Numidian king, Micipsa, sent his nephew Jugurtha to the Romans at the siege of Numantia because he was worried about Jugurtha's ambition and hoped he would be killed in battle; the notion of the hated heir thus prevails early in the work.[66] Later, on the other hand, Sallust observes that Jugurtha's tenure among the Romans only catapulted him to the top of Micipsa's choices of successors, as Scipio Aemilianus expressed his support of Jugurtha in a letter of recommendation.[67] It is unlikely that Scipio's promotion of Jugurtha came as a surprise to Micipsa: the king himself had been hand-picked as heir to Masinissa by Scipio Africanus in the previous generation.[68] It seems preposterous, then, for Sallust to allege that Micipsa sent Jugurtha to Rome – the land of the kingmakers – in order to get rid of him; rather, the mission marked

---

[66] Sall. *Jug.* 6.3.

[67] In Sall. *Jug.* 9.3, Sallust implies that Micipsa adopted Jugurtha the moment he heard of Scipio's approval (around 132 BCE), but in *Jug.* 11.6, he says that Micipsa adopted him under duress and only within three years of his death, making 121 the earliest possible date for adoption. Coltelloni-Trannoy 1997, 38 compares Jugurtha's stint at Numantia with Juba II's participation in Augustus's Spanish campaigns.

[68] App. *Pun.* 105; cf. Polyb. 35.18.10; Livy, 30.15.11. See also Paul 1984, 26–27.

Jugurtha as Micipsa's potential replacement. In general, however, the historian is clearly interested in demonizing Jugurtha (and his Roman friends). It would seem that here he selectively deployed one of the many stereotypes of the hostage – the hated heir – even though it makes little sense.[69] For our purposes in this chapter, the trope itself is of interest: in this conception, hostage-taking in effect created multiple "fathers" who might compete or collude in the future of the donor state's politics.

[69] For a revision of Sallust's polemic against Jugurtha, see Claassen 1992–1993.

6

TEACHER-STUDENT

Multiple texts from Roman antiquity describe situations and episodes where hostages became acculturated to the behaviors, routines, and lifestyles of their overseers. Several literary sources imply that it was nothing short of imperial policy for the Romans to offer their hostages a formal, controlled education. Three episodes suggest that the effort to assimilate hostages was a means of reaching, through them, entire tribes. First, Tacitus describes the policies of Agricola, his father-in-law and governor of Britain under Domitian, as follows:

[Agricola] allowed no break for the enemy from sudden assaults, and when he had frightened them enough, he demonstrated the benefits of peace through leniency. As a result many states which until that day had been autonomous set aside their anger, having given hostages (*datis obsidibus*). . . . In order that these scattered and savage men, who had always been liable to wage war, might become accustomed to leisure through pleasant distractions, he encouraged them privately and helped them publicly in building temples, marketplaces, and houses, praising the industrious and castigating the slothful; thus the rivalry for his respect stood in for compulsion. He also brought up the sons of the leaders [most likely, the hostages mentioned above] in liberal studies (*liberalibus artibus*). . . such that those who recently had disdained the Latin language longed for eloquence themselves. Our dress became a mark of distinction as the toga came into vogue. Little by little they slipped into the distractions of vices: the porticos, the baths, the elegance of banquets. Among the inexperienced, it was called culture when it was truly a part of their enslavement.[1]

---

[1] Tac. *Agr.* 20.2–21.2. Ogilvie 1967 presents a positivistic reading of the passage, but on the rhetorical nature of the claim of reeducation, see Woolf 1998, 69–71; Rutledge 2000,

Plutarch pictures a similar Romanizing agenda for Sertorius's conduct on the Iberian peninsula in the seventies BCE:

Having impressed them by these accomplishments, Sertorius was adored by the barbarians, and by demonstrating Roman defenses, formations, and coordination, he made a powerful army out of a large gang of bandits, and did away with their disorganized and savage acts of courage. He generously decorated their helmets and shields with silver and gold and taught them to wear flowered cloaks and tunics, giving them the necessary supplies and sharing their love of array; he was thus welcomed there. Most of all they liked what he did with their children: assembling the highest born of their tribes at Osca, a large city, he assigned to them tutors of Greek and Roman education, in effect making them hostages as, ostensibly, he taught them (ἔργῳ μεν ἐξωμηρεύσατος, λόγῳ δὲ ἐπαίδευεν). He promised them citizenship and power when they grew to manhood. The fathers were pleased to see their boys dressed in purple-bordered togas going proudly to school as Sertorius took care of the fees and tested them often, awarded prizes to those who earned them, and made gifts of the gold necklaces that the Romans call *bullae*.[2]

Third, in his biography of Caligula, Suetonius says that the emperor, desperate from his lack of suitable accomplishments and eager to show some sign of courage no matter how contrived, had hostages "removed from a grammar school" and set free for him to capture as runaways.[3] Taken together these three episodes, all written around the start of the second century CE, lend credence to the notion that the Romans sought to manage their empire with more subtlety and forward-looking strategy than with brute force after the final battles were over.[4] The episodes all imply an education in the Latin language,

---

85–86; and Clarke 2001, 105–106. On the archaeological evidence for Agricola, see Hanson 1987 and 1991. On the inertia of native architectural styles in Roman Britain, see Hingley 1997.

[2] Plut. *Sert.* 14. For a positivistic view of the passage, see Konrad 1994, 144, but also see Swain 1989, 66–68 and García Moreno 1992, 136 on its rhetorical nature. Cf. Lécrivain 1916, 131 and Elbern 1990, 119.

[3] Suet. *Calig.* 45.2: *abductos e litterario ludo.* Cf. Lécrivain 1916, 131 and Scardigli 1994, 149.

[4] There are some problems with citing these passages in relation to Roman initiatives in hostage education. With Tacitus, for example, the historian says that hostages were taken and sons of chieftains were educated by Romans, but it is unspecified whether he meant that both groups of boys were the same, although context allows for that conclusion. Moreover, in Plutarch's biography, Sertorius invites the boys to attend a school of sorts

and the stories in Plutarch and Tacitus also mention concomitant changes in styles of dress; Tacitus adds references to architecture and eating habits.[5] Most important, Tacitus and Plutarch both believe that the transformation of the hostages played an important part in the transformation of the indigenous, non-Roman, nonhostage adults as styles changed and a positive impression of Rome emerged simultaneously. All three of these cases deal with the Roman West, perhaps not surprisingly given the limited extent of Hellenistic-style urbanization there, but as we shall see, the idea of young hostages undergoing some kind of training during their captivity was a common rhetorical motif with respect to the East as well, whether the "students" were Parthians, Armenians, or Greeks themselves, either from the mainland or the Hellenistic kingdoms.[6]

The notion was widespread enough to draw the attention of Lucian's satire in the second century. At one point, the speaker in his fantasy, *True Histories*, describes a meeting that he had with the poet Homer, which indirectly raises questions about the theme of hostage reeducation in historiography:

Not two or three days had passed and I went up to Homer the poet when we were both unoccupied, and I asked him about this and that and about

---

and only afterward uses them as hostages. Suetonius, however, is unequivocal in his reference to a school for hostages.

[5] For a discussion of the significance of clothing in characterization in Roman literature (in this case, Cicero), see Dyck 2001. Note also Vergil's interest in dress and language as indicators of foreign-ness in his ekphrasis of Augustus's triple triumph on the shield of Aeneas: *Aen.* 8.714–728.

[6] In general, on the reeducation of hostages, see also Matthaei 1905, 243; Lécrivain 1916, 131; Aymard 1961, 445; Walker 1980, 42; Braund 1984a, 13–17; Elbern 1990, 118; Ndiaye 1995, 154–155; and Burns 2003, 101. See also Lee 1991, 367, who points out similar cases in late antiquity: in Amm. Marc. 16.12.25, an Alamannic king changed his name from Agenaric to Serapio because his father was initiated into the cult while a hostage in Rome; and in Amm. Marc. 18.6.20, a certain Jovinianus learns Greek culture while a hostage in Antioch. See also Matthews 1989 for the phenomenon in late antiquity. On the interesting related issue of the extent to which the Romans were said to learn from their hostages, there is little evidence, although Austin and Rankov 1995, 69 and Bertrand 1997, 114 note that Caesar relied on the information about Gallic topography from his prisoners of war (*BGall.* 2.16.1). Also, Palombi's entry on the *Vicus Africus* in the *Lexicon Topographicum Urbis Romae* suggests that a dedication to Dea Caelestis found on the Esquiline Hill represents a Romanization of the Punic goddess Tanit – a vestige of the Carthaginian hostages in that region.

where he was from, since this is especially of interest now among us. He said the he was not unaware that some believed he was from Chios, some from Smyrna, and even more from Colophon, but he said he was from Babylon and that among his own people his name was not Homer but Tigranes – later when he was a hostage (ὁμηρεύσας, and so a *homeros*) among the Greeks, he changed his name.[7]

Any reader of the history of Roman relations with the East will know of the seeming ubiquity of eastern hostages named Tigranes. At least five can be found in the surviving, fragmentary record: a Tigranes detained by Pompey following his eastern campaign and stolen by Clodius in 58 BCE;[8] Tigranes II, taken by Octavian in 30 BCE from among Antony's Alexandrian entourage and sent back to Armenia in 20;[9] his son, Tigranes III, who may have been detained with him and who ruled with his sister Erato around 7 BCE;[10] another, shadowy Tigranes, called a former king by Josephus and Tacitus, about whom all is known is that he ran into trouble with a paranoid Tiberius in 36 CE;[11] and, finally, a Tigranes who was installed on the throne of Armenia by Corbulo, on Nero's orders, around 60 CE, and who is said to have adopted Roman habits while a hostage.[12] The family tree of these Tigraneses is a notorious puzzle, with their parentage, dates, and even the Roman numerals following their names not completely secure

---

[7] Lucian, *Ver. hist.* 2.20.

[8] See Chapter 3, note 73.

[9] *Mon. Anc.* 27.2; Vell. Pat. 2.94.4; Joseph. *AJ* 15.105; Tac. *Ann.* 2.3; Suet. *Tib.* 9.1; Cass. Dio, 54.9.4–5.

[10] Tac. *Ann.* 2.3; Cass. Dio, 55.10a.5, 55.10.20–21. There seems to have been a struggle for power between this Tigranes (III) and his uncle Artavasdes II. Pani 1972, 25–26 suggests that Artavasdes II never entered Armenia but was an absent king, "ruling" simultaneously and at odds with Tigranes III. Chaumont 1976, 76 argues that the reason that this Tigranes is absent from the *Res Gestae* is that he did not last long. See also Sherwin-White 1984, 325–326.

[11] Joseph. *AJ* 18.139; Tac. *Ann.* 6.40. This may be the second Tigranes mentioned at *Res Gestae* 27, now at the end of his career and (unluckily) in Rome for some unknown reason. Josephus says that he was a grandson of Herod the Great through his father Alexander and a grandson of Archelaus of Cappadocia through his mother Glaphyra; he also says in *BJ* 2.222 that the offspring (ἡ γενεά) of Alexander and Glaphyra became kings of Armenia. It is the same Glaphyra who later married Juba II, so Tigranes would have been Juba's stepson. See Pani 1972 and Chaumont 1976.

[12] Joseph. AJ 18.140; Tac. *Ann.* 14.26; Cass. Dio, 62.20.2–3: the great-grandson of Alexander and Glaphyra. See Wheeler 1997, 384 n. 7 for the evidence for his dates.

today.[13] It was perhaps just as confusing in Lucian's day, such that the name Tigranes, combined with hostageship, became an opportunity for sarcasm: Lucian makes the joke that Homer himself, whose name is Greek for hostage, was yet another of them, adopting a new name and outlook when he was stranded far from his home in Babylon, also a symbol of the exotic East.[14] He expects the reader to roll his eyes: the figure of the hostage/student had become a stock character in historiography, and the hostage's total acceptance of the hostage-taker's culture, a cliché.[15] The name "homer" became a watchword, ridiculous at that, for "brainwashing."

By holding his tongue in cheek as he recounts a fictional hostage episode, Lucian implicitly casts doubt on the validity of the model and raises a series of issues to be addressed in this chapter. The Romans seem to have had an innate obsession with the impressionable nature of youth and thus valued the taking of hostages as an opportunity to mold the attitudes of foreign adolescents toward Rome. At times, however, hostages can be proven to have been less than accommodating of Roman culture: archaeological evidence on occasion presents a more nuanced picture than that of the literary record, suggesting that Rome was not as irresistible as it is portrayed or that Romanization proceeded in a piecemeal fashion, at odds with Roman rhetoric. In the literary testimonies, then, the Roman trust in hostage education is shown to be not only simplistic but also overly optimistic, or deliberately misleading. The fact that the complex, polyvalent phenomenon of "Romanization" was reduced to a story of stooges eagerly embracing Roman culture betrays the essence of ethnic hegemony and the imperialist tendencies of the Roman center and its writers. Keeping in mind Lucian's irreverent approach to hostage-taking, the modern

---

[13] Romer 1979, 202 discusses the silence of the sources for 6–2 BCE. Our Tigranes II and III sometimes appear as III and IV in modern treatments, such as the *Oxford Classical Dictionary*, third edition. But see Chaumont 1976, 74–77.

[14] For references in literature to Homer's contested birthplace, see Georgiadou and Larmour 1998, 201. On the meaning of Homer's name, see also Birt 1932; Deroy 1972; and Thesleff 1985. Zeitlin 2001, 246–247 discusses the significance of the interview for the Second Sophistic.

[15] Cf. Strabo, 11.14.15, C532 commenting on the replacement of eastern kings with Roman candidates as a rote pattern and discussing another Tigranes who was a hostage in Parthia. Cf. Flor. 2.32.

reader is confronted with the challenge of separating rhetoric from reality. As usual in this book, the rhetoric is what draws our attention, given that it can demonstrate another possible role that hostages were expected to play in ancient Rome. When a Roman saw a hostage in the street, he might think of him as a student of his surroundings, which necessarily implied, to the viewer at least, that Rome was worth learning, worth respecting, and therefore, in a sense, worth fearing.

THE RHETORIC OF INDOCTRINATION

One of the reasons given by Polybius for the virulence of Hannibal's hatred of Rome in the Second Punic War is that when the Carthaginian was nine years old, his father brought him before an altar and made him swear to be Rome's eternal enemy. As the argument goes, Hannibal's determination to annihilate the Romans was all the more severe because, uniquely when compared with all of Rome's other enemies, it had been ingrained in him when he was still a boy.[16] Whether such an event ever took place or not, the anecdote demonstrates the belief commonly held in antiquity that the events of one's early life had a profound influence on his or her later development. Children, adolescents, and young adults were thought to be susceptible to new ways of thinking, which could set them apart from their relatives, their countrymen, and even their species or gender.[17] Greco-Roman mythology is full of such stories, where a hero's unusual traits are explained by an unusual upbringing: Achilles's outstanding qualities came from the tutelage of Chiron, the enlightened centaur, and the reason behind Atalanta's superhuman (and, to the mind of the ancient reader, supergender) hunting instincts lay in her being reared

---

[16] Polyb. 3.11.7. Lazenby 1978, 20 and Walbank 1957, 314–315 make a case for the rumor being true.

[17] On adulthood and childhood as categories in Rome, see Wiedemann 1989; Eyben 1991, 125–126 and 1993; and Rawson 1991, 17–23. Evans 1991, 195–199 discusses the tension surrounding surrogate parenting. On the mechanics of teaching, see Cribiore 2001. Golden 1997 argues against looking for continuity and change in the way children were viewed in antiquity, implying it was common throughout. Much of these argue implicitly against Kleijwegt 1991, who denies that adolescence was a distinct category of childhood in antiquity. On the emergence of the idea of adolescence, see Demos and Demos 1969.

by a bear.[18] Early prose history includes similar legends, but replaces the animals with animal-named humans: Herodotus says that Cyrus the Great of Persia was raised by a shepherdess whose name, Spako, was Medean for dog, and Livy, of course, recounts the old story of the infants Romulus and Remus being rescued by Lupa, whose name means wolf.[19] The plot of ancient drama, both comedy and tragedy, was often driven by a youth's separation from his family and by his subsequent foreign education. Oedipus, abandoned by his birth father, rescued by shepherds, and raised by a foreign king, could not recognize his family, with well-known tragic results, whereas Agorastocles, the boy hero of Plautus's *Poenulus*, or "Little Carthaginian," generated laughs as a kidnapped and utterly transformed Carthaginian, now speaking Greek.[20] Historians recording biographical vignettes found meaning in the way their subject spent his or her childhood. The fact that Alcibiades cut the tail off of a puppy when he was a boy, to Plutarch, foretold a life of restlessness, cruelty, and ambition; Suetonius found a kind of genius in Titus, the son of Vespasian, because of his adolescent skills in speed writing, shorthand, and forgery, which were interpreted as portents of diligence and craft.[21] Youthful games and rituals in Rome were thought to be effective ways to teach ethics, as allusions to boys pretending to be generals or senators also attest.[22] Cicero believed one's environment, and not his race, shaped his demeanor, and Horace, in his *Carmen Saeculare* of 17 BCE, prayed that the gods "give sound character to youth while they are teachable (*docili*)."[23] The very existence in Latin of the verb *dedisco*, meaning something

---

[18] See Grimal 1963 for references. Abbondanza 1996 discusses images of Achilles and Chiron in the Roman era, noting the greater interest in Achilles's *paideia*, relative to Hellenistic depictions. On the casting of Chiron as teacher, father, and host simultaneously in Ovid's *Fasti*, see Boyd 2001; note also Ovid, *Ars Am.* 1.12 on how Chiron's training of Achilles soothed his "savage spirit" (*animos feros*). On Atalanta as "the embodiment of ambiguity and liminality, combining aspects of male and female," see Barringer 1996, 49.

[19] Hdt. 1.110; Livy, 1.4.7. On the folkloric qualities of the stories, see Cornell 1995, 61–63.

[20] Rather, Latin, which Plautus's characters naturally speak for their audience despite Greek settings. On the link between hostage-taking and the *Poenulus*, see later.

[21] Plut. *Alc.* 9; Suet. *Tit.* 3.2.

[22] See Wiedemann 1989, 143–170 and Rawson 2003, 126–129. On the *collegia iuvenum*, see Eyben 1993, 112–114.

[23] Cic. *Leg. Agr.* 2.95. Hor. *Carm. Saec.* 45.

like to "unlearn," shows that the Romans believed education to be fluid and reversible: early in his work on oratory, Quintilian urges parents to ensure that the nurses employed to watch their children are able to speak with proper grammar, lest their children, in their impressionable state of mind, pick up modes of speech that they may later have to "unlearn."[24] A child's upbringing was closely guarded and valued, but even more important for our purposes, the chance always existed that the child could be reeducated and molded into an entirely different creature based on the whims of the teacher.

In terms of international relations, the education of youth was seen as one way of building alliances with neighbors with whom Rome was at peace. Notably, the Temple of *Fides* on the Capitoline Hill, where Romans set up copies of foreign treaties and near which foreign kings made honorary dedications, displayed a painting of an old man with a lyre teaching a boy.[25] The *Atrium Libertatis*, where hostages were kept during the Second Punic War, was an archive and later expanded as a library by Gaius Asinius Pollio, the same man who shepherded the education of the sons of Herod. Ruling families on the fringes of Roman territory are said to have sent their sons to Rome voluntarily, as Braund has shown.[26] Livy says that Ariarathes IV sent his son to Rome so that he might "become accustomed to Roman men and their way of life and so that he might be under the guardianship not only of private hosts but also under public care just as under protection."[27] Polybius says that Charops of Epirus was sent to Rome to learn Latin.[28] Jugurtha, too, may have been sent to Scipio Aemilianus at Numantia (before he became Rome's enemy) in order to learn Roman tactics and language; Sallust does not say as much explicitly, but one of Jugurtha's greatest moments on the battlefield against Rome was when he spoke to Roman soldiers in Latin, spreading the

---

[24] Quint. *Inst.* 1.1.4: *discendus sit.* See Rawson 2003, 136–145 on Roman conceptions of the stages of childhood when education was seen as especially important.

[25] Pliny, *HN* 35.100.

[26] Braund 1984a, 9–11. Roller 2003, 60 suggests that the trend "died out" in 153/2 and was not "reinstated" until a century later.

[27] Livy, 42.19.4–5: . . . *assuesceret moribus Romanis hominibusque. Petere ut eum non sub hospitum modo privatorum custodia, sed publicae etiam curae ac velut tutelage vellent esse.*

[28] Polyb. 27.15.4.

false rumor that Marius was dead and that their efforts were thus in vain.[29] Moreover, as we have seen, the heirs of Herod the Great were cycled through Rome for what Josephus at one point calls their "studies."[30] This act of reeducation was not accidental, nor futile: Rome's alliances allegedly grew stronger through the practice. Braund suggests that Ariarathes's later success in obtaining Rome's recognition of his crown in 169/8 stemmed from his personal relationships.[31] Charops was an ally of Rome until his betrayal of his countrymen became so nefarious that even the senate turned on him.[32] Jugurtha was supported by a faction of senators who probably knew him from prior contacts; Sallust believes this support was the result of massive bribery, but it could have simply been loyalty and even admiration, as Scipio Aemilianus showed in writing Jugurtha's letter of recommendation to Jugurtha's uncle Micipsa.[33] And the sons of Herod who reached the throne were effectively Roman puppets, moved around and reassigned at the behest of Augustus.[34] To the Roman mind-set, the fundamental notion that the education of youth could bring foreign cultures closer together, or rather, bring a less advanced culture up to speed with a hegemon, was taken for granted.

The four examples above are of voluntary students; by extension it would be reasonable for Roman writers and readers to assume that involuntary hostages could also face systematic reeducation in a similar fashion. They, too, could be used to achieve objectives in international relations, despite the origins of their internment in compulsion and, perhaps, hostility. The Romans notoriously targeted the very young in their hostage-taking. For the hostages of Carthage, Antiochus III, and the Aetolian League, all in the early second century, the age requirements were as low as fourteen, eighteen, and twelve, according to recorded stipulations. In the case of the Seleucids, exceptions were

[29] Sall. *Jug.* 101.6. cf. Braund 1984a, 15–16.
[30] Joseph. *AJ* 16.6: μαθήμασιν, in reference to Herod's Hasmonaean heirs. See also Joseph. *AJ* 15.342–343. Cf. Bickerman 1988, 161–178, who discusses the foundation of Jewish schools to compete with the spread of Hellenism.
[31] Braund 1984a, 9.
[32] Polyb. 27.15. See Gruen 1984, 165–166.
[33] Sall. *Jug.* 9.3. For a revision of Sallust's demonization of Jugurtha, see Claassen 1992–1993 and Chapter 5.
[34] See Chapter 5.

made for Antiochus IV Epiphanes and later his nephew Demetrius Soter, who were both younger than the cutoff age of eighteen.[35] We have already seen that Demetrius of Macedon was very young when he marched in Flamininus's triumph following the defeat of Macedon at Cynoscephalae in 197 BCE. Plutarch also says that his brother Perseus's children were little different: in the course of the triumph after Pydna, tutors were said to be on hand to teach them to beg, and the spectators pitied them because of their tender ages.[36] Plutarch again had in mind the susceptibility of youthful hostages to indoctrination when he recorded the anxiety felt by a Spartan king who had been asked to submit youths as hostages as part of an agreement:

After Agis was defeated and Antipater had called for 50 boys as hostages, the ephor Eteocles said that they would not surrender boys so that they would grow up outside of training, thus missing their country's *agoge* and becoming unsuitable as citizens. If he wanted, they would give twice as many old men or women. When Antipater threatened harsh penalties if he should not receive the boys, they answered together, "if you sentence us to a fate more heinous than death, we are satisfied with death."[37]

Sparta's system of education – the vaunted *agoge* – was notoriously regimented, and its successful completion was critical to Spartan identity, such that the boys' detention was worrisome not because they could be harmed, but that they could not become Spartans in the first place. In this sense, the hostages' minds were in jeopardy rather than their bodies, a sentiment Livy expresses when he says that Flamininus held Demetrius's soul hostage, not his body.[38]

It was a common historical trope among Roman authors for an uncivilized person to encounter and adopt a new, civilized lifestyle during his hostageship. Examples are plentiful. A passage from Diodorus Siculus in reference to the transformation of Philip II from an unruly Macedonian to a refined Theban serves as a template by which other episodes can be measured:

[35] See Chapter 1.
[36] Plut. *Aem.* 33.4.
[37] Plut. *Mor.* 235B.
[38] Livy, 39.47.10.

When Amyntas had been conquered by the Illyrians and compelled to pay tribute to the conquerors, the Illyrians took Philip, the youngest of his sons, and turned him over to the Thebans. They then gave him to the father of Epaminondas and instructed him to guard the youth and supervise his education and training (τῆς ἀγωγῆς καὶ παιδείας). Because Epaminondas had a Pythagorean philosopher as his teacher, Philip, his companion, learned much about Pythagorean beliefs.[39]

Vegetarianism, reincarnation, sexual abstinence – readers of Diodorus might be expected to delight in the image of an urchin of the "savage" Macedonians, with his head cocked and quizzical, trying to figure out Pythagorean lecturers. In other words, the more barbaric the hostage was, the more radical his acculturation. But it was more than simply humorous irony: the reeducation of this one man was thought to have an effect on an entire population, as Diodorus goes on to recount how Philip's eventual rule brought Macedon to new heights: he reportedly organized political assemblies, in the style of Thebes, and introduced the phalanx, bringing Macedonian weaponry up to date as well.[40]

Polybius envisions a similar scenario for Antiochus IV Epiphanes of Syria. After having lived in Rome as a hostage from 188 to 178/7, he assumed the throne back home (removing a young nephew first) and took to wearing the toga, frequenting the forum like a Roman magistrate, gladhanding for votes that he, as a king, did not need, and sitting in judgment on a Roman magistrate's chair.[41] Livy adds that he built a temple to Jupiter Optimus Maximus in the heart of Antioch, and staged gladiatorial exhibitions. His description of how the people of Antioch received the changes recalls the notion in Diodorus's account of Philip II of how one former hostage could steer his people in a completely new and astonishing direction:

He put on a gladiatorial exhibition according to the Roman custom, which at first caused greater terror than pleasure among those not used to such

---

[39] Diod. Sic. 16.2.2–3. Cf. Just., *Epit.* 6.9.7 and Dio Chrys., *Or.* 49.5 who imply that Philip was trained by, not with, Epaminondas. On Philip's education see Aymard 1954; Chatzopoulos 1985–1986; and Hammond 1997.

[40] Diod. Sic. 16.3.1–3.

[41] Polyb. 26.1.1–7 = Athen. 10.439a. Cf. Diod. Sic. 29.32 and Livy, 41.20.1. Grainger 1990, 156 views Antiochus's transformation as radically altering the Seleucid political system.

a spectacle. But then, by putting them on more often and by sometimes stopping the fighters at the point of wounding each other and at other times letting them fight without interruption, he made the event commonplace and even pleasing to the eyes.[42]

After taking the throne, Antiochus is also said to have sent flattering embassies to Rome, which asserted his loyalty, specifically in return for his excellent treatment as a hostage.[43]

Roman authors seem to appreciate that children of Rome's enemies were tamed through reeducation. As we have seen, Juba II was remembered for his advanced education and interest in Hellenistic science, arts, and history. Tacitus tells of the drastic reeducation of Parthian and other eastern hostages in Rome, although as will be seen in Chapter 9, he questions its value as a device of empire. In Plutarch's biography of Aemilius Paullus, he includes an anecdote about the otherwise unknown Alexander, son of the defeated Perseus, who grew up in Rome and learned metalworking as well as the Latin language, becoming a secretary to a magistrate. His career is recounted by Plutarch in sharp contrast with the menacing quality of his father.[44] That the Romans expected their hostages to change somehow is also indicated by a second-century law preserved in the *Digest*, which makes special provisions for hostages who toe the line and adopt Roman customs:

Marcian, *Institutes* 4: The deified Commodus wrote back that the goods of hostages, just as those of prisoners of war, must be entirely collected for the treasury [upon their death]. Marcian, *Institutes* 14: But if, having donned the toga, they always conduct themselves as Roman citizens, the deified brothers (Marcus Aurelius and Lucius Verus) wrote to the procurators of estates that without a doubt the right of their children was different from the status of hostage (*ab obsidis condicione*) by virtue of the emperor's beneficence. Therefore the same right is held for them as they would have if they had been appointed heirs by full Roman citizens.[45]

The cultural demeanor of the hostage parents thus determined the status of their children: failure to abide by Roman conventions led

[42] Livy, 41.20.11. Kondoleon 2000, 155 reads the passage positivistically.
[43] In 173: Livy, 42.6.6–11. In 172: Livy, 42.36.7–8; App. *Mac.* 11.4.
[44] Plut. *Aem.* 37.
[45] *Dig.* 49.14.31–32. See also Lécrivain 1916, 132.

to the confiscation of their property on death, whereas the reverse –
indicated, again, by dress – guaranteed the future citizenship of any
children who were in captivity with them. Marcus Aurelius and Lucius
Verus thus actively installed incentives for the cultural change of
hostages; in short, hostage-taking was thought to be a means of creating new citizens.[46] Some historians have denied that the Romans had
any interest in what we might call "cultural imperialism";[47] but the
targets of Romans working overseas were clearly not only the wealth
and land and labor of the newly conquered, but also their "hearts and
minds," especially in the case of the younger generation.

A piece of Roman popular culture from the mid-Republic suggests
circumstantially that the reeducation of hostages was expected at an
early period in Roman history, if not proactively encouraged by the
state, and more importantly, that it could be demeaning to the "student" in question. Plautus's *Poenulus*, or, "The Little Carthaginian,"
was staged around 191 BCE, at the end of the first decade of the fifty-
year settlement with the defeated Carthaginians of the Second Punic
War.[48] The play includes many of the stock situations of New Comedy borrowed from the Greeks, such as a kidnapped child who was
taken far from his family, mistaken identity, and a final revelation of
his parentage, with the attendant epiphanies for each of the characters

---

[46] A few inscriptions from the Principate may reveal the creation of these "new Romans":
Dessau, 846 reads, in its entirety: "Sitalces, hostage of Augustus from Thrace, and his
sister Julia Phyllis" (*Sitalces divi / Augusti / opses Thracum / Iulia Phyllis / soror eius*). Dessau,
842 simply records names of two sons of Phraates IV in the nominative: *Seraspadanes,
Phraatis / Arsacis regum regis f. / Parthus / Rhodaspes, Phraatis / Arsacis regum regis f. /
Parthus*. It is odd that these are precisely the two sons from Strabo's list of four (16.1.28,
C 749) that do not appear in any other sources. I am reluctant to include Dessau 843
in this study, which refers to the Parthian Arsacids, given the extent to which it is
restored. It comes from a temple to Isis near Lake Nemi: *[imp. Caesar divi Traiani Parthici
fil. divi] Nervae nepos Traianus / [Hadrianus Augustus pont. max. trib]unic. potest. VI cos. III
/ [fanum quod . . . Phraatis regis regu]m Parthorum fil. Arsacides / [fecerat, vetustate collaps]um
restituit*. On both of the inscriptions dealing with the Parthians, see Gardthausen 1906;
Nedergaard 1988, 108–109; and Noy 2000, 107.
[47] E.g., Galinsky 1996, 330. See also MacMullen 2000, 89, in which cultural change is
"left to the natives" and proceeds "at its own pace." By contrast, Sicker 2001, 91 speaks
directly of Augustus's "cultural imperialism," and Toll 1997, 41–48 discusses Vergil's
active interest, visible in the *Aeneid*, of portraying the openness of Rome, perhaps with
the intent of forging a new, hybrid Roman identity.
[48] On the date of the *Poenulus*, see Woytek 2004.

delivered at the climax. In this case, the lost child is a Carthaginian boy who ends up in Greece, forgets how to speak Punic, and can later recognize neither his female first cousins nor his uncle.[49] Spectators of the comedy in the early second century must have been reminded of the momentous settlement with Carthage as they watched and laughed. They would have been aware that Scipio had won at Zama; that the overwhelming sum of 200 talents were paid to the Roman treasury each year, scheduled for fifty years in all; that Punic lands in Iberia and Africa were in Roman hands or in the hands of their friends; and that the once-terrible Hannibal was on the run in Asia Minor. They also would have grown accustomed to the hundreds of Carthaginian boys who themselves had been living in Rome and in surrounding cities as hostages for at least the past decade. The hostages had been repeatedly in the public eye, for both good and bad. As we have seen, embassies had arrived from Carthage asking that their accommodations be improved and that they be moved to more suitable cities.[50] The staging of the comedy followed closely the rebellion of Carthaginian slaves, in which the hostages were implicated but acquitted. Suspicion of the hostages remained strong, and the Roman attitude toward them had changed: their freedom to appear in public places at will became limited.[51] The humor of the play would have been animated by the figurative similarity and the literal proximity of these Carthaginian hostages, who were themselves in an unfamiliar setting, speaking a strange language that few Romans could understand, and who would have been the age of the comedy's protagonist. The jokes would have fallen flat unless there had been a ready understanding among viewers of the possibility of reeducation of those same hostages. The comedy is thus an implicit celebration of Roman imperial success, not only in their military but in their culture as well.[52] The play's very title,

---

[49] For the protagonist's ignorance of Punic, see Plaut. *Poen.* 985–1031. On Punic words in the play, see Faller 2004.

[50] Livy 32.2.4; 32.26.5.

[51] Livy, 32.26.18.

[52] For a full discussion of the play, see the first chapter in Henderson 1999. Gruen 1990, 129–140 discusses Plautus's interest in triumph-hungry generals in other plays. For the reverse argument, that the Punic hostages had a cultural influence *on Rome*, see Kolendo 1970 and earlier.

Poenulus, reveals two anxieties and desires on the part of the Roman audience: not only does it register the fact of Carthage (*Poen-*), now downtrodden and to be mocked, but it also identifies the Carthaginian as little, or, young (*-ulus*). As such he is understood by the audience as weak, ridiculous, and able to be manipulated in ways that were, to the Roman victors, both typical and hilarious. The comedy's long speeches in Punic, as the uncle speaks but is not understood by his refashioned nephew, are dehumanizing riffs on the strangeness and helplessness of the Carthaginians back home in Africa and on the radical transformation that their hostage children will undergo. The play essentially affirmed for the audience that they were preventing the rise of another Hannibal and his deadly childhood oath.

In one case, archaeological evidence describes the setting of a "school" for foreign youth and suggests that reeducation was one part of a larger cultural strategy for maintaining empire and that it must have met with resistance. Both Tacitus and Eumenius, an orator of the late third century, refer to a school or schools at the town of Augustodunum, modern Autun, France. Tacitus says that when Julius Sacrovir began a rebellion against Rome in 21 CE, his first step was to take the Gallic children out of some classes where they were receiving an education in "liberal studies" and detain them in order to secure the loyalty of their families against Rome.[53] The staunch opposition to the school, evident with Julius Sacrovir's rebellion, seems to have ebbed over the course of generations, as Eumenius, himself a resident of Augustodunum, is proud of the institution when he addresses a speech to the governor of Lugdunensis I: Eumenius's grandfather had taught there before him, and he feels honored to carry on the family tradition.[54] Apparently, the school had been destroyed along with much of the rest of the city in 269/70, when it was sacked by "the thievery of a Batavian rebellion"; the purpose of Eumenius's oration is to ask the Roman prefect if he may redirect his salary as professor to the rebuilding of the school.[55] Eumenius reveals that the facility stood

---

[53] Tac. *Ann.* 3.42–43: *liberalia studia*. Hostages of the teacher-student paradigm thus shift to one of creditor-collateral.

[54] *Pan. Lat.* 9.17.3–4. On the date and addressee of the speech, see Nixon and Rodgers 1994, 145–150; the speech is also discussed by Woolf 1998, 1–2.

[55] *Pan. Lat.* 9.4.1: *latrocinio Batavicae rebellionis.*

on the main thoroughfare between the Capitolium and a temple to Apollo; the building has not been securely identified, but archaeologists surmise that it was located between the remains of two round temples in the center of town.[56]

The school seems to have gone up at the same time as the town itself, which was established by Augustus either by 12 or 7 BCE as a new center for Roman administration of the Aeduans. In effect, Augustodunum took the place of Bibracte, a Gallic city only fifteen miles to the west, which had been the former Aeduan "capital."[57] Because Augustodunum was so close by, it could not have been created to present a better geographic, economic, or strategic position than had already existed in Bibracte. Rather, the old capital had been the location of the convention of Gallic chieftains who supported Vercingetorix's rebellion and must have had strong patriotic associations.[58] Augustus may have supported the new city for no other reason than to present the attractions of Roman culture in a historically unfriendly, or at least unsettled, region, antithetical to the symbolism of Bibracte.[59] The town has been called a "store window" for all that Rome had to offer, with impressive walls, temples, and later, the largest theater and amphitheater in the West.[60] Eumenius's speech hints at the type of studies that went on at the school: he says that the students might someday "be promoted to the expectation of every tribunal or to the employ of the sacred judiciary or perhaps even to the magistracies of the palace"[61] and through their education they may "mature into the

---

[56] MacKendrick 1971, 118; Bedon 2001, 90.

[57] Excavations have shown that Bibracte practically ceased to exist under Augustus: Rebourg 1991, 101; Woolf 1998, 113. The last reference to the town is Strabo, 4.3.2, C192. Béal 1996 objects to the term "capital city" for Bibracte, given that there is no evidence that Gauls thought of cities in such terms.

[58] Caes. BGall. 7.63.

[59] Woolf 2000, 119 argues that "the impetus [to build the new city] came from the aristocracy of the Aedui." But see Whittaker 1997, 152–160 on the "Roman initiative" in general terms.

[60] Pinette and Rebourg 1986, 22: une vitrine de Rome. Cf. Woolf 2000, 119: "a monumental kit" and Potter 1988 who calls Juba's Iol-Caesarea "une ville-vitrine." MacKendrick 1971 notes that Chaumar, the name of a district of the modern town, is a corruption of Campus Martius.

[61] Pan. Lat. 9.5.4: hi quos ad spem omnium tribunalium aut interdum ad stipendia cognitionum sacrarum aut fortasse ad ipsa palatii magisterial provehi oporteret. The translation owes a debt

service of the military and the camps."[62] The education at Augustodunum in this late third-century context may have had a different purpose from in the period that concerns us, but in any case, the Romanizing agenda is undeniable. That the city and the school were the locus of the first organized resistance in Gaul, as recorded by Tacitus, some thirty years after they were founded, implies that it was both acknowledged as effective and despised by the independently minded. Eumenius's more admiring view, coming centuries later, demonstrates that a profound shift had taken place over time.

RESISTANCE AND ACCOMMODATION: ANTIOCHUS IV, JUBA II, AND VONONES

Whether it is just a rhetorical claim or a *bona fide* policy, the reeducation of hostages was politically charged. Playing the role of student under another's tutelage obviously had the potential to be shameful, in spite of (or because of) the appeal of the rhetoric to the Romans. It implies powerlessness, a weakness of will, and a denial of one's past. On the Roman side, there existed excessive hubris concerning the success of their culture, most potently realized in the jokes told in the *Poenulus*; on the non-Roman side, as seen in Sacrovir's revolt at the school in Augustodunum, sharp resistance challenged the model. The division begs the question of how effective the policy of reeducating hostages was, beyond the optimism of the Roman writers. As clear as the Roman intentions in reeducating hostages were, their success is not so easy to measure. We have examples of hostages rejecting all or some aspects of their "mentor's" culture, as well as accounts of the hostages' native society rejecting them on the basis that they were no longer familiar. Briefly, Plutarch believed that Philip II fell short of a complete transformation during his hostageship in Thebes, mentioning that he did not acquire all the good qualities of Epaminondas. But still, these are Plutarch's words, not Philip's. In three case studies – Antiochus IV,

---

to Nixon and Rodgers 1994. See *ibid.*, 157, note 24 on education and public careers in the Principate. Nicolet 1991, 111–112 discusses a map that was apparently displayed in the school in Eumenius's day, which located conquered peoples, among other things.
[62] *Pan. Lat.* 9.8.2: *militiae atque castrorum munia convalescunt.*

Juba II, and Vonones – we may "read," to an extent, the responses of hostages themselves, whether in archaeological evidence for their careers or in their conduct in international affairs.

For all of the cultural changes alleged for Antiochus IV Epiphanes by Polybius and Livy, both historians demonstrate that a new cultural outlook, if true, did not translate into policies that were necessarily favorable to Rome. In spite of the fanciful and gossipy records of Antiochus IV becoming a quisling of the Romans, supposedly demonstrated by his temple, his banquets, his politicking, his toga, his gladiators, and his flattering embassies, one school of thought holds that Antiochus pursued an independent, even aggressive, foreign policy.[63] These scholars note that Antiochus did not send an embassy to Rome until 173, two years after he took the throne,[64] and that he tested the limits of the treaty of Apamea, imposed by Rome in the previous generation, by maintaining both a fleet and a corps of war-elephants.[65] Moreover, some see his war with Egypt over Coele-Syria as opportunistic, given that Rome was involved with Perseus and could not intervene; Antiochus invaded twice, and while he did not take Alexandria, he established a garrison at Pelusium in the northeast Nile Delta; seized Cyprus; and tried to manipulate Ptolemy Philometor, his nephew, as a puppet-king.[66] Antiochus finally withdrew after the famous show of

[63] Tarn 1951, 190 believes Antiochus sought to replicate Rome's system of centralized empire with a view toward creating Rome's "counterpoise." Mørkholm 1966, 68 says that when hostilities between Syria and Egypt broke out in 169, Antiochus "followed a premeditated plan with a clear political aim." Swain 1944, 75 argues Antiochus feared the encroaching nationalism of indigenous Egyptians abroad and Asians in his own realm. Briscoe 1969, 49 refers to Antiochus's "independent foreign policy" before the Day of Eleusis. On challenges to these notions, see later.

[64] Livy, 42.6.6–12. Mørkholm 1966, 64–65 sees this as Antiochus's independence. Passerini 1935, 332; Swain 1944, 80; and Gruen 1984, 648 suggest that the embassy sought to mollify Rome because the war with Egypt was imminent.

[65] Antiochus used a navy to attack Egypt (Livy, 44.19.9) and Cyprus (Livy, 45.11). He apparently offered elephants to Rome (Polyaenus, *Strat.* 4.21) and elephants were present at his parade at Daphne (Polyb. 30.25). After Antiochus's death, a Roman envoy sought to burn the Seleucid fleet and hamstring their elephants (App. *Syr.* 46). Paltiel 1979a, 34 also notes that Antiochus's use of mercenaries from certain Greek islands went against the settlement at Apamea. Ibid. 31–34 notes that these are infractions of the treaty; he takes it as evidence that it did not apply to this generation, but see Morgan 1990, 47.

[66] On Antiochus's opportunism in light of Rome's war with Macedon: Tarn 1951, 192; Swain 1944, 88; Mørkholm 1966, 96. Note that Popillius delayed his mission to

power by the Roman legate, Popillius Laenas, who drew a line around Antiochus, issuing a vague but ominous threat that he could not leave the spot unless he called off the invasion.[67] Along the lines of this interpretation of Antiochus, the parade of his troops in a Roman-style triumph after his disengagement from Egypt is seen as an attempt to flaunt his power before the Romans; Polybius, for example, says that his ambition was to surpass the games celebrated by Aemilius Paullus in Macedonia.[68] Of course, many scholars have rightly challenged this reading of Antiochus at nearly every turn; most of his suppos-edly aggressive acts can be explained: his invasion of Egypt was in self-defense; he sent embassies to Rome all the while to gauge their opinion; and he proceeded cautiously and with restraint, tarrying in Gaza during his second invasion and not moving on Alexandria as fast as he could have.[69] Seen this way, the "Day of Eleusis" was not as momentous as Polybius described, and Antiochus's parade of troops in the Roman style is more of a pledge of allegiance than a show of defiance.[70] These matters are likely to be debated for a long time, but

---

Antiochus until after Pydna: Livy, 45.10.2–3. Cyprus: Livy, 45.11.8 and 45.12.7. Pelu-sium: Livy, 45.11.1; cf. Polyb. 28.18 and Diod Sic. 30.18.2. Philometor: Polyb. 28.23.4; Diod. Sic. 31.1; Livy, 44.19.8 and 45.11.1; with Mørkholm 1966, 80–81. Polybius's general opinion on the so-called Sixth Syrian War was that Antiochus was aiming at total conquest: Polyb. 28.17.5; 28.19.1; 29.2.1; 29.27.11–13.

[67] Popillius's mission: Polyb. 28.17.5 and 29.2.1–3; Livy, 44.19.3 and 44.20.1. Antiochus's withdrawal: Polyb. 28.22. The episode is called the "Day of Eleusis" after the suburb of Alexandria where it takes place. See Polyb. 29.27.1–8 and Livy, 45.12.1–6 and Morgan 1990, 37 for nearly a dozen further references. Swain 1944, 87 says that Popillius's act had the effect of removing Hellenistic Egypt as a major power for the rest of its independent life. Mørkholm 1966, 97 points out that Antiochus still got what he was after – control of Coele-Syria.

[68] Polyb. 30.25.1. See also Downey 1961, 97–98; Mørkholm 1966, 98–99; Briscoe 1969, 51–52; Gruen 1984, 660; Morgan 1990, 47; Sherwin-White and Kuhrt 1993, 220–221; and Takács 2000, 199.

[69] See especially Morgan 1990, 65–66. On Antiochus's embassy to Rome: Polyb. 27.19 and 28.1; Diod. Sic. 30.2. He also refused to help Perseus (Livy, 42.29.5–6), instead donating funds for the war against him (Polyb. 28.22; Livy, 45.11.8), and he still later received embassies from Rome (Polyb. 28.23). On Antiochus's delay in Gaza: Livy, 45.11.9–11. Passerini 1935, 336 and Swain 1944, 79–80 say that Antiochus did not fully expect to control Egypt outright.

[70] Downplaying the Day of Eleusis are, for example, Gruen 1984, 660 and Morgan 1990, passim. Morgan 1990, 53 sees the Roman aspect of the parade as proof that Antiochus was not alienated from Rome. Note that ultimately, Antiochus departed on good terms: Polyb. 29.27.2–6; Diod. Sic. 31.2.1–2; Livy, 45.12.6. Livy, 45.12.6 sees Popillius's action

there is common ground in observing that while Antiochus is never seen as specifically *anti*-Roman in our sources (with the exception of an obscure annalist's claim that he sought war with Rome), he is clearly not a lackey of the empire.[71] Despite the fanfare surrounding his allegedly Roman demeanor, especially evident in Livy, he was naturally more concerned with his reputation as a Seleucid and with his kingdom's future and security, even if this might defy Rome.

Apart from Antiochus's policies, his capital city at Antioch, as far as excavations can reveal for the early second century BCE, looked nothing like the literary accounts of his building activity there. As for Livy's assertion that Antiochus built a temple to Jupiter Optimus Maximus, complete with a gilded ceiling, no trace of it has been found, and John Malalas, the only other literary source on Antiochene topography to have mentioned its existence, assigned it to the reign of Tiberius two hundred years after Antiochus.[72] It is possible that Malalas is recording a renovation project, such that Tiberius was only commissioning improvements for a preexisting temple,[73] but even if the temple was ordered by Antiochus, it may be a mistake to attribute it to his Romanization. Livy's story of a temple dedication to Jupiter has been interpreted as the Roman syncretic interpretation of an honor that was really meant for Zeus Olympios, which would be in keeping with Antiochus's temple commissions in Athens and Jerusalem and with his devotion to that god in his coinage.[74] As Rigsby has shown, Antiochus's public references to Zeus Olympios constituted an attempt to hearken back to the reign of his ancestor, Seleucus Nicator, who had imported the Greek cult to his own capital, Seleuceia.[75] In this scenario, Antiochus's temple to Jupiter/Zeus is more of a wedge separating him from Rome than a mark of a new identity.

---

as the legate's own idea and thus not indicative of larger geopolitics. For a prosopography of other Popillii, viewed as "hawks" in Roman foreign policy, see Paltiel 1982, 234.

[71] Cf. Swain 1944, 78. On the annalist: Martina 1984.

[72] Livy, 41.20. Malalas, 230.10–11.

[73] Downey 1961, 100 and 174–175.

[74] For the conversion of the Temple in Jerusalem into a shrine to Zeus: 2 Macc. 6.2. For Zeus on Antiochus's coins, see Downey 1961, 96; Mørkholm 1966; and Pollitt 1986, 282–283. For the syncretism, see Pollitt 1986, 283 and Rigsby 1980, 234–235, with references.

[75] Rigsby 1980, 237–238.

Ancient Antioch has not been well excavated, but the little work that has been done would seem to indicate that Antiochus's (provable) imprints on the city – a residential district called the Epiphania that included a bouleuterion and several temples – have more to do with Hellenistic models than with Roman.[76] Some archaeologists working on Antioch have sought out signs of Romanization under Antiochus's regime, influenced by the literary record of Antiochus's acculturation, but the evidence is scanty at best, even dubious. One scholar has presumed that some kind of amphitheater was present in Antioch at an early stage, given Livy's claim of Antiochus's interest in gladiators, although no evidence of one has come to light.[77] Another archaeologist reported that he found scratched into the interior surface of an aqueduct the name "Cossutius," apparently a reference to Decimus Cossutius, a famous Roman architect who worked for Antiochus on his temple to Zeus Olympios at Athens; the inscription has been cited as proof that Antiochus commissioned him to build the aqueduct along Roman lines.[78] However, the inscription is problematic: editors have doubted that the texts were ancient; in any case, it would be very odd given the habits of ancient epigraphy that only the cognomen would be "scratched" with a trowel on a surface of wet cement that was not visible to passers by.[79] Thus, the Roman aspect of Antiochus's aqueduct has not been sufficiently proven.

[76] On the Epiphania: Strabo, 16.2.4. Downey 1961, 99–100 and Grainger 1990, 125 place the district in Hellenistic traditions. Downey 1961, 116–117 dismisses the claim that the Antiochene constitution, evident in references to magistrates in epigraphy and the Gurub papyrus, was influenced by his stay in Rome. Another commission attributable to Antiochus is the Charonion, a monumental portrait carved in the living rock above the city. Malalas 205.8–13 tells the story that at the time of a citywide plague, Antiochus built it for divine protection.

[77] Kondoleon 2000, 159, who notes that the evidence for a later amphitheater, build under Julius Caesar in 47–46 BCE, is better, but it is also only literary (Malalas). Braund 1984a, 77 discusses buildings of Agrippa, Tiberius, and Herod at Antioch.

[78] On Antiochus's connection to Cossutius at Athens: Vitr. De Arch. 7.praef.15 and 17. Rawson 1975, 44 n. 21; Downey 1961; and Grainger 1990, 125 all accept the inscription. Downey 1961, 103, n. 81 suggests that the inscription was a workman's "construction mark" or a "compliment to his master."

[79] Campbell 1938, 206, in the initial publication of the excavation season, says that A.H. Athanassiou, the team's civil engineer, "came to a covered section near a change in the course and found the name COSSUTIUS scratched into the cement of the wall with a sharp instrument, probably a trowel, before the cement was dry," which would make

It may be that Livy's anecdotes concerning the temple and, possibly, an arena, which have been so influential in Antiochene archaeology, are better viewed as part of a trend among his Augustan contemporaries: under a peaceful hegemony, the construction of new cities was seen as the first foray of civilization into barbarism. In such a way does Vergil's Dido build her Carthage out of the wilds of North Africa in the *Aeneid,* and in his fourth *Georgic,* the bees in their hive similarly inhabit nature's city, demonstrating metaphorically the capacity for order in the cosmos.[80] Augustus's celebrated discovery of Rome as a "city of brick" and his creation of a "city of marble" are meant to signal an end to more chaotic times, even within the center of the civilized world.[81] The motif of the city as a civilizing force was widespread in Livy's day; the historian, however, has altered the formula by applying it to a Hellenistic kingdom, which was already known as conventionally, or even hyperbolically, civilized. The implication is that even with the magnificent cultural reputation of the Greek world, there was still room for improvement as Rome emerged onto the scene. Written during the reign of Augustus, Livy's histories may be seen as part of a culture and philosophy of expansion by peaceful means, whether or not it was effective: the Ara Pacis and the mausoleum of Augustus with its inscribed *Res Gestae* highlighted the foreign youths who had come under Rome's care, and Livy's story of Antiochus's acculturation fits nicely in such an agenda. Livy's Antiochus IV is depicted as the very model of Romanization, but given the nature of the archaeological evidence for his capital city, the extent of his transformation when in Rome must be questioned.

A look at another city, Iol/Caesarea, sheds more light on the part played by the hostage in the Romanization of the periphery, although here, too, the excavation of the city is limited. Strabo tells us that in 25 BCE, when Juba II received the kingdom of Mauretania from Augustus, he made his capital at Punic Iol on the coast, rebuilding it (ἐπικτίσας)

---

the inscription unusual in both location and aspect. The editor of *IGLS* 825 wonders, "mais les caractères sont-ils si anciens?"

[80] Verg. *Aen.* 1.421–449; Verg. *Geor.* 4.
[81] Suet. *Aug.* 28. Other references to the civilizing roles of cities for the Romans are collected at Woolf 2000, 120.

1 and 2. Northwest frieze of the Ara Pacis (Figure 1, fragmentary, abuts Figure 2 on the left). Note the child in "western" dress in the lower left corner of Figure 2 with children of the imperial family filing behind him in Figure 1. (Figure 1 courtesy of Erich Lessing/Art Resource, NY. Figure 2 courtesy of Alinari/Art Resource, NY; Museum of the Ara Pacis, Rome.)

3. (Above.) Southeast frieze of the Ara Pacis. The left-most child is in "eastern" dress; again, with children of the imperial family lined up behind him. (Photo courtesy of Fototeca Unione, AAR.)

4. (Right.) Detail of Figure 3 showing the "eastern child" to the right of Agrippa. (Photo courtesy of Lisa R. Brody.)

5. (Left.) Portrait of Juba II. (Photo from Ny Carlsberg Glyptotek, Copenhagen.)

6. (Below.) Plan of Iol/Caesarea (from Potter 1995, 10). (Photo courtesy of the Ian Sanders Memorial Fund.)

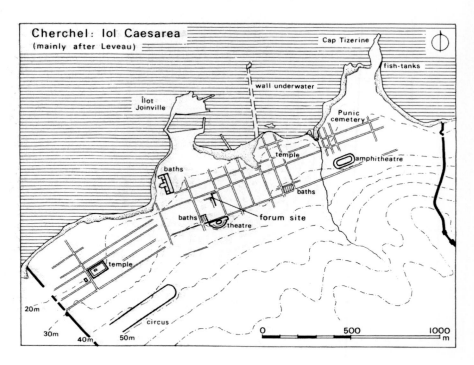

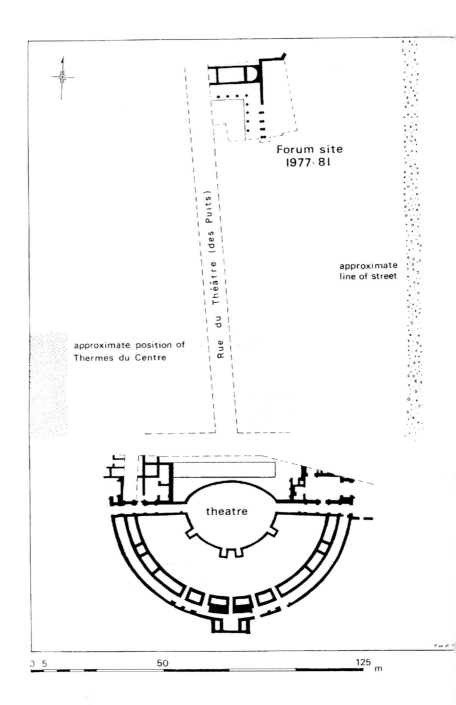

Forum site
1977-81

Rue du Théâtre (des Puits)

approximate
line of street

approximate position of
Thermes du Centre

theatre

0 5   50   125
                                                          m

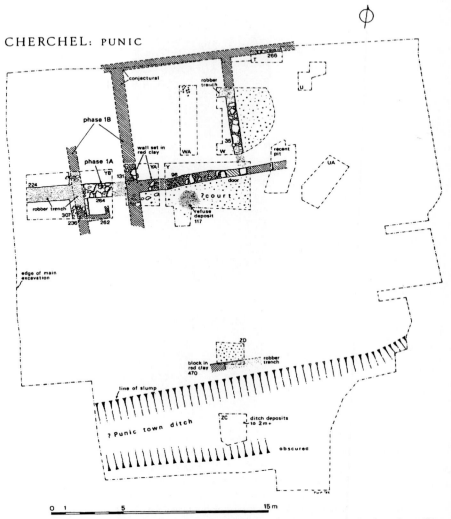

7a and 7b. The plan of the forum of Iol/Caesarea with a detail of the Punic/Juban phase (from Potter 1995, 24 and 28). Figure 7a shows the excavated section of the forum, approximately 115 meters north of the theater. The theater dates to Juba II, but in this plan, the walls and columns of the forum-section are of Severan date. Figure 7b is a detail of the Punic and Juban phase of this section of the forum. Running across the bottom are the remains of the "town defences" – a wall and ditch – filled in under Juba II (Potter 1995, 29). North of them, the walls marked with shading ("phase 1B") indicate the slight reorientation of buildings to fit the Juban grid (Potter 1995, 29). (Photo courtesy of the Ian Sanders Memorial Fund.)

a

b

c

8. Coins of Vonones. From top to bottom: a) tetradrachm, obverse (ANS 1944.100.82997); b) drachm, obverse (ANS 1944.100.83000); c) drachm, reverse (ANS 1977.158.795). The portrait on the tetradrachm is typical of Arsacid monarchs preceding Vonones, but that of the drachm departs from the norm, most notably with its shorter hair. The legend of the reverse also constitutes a departure, in that Vonones's name is present (on the right side) along with a reference to his victory over Artabanus (on the lower – NEIKHΣAΣ – and left sides). (Photo courtesy of the American Numismatics Society.)

9. The death of Decebalus, Trajan's Column. (Photo courtesy of Peter Rockwell.)

10. The detention of Dacian princes, Trajan's Column. The scene comes shortly after Figure 9 on the frieze. (Photo courtesy of Peter Rockwell.)

and renaming it Caesarea (Figure 6).[82] It has obvious Roman elements: significant improvements to the harbor have been dated to Juba's reign, including a lighthouse on the small island off the coast and a jetty sheltering the harbor at its eastern end. Juba is also credited with a network of centuriated roads and with a seven-kilometer circuit of walls enclosing the highlands to the south of the new town.[83] A wealth of fine sculpture at Caesarea has been attributed to Juba, owing to his known interest in the arts as well as to findspots and excavations; examples include the Cherchel torso, discussed earlier in Chapter 5, a copy of the "Albani *kore*," a Caryatid statue, a personification of Africa, a relief of a sphinx, and fragments of colossal statues of deities.[84] Numismatic evidence suggests that he built a temple to Augustus, and white marble columns found in second century contexts were possibly reused from that original structure.[85] Isis imagery on Juba's coins suggests some kind of building activity for that cult as well, which may be plausibly linked with his wife, Cleopatra Selene.[86] The theater and amphitheater of Iol/Caesarea have also both been dated to Juba's reign, as well as the adjoining forum north of the theater (Figure 7a).[87] The city has been viewed as a model of Romanization and as the necessary proof to substantiate claims of hostage-based strategies

[82] Strabo, 17.3.12. On the date of renaming the city, see Braund 1984a, 108 and Roller 2003, 119–120.

[83] On the harbor improvements: Leveau 1982, 707–708; Roller 2003, 124. For a discussion of the centuriation, as well as a survey of the hinterland, see Leveau 1982, 700–702; Potter 1995, 8; and Coltelloni-Trannoy 1997, 148–149. Roller 2003, 125 argues that the evidence for centuriation under Juba is insufficient. On the grid as a means of control, see Hingley 1997 and Woolf 1998, 119. On the aqueduct and mausoleum in the hinterland, also likely to be Juban, see Roller 2003, 128–130. Roller 2003, 127 compares the city wall with that of Herod's Caesarea.

[84] Fittschen 1979 is a thorough survey of the finds. See also Albertini 1950, 80; Potter 1995, 8; Coltelloni-Trannoy 1997, 155–159; Roller 2003, 139–151.

[85] On the temple, see Fishwick 1983; Coltelloni-Trannoy 1990; Coltelloni-Trannoy 1992, 69–81, with discussants; Potter 1995, 8; and Roller 2003, 126–127. On the reused columns, see Potter 1983, 462; cf. Potter 1995, 32.

[86] Coltelloni-Trannoy 1997, 40–43; Grenier 2001, 111; Roller 2003, 126.

[87] There remains some controversy about the dating of the amphitheater, which may be later. See Picard 1975; Golvin and Leveau 1979; and Potter 1988, 191. On the theater, see Picard 1975; Golvin and Leveau 1979; Leveau 1982, 702–705; Coltelloni-Trannoy 1997, 151–153; Cooley 1999, 178; and Roller 2003, 122–123. Roller 2003, 123 argues that the location of the Juban forum is unknown, although it is placed north of the theater by Albertini 1923; Fittschen 1979; Leveau 1982; Potter 1995, 29–32; and

of cultural imperialism, such as made by Tacitus and Plutarch, quoted earlier.[88]

But to what extent was Iol really "Romanized"? At the time of Juba's reign, the city still retained elements of the indigenous Punic culture, resulting in a hybrid mix that respected the old, pre-Roman town. It is interesting to note that all of Juba's most significant projects came outside the old city walls, with the exception of the harbor improvements. The forum was located on the southern edge of the old town. The only thorough excavation of the site is of a patch of nine hundred square-meters about 115 meters north of the theater (Figures 7a and b). Extensive evidence of paving and construction date to the Severan era; beneath this, the scant remains, supposedly of the Punic and Juban periods, suggest that the patch of land was bifurcated by a wall and ditch combination running east-west (Figure 7b). North of this wall, on the seaward side, remains of industrial activity were found. On the southern, inland side, however, there was very little, leading Potter to suggest that the city's defenses were removed at the same time as the construction of the theater under Juba, turning the path of the rampart into a kind of Wall Street.[89] The industrial activities north of this line continued apace under Juba, although the buildings housing them were slightly reoriented to fit a new grid of streets, but to the south, the empty space, presumably formerly fields, became the new forum.[90] Juba's choice of this location for the forum is significant: Vitruvius, a contemporary of Juba's and probably an acquaintance in the scientific and literary community of Augustan Rome, wrote in his multivolume *On Architecture* that the forum of a harbor town belonged by the sea, whereas inland towns call for them in the

---

Coltelloni-Trannoy 1997, 82. For more on the controversy surrounding the forum, see later.

[88] Potter 1995, 29. cf. Roller 2003, 131, who also compares Juba's Caesarea with that of Herod (p. 124; 127, n. 42).

[89] Potter 1983, 459; Potter 1995, 29–32, conclusions that are overlooked at Roller 2003, 123, note 18.

[90] Potter 1995, 29–31. On the industrial activity, see Potter 1983, 460, citing pottery and animal bones. New finds in the Juban period include bronze and iron waste, and pastry molds. Trial excavations under the theater have shown that it was the first building to occupy the site: Picard 1975, 394–395. The Severan buildings, then, according to Potter 1995, 32, represent a northward expansion of the forum centuries after Juba's reign.

center.[91] Juba established the forum here, instead, because it was a blank space.

The evidence is slight, as fewer than a thousand square meters of a much larger space have been excavated, but the image that emerges is of a town that has been "creolized" rather than "Romanized," where old habits were slow to change, despite the introduction of outside influences.[92] Punic inscriptions continued to be posted and the indigenous goddess Tanit continued to be worshipped along side the imported gods.[93] Thinking of Juba's work at Iol, one imagines a city where the half-mile or so between the docking points in the harbor and the old city walls remained as it had been. Were a visitor to arrive at the harbor late in Juba's reign, he would notice a mélange of imported and indigenous activities and structures. Disembarking and heading south, he would not encounter any appreciable change in the use of space or the location of certain activities.[94] The shops (at least those at the northern edge of the forum, which is all that has been excavated) still stood in their long-held positions. When he reached the southern extent of the old town, he would note that the wall was gone; now there was a road. And where there used to be fields, now there was a forum, and looming before him was the new Roman theater. The location of the forum on the fringe of the old town reinforced its

---

[91] Vitr. De Arch. 1.7.1. On Juba's possible connection with Vitruvius, see Roller 2003, 70.

[92] On the implications of using creolization for the more conventional Romanization, see Webster 2001. cf. D. J. Mattingly 1997, discussing the African hinterland.

[93] Coltelloni-Trannoy 1997, 200 discusses the presence of Punic and Greek names in inscriptions at Iol; ibid. 69 discusses the survival of a North African heritage; and ibid. 172 discusses the worship of Tanit. See also Leveau 1975; Leveau 1982, 691–692 and 709–710. Potter 1995, 9 points out that the Greek names became more prominent after the Roman annexation in 40 CE, well after Juba's death. Decret and Fantar 1998, 272–273 refer to Roman gods being "Africanized" rather than indigenous populations becoming Romanized.

[94] Roller 2003, 125 and Map 3 and Figures 6 and 7 argues for a palace by the harbor, apparently citing comparison with Alexandria and architectural ornaments found nearby, but no such palace appears in maps in Fittschen 1979, 229; Leveau 1982, figure 7; Potter 1995, 10; and Coltelloni-Trannoy 1997, 82. Fittschen 1979, whom Roller 2003 cites, admits of the possibility of a palace near the harbor, but, repeatedly lamenting the poor state of excavation of the city (pages 229, 230, 242), he stops short of a certain identification and calls for further research on the architectural fragments in the Cherchel Museum. Coltelloni-Trannoy 1997, 78 discusses the itinerant nature of the court and absence of a formal "capital."

newness; it had the quality of being added on rather than necessarily dominating the old town. Even with all the expensive new building at Iol, there were still limits to what the Romans could achieve. The Juban city was a binary one, with Roman additions coming, at first, only on the outskirts, and a Punic identity surviving for years afterward.

An explanation of the inertia of indigenous elements at Iol/Caesarea can begin with a look at the history of the Roman presence in the region. Mauretania, at the time of Juba's succession, had nominally been without a ruler since the death of Bocchus II in 33; by 25, then, it was under an ambiguous Roman government.[95] Mackie has argued that the region was headed down the path of outright annexation, with three veteran colonies having been founded in 33 BCE (or slightly later) in the west, near the Straits of Gibraltar, and nine more in eastern Mauretania, just before Juba's accession. These conclusions are not without problems, but Strabo portrays the pre-Juban situation as somewhat chaotic when he says that "the country was divvied up in various ways since there were many residents and the Romans had treated them in different ways at different times, both friends and enemies."[96] As for the enemies, the methods used by the Romans to

---

[95] Mauretania is not on the lists of provinces of 32 BCE and 27 BCE (*Mon. Anc.* 25.2; Cass. Dio 50.6.3–4, 53.12.4–7). Mackie 1983 argues that the region was effectively controlled through veteran colonies, which were in turn under the jurisdiction of the governor in Spain. Whittaker 1996, 610–615 disagrees, arguing that the region simply went without Roman political involvement, owing to the civil war and the expense of maintaining troops there. See the following note.

[96] Strabo, 17.3.12, C831: πολυτρόπως γὰρ οἱ μερισμοὶ γεγένηνται τῆς χώρας, ἅτε τῶν νεμομένων αὐτὴν πλειόνων γενομένων καὶ τῶν Ῥωμαίων ἄλλοτ' ἄλλως τούτων τοῖς μὲν φίλοις χρωμένων, τοῖς δὲ καὶ πολεμίοις. See Mackie 1983, 337–342, who assumes that the eastern colonies had to be founded before Juba's accession, because there is no evidence elsewhere of colonies being founded within client kingdoms (cf. Braund 1984a, 95). Given the oddity of the Mauretanian case and the lack of evidence for any uniform Roman policy concerning so-called client kingdoms, however, the settlement of veterans after Juba's accession should not be ruled out. Second, the division in dating is based on the observation that the western colonies had "Julia" included in their names, while those of the eastern region were called "Julia Augusta" and therefore must have come after 27. Braund 1984a, 95 suggests all colonies predated Juba. Decret and Fantar 1998, 163–164 believes the "Augusta" colonies were founded by Augustus; Roller 2003, 96 suggests they are Claudian, whereas the non-"Augusta" date to the 30's BCE. The problem is discussed further at Coltelloni-Trannoy 1997, 125, but for our purposes, Mackie's underlying observation – simply that the region was unsettled – is sufficient.

infiltrate and secure the territory, whether before Juba or after, suggest an expensive and difficult process: two of the Augustan colonies were founded on established Mauretanian sites, Zulil and Icosium, whose native inhabitants were transplanted to Spanish towns to make room.[97] Such forced migrations imply, at the least, a general discontent in the region and most likely required violence to effect. Unable to rule on their own, yet not wanting to abandon the wealthy coast, the Romans arrived at Juba's candidacy as a half-way settlement.[98] Hastily, the Roman bite became a bark, and Juba's new city – Iol first and then Caesarea – reflects, in part, the tenuousness of Roman control. Horace, in perhaps the earliest written reference to Juba, describes his realm as "the dry nurse of lions," and well into Juba's reign, the region was far from stable, as numerous reports of battles with the interior populations attest.[99] Although one can make the case that Juba was fairly well "Romanized," citing his Julio-Claudian visage in his public portraiture, his interest in Hellenistic scholarship, and his extensive building program outside the old city walls, one cannot assume, as Tacitus does in his *Agricola*, and Plutarch in his *Sertorius*, that the hostage's cultural decisions translated automatically, or quickly, to the population at large beneath him. The literary assertions of utter Romanization via hostages should not necessarily be rejected based on this slight evidence, but the timetable for the phenomenon, as envisioned by Tacitus, Plutarch, and the rest, ought to be slowed down considerably. The thorough Romanization of Iol/Caesarea took many generations to achieve, and it happened not without resistance.

[97] Zulil: Strabo, 3.1.8, C140; Plin. *HN* 5.2. Icosium: Plin. *HN* 5.19, where the destination of the transplants is identified as Ilici in Spain. Cf. Pompon. 2.96, who says that his Spanish hometown, Tingetera, was inhabited by "Phoenicians brought over from Africa" (*transvecti ex Africa Phoenices*). Mackie 1983, 341 argues that the colonization and resettlement only ceased when the legions were drawn to the other side of the empire by a disturbance surrounding the death of Amyntas in Galatia; note also Cass. Dio, 53.26.1–3.
[98] Cf. Gsell 1952, 12, arguing that Augustus resorted to Juba because Mauretania was not yet ready ("*mûre*") for annexation.
[99] Hor. *Carm.* 1.22.15–16: *leonum arida nutrix*. It is also possible that Vergil's depiction of Dido building her city from the wilds of North Africa has Juba's new kingdom in mind. On resistance in Mauretania, see Fishwick and Shaw 1976; Whittaker 1996, 591; Coltelloni-Trannoy 1997, 47–54; Decret and Fantar 1998, 166; Roller 2003, 107–114. On Juba's bodyguard, see Speidel 1979.

Archaeological evidence can also be brought to bear upon literary accounts of the Parthian Vonones's Romanization during his hostage-ship. Vonones had been sent to Rome by Phraates IV in 10/9 BCE along with three of his brothers.[100] In 6 CE, according to Josephus and Tacitus, ambassadors from Parthia asked for Vonones to be given to them to place on the throne because he was the eldest surviving heir.[101] Both historians claim that Vonones had adopted a Roman lifestyle while a hostage: Josephus says that Vonones's education in Rome (τῆς ἐν Ῥώμῃ κομιδῆς) sustained him as an ally even when he was on the run later on; Tacitus goes further, saying that the Parthians complained that he was "infected with the arts of the enemy" (*hostium artibus infectum*), as manifested by his disdain for hunting and equestrian exercises and his affection for luxury and Greek culture.[102] But the coins of his reign, particularly the tetradrachms, the highest denomination of coin, few though they are, imply something rather more ambiguous. Vonones's tetradrachm portraits are highly stylized, with details of his beard, hair style, diadem, torque, and cuirass all fully in keeping with the norms of Parthian numismatics such that he is indistinguishable from other Arsacid kings who came before him (Figure 8a).[103] The legends are identical, proclaiming a generous king of the Arsacid line, and nowhere do these issues refer to his Roman connections. Departures from his predecessors, however, come in Vonones's issues of drachms, in which he, uniquely among his Parthian predecessors, is depicted with short hair that does not reach the nape of his neck and does not cover his ears (Figure 8b). Moreover, although he does not explicitly mention the Roman support that Tacitus and Josephus say he received, the legend on the drachms uniquely includes his own name in the nominative case and refers to his victory (ΝΙΚΗΣΑΣ) over his cousin Artabanus III

---

[100] The brothers are named in Strabo, 16.1.28, C749: Seraspadanes, Rhodaspes, and Phraates V.

[101] Joseph. *AJ* 18.46; Tac. *Ann.* 2.2. For more on the Parthian hostages and, especially, Tacitus's treatment of them, see Chapter 9.

[102] Joseph. *AJ* 18.47 and 18.52; Tac. *Ann.* 2.2.

[103] Note the tables at Wroth 1964, covering the coins for Orodes I, Phraates IV, Phraataces, and Orodes II. Vonones's tetradrachms are at Wroth 1964, 143, numbers 1–5. See also Colledge 1967, 48 and pl. 6ii and Sellwood 1971, 182. The dates of Vonones's coins are discussed at Gonella 2001, correcting McDowell 1935, 102–104.

in his campaign to take the throne.[104] The drachms, naturally more plentiful than the tetradrachms, clearly express Vonones's difference from his forebears. In overall aspect, however, his numismatic issues are still unmistakably Parthian, as one would expect. If we, like the Parthians at the time, did not have Josephus's and Tacitus's accounts of Vonones's adventures on returning from Rome, we would conclude, at least from the coins, that he, somehow, defeated a rival, yet otherwise differed little from other Arsacid kings. Given that we do have more than the coins, a decision must be made – either Josephus and Tacitus have it wrong and Vonones was *not* irremediably Romanized during his hostageship, or they have it right, and Vonones was simply savvy enough in the manipulation of his public image to foreground his Parthian qualities at the expense of any "new identity," at least in his coins. One suspects the latter, but in either case, we see that the hostage's acculturation, as idealized as a device of empire in certain literary sources, was not so easy to read elsewhere. Vonones, like Antiochus and Juba, had to pay attention to the realities of strong resistance to the imperial culture, or cultural imperialism, of outsider Romans.

[104] Vonones's coins are at Wroth 1964, 144, numbers 6–13. All but one of Vonones's predecessors, going back to Orodes I (ruled 57–37 BCE), have longer hair in their coins; the exception is Pacorus I, who ruled briefly in 37 BCE: see Wroth 1964, 97–98, numbers 1–2. Sellwood 1971, 193 calls Vonones's hair in this coins "westernized" and sees Vonones's peculiar use of his own name as "customary for Roman issues."

7

MASCULINE-FEMININE

In Lucian's *True Histories* – the ironically titled parody of sensational historians, which was encountered in the previous chapter – the author seems to satirize another of the expectations of hostages in antiquity. In an extended episode the speaker assigns a sexual role to a hostage who is submitted to him during one of his escapades.[1] He tells of how he sailed his ship up from the sea, traveled through the air, and put in on a large "island" which he later discovered to be the moon. He soon made an alliance of sorts with the king there, named Endymion, and helped him in an outrageous battle with the people of the sun, led by Phaethon, for control over the morning star, which both "states" had hoped to colonize. (For the sake of brevity, we omit summary of the battle waged among giant fleas, men riding three-headed vultures, and birds with grass for feathers and lettuce leaves for wings – the characteristic untruths of the *True Histories*.[2]) After the conflict was resolved with the sun and the moon sharing the morning star, Endymion offered his son to the speaker both as a sign of friendship and as an inducement for the speaker to be among the first colonists of the star.[3] Although the boy is not formally called a hostage, the proposal is reminiscent of many hostage transactions in less fanciful

---

[1] Lucian, *Ver. hist.* 1.10–26.
[2] Anderson 1976a, 3 believes Lucian is sending up Aristophanes's *Peace*; Robinson 1979, 25 compares the passage with Thucydides and Homer; Bowersock 1994, 20–21 refers to Aristophanes's *Birds;* on the question of the passage's debt to Arrian, see Anderson 1980 and Macleod 1987; on Lucian's use of Herodotus, see Avery 1997. Fusillo 1999 discusses Lucian's satiric method, involving "amplification" and "concretization."
[3] Lucian, *Ver. hist.* 1.21.

histories: the boy was under twenty-five years of age and the act of his transfer betokened a new relationship between the donor and the recipient. In essence, the speaker was offered a critical dynastic asset with the hopes that it would strengthen his friendship with Endymion. In this case, however, the record of the transaction also includes, in addition to allusions to hostage-taking, obvious references to the practice of marriage alliance: Endymion specifically says that the boy will be given "in marriage" to the speaker.[4] Moreover, the speaker's ensuing description of the reproductive habits of the Moon people seems to indicate that the union was meant to result in offspring: he explains that there are no women on the moon, that boys reproduce until the age of twenty-five (the top limit given as the age of Endymion's son), and that children are born from the calf of the "mother's" leg.[5] In the end, the speaker declines the offer and continues his voyage. To the modern reader, the story may be strange, even by Lucian's standards, but for the ancient reader, although the episode is clearly meant to be humorous, it would not have been unfamiliar; Lucian's story, in infusing the submission of a hostage with the aura of an arranged marriage, spoofs a characteristic of hostage-taking that can be found elsewhere.

Repeatedly in the literature leading up to Lucian, records of hostage submissions refer to a sexual role for the hostage, especially, but not only, if the hostage was female.[6] The descriptions may be literal: for example, hostages are sometimes said to be the victims of rape. Or the language may be figurative: a writer may employ a metaphor involving sex and gender to construct the identity of a hostage as inferior to his or her captor. In simplistic terms, it was considered masculine to take hostages and feminine to be a hostage, even though in the preponderance of cases hostages were male; hostages in such scenarios typically, of course, play the passive role, just as in Lucian's comic

---

4   Anderson 1976a, 13 argues that Lucian is alluding to both Herodotus and Plato. Georgiadou and Larmour 1998, 122–123 compare the scene with marriage alliances as told by Homer and with stories of Zeus and Ganymede.

5   Lucian, *Ver. hist.* 1.22. That this was the mode of delivery for the god Dionysus may mean something about the character of the Moon people, as imagined by Lucian, but it is a question not to be taken up here.

6   Walker 1980, 131 notes the frequency of the molestation of hostages in other cultures, not Roman.

treatment, Endymion's son is able to reproduce. As with other notions of hostageship described in this book – coercion, hospitality, prestige, "family," education – the expectation of a sexual role for a hostage places the captor in a recognizable position of power. That conquest was considered a manly pursuit comes as little surprise, but the inclusion of young hostages in the formula, however, implicitly extends the sexual, or gendered, domination of the moment of the battle into the future and into the realm of the "overclass," even after, so to speak, the final sword is thrust. In most, but not all, contexts the sexualization of the hostage is cast in a negative light. Flying in the face of the rhetoric of hospitality or family or education, sexual vocabulary in hostage episodes at times allowed writers to villainize any of the various characters in their narrative: depending on the historian's agenda, the hostage recipient could become a rapist; the hostage donor could act as a pimp; or the hostage herself could come off as a slut. If the basic syllogism posited in this book holds true – that a hostage may stand as a representative in Rome of a faraway place – then the articulation of power over a hostage in sexual terms helps us to understand another dimension of the Roman ethic of imperialism: in Rome, to see a hostage in the street was to be reminded of the new exposure and powerlessness of that hostage's peripheral community as well as its ability to provide Roman overlords – nefarious or not – with a kind of cruel gratification. That Lucian, through the story of Endymion's son, holds the notion up for ridicule demonstrates not only that his readers were aware of the phenomenon but also that it was at least being questioned in his second-century context.

WOMEN AS HOSTAGES

In his biography of Augustus, Suetonius credits the emperor with being the first to take "a new kind of hostage – women."[7] He explains that the decision came in dealing with Germanic tribes at the moment when the Romans realized that male hostages held less sway in securing

---

[7] Suet. *Aug.* 21.2: *vero novum genus obsidum feminas.* Cf. Lica 1988, 42 and Elbern 1990, 108. Kellum 1997, 167–168 interprets the Caryatids in Augustus's forum as referring to the German female hostages.

agreements. He may have developed this idea from the German ethnography of his contemporary, Tacitus, who observed that Germans placed a higher value on female family members because of their role in propagating a legitimate family line.[8] Nonetheless, a review of sources on hostage-taking would reveal that Suetonius was wrong in labeling the detention of women by Augustus as a revolution in diplomacy.[9] Polybius and those who followed him reported on Iberian women who were held, and well treated, on two occasions by members of the Scipionic family during the Second Punic War, first by the brothers Gnaeus and Publius in 218 BCE, and then by Scipio Africanus in 209.[10] As we have seen, Scipio Africanus gained a reputation for honor in protecting the daughters of the wife of Mandonius from abuse and in returning an Iberian bride to her fiancé when he took charge of them from the defeated Carthaginians. Moreover, Augustus found female hostages at the court of Antony and Cleopatra in Alexandria on his arrival in 30 BCE; some of these were paraded in Rome in his triumph a year later.[11] If Suetonius were to raise the objection that in these cases the Romans acted as a third party, assuming control of someone else's female hostages rather than taking them on their own initiative, one could point to records of Pompey's triple triumph, in which Appian and Plutarch record not only hostage daughters and wives from royal dynasties in the East, but also Amazon, or "Scythian," women.[12] Strabo says that two of the four famous Parthian hostages of Phraates IV traveled with their wives.[13] It should be added that when the detention of women is recorded for contexts after Augustus, it does not draw special comment: Tacitus says that before Tiridates of

---

8 Tac. *Germ.* 8.1, cf. 20.4. For references to episodes of active women in Germany and Gaul in Caesar, Tacitus, and Plutarch, see Rives 1999, 152–153. For the Roman view of societies with powerful women as barbaric, see Saavedra 1999. Benario 1999, 73 discusses the passage in light of the Pergamene statue of the dying Gaul who has killed his wife.

9 Phillipson 1911, 401; Aymard 1961, 137–138.

10 Gnaeus and Publius: Polyb. 3.98–99; cf. Livy, 22.22.4–21. Africanus: Polyb. 10.18; cf. Diod. Sic. 26.21; Livy, 26.49.11–16; App. *Hisp.* 23.

11 Cass. Dio, 51.16.1–2.

12 App. *Mith.* 103, 117; Plut. *Pomp.* 45.4. In Appian detainees from the Amazons are hostages whereas in Plutarch they are prisoners. See Chapter 4. Cf. Walker 1980, 33–34.

13 Strabo, 16.1.28, C 748.

Armenia left to go to Rome to receive his crown from Nero in 63 CE, he gave his daughter as a hostage to Gnaeus Domitius Corbulo.[14] The Roman reader in the empire could also learn of female hostages in other contexts where non-Romans were the hostage recipients.[15] The Etruscans led by Lars Porsenna received female hostages in addition to males; Cloelia, arguably the most famous female hostage in Roman history, performed her heroic escape and rescue in this setting.[16] Contrary to Suetonius's understanding of Augustan innovation, many writers do not seem to think that the detention of women in the Republic and afterwards was out of the ordinary. Given that a target of diplomacy naturally would have had women as relatives, it is not odd that they could have been attractive candidates for hostageship.

The Romans believed that when necessary women could be used as hostages in a menacing and coercive fashion. According to Dionysius of Halicarnassus, during the first secession of the plebs the patricians in Rome considered threatening the wives who had been left behind in order to compel the dissenters to return.[17] Dionysius also says that when the consul Coriolanus was exiled from Rome and marched back to lay siege to his former home city, some of the Romans trapped inside the walls argued that they should threaten to harm the women of Coriolanus's family.[18] The senate voted for the counterargument, that the same women – Veturia, Coriolanus's mother, and Volumnia, his wife – should persuade Coriolanus to stand down on the basis of duty to family, as well as to country, but it is interesting to note that, as recorded by Dionysius, the senate's decision to abandon the hostage plan was not made out of a sense of impropriety concerning

---

[14] Tac. *Ann.* 15.30.

[15] For example, Polyb. 1.68.3 says the Carthaginians ought to have held the wives and children of their mercenaries with whom they were at war. In Curt. 7.2.18, Alexander the Great held the wives and children of two Arab guides as hostages. Joseph. *BJ* 1.118 and 121 records that Hyrcanus held the wife and children of his brother as hostages in their civil war. Plut. *Mor.* 215B says that Agesipolis of Sparta was relieved when he was taken hostage and not Spartan women, who were evidently eligible. Cf. Walker 1980, 13.

[16] For the references concerning Cloelia, see Chapter 3.

[17] Dion. Hal. *Ant. Rom.* 6.62.5, quoted in Chapter 2.

[18] Dion. Hal. *Ant. Rom.* 8.43.4. On Plutarch's reliance on and adaptation of Dionysius for his *Coriolanus*, see Russell 1995. Note that Plutarch gives different names for the women: the mother is Volumnia; the wife is Verginia.

female hostages but simply because the coercive approach was deemed ineffective in this case. By comparison, in an episode in Appian, when senators are faced with a similar decision concerning a rebellion by one of their own, they are easily persuaded to threaten women: when Octavian was marching on Rome in 43 BCE to secure the consulship, the opposing faction of senators attempted to detain his mother and sister as hostages.[19] They failed, according to Appian, only because the women were hiding in the Temple of Vesta and the house of the Vestal Virgins, but of the senators' determination Appian is certain: holding women as coercive hostages was not taboo, especially when it was expedient.

A passage in Josephus provides slight evidence that when hostages were described as nebulous family groupings of unnamed hostages in which women took part – "the wives and children of so-and-so" – a hierarchy existed in which the women held less value than their children. In his account of Moses's attempts to free the Hebrews from Egypt, Josephus records the obstinacy of the pharaoh, which weakened only gradually in response to a series of famous plagues.[20] As Moses consistently called for the release of all hostages (ὅμηρα), time and again the pharaoh met his demands only in part, holding back the more prized detainees each time. Following a plague of lice, according to Josephus, the pharaoh agreed to free all the Hebrews, but then retook the women and children. After an infestation of "beasts of all walks of life," he released the women, but recaptured the children.[21] Only after an outbreak of ulcers, a downpour of hail, and a swarm of locusts did he agree to release the children. Josephus's linking of groups of hostages with the succession of plagues in a sense sets up a convenient, albeit absurd, scale of their perceived values. The pharaoh's determination to hold on to the children trumped his desire to detain the women; his desire to hold both women and children trumped his desire to hold the men. Likewise, Josephus's Moses stepped up his resistance in order not to leave without the youths, the most prized contingent. Admittedly this is an account of early, legendary Jewish history, and even if it is

[19] App. *BCiv* 3.91–92.
[20] Joseph. *AJ* 2.300–306.
[21] Joseph. *AJ* 3.303.

told by a historian living in Rome, it may not represent commonly held views of the Romans during first century CE, but the high value placed on the progeny in the story, relative to their mothers, is in keeping with the vastly greater proportion of all hostage episodes that involve youths rather than adult women.[22] Although it is clear that women were taken hostage from time to time, retaining female hostages may not generally have been the preferred course of action by the recipient.

In most of these cases, female hostages are anonymous, with no voice or any kind of agency in the sequence of events. A more significant category of female hostage, in which the principal players are not anonymous, includes those who came into the custody of their recipient on a permanent basis as brides: on several occasions in our sources, the women in marriage alliances, whether international or domestic, were said to serve a secondary role as hostages between groom and in-laws.[23] The marriage alliance in Roman antiquity bears many similarities to the institution of hostage-taking. In general terms, both practices helped to create the same artificial circumstance whereby two parties would develop a shared interest, centered on the person of either the detainee or the bride. In both cases, there is a concomitant payment of resources, either tribute or dowry. One of the most coveted assets of the hostage was his name and his legitimacy to rule, which was an advantage provided by elite women as well when they produced heirs. Most important for a study of empire, the bride's presence abroad, like that of a hostage, articulated an alliance and hierarchy between states. This is not to say that obvious differences did not exist: brides automatically became bound to the states of their new "families," unlike in hostage-taking, where the status was seen as temporary. Moreover, male hostages had closer and more direct access to power in both donor and recipient states by virtue of their sex, and thus might be subject to a different kind of scrutiny. Not quite the same as

---

[22] See the chart in Walker 1980, 29: of the sixty-nine cases of Hellenistic and Roman hostage-taking that give some clue as to the sex of hostages, only fifteen (22 percent) either specifically mention women, or, in referring to entire groups in an ambiguous way, allow the possibility that women were detained. In all the other cases, the sex is identified directly as male.

[23] For seeing brides as hostages, see also Lécrivain 1916, 116 and Elbern 1990, 124–125.

hostage-taking, match-making nevertheless was in the same category of methods for forging international, filial alliances.

In Quintus Curtius's history of Alexander the Great, written in the first century CE, the submission of a son as hostage is specifically linked with the betrothal of a daughter in a marriage alliance as simultaneous, equivalent practices in a diplomatic arrangement. Curtius describes the attempt by Darius to reach a settlement with Alexander the Great following the Battle of Issus. Darius was on the run and he made a generous offer of peace, which is reported to Alexander in the second person:

Before now he had designated the river Halys as the boundary of your king-dom, where Lydia ends. Now he offers all land between the Hellespont and the Euphrates as the dowry for his daughter whom he hands over to you. Keep Ochus, his son, whom you have, as a hostage of peace and trust (*pacis et fidei obsidem*), yet return his mother and two maiden daughters. He asks that you accept 3,000 talents of gold in exchange for these.[24]

Alexander ultimately rejected the offer, but Darius's proposal is worth considering as a hypothetical situation that was believed to be a plau-sible solution to an international conflict. Darius's daughter, Statira, and son are offered to Alexander as a sort of package deal where both would be held by the Macedonians as tokens of a new peace.[25] By mentioning them in the same breath, Curtius betrays the similarities of hostage submission and marriage alliance and demonstrates the sim-ilar opportunities for both male and female progeny in striking such alliances.

A similar proximity occurs in Livy, when he describes the rela-tions between Capua and Rome during the Second Punic War. Rome's weakest moment famously came in the aftermath of the Battle of Cannae in 216 BCE in which nearly fifty thousand Romans were killed.[26] The southern Italian allies in whose midst the disaster occurred were tempted, we are told, to abandon their support for

---

[24] Curt. 4.11.5–6.
[25] For commentary on the nature of Darius's offer and the validity of Curtius's account, see Atkinson 1980, 395–396.
[26] Lazenby 1978, 84–85 accepts Livy's figures (22.49.15) over Polybius's (3.117.1–4).

Rome. According to Livy, the Capuans at first were reluctant to switch sides for two reasons:

> One thing that delayed them from defecting immediately was the ancient rite of intermarriage, which had joined many distinguished and powerful families to the Romans; also, since some men were serving as soldiers among the Romans, the greatest link was the 300 *equites*, the noblest of the Campanians who had been chosen by the Romans to guard the cities of Sicily and who had been sent there accordingly.[27]

As in Curtius's description of Darius's plea, Livy raises the possibility that sons in a kind of hostageship were viewed in a comparable way with daughters in marriage: the concern of the elite decision-makers was for both sets of children.[28] In the end, Capua decided to revolt in spite of its worries, and the youths were detained in Sicily and the brides forsaken. Nevertheless, the Capuans continued to exhibit anxiety over the three hundred: when they were negotiating the terms of alliance with Hannibal, one of their demands was that the Carthaginians give them three hundred Roman captives, which they could use for a trade, an exchange that ultimately never took place.[29] After Capua fell to Rome and Hannibal was forced to leave Italy, the status of the Capuan youths remained unresolved. Livy says that a proposal was introduced in the senate that they be given citizenship, but in an unusual capacity: first they should be enrolled in Cumae, not their hometown, and second, their citizenship should be retroactive to the day before the Capuans declared their independence.[30] According to Livy, the reason for reassigning them to Cumae, was that "they themselves said they did not know to which community (*quorum hominum*) they belonged, now that they had abandoned their old fatherland (*vetere patria relicta*) and had not yet been enrolled in the one to which they had returned."[31] The retroactive quality of their citizenship essentially proclaimed that when Capua rebelled without them, thereafter the hostages had been deprived of their state and shifted to the population

---

[27] Livy, 23.4.7–8.
[28] On known marriages between Capuans and Romans, see Lazenby 1978, 89.
[29] Livy, 23.7.2.
[30] Livy, 23.31.10.
[31] Livy, 23.31.11.

of Rome. The sons, as hostages, were thus initially in a Limbo that differed from the daughters who left Capua under marriage contracts, even though both had a (failed) coercive value in keeping Capua in line. Hostage-taking's place in cross-national family structures, relative to the marriage alliance, was more flexible and as a result potentially more anguished. The Capuans were said to have tried to retrieve their sons, and the Romans were said to go to extraordinary lengths to keep them on a permanent basis.

As for brides specifically being labeled as hostages themselves, rather than simply in the orbit of simultaneous male hostages, Josephus records that Sanaballetes, a Persian satrap, gave his daughter Nikaso in marriage to Manasses, the brother of the High Priest, thinking that she would be a hostage who could secure the goodwill of the entire Jewish nation.[32] In one of the *Controversiae* of Seneca the Elder, the Athenian Iphicrates must defend himself, in part, for marrying a daughter of the king of Thrace when the two states were supposed to be at war; his defense was that the woman doubled as a hostage as well as a wife.[33] Twice in Plutarch's biographies the contentious relationships of the last years of the Roman Republic were potentially reparable by what he calls hostage-taking in the disguise of marriage alliances. Plutarch says that Pompey viewed Julia, the daughter of Julius Caesar, as a hostage who could secure Caesar's allegiance.[34] A similar motivation led Pompey next to shift his attention to two nieces of Cato the Younger to be brides for himself and his son, but Cato rejected the proposal, according to Plutarch, on the grounds that it was an attempt by Pompey to make Cato beholden to him.[35] In his take on the myth of Phaedra and Theseus, Seneca the Younger gives his heroine a lament that sums up the anxiety of wives who enter a marriage to satisfy the exigencies of international relations. Here is

[32] Joseph. *AJ* 11.303.
[33] Sen. *Controv.* 6.5.
[34] Plut. *Pomp.* 70.4.
[35] Plut. *Cato*, 30.3–4. Compare Plut. *Cam.* 33 and *Rom.* 29 where the Latins demand the women of Rome as new wives who could also function as their hostages. It was an obligation that the Romans avoided by dressing up slave women as free born, who then surprised their new Latin husbands as they slept. Plutarch includes the theme in his *Parallel Stories* where the women of Sardis pull the same ruse against the men of Smyrna after a siege: *Mor.* 312E–313A.

Phaedra, who had been given in marriage to Theseus from her native Crete so that she could patch the conflict between the two warring sides:

O Crete, powerful mistress of the wide sea, whose countless ships have taken to wave along every coast, even as far as Assyria where Nereus cleared a path for your prows, why do you compel me to be given as a hostage to hated gods (*in penates obsidem invisos datam*), the wife to an enemy, wasting her life in unhappy tears?[36]

Women such as the mythical Phaedra and the more historical Nikaso, Julia, and the rest, who traveled abroad first as wives and then, secondarily but simultaneously, as hostages, seem to have had a higher profile in the transactions and were closer in status to conventional male hostages than to the donors' unnamed female relatives who often traveled with children and who were simply detained on a temporary basis. Unaccompanied by children, a bride alone was the cause for concern which should, ideally, keep the two sides from quarreling, and thus she drew more attention. In that she formally entered a new family through marriage, the bride-hostage had as much bearing on the recipient as on the donor and therefore may have effected a stronger bond.

RAPE

Women and girls were certainly liable for hostageship in Roman antiquity, but their role as hostages differed from that of men or boys in one crucial respect: as women, their value for either sex or reproduction altered the dynamic of the negotiation. Viewed as sexually vulnerable as well as politically symbolic, female hostages generated a different kind of anxiety among hostage donors. The expectation among Roman authors that hostages could be raped during their internments was common, especially if they were seized in a haphazard way and were not backed by formal diplomacy. There was a dichotomy, however, in how such a practice was received and evaluated; judgments

---

[36] Sen. *Phaedra*, 85–91. The strange reference to Nereus clearing a path for Cretan prows to cut across may be an ironic sexual reference, playing on the rhetoric of gender in hostage-taking: Crete is the one that usually breaks the waves, but now Phaedra is the one who, as a hostage, is "broken" in a sexual sense.

of the perpetrators of hostage rape vary from case to case. In some episodes the rape of hostages is seen as a right of the recipient, even heroic, while in most it is portrayed as a vicious assault. In all cases, however, the powerlessness of the hostage is taken for granted; even when the rape of a hostage is given a negative assessment, for example, it is not the crime of rape or the plight of the victim that draws comment, but the lack of control on the part of the assailant.[37] The rape of hostages was thought to be a compelling vice, which was understood by Roman audiences as natural, but at the same time rejected as uncivilized.

In some cases, the sexual assault of a hostage – particularly when that hostage was a woman – was viewed as a privilege of the hostage-taker. The rape of hostages appears in Roman epic mythology with little by way of negative treatment of the perpetrators. According to Dionysius of Halicarnassus, Heracles raped a Hyperborean hostage girl under his care while they were traveling to Italy.[38] The union led to the birth of king Latinus, Aeneas's principal ally in Italy and a respected ancestor of the Roman people; the rape of a hostage was thus a first act of sorts in the foundation of Rome. Moreover, Romulus's abduction of the Sabine women famously explained how the all-male community of early Rome managed to perpetuate itself into a second generation and beyond. Plutarch's biography refers to the women as Romulus's hostages, at first wielded against the Sabines for their bargaining potential and only later incorporated into Roman society through the proper ritual of marriage.[39] In both of these cases, Dionysius and Plutarch allow their readers some amount of circumspection of their heroes' actions: Dionysius says that Heracles at first managed to control his lust and only succumbed to it after a time, and Plutarch gives the Sabines a voice in protesting the violence done to the abducted women.[40]

---

[37] Recent scholarship on rape in Roman antiquity discusses its significance as an expression of power. For examples, with the rape of Lucretia, see Joplin 1990, Joshel 1992, Arieti 1997; with rape as a theme in Ovid, see Curran 1978, Richlin 1992, and James 1997. On rape's affirmation of a young man's masculinity in Roman comedy, see James 1998.

[38] Dion. Hal. *Ant. Rom.* 1.43.1.

[39] Plut. *Rom.* 16.2.

[40] Comparing the various accounts of the rape of the Sabines in Livy, Dionysius, Ovid, and others are Hemker 1985; Joplin 1990, 56–57; Miles 1995; and Fox 1996.

Nevertheless, both heroes ultimately make the grade for the Roman pantheon; the rapes, after all, were critical in advancing Rome's destiny.

By contrast, in episodes involving mere mortals of Rome's past, the rape of female hostages is often criminalized; in the cases of historical personages and not epic heroes, good leadership could be marked by restraint in the consideration of a hostage's sexuality. As we have seen in Chapter 5, Scipio Africanus was thought to be exceedingly honorable for promising the mother of Iberian hostages in his possession that he would not let his soldiers abuse them, which, we are led to assume, would have been inevitable otherwise. Similarly, king Cleonymus of Sparta was vilified by Diodorus and others in stories about his taking of female hostages from Metapontum in southern Italy in 303 BCE:

Entering the city as its ally, he drew off more than 600 talents of silver and took the 200 most beautiful girls as hostages, although they were not so much guarantees of good faith as objects of lust (ὡς τῆς ἰδίας ἕνεκεν λαγνείας). Casting off the trappings of Sparta, he continued in his luxury and enslaved those who had trusted him. Although he had a powerful army and stores of supplies, he did not act in a way worthy of Sparta.[41]

In this case, Cleonymus is accused of ignoring the essence of hostage-ship – the articulation of good faith – in favor of sexual gratification. Still, rape is not portrayed as something that is condemned by the signatories of the deal. In both this case and Polybius's story of Scipio in Iberia, neither author denies that a hostage could be sexually violated without committing a breach in the *letter* of the contract. Scipio's restraint is an exception in hostage policies, which only proves the rule of the admissibility of rape; and with Diodorus's Cleonymus, rape comes across as a subsidiary benefit of hostage-taking, which was always beneath the surface and only now is wrongfully elevated to the hostage's primary role. In Appian's tale of Octavian and the senators who wanted to take his mother and sister hostage, recounted above, it is appropriate, then, that the author places their hiding place at the temple of Vesta, the protector of chastity and the household.[42] To be

[41] Diod. Sic. 20.104.3–4. Cf. Ath. 13.605e.
[42] App. BCiv 3.91.

taken hostage as a woman could be seen as tantamount to rape; even if it was abhorred, it was still expected.

An episode in Polybius, which is followed by Livy, confirms that for all the repugnance of rape, the rights of the victim were less compelling than the realization of the contract for which she was a hostage. Polybius, apparently in a book that is now lost, told the story of Chiomara of the Asiatic Gauls, who was taken prisoner by a Roman centurion.[43] The centurion held her hostage for a ransom from her husband, and raped her in the interim. Eventually a time, place, and price were set for her release, but when the centurion went to embrace her a final time, Chiomara motioned to her stewards to kill and behead him. When she presented the head to her husband, though, his first reaction was one of horror, and he reprimanded her for violating the sworn ransom. He was ignorant of the rapes, and the story ends with Chiomara justifying her act by referring to them. Polybius then reveals that he met the woman herself, and he praises her "dignity and intelligence," but the husband's first response – repugnance at Chiomara's sacrilege – as so recorded, demonstrates the dilemma of the hostage as a powerless figure who carries the burden of proof.[44] The setting here is not an international alliance but, rather, an *ad hoc* transaction between two men; nevertheless, Chiomara's description as the chattel that shifts hands is reminiscent of other accounts dealing with agreements between states; such situations likely did not preclude rape.

So far, we have only seen episodes in which victims were female; a smaller body of evidence suggests that a similar fate could be in store for male hostages. In most cases, sexual assaults on male hostages come from male overseers; the only near exception is the mythological story told by Parthenius, which was encountered in Chapter 5, in which queen Cleoboea attempted to seduce a boy hostage, Antheus, but failed and drowned him as a result.[45] In examples in which adult men

---

[43] Polyb. 21.38, preserved at Plut. *Mor.* 258E-F. Cf. Livy, 38.24.

[44] Polyb. 21.38: τό τε φρόνημα καὶ τὴν σύνεσιν. Cf. Livy, 38.24.10 who refers to Chiomara's action as a *facinus*, or moral crime. For discussion of this episode in the context of Polybius's historiography, see Chapter 8.

[45] Parth. *Amat. narr.* 14. On sexual aggression among women as abnormal in Roman conceptions of sexuality, see Parker 1997, 58–59.

target male youth, hostage-taking could intersect with commonly held notions in antiquity concerning the sexual dimensions of mentoring relationships between the old and the young. It is in this spirit, and not one of rape, that Dio Chrysostom reports that Philip II, while serving as both a hostage and a student in Thebes during his adolescence, was a lover of Pelopidas, his mentor.[46] Chrysostom, who is the only source for an erotic quality to Philip's hostageship, understands the relationship to be consensual and even edifying. In other examples, however, the boys in question are believed to be in jeopardy. The mini-biography of Lars Porsenna in the *De Viris Illustribus* includes a unique anecdote in the otherwise oft-told story of Cloelia, the Roman hostage who escaped from the Etruscans in the early Republic. After Cloelia fled across the Tiber and was returned by the Romans to Porsenna in keeping with their contract, the king offered her a reward for her bravery by allowing her to return home with any other hostages of her choosing. Although the original hostage contingent included both boys and girls, we are told in this version that Cloelia thought that the ages of the boys made them particularly susceptible to sexual assault and so selected them for freedom.[47] The boys are thus rescued from what is portrayed as an inevitable fate, and the girls are left behind to suffer it. In an anecdote about Agathocles the tyrant of Syracuse, Polyaenus describes a similar deliverance. In the story, Agathocles deliberately sent his son, Heraclides, as a hostage to Ophelas of Cyrene, who was marching against him. The reason, we are told, was that Ophelas had a reputation as a lover of boys, and so Heraclides had been instructed by his father to seduce Ophelas while Agathocles organized a counterattack.[48] The plan allegedly worked, with Agathocles defeating and killing Ophelas and retrieving his son in the nick of time. Given Agathocles's instructions for his son to seduce his captor, rape is not so much the problem here as penetration, generally, which, of course, already carried a negative stigma in Roman attitudes toward male sexuality. But Agathocles's strategy, like Cloelia's rationale for rescuing the youths

---

[46] Dio Chrys. *Or.* 49.5.
[47] *De vir. ill.* 13. On the rape of both sexes as equivalent horrors in the Roman mentality, see Williams 1999, 104–107.
[48] Polyaenus, *Strat.* 5.3.4.

from Lars Porsenna, counted on the fact that young male hostages would likely draw the sexual attention of their captors. As usual, we are not commenting on whether events unfolded just as Polyaenus so dramatically relates; it is the way in which he describes Agathocles's gamble that betrays a general understanding of a hostage's sexuality.

The expectation of male rape can also be seen in an episode in Josephus concerning the tense relationship between Herod the Great and Mark Antony in 36 BCE.[49] At the time Herod's position in Judaea was in peril, as he had taken the throne only a year before and was facing opposition from the old Hasmonaean aristocracy as a result of both his close ties to Rome and his execution of the elderly king Hyrcanus on charges of conspiracy. Herod was now at odds with Alexandra, Hyrcanus's formidable daughter and the mother of Herod's first Hasmonaean wife, Mariamme. Josephus tells us that Alexandra tried to use her friendship with Cleopatra to convince Antony to support her son, Aristobulus (Herod's brother-in-law), in a bid for the high priesthood. Josephus says that Antony was not interested in helping her until Alexandra sent him a painted portrait of the boy. When he saw the beauty of Aristobulus, so the story goes, Antony asked Herod to send him along, the implication being that Antony was motivated by lust. According to Josephus, Herod sent a letter to Antony explaining that he could not release Aristobulus because the Jewish people would surely instigate a rebellion in order to protect him. The entire episode is complicated by a number of inconsistencies. First, Antony had always managed the East very carefully, and it is unlikely that his sole objective in calling Aristobulus to his side was so that he could have sex with him. Second, far from having the interests of Aristobulus's safety in mind, rather, Herod was jealous and suspicious of the youth; his contempt for Aristobulus was unequivocally revealed in the following year when he had Aristobulus drowned in a palace swimming pool. Third, Josephus notoriously held Cleopatra in low esteem, and the negative impression that arises for her in a story where she assists in a plot to rape a youth seems part and parcel of a larger campaign to tar her reputation.[50] It seems more likely that

[49] Joseph. *AJ* 15.25–30.
[50] Cf. Pelling 2001, 298.

Antony had asked for Aristobulus purely for the purposes of political maneuvering – according to the conventions of hostage-taking and its related institutions of fosterage, Alexandra offered a political alliance, Antony accepted, and Aristobulus was to be the token of the agreement. It is the same type of submission of sons that would be the method of choice for Herod himself and the various factions of his family in trying to win over Augustus a few years later, as one son after another was sent to Rome for an "education."

Two options exist for the origin of the misinterpretation of Antony's intentions: either Herod, feeling the pressure from both Alexandra and Antony, refused to send Aristobulus and instead spread a rumor about the possibility of Aristobulus's rape at the hands of Antony, or else Josephus, eager to discredit Cleopatra, included a polemical version of events, either self-created or borrowed, as part of a larger historiographical agenda.[51] In either case, at the center of the ploy, be it Herod's attempt to survive against the arrayed opposition of Alexandra, Antony, and Cleopatra, or Josephus's determination to cast Cleopatra in a negative light, was the understanding that Herod's people, or Josephus's readers, would assume that the rumor was credible. There must have been some population in Roman antiquity that naturally suspected that Antony's request for Aristobulus was primarily or even partially an opportunity for slaking his libido. When an adult man sought control over the son of another as part of a political strategy – a commonplace in diplomatic hostage-taking – his motives could be questioned and misidentified in a war of propaganda. Fears and anxieties in geopolitics provided the incentive for scandal mongering, whose weapon could be allegations of hostage rape. As Josephus tells it, the fear of the violation of hostages could move entire populations.

THE RHETORIC OF GENDER

The language of gender often infuses descriptions of hostage-taking, regardless of the sex of the characters involved or sexual events in the narrative. The hierarchical relationship between a hostage-taker and a

---

[51] Sicker 2001, 80–81 argues the former.

hostage-donor or the hostage himself gave writers an opportunity to use sexual vocabulary in discussing their views on any given episode. Descriptions of the gender of hostages typically match the commonly perceived power discrepancies between male and female: hostage-taker equals strength equals male, while hostage equals weak equals female.[52] To fight back is to be a man, and if a man succumbed to hostage obligations, his gender had to be shifted by writers who imbued him with feminine characteristics. For example, the comic poet Antiphanes, as he is quoted by Athenaeus, a Greek writer in the Roman empire, matches the submission of hostages with a gendered quality when he comments on the decline of Sparta in mid-fourth century BCE:

The comic playwright Antiphanes said the following [about the Spartans] in his *Harp Player:* "Did not the Spartans say that they would never be conquered? Yet now they give hostages and wear purple headbands."[53]

The wearing of purple hair coverings was a signifier of femininity, and by equating the surrender of hostages with a gender swap for the formerly manly Spartans, Antiphanes (abetted by his medium, Athenaeaus) found a new way of describing their unqualified powerlessness. Assigning gender roles to the characters in a story of hostage-taking was an effective way of passing judgment on that episode. Tacitus at one point viewed a Parthian hostage as being marked by "softness" (*mollitia*), an unmistakable marker of femininity.[54] Calling a hostage feminine, in addition to, or instead of, spelling out the consequences of that hostage in geopolitical terms, conveyed an added dimension to international relations, which could resonate with a broader spectrum of readers, or evoke more intense emotions.

Reversing the terms, if a female resisted hostageship, to Roman eyes she must really be a kind of male; Roman writers made sense of a woman's courage in hostageship by switching her gender. Cloelia,

---

[52] On masculinity and impenetrability, see Edwards 1993, 73–75; Walters 1997; Parker 1997; Kellum 1997, 113; James 1998; and especially Williams 1999. Gleason 1990 discusses physiognomy in the second century CE and beliefs in a state of flux for sex as well as gender. For a macroscopic view of masculinity and warfare throughout history, see Braudy 2003.

[53] Ath. 15.681c. Cf. Aeschin. *In Ctes.* 133; Diod. Sic. 17.73.5.

[54] Tac. *Ann.* 6.43. On the gendered associations of *mollitia*, see Edwards 1993, 68–70 and Parker 1997, 51.

the Roman maiden who escaped hostageship among the Etruscans by swimming across the Tiber, was repeatedly described as acting beyond the capacity of her gender.[55] Dionysius of Halicarnassus describes the reaction of Lars Porsenna to Cloelia's heroism:

Referring to the girl from the group of hostages by whom the rest had been persuaded to swim across the river as having greater wisdom than her sex and age would suggest, he honored the city not only for producing noble men but also maidens who are their equal.[56]

The preponderance of gendered language is obvious: Cloelia cannot have been just a woman if she fled a status that was one of humiliation and weakness. The same sentiment of Cloelia's triumph over her sex appears also in Seneca the Younger, who says her statue is a foil for effeminate men in the city; in Pliny the Elder, who notes she was remembered as wearing a man's toga; in Silius Italicus, who wonders how much more she could have accomplished had she actually *been* a man rather than merely acted like one; in Polyaenus, whose Cloelia impressed Lars Porsenna by her "manliness"; and in Plutarch, one of whose characters says that Cloelia's courage was "greater than a woman's."[57] Cicero, in his *De Officiis*, appears to be the earliest literary source for this mode of thinking on Cloelia when he quotes a line of poetry, which comes as a lesson to Roman men to fight harder: "for you, young men, betray a womanish soul, but that maiden displays a man's."[58] This way of reconceiving Cloelia was not, however, limited to literary commentators. As seen in Chapter 3, five sources – Livy, Dionysius of Halicarnassus, Seneca, Pliny the Elder, and Plutarch – record that a bronze statue was erected in Rome depicting Cloelia; all but Dionysius say it was equestrian, and Pliny adds that she wore a toga.[59] Plutarch, presenting the episode in keeping with a host-guest

---

[55] Cf. Walker 1980, 263–274.

[56] Dion. Hal. *Ant. Rom.* 5.34.3.

[57] Sen. *ad Marc. de cons.* 16.2; Plin. *HN* 34.13.28; Sil. *Pun.* 10.496–500, cf. 13.828–830; Polyaenus, *Strat.* 8.31: τὸ ἀνδρεῖον; Plut. *Mor.* 250F: τὴν τόλμαν αὐτῆς ὡς κρείττονα γυναικὸς cf. *Publicola*, 19.4. Compare Livy 38.24.10, whose Chiomara, in attacking her captor, acts "in a way unlike a woman" (*haudquaquam mulieris*).

[58] Cic. *Off.* 1.61: *vos enim, iuvenes, animum geritis muliebrem, illa virgo viri.*

[59] For references, see Chapter 3. On statues of women in Rome and Livia's commissions, see Flory 1993.

paradigm, interprets the statue differently from the others, especially Livy, but in either case, the very people who set up the statue had emphasized her ability to act in a way that was atypical of women. The statue itself is the earliest known "text" of a gendered reading of a hostage episode in Rome: its very casting in a durable, valuable material, and its placement in a highly trafficked area in the pose and dress of a soldier-statesman effectively reimagined Cloelia as a veritable man by virtue of her resistance to hostageship.

Just as the gendered qualities of hostage-taking required half a dozen authors to explain Cloelia as an aberration, the way of thinking also led Suetonius to discuss Caligula's atypical treatment of his hostages as evidence of his monstrosity and of his subversion of universal norms. In a vituperative anecdote, Suetonius alleges that Caligula played the passive role in sexual relations with his foreign hostages, just as he did with an actor, Mnester, and a youth of the senatorial aristocracy.[60] Moreover, as seen in Chapter 4, rather than leading hostages in his mock triumph over the Bay of Naples, Caligula took the reins of the chariot himself, playing the charioteer, or servant, to Darius, who, despite being a Parthian hostage at the time, was dressed as the conqueror.[61] Caligula's slavish demeanor with this hostage intensifies the sexual depravity to which the biographer also alludes. As the emperor with overarching *imperium*, Caligula ultimately bore the responsibility for taking hostages, and as such, he should have played a masculine role. In making his subject do precisely the opposite on two occasions, Suetonius depicts Caligula as inhabiting a warped universe, and readers can more easily comprehend his (alleged) villainy. Like Antiphanes's (and Athenaeus's) Spartans and their purple hair coverings, Caligula here is an inversion of a natural order, as proven by his practices in hostage-taking.

We have seen so far how being or giving a hostage was compared in antiquity to playing a passive role in sex; this conceit of hostage-taking was understood and anticipated sufficiently by ancient audiences that the metaphor could be switched. Writers who wanted to portray their characters as craving an immoral sexual role could describe them with

[60] Suet. *Calig.* 36; cf. Elbern 1990, 106.
[61] Suet. *Calig.* 19; cf. Cass. Dio, 59.17. See Chapter 4.

the metaphor of hostageship. In his *Metamorphoses*, Ovid tells the story of Scylla, a daughter of Nisus and princess of Megara.[62] When her city was under siege by Minos, Scylla conceived a passion for him as she watched the battle from the walls. As Ovid tells it, she longed to become Minos's hostage so that she could bring about an affair.[63] Hostage-taking, to Ovid's Scylla, was assumed to be a sexual opportunity, a stand-in term for intercourse. The completion of Ovid's story demonstrates that the sexual aspect of hostage-taking was open to scorn: Scylla betrays her father by cutting the lock of hair that made him invulnerable, but as she is on the verge of realizing her dream of hostageship, Ovid's Minos reproaches her as wretched and sacrilegious. Notably, Scylla is a hypersexual being first, who secondarily seeks hostageship in pursuit of her objective.[64] The crime of sexual immorality is made more intense by the criminal motivation of treason; to long for hostageship is both perverted *and* treacherous.

A similar opprobrium, expressed in the language of both sex and hostage-taking, is felt by one character for another in Achilles Tatius's novel, *Leucippe and Clitophon*. In the story, Thersander, a pirate and the principal villain in the melodrama, is on trial, and a bishop who knew him as a boy is called to speak against him. The bishop begins to dress down the defendant by pointing out that when he was a youth, he led the decadent lifestyle of a passive homosexual; more specifically, the bishop says that Thersander "played the hostage" to a number of older men.[65] In this context the verb also makes reference to the pedagogical quality of hostage-taking, which was explored in Chapter 6. Thersander was not only having sex with the "hostage-takers," but he

---

[62] Ov. *Met.* 8.1–151.

[63] Ov. *Met.* 8.48: *obside* (hostage) begins the line, followed in apposition by *comitem* (companion) and *pignus* (security). On the abruptness and surprise of the word, see Anderson 1972, 338.

[64] The fact that Minos is compared with Apollo (line 31) and that he justly imposes laws on the defeated (line 102) suggests that he may be yet another stand-in for Augustus. Minos's rejection of a negative quality of hostageship could be compared with Jupiter's rejection of Lycaon's cannibalistic feast of a hostage in *Met.* 1. Also, Tissol 1996, 143 compares Ovid's Scylla with Propertius's Tarpeia.

[65] Achilles Tatius, *Leucippe and Clitophon*, 8.9.3: ὁμηρίζων. This translation disagrees with other proposals, such as "to do joint work," of the Loeb (Gaselee 1984); and to "specializ[e] in the old Greek lays (Homer, I mean)" of Reardon 1989, 276. On Thersander lacking control, see Haynes 2003, 140.

was also said to be learning technique from them, which enabled him to continue his debauchery into adulthood. "Playing the hostage" in this context thus meant both having sex and perfecting it. Although the verb, "to play the hostage," is a *hapax legomenon*, coined in this novel and not used anywhere else in Greek literature, it effectively illustrates what might be called the sexualization of hostage-taking in the second century CE, the time when Lucian also imagined the hostage exchange between Endymion and the speaker of the *True Histories*. To Athenaeus (who excerpted Antiphanes, quoted earlier) and Achilles Tatius, both of the second century CE, sexual intercourse and the taking of hostages could each serve as explanatory metaphors for the other; in Antiphanes's example of the Spartans and their feminine, purple bandannas, a metaphor of gender explained the nature of hostage-taking; in the case of Achilles Tatius's novel, the metaphor of hostage-taking explained a character's sex life and gender identity.

Achilles Tatius, Athenaeus, Suetonius, Tacitus, and Lucian, all writing in the second century CE, were preceded in blending the pedagogical with the sexual as an equation of decadence in hostage-taking by Juvenal's second satire, written around the early second century. The satire is a catalog of the different stereotypes of effeminate men in Juvenal's day: drag queens, prostitutes, castrated priests of Cybele, male-male "domestic partners," and men who prefer weaving to warfare are all scorchingly vilified.[66] The satire is simultaneously a diatribe against those who preach high morals yet themselves engage, hypocritically, in the same behavior they proscribe. As an *exemplum*, the poem ends with a passage about an Armenian hostage (probably fictional) named Zalaces who has been buggered by an unnamed magistrate.[67] The speaker of the satire, in reference to the degradation of the hostage, laments the implications for Rome's place in geopolitics:

[66] "Domestic partners" refers to lines 117–136 about marriage among men. On the emphasis on the "inversion of social relations," with attacks on "passive homosexuality" in a "secondary" role, see Nappa 1998, 91. The reversal of roles yields "a greater portrait of debasement and enervation" (Nappa 1998, 106); Juvenal's treatment of hostages fits well with Nappa's arguments. On the "visual quality" of the satire, see Walters 1998. For the inclusion of women in the shooting gallery in the form of Laronia's speech, see Braund 1995.
[67] Courtney 1980, 149 suggests that the tribune was the hostage's caretaker.

Look at what happens as a result of such trysts: a hostage had come [to Rome], for here they are made human. But if a longer stay in the city opens him up to boys, a lover is never wanting. His pants and knives and reins and whips are cast off, and Armenia will become Obscenia.[68]

The satire effectively deflates the common rhetoric in accounts of hostage-taking discussed in the previous chapter – that of reeducation, the creation of civilized human beings, and the pacification of the periphery through hostage-taking.[69] As Juvenal's reader approaches the end of the poem, he finds a failed cliché about the glory of Rome: the trappings of barbarism, such as knives instead of swords and pants instead of togas, will indeed be thrown away by the former hostage, but that which has been taught by the Roman men is a "lifestyle" that will ultimately undo them all, both center and periphery. As a hostage, he will lose his pants and in so doing, drop the phallic knife and the controlling reins and whip, and become feminine; the problem is that another part of the equation of the hostage's experience is that, given his impressionable nature, he will broadcast his new immorality to the world and transform it.

---

[68] Juv. 2.166–170: *aspice quid faciant commercia: venerat obses, / hic fiunt homines. Nam si mora longior urbem / indulsit pueris, non umquam derit amator. / Mittentur bracae cultelli frena flagellum; / sic praetextatos referunt Artaxata mores.* The above translation of the last line is an attempt to preserve the Latin rhyme and juxtaposition of the original *praetextatos* and *Artaxata* – a more literal translation would be "...and the Artaxians would take to wearing the toga *praetexta*." Not very funny to the modern speaker of English, but the Romans would understand a pun: *Artaxata* refers to a place-name in Armenia, probably with an exotic flavor; *praetextatos*, to the Roman understanding, would signify youths under the age of sixteen, the period of life when males wore the toga *praetexta*. More specifically, in this context the clothing of young boys is a metaphor for their passive sexuality. For the rhyming "echo" or "mirror" of *praetextatos* and *Artaxata*, see Henderson 1999, 315, note 91. For taking Artaxata as a nominative and the subject of *referunt*, see Courtney 1980, 130. On Roman beliefs in methods of transforming men into *cinaedi*, see Gleason 1990, 397.

[69] Cf. Braund and Cloud 1981, 204.

8

POLYBIUS AS A HOSTAGE

In the study of hostage-taking in the Roman world, Polybius presents an undeniable opportunity. Not only does he include several extensive and detailed commentaries on episodes of hostage-taking, but also he himself wrote from the perspective of one detained among the Romans. So far, we have had only slight, oblique glimpses of a hostage's opinion of his own unique status and identity, most of it coming from archaeological evidence: Juba II's portraiture, plus his new city at Iol/Caesarea, Antiochus IV's commissions (or lack thereof) at the city of Antioch, in addition to his conduct in foreign policy (as reported by Roman authors), and Vonones's coins have all suggested, albeit indirectly, varying degrees of accommodation of Roman culture on the part of the hostage. By contrast, Polybius and his *Histories* – his study of Roman institutions and his pseudo-autobiographical passages about life in Rome – offer a more nuanced and sophisticated understanding, firsthand, of the experience of hostageship and the hostage's relationship to Rome and to individual Romans. Coming from an oligarchy and not a royal dynasty and arriving in Rome in his mid-thirties and not his adolescence, Polybius was clearly different from princes like Antiochus IV, Juba II, Vonones, and others. But his experience with the Romans still overlapped with theirs in critical ways, and more important, his writing demonstrates that he was profoundly affected by his stay. Whether Polybius is called *obses* or ὅμηρος or something else, his reflections on his experience as an elite outsider in Rome, with access to power and the hope of release, can reveal some of the anxieties and pressures confronted by more conventional hostages; equipped with his writings, we are better able to gauge a non-Roman's response to the withering rhetoric that placed him in a position of inferiority.[1] On balance, as we shall see, the historian's message is a combination of acceptance of Rome's dominance, at least on the surface, and a determination, simmering underneath, to maintain dignity.[2]

Before examining Polybius's reaction to Rome, it is useful to consider the circumstances and nature of his status as a hostage, something discussed briefly in the Introduction. In the years leading up to the Battle of Pydna, the Achaean League, of which Megalopolis, Polybius's home *polis*, was a part, was divided into factions that were defined by their opinions concerning Achaean autonomy in the face of Roman expansion. Polybius and his father, Lycortas, were associates of Philopoemen who advocated the independence of the League from Roman interference.[3] Within this group, Polybius, at least by his own account, stood out as being particularly adept at keeping Rome at bay and preserving Achaea's autonomy. He records that in a meeting of his political allies concerning the best policy for dealing with Rome during the conflict with Perseus, his own argument, which carried the day, was that it would be prudent to give outward pledges of support, but in practice, to act only in ways that benefited their league.[4] He was then elected hipparch for 170/169 and, as he relates in the *Histories*, promptly put the strategy into action: the League promised to send troops to help the Roman legate Quintus Marcius Philippus against Perseus, but Polybius held back, as he says, until a Roman victory was assured and he could no longer feasibly avoid this

---

[1] One also could consider Josephus and Juba II as "hostage historians." Eckstein 1990b has already noted similarities between Polybius and Josephus in style and method. Cf. Henderson 2001, 43. Juba's writings exist only in fragments, collected at Roller 2003.

[2] For a full discussion of Polybius's method, see the classic studies of Pédech 1964; Petzold 1969; Eckstein 1995; and Champion 2004, which are cited later *passim*.

[3] In general, see Errington 1969; Derow 1970, 16–17. Eckstein 1985, 278–281 points out that it is overly schematic to say Philopoemen's faction was "anti-Roman" or even that he had a "faction" at all. Notably, Philopoemen had *supported* Rome in its war against Antiochus III. The conduct of his allies, however, when juxtaposed with that of Callicrates, was less tolerant of Roman interference on a permanent basis.

[4] Polyb. 28.6. On Polybius's role in Philopoemen's funeral, see Plut. *Phil.* 21; on his now lost encomium, see Henderson 2001, 33. See also Pédech 1964, 517–521 and Champion 2004, 16. Walbank 1979, 333–334 argues that Polybius was aligning himself with Archon who, as a statesman, was in ascendancy.

obligation.[5] Direct support of Rome was given only when there was no alternative, and even then, dissimulation was the order of the day. The principal opposition to this policy toward Rome came from Callicrates, who favored subordination and who is said to have curried senatorial favor with abandon.[6] Polybius lets his opinion be known about Callicrates on multiple occasions: he takes notoriously cheap shots, alleging, in addition to political malfeasance, that he was physically repulsive, filthy, and the object of ridicule for children on the street. At one point, he says that celebrants at a festival refused to bathe in the same basin as Callicrates until it had been drained, cleaned, and filled with fresh water.[7] Polybius's hatred for Callicrates, of course, was fueled by the fact that the Romans eventually won at Pydna, came to hold tremendous influence over Greek affairs, and backed those who had supported Rome the most. In 167, Polybius and his allies had become unwelcome by virtue of the new settlement, and Callicrates eventually was successful in accusing many of them of abetting Perseus and accordingly had them – by most accounts, over a thousand – removed to Italy without a trial.[8]

Unlike the earlier internments of the Carthaginians, Macedonians, and Seleucids during the previous generation, the deportation of the Achaeans was the result of political infighting within the League and was apparently not stipulated by a treaty. As we have seen, the Achaeans who were sent to Rome are not categorically defined in the

---

[5] Polyb. 28.13. On Polybius's career as hipparch, see Pédech 1964, 123 and Eckstein 1995, 5–6.

[6] E.g., Polyb. 24.8; 30.29. On Polybius's antipathy for Callicrates, see Derow 1970; Eckstein 1985, 278–281; Eckstein 1995, 204–205; Golan 1995, 75–94; and Champion 2004, 156. Arguing that Callicrates was not as strong politically as Polybius led on is Gruen 1976, 49.

[7] Polyb. 30.13.9 discusses false accusations leveled by Callicrates; Polyb. 30.29 suggests the popular attitude toward him was as to a traitor. On the bath, see Polyb. 30.29.4.

[8] Polyb. 30.13.1–11; 30.32.1–12; Livy, 45.31.9; Paus. 7.10.10. The detainees also included Thessalians and Perrhaebians (Livy, 30.7.5); Boeotians, Acarnanians, and Epirotes (Livy, 45.31.9, 45.34.9); and Aetolians (Livy, 45.31.1). Shimron 1979–1980 views the detention as a "brutal and unjust" decision by the Romans, but the diplomatic norms of hostageship and the agency of Callicrates might argue against such a reading. Gruen 1976, 49 argues that Polybius exaggerated Greek despair over the loss of the thousand. On the nature and purpose of the detention, see also Pédech 1964, 360–367 and Edlund 1977, 129.

ancient sources as hostages; rather they are usually referred to with a periphrastic description, such as "those detained in Rome,"[9] or "those accused of conspiring against Rome."[10] In one case, they are called exiles (φυγάδες).[11] In part the latter designation is not unexpected – to the *Callicratean* faction in power, which supported Rome, the assertion of Achaean autonomy on the part of the thousand constituted a form of treason, and exile would have been an appropriate response. Nevertheless, the label of exile obscures the coercive nature of the Achaeans' detention: Polybius implies that some of his allies remained in Greece, despite the large purge of the thousand, and to them, the Roman possession of Polybius and his companions would have a force different from punishment. The detention of the thousand instead could be wielded as a device to "silence the people in Greece and to make them obey Callicrates."[12] Apart from coercion, a number of other features of conventional hostage-taking are present in accounts of the Achaeans. For example, although Polybius stayed in Rome, the rest of the thousand Achaeans were scattered throughout towns in Rome's environs.[13] As with other hostage groups, occasional attempts to secure their release were made by their countrymen in the form of embassies to the senate.[14] Moreover, Polybius spent time with other Greek-speaking hostages in Rome, most notably Demetrius, the young hostage of the Seleucids.[15] In all, the Achaeans were held for seventeen years, finally released in 150 BCE when, according to Plutarch,

---

[9] Polyb. 31.23.5; 32.6.4; 33.1.3.

[10] Polyb. 30.5–7; 30.32.1–9; 32.3.14; Livy, 45.35.2; Paus. 7.10.10–11. Cicero once refers to Polybius as "our guest" (*noster hospes*): *Rep.* 4.3.3. Champion 2004 calls them political hostages (17), political prisoners (18; cf. Derow 1970, 18), and political exiles (28). Henderson 2001, 37 captures the essential ambiguity in saying that they were "in a Kafkaesque limbo of indeterminate status and shape."

[11] Polyb. 35.6 = Plut. *Cato*, 9.2–3.

[12] Polyb. 30.32.8: ἵνα συμμύσαντες πειθαρχῶσιν ἐν μὲν Ἀχαίᾳ τοῖς περὶ τὸν Καλλικράτην. Walbank 1979, 461 argues that the line refers to an attempt to force the *detainees* to obey Callicrates. Gruen 1976, 50–53 points out that many of Polybius's faction were still in power and argues that the Romans did not seek to influence Achaean policy directly.

[13] Polyb. 31.23.5; Paus. 7.10.11.

[14] In 164: Polyb. 30.32.1–9; in 159: Polyb. 32.3.14–17; in 155: Polyb.33.1.3–8 and 33.3.1–2; in 153: Polyb. 33.14.

[15] Polyb. 31.11–15.

Cato the Elder personally granted Scipio Aemilianus's request that Polybius and his fellow Achaeans be allowed to return to Greece.[16] Pausanias says that of the original thousand, approximately three hundred were still living in Italy at the time; some had managed to escape, but most of the remainder had died while in custody.[17]

Certain milestones in Polybius's life as a hostage and afterward can be recovered from autobiographical vignettes in his extant history as well as from other sources, which themselves probably drew from those parts of his history that are missing today. He kept frequent company with Scipio Aemilianus, who was the grandson by adoption of Scipio Africanus and the son of Aemilius Paullus, the victorious general at Pydna. They met at the start of Polybius's detention, when Scipio Aemilianus was about seventeen years old and Polybius in his mid-thirties.[18] Polybius says that they shared a fondness for hunting and grew increasingly close over the years; it was perhaps in Scipio's company that Polybius visited Gaul, Spain, and Africa while still a hostage.[19] Polybius appears to have been a close observer of events in Greece following his release, but it is unclear what his formal position was, or if he had one at all.[20] Pliny the Elder implies that while the Third Punic War was being waged Scipio lent Polybius a ship so that he could visit the rest of northern Africa as well as the Atlantic coast of the Iberian peninsula beyond the Straits of Gibraltar, but in any case, they were together at Carthage where Polybius witnessed the sack of the city in 146.[21] After the sack of Corinth later that same year, Polybius's

[16] Plut. *Cato,* 9.2–3 = Polyb. 35.6.

[17] Paus. 7.10.12. cf. Polyb. 32.3.15.

[18] The date of Polybius's birth is not known. Walbank 1972, 7 suggests approximately 202 to 200, which is generally accepted.

[19] Hunting: Polyb. 31.29.8. Polyb. 10.11.4 says that he had visited New Carthage; Polyb. 3.48.12 refers to a visit to the Alps. Pédech 1964, 560 discusses Polybius's role in an embassy to Masinissa with Scipio Aemilianus.

[20] Polybius expresses disgust at the radical government in Achaea on several occasions, seemingly as an outsider and not as one holding any kind of official power: Polyb. 38.3.8–13; 38.11.7–11; 38.13.8–9. Walbank 1965, 4 argues that the change in Polybius's status from detainee to freed representative of Rome was reflected in his work. Cf. Henderson 2001, 41.

[21] Plin. *HN* 5.9. Pédech 1964, 560 and Eckstein 1995, 14 date the expedition to the Third Punic War, whereas Walbank 1972, 10 suggests it happened after the sack of Corinth in the same year because returning to Greece would have been "awkward." Polybius

role is better defined as he seems to have been a kind of representative of Rome's interests in Greece: again, according to his own account, after the Roman commissioners departed Achaea, they asked Polybius to visit various cities, explain Rome's new laws and constitution to them, and oversee their enactment.[22] The latest date when we can tentatively locate the historian – we do not know when he died – is 133, when it appears that he was again with Scipio Aemilianus, this time at the siege of Numantia, when he would have been approximately seventy years old.[23] Some have argued based on these contacts that Scipio was Polybius's literary patron, although the evidence is not conclusive.[24] In any case, at one point Polybius himself admits that his closeness to Scipio was well known, even widely discussed, and that people beyond Italy and Greece were aware of it.[25] As a detainee in Italy and companion of the well-connected consular, Polybius had close access to Roman power at home and abroad, and he clearly developed important friendships.

It is important to note that Polybius's exposure to Roman politics and culture did not spell an unquestioning loyalty or dependence. In

appears to have published a work on geography and natural history, which is thoroughly mocked by Strabo, Pliny the Elder, and Athenaeus for its inaccuracies (Strabo, 5.2.5, C222; 10.3.5, C465; Pliny, *HN* 4.121; 31.131; Athen. 7, p. 302e). On the significance of the geography to Polybius's larger history, see Pédech 1964, 515–597. For Polybius and Scipio at the sack of Carthage, see Plut. *Mor.* 200 and App. *Pun.* 132; both are also conventionally found at Polyb. 38.21.1–22.3. See also Diod. Sic. 32.24 and Amm. Marc. 24.2.16. Many scholars discuss Polybius's famous account of his conversation with Scipio as they overlooked the burning city: Pédech 1964, 195; Henderson 2001, 40; Champion 2004, 159.

[22] Polyb. 39.5.

[23] Numantia: Walbank 1972, 12, notes 59–60, 63. The year of his death is not known, despite [Lucian], *Macr.* 22, who says that he died after a fall from a horse. Champion 2004, 11 sees Polybius's description of a road through Gaul at 3.39.8 as establishing a *terminus post quem* for his death of 118 (after the Via Domitia had been completed). For a thorough discussion, see Eckstein 1992.

[24] Foulon 1992, 16 argues Polybius was a kind of client, pointing out the frequency with which Polybius compares Scipio with Alexander the Great. See also Pédech 1964, 352–353 and Edlund 1977. Astin 1967, 3 suggests Polybius admired Scipio. Walbank 1965 sees an equitable relationship between the two, although Walbank 1979, 499 notes that the reader would expect the patron–client relationship. Eckstein 1995, 9 argues that Polybius's ties to Scipio should not be exaggerated.

[25] Polyb. 31.23.3. The friendship is also attested at Diod. Sic. 31.26.5; Vell. Pat. 1.13.3; Plut. *Mor.* 659F.

many ways, a close reading of Polybius's *Histories* demonstrates that he was conscious of the various expectations of hostages and was anxious to refute them, either by denying explicitly that the types of binary power relationships described in this book applied to his own situation, or by reversing the roles and effectively redeploying the rhetoric to articulate the extent of his independence of mind and, ultimately, his triumph over his captors. Polybius's attitude toward hostageship and its relation to empire can be best recovered from the passages where he tells his own life story during his time in Rome and thereafter. Hostage-taking clearly was important to him: in most of his references to himself (usually recounted in the third person), hostages and hostage-taking figure prominently – his introduction to Scipio Aemilianus, his friendship with Demetrius of Syria, his acquaintance with the Galatian woman Chiomara, and his role in the origins of the Third Punic War, among other events. In every case, the hostages in question or their donors overcome Roman captors, and Polybius, as the narrator, departs from his typically clinical reportage to offer his own opinion, expressing either approval for the stereotype-defying hostages or disgust at Roman abuse.[26] When viewed in the light of the rest of his *Histories*, his account of his own experience of hostageship in these cases seems to go beyond mere pride or personal ambition: if it can be argued that the Romans viewed hostages as symbols of the periphery – by their understanding submissive, in a variety of ways, to Roman power – then Polybius's redefinition of his career as a hostage, symbolic as it was, communicates a larger message of resistance to hegemony, elevating his own struggle to that of greater geopolitics.

REDEFINING THE HOSTAGE

Polybius's first reported contact with a Roman following the Battle of Pydna was with Aemilius Paullus, the victorious general. The text describing the meeting is no longer extant, but Polybius, at the start of a later, abrupt digression on his detention, reminds his readers that

---

[26] Notably, as will be seen, these criticisms are delivered in oblique and subtle ways and may be described as the "politics of cultural alienation," to use the term of Champion 2004, 3 and *passim*.

he had already mentioned how he and Aemilius Paullus had happened to discuss literature.[27] As Polybius describes it, one of them lent the other some books; the direction of the loan is not stated, although it seems likely that Polybius, the literary figure who was at home in Greece, provided services to the general who was far from Italy and any library he may have had. A friendship reportedly grew from there, and Polybius says that Paullus's sons begged the praetor in charge of the detainees to let Polybius stay in Rome while the others were sent to other towns in Italy. In a long and peculiarly personal aside, Polybius discusses how he first grew close to Scipio Aemilianus. He says that Scipio approached him shyly once his older brother Fabius had left them alone and "in a mild and gentle voice, blushing slightly," asked why Polybius spoke more frequently with Fabius than with him.[28] Polybius, referring to himself in the third person, says he responded, delicately, that he had done so only because Fabius was older and that he would be happy to help Scipio with his "studies" and to train him "to speak and act in a way worthy of his ancestors."[29] Scipio then is said to have interrupted Polybius and excitedly accepted his offer:

Before Polybius finished speaking, Scipio, taking Polybius's right hand in both of his and holding it with affection (ἐμφαθῶς), said, "I hope I see the day when you, viewing all other things as secondary, turn all your thoughts to me and share your life with me (μετ ἐμοῦ συμβιώσεις), for from that moment I will feel I am worthy of my house and my ancestors." Polybius was pleased at this, noting the passion and respect of the young man, but he was at a loss when he considered the eminence of his house and the opportunities available for its members. Having addressed his sentiment, the youth was never far removed from Polybius and deemed all else secondary to his companionship (πάντα δ ἦν αὐτῷ δεύτερα τῆς ἐκείνου συμπεριφορᾶς); from that moment, they constantly sought to please each other with their deeds of mutual affection (φιλοστοργίαν), thinking of each other as a father and a son.[30]

[27] Polyb. 31.23.4.
[28] Polyb. 31.23.8: ἡσυχῇ καὶ πράως τῇ φωνῇ φθεγξάμενος καὶ τῷ χρώματιγενόμενους ἐνερευθής.
[29] Polyb. 31.24.5–6: τὰ μαθήματα . . . τὸ καὶ λέγειν τι καὶ πράττειν ἄξιον τῶν προγόνων.
[30] Polyb. 31.24.9–25.1.

In this passage, Polybius addresses – and reverses – several of the common understandings of the vulnerability of hostages; contrary to common expectations of hostages, Polybius says that *he* will be the teacher, the father, even the "male." In a role reversal, he speaks of the boy's naïveté and seems to go to great lengths to convince his readers of his pedagogical role in Scipio's life.[31] The very reason for Polybius's privilege of staying in Rome was attributed to his literary acumen, which drew Paullus's eye in the first place when they met after Pydna; now the hostage will ironically help the captor in his studies and train him in oratory. Much later in his narrative, Polybius seems to have returned to this theme: Appian, in describing the sack of Carthage of 146, is assuredly paraphrasing the lost text of Polybius when he says that Scipio turned to Polybius as to a "teacher" in order to inquire about the role of Fortune in warfare and to contemplate the meaning and nature of Rome's success.[32] Scipio is thus repeatedly portrayed as the one in need of instruction, eagerly learning from the man who should have been his underling. Moreover, in the passage quoted above Polybius explicitly compares their relationship as it ensued with that of a father and son, only in this case with the hostage in the pater- nal role. The relationship is portrayed as especially odd because not only is the defeated Greek the father figure to his conqueror, but he also takes the place of ancestors who are hyperbolically illustrious: on five occasions in this single anecdote Polybius refers to Scipio's lin- eage. As described earlier in Chapter 5, once Scipio's and his brother's adoptions are accounted for, Scipio was related to Aemilius Paullus, Scipio Africanus, and Fabius Maximus Cunctator.[33] By ending the digression, then, with himself as Scipio's new role model, Polybius subtly puts nearly all of Rome beneath him. Finally, there may also

---

[31] Astin 1967, 298 and Walbank 1979, 498 believe the anecdote distorts Polybius's influence over Scipio. But see Eckstein 1995, 79–82. Here, of course, our concern is more with the representation than with the reality.

[32] App. *Pun.* 132: διδάσκαλος. Cf. Paus. 8.30.9 who, on describing a monument to Polybius at Megalopolis, says that "whenever the Romans obeyed the advice of Polybius, things went well with them."

[33] Five times: Polyb. 31.23.1; 31.23.12; 31.24.5; 31.24.10; 31.24.11. On the adoptions of the brothers, see Chapter 5.

be a slight reference to a feminine quality in the adolescent Scipio, in that his voice is described as mild and gentle, he blushes, and he takes Polybius by the right hand – a gesture also used in Roman weddings – and longs for a "shared life."[34] The reversal of the masculine-feminine metaphor for hostage-taker and hostage may be the least obvious in this case, but overall, Polybius's claim of utter mastery over Scipio Aemilianus is remarkable.

Polybius's statement of independence in his relationship with Scipio in spite of his subordinate status as a hostage comes shortly after a much longer digression on Demetrius Soter, the hostage from the Seleucids of Syria, in which Polybius presents a similarly irreverent attitude toward detention among the Romans. By the time Polybius arrived in Rome, Demetrius had already been serving as a hostage for about eight years and was now in his late teens. Polybius says that the two became friends over the next several years during boar hunting expeditions, just as he and Scipio Aemilianus had.[35] At one point, the hostage/historian describes Demetrius's detention as "unjust," considering that both Demetrius's father Seleucus IV and his uncle Antiochus IV were deceased; as quoted in Chapter 5, Polybius says that Demetrius asked to be released and pleaded with the senate by both citing the justice of his case and, according to Polybius, parroting what he believed the Romans wanted to hear, namely that the senators had become like fathers to him and their sons like his brothers.[36] Polybius takes pains to point out that none of these emotions were sincere in Demetrius: despite a life spent almost entirely among the Romans, Demetrius had grown into his own man and longed to return to Syria. Demetrius's request, of course, was rejected and he remained a hostage. Later, he was eager to try again, believing that the senate would be more amenable to a change of regime after a Roman legate had been assassinated during a mission to Syria. Polybius now reports that he himself began to play a greater role in events: he urged Demetrius not to appear before the senate again but "to have faith in himself and

---

[34] Polyb. 31.24.9.
[35] Polyb. 31.24.3. Cf. Champion 2004, 17.
[36] Polyb. 31.1.2–5: παρὰ τὸ δίκαιον κατέχεσθαι. See Chapter 5.

attempt a bold action worthy of a monarch."[37] But Polybius, as he portrays himself, is playing a Cassandra: Demetrius does not heed his advice, goes before the senate a second time to make a formal plea, and again is rejected.[38] Polybius then says that Demetrius wished that he had listened to him and soon decides to "attempt the bold action" by escaping from captivity.

The story of Demetrius's flight is well known, but for our purposes it is important to note the extent to which Polybius himself takes the credit. From the start, Polybius is instrumental in hatching the plot. By his account, Demetrius begs him to help, and Polybius obligingly convinces an ambassador from Egypt – an old friend from his days as a hipparch in Achaea – to provide a ship for Demetrius and to cover for him by falsely claiming that the ship was his own transport back to Alexandria.[39] On the appointed day of the escape, Demetrius was to pretend to be visiting a friend's house for dinner, with (false) plans to go to Cerceii where he and Polybius used to hunt together. As it turned out, Polybius happened to be sick in bed when Demetrius made his move, and so could not accompany him to the banquet, nor from there to the port at Ostia, but as he tells it, he still was responsible for the success of the escape: he says that he feared lest Demetrius, being young, would drink too much and somehow botch the plans, and so although he was ill, he wrote a cryptic note to Demetrius reminding him to act quickly and to take advantage of the cover of night.[40] We are told that the message arrived in the nick of time, and Demetrius just managed to escape undetected, such that it was five days before his absence was noticed by the senate. Although Demetrius succeeded in his flight, it would seem that this is really a story about

---

[37] Polyb. 31.11.5: ἀλλ ἐν ἑαυτῷ τὰς ἐλπίδας ἔχειν καὶ τολμᾶν τι βασιλείας ἄξιον. On Polybius's disapproval of the prolonged detention, note Champion 2004, 161.

[38] Cf. Henderson 2001, 33, noting that Polybius was a "warner-figure" in his accounts of his own foreign policy before his detention.

[39] Polyb. 31.12.8–13. For Polybius's participation in an embassy to Egypt in 181/0: Polyb. 24.6.1–7. Polyb. 34.14 reveals that he had visited Alexandria. Walbank 1979, 479 suggests Polybius met Menyllus in Rome.

[40] Polyb. 31.13.7–14. The note appears to be a series of lines of poetry stitched together from different sources. Walbank 1979, 482 identifies one as coming from Eur. Phoen. 726.

Polybius: the historian inserts himself into the narrative five times. Advising Demetrius on two occasions, finding the Egyptian, choosing the decoy of a hunting trip at Cerceii, and writing the note sending Demetrius on his way, Polybius comes off as the very soul of the operation. The obvious irony after all of this – that *Polybius* is the one who remained a hostage – serves to reveal to his readers that his own hostageship is atypical and that he feels no allegiance to Rome.[41] The way in which he reminds his readers that the Egyptian who abetted his plans was an associate from his days as an opponent of Rome before Pydna hearkens back to the days of Achaean independence and intensifies the level of his inner resistance. Polybius will, by necessity, stay in Rome, yet as he always did in the past, he will help those who are justified in fleeing and who, like Demetrius, might deny the common expectations of hostage-taking and refuse to play the son to new fathers.

Polybius also inserts himself, albeit obliquely, into another hostage episode that went awry for Rome – that of Chiomara of Galatia in Asia Minor, which was encountered in Chapter 7. We do not have Polybius's own words on this event, but, rather, a paraphrase by Plutarch, who included the anecdote in his collection of "the virtuous deeds of women," citing Polybius as his source.[42] It will be remembered that Chiomara was taken hostage by a Roman centurion and held for ransom, during which time she was raped by her captor. Chiomara did not passively accept the crime: she had the centurion killed and beheaded on the day when the ransom arrived and presented the head to her husband. Polybius himself was not involved in the hostage-taking or in the act of defiance, as he was with Demetrius; the important part of the passage for our purposes comes in how Plutarch ends his summary: "Polybius says he spoke at length [with Chiomara] at Sardis and was amazed at her pride and intelligence."[43] One longs to have Polybius's own account of this story. Editors have placed it in Polybius's Book 21, because that is where Rome's campaigns in Galatia

---

[41] Eckstein 1995, 12 notes Polybius's independence in arranging Demetrius's escape.
[42] Plut. Mor. 258 E-F = Polyb. 21.38. cf. Livy, 38.24.2. See Eckstein 1995, 151 on Plutarch's use of Polybius.
[43] Conventionally cited as Polyb. 21.38.7.

are recorded, but it is possible that the story came in a later book, when Polybius may have described his own travels to Sardis after his release.[44] When Polybius records that he met a character in his history and shifts into the first person in order to declare his approval for her actions, the larger history becomes, again, at least in part, a history of Polybius himself: by inserting his own voice in order to comment on the episode and its protagonist, Polybius in effect makes himself a participant in Chiomara's resistance to Rome, as well as in her resistance to the expectations of detention. The message is that one who approves of Chiomara's boldness and even of her masculinity himself would not fall into the trap of a hostage's identification with his captor.

Like the story of Chiomara, Polybius's original account of the release of the Achaeans in 150 BCE is lost yet preserved as a summary in Plutarch, and Polybius again seems to have emphasized his own primary role in contravening detention. In his biography of Cato the Elder, Plutarch says that it was at Polybius's instigation that Scipio Aemilianus came to Cato to plead for the release of the Achaeans. Readers of the original passage, wherever it occurred in Polybius's narrative, would have been reminded of Scipio's devotion to Polybius, and thus the years of Scipio's "education" under Polybius would seem to have paid dividends. As Plutarch tells it, the senate finally voted for their release, but Polybius had more to say: he visited Cato again to make the additional demand that the Achaeans be restored their honorable status upon their return. Cato's response, according to Plutarch and probably Polybius as well, was to quip that Polybius was like Odysseus returning to the Cyclops's cave to retrieve his clothes. Plutarch's intent as a biographer was to showcase Cato's wit; Polybius, however, may have sought the reflexive prestige of being compared with Greece's archetypal "wily" hero.[45] Moreover, by means of the

---

[44] Walbank 1979, 151–152 discusses the potential dates for Polybius's visit to Sardis, arguing that it took place either before his detention in 168 or perhaps in 140/39 when he may have accompanied Scipio Aemilianus on a mission there. Walbank points out that Chiomara would have been very old at that point, and that Polybius's language could imply respect for an elder.

[45] Polyb. 35.6 = Plut. *Cato mai.* 9. On Polybius's general interest in Odysseus, see Eckstein 1995, 281.

anecdote, once Polybius returned to Greece with Rome's backing, he could assert that he was not now a puppet of the Romans, as might be expected of a hostage, but had won his restitution in his own way, even in a gesture of defiance. Again, one wishes to have Polybius's own account, but the credit that Plutarch gives to his source at least communicates Polybius's understanding of his own heroic status.

After he was released, Polybius had another brush with significant hostages, this time from Carthage, which he discusses at length. We have already seen in Chapter 2 that when the Carthaginians fought against Masinissa, Rome's ally in Numidia, the Romans ordered them to desist and threatened to declare war otherwise. Polybius says that Manius Manilius, the consul at the time, sent a letter *to the Achaeans* asking them to send Polybius to Sicily to act as a kind of broker in the conflict, and *the Achaeans* voted accordingly.[46] Polybius goes on to say that while on his way to Sicily, he read a letter from the consul *to the people of Corcyra* in which the news was delivered that the Carthaginians had surrendered hostages. Polybius says that he assumed that this meant that both sides had thus backed away from the brink of war – hostages, after all, were a sign of peace – and he returned home.[47] Contemporary readers of Polybius would have known without reading further that the war certainly was not over, and that the Romans famously disregarded the spirit of the hostage-based deal, broke their own word, and forced Carthage into a final confrontation. The justification for Rome's action was much discussed in Polybius's day; Polybius goes into some detail about the various arguments in the debate: a significant number of people believed the Romans had betrayed Carthage and manipulated the hostages to their advantage, in opposition to international justice. Ultimately, his account of the debate ends with him siding *with* Rome, noting that the Romans did not disobey the letter of the treaty.[48] Yet in subtle ways, in describing his own conduct in events leading up to war, he condemns the Romans for their deceit.[49]

[46] Polyb. 36.11.1.
[47] Polyb. 36.11.4.
[48] Polyb. 36.9.16–17.
[49] Cf. Champion 2004, 164–166.

In returning to Greece when he read the letter at Corcyra, Polybius guilelessly assumes the Romans will keep their word; when they do not, he has thus absolved himself of all guilt. Polybius's history of this prelude to the Third Punic War makes two points about hostage-taking in Rome. First, one notes further that Polybius repeatedly points out that he was not involved in any of the correspondence in this affair: it was the Romans, the Achaeans, and the Corcyraeans who are said to be exchanging letters; thus the Achaeans sent him on their own, not his, initiative. In other words, Polybius tells his readers implicitly that he is not active in Roman service, and that it was not his desire to become involved in this war. Second, as Polybius describes it, the Punic hostages' sole purpose was as collateral; all that they were meant to do, to Polybius's understanding, was to stop the war. Polybius thus indirectly asserts that any of the other residual benefits of hostage-taking that might be expected, such as a cultural transformation or a shift in loyalty, are unattainable for the Romans. In this way, Polybius, who was himself a hostage for so long, moves further from any possible accusation of collaboration with Rome and reveals his own resolve. It is interesting to find, furthermore, that Polybius's account of his role (or lack thereof) in the Romans' brutal behavior concerning the Carthaginian hostages is followed immediately by his famous defense of his decision as a historian to highlight his own presence in events throughout his work. Evidently, Polybius felt that his place at center stage in the episode could potentially elicit criticism. And immediately following this statement, Polybius records that after the affair of the Punic hostages, where he displayed patent indifference to the Romans, the Achaeans removed public statues of Callicrates in the dead of night and replaced them with images of Lycortas.[50] Polybius says this was the stuff of revolution: past supporters of Rome were replaced by an Achaean champion, not coincidentally Polybius's own father. Again, the string of events is chiefly concerned with Polybius, and the emphasis is on his distance from Rome.

On a number of occasions, Polybius thus redefines hostage-taking as it relates to his own career and experiences. This chapter is focusing on

[50] Polyb. 36.12–13.

Polybius's direct fashioning of his own character, but it is important to note briefly that in other episodes of hostage-taking concerning previous generations, Polybius also interprets hostages in unique ways. To take two prominent examples, with Demetrius of Macedon, Polybius, compared with Livy, describes Flamininus as more determined to wield influence against Philip and meddle in Greek affairs by means of his hostage.[51] Moreover, with Antiochus IV, Polybius falls short of Livy in describing the king's Romanization: while he does say that Antiochus wore the toga and canvassed, Roman-style, for votes, he does not mention gladiators or a temple to Jupiter in Antioch; his disdain for Antiochus's Roman vestiges is apparent in his reporting that Antiochus's subjects called him *epimanes* (crazy) as a result.[52] In both these cases, we still find determined Romans and resistant non-Romans, but in reference to himself, the redefinition of hostageship is especially clear. He says that from the start, when he first met Scipio Aemilianus, he was neither son nor student, but occupied the opposing positions, and whenever he was personally involved with Roman hostage-taking or had the opportunity to comment on it directly, he praised and assisted those who sought their freedom and revealed, however subtly, Rome's abuses.

TRAITORS AND RECONCILIATION

Polybius's *Histories* seems an odd project for an associate of Philopoemen to have undertaken: at the start of his work, he says that his objective is to explain how Rome grew as quickly as it did to become the dominant power in Mediterranean geopolitics. In addition to observation, the work also has a strong persuasive quality.[53] As he tells his readers what the Romans have done in the past, he is also suggesting

---

[51] Polyb. 23.3.7–8: Flamininus tells Demetrius that Rome would help to secure the throne for him, an aspect of their relationship not present in Livy, except in Perseus's paranoia (cf. Livy, 39.46.6).

[52] Polyb. 26.1.5–7; cf. Livy, 41.20.9–13. See also the earlier discussion in Chapter 6 concerning the problems of interpreting the various accounts of the so-called Day of Eleusis.

[53] Petzold 1969 discusses the comparative method of Polybius and his interest in writing history that has a practical application. Walbank 1964, 245 says that Polybius was "driven by didacticism." On Polybius's audience, see Eckstein 1995, 118–119.

what would be the best course of action for the Greeks in the future. His narrative is frequently disrupted by asides on Roman culture that serve as both models for the Greeks to follow and proof that they must respect Rome's authority. His Book 6 is particularly famous with its long description of the Roman military camp and its expert design and discipline, the Roman political constitution in relation to other Greek systems, and the inspirational quality of the Roman funeral. Perhaps most effectively, Polybius's theory of the cycle of constitutions and the system of checks and balances in the Roman Republic demonstrated that Rome was unique in its ability to prosper endlessly without experiencing a period of decline. The historian's judgment in every case is that the Romans have developed a culture that sets them apart and makes them difficult to resist.[54] In light of these superb institutions, Polybius repeatedly decries Greek attempts at rebellion as inherently foolish and futile.[55] In that Polybius's objective is to persuade, large parts of the *Histories* presuppose a target audience of dissenters, or, the faction with which Polybius was formerly associated. Rather than adhering to assertions of independence, which, Polybius argues, can be self-destructive, Polybius recommends behavior that may have characterized his rivals, the Callicrateans.

Polybius's readers in Greece thus may have been surprised to find Lycortas's very son arguing against rebellion and would have wondered about the reason for the shift. Searching for clues, they might blame the *volta face* on the fact that Polybius wrote his initial work with Scipio's support. The Scipionic clan had a long reputation as especially effective hostage-takers; as seen in Chapter 4, many members of the

---

54 For a fuller discussion of the ambiguities of Book 6 from the standpoint of the "politics of indeterminacy," see Champion 2004, 84–98.

55 A famous example is Polybius's record of Critolaus's resistance of Rome leading up the Achaean war (38.10.6–8; 38.11.7–11; 38.12.6–7). On Polybius's criticism of Achaean statesmen during the war, see Pédech 1964, 293–295; Gruen 1976, 62–65; Shimron 1979–1980, 100; Eckstein 1995, 142–146; and Champion 2004, 166–167. Petzold 1969, 43 notes the irony of Polybius's arguments against rebellion. Note Henderson 2001, 38 that a "lesson of [Polybius's] lifetime is the incomensurability of Roman power"; his past heroes, such as Philopoemen, thus become "dinosaur species." For the related question of Polybius's attitude toward social movements, see Mendels 1982, who distinguishes between radical and moderate revolutions in Polybius's histories. On the Roman side, Derow 1979 argues that Polybius's record of Rome's imperial ambition is at odds with the Holleaux thesis of defensive maneuvering.

family were taking hostages between 218 and 188, and an inscription in the tomb of the Scipios cast new light on similar accomplishments of their long-dead ancestor of the early third century. When Polybius wrote what might be considered at first inspection to be a flattering history of Rome and when he served as a Roman representative after being released, he would seem to be just like a son, just like a student; "typical hostage," they might complain.[56] Polybius describes just such a reception in his account of his associate Stratius's post-hostageship career in Greece, to be discussed shortly. It may have seemed that the Aemilian and Scipionic families had kept close tabs on the author, had convinced him over time of Rome's superiority, and had supported him in his project of writing a long treatise on the morality of Roman rule and, more importantly, on the futility of continued resistance.

In the face of such challenges, Polybius worked hard to clarify his purpose and to salvage his reputation. His long, complex story of Rome's rise includes several cautionary asides and occasionally negative assessments of Rome's methods, and it defies easy categorization. Polybius repeatedly shows that although he was a student of Rome, he was not necessarily its disciple. For example, although he believed some resistance movements were foolish, Polybius also clearly resented those who bowed to Roman authority as a matter of course. Displays of slavish behavior and sycophancy were to be avoided. After he had been in Rome and had met Scipio, he witnessed the arrival of another Greek from the East, Prusias of Bithynia, who brought his son to be presented formally before the senate – an episode that Polybius treats as an example of what not to do when dealing with Rome. The king, he says, was dressed in the clothing of a freedman, and his entrance to the curia was appalling:

Standing in the doorway opposite the senate and laying both his hands on the ground, he fell down in adoration of the threshold and the seated senators calling out, "Bless you, my savior gods," not at all abandoning his extremes

---

[56] Henderson 2001, 39 notes that Polybius worked against the image that he was "a *Graeculus*, re-educated in the house of Roman generals." Note also Champion 2004, 228–232.

of unmanliness, and second to no-one in womanishness and servility (καὶ γυνασκισμοῦ καὶ κολακείας).[57]

Polybius says that the rest of Prusias's behavior was too shameful even to mention, even though the senate looked kindly on him as a result.[58] The reversal of Prusias's gender makes use of the same conceptions of hostage-taking explored in Chapter 7, and serves to deposit Prusias in the same vile category as occupied by Callicrates. By condemning abject subservience, Polybius distances his own acceptance of Rome from that of his Hellenic contemporaries, and thus seeks to define a compromise.

Polybius seems to be trying to extricate his Greek readers from a trap between irreconcilable extremes: on one side is the Greeks' long history of autonomy and of their sacrifices to maintain that autonomy, which Polybius once championed, and on the other is the unavoidable reality of Roman power, which threatened to swallow up the Achaean League no matter how stubborn the resistance. In steering a middle course, Polybius encourages a measured acceptance of Roman rule as the only rational solution – submit, but do so with dignity and with the hope of regaining an advantage at some point in the future. Polybius's criticism of Roman hostage-taking consistently dwells on the dichotomy between what is portrayed "on the surface" in hostage-taking and what exists behind the façade: Demetrius Soter's hatred of Rome is concealed; Chiomara must deceive her captor into a fatally compromising position; the Romans in possession of Punic hostages go back on their word. The historian's interest in autonomy and deceit is in keeping with larger themes throughout his work having to do with the dignified, even duplicitous, accommodation of Roman power.[59] A succinct explication of his agenda of accommodation takes the form of an apology for those who shift allegiances

---

[57] Polyb. 30.18.5. Cf. Diod. Sic. 31.15; Livy, 45.44.4–21; Val. Max. 5.1.1; App. *Mithr.* 2.

[58] Cf. Eckstein 1995, 155–156 and 222–225. Walbank 1979, 442 argues that the reference to the senators as "savior gods" refers to Flamininus's deification following the Battle of Cynoscephalae.

[59] Eckstein 1995, 89–117, by contrast, notes cases in which Polybius condemns acts of deception in geopolitics.

in the interest of their state's survival. In a passage that has come to be called Polybius's treatise "On Traitors," the historian suggests that what has the appearance of treason is often in reality the best policy available:

It is evident that one must not . . . immediately consider men to be traitors (προδότας) who, because of circumstances, induce their countries to exchange their established relations for other friendships and alliances. Far from it, since such men have often been the source of the greatest benefits for their country.[60]

The "treatise" goes on to identify the repercussions of rejecting this prescription by recounting the destruction of Athens that was brought on by Demosthenes's resistance of Philip II: there was no honor in ruining the state entirely for the sake of the preferred way of life. As Eckstein has put it, Polybius has recast the debate away from freedom versus submission and replaced it with a discussion of rationality versus irrationality.[61] For the Achaeans of his own day, submission was, for now, on the side of rationality, but it could change and one should be prepared for change. The defense of a productive brand of treason is carried out repeatedly in the *Histories,* not least in Polybius's story of this own trick of offering to support Rome during the war with Perseus, but then withholding his troops as late as possible. Especially pertinent here is Polybius's account of the debate between Philopoemen and Aristaenus about the value of assertions of autonomy in the face of overwhelming power. Polybius ultimately compliments both Aristaenus's strategy of double-dealing and Philopoemen's bolder statements of independence, but points out that the people mistook Aristaenus's plan for pro-Roman sentiment.[62] Moreover, Hiero of Syracuse is first praised for his acknowledgement of Roman superiority at the start of the First Punic War in 263, but then for his

---

[60] Polyb. 18.13.4–5. Eckstein 1987b and 1990a are convincing in arguing (*contra* Aymard 1940) that the fragment refers to Aristaenus. Compare the debate between Philopoemen and Aristaenus at Polyb. 24.11–13. In any case, the tone of the passage implies its universal application: Pédech 1964, 200–201; Walbank 1979, 564–565; and Piatkowski 1991, 400.

[61] Eckstein 1995, 195–197 and 233–235.

[62] Polyb. 24.11–13, especially 24.13.8–10.

assistance of Carthage later in 241 with their mercenaries.[63] Hiero's conduct is an example of how to handle life under another state's hegemony: as Eckstein summarizes Polybius's view, "a weak state, if it can avoid it, should not by its own behavior abet the strengthening of that hegemony."

The same kind of conduct was ascribed by Polybius to his colleague Stratius of Tritaea, who is the only other detainee of the thousand Achaeans known by name. Polybius reports that in the discussion among his fellow statesmen before the war with Perseus concerning how to deal with Rome, Stratius held the most extreme position in arguing that they should not send the Roman army help and, what is more, they should confront anyone who openly courts Roman leaders.[64] Stratius was detained by the Romans after Pydna and seems to have remained, along with Polybius, one of the most sought after of the detainees when the Achaeans sent an embassy to win their release.[65] Yet once Stratius was released, he, like Polybius, maneuvered prudently in the new *Realpolitik* between Greece and Rome: at one point after the restoration, a crowd of Achaeans, furious with Rome's encroachment, targeted Stratius as a spy, but as Polybius records it, Stratius was resolutely pro-Achaean, despite appearances to the contrary:

Stratius admitted that he had communed with [the Romans], and he declared that he would still associate with them as friends and allies in the future. But he also swore that he had never informed them of the proceedings of their magistrates. A few people believed him, but most believed the accusations.[66]

Stratius thus acts in accordance with the behavior prescribed in Polybius's "On Traitors," doing just barely what was necessary to survive under Rome's hegemony and keeping his own land foremost in his mind. As Polybius tells it, most people did not believe Stratius; by extension, we might reasonably assume that most people also did not trust Polybius. By characterizing Stratius (and himself) as something different from the expected quisling and instead as a kind of double

---

[63] Polyb. 1.16.4 and 1.83.2–4. See Eckstein 1985, 271–272.
[64] Polyb. 28.6.6. On Stratius's background and the other Achaeans who may have been taken hostage, see Pédech 1964, 360 and note 33.
[65] Polyb. 32.3.14.
[66] Polyb. 38.13.5.

agent like Hiero, Polybius seeks to put them all in the same company as heroes. His conduct *as a hostage* is made to match his record *as a hipparch* of the Achaean League: Polybius was already revealed as a model practitioner of self-serving dissimulation, and his irreverence toward hostage-taking then is just an extension of previously acknowledged acts of resistance. By including himself as a player in a game of deceit and accommodation, Polybius effectively defends himself *as a historian*, while also serving as an *exemplum* of the behavior that he prescribes in other parts of his *Histories*.

In conclusion, Polybius seems to have been aware of the connection between reeducation, hostageship, and a debilitating surrender of power and personal identity. In order to remain influential with his native colleagues, he had to declare that in this case, it was the Greeks who were the teachers, the fathers, and the males, even as hostages. An important key to understanding Polybius's self-presentation with respect to the expectations of hostages is that the unusual lapse into memoir in discussing his assistance of Demetrius and his first meeting with Scipio Aemilianus comes in Book 31, near the beginning of Polybius's final books, which some have suggested were written after his release and after the publication of the first thirty books.[67] Polybius's first thirty books, it would be explained in some imaginary indictment, present Rome as invincible simply because Polybius was working under a new power. Confronted with such a reputation Polybius's task of salvaging his own dignity was urgent, and he carried it out in his later historical installment with new rhetorical arrangements of the empowered now surprisingly subjected to the powerless. It is a compelling message, this turning of the tables, which must have helped to defend Polybius from charges of collaboration with Rome in both his politics and his writing. That he did so with the vocabulary of family and education not only demonstrates the prevalence of

---

[67] Polyb. 3.4.12–13 discusses his decision to extend the work to 146. See Walbank 1977 and Eckstein 1995, 10–11. Cf. Henderson 2001, 41: "in his last ten books, world history even metamorphosed, progressively, into autobiography." Champion 2004, 9–11 is rightly suspicious of the evidence for any "chronological map" of Polybius's composition, but notably, he points out that two of these episodes – Demetrius's flight and Chiomara's escape – were later additions to the work (although he suggests the Chiomara story was plotted before even his own detention).

the perception of hostages as both virtual sons and students, but also suggests that the power relationship of the metaphors could be denied on their own terms. The surest indication that a brand of rhetoric was effective and widespread is for those who are targeted, or victimized, by it to redeploy it against the powerful. Notably, Polybius never calls himself a ὅμηρος, which, although appropriate, would have been demeaning.

TACITUS ON HOSTAGE-TAKING
AND HEROISM

At the time when Tacitus was writing the *Annals*, the theme of
the Romanized, benignly subservient, quasi-filial hostage was
deeply ingrained in Roman literature. It could be found in multiple
authors regardless of literary genre, as writers of the Republic and early
Principate used it as one of the explanations for Rome's prodigious
success at the dawn of its empire. As we have seen repeatedly, hostage-
taking appeared in new legends for Rome's foundation and accounted
for triumphs over one impressive enemy after another. The fact that
Polybius had done much to debunk the stereotype of the quisling
hostage in his own case in order to gain some amount of credibility
with his audience shows the extent to which it was conventional wisdom. Plautus joked about it; Julius Caesar bragged about it; and in the
case of Augustus, it was literally carved in stone, if one is to judge by
the words and images on the *Res Gestae* and Ara Pacis. Hostage-taking
had become an attractive endeavor: transforming a young hostage and
exercising influence over him in his later life constituted an inex-
pensive, low-risk method of winning ever more territory, or at least
extending Rome's sphere of influence. Long after Tacitus, belief in the
tactic continued apace, the most telling evidence for which would be
the law of Marcus Aurelius and Lucius Verus, described in Chapter 6,
commanding special privileges for the families of compliant detainees.

But Tacitus, as we shall see, expressed some objections. Most
prominently in the *Annals*, Tacitus demolished the model of peaceful expansion through the device of hostage-taking. Repeatedly he
tells stories where foreign hostages and the Romans who rely on
them fail utterly, while those who reject such a device are vastly more

effective.[1] Figures such as Germanicus and Corbulo handle hostages in what he views as properly heroic ways, often specifically working against the commonly understood roles for hostages outlined in this book, whereas criticism is leveled, sometimes implicitly, sometimes explicitly, against Augustus, Tiberius, Claudius, and Nero, whose policies in geopolitics and dependence on hostages are seen as insufficient measures not in keeping with old Roman values of sheer destruction and humiliation of the enemy.[2] Tacitus consciously plays on his readers' expectations concerning hostages in order to achieve his purpose: he will often first describe the deployment of a hostage in accordance with the various themes of hostage-taking – most notably those of reeducation and quasi-adoption – recording excessive optimism on the part of those who control the hostage, but then undermine these expectations by revealing that the hostage in question soon disappoints, and matters must be set aright by one of the historian's heroes. Tacitus's negative evaluation of certain aspects of hostage-taking is different from that of Polybius discussed in the preceding chapter: whereas Polybius denied the assimilative quality of hostage-taking in his case, Tacitus accepted that foreign hostages could be thoroughly reformed but denied that such a process had any value for Rome in the long run. The historian instead repeats certain criticisms of hostage figures, recasting them as illusory, dilatory, decadent, or weak, usually because of their indoctrination. Four cases from Tacitus's *Annals* are considered in this chapter as examples of the historian's view that those who manipulate hostages by focusing on their coercive value and ignoring their role as vassals are model Romans whose success served to cast the villainy and ineptitude of the Julio-Claudian emperors in sharp relief.

TIBERIUS, GERMANICUS, AND THE EAST

Throughout his record of Tiberius's policies with regard to Parthia and Armenia, Tacitus performs a thorough character assassination of

---

[1] For a similar study of Tacitus's use of the figure of the client king in developing his characters, see Keitel 1978 and especially Gowing 1990. Campbell 1993, 218 sees Tacitus's accounts of the failure of the hostages as an indictment of Parthia as an uncivilized land.

[2] See Mattern 1999, 176 on the importance of the perception of victory over Parthia. For a survey of scholarship on Tacitus's opinion of the *Pax Romana*, see Benario 1991.

Vonones, a former Parthian hostage to whom, evidently, great hopes for Roman vassalage were attached, with the result that Tiberius and even Augustus are revealed as unworthy of their power. Tacitus begins the second book of the *Annals* with a quick summary of the submission of the sons of Phraates IV, in which he challenges the notion that the hostages constituted a benevolent show of respect or a sign of Augustus's international prowess.[3] As we have seen, some prior explanations for Phraates's motives – those of Velleius Paterculus and Suetonius, for example – were influenced by Augustus's own interpretation, namely that the Parthians were intimidated by Roman arms and were attempting to forestall an invasion by offering hostages and by making a show of obsequiousness. In his *Res Gestae*, Augustus declares that force had not been necessary and that his own *auctoritas* had made the eastern king beholden to him.[4] At first, Tacitus admits that Phraates sought to pay respect to Augustus, but he then defuses this motivation by pointing out that Phraates had defeated Rome in the past and by repeating the alternate version, espoused by Strabo and Josephus, that Phraates was hardly in awe of Augustus, but only feared an uprising among his own people and accordingly removed the princes from contention for his throne.[5] In combining both explanations at once, Tacitus emphasizes the preexisting tensions in Parthia and in effect argues, even in quick summary, that the submission of the hostages was more complex than Augustus allowed: the princes may have betokened the king's loyalty, but it was only on the surface, and in any case, there were many others in Parthia who were not like-minded. Still only summarizing events, Tacitus then passes over some sixteen years of Parthian politics, which had seen the death of Phraates IV in 2 BCE and the brief reigns of Phraates's successors, Phraataces and Orodes.[6] He resumes his account in 6 CE, when a faction of Parthian nobility arrived in

---

3 Tac. *Ann.* 2.1.
4 *Mon. Anc.* 32.2. Cf. Strabo 6.4.2. Vell. Pat. 2.94.4; Suet. *Aug.* 21.3.
5 Tac. *Ann.* 2.1. Cf. Strabo, 16.1.28; Joseph. *AJ* 18.42. Some see this view as more plausible: Ziegler 1964, 51–52; Goodyear 1981, 190 ("more accurate"). On the trope of the unwanted heir, see Chapter 5.
6 For a history of Roman and Parthian relations in the intervening years (10/9 BCE to 6 CE), see Debevoise 1938, 144–151; Koestermann 1963, 259–260; Ziegler 1964, 51–56; and Goodyear 1981, 190.

Rome to ask Augustus to send Vonones, the eldest of Phraates's hostage sons, to take the throne. Augustus is said to have taken this as a sign of his own magnificence (*magnificum sibi*), yet the reader's knowledge of Phraates's insincerity renders the assertion almost laughable.[7] In the space of a single sentence, Tacitus then records that Vonones first encountered goodwill, but that it quickly deteriorated into hostility tinged with embarrassment. According to Tacitus, after Vonones returned to Parthia, his people had two complaints: that Rome had been the one to choose their king, and that the king they chose was unacceptable:

Soon it became a source of shame (*subiit pudor*) that the Parthians had degenerated; that a king had been sought from a foreign nation; that he had been infected by the education (*artibus*) of the enemy; that the throne of the Arsacids was given away and [Parthia was] considered among the Roman provinces. What would become of the glory of the men who slaughtered Crassus and drove out Mark Antony, if this possession (*mancipium*) of Caesar, who suffered in slavery (*servitutem perpessum*) for so many years, came to rule the Parthians?[8]

Tacitus goes on to say that Vonones, a Roman possession and slave, was disliked because he had neglected the traditional customs of an Arsacid monarch, such as hunting and horsemanship, and had taken up the Roman habits of riding in a litter, listening to Greeks, and receiving guests openly. According to Tacitus, Vonones's opponents then supported Artabanus, another Arsacid prince, under whose leadership they drove Vonones off the throne and into neighboring Armenia.[9] Tacitus then implies that Artabanus would have declared war if the Romans sought to defend Vonones's claim to power in Armenia, and so the governor of Syria, Creticus Silanus, removed him and put him under guard in his province; Vonones was still sustained in luxury and ambiguously held the title of king, but now it was what Tacitus calls a "sham."[10]

[7] Tac. *Ann.* 2.2.
[8] Tac. *Ann.* 2.2.
[9] Tac. *Ann.* 2.3.
[10] Tac. *Ann.* 2.4: *ludibrium*.

Tacitus's account passes over many details of Vonones's reign which can be recovered from, or at least compared with, other sources. Vonones's coins, for example, whose portrait types have been discussed in Chapter 6, indicate a reign of nearly four years, from 8 to 12 CE.[11] After leaving Parthia around 12 CE, Vonones seems to have lasted in Armenia until as late as 16 CE before he fled capture.[12] It was not a long reign in either realm, but it is considerably more substantial than what Tacitus's breathless pacing in the Vonones story implies: Tacitus moved directly from Vonones's arrival in Parthia to his flights from opponents. Moreover, while Tacitus implies a widespread negative reaction to Vonones on the part of the Parthians, Josephus's account reveals that this was a minority point of view and says that most of Parthia supported Vonones against the usurper Artabanus.[13] Neither historian is flattering in their stories of Vonones, but they both differ in details of his career following his expulsion from Parthia and flight to Armenia. Tacitus's Vonones is a creature of the Romans, who is shuffled about as a pawn in the East; Creticus Silanus himself moves Vonones to Syria. Josephus affords Vonones more independence and reports that he fled Armenia of his own volition when the faction in support of Artabanus became more powerful; according to him, Tiberius pointedly refused to help him owing to Vonones's cowardice.[14] Josephus's Silanus then offered him asylum "in acknowledgement of his Roman education."[15] One could argue that Tacitus's hurried tempo can be attributed to the fact that he was simply providing a summary in order to bring events up to Tiberius's reign in the late teens CE, which is when the digression is set. But in these passages, Tacitus is clearly interested in the nature and effect of Roman meddling in Armenian affairs: amid his discussion of Vonones, he briefly surveys the history of four ill-advised or immoral attempts by the Romans to back their

---

[11] Ziegler 1964, 56; Gonnella 2001, 69–72. Gowing 1990, 319 also argues that Tacitus abbreviated Vonones's reign for effect.

[12] Ziegler 1964, 57; Gonnella 2001, 73. Cf. Karras-Klopproth 1988, 213.

[13] Joseph. *A.J.* 18.48. For the comparison of Tacitus with Josephus, see Kahrstedt 1950, 11–12; Chaumont 1976, 85, n. 69; Koestermann 1963, 262–264; Gowing 1990, 317–318. Paltiel 1991, 124 prefers the Josephan version.

[14] Joseph. *A.J.* 18.51. Suet. *Tib.* 49 says that Tiberius put Vonones to death at this point, which differs, as we shall see, from Tac. *Ann.* 2.68.

[15] Jos. *AJ* 18.52: κατὰ αἰδῶ τῆς ἐν Ῥώμῃ κομιδῆς.

own candidates in that reign; Vonones is viewed as fitting the same pattern.[16] Skimming over much of what happened to Vonones, Tacitus devotes serious attention only to a single part of his tenure, namely his cultural transformation, which stemmed from his hostageship and which he describes as the very source of the Parthians' (alleged) disgust. Tacitus has deliberately chosen to accentuate certain unflattering aspects of Vonones's career, which paint him as incompetent and the Romans who manipulated him, which include Augustus, as misguided.

The Josephan account of Vonones ends with his asylum in Syria, but Tacitus carries through to Vonones's death and continues to denigrate his character along the way. He says that in 18 CE, Vonones's presence in Syria was a sticking point for negotiations between Rome and Artabanus.[17] According to Tacitus, Vonones still had some support among Parthians and was gathering allies along the Syrian border, and Artabanus therefore asked the Romans to remove him. (This account of Vonones's popularity contradicts the historian's previously stated view that Vonones's downfall was the result of universal Parthian hatred for his Roman nature, and instead is in keeping with Josephus's story of factional rivalry.) The Romans now had a new general on the scene – Germanicus, the nephew of Tiberius and, according to Tacitus, a beloved and capable soldier.[18] Tacitus says that Germanicus withdrew Vonones into Cilicia and further from Parthia, partly in keeping with Artabanus's request, but also in order to thwart Gnaeus Calpurnius Piso "to whom [Vonones] was most pleasing on account of the many services and gifts (*officia et dona*) by which he had bound Plancina (Piso's wife) to him."[19] Piso and Plancina are well known

[16] Tac. *Ann*. 2.3–4: the four examples are (1) Mark Antony's treacherous deception and execution of Artavasdes, (2) Augustus's subsequent support of Tigranes and (3) of another Artavasdes, both of whom were deposed, and (4) Augustus's donation of the throne to Ariobarzanes of Media Atropatene, who died in some kind of unspecified accident. On the history of Roman involvement in Armenia, see Debevoise 1938, 152–153; Ziegler 1964, 60; Chaumont 1976, 73–84; Goodyear 1981, 195–196; and Paltiel 1991, 123–124.

[17] Tac. *Ann*. 2.58.

[18] On the characterization of Germanicus, see Walker 1952, 118–120; Syme 1958, 392–395; Shotter 1968; Bird 1973; Goodyear 1981, 199; and especially Pelling 1993.

[19] Tac. *Ann*. 2.58. Shotter 1974, 237 suggests Piso contrived Vonones's escape.

as villains in Tacitus's narrative.[20] As Tacitus recounts, they were sent by Tiberius and by his mother Livia to the East in order to "impede Germanicus's aspirations,"[21] and they perpetually exhibit disgraceful habits: the historian accuses Piso of insulting Germanicus in spite of the fact that Germanicus rescued him from a near shipwreck, and his Piso proceeds to lead the army in the East in unacceptable ways, by pandering to the meek, removing the experienced, and encouraging corruption. Plancina is equally as shameful in Tacitus, as she attended military exercises (for what reason Tacitus does not specify) and insulted Germanicus's wife Agrippina the Elder, as well as Germanicus himself.[22] Notoriously, the pair allegedly went on to poison Germanicus, for which crime, among others, Piso was charged before the senate and ultimately committed suicide.[23] By connecting Vonones with this quintessentially evil pair as a provider of bribes, Tacitus manages to degrade the hostage's reputation even further and also to implicate Tiberius once again. By contrast Germanicus's decision to sweep Vonones aside accentuates his own dignity.[24]

Tacitus further indicts the Principate's brand of hostage-taking when he identifies the reason for Germanicus's eventual diplomatic success with Artabanus. Germanicus is said to have immediately set about reversing the failures wrought by the policy behind Vonones. In Armenia, after Vonones had been removed, he promoted to the throne Zeno, a son of king Polemo of Pontus, who had been raised as a hostage *in Armenia*.[25] Like Vonones, Zeno was a royal heir kept in a land far from home, but his situation was obviously different: whereas Vonones had learned to live like a Roman, Zeno is said to have learned to live

---

[20] For example, Tac. *Ann.* 2.43; 2.69; 6.26. See Walker 1952, 114–123; Martin 1981, 123; and Pelling 1993, 82–85. Shotter 1974 discusses Piso's full career and argues that Tacitus distorted the character of Piso in order to pass a negative judgment of Tiberius. Griffin 1995 sees Tacitus's criticism of Tiberius as directed toward the system of the Principate. Smith 1972, 84–85 seeks to rehabilitate Piso's memory.

[21] Tac. *Ann.* 2.43: *ad spes Germanici coercendas.*

[22] Tac. *Ann.* 2.55.

[23] Tac. *Ann.* 3.12–15.

[24] Gowing 1990 discusses Tacitus's disdain for the personal relationships between the Parthian candidates and the emperors.

[25] Tac. *Ann.* 2.56. For the circumstances of Zeno's lineage and career, see Kahrstedt 1950, 18; Koestermann 1963, 359–360; and Chaumont 1976, 86.

like an Armenian, the very people he was called on to rule. Tacitus says that Zeno made a more suitable candidate because he had endeared himself to the locals by wearing Armenian clothes and by demonstrating an appreciation for Armenian culture, including the customs of hunting and banqueting; he also changed his name to Artaxias, an obvious Armenian moniker.[26] To Tacitus, this was the perfect compromise: it is only after Germanicus ignores Vonones, pushing him further west in the direction of Rome where he belongs, that the two sides arrive at an agreement. For Armenians, Zeno's lack of direct contact with the imperial court made him more attractive. The Parthians were also clearly pleased: Artabanus abruptly withdrew his son Orodes, who had been sent to take the throne, and offered a treaty to Germanicus right after Zeno's coronation.[27] The Romans also were content, as Zeno was an outsider, linked by birth to the regime of Pontus, which was a reliable ally.[28] The Romans made a spectacle of their own superiority at the coronation, according to Tacitus, in that they alone did not bow.[29] Tacitus's Germanicus thus is made to correct the very essence of Vonones's failure, which was his Romanized cultural demeanor resulting from his hostageship, and pointedly repaired it with Vonones's opposite, effected by a different kind of acculturation.[30] Unlike Augustus and Tiberius who sent the wrong man for the job, Germanicus was able to display Rome's authority over the realm, claim the new monarch's loyalty, and stave off Parthian opposition.

Ultimately, the decription of Vonones's death drives Tacitus's point home: supposedly bristling at his station in Cilicia, Vonones bribed his guards and tried to escape when on a hunting expedition. But word of

---

[26] Tac. *Ann.* 2.56 attributes the name to the capital city.

[27] Joseph. *AJ* 18.52; Tac. *Ann.* 2.58. Chaumont 1976, 85 rejects the Josephan account on the basis that Tacitus says that an Orodes was sent to the throne in 35 (*Ann.* 6.33), but there may have been more than one son of Artabanus with that name. See Kahrstedt 1950; Ziegler 1964, 59; and Karras-Klopproth 1988, 110–111.

[28] On Rome's history of diplomacy with Pontus, see Barrett 1978, 439 and Paltiel 1991, 44. Goodyear 1981, 364–365 discusses the possible family link, through Mark Antony, of Germanicus and Zeno.

[29] Moreover, Zeno's (Artaxias's) coinage advertised his links to Rome with the legend, "Germanicus Artaxias" (*RIC* 104). See also Chaumont 1976, 87–88; Goodyear 1981, 365.

[30] Gowing 1990, 325 sees the downfall of Vonones and the ascension of Zeno as frames for Tacitus's account of king Maroboduus.

his attempt preceded him, and the bridge that would have carried him beyond Rome's reach was knocked down in time; Vonones became trapped; and the very guard who had accepted the bribe in the first place ran him through.[31] It is immediately after this story that Tacitus begins to recount Germanicus's slow death and the rumors, entirely amplified by the historian, that poison had been administered by Piso.[32] The irony is evident, as the proper Roman hero who removed a worthless hostage came to be murdered by that hostage's equally worthless champions, who were, as far as Tacitus saw it, agents of an evil emperor. Mellor's general observation that "a central theme of Tacitus's history is the link between the decline of *virtus* and the loss of freedom at Rome" can thus be applied to Tacitus's account of Vonones, Tiberius, and Germanicus: the absence of Roman military prowess and tradition, exhibited by Vonones, coincides with an imperial abuse of power, also evident in Vonones through his ties with Piso and Tiberius.[33]

Tacitus continues to excoriate Tiberius and his reliance on former hostages in conducting diplomacy and foreign policy when he describes the next attempts by the Romans to put descendants of Phraates IV on the throne in Parthia.[34] In 34 CE Artabanus, the king who upset Vonones, was challenged by a faction, which turned to Rome for support. Cassius Dio mentions briefly that Tiberius chose to send Phraates V, who had by then been living in Rome for over forty years.[35] Tacitus's account is more elaborate, but also brief, in reporting Phraates V's campaign; again he takes the opportunity to comment explicitly on the tactic of promoting a former hostage to a foreign throne. According to him, all that the ambassadors sought upon appearing before Tiberius was "a name and the emperor's

---

[31] Tac. *Ann.* 2.68. There is an obvious temptation to compare Vonones's attempted escape with that of Demetrius, hostage of the Seleucids, whom Polybius says escaped while pretending to be on a hunting party. On Vonones's objectives in fleeing, see Cernjak 1986.

[32] Tac. *Ann.* 2.69–84.

[33] Mellor 1993, 48. Cf. Gowing 1990, 325, who argues that the entire purpose in discussing Germanicus, and also Corbulo to be discussed later, is to comment on the emperors.

[34] On the notion that the stories of the next returned hostages, Phraates V and Tiridates, follow a deliberate pattern, see Gowing 1990, 320. Cf. Kahrstedt 1950, 35; Ziegler 1964, 60–63; and Paltiel 1991, 150.

[35] Cass. Dio, 58.26.

permission," disregarding Phraates V's leadership completely.[36] The emperor obliged, demonstrating, as Tacitus complains, "his rule of manipulating foreign affairs by policy and craft without a resort to arms."[37] According to Tacitus, Phraates V learned from the failure of his older brother Vonones and dropped the Roman mannerisms and culture that would no doubt be used against him in the East. His new, pseudo-Parthian disguise, however, according to Tacitus, was not enough to sustain him, as his true, weakened self, hidden behind false manners, proved "unequal to his native customs," and he died of an illness in Syria.[38] An illness, of course, could stop the strongest of generals, even had he been reared in his native Parthia, and Tacitus's description of Phraates's disease, whatever it was, as an indication of his innate incompetence demonstrates more clearly the historian's *a priori* disdain for reformed hostages. If, judging by the Vonones episode, the reader were to conclude mistakenly that the only problem with hostage-based strategies was in outward appearances of cultural demeanor, Tacitus here offers a correction: the transformation of a hostage certainly did take place, altering his very being; it was not just a façade.

Tacitus records another attempt to manipulate the Parthian throne under Tiberius immediately thereafter, this time with a grandson of Phraates IV named Tiridates.[39] Lucius Vitellius was the Roman general for the campaign, and according to Tacitus, before arriving in Parthia, he acted with "old-fashioned excellence," advising Tiridates to take as his role models both his grandfather, Phraates IV, and his "foster father," Tiberius.[40] Tacitus's readers would have understood the use of filial language in connection with hostage-taking as another way of expressing Rome's absolute control, as with education. Tiridates enjoyed some initial success, but according to Tacitus, once again the hostage met his demise through the recognition on the part of the Parthians of his compromised identity as a hostage. Tiridates's opponents are made to comment that "it was no Arsacid that held sway,

---

[36] Tac. *Ann.* 6.31: *nomine tantum et auctore opus.*
[37] Tac. *Ann.* 6.32: *destinata retinens consiliis et astu res externas moliri, arma procul habere.*
[38] Tac. *Ann.* 6.32: *patriis moribus impar.*
[39] On Tiridates's age, see Chapter 5.
[40] Tac. *Ann.* 6.37: *prisca virtute; altor.*

but an empty name housed in an unwarlike man who was weak from foreign softness."[41] Not surprisingly, at this point Tiridates goes on to fail, forced to flee to Syria for refuge with the Romans. The debacle seems designed by Tacitus to reflect poorly on the boast that Rome exercised paternal authority over the East. Tacitus's *Annals* breaks off in a long lacuna before we can find out what became of Tiridates, but the historian's disapproval is apparent: Augustan notions of ruling the world like his extended clan, as trumpeted, for example, on the Ara Pacis, were thus denied by Tacitus to have any substance in practice.

CLAUDIUS, CORBULO, AND THE WEST

Tacitus again articulates the problems with relying on a former hostage – or one like a hostage – when he tells the story of an attempt by Claudius to influence the Cheruscan throne by means of a re-formed vassal, just as Tiberius had done in Parthia with Vonones and the rest.[42] The pattern by now will be familiar: by 47 CE, a civil war that had lasted for over twenty years among the Cheruscans had resulted in the murders of the members of their ruling dynasty, and a faction thus appealed to Claudius, asking him to send as the next king the son of Flavus, a Cheruscan nobleman living in Rome since his service as an auxiliary. The young Cheruscan, with the revealingly Roman name of Italicus, had been raised, according to Tacitus, in the traditions of both German and Roman warfare. Tacitus has the emperor explic-itly compare Italicus with a hostage: his Claudius remarks that the occasion was memorable because Italicus was the first man to claim a foreign throne, who was raised "not as a hostage but as a citizen."[43] As the story continues, Italicus takes his place among the Cherusci, but his experiences follow those of Vonones: he made occasional missteps among his subjects owing to the cultural demeanor he had acquired in Rome, such as when he acted "in an affable and restrained way"

---

[41] Tac. *Ann.* 6.43: *neque penes Arsaciden imperium, sed inane nomen apud inbellem externa mollitia.* Note the feminine quality of hostage-taking deployed by Tacitus as a criticism of the hostage.

[42] In general, see Vessey 1971; Keddie 1975; and again, Gowing 1990, 321–322.

[43] Tac. *Ann.* 11.16: *nec obsidem sed civem.* Koestermann 1967, 58 views Italicus as a pendant to Arminius.

(*comitatem et temperantiam*); by and large, however, Tacitus says that he was just rude enough to endear himself with the Germans, plus his status as nephew of Arminius, Flavus's brother, won him, at first, an opportunity to prove himself.[44] Eventually, a faction rose that challenged Italicus, regardless of his ties to Arminius, as the indirect speech that Tacitus ascribes to one of his native opponents attests:

Roman power had surmounted Germany's past liberty. Was there no-one raised in the region who could take the king's place except the offspring of the scout Flavus, uniformly exalted? To mention Arminius means nothing: even if his own son were to rule after attaining adulthood in a hostile territory (*hostili in solo adultus*), one could still fear that he was infected with foreign money, servitude, and upbringing (*infectum alimonio, servitio, cultu, omnibus externis*). If Italicus has his father Flavus's mentality (*paterna mens*), [the situation is all the worse because] no-one has fought against his country and ancestral gods more implacably than Flavus.[45]

As Tacitus tells it, Italicus then defends himself, methodically pointing out that he was a suitable king: his father Flavus had fought for Rome with the approval of the Cherusci, not as a traitor; Italicus entered Germany at the request of the Cherusci, not at the behest of the emperor; and he had proven in battle that he was brave, not a coward. His defense, according to Tacitus, ends with the accusation that those who oppose him are opportunists, preying upon the common expectations that one raised abroad would automatically support Rome.[46] Tacitus's Italicus thus differs from Vonones in his independent spirit and demonstrable courage, but as the historian tells it, the people did not respond favorably: Tacitus summarizes the rest of Italicus's reign in one short sentence, reporting that he lurched into civil war, won at first, but was later expelled, followed by another comeback. In the end, Tacitus says that Italicus, on balance, "beleaguered" his Cherusci.[47]

With all the significance attached to Italicus's family in this episode and in the quote above, readers of the controversy surrounding his

---

[44] Tac. *Ann.* 11.16.
[45] Tac. *Ann.* 11.16.
[46] Tac. *Ann.* 11.17.
[47] Tac. *Ann.* 11.17: *adflictabat*.

cultural demeanor at this point in *Annals*, Book 11, would have been reminded of the momentous, even picturesque debate between Italicus's father Flavus and his uncle Arminius, which appeared earlier in the text, in Book 2. In a set piece designed to comment on the state of Rome's relations with Germany and the general nature of Roman imperial rule, Tacitus staged a debate between the two brothers at the Weser River which separated Roman territory from the Germanic tribes. The brothers Flavus and Arminius had both initially joined the Romans as auxiliaries, probably during the reign of Augustus, but they were now on opposite sides owing to Arminius's defection and spectacular slaughter of three Roman legions at the Battle of the Teutoberg Forest in 9 CE.[48] In Tacitus's dramatic scene of their reunion, the two shout in order to be heard over the rumble of the current. Tacitus's Flavus rattles off the benefits that he has encountered on the Roman side – increased pay, military decorations, status, comfort. In response, Arminius declares Flavus to have succumbed to slavery, to have forsaken his land, liberty, gods and family, and to have become in essence, a "deserter and traitor."[49] In Tacitus's crafting of the exchange, Arminius is meant to be the sympathetic figure: his speeches are longer than Flavus's and he gets the final word. Moreover, after a long record of Arminius's career, which is marked by courage and conviction, Tacitus punctuates the story of his death with a lavish eulogy, in which he is called the liberator of Germany.[50] In the end, Tacitus says that his heroism was fitting for the Rome of old. The words mark the end of the *Annals*, Book 2, which had opened with the story of the pathetic Vonones; the contrast could not have been accidental: Vonones and Arminius both spent significant periods of time in Rome and had served the emperor, but obviously with very different endings.[51] The reader would come to find similarities between Flavus and Vonones; reading of Italicus, Flavus's son, later in

---

[48] Wells 1999, 231 suggests that Arminius may have still been on the Roman side as late as 7–8 CE during the Pannonian revolt.

[49] Tac. *Ann.* 2.9-10: *desertor et proditor.*

[50] Tac. *Ann.* 2.88. On Tacitus's sympathetic treatment of Arminius, see Walker 1952, 30 and Mellor 1993, 26 and 109.

[51] Cf. Walker 1952, 124 who sees the death scene of Arminius as a complement to that of Germanicus.

Book 11 and of his reeducation, one is led to think of him along similar lines as well, with the formidable Arminius as a foil to them all.

Returning to the story of Italicus, in its aftermath one finds that the failure of Italicus (and, thus, of Claudius) is followed by the success of a new Roman general appointed to the region – Gnaeus Domitius Corbulo – with a different, "more Roman" brand of hostage-taking highlighted by the historian. Immediately, Corbulo is said to have reversed the damage done by Italicus to both the Cherusci and to Roman interests in Germany. The region was being tormented by the pirate Gannascus, who had been recruited by Rome like Flavus and Arminius but had deserted and used his knowledge of Roman territory to target the wealthiest victims.[52] The reeducation of Gannascus thus had backfired on the Romans, and true military acumen, here provided by Corbulo, was needed to correct it. Corbulo moved against the neighboring Frisians; Tacitus records that he compelled them to submit hostages, and then imposed on them a Roman style of government, complete with senate, elected magistrates, and new laws.[53] Tacitus seems deliberate in this juxtaposition of Corbulo's bold seizure of hostages with Claudius's failure in trying to reinstate a near-hostage whom he had inherited; Tacitus's Corbulo comes across as a countervailing type to the emperor. Moreover, Corbulo's forthright method of conquest proved the folly of Italicus's Romanization: cultural assimilation of the Germans *does* ultimately take place, according to Tacitus, in that Corbulo imposed a new system of politics along the lines of the Roman model, but as he tells it, force is crucial to its success, not the indirect, failing method of hostage-taking. Given that Tacitus used Corbulo's memoirs as a source for the *Annals*,[54] one wonders the extent to which the general himself drew attention to his hostages and compared them with the emperor's. In any case, Tacitus ends the story of Corbulo's accomplishments in Germany with a final dig at Claudius: the emperor is said to have been nervous about Corbulo's success and therefore withdrew him from the region. Before his reassignment,

---

[52] Tac. *Ann.* 11.18.
[53] Tac. *Ann.* 11.19. On Corbulo's campaign against the Frisii, see Koestermann 1967, 61–67 and Levick 1990, 153.
[54] Tac. *Ann.* 11.20: *beatos quondam duces Romanos.* Corbulo's longing for the past is also in Cass. Dio, 60.30.5. See Walker 1952, 207 and Martin 1981, 155.

Tacitus's Corbulo proclaims, "Happy were the generals before my day."[55] Tacitus's alignments of Corbulo with Rome's glorious past and of the emperor with its lackluster present, echo the discrepancy between Vonones's current weakness and his people's past accomplishments, quoted above. Once again, Tacitus paints the policy of benevolent hostage-taking as a recent phenomenon, simultaneously associating it with Julio-Claudian decadence.

CLAUDIUS, LONGINUS, AND THE EAST

Tacitus resumes his discussion of the Parthian hostages in Book 12, and the familiar outline is retraced: an emperor's policy of reinstating a former hostage fails because of the hostage's fatal reeducation, and a better Roman – specifically an "old-fashioned" one – is required to fix the damage.[56] In 47 CE, Claudius tried to send Meherdates, another grandson of Phraates IV presumably born in captivity, at the request of Parthian envoys, who are said to have come to Rome out of their tradition of respect. Tacitus has the envoys explain that the "children of the kings were given as hostages [in the first place] so that if they disapproved of their regime at home, one could return to the emperor and senate, and a better king, accustomed to [Roman] *mores*, could be summoned."[57] According to Tacitus, Claudius then responded by equating himself with Augustus for taking advantage of the deference of the Parthians and for sending out a king when his own subjects requested him.[58] As we have seen earlier, Augustus is precisely the company which the emperor should eschew on the question of former hostages, and Tacitus's reader comes to await an uninspiring denouement. Claudius advises Meherdates, who is called a "foster child" of the city, that he should reject the traditional political relationship that existed between ruler and ruled in Parthia – that of

---

[55] Tac. *Ann.* 15.16.

[56] Keitel 1978, 466 reads Meherdates in light of the civil war between Mithridates and Vardanes. On the pattern followed by Meherdates, see Ziegler 1964, 65; Martin 1981, 153–154; and Gowing 1990, 320–321.

[57] Tac. *Ann.* 12.10: *ideo regum liberos obsides dari, ut, si domestici imperii taedeat, sit regressus ad principem patresque, quorum moribus adsuefactus rex melior adscisceretur.*

[58] Tacitus also notes that Claudius chose not to equate himself with Tiberius, who also had sent out hostages.

"despot to slave" – in favor of the Roman approach – that of "governor to citizen."[59]

After setting up the ideal of a hostage who is viewed as a kind of Roman son and who has been enlightened by lessons in Roman statecraft, Tacitus quashes it with the ensuing narrative of Meherdates's collapse. Gaius Cassius Longinus was instructed to lead the young Meherdates back to Parthia; he is said by Tacitus to have "exhibited an old-fashioned morality" and to have been "worthy of his ancestors."[60] In keeping with Tacitus's conception of past virtues being at odds with new attitudes toward hostages, he portrays Longinus as nervous about the mission: his Longinus admonishes Meherdates to move quickly and to press his advantage. According to Tacitus, Meherdates then did precisely the opposite, lingering for too long in one place and, like his hostage relatives before him, "equating his great fortune with excess."[61] He is eventually captured by the Parthian king Gotarzes, who according to Tacitus, "rebuked him as no member of the Arsacid family, but a foreign-born Roman (*aliengenam Romanum*), and ordered that he be allowed to live but with his ears chopped off as a sign of his own clemency and as an insult against [the Romans] (*in nos dehonestamento*)."[62] Longinus here represents the same virtues as the foiled Germanicus and Corbulo – brave, fast, practical, even moral. The fact that his course of action was disregarded by the hostage demonstrates, yet again, the poor state, as Tacitus sees it, of Julio-Claudian foreign policy, characterized by an overzealous trust in hostage-taking.

NERO, CORBULO, AND THE EAST

Meherdates was the last of the Phraatean hostages mentioned by our sources, but as Tacitus describes it, the practice of taking hostages, with

---

[59] Tac. *Ann.* 12.10: *alumnus urbis . . . dominationem et servos . . . rectorem et cives.*

[60] Tac. *Ann.* 12.12: *revocare priscum morem . . . dignum maioribus suis.* On the character of Longinus, see Koestermann 1967, 127–128; Keitel 1978, 467–468; and Martin 1981, 169.

[61] Tac. *Ann.* 12.12: *summam fortunam in luxu ratum.*

[62] Tac. *Ann.* 12.14. Gowing 1990, 321 argues that the punishment and especially Gotarzes's vaunted *clementia* are meant to recall ironically Claudius's speech. Cf. Martin 1981, 154. Ziegler 1964, 66 n. 150 draws a comparison with the punishment of the pseudo-Smerdis in Herodotus 3.69. Cf. Hyrcanus, the Hasmonaean king captured by the Parthians.

the expectation of manipulating them for their symbolic and political value continued, still to no avail. As Corbulo's command shifts from Germany to Armenia, Tacitus continues to set his military accomplishments against the contrasting background of emperors dependent on wielding former hostages, rather than fighting to achieve Rome's interests.[63] By 51 CE, an Arsacid, Vologaeses, eliminated his rivals in Parthia and ruled alone; his family background (he was born of a Greek woman) suggests that he may have been acceptable to the Romans.[64] He entered Armenia and deposed Rhadamistus, who had exhibited a virulent hatred for Rome. Vologaeses apparently, had encountered little objection both from the natives and from Rome.[65] He appointed his brother, another Tiridates, to the Armenian throne, but by 54 CE, this settlement had become unacceptable to the Romans. According to Tacitus, Nero decided to act, ordering legions to be stationed along the Armenian border, instructing nearby allied kings to prepare themselves for a campaign, and sending Corbulo to join Gaius Ummidius Quadratus, the governor of Syria, as the joint leaders of the effort.[66]

Tacitus lays the groundwork for the discrepancies between Corbulo and Nero right away. He begins by reporting rumors that the people of Rome were skeptical of Nero's ability, given that he was under the control of a woman (his mother, Agrippina the Younger) and his "teachers" (Burrus and Seneca).[67] Moreover, Tacitus derides the senate for falling into its "customary sycophancy" (*suetam adulationem*) by offering Nero triumphal decorations, public commemorations, and

---

[63] On the heroism of Corbulo, see Gilmartin 1973, 583 and Martin 1981, 180–181, who attributes the praise to Tacitus's use of Corbulo's memoirs as a source. For a reassessment of Corbulo, see Walker 1952, 29. On Tacitus's criticism of Nero, both subtle and overt, in his Armenian policy, see Walker 1952, 221; Classen 1988, 112; and Gowing 1990, 322. Chaumont 1976, 101–116 notes its adherence to Tacitean pattern. Syme 1958, 492–497 views the account has meant to have a bearing on contemporary policy in the early second century; cf. Vervaet 1999a.

[64] Tac. *Ann.* 12.44. For the historical background of Vologaeses's accession, see Debevoise 1938, 176–177; Kahrstedt 1950, 24–36; and Ziegler 1964, 66–67.

[65] Tac. *Ann.* 12.44–47 describes how Rhadamistus drove out Mithridates, who had been made king by Rome.

[66] Tac. *Ann.* 13.7–8. For a discussion of Corbulo's allies in the campaign, see Barrett 1979 and Paltiel 1991. For Corbulo's career and the nature of his *imperium*, see Vervaet 1999 b. For a general history of the campaign, see Ziegler 1964, 72–77 and Millar 1993, 54–66.

[67] Tac. *Ann.* 13.6. Cf. Gilmartin 1973, 586.

a larger than life statue in the Temple of Mars the Avenger after Vologaeses simply retired in order to deal with civil unrest at home, and not because of Nero's maneuvers.[68] By contrast, Tacitus says that what *sincerely* pleased the senate, beyond their empty praise of Nero, was when Corbulo was put in charge. Similarly when Corbulo arrives in the East, he is likewise depicted as the one whom the allied kings respect, and not his co-commander Quadratus.[69] Tacitus thus draws attention to the difference between the illusory and the real, between Nero and Corbulo, an interest that he retains in the ensuing descriptions of the campaigns in Armenia and the function of the hostages.

At the start of the campaign Corbulo and Quadratus demand that Vologaeses back down, submit hostages, and continue "the reverence for the Roman people in keeping with their ancestors' customs."[70] According to Tacitus, Vologaeses agreed, but only so that he could "prepare for war, or expel suspected pretenders in the name of hostageship."[71] In deploying the familiar trope of hostages as hated heirs, Tacitus suggests that the submission is similar to that of Phraates IV's sons generations before, under Augustus: once again, the respect embodied by the hostages was only rhetorical, and in reality, the Parthian king was taking advantage of the Romans. Nevertheless for the moment, the hostages are sought after by both Quadratus and Corbulo as symbols of their own role in the diplomatic *coup*. As seen in Chapter 4, the two competed for the right to hold the hostages, a dispute settled by putting the issue to a vote by the hostages themselves, which came out in Corbulo's favor.[72] Again, the focus is on truth versus illusion: Corbulo is said to have earned the hostages' respect through his prior glory, just as the senators and allied kings had thought more highly of him than of Nero.

When it becomes clear that Vologaeses's hostages were insincere and meaningless, Tacitus's Corbulo, ever painted as a man of action, again

---

[68] Tac. *Ann.* 13.8.

[69] Tac. *Ann.* 13.8. cf. Gilmartin 1973, 587–589.

[70] Tac. *Ann.* 13.9: *solitam prioribus reverentiam in populum Romanum continuaret.*

[71] Tac. *Ann.* 13.9: *quo bellum ex commodo pararet an ut aemulationis suspectos per nomen obsidum amoveret.*

[72] Tac. *Ann.* 13.9. Koestermann 1967, 252 attributes the record of the 'victory' to Corbulo's memoirs.

probably because his own memoirs were one of Tacitus's sources, does not hesitate to resort to arms: Tacitus compares Corbulo with Lucullus and Pompey as he marches his armies down their familiar paths into Armenia.[73] Ignoring the hostages, Corbulo sharpens discipline among his troops, raises auxiliaries, sleeps in tents even in the dead of winter, and kills those who try to desert. In a telling contrast, Tacitus's Corbulo "seeks out a battle" while Tiridates manages to avoid committing his troops.[74] Tacitus enhances Corbulo's initiative by emphasizing the fact that he is doing all of this against the conventions of peaceful hostage-taking: he says that Tiridates sent envoys to ask Corbulo why he was attacking even after they had given hostages. Tacitus, of course, has already let the reader know that the hostages were of no value, and Corbulo's foresight and initiative is thus increasingly valorized. Tiridates continues to fall back and Tacitus continues to describe numerous feats of Corbulo's courage and ingenuity, building up considerable momentum in his report: Corbulo takes a well-defended fortress without losing a single man; he is hard-pressed by poor rations and harsh conditions yet still captures two strongholds; he orders a forced march to push Tiridates even further to the border even after he is already on the run.[75]

When Tacitus has reached a point where Corbulo is in total control of Armenia after many sacrifices and struggles, he abruptly brings the story to a halt when he reintroduces Nero:

By slaughter and arson [Corbulo] destroyed every place where he observed that men opposed us, and he usurped control of Armenia. Then Tigranes arrived (*cum advenit Tigranes*). He had been chosen by Nero to take up the command...but because he had been a hostage in the city for a long time, he had deteriorated to a slavish passivity.[76]

---

[73] Tac. *Ann.* 13.34. On the comparison of Corbulo with Lucullus and Pompey, see Koestermann 1967, 301 and Gilmartin 1973, 591.

[74] Tac. *Ann.* 13.35–37: *quaesito diu proelio.* The account is clearly exaggerated, as demonstrated by the story of the soldier whose arms fell off from cold when he was carrying firewood.

[75] Tac. *Ann.* 13.38–41; 14.23–26. Cf. Isaac 1990, 25 on Tacitus's characterization of the acclimatization of the army. See also Barrett 1979.

[76] Tac. *Ann.* 14.26.

Right away, Corbulo – the man who by pursuing an all out campaign against Tiridates had resisted, to enormous acclaim, the institution of hostage-taking as it had been practiced with Vologaeses – cedes authority and is reassigned to Syria to take over the province after the recent death of his co-commander, Quadratus. As Tacitus describes it, the hard-won advantages of Corbulo in Armenia immediately begin to unravel. Vologaeses's subjects complain that "they had descended to the level of contempt when they were assaulted not even by a Roman general but by the rashness of a hostage who was detained for so many years among chattel slaves (*mancipia*)."[77] Tacitus's reference to chattel is significant as it mirrors the label he first gave to Vonones when describing the Parthian reactions to him. Another war erupts as Vologaeses and Tiridates press their new advantage in Armenia, taking the opportunity of Corbulo's departure. Tacitus devotes much attention to this second conflict: Caesennius Paetus leads the Roman forces poorly and squanders their manpower; ultimately Corbulo must return to rescue trapped Roman armies and drive Vologaeses out a second time.[78] The campaign ends with Tigranes deposed and Corbulo offering new terms to Tiridates, so long as he admits Rome's hegemony and, famously, goes to Rome in person to be crowned in public by Nero himself.[79]

By this point, Tacitus's disdain for the reformed hostage given in peace is unmistakable. But the *idea* of "reformation" is not entirely jettisoned: in the ensuing narrative of Corbulo, he demonstrates that reeducation, if done correctly after physical subjugation, can bear fruit. As Tacitus tells it, once Corbulo is back in charge, he is said to act as a teacher to Tiridates: when the two are in a conference, Corbulo answers Tiridates's questions about the impressive Roman military,

---

[77] Tac. *Ann.* 15.1.

[78] Tac. *Ann.* 15.6–18. Paetus's failure is compared with the Roman defeat at the Caudine Forks (15.15). On Tacitus's characterization of Paetus, see Gilmartin 1973, 610–619; Chaumont 1976, 111–113; Paltiel 1991, 253–254; and Mattern 1999, 177. Gowing 1990, 328 notes the antithetical quality between Paetus and Corbulo.

[79] Tac. *Ann.* 15.24–28. In portraying Corbulo's return, Tacitus hearkens back to the successful Lucullus (15.27). For Tiridates's coronation in Rome, see Suet. *Nero* 13; Cass. Dio, 43.1.2; and on its importance as an expression of Roman values, see Mattern 1999, 177.

explaining the system of watches, signals, and expressions of honor.[80] Notably, the lesson Corbulo gives is nothing like that received by the hostages who were freely given to Augustus and his successors, at least as Tacitus describes it: the emphasis is not on banqueting, nor on philosophy, nor on government, but on the irresistible nature of Roman arms, and the "student" has been forcibly reduced beforehand.[81] The punctuation comes when Tiridates submits his daughter as a hostage to Corbulo, just before setting off for Rome. The story thus ends well for Rome, but only as a direct result of, first, Corbulo's realization that Vologaeses's hostages were insincere and, second, his return to battle after a former hostage, appointed by Nero, had failed.

The norms of Roman hostage-taking are critical in Tacitus's attempts to develop his characters and articulate his thesis on the shortcomings of the Julio-Claudian emperors. He takes a dim view of hostage-taking when it is done irresponsibly as the only method of entry into a foreign territory. Repeatedly, he presents a number of dichotomies between, on the one hand, hostages and hostage-takers, and, on the other hand, the proper Roman soldier – passive versus active, decadent versus old-fashioned, slave versus free, slow versus fast. He rejects the value of the host–guest, father–son, teacher–student paradigms in explicit terms, recasting the act of education and fosterage as tantamount to disrespectful and fruitless enslavement. These are constructs that, according to Tacitus, the enemy never fails to detect, and that thus only breed resentment and foment further resistance. The resistance is all the more successful because the guard set against them – the former hostage himself – is not up for the challenge. The figure of the hostage and his malleability were thus seized on by the historian as opportunities to comment on Roman order, both at home and abroad.

---

[80] Tac. *Ann.* 15.30. cf. Gilmartin 1973, 624 and Chaumont 1976, 117–118.

[81] In this sense, Corbulo's mode of reeducating Tiridates is similar to that of Tacitus's father-in-law, Agricola, about whom Tacitus wrote much earlier in his career. In that case (*Agr.* 20.1), Tacitus describes a process of hostage acculturation that meets with extraordinary success under Agricola's watch. By contrast with the Julio-Claudians, Agricola, after receiving the hostages, surrounded the donor tribes with garrisons and forts, and only then promoted their Romanization. See Chapter 6.

EPILOGUE: THE ALTAR AND THE COLUMN

Wars are terrifying to most people; realizing this, leaders may choose either of two options: they can say that they win them, or they can say that they avoid them. Whatever his policies are in practice, a leader may manipulate his image either as universal friend or as conquering hero in order to calm the nerves of his followers and to win them over to his side. In ancient Rome, Augustus's Altar of Peace and Trajan's victory column are vivid examples of the two extremes. The former, as we have seen, displays a quiet march forward, with children, women, priests, and senators; facial expressions are serene and dignified, and none of them seems fierce. A figure even holds a finger to the mouth, seemingly hushing both fellow statues and the people watching them. Trajan's column also depicts a procession of sorts, but it is clearly radically different; it is a military campaign that lasts for a long time, covers many miles, makes lots of noise, and spirals skyward out of sight. All the while, Roman soldiers demonstrate grit and determination, and the onlooking emperor is cool and in control. The architectural forms alone tell of vastly different ways of thinking. The former: a generous sanctuary, open to the sky, with big wide doorways inviting a breeze; the latter: an upward thrust, towering over its foundation, a metaphor of aggression. One is low, the other tall; one may shade the viewer; the other makes him squint.[1] Yet for all their differences, the two monuments deliver a similar message: Rome is safe. In both cases, the Romans move in tandem; on the column, the

---

[1] For other readings of the monuments side by side, see Huet 1996; Campbell 2002, 122–146; and Clarke 2003, 19–41.

order and symmetry of Rome is especially contrasted with the chaos of the Dacians. Both of these emperors – long-lived, successful, and for the most part fondly remembered by history – sought to convey a sense of prosperity and security; it is just that they had different ideas about how to get there.

In addition to the monuments both making the viewer feel like he is out of harm's way, they have something else, more specific, in common: they are the only monuments from the ancient city (extant, that is) that show Romans alongside the children of an outsider-leader.[2] As we have seen, the two foreign children on the Ara Pacis are arranged in correspondence with the compass direction of their homelands: the "Gallic" child faces the northwest; the one dressed in a tunic and eastern-style slippers looks homeward to the south and east (Figures 1– 4). Their most important attribute is that they are not Roman, but they are also shown young, happy, under control, and alone for the Romans to supervise. The periphery that they represent, it would be understood, was in virtually the same state. These two children have appeared so many times in this book that one might think that they were a bigger presence on the altar than they really are. Being a toddler and a preadolescent, they do not take up much room, but that also seems to be part of the point: it literally goes without saying in this regime that the borders are taken care of. This is Augustus avoiding a war.

On Trajan's column, the foreign children are also difficult to see, but their location is equally critical to the overall composition of the monument. They are at the very top; toward the arrow's head, so to speak. The culminating scene of the long, twisty epic-in-stone is of the sons of Decebalus being forcibly detained, but not harmed, by Roman centurions, as their father, petrified, is knocked down, humiliated, and slaughtered before them (Figures 9 and 10). It is possible that the apparent gash in Decebalus's throat was self-inflicted, but the scene is still one of utter violence; the next image to the right is of his decapitated head being shown to the troops.[3] As far as the children are

---

2 Kuttner 1995 makes a thorough case for a now lost monument that depicted the surrender of the same "Gallic" child as appears on the Ara Pacis, an image that one of the Boscoreale cups preserves in miniature.

3 See the chapter in Lepper and Frere 1988 appropriately titled "Mopping up," esp. 177. Lica 2000, 202–208 discusses the oblique evidence for Dacian hostages, suggesting,

concerned, gone are the smiles and the playful tugs on the togas that characterized those on the Ara Pacis. These children are not guests in Rome, not students of Roman culture, nor participants in Roman religion; rather, they are the embodiment of the helplessness and despair of any Dacians who somehow managed to survive. In other words, this is Trajan winning a war.

I would argue that the depiction of the children of the non-Roman ruling class on both of these monuments, as well as in works of other media, made critical contributions to the Romans' sense of their place in the Mediterranean. The ways in which the children of the foreign elite were treated in Rome, be they hostages or students, refugees or recruits, explained the strength and character of Rome's preeminent position in an international hierarchy. It may be useful to think of the practice of hostage-taking in Roman antiquity as analogous to early notions of scapegoating. Whereas in Greek religion some kind of being, either human or animal (a *pharmakos*), was ritually assigned as a vessel for a communal evil (a *miasma*) and then ceremoniously driven from the human realm, taking his "cargo" with him, likewise the diplomatic hostage bore the intensity of the former hatred of two worlds. He carried a *miasma* of conflict; all tension was piled on him so that, once he was moved to the side, friendlier relations could ensue. When these friendlier relations became normalized, and warfare forgotten, the intensity of the hostage's *miasma* accordingly faded. But if these relations broke down, the hostage was, in theory if not in practice, to suffer the consequences, shedding alone the blood of war. In the negotiations preceding the submission of hostages, the two sides defined and articulated what was to become a new order of business between them – by means of a treaty, usually – which was intended to bring an end to the alternation between diplomacy and warfare. After hostages had been given, the two populations would be able to interact according to a set of rules, on a day-to-day basis, predictably. The hostage effectively froze the new *status quo*, arrived at through war and other interactions, and made it reliable. Nevertheless, it was always

generally, that they appear on the column, but not isolating this scene in particular. No hostages are mentioned in Cassius Dio's account of Trajan's wars, but Cass. Dio, 79.27.5 mentions hostages detained by Caracalla but recovered angrily by the Dacians.

a uniquely Roman brand of peace that quickly admitted that the pain of war could easily return some time in the future, only exercised at that point on the person of the hostage. As the hostage passed from one world into the Limbo bordering another, he removed war to a different place, but he did not eliminate it. The range of human responses to victory and defeat included too many powerful anxieties – greed, ambition, fear, resentment – to trust that feelings of hostility would dissipate on their own, or abide by the economy of superior strength over relative weakness, or yield to the weight of promises. Hostage-taking was a means of harnessing those same, powerful human anxieties and driving them in a different direction. In theory, the life and well-being of one or a few people were in jeopardy, and the threats against them had the effect of distracting an entire society, or at least the ruling class that made the decisions, from acting in larger interests; in theory, the hostage donors would act to preserve the hostages.

All eyes, then, were on the hostage. Was he happy? Was he uncomfortable? Was he safe? Was he threatened? Talking about the hostage in different ways, writers and artists – and this includes emperors whose art form was their public image – could express their opinions and make their cases about the nature of the peace at hand. The children on the Ara Pacis suggest that a willingly submissive periphery was already in place; the princes on Trajan's Column, however, were detained, it would seem, because Rome had to hold its heel on the downtrodden north. The various motifs discussed in the chapters of this book might be said to line up under the headings of the two monuments. The Ara Pacis children are certainly guests in Rome; their proximity to the biological children of the ruling family also implies that they had a filial association. Moreover, when a Roman "read" the youth on their faces, they would think of their impressionability and of the potential for teaching them a new, less dangerous opinion of their capital city. A century later, however, on Trajan's column, the boys are taken against their will, and their faces are marked by anguish. These will be hostages of the variety found in our modern popular culture: a gun held to their heads, or rather knife to their throats, in effect challenging the Dacians, daring them to make a move while also congratulating the Romans. They serve to expand on the defining theme of the whole monument: Rome's overwhelming, pitiless military prowess. They will be the walking, talking trophies of the Dacian wars.

Although the two monuments and the different ethics of security that they connote can be useful in dividing up the seemingly conflicting images of hostage-taking described in this book, it should be remembered that the categories are not exclusive: the image of a student learning Roman culture could be wielded as evidence of that hostage's humiliation rather than his opportunities. For example, to Tacitus, when Agricola combined the right amount of force and physical intimidation with the reeducation of the hostages in Britain, he was showing the way to the enslavement of the population. Moreover, when Dio Chrysostom alluded to a sexual relationship between Philip II and his overseer, it was in the vein of mentoring, even charity, and not at all the horror show of rape or the comedy of decadence that appear in most accounts of a hostage's sexuality. Depending on a number of factors – author, genre, era – the motifs of hostage-taking could be used for different agendas. Over time, certain ways of thinking about hostages fell in and out of fashion, and the motif of one regime could be appropriated and redeployed in another with a new meaning.

Do the two monuments reflect different ways of thinking that were current and predominant in their eras? Can we fill in the century that separated them with a story of general attitudes toward hostages changing over time? If so, what is that story? Trying to track continuity and change in Roman antiquity can easily seem like a fool's errand. Naturally, our evidence is fragmentary. All we receive are flashes of light, interspersed sporadically, some times shining together, other times faint and thin. Moreover, attempts to fill the gap between the altar and the column are hazardous because the foreign boys may just reflect context, as opposed to trend: perhaps Augustus's periphery *was* peaceful; Trajan's certainly was restless. But other scenarios also could explain the images: Augustus wanted to *seem* in blissful control for obvious reasons having to do with the long civil war, which perhaps had little to do with the actual periphery; and Trajan, not a part of the old Flavian dynasty, perhaps wanted to *seem* to be ready and willing to use overwhelming force, and not just against the Dacians. With fragmentary and contentious evidence, one turns to ancillary sources in the hope that clusters of references from the same or similar contexts as the monuments can attain a critical mass whereby we can discern a pattern.

The Augustan period seems to be among the best illuminated by these "flashes of light." Three trends can be traced in the evidence of the Augustan age as we have it. First, there seems to have been a general acceptance of the taking of hostages as a form of victory in and of itself. The rest of the Augustan complex near the altar spells it out: the emperor's *Res Gestae* to the north trumpets his ability to win without fighting as proven by the sons of Phraates IV under his care; his and Agrippa's map of the world to the south makes the extent of his dominion quantifiable, as much furthering the cause of empire as merely reflecting it. On this score, Augustus may have been taking a page from his adoptive father's playbook: Caesar's commentaries with their records of the unflappable detention of hostages were meant to persuade the Romans at home that his grip on Gaul, and even Britain, was secure. What is more important is that Caesar's *report* of the detention of those hostages was taken up and repeated by subsequent historians. The hostage could connote victory regardless of how he was acquired. Livy's version of the Lucanian hostages held by Scipio Barbatus suggests that the consul received them without a fight; it is a revision of the older story told on the tomb of the Scipios, where Barbatus is portrayed as more of a conqueror, but it does not diminish his prestige. For the motif of the efficacy of peaceful submission to work, it calls for another, second motif: Augustan stories of hostage-taking often declare that hostages learn something about Rome while they are there. In keeping with the notion that willing submission was tantamount to physical domination, hostages were expected to *become* Roman and through their vassalage give a return on an initial investment, as the economic and emotional expenses of war were avoided. For example, Livy goes above and beyond Polybius's story of Antiochus IV's acculturation to include a unique record of new gladiatorial exhibitions in Antioch and a temple to Jupiter Optimus Maximus, the latter of which is surely a misrepresentation, at best an exaggeration. The tradition of Juba's transformation, which can be corroborated by his portraits and his efforts, if not his successes, at urban reform in Mauretania, has its earliest literary testimony in Strabo, who is happy to report of Rome's absorption of the known world. The emperor himself claims a personal responsibility for this success: a third aspect of what might be called the Augustan view of hostages is that the enterprise was honorable, with a protocol and code of ethics that bound the periphery to Rome while also signaling the moral superiority of the hostage-taker. In Livy, Scipio Africanus in Spain acted with decorum in returning Iberian hostages to their homes. Again, he goes beyond the Polybian account when he says a dowry was provided to one of them. Along this line of thinking, the slaughter of hostages becomes unconscionable. Only the horrible Samnites of the Caudine Forks would be capable of executing their hostages; Livy is sure to point out that when the Romans killed hostages, as in the case of the Thurians and Tarentines in the Second Punic War, it was because Rome was the victim: the Thurians and Tarentines had tried to escape, even though the Romans were housing them in the *Atrium Libertatis*, or Hall of Freedom. Moreover, Ovid drew a line under the sacrosanctity of the hostage when he replaced Lycaon's son with Lycaon's hostage and replaced Jupiter with a thinly disguised Augustus in the story of the moral transgression that led to the great flood. Hostages were clearly respected figures, such that Rome's very founders, Romulus and Remus, may have been hostages themselves, given by Aeneas to Latinus in a friendly agreement that, according to a source of Dionysius of Halicarnassus, also of the Augustan age, melded the two races into one, harmonious whole. This encapsulation of Augustan attitudes is not meant to imply that the man who was honored by the Ara Pacis also commissioned the literature; it is fruitless to look for clues that Augustus meddled directly in Livy's, or in Ovid's, or in Dionysius's literary lives. Nevertheless, the trend of benign thinking on hostages is inescapable. Even if Livy and Dionysius of Halicarnassus are quoting others, they are still preserving traditions, and their decisions on what to amplify and sustain reflect the climate in which they worked. Vergil's famous dictum that Rome will humble the haughty and give laws to the rest of the world is a capstone of sorts: hostages at this time were thought to be agents of change on the periphery, both for good and for the better.

It is fair to say that this notion was demolished in the Trajanic period. A host of writers during the early second century CE betray their cynicism with respect to all three trends outlined earlier: to them, hostage-taking alone did *not* equal a military victory; hostages learned *nothing* in Rome, or if they did learn something, it was not pretty; and the emperors who played this game were *not* worthy of respect but instead deserved contempt. Most of these critiques are delivered in the form of negative assessments of the Julio-Claudians, Augustus included. Tacitus's *Annals*, in presenting its parade of Parthian losers, points out both that the gains measured by the hostages were illusory and that the manners they learned in Rome only served to make them effete, unwarlike, lazy, and ultimately worthless. Juvenal, too, makes the acquired effeminacy of hostages clear enough in his second *Satire* about a buggered and debauched Zalaces from Armenia, and Achilles Tatius's understanding of hostage-taking as analogous to a veritable seminar in sexual immorality also bears it out. Tacitus goes on to imply that perhaps if the hostages had been detained and indoctrinated with the right admixture of force, as proven by his heroes, Germanicus, Corbulo, Agricola, and others, then the strategy may have been a profitable one. But the blind faith in hostages, it was argued, did little more than provide the masses with a good show, as Suetonius claims was the case with Caligula and Tacitus with Domitian; it was an expensive deception at that, as suggested by Pliny's *Panegyric* to Trajan. Just as Livy was a product of his time (if not of the emperor's patronage directly), so too are these others writing under a new Rome: as Trajan self-consciously marched on Dacia and then Armenia and Mesopotamia and received the submission of Arabia, he reinvigorated Rome's military ethos. New stories of hostage-taking and contrasts between the brave and the cowardly, the active and the passive, the tough and the meek were deliberately sketched at the dawn of what Trajan preferred to herald as a new day. As the emperor gathered his armies, he acquired a sort of intellectual fuel from writers and artists who created foils out of the preceding emperors; the Julio-Claudians were refashioned as antitheses of proper Roman values. Hostage-taking of the benevolent, pacifying sort, it was decided, was not in the Roman blood after all.

In conclusion, it would seem that between the reigns of Augustus and Trajan, the Roman attitude toward the periphery, as gauged by its attitudes toward hostages, shifted from one of welcoming condescension to that of stampeding military ambition. It would be too simplistic to say, of course, that the discrepancy between the monuments is a result of the Romans, in the interval, moving from avoiding wars to winning them. It is important to note that we are not saying that the hostages themselves under Trajan were less malleable, or more threatened, or more decadent, or less liked. With all the rhetorical constructions and oft-used tropes of hostage-taking, the act of recovering the "lived experience" of the hostages becomes problematic. The trends assigned earlier to both periods, for example, have their outliers: Ovid's stories of hostages in his lines on Lycaon and Scylla may have been spoofing the emperor as much as respecting him, and Oppian, in using hostage exchange to explain marine biology and amphibians in a second-century context, necessarily subscribes to the rosy picture of hostage utopia that his contemporaries by and large seemed to despise. But not only are the trends described here porous and nonexclusive, but in addition the sources that constitute the trends do not necessarily represent the truth about the hostages and those who took them. Trajan's gains in Dacia had to be shored up by later emperors, which is not the impression left by the column or by the violent detention of the hostages.[4] Ordering the sculptors to depict him as a general and to highlight the bloody slaughter of Decebalus could be a case of protesting too much. Should we think of Augustus, then, as all that different from Trajan, even though he was not remembered for his soldierly skills? Our information is incomplete and it is difficult to know for certain "what happened." The truth is that we do not see only the hostages on Trajan's Column or on the Altar of Peace; we also see the Romans seeing them, or creating them, and in the end, that is just as important.

---

[4] In general, see Bennett 1997, 85–103. On the retrenchment under Hadrian, with the buffer of so-called free Dacia, see Ellis 1998, 221 and Diaconescu 2004, 126. On revolts by the free Dacians in 138–140 and 156–157, see Musat and Ardeleanu 1985, 58. Cass. Dio, 79.27.5 discusses a war under Caracalla. Ellis 1998, 229–233 doubts the feasibility of widespread genocide of the Dacians under Trajan, which is suggested by passages in Eutropius's *Breviarium*; Ellis argues instead that the absence of Dacian names in existing epigraphy reflects cultural difference rather than radical demographic changes.

BIBLIOGRAPHY

Abbondanza, L. 1996. Immagini dell'infanzi di Achille in età imperiale: continuità di un paradigma educativo. *Ocnus* 4: 9–33.

Affortunati, M. and B. Scardigli. 1992. Aspects of Plutarch's *Life of Publicola*. In *Plutarch and the historical tradition*, ed. P. A. Stadter. London and New York: Routledge, 109–131.

Ager, S. 1998. Thera and the pirates: An ancient case of the Stockholm Syndrome? *The ancient history bulletin* 12.3: 83–95.

Albertini, E. 1923. Êtudes sur quelques milliaires de Cherchel. *Bulletin archéologique du comité des travaux historiques et scientifiques* 38.

Albertini, E. 1950. *L'Afrique romaine*. Algiers: Direction de l'interieur et des beaux-arts.

Albertson, F. C. 1990. The Basilica Aemilia frieze: Religion and politics in late Republican Rome. *Latomus* 49.4: 801–815.

Allen, A. 1972. Catullus' English Channel. *Classical world* 66: 146–147.

Allison, J. W. 1997. Corbulo's Socratic shadow. *Eranos* 95: 19–25.

Alonso-Nuñez, J. M. 1987. An Augustan world history: The *Historicae Philippicae* of Pompeius Trogus. *Greece and Rome* 34: 56–72.

Amit, M. 1970. Hostages in ancient Greece. *Rivista di filologia* 98: 129–147.

Anderson, G. 1976a. *Studies in Lucian's comic fiction*. Leiden: Brill.

Anderson, G. 1976b. *Lucian: Theme and variation in the Second Sophistic*. Leiden: Brill.

Anderson, G. 1980. Arrian's *Anabasis Alexandri* and Lucian's *Historia*. *Historia* 29: 119–124.

Anderson, W. S. 1972. *Ovid's Metamorphoses, Books 6–10*. Norman: University of Oklahoma Press.

Anderson, W. S. 1989. Lycaon: Ovid's deceptive paradigm in *Metamorphoses* I. *Illinois classical studies* 14: 91–101.

Anderson, W. S. 1997. *Ovid's Metamorphoses, Books 1–5*. Norman and London: University of Oklahoma Press.

Ando, C. 2000. *Imperial ideology and provincial loyalty in the Roman empire*. Berkeley: University of California Press.

Arieti, J. A. 1997. Rape and Livy's view of Roman history. In *Rape in antiquity*, ed. S. Deacy and K. F. Pierce. London: Duckworth, 209–229.

Arjava, A. 1998. Paternal power in late antiquity. *Journal of Roman Studies* 88: 147–165.

Astin, A. E. 1967. *Scipio Aemilianus*. Oxford: Clarendon Press.

Atkinson, J. E. 1980. *Q. Curtius Rufus' Historiae Alexandri Magni, Books 3 and 4*. Amsterdam: J. C. Gieben.

Austin, N. J. E. and B. Rankov. 1995. Exploratio: *Military and political intelligence in the Roman world from the Second Punic War to the Battle of Adrianople*. London and New York: Routledge.

Avery, J. R. 1997. *Herodotean presences in Lucian*. Yale University Ph.D. dissertation.

Aymard, A. 1940. Le fragment de Polybe "Sur les traîtres" (xviii, 13–15). *Revue des études anciennes* 42: 9–19.

Aymard, A. 1953. Les ôtages Carthaginois à la fin de la deuxième guerre punique. *Pallas* 1: 47–56.

Aymard, A. 1954. Philippe de Macédonie, ôtage à Thèbes. *Revue des études anciennes* 59: 15–36.

Aymard, A. 1961. Les ôtages barbares au debut de l'Empire. *Journal of Roman studies* 51: 136–142.

Badian, E. 1958. *Foreign clientelae (264–70 BC)*. Oxford: Oxford University Press.

Bannon, C. J. 1997. *Brothers of Romulus: Fraternal pietas in Roman law, literature, and society*. Princeton: Princeton University Press.

Barber, B. 1996. *Jihad vs. McWorld: How globalism and tribalism are reshaping the world*. New York: Ballantine Books, repr.

Barlow, J. 1998. Noble Gauls and their other in Caesar's propaganda. In *Julius Caesar as artful reporter: The war commentaries as political instruments*, ed. K. Welch and A. Powell. London: Duckworth, 139–170.

Barnes, T. D. 1974. The victories of Augustus. *Journal of Roman Studies* 64: 21–26.

Baronowski, D. W. 1983. A reconsideration of the Roman approval of peace with Macedonia in 196 B.C. *Phoenix* 37.3: 218–223.

Baronowski, D. W. 1990. *Sub umbra foederis aequi:* The history of the majesty clause. *Phoenix* 44: 345–369.

Baronowski, D. W. 1995. Polybius on the causes of the Third Punic War. *Classical Philology* 90.1: 16–31.

Barrett, A. A. 1978. Polemo II of Pontus and M. Antonius Polemo. *Historia* 27: 437–448.

Barrett, A. A. 1979. *Annals* 14.26 and the Armenia settlement of A.D. 60. *Classical Quarterly* 29.2: 465–469.

Barrett, A. A. 1989. *Caligula: The corruption of power*. New Haven and London: Yale University Press.

Barrett, A. A. 2001. Tacitus, Livia, and the wicked stepmother. *Rheinisches Museum für Philologie* 144.2: 171–175.

Barringer, J. M. 1996. Atalanta as model: The hunter and the hunted. *Classical Antiquity* 15.1: 48–76.

Barton, C. A. 1993. *The sorrows of the ancient Romans: The gladiator and the monster.* Princeton: Princeton University Press.

Bassler, J. M. 1985. Philo on Joseph: The basic coherence of *De Iosepho* and *De somniis II. Journal for the study of Judaism* 16: 240–255.

Béal, J.-C. 1996. Bibracte-Autun ou le "transfert de capitale": Lieu-commun et réalités archéologique. *Latomus* 55.2: 339–367.

Beard, M. 2003. The triumph of the absurd: Roman street theatre. In *Rome the Cosmopolis*, ed. Catharine Edwards and Greg Woolf. Cambridge: Cambridge University Press, 21–43.

Bedon, R. 2001. *Atlas des villes, bourgs, villages de France au passé romain.* Paris: Picard.

Benario, H. W. 1991. Tacitus' view of the empire and the *Pax Romana. Aufstieg und Niedergang der römische Welt* 2.33.5: 3332–3353.

Benario, H. W. 1999. *Tacitus: Germany.* Warminster: Ares and Phillips.

Benediktson, D. T. 1988–1989. Caligula's madness: Madness or interictal temporal lobe epilepsy? *Classical World* 82: 370–375.

Bennett, J. 1997. *Trajan, Optimus Princeps.* Bloomington: Indiana University Press.

Bergmann, B. 1995. Greek masterpieces and Roman recreative fictions. In *Greece in Rome: Influence, integration, resistance*, ed. C. P. Jones, C. Segal, R. J. Tarrant, and R. F. Thomas. *Harvard Studies in Classical Philology* 97: 79–120.

Bertrand, A. C. 1997. Stumbling through Gaul: Maps, intelligence, and Caesar's *Bellum Gallicum. Ancient History Bulletin* 11.4: 107–122.

Bhabha, H. K. 1994. *The location of culture.* London and New York: Routledge.

Bickerman, E. J. 1988. *The Jews in the Greek age.* Cambridge, MA. and London: Harvard University Press.

Billows, R. 1993. The religious procession of the Ara Pacis Augustae: Augustus's *supplicatio* in 13 BC. *Journal of Roman Archaeology* 6: 80–92.

Bird, H. W. 1973. Germanicus mytheroicus. *Echos du monde classique* 17: 94–101.

Birt, T. 1932. Über ὅμηρος und den Namen Homer. *Philologus* 87: 376–382.

Boisacq, E. 1950. *Dictionnaire étymologique de la langue Grecque.* 4th edition. Heidelberg: Carl Winter, Universitätsverlag.

Bolchazy, L. J. 1977. *Hospitality in early Rome: Livy's concept of its humanizing force.* Chicago: Ares Publishers.

Bowersock, G. W. 1994. *Fiction as history: From Nero to Julian.* Berkeley: University of California Press.

Boyd, B. W. 2001. Arms and the man: Wordplay and the catasterism of Chiron in Ovid's *Fasti* 5. *American Journal of Philology* 122.1: 67–80.

Braudy, L. 2003. *From chivalry to terrorism: War and the changing nature of masculinity.* New York: Knopf.

Braund, D. 1984a. *Rome and the friendly king: The character of the client kingship.* New York: St. Martin's Press.

Braund, D. 1984b. *Anth. Pal.* 9.235: Juba II, Cleopatra Selene and the course of the Nile. *Classical quarterly* 84: 175–178.

Braund, D. 1989. Function and dysfunction: Personal patronage in Roman imperialism. In *Patronage in ancient society,* ed. A. Wallace-Hadrill. London and New York: Routledge, 137–152.

Braund, D. 1996a. River frontiers in the environmental psychology of the Roman world. In *The Roman army in the East,* ed. D. L. Kennedy. Ann Arbor: *Journal of Roman archaeology,* 43–48.

Braund, D. 1996b. *Ruling Roman Britain: Kings, queens, governors, and emperors from Julius Caesar to Agricola.* London and New York: Routledge.

Braund, S. H. 1995. A woman's voice: Laronia's role in Juvenal *Satire 2.* In *Women in antiquity: New assessments,* ed. R. Hawley and B. Levick. London and New York: Routledge, 207–219.

Braund, S. H. and J. D. Cloud. 1981. Juvenal: A diptych. *Liverpool Classical monthly* 6.8: 195–208.

Brennan, T. C. 1994. M.' Curius Dentatus and the praetor's right to triumph. *Historia* 43: 423–439.

Brennan, T. C. 1996. Triumphus in Monte Albano. In *Transition to empire: Essays in Greco-Roman History, 360–146 BC, in honor of Ernst Badian,* ed. R. W. Wallace and E. M. Harris, Norman: University of Oklahoma Press. 315–337.

Briscoe, J. 1969. Eastern policy and senatorial policy, 168–146. *Historia* 18: 49–70.

Briscoe, J. 1973. *A commentary on Livy, Books 31–33.* Oxford: Clarendon Press.

Brizzi, G. 1982. *I sistemi informativi dei Romani: Principi e realta nell'eta delle conquiste oltremare (218–168 a. C.).* Stuttgart: Steiner.

Brunt, P. A. 1971. *Social conflicts in the Roman Republic.* London and New York.

Brunt, P. A. 1990. The Romanization of the local ruling classes in the Roman empire. In *Roman imperial themes,* P. A. Brunt. Oxford: Clarendon Press, 267–281.

Burns, T. S. 2003. *Rome and the barbarians, 100 B.C.–A.D. 400.* Baltimore and London: Johns Hopkins University Press.

Byrne, S. 1998. Flattery and inspiration: Cicero's epic for Caesar. In *Studies in Latin literature and Roman history 9,* ed. P. Deroux. Brussels: Latomus, 129–137.

Campbell, B. 1993. War and diplomacy: Rome and Parthia, 31 B.C.–A.D. 235. In *War and society in the Roman world,* ed. J. Rich and G. Shipley. London and New York: Routledge, 213–240.

Campbell, B. 2002. *War and society in imperial Rome.* London and New York: Routledge.

Campbell, W. A. 1938. The fourth and fifth season of excavation at Antioch-on-the-Orontes: 1935–1936. *American Journal of Archaeology* 42: 205–217.

Card, C. 2002. *The atrocity paradigm.* Oxford: Oxford University Press.

Cernjak, A. B. 1986. Die Flucht des Vonones: Tac. *Ann.* 2.68. *Philologus* 130: 198–209.

Champion, C. B. 2004. *Cultural politics in Polybius's* Histories. Berkeley: University of California Press.

Chantraine, P. 1984. *Dictionnaire étymologique de la langue Grecque.* Paris: Klincksieck.

Chaplin, J. D. 2000. *Livy's exemplary history.* Oxford: Oxford University Press.

Chatzopoulos, M. V. 1985–1986. Philippe fils d'Amyntas, otage à Thèbes. *Archaiognosia* 4: 37–58.

Chaumont, M.-L. 1976. L'Arménie entre Rome et l'Iran: De l'avènement d'Auguste à l'avènement de Dioclétien. *Aufstieg und Niedergang der römische Welt* 2.9.1: 71–194.

Chilver, G. E. F. 1979. *A historical commentary on Tacitus's* Histories *I and II.* Oxford: Clarendon Press.

Chiranky, G. 1982. Rome and Cotys, two problems. *Athenaeum* 60.3–4: 461–482.

Claassen, J.-M. 1992–1993. Sallust's Jugurtha – rebel or freedom fighter? On crossing crocodile-infested waters. *Classical World* 86: 273–297.

Clarke, J. R. 2003. *Art in the lives of ordinary Romans: Visual representation and non-elite viewers in Italy, 100 BC–315 AD.* Berkeley: University of California Press.

Clarke, K. 1999. *Between geography and history: Hellenistic constructions of the Roman world.* Oxford: Clarendon Press.

Clarke, K. 2001. An island nation: Re-reading Tacitus's Agricola. *Journal of Roman Studies* 91: 94–112.

Classen, C. J. 1988. Tacitus: Historian between Republic and Principate. *Mnemosyne* 41: 93–116.

Coarelli, F. 1973. Il sepolcro degli Scipioni. In *Roma medio repubblicana.* Rome: L'Erma di Bretschneider, 234–236.

Coarelli, F. 2000. *The column of Trajan.* Rome: Editore Colombo, in collaboration with the German Archaeological Institute.

Colledge, M. A. R. 1967. *The Parthians.* New York: Praeger.

Coltelloni-Trannoy, M. 1990. Le monnayage des rois Juba II et Ptolémée de Maurétanie: Image d'une adhesion réitérée à la politique romaine. *Karthago* 22: 45–53.

Coltelloni-Trannoy, M. 1992. Le culte royal sours les règnes de Juba II et de Ptolémée de Maurétanie. In *Actes du Ve colloque international sur l'histoire et l'archèologie de l'Afrique du Nord.* Paris: Comité des travaux historiques et scientifiques: 69–81.

Coltelloni-Trannoy, M. 1997. *Le royaume de Maurétanie sous Juba II et Ptolémée.* Paris: CNRS Editions.

Conole, P. and R. D. Milns. 1983. Neronian frontier policy in the Balkans. *Historia* 32.2: 183–200.

Cooley, A. 1999. A new date for Agrippa's theatre at Ostia. *Papers of the British School at Rome* 67: 173–182.

Corbier, M. 1991a. Divorce and adoption as familian strategies (Le divorce et l'adoption "en plus"). In *Marriage, divorce, and children in ancient Rome*, ed. B. Rawson. Oxford: Clarendon Press, 47–78.

Corbier, M. 1991b. Constructing kinship in Rome: Marriage and divorce, filiation and adoption. In *The family in Italy from antitquity to the present*, ed. D. I. Kertzer and R. P. Saller. New Haven and London: Yale University Press, 127–144.

Corbier, M. 2000. Adoptés et nourris. In *Adoption et fosterage*, ed. M. Corbier. Paris: de Boccard, 5–41.

Cornell, T. J. 1995. *The beginnings of Rome: Italy and Rome from the Bronze Age to the Punic Wars (c. 1000–264 BC)*. London and New York: Routledge.

Courtney, E. 1980. *A commentary on the* Satires *of Juvenal*. London: Athlone Press.

Crawford, M. H. 1973. *Foedus* and *sponsio*. *Papers of the British School at Rome* 41: 1–7.

Cribiore, R. 2001. *Gymnastics of the mind: Greek education in Hellenistic and Roman Egypt*. Princeton: Princeton University Press.

Curran, L. C. 1978. Rape and rape victims in the *Metamorphoses*. *Arethusa* 11: 213–241.

Debevoise, N. C. 1938. *A political history of Parthia*. Chicago: University of Chicago Press.

Decret, F. and M. Fantar. 1998. *L'Afrique du Nord dan l'antiquité*. Paris: Éditions Payot et Rivages.

Demos, J. 1994. *The unredeemed captive*. New York: Vintage Books.

Demos J. and V. Demos. 1969. Adolescence in historical perspective. *Journal of marriage and the family* 31.4: 632–638.

Derow, P. S. 1970. Polybius and the embassy of Kallikrates. In *Essays presented to C. M. Bowra*. Oxford: Alden Press for Wadham College, 12–23.

Derow, P. S. 1979. Polybius, Rome and the East. *Journal of Roman studies* 69: 1–15.

Deroy, L. 1972. Le nom d'Homère. *L'Antiquité classique* 41: 427–439.

Desanges, J. 1984–1985. L'hellénisme dans le royaume protégé de Maurétanie. *Bulletin archéologique du comité des travaux historiques et scientifiques, série B, Afrique du Nord* 20–21: 53–61.

Develin, R. 1994. Introduction. In *Justin: Epitome of the Philippic History of Pompeius Trogus*, trans. J. C. Yardley. Atlanta: Scholars Press, 1–11.

Diaconescu, A. 2004. The towns of Roman Dacia: An overview of the recent research. In *Roman Dacia: The making of a provincial society*, ed. W. S. Hanson and I. P. Haynes. *Journal of Roman archaeology supplementary series* 56: 87–142.

Dixon, S. 1986. Family finances: Terentia and Tullia. In *The family in ancient Rome: New perspectives*, ed. B. Rawson. Ithaca, NY: Cornell University Press, 93–120.

Dixon, S. 1997. Continuity and change in Roman social history: Retrieving "family feeling(s)" from Roman law and literature. In *Inventing ancient culture: Historicism, periodization, and the ancient world*, ed. M. Golden and P. Toohey. London and New York: Routledge, 79–90.

Dixon, S. 2000. The circulation of children in Roman society. In *Adoption et fosterage*, ed. M. Corbier. Paris: de Boccard, 217–230.

Donlan, W. 1989. The unequal exchange between Glaucus and Diomedes in light of the Homeric gift economy. *Phoenix* 43: 1–15.

Dorey, T. A. and D. R. Dudley. 1971. *Rome against Carthage*. London: Seeker and Warburg.

Downey, G. 1961. *A history of Antioch in Syria*. Princeton: Princeton University Press.

Drijvers, H.J.W. 1998. Strabo on Parthia and the Parthians. In *Das Partherreich und seine Zeugnisse*, ed. J. Wieschöfer. Stuttgart: Steiner, 279–293.

Dubuisson, M. 1989. "*Delenda est Carthago*": Remise en question d'un stereotype. In *Punic Wars: Proceedings of the conference held in Antwerp 23–26 November 1988*, ed. H. Defijver and E. Lipinski. Leuven: Uitgeverij Peeters, 279–288.

Duff, T. 1999. *Plutarch's Lives: Exploring virtue and vice*. Oxford: Clarendon Press.

Dyck, A. R. 2001. Dressing to kill: Attire as proof and means of characterization in Cicero's speeches. *Arethusa* 34.1: 119–130.

Dyer, R.R. 1990. Rhetoric and intention in Cicero's *Pro Marcello*. *Journal of Roman Studies* 80: 17–30.

Eck, W. 1984. Senatorial self-representation: Developments in the Augustan period. In *Caesar Augustus: Seven aspects*, ed. F.G.B. Millar and E. Segal. Oxford: Clarendon Press, 129–167.

Eckstein, A.M. 1985. Polybius, Syracuse, and the politics of accommodation. *Greek, Roman, and Byzantine studies* 26: 265–282.

Eckstein, A.M. 1987a. *Senate and general: Individual decision-making and Roman foreign relations, 264–194 BC*. Berkeley and Los Angeles: University of California Press.

Eckstein, A.M. 1987b. Polybius, Aristaenus, and the fragment "On Traitors." *Classical quarterly* 37: 140–161.

Eckstein, A.M. 1990a. Polybius, the Achaeans, and the "freedom of the Greeks." *Greek, Roman, and Byzantine studies* 31: 45–71.

Eckstein, A.M. 1990b. Josephus and Polybius: A reconsideration. *Classical antiquity* 9.2: 175–208.

Eckstein, A.M. 1992. Notes on the birth and death of Polybius. *American journal of philology* 113.3: 387–406.

Eckstein, A.M. 1995. *Moral vision in the histories of Polybius*. Berkeley and Los Angeles: University of California Press.

Eder, W. 1986. The political significance of the codification of law in archaic societies: An unconventional hypothesis. In *Social struggles in archaic Rome: New perspectives on the struggle of the orders*, ed. K. Raaflaub. Berkeley and Los Angeles: University of California Press, 262–300.

Edlund, I. 1977. Invisible bonds: Clients and patrons through the eyes of Polybius. *Klio* 59: 129–136.

Edmondson, J. 1992. *Dio: The Julio-Claudians*. London: London Association of Classical Teachers.

Edson, C. F. Jr. 1935. Perseus and Demetrius. *Harvard studies in classical philology* 46: 191–202.

Edwards, C. 1993. *The politics of immorality in ancient Rome*. Cambridge: Cambridge University Press.

Edwards, C. 2003. Incorporating the alien: The art of conquest. In *Rome the cosmopolis*, ed. Catharine Edwards and Greg Woolf. Cambridge: Cambridge University Press, 44–70.

Eilers, C. 2002. *Roman patrons of Greek cities*. Oxford: Oxford University Press.

Elbern, S. 1990. Geiseln in Rom. *Athenaeum* 68: 97–140.

Ellis, L. 1998. *Terra deserta*: Population, politics, and the [de]colonization of Dacia. *World archaeology* 30.2: 220–237.

Ellis, P. B. 1980. *Caesar's invasion of Britain*. New York: New York University Press.

Elsner, J. 1996. Inventing *imperium*: Texts and the propaganda of monuments in Augustan Rome. In *Art and text in Roman culture*, ed. J. Ellsner. Cambridge: Cambridge University Press, 32–53.

Ernout, A. and J. Andre. 1985. *Dictionnaire etymologique de la langue latine: Histoire des mots*. Paris: Klincksieck.

Errington, R. M. 1969. *Philopoemen*. Oxford: Clarendon Press.

Evans, J. K. 1991. *War, women, and children in ancient Rome*. London and New York: Routledge.

Eyben, E. 1991. Fathers and sons. In *Marriage, divorce, and children in ancient Rome*, ed. B. Rawson. Oxford: Clarendon Press, 114–143.

Eyben, E. 1993. *Restless youth in ancient Rome*. Trans. P. Daly. London and New York: Routledge.

Faller, S. 2004. Punisches im *Poenulus*. In *Studien zu Plautus' Poenulus*, ed. T. Baier. Tübingen: Gunter Narr Verlag, 163–202.

Favro, D. 1996. *The urban image of Augustan Rome*. Cambridge: Cambridge University Press.

Feldman, L. H. 1985. Asinius Pollio and Herod's sons. *Classical Quarterly* 35: 240–242.

Fineberg, S. 1999. Blind rage and eccentric vision in *Iliad* 6. *Transactions of the American Philological Association* 129: 13–31.

Fishwick, D. 1983. Le culte imperial sous Juba II et Ptolémée de Maurétanie: Le témoignage des monnaies. *Bulletin archéologique du comité des travaux historiques et scientifiques, série B, Afrique du Nord* 19: 225–233.

Fishwick, D. and B. D. Shaw. 1976. Ptolemy of Mauretania and the conspiracy of Gaetulicus. *Historia* 27: 491–494.

Fittschen, K. 1974. Die Bildnisse der mauretanischen Könige und ihre stadtrömische Vorbilder. *Mitteilungen des Deutschen Archäologischen Instituts, Abteilung Madrider* 15: 156–173.

Fittschen, K. 1979. Juba II. und seine Residenz Iol/Caesarea. In *Die Numider: Reiter und Könige nördlich der Sahara*, ed. H. G. Horn and C. B. Rüger, Cologne: Rheinland-Verlag, 227–242.

Flory, M. B. 1988. Pearls for Venus. *Historia* 37: 498–504.

Flory, M. B. 1993. Livia and the history of public honorific statues for women in Rome. *Transactions of the American Philological Association* 123: 287–308.

Foulon, E. 1992. Βασιλευς Σκιπιων. *Bulletin de l'association Guillaume Budé* 16: 9–30.

Fox, M. 1996. *Roman historical myths: The regal period in Augustan literature*. Oxford: Clarendon Press.

Fox, M. 2001. Dionysius, Lucian, and the prejudice against rhetoric in history. *Journal of Roman Studies* 91: 76–93.

Frank, T. 1921. The Scipionic inscriptions. *Classical Quarterly* 15: 169–171.

Freyburger, G. 1986. *Fides: Étude sémantique et religieuse depuis les origines jusqu'à l'époque augustéenne.* Paris: Société d'Édition les Belles Lettres.

Freyburger-Galland, M. 1997. *Aspects du vocabulaire politique et institutionnel de Dion Cassius.* Strasbourg: Groupe de recherché d'histoire romaine.

Fuhrmann, M. 1992. *Cicero and the Roman Republic.* Trans. W. E. Yuill. Oxford: Blackwell.

Furneaux, H. 1896. *P. Cornelii Taciti Annalium ab excessu divi Augusti libri*, second edition. London: Oxford University Press.

Fusillo, M. 1999. The mirror of the moon: Lucian's *A True Story* – from satire to utopia. In *Oxford readings in the Greek novel*, ed. S. Swain. Oxford: Oxford University Press, 60–82.

Gagé, J. 1988. Les otages de Porsenna. In *Hommages à Henri Le Bonniec*, ed. D. Porte et J.-P. Néraudau. Brussels: Latomus, 236–245.

Galinsky, K. 1969. *Aeneas, Sicily, and Rome.* Princeton: Princeton University Press.

Galinsky, K. 1996. *Augustan culture.* Princeton: Princeton University Press.

García Moreno, L. A. 1992. Paradoxography and political ideals in Plutarch's *Life of Sertorius*. In *Plutarch and the historical tradition*, ed. P. A. Stadter. London and New York: Routledge, 132–158.

Gardner, J. F. 1998. *Family and familia in Roman law and life.* Oxford: Clarendon Press.

Gardner, J. F. 2000. Status, sentiment, and strategy in Roman adoption. In *Adoption et fosterage*, ed. M. Corbier. Paris: de Boccard, 63–79.

Gardthausen, V. 1906. Die Parther in griechisch-römischen Inschriften. In *Orientalische Studien Theodor Nöldeke zum siebzigsten Geburtstag.* Gieszen: Töpelmann, 839–859.

Garnsey, P. 1978. Rome's African empire under the Principate. In *Imperialism in the ancient world*, ed. P. Garnsey and C. Whittaker. Cambridge: Cambridge University Press, 223–354.

Gazda, E. 1995. Roman sculpture and the ethos of emulation: Reconsidering repetition. In *Greece in Rome: Influence, integration, resistance*, ed. C. P. Jones, C. Segal, R. J. Tarrant and R. F. Thomas. *Harvard Studies in Classical Philology* 97: 121–156.

Georgiadou, A. and D. H. J. Larmour. 1994. Lucian and historiography: *De historia conscribenda* and *Verae historiae*. *Aufstieg und Niedergang der römische Welt* 2.34.2: 1448–1509.

Georgiadou, A. and D. H. J. Larmour. 1998. *Lucian's science fiction novel*, True Histories: *Interpretation and commentary*. Leiden: Brill.

Gilmartin, K. 1973. Corbulo's campaigns in the East. *Historia* 22: 583–626.

Gleason, M. W. 1990. The semiotics of gender: Physiognomy and self-fashioning in the second century C. E. In *Before sexuality*, ed. D. M. Halperin, J. J. Winkler, and F. I. Zeitlin. Princeton: Princeton University Press, 389–415.

Golan, D. 1995. *The* res Graeciae *in Polybius: Four studies*. Como: Edizioni New Press.

Golden, M. 1997. Change or continuity? Children and childhood in Hellenistic historiography. In *Inventing ancient culture: Historicism, periodization, and the ancient world*, ed. M. Golden and P. Toohey. London and New York: Routledge, 176–191.

Golvin, J. C. and P. Leveau. 1979. L'amphithéâtre et le théâtre-amphithéâtre de Cherchel: Monuments à spectacle et histoire urbaine à Caesarea de Maurétanie. *Mélanges de l'École française de Rome* 91: 817–843.

Gonnella, R. 2001. New evidence for dating the reign of Vonones I. *Numismatic Chronicle* 161: 67–73.

Goodyear, F. R. D. 1981. *The* Annals *of Tacitus, Books 1–6, volume II*. Cambridge: Cambridge University Press.

Gowing, A. M. 1990. Tacitus and the client kings. *Transactions of the American Philological Association* 120: 315–331.

Grainger, J. D. 1990. *The cities of Seleucid Syria*. Oxford: Clarendon Press.

Grainger, J. D. 2002. *The Roman war of Antiochos the Great*. Leiden: Brill.

Gray-Fow, M. J. G. 1988. The wicked stepmother in Roman literature and history: An evaluation. *Latomus* 47: 741–757.

Grenier, J. 2001. Cléopâtre Séléné, reine de Maurétanie. In Ubique amici: *Mélanges offerts à Jean-Marie Lassère*, ed. C. Hamdoune. Montpellier: Centre d'études et de recherches sur les civilizations antiques de la Méditerranée: 101–116.

Griffin, M. T. 1982. The Lyons tablet and Tacitean hindsight. *Classical Quarterly* 32.2: 404–418.

Griffin, M. T. 1995. Tacitus, Tiberius, and the principate. In *Leaders and masses in the Roman world: Studies in honor of Zvi Yavetz*, ed. I. Malkin and Z. W. Rubinsohn. Leiden: Brill, 33–58.

Grimal, P. 1963. *Dictionnaire de la mythologie Grecque et Romaine*. Paris: Presses Universitaires de France.

Gruen, E. S. 1973. The supposed alliance between Rome and Philip V of Macedon. *California Studies in Classical Antiquity* 6: 123–136.

Gruen, E. S. 1974. The last years of Philip V. *Greek, Roman and Byzantine Studies* 15: 221–246.

Gruen, E. S. 1976. The origins of the Achaean War. *Journal of Hellenic Studies* 96: 46–69.

Gruen, E. S. 1984. *The Hellenistic world and the coming of Rome*. 2 vols. Berkeley and Los Angeles: University of California Press.

Gruen, E. S. 1990. *Studies in Greek culture and Roman policy*. Leiden: Brill.

Gruen, E. S. 1992. *Culture and National Identity in Republican Rome*. Ithaca, NY: Cornell University Press.

Gruen, E. S. 1995. The "fall" of the Scipios. In *Leaders and masses in the Roman world: Studies in honor of Zvi Yavetz*, ed. I. Malkin and Z. W. Rubinsohn. Leiden: Brill, 59–90.

Gruen, E. S. 1996. The expansion of the empire under Augustus. *The Cambridge Ancient History, volume 10* (second edition): 147–197.

Gruen, E. S. 1999. The Hellenistic images of Joseph. In *The eye expanded: Life and the arts in Greco-Roman antiquity*, ed. F. B. Titchener and R. F. Moorton. Berkeley and Los Angeles: University of California Press, 113–146.

Gsell, S. 1952. *Cherchel, antique Iol-Caesarea*. Algiers: Direction de l'intérieur et des beaux-arts.

Guidobaldi, M. P. 1993. I *magalia* di Sinuessa e gli ostaggi cartaginesi. *Ostraka* 2: 73–79.

Gurval, R. A. 1995. *Actium and Augustus: The politics and emotions of civil war*. Ann Arbor: University of Michigan Press.

Hallett, J. P. 1984. *Fathers and daughters in Roman society: Women and the elite family*. Princeton: Princeton University Press.

Hammond, N.G.L. 1996. Sparta at Thermopylae. *Historia* 45.1: 1–20.

Hammond, N.G.L. 1997. What may Philip have learnt as a hostage in Thebes? *Greek, Roman, and Byzantine Studies* 38.4: 355–372.

Hanson, A. E. 1999. The Roman family. In *Life, death, and entertainment in the Roman empire*, ed. D. S. Potter and D. J. Mattingly. Ann Arbor: University of Michigan Press, 19–66.

Hanson, V. D. 2001. *The soul of battle: From ancient times to the present day, how three great liberators vanquished tyranny*. New York: Anchor.

Hanson, W. S. 1987. *Agricola and the conquest of the north*. London: B. T. Batsford.

Hanson, W. S. 1991. Tacitus' *Agricola*: An archaeological and historical study. *Aufstieg und Niedergang der römische Welt* 2.33.3: 1741–1784.

Hardt, M. and A. Negri. 2000. *Empire*. Cambridge, MA: Harvard University Press.

Harkis, B. A. 1986. The psychopathology of the hostage experience: A review. *Medicine, science, and the law* 26.1: 48–52.

Harris, W. V. 1979. *War and imperialism in Republican Rome*. Oxford: Clarendon Press.

Haynes, K. 2003. *Fashioning the feminine in the Greek novel*. London and New York: Routledge.

Heald, M. and L. S. Kaplan. 1977. *Culture and diplomacy: The American experience*. Westport, CT: The Greenwood Press.

Hemker, J. 1985. Rape and the founding of Rome. *Helios* 22.1: 41–48.

Henderson, J. 1999. *Writing down Rome: Satire, comedy, and other offenses in Latin poetry*. Oxford: Clarendon Press.

Henderson, J. 2001. From Megalopolis to Cosmopolis: Polybius, or there and back again. In *Being Greek under Rome*, ed. S. Goldhill. Cambridge: Cambridge University Press, 29–49.

Hickson, F. V. 1991. Augustus Triumphator: Manipulations of the triumphal theme in the political program of Augustus. *Latomus* 50: 124–138.

Hingley, R. 1996. The 'legacy' of Rome: The rise, decline, and fall of the theory of Romanization. In *Roman Imperialism: Post-colonial perspectives*, ed. J. Webster and N. Cooper. Leicester: Leicester Archaeological Monographs, 35–48.

Hingley, R. 1997. Resistance and domination: Social change in Roman Britain. In *Dialogues in Roman imperialism: Power, discourse, and discrepant experience in the Roman Empire*, ed. D. J. Mattingly, Portsmouth, RI: *Journal of Roman Archaeology*, 81–100.

Hoehner, H. W. 1972. *Herod Antipas*. Cambridge: Cambridge University Press.

Hofmann, J. B. 1971. *Etymologisches Wörterbuch des griechischen Sprache*. Munich: R. Oldenbourg Verlag.

Hölkeskamp, K. J. 1993. Conquest, competition, and consensus: Roman expansion in Italy and the rise of the *nobilitas*. *Historia* 42: 12–39.

Holliday, P. J. 1997. Roman triumphal painting: Its function, development, and reception. *Art bulletin* 79.1: 130–147.

Hopkins, K. 1983. *Death and renewal*. Cambridge: Cambridge University Press.

Horsfall, N. 1982. The Caudine Forks: Topography and illusion. *Papers of the British School at Rome* 50: 45–52.

Hoyos, D. 2001. Generals and annalists: Geographic and chronological obscurities in the Scipios' campaigns in Spain, 218–211 BC. *Klio* 83.1: 68–92.

Huet, V. 1996. Stories one might tell of Roman art: Reading Trajan's column and the Tiberius cup. In *Art and text in Roman culture*, ed. J. Elsner. Cambridge: Cambridge University Press, 9–31.

Isaac, B. 1990. *The limits of empire: The Roman army in the East.* Oxford: Clarendon Press.

James, S. L. 1997. Slave-rape and female silence in Ovid's love poetry. *Helios* 24.1: 60–76.

James, S. L. 1998. From boys to men: Rape and developing masculinity in Terence's *Hecyra* and *Eunuchus. Helios* 25.1: 31–47.

Jones, B. W. 1992. *The emperor Domitian.* London and New York: Routledge.

Jones, C. P. 1986. *Culture and society in Lucian.* Cambridge, MA and London: Harvard University Press.

Jones, R. 1991. Cultural change in Roman Britain. In *Britain in the Roman period: Recent trends,* ed. R. Jones. Sheffield: J. R. Collis Publications, 115–120.

Joplin, P. K. 1990. Ritual work on human flesh: Livy's Lucretia and the rape of the body politic. *Helios* 17: 51–70.

Joshel, S. R. 1992. The body female and the body politic: Livy's Lucretia and Verginia. In *Pornography and representation in Greece and Rome,* ed. A. Richlin. Oxford: Oxford University Press, 112–130.

Kahrstedt, U. 1950. *Artabanos III und seine Erben.* Bern: A. Francke.

Karras-Klopproth, M. 1988. *Prosopographische Studien zur Geschichte des Partherreiches auf der Grundlage antiker literarischer Überlieferung.* Bonn: R. Habelt.

Keddie, J. N. 1975. Italicus and Claudius. Tacitus, *Annales* 11.16–17. *Antichthon* 9: 52–60.

Keitel, E. 1978. The role of Parthia and Armenia in Tacitus Annals 11 and 12. *American Journal of Philology* 99: 462–473.

Kellum, B. 1997. Concealing/revealing: Gender and the play of meaning in the monuments of Augustan Rome. In *The Roman cultural revolution,* ed. T. Habinek and A. Schiessaro. Cambridge: Cambridge University Press, 158–181.

Kennedy, D. 1996. Parthia and Rome: Eastern perspectives. In *The Roman army in the East,* ed. D. L. Kennedy. Ann Arbor: *Journal of Roman Archaeology,* 67–90.

Kertzer, D. I. 1997. *The kidnapping of Edgardo Mortara.* New York: Vintage Books.

Kleijwegt, M. 1991. *Ancient youth: The ambiguity of youth and the absence of adolescence in Greco-Roman society.* Amsterdam: Gieben.

Kleijwegt, M. 1994. Caligula's "triumph" at Baiae. *Mnemosyne* 47: 652–671.

Kleiner, D.E.E. 1978. The great friezes of the Ara Pacis Augustae: Greek sources, Roman derivatives, and Augustan social policy. *Mélanges de l'École française de Rome* 90: 753–785.

Klotz, A. 1936. *Appians Darstellung des zweiten Punischen Krieges: Eine Untersuchung zur Quellenanalyse der dritten Dekade des Livius.* Paderborn: F. Schöningh.

Koestermann, E. 1963. *Cornelius Tacitus, Annalen, Band I: Buch 1–3.* Heidelberg: Carl Winter.

Koestermann, E. 1967. *Cornelius Tacitus, Annalen, Band III: Buch 11–13.* Heidelberg: Carl Winter.

Kokkinos, N. 1992. *Antonia Augusta: Portrait of a great Roman lady.* London: Routledge.

Kolendo, J. 1970. L'Influence de Carthage sur la civilization matérielle de Rome. *Archeologia* 21: 8–22.

Kondoleon, C. (ed.) 2000. *Antioch: The lost ancient city.* Princeton: Princeton University Press.

Konrad, C. F. 1994. *Plutarch's* Sertorius*: A historical commentary.* Chapel Hill and London: University of North Carolina Press.

Kruschwitz, P. 1998. Die Datierung der Scipionenelogien CLE 6 und 7. *Zeitschrift für Papyrologie und Epigraphik* 122: 273–285.

Künzl, E. 1988. *Der römische Triumph: Siegesfeiern in antiken Rom.* Munich: C. H. Beck.

Kuttner, A. L. 1995. *Dynasty and empire in the age of Augustus: The case of the Boscoreale cups.* Berkeley: University of California Press.

La Regina, A. 1968. L'elogio di Scipione Barbato. *Dialoghi di archeologia* 2: 173–190.

La Rocca, E. 1983. *Ara Pacis Augustae.* Rome: L'Erma.

Lacey, W. K. 1986. Patria potestas. In *The family in ancient Rome: New perspectives,* ed. B. Rawson. Ithaca, NY: Cornell University Press, 121–144.

Lacey, W. K. 1998. Augustus' *auctoritas* and other aspects of government. *Prudentia* 30.2: 16–32.

Lazenby, J. F. 1978. *Hannibal's war.* Warminster: Aris and Phillips.

Lécrivain, M. C. 1916. L'institution des ôtages dans l'antiquité. *Mémoirs de l'Académie des Sciences de Toulouse* 11.4: 115–139.

Lee, A. D. 1991. The role of hostages in Roman diplomacy with Sasanian Persia. *Historia* 40: 366–374.

Lendon, J. E. 1997. *Empire of honour: The art of government in the Roman world.* Oxford: Clarendon Press.

Lepper, F. and S. Frere. 1988. *Trajan's column: A new edition of the Cichorius plates.* Gloucester, UK: Alan Sutton.

Leveau, P. 1975. Paysans maures et villes romaines en Maurétanie césarienne centrale. *Mélanges de l'école française de Rome* 87: 857–871.

Leveau, P. 1982. Caesarea de Maurétanie. *Aufstieg und Niedergang der römische Welt* 2.10.2: 683–738.

Levick, B. 1990. *Claudius.* New Haven and London: Yale University Press.

Lica, V. 1988. Die daksichen Geisel im römischen Reich. *Studii clasice* 26: 35–44.

Lica, V. 1993. Römische Kriegsgefangene und "Geiseln" in Dakien. *Bonner Jahrbücher des Rheinischen Landesmuseums in Bonn und des Vereins von Altertums freunden im Rheinlande* 193: 161–163.

Lica, V. 2000. *The coming of Rome in the Dacian world.* Trans. C. Patac and M. Neagu; revised by A. R. Birley. Konstanz: Universitätsverlag Konstanz.

Lind, M. 1995. *The next American nation: The new nationalism and the fourth American revolution.* New York: The Free Press.

Linderski, J. 1984. *Si vis pacem, para bellum*: Concepts of defensive imperialism. In *The imperialism of mid-Republican Rome*, ed. W. V. Harris. Rome: Papers and monographs of the American Academy in Rome, 133–164.

Lightfoot, J. L. 1999. *Parthenius of Nicaea: The poetical fragments and the Ἐρωτιμά Παθήματα*. Oxford: Clarendon Press.

Lossmann, F. 1962. *Cicero und Caesar im Jahre 54: Studien zur Theorie und Praxis der römischen Freundschaft*. Stuttgart: Steiner.

Luetcke, K. H. 1968. *Auctoritas bei Augustin, mit einer Einleitung zur Vorgeschichte des Begriffs*. Stuttgart: Steiner.

Mackie, N. 1983. Augustan colonies in Mauretania. *Historia* 32: 332–358.

MacKendrick, P. 1971. *Roman France*. New York: St. Martin's Press.

Macleod, M. D. 1987. Lucian's relationship to Arrian. *Philologus* 81: 257–264.

MacMullen, R. 2000. *Romanization in the Age of Augustus*. New Haven: Yale University Press.

MacWillson, A. C. 1992. *Hostage-taking terrorism: Incident-response strategy*. New York: St. Martin's Press.

Malloch, S.J.V. 2001. Gaius on the Channel coast. *Classical Quarterly* 51.2: 551–556.

Marcotte, D. 1985. *Lucaniae*: Considérations sur l'Éloge de Scipion Barbate. *Latomus* 44.4: 721–742.

Marincola, J. M. 1994. Plutarch's refutation of Herodotus. *Ancient World* 25: 191–203.

Marks, S. 1987. *Not either an experimental doll*. Bloomington: Indiana University Press.

Marshall, B. A. 1985. *A historical commentary on Asconius*. Columbia: University of Missouri Press.

Martin, R. 1981. *Tacitus*. London: Batsford.

Martina, M. 1984. La *vita Antiochi* dell'annalista Liciniano. *Athenaeum* 62: 190–209.

Marvin, M. 1993. Copying in Roman sculpture: The replica series. In *Roman art in context*, ed. E. D'Ambra. Englewood Cliffs, NJ: Prentice Hall, 161–188.

Mattern, S. P. 1999. *Rome and the enemy: Imperial strategy in the Principate*. Berkeley and Los Angeles: University of California Press.

Matthaei, A. 1905. Das Geiselwesen bei den Römern. *Philologus* 64: 224–247.

Matthews, J. F. 1989. Hostages, philosophers, pilgrims, and the diffusion of ideas in the late Roman Mediterranean and Near East. In *Tradition and innovation in late antiquity*, ed. F. M. Clover and R. S. Humphreys. Madison: University of Wisconsin Press, 29–49.

Mattingly, D. J. 1997. Africa: A landscape of opportunity? In *Dialogues in Roman imperialism: Power, discourse, and discrepant experience in the Roman empire*, ed. D. J. Mattingly. Portsmouth, RI: *Journal of Roman Archaeology*, 117–139.

Mattingly, H. B. 1997. The date and significance of the *Lex Antonia de Termessibus*. *Scholia* 6: 68–78.

McDougal, I. 1991. Dio and his sources for Caesar's campaigns in Gaul. *Latomus* 50: 616–638.

McDowell, R. H. 1935. *Coins from Seleuceia on the Tigris*. Ann Arbor: University of Michigan Press.

Mellor, R. 1978. The dedications on the Capitoline Hill. *Chiron* 8: 319–330.

Mellor, R. 1993. *Tacitus*. London and New York: Routledge.

Mendels, D. 1982. Polybius and the socio-economic revolution in Greece (227–146 BC). *L'Antiquité classique* 60: 86–110.

Miles, G. B. 1995. *Livy: Reconstructing early Rome*. Ithaca, NY: Cornell University Press.

Millar, F. 1993. *The Roman Near East: 31 B.C. to A.D. 337*. Cambridge, MA: Harvard University Press.

Millar, F. 1998. *The crowd in Rome in the late Republic*. Ann Arbor: University of Michigan Press.

Miller, A. H. 1980. *Terrorism and hostage negotiation*. Boulder, CO: Westview Press.

Miller, J. F. 2000. Triumphus in Palatio. *American Journal of Philology* 121.3: 409–422.

Millett, M. 1990. Romanization: Historical issues and archaeological interpretations. In *The early Roman empire in the West*, ed. T. Blagg and M. Millett. Oxford: Oxbow Books, 35–44.

Mitchell, R. E. 1986. The definition of *patres* and *plebs*: An end to the struggle of the orders. In *Social struggles in archaic Rome: New perspectives on the conflict of the orders*, ed. K. A. Raaflaub. Berkeley: University of California Press, 130–174.

Mitchell, T. N. 1991. *Cicero: The senior statesman*. New Haven: Yale University Press.

Morgan, M. G. 1990. The perils of schematism: Polybius, Antiochus Epiphanes and the "Day of Eleusis." *Historia* 39.1: 37–76.

Mørkholm, O. 1966. *Antiochus IV of Syria*. Copenhagen: Gyldendal.

Morstein-Marx, R. 2004. *Mass oratory and political power in the late Roman Republic*. Cambridge: Cambridge University Press.

Moscovich, M. J. 1974a. Hostage regulations in the treaty of Zama. *Historia* 23: 417–427.

Moscovich, M. J. 1974b. A note on the Aetolian treaty of 189 BC. In *Polis and imperium: Studies in honor of Edward Togo Salmon*, ed. J. A. S. Evans. Toronto: Hakkert, 139–144.

Moscovich, M. J. 1979–1980. Obsidibus traditis: Hostages in Caesar's *De Bello Gallico*. *Classical Journal* 75: 122–128.

Moscovich, M. J. 1983. Hostage princes and Roman imperialism in the second century BC. *Echos du monde classique* 27: 297–309.

Moscovich, M. J. 1997. Cassius Dio on the death of Sophonisba. *Ancient History Bulletin* 11.1: 25–29.

Mossman, J. M. 1992. Plutarch, Pyrrhus, and Alexander. In *Plutarch and the historical tradition*, ed. P. A. Stadter. London and New York: Routledge, 90–108.

Mueller, D. 1987. Ovid, Iuppiter, und Augustus: Gedanken zur Götterversammlung im ersten Buch der Metamorphosen. *Philologus* 131: 270–288.

Musat, M. and I. Ardeleanu. 1985. *From ancient Dacia to modern Romania.* Bucharest: Editura Stiintifica Si Enciclopedica.

Nappa, C. 1998. Praetextati mores: Juvenal's second satire. *Hermes* 126.1: 90–108.

Ndiaye, S. 1995. Le recours aux otages à Rome sous la république. *Dialogues d'histoire ancienne* 21.1: 149–165.

Nedergaard, E. 1988. The four sons of Phraates IV in Rome. In *East and west: Cultural relations in the ancient world,* ed. T. Fischer-Hansen. Copenhagen: Museum Tusculanum Press, 102–115.

Néraudau, J-P. 1993. La fama dans la Rome antique. *Médiévales* 24: 27–34.

Nicolet, C. 1991. *Space, geography and politics in the early Roman empire.* Ann Arbor: University of Michigan Press.

Nisbet, R.G.M. and M. Hubbard. 1978. *A commentary on Horace: Odes Book II.* Oxford: Clarendon Press.

Nixon, C.E.V. and B. S. Rodgers. 1994. *In praise of later Roman emperors: The* Panegyrici Latini. Berkeley and Los Angeles: University of California Press.

Noy, D. 2000. *Foreigners at Rome: Citizens and strangers.* London: Duckworth.

Ogilvie, R. M. 1967. *Cornelii Taciti de vita Agricolae.* Oxford: Clarendon Press.

Oltramare, A. 1938. Auguste et les Parthes. *Revue des études latines* 16: 121–138.

Paltiel, E. 1979a. The treaty of Apamea and the later Seleucids. *Antichthon* 13: 30–41.

Paltiel, E. 1979b. Antiochos IV and Demetrios I of Syria. *Antichthon* 13: 42–47.

Paltiel, E. 1982. Antiochos Ephiphanes and Roman politics. *Latomus* 41: 229–254.

Paltiel, E. 1991. *Vassals and rebels in the Roman empire.* Brussels: Latomus.

Panagopoulos, A. 1978. *Captives and hostages in the Peloponnesian War.* Athens: Grigoris Publications.

Pani, M. 1972. *Roma e i re d'oriente da Augusto a Tiberio.* Bari: Adriatica.

Parker, H. N. 1997. The teratogenic grid. In *Roman sexualities,* ed. J. P. Hallett and M. B. Skinner. Princeton: Princeton University Press, 47–65.

Parrish, E. J. 1973. Crassus' new friends and Pompey's return. *Phoenix* 27: 357–380.

Passerini, A. 1935. Roma e l'Egitto duranta la terza guerra macedonica. *Athenaeum* 13: 317–342.

Paul, G. M. 1984. *A historical commentary on Sallust's* Bellum Jugurthinum. Liverpool: Francis Cairns.

Pédech, P. 1964. *La méthode historique de Polybe.* Paris: Les Belles Lettres.

Pelling, C.B.R. 1986. Plutarch and Roman politics. In *Past perspectives: Studies in Greek and Roman historical writing,* ed. I. S. Moxon, J. D. Smart, and A. J. Woodman. Cambridge: Cambridge University Press, 159–187.

Pelling, C.B.R. 1993. Tacitus and Germanicus. In *Tacitus and the Tacitean tradition*, ed. T. J. Luce and A. J. Woodman. Princeton: Princeton University Press, 59–85.

Pelling, C.B.R. 2001. Anything truth can do, we can do better: The Cleopatra legend. In *Cleopatra of Egypt, from history to myth*, ed. S. Walker and P. Higgs. Princeton: Princeton University Press, 292–301.

Perry, E. 2005. *The aesthetics of emulation in the visual arts of ancient Rome.* Cambridge: Cambridge University Press.

Petzold, K. 1969. *Studien zur Methode des Polybios und zu ihrer historischen Auswertung.* Munich: C. H. Beck.

Phillips, J. E. 1974. Form and language in Livy's triumph notices. *Classical philology* 69: 265–273.

Phillips, K. 2002. Dynasties! *The Nation.* July 8: 11–14.

Phillipson, C. 1911. *The international law and custom of ancient Greece and Rome.* 2 vols. London: Macmillan.

Piatkowski, A. 1991. *Eleutheria kai autonomia chez Polybe. Klio* 73: 391–401.

Picard, G. C. 1975. La date du theater de Cherchel et les débuts de l'architecture théâtrale dans les provinces romaines d'Occident. *Comptes-rendus des séances de l'academie des inscriptions et belles-lettres*: 386–397.

Pinette, M. and A. Rebourg. 1985. *Autun-Augustodunum, capitale des Éduens: Guide de l'exposition.* Autun: Hotel de Ville.

Plescia, J. 1976. *Patria potestas* and the Roman revolution. In *The conflict of the generations in ancient Greece and Rome*, ed. S. Bertman. Amsterdam: B. R. Grüner, 143–170.

Pollini, J. 1986. Ahenobarbi, Appuleii, and some others on the Ara Pacis. *American journal of archaeology* 90: 453–460.

Pollini, J. 1987. *The portraiture of Gaius and Lucius Caesar.* New York: Fordham University Press.

Pollitt, J. J. 1986. *Art in the Hellenistic Age.* Cambridge: Cambridge University Press.

Potter, T. W. 1983. Models of urban growth: The Cherchel excavations, 1977–1981. *Bulletin archéologique du comité des travaux historiques et scientifiques, série B, Afrique du Nord* 19: 457–468.

Potter, T. W. 1988. City and territory in Roman Algeria: The case of Iol-Caesarea. *Journal of Roman Archaeology* 1: 190–196.

Potter, T. W. 1995. *Towns in late antiquity: Iol Caesarea and its context.* Oxford: Oxbow Books.

Poucet, J. 1976. Fabius Pictor et Denys d'Halicarnasse: Les enfances de Romulus et Rémus. *Historia* 25.1: 201–216.

Poulsen, F. 1951. *Catalogue of ancient sculpture in the Ny Carlsberg Glyptothek.* Copenhagen: Ny Carlsberg Foundation.

Pratt, M. L. 1992. *Imperial eyes: Travel writing and transculturation.* London and New York: Routledge.

Purcell, N. 1993. Atrium Libertatis. *Papers of the British School at Rome* 61: 125–155.

Raaflaub, K. 1986. From protection and defense to offense and participation: Stages in the conflict of the orders. In *Social struggles in archaic Rome: New perspectives on the struggle of the orders*, ed. K. Raaflaub. Berkeley and Los Angeles: University of California Press, 198–243.

Radke, G. 1991. Beobachtungen zum Elogium auf L. Cornelius Scipio Barbatus. *Rheinisches Museum für Philologie* 134: 69–79.

Ramage, E. S. 1987. *The nature and purpose of Augustus' Res Gestae*. Stuttgart: Steiner.

Randall, D. 2000. *Kipling's imperial boy: Adolescence and cultural hybridity*. Basingstoke, UK: Palgrave.

Rawson, B. 1991. Adult-child relationships in Roman society. In *Marriage, divorce, and children in ancient Rome*, ed. B. Rawson. Oxford: Clarendon Press, 7–30.

Rawson, E. 1975. Architecture and sculpture: The activities of the Cossutii. *Papers of the British School at Rome* 43: 36–47.

Rawson, E. 1990. The antiquarian tradition: Spoils and representations of foreign armour. In *Staat und Staatlichkeit in der frühen römischen Republik*, ed. W. Eder. Stuttgart: Steiner, 158–173.

Rawson, E. 2003. *Children and childhood in Roman Italy*. Oxford: Oxford University Press.

Reardon, B. P. 1989. *Collected ancient Greek novels*. Berkeley: University of California Press.

Rebourg, A. 1991. Les origines d'Autun: L'archéologie et les texts. In *Les villes augustéennes de Gaule*, ed. C. Goudineau and A. Rebourg. Autun: Société Éduenne des Lettres, Sciences et Arts, 99–106.

Reiter, W. 1988. *Aemilius Paullus: Conqueror of Greece*. London: Croon Helm.

Rich, J. 1989. Patronage and international relations in the Roman republic. In *Patronage in ancient society*, ed. A. Wallace-Hadrill. London and New York: Routledge, 117–136.

Rich, J. 1998. Augustus's Parthian honours, the temple of Mars Ultor and the arch in the Forum Romanum. *Papers of the British School at Rome* 66: 71–128.

Richardson, J. S. 1975. The triumph, the praetors, and the senate in the early second century B. C. *Journal of Roman Studies* 65: 50–63.

Richardson, J. S. 2000. *Appian: Wars of the Romans in Iberia*. Warminster: Ares and Phillips.

Richardson, L., Jr. 1992. *A new topographical dictionary of ancient Rome*. Baltimore and London: Johns Hopkins University Press.

Richardson, P. 1996. *Herod, king of the Jews and friend of the Romans*. Columbia: University of South Carolina Press.

Richlin, A. 1992. Reading Ovid's rapes. In *Pornography and representation in Greece and Rome*, ed. A. Richlin. Oxford: Oxford University Press, 158–179.

Rigsby, K. 1980. Seleucid notes. *Transactions of the American Philological Association* 110: 233–254.

Rives, J. B. 1999. *Tacitus: Germania.* Oxford: Clarendon Press.

Robinson, C. 1979. *Lucian and his influence in Europe.* Chapel Hill: University of North Carolina Press.

Roller, D. W. 2003. *The world of Juba II and Kleopatra Selene.* London and New York: Routledge.

Romer, F. E. 1979. Gaius Caesar's military diplomacy in the East. *Transactions of the American Philological Association* 109: 199–214.

Rose, B. 1990. "Princes" and barbarians on the Ara Pacis. *American Journal of Archaeology* 94.3: 453–467.

Russell, D. A. 1995. Plutarch's *Life of Coriolanus.* In *Essays on Plutarch's Lives,* ed. B. Scardagli. Oxford: Clarendon Press, 357–362.

Rutherfurd, D. R. 1989. Vergil's *Fama:* A new interpretation of *Aeneid* 4.173ff. *Greece and Rome* 36: 2–32.

Rutledge, S. H. 2000. Tacitus in tartan: Textual colonization and expansionist discourse in the *Agricola. Helios* 27.1: 75–95.

Saavedra, T. 1999. Women as focalizers of barbarism in conquest texts. *Echos du monde classique* 18.1: 59–77.

Saller, R. P. 1982. *Personal patronage under the early empire.* Cambridge: Cambridge University Press.

Saller, R. P. 1984. Roman dowry and the devolution of property in the principate. *Classical Quarterly* 34: 195–205.

Saller, R. P. 1987. Men's age at marriage and its correspondence in the Roman family. *Classical Philology* 82: 21–34.

Saller, R. P. 1991a. Corporal punishment, authority, and obedience in the Roman household. In *Marriage, divorce, and children in ancient Rome,* ed. B. Rawson. Oxford: Clarendon Press, 144–165.

Saller, R. P. 1991b. Roman heirship strategies in principle and practice. In *The family in Italy from antiquity to the present,* ed. D. I. Kertzer and R. P. Saller. New Haven: Yale University Press, 26–47.

Saller, R. P. 1994. *Patriarchy, property, and death in the Roman family.* Cambridge: Cambridge University Press.

Saller, R. P. and B. D. Shaw. 1984. Tombstones and Roman family relations in the principate: Civilians, soldiers, and slaves. *Journal of Roman Studies* 74: 124–156.

Salomies, O. 2000. Names and adoptions in ancient Rome: The possibility of using personal names for the study of adoption in Rome. In *Adoption et fosterage,* ed. M. Corbier. Paris: de Boccard, 141–156.

Savunen, L. 1993. Debt legislation in the fourth century, BC. In *Senatus populusque Romanus: Studies in Roman Republican legislation,* ed. U. Paananen et al. Helsinki: Acta Instituti Romani Finlandiae, 143–170.

Scardigli, B. 1994. Germanische Gefangene und Geiseln in Italien (von Marius bis Konstantin). In *Germani in Italia*, ed. B. Scardigli and P. Scardigli. Rome: Consiglio nazionale delle ricerche, 117–150.

Scodel, R. 1992. The wits of Glaucus. *Transactions of the American Philological Association* 122: 73–84.

Seavey, W. 1991. Forensic epistolography and Plutarch's *de Herodoti malignitate*. *Hellas* 2: 33–45.

Segal, C. 2001–2002. Jupiter in Ovid's *Metamorphoses*. *Arion* 9.1: 78–99.

Sellwood, D. 1971. *An introduction to the coinage of Parthia*. London: Spink and Sons.

Severy, B. 2003. *Augustus and the family at the birth of the Roman empire*. London and New York: Routledge.

Shaw, B. D. 2001. Raising and killing children: Two myths. *Mnemosyne* 54: 31–77.

Sherwin-White, A. N. 1984. *Roman foreign policy in the East, 168 BC to AD 1*. London: Duckworth.

Sherwin-White, S. and A. Kuhrt. 1993. *From Samarkhand to Sardis: A new approach to the Seleucid empire*. Berkeley and Los Angeles: University of California Press.

Shimron, B. 1979–1980. Polybius in Rome: A re-examination of the evidence. *Scripta classical Israelica* 5: 94–117.

Shotter, D.C.A. 1968. Tacitus, Tiberius, and Germanicus. *Historia* 17: 194–214.

Shotter, D.C.A. 1974. Gnaeus Calpurnius Piso, legate of Syria. *Historia* 23: 229–245.

Sicker, M. 2001. *Between Rome and Jerusalem*. Westport, CT: Praeger.

Sigismund Nielsen, H. 2000. Quasi-kin, quasi-adoption and the Roman family. In *Adoption et fosterage*, ed. M. Corbier. Paris: de Boccard, 249–262.

Silvestri, D. 1978. Taurasia, Cisauna, e il nome antico del Sannio. *La parola del passato* 33: 167–180.

Simon, E. 1967. *Ara Pacis Augustae*. Greenwich, CT.: New York Graphic Society.

Simon, E. 1986. *Augustus: Kunst und Leben in Rom um die Zeitenwende*. Munich: Hirmer Verlag.

Simpson, C. J. 1992. On the unreality of the Parthian arch. *Latomus* 51: 835–842.

Skard, S. 1961. *The American myth and the European mind: American studies in Europe, 1776–1960*. Philadelphia: University of Pennsylvania Press.

Sklenár, R. 2003. *The taste for nothingness: A study of virtus and related themes in Lucan's* Bellum Civile. Ann Arbor: University of Michigan Press.

Slater, N. W. 1988. The fictions of patriarchy in Terence's *Hecyra*. *Classical World* 81.4: 249–260.

Smith, C. E. 1972. *Tiberius and the Roman empire*. London: Kennikat Press.

Solodow, J. B. 1988. *The world of Ovid's* Metamorphoses. Chapel Hill and London: University of North Carolina Press.

Speidel, M. P. 1979. An urban cohort of the Mauretanian kings? *Antiquités africaines* 14: 121–122.

Speidel, M. P. 1998. The slaughter of Gothic hostages after Adrianople. *Hermes* 126.4: 503–506.

Spivak, G.C. 1988. Can the subaltern speak? In *Marxism and the interpretation of culture*, ed. C. Nelson and L. Grossberg. Urbana and Chicago: University of Illinois Press: 271–313.

Stadter, P. A. 1989. *A commentary on Plutarch's* Pericles. Chapel Hill and London: University of North Carolina Press.

Steel, C.E.W. 2001. *Cicero, rhetoric, and empire.* Oxford: Oxford University Press.

Stewart, A. 2004. *Attalos, Athens, and the Akropolis.* Cambridge: Cambridge University Press.

Strentz, T. 1982. The Stockholm Syndrome: Law enforcement policy and hostage behavior. In *Victims of terrorism*, ed. F. M. Ochberg and D. A. Soskis. Boulder, CO: Westview Press: 149–163.

Sullivan, R. D. 1990. *Near Eastern royalty and Rome, 100–30 BC.* Toronto: University of Toronto Press.

Swain, J.W. 1944. Antiochus Epiphanes and Egypt. *Classical Philology* 39: 73–94.

Swain, S.C.R. 1989. Character change in Plutarch. *Phoenix* 43: 62–68.

Syme, R. 1958. *Tacitus.* Oxford: Clarendon Press.

Symonds, M. 1982. Victim responses to terror: Understanding and treatment. In *Victims of terrorism*, ed. F. M. Ochberg and D. A. Soskis. Boulder, CO: Westview Press, 95–103.

Takács, S.A. 2000. Pagan cults at Antioch. In *Antioch: The lost ancient city*, ed. C. Kondoleon. Princeton: Princeton University Press: 198–200.

Talbert, R.J.A. (ed.) 2000. *Barrington atlas of the Greek and Roman world.* Princeton and Oxford: Princeton University Press.

Tarn, W. W. 1932. Tiridates and the young Phraates. In *Mélanges Gustave Glotz*, volume 2. Paris: Les Presses universitaires de France, 831–837.

Tarn, W. W. 1951. *The Greeks in Bactria and India*, second edition. Cambridge: Cambridge University Press.

Tatum, W. J. 1999. *The patrician tribune: Publius Clodius Pulcher.* Chapel Hill: University of North Carolina Press.

Thesleff, H. 1985. Notes on Homer and the Homeric question. In *Studia in honorem Iiro Kajanto.* Helsinki: Classical association of Finland, 293–314.

Timpe, D. 1975. Zur augusteischen Partherpolitik zwischen 30 und 20 v. Chr. *Würzburger Jahrbücher für die Altertumswissenschaft* 1: 155–169.

Tissol, G. 1996. *The face of nature: Wit, narrative, and cosmic origins in Ovid's* Metamorphoses. Princeton: Princeton University Press.

Toll, K. 1997. Making Roman-ness and the *Aeneid. Classical Antiquity* 16.1: 34–56.

Torelli, M. 1982. *Typology and structure of Roman historical reliefs.* Ann Arbor: University of Michigan Press.

Traill, D. 1989. Gold armor for bronze and Homer's use of compensatory τιμή. *Classical Philology* 54: 301–305.

Treggiari, S. 1991. *Roman marriage:* Iusti coniuges *from the time of Cicero to the time of Ulpian.* Oxford: Clarendon Press.

Tucker, T. G. 1985. *Etymological Dictionary of Latin.* Chicago: Ares.

Turner, J. T. 1985. Factors influencing the development of the hostage identification syndrome. *Political psychology* 6.4: 705–711.

van Sickle, J. 1987. The elogia of the Cornelii Scipiones and the origin of the epigram at Rome. *American Journal of Philology* 108: 41–55.

Verbrugghe, G. P. 1981. Fabius Pictor's "Romulus and Remus." *Historia* 30: 236–238.

Versnel, H. S. 1970. *Triumphus: An inquiry into the origin, development and meaning of the Roman triumph.* Leiden: Brill.

Vervaet, F. J. 1999a. Tacitus, Domitius Corbulo, and Traianus' *Bellum Parthicum. L'Antiquité classique* 68: 289–297.

Vervaet, F. J. 1999b. *CIL* IX.3426: A new light on Corbulo's career, with special reference to his official mandate in the East from AD 55 to AD 63. *Latomus* 58: 574–599.

Vessey, D.W.T.C. 1971. Thoughts on Tacitus's portrayal of Claudius. *American Journal of Philology* 92: 385–409.

Viswanathan, G. 1989. *Masks of conquest: Literary study and British rule in India.* Delhi: Oxford University Press.

Wachter, R. 1987. *Altlateinische Inschriften: Sprachliche und epigraphische Untersuchungen zu den Dokumenten bis etwa 150 v. Chr.* Bern: Peter Lang.

Walbank, F. W. 1938. Φίλιππος Τραγωιδούμενος. *Journal of Hellenic Studies* 58: 55–68.

Walbank, F. W. 1940. *Philip V of Macedon.* Cambridge: Cambridge University Press.

Walbank, F. W. 1957. *A historical commentary on Polybius, volume 1.* Oxford: Clarendon Press.

Walbank, F. W. 1964. Polybius and the Roman state. *Greek, Roman, and Byzantine Studies* 5: 239–259.

Walbank, F. W. 1965. Political morality and the friends of Scipio. *Journal of Roman studies* 55: 1–15.

Walbank, F. W. 1967. *A historical commentary on Polybius, volume 2.* Oxford: Clarendon Press.

Walbank, F. W. 1972. *Polybius.* Berkeley: University of California Press.

Walbank, F. W. 1977. Polybius' last ten books. In *Historiographia Antiqua: Commentationes Lovanienses in honorem W. Peremans septuagenarii editae.* Leuven: Leuven University Press, 139–162.

Walbank, F. W. 1979. *A historical commentary on Polybius, volume 3.* Oxford: Clarendon Press.

Walker, B. 1952. *The Annals of Tacitus: A study in the writing of history.* Manchester: Manchester University Press.

Walker, C. L. 1980. *Hostages in Republican Rome.* University of North Carolina Ph.D. dissertation.

Walsh, P. G. 1961. *Livy: His historical aims and methods.* Cambridge: Cambridge University Press.

Walters, J. 1997. Invading the Roman body: Manliness and impenetrability in Roman thought. In *Roman sexualities,* ed. J. P. Hallett and M. B. Skinner. Princeton: Princeton University Press, 29–43.

Walters, J. 1998. Juvenal, *Satire* 2: Putting male sexual deviants on show. In *Thinking men: Masculinity and its self-representation in the classical tradition,* ed. L. Foxhall and J. Salmon. London and New York: Routledge, 148–154.

Wardman, A. 1974. *Plutarch's* Lives. Berkeley and Los Angeles: University of California Press.

Warren, L. B. 1970. Roman triumphs and Etruscan kings. *Journal of Roman Studies* 60: 49–66.

Warrior, V. 1988. The chronology of the movements of M. Fulvius Nobilior. *Chiron* 18: 325–376.

Watson, A. 1975. *Rome of the Twelve Tables.* Princeton: Princeton University Press.

Webster, J. 2001. Creolizing the Roman provinces. *American Journal of Archaeology* 105.2: 209–225.

Welch, K. 1998. Caesar and his officers in the Gallic War commentaries. In *Julius Caesar as artful reporter: The war commentaries as political instruments,* ed. K. Welch and A. Powell. London: Duckworth, 85–110.

Wells, P. S. 1999. *The barbarians speak: How the conquered peoples shaped the Roman empire.* Princeton: Princeton University Press.

Welwei, K.-W. 1989. Zum *metus Punicus* in Rom um 150 v. Chr. *Hermes* 117.3: 314–320.

West, D. 1995. *Carpe diem: Horace Odes I.* Oxford: Clarendon Press.

Wheeler, E. 1997. The chronology of Corbulo in Armenia. *Klio* 79.2: 383–397.

Wheeler, S. M. 1999. *A discourse of wonders: Audience and performance in Ovid's* Metamorphoses. Philadelphia: University of Pennsylvania Press.

White, P. 1997. Julius Caesar and the publication of *acta* in late Republican Rome. *Chiron* 27: 73–93.

Whitmarsh, T. 2001. *Greek literature and the Roman empire: The politics of imitation.* Oxford: Oxford University Press.

Whittaker, C. R. 1996. Roman Africa: Augustus to Trajan. In *Cambridge ancient history, volume 10* (second edition). Cambridge: Cambridge University Press, 586–618.

Whittaker, C. R. 1997. Imperialism and culture: The Roman intitiative. In *Dialogues in Roman imperialism: Power, discourse, and discrepant experience in the Roman Empire,* ed. D. J. Mattingly, Portsmouth, RI: *Journal of Roman Archaeology,* 143–163.

Wiedemann, T. 1989. *Adults and children in the Roman empire.* New Haven and London: Yale University Press.

Williams, C. A. 1999. *Roman homosexuality: Ideologies of masculinity in Classical antiquity.* Oxford: Oxford University Press.

Williams, J. H. C. 2001. *Beyond the Rubicon: Romans and Gauls in Republican Italy.* Oxford: Oxford University Press.

Wiseman, T. P. 1995. *Remus: A Roman myth.* Cambridge: Cambridge University Press.

Wölfflin, E. 1890. De Scipionum elogiis. *Revue de philologie, de littérature et d'histoire anciennes* 14: 113–122.

Woods, D. 2000. Caligula's seashells. *Greece and Rome* 47.1: 80–87.

Woolf, G. 1992. The unity and diversity of Romanization. *Journal of Roman Archaeology* 5: 349–352.

Woolf, G. 1993. Roman peace. In *War and society in the Roman world,* ed. J. Rich and G. Shipley. London and New York: Routledge, 171–194.

Woolf, G. 1998. *Becoming Roman: The origins of Roman provincial civilization in Gaul.* Cambridge: Cambridge University Press.

Woolf, G. 2000. Romanization and its discontents. In *Romanization and the city: Creations, transformations, and failures,* ed. E. Fentress. Portsmouth, RI: *Journal of Roman Archaeology,* 115–131.

Woytek, E. 2004. Zur Datierung des *Poenulus.* In *Studien zu Plautus' Poenulus,* ed. T. Baier. Tübingen: Gunter Narr Verlag, 113–137.

Wroth, W. W. 1964. *Catalogue of the coins of Parthia.* London: British Museum.

Wu, F. H. 2003. *Yellow: Race in America beyond black and white.* New York: Basic Books, repr.

Yavetz, Z. 1974a. Rome and Carthage: A gesture towards peace. *History today* 24: 874–877.

Yavetz, Z. 1974b. *Existimatio, fama,* and the Ides of March. *Harvard Studies in Classical Philology* 78: 35–65.

Yavetz, Z. 1984. The *Res Gestae* and Augustus' public image. In *Caesar Augustus: Seven aspects,* ed. F. Millar and E. Segal. Oxford: Clarendon Press, 1–36.

Yohannan, J. D. 1968. *Joseph and Potiphar's wife in world literature: An anthology of the story of the chaste youth and the wicked stepmother.* New York: New Directions Books.

Zanker, P. 1988. *The power of images in the Age of Augustus.* Trans. H. A. Shapiro. Ann Arbor: University of Michigan Press.

Zecchini, G. 1996. Il cognomen "Augustus." *Acta classica Universitatis Scientiarum Debreceniensis* 32: 129–135.

Zeitlin, F. I. 2001. Visions and revisions of Homer. In *Being Greek under Rome: Cultural identity, the Second Sophistic and the development of empire,* ed. S. Goldhill. Cambridge: Cambridge University Press, 195–266.

Ziegler, K. 1964. *Die Beziehungen zwischen Rom und dem Partherreich.* Wiesbaden: Franz Steiner.

INDEX OF PASSAGES DISCUSSED

GENERAL INDEX

Achaean League, hostages from, 11, 19, 90, 203–205, 213. *See also* Polybius

Achilles Tatius, *Leucippe and Clitophon*, 198–199, 252

Adherbal (son of Micipsa of Numidia), 21

adolescence, 154–156

adoption, 127

Adrianople, Battle of, 21, 53

Aemilius Paullus, Lucius, 97, 127, 167

Aeneas, 9, 78

Aetolian League, hostages from, 2, 10, 13, 15, 41, 157

Agathocles (tyrant of Syracuse), 192

Agenaric (Alamannic hostage in Rome), 151

Agricola, Gnaeus Julius (governor of Britain), 72, 120, 121, 149, 244, 249

Alexander the Great, 43, 48, 58, 61, 185

Antioch, alleged Romanization of, 168–169, 250

Antiochus III (Seleucid king), 13, 103, 144, 157. *See also* Seleucid monarchy

Antiochus IV (Seleucid king)
 as hostage in Rome, 13, 16, 89, 158
 as king of the Seleucids, 62, 159–160, 166–170, 216

Appian
 on Iberian hostages, 65
 on origins of Third Punic War, 64

Appius Claudius (consul of 495 BCE), 44, 53

Ara Pacis (Altar of Peace), 105–108, 133–134, 170, 238–239, 245–246, 248

Ariarathes V of Cappadocia, 20–21, 156

Ariovistus, 57

Armenes (son of Nabis of Sparta), 3

Armenia. *See* Tacitus, Juvenal, Tigranes (three entries), Tiridates (king of Armenia), Zeno

Arminius (chieftain of Cherusci), 20–21, 236

Artabanus (king of Parthia). *See* Parthia

Atrium Libertatis, 87, 156, 251

auctoritas, 95

Augustodunum (Autun, France), school for Gallic children in, 163–165

Augustus (also Octavian)
 and Britain, 116
 and German hostages, 180
 and Herod the Great, 142–144
 and Illyrian hostages, 11, 65
 and Juba II, 138
 and Parthian hostages, 84–87, 104–108, 135, 226
 appears obliquely in Ovid, *Metamorphoses*, 92, 198
 as imperial *paterfamilias* in Strabo, 140
 autobiography (non-epigraphic) of, 104
 commandeers hostages in Alexandria, 61
 nearly loses Octavia as hostage, 183

Bithys (son of Cotys of Thrace), 61, 80–81, 89

Boii, hostages from, 4, 99

Britain, hostages from, 114. *See also* Agricola; Julius Caesar

286

Lex Antonia de Termessibus, 74
Livy, 22–24, 80–81, 98–99. *See also index of passages discussed*
  on Antiochus IV Epiphanes, 159, 170, 250
  on Demetrius of Macedon, 59
  on Scipio Africanus in Spain, 134, 251
Longinus, Gaius Cassius, as characterized by Tacitus, 239, 248
Lucan, *Pharsalia*, 73
Lucania, hostages from, 71, 102, 250
Lucian, *True Histories*, 27, 151, 178–179
Lycian League, 75

maiestas, 119
Mandonius, wife of, 130, 181, 190
map of the world, Agrippa's, 107, 250
Marcius Philippus, Quintus, 48, 70, 100, 202
Marcus Aurelius (emperor of Rome), 161
Mark Antony
  and Herod the Great, 193–194
  holds hostages in Alexandria, 11, 61, 99, 181
  gives son to conspirators, 48
marriage alliance, and hostage-taking, 184–188
Mauretania, Roman control of, 174–175
Meherdates (Parthian hostage in Rome), 136. *See also* Tacitus
Minucius Rufus, Quintus (consul of 197 BCE), 98–99
Moesia, hostages from, 109
"monument of the Asian kings," so-called, 74

Nabis (tyrant of Sparta), 91, 145. *See also* Armenes
Nero (emperor of Rome), 119. *See also* Tacitus
  and hostages from Vespasian, 46
  fails to honor Tiberius Plautius Aelianus, 109
nexum (debt bondage), 38
Numidia, hostages from, 11, 43

Octavia (sister of Augustus), 139, 183, 190

Octavian. *See* Augustus
Octavius, Gnaeus (legate to Seleucids), 56, 63
Oppian, *Halieutika*, 79
Otho (emperor of Rome), 47
"overclass," in imperial contexts, 33
Ovid
  Heroides (Canace and Medea), 75
  Metamorphoses (Lycaon), 91–93, 137, 251
  Metamorphoses (Scylla), 198

Pannonia, hostages from, 109
Parthenius, 137, 191
Parthia, 252. *See also* Tacitus
  hostages from Artabanus, in 37 CE, 117, 122
  hostage from Phraates IV, in 20s BCE, 84–87
  hostages from Phraates IV, in 10/9 BCE, 17, 72, 104–108, 135, 145, 160, 161, 176, 181, 195, 226, 250
  hostages from Vologaeses, in 54 CE, 73, 118, 146, 249
  retrieval of standards from, 86, 105
paterfamilias, 126
pax (peace), as defined by hostages, 42–44, 58, 237, 247
Penestae (and Parthini), 81, 89
Perseus (king of Macedon), 7, 48, 80, 97, 100, 132
  children of, in Rome, 158, 160
Philip II (king of Macedon), 10, 68, 144, 158, 165, 192, 241, 249
Philip V (king of Macedon), 1, 6, 48, 144
Philo, *On Joseph*, 48, 57
Phraates IV (king of Parthia). *See* Parthia
Phraates V (Parthian hostage in Rome). *See* Tacitus
Pineus (king of Illyria), 40
Piso, Gnaeus Calpurnius, and connections to Vonones, 229
Plautius Aelianus, Tiberius (consul of 45 and 74 CE), 108–110
Plautus, *Poenulus*, 52, 155, 161–163
Pliny the Younger, *Panegyric*, 124, 252

Suetonius
on Caesar's hostages from Britain, 115
on Caligula's alleged perversions, 197,
252
on female hostages from Germany, 181
Struggle of the Orders, 44–45, 55, 182

Tacitus, 252
on Agricola, 149, 239–244, 249
on Claudius and Italicus, 234–235
on Claudius and Meherdates, 238–239,
248
on feminine qualities of hostages, 195
on Nero and Tigranes, 239–244, 249
on Tiberius and Phraates V, 232–233
on Tiberius and Tiridates, 233–234
on Tiberius and Vonones, 226–232
Tampius Flavianus (governor of Pannonia),
109
Tarentum. See Thurii
Thucydides, 10
Thurii (and Tarentum), hostages from, 53,
87, 251
Tiberius (emperor of Rome), 44, 117, 135.
See also Tacitus
Tigranes (detainee of Pompey), 90, 117,
152
Tigranes (name parodied by Lucian), 152
Tigranes (Neronian hostage). See Tacitus
Tiridates (king of Armenia), 181, 243, 249
Tiridates (Parthian hostage in Rome), 136.
See also Tacitus
Tiridates (renegade Parthian nobleman),
84

Titus (emperor of Rome), as hostage in
domestic politics, 46
Trajan, 124, 244, 249
victory column of, 237–238, 239,
245–247, 248
triumphal processions
significance of hostages in, 1–4, 96–101
on the Alban Mount, 99
Tusculum, rebellion of, 58
Twelve Tables, Laws of, 38

Valeria (co-hostage with Cloelia), 82
Vergil, *Aeneid*, 170
Vespasian
sons of, 46
honors Tiberius Plautius Aelianus, 109
Vicus Africus, 88
violence
absence of, in hostage-taking, 52–55
presence of, in hostage-taking, 55–57
Vitellius (emperor of Rome), 46
Vitellius, Lucius (governor of Syria)
as characterized by Tacitus, 233
escorts Tiridates to Parthia, 135
receives hostages from Artabanus, 44,
117–118, 120
Vitruvius, 172
Vologaeses (king of Parthia). See Parthia
Volsci, hostages from, 53
Vonones (Parthian hostage in Rome). See
also Tacitus; Piso
coinage of, 176–177

Zeno (Pontic hostage in Armenia), 230